Christian Labor and the Politics of Frustration in Imperial Germany

Christian Labor and the Politics of Frustration in Imperial Germany

by

Eric Dorn Brose

The Catholic University of America Press
Washington, D.C.

Library of Congress Cataloging in Publication Data

Brose, Eric Dorn, 1948–
Christian labor and the politics of frustration in imperial Germany.
Bibliography: p.
1. Trade-unions and Christianity—Germany—History.
2. Trade-unions, Catholic—Germany—History.
3. Church and social problems—Germany—History.
4. Trade-unions—Miners—Germany—History. I. Title.
HD6481.2.G3B76 1984 331.88′0943 83-25172
ISBN 0-8132-0589-1

FOR CHRIS

Contents

Preface

This study is primarily a history of the politics of the Christian trade unions and other associations which made up the Christian labor movement in Imperial Germany. The book also pays considerable attention to the socio-economic side of the movement, but offers no exhaustive treatment here, focusing mainly on the miners of western Prussia. The *Leitmotiv* of the work is the long, arduous and unsuccessful attempt to promote Christian social reform and supplant the Social Democrats from the labor movement. Thus the study is an anatomy of failure and the resulting frustration.

Considerable research barriers had to be overcome in preparing this study. During the first bombing raids over Cologne in 1942 the archives of the general secretariat of the Christian trade unions and the Rhenish Center Party were totally destroyed. Consequently, thirty repositories in Germany had to be visited before sufficient material could be collected. With most pieces of the mosaic now in place, one of the only studies of Christian labor based on archival evidence can be presented.

My work would not have been possible without generous assistance from many different sides. Thanks are due the German Academic Exchange Service, which provided travel funds, living costs and health expenditures from August 1974 to July 1976, and again from May to July 1979. Throughout this period I also received invaluable advice on source material from the staffs of the numerous archives and libraries I visited. I would particularly like to thank Dr. Löhr of the Stadtarchiv in Mönchen-Gladbach, Dr. Wermter of the Stadtbibliothek in Mönchen-Gladbach, Dr. Trumpp and his associates at the Bundesarchiv in Coblence, Dr. Romeyk of the Hauptstaatsarchiv in Düsseldorf, Frl. Ellen Giesberts of the KAB Haus in Cologne, and Herr Glaser of the Zentrales Staatsarchiv in Potsdam. Thanks are also due to Professor John K. Zeender, whose detailed comments on the manuscript were a tremendous asset, Professor Hans Mommsen, who offered many helpful criticisms, and

Professor Vernon Lidtke, who kept me informed of his own relevant research. The Graduate School at Ohio State University, which enabled me to purchase some expensive research materials from Poland in 1976, and the College of Humanities and Social Sciences at Drexel University, which reduced my teaching load in 1980 and 1981 so that I could complete the revisions of the manuscript, should also not be forgotten. I owe a very special debt of gratitude, finally, to my *Doktorvater*, the late Andreas Dorpalen, who gave me indispensable advice and criticism from the proposal stage in 1972 until only weeks before his passing last year. Without his help over these ten years, a product of much greater length and far inferior quality would have resulted. Those defects that remain, of course, are solely my responsibility.

ERIC DORN BROSE

Philadelphia
June 1983

Introduction: Christian Labor in the Literature

Throughout the Imperial period many Christian workers remained aloof from the "free" and Hirsch-Duncker trade unions, the organizations, respectively, of Socialist and Liberal laborers. The latter were opposed as agents of secularism and enemies of the Christian *Weltanschauung*, while the Socialist unions were criticized as the shock troops of an atheistic, revolutionary Social Democratic Party (S.P.D.) and the proponents of an "unnatural" socialization of the means of production. Christian labor leaders, on the contrary, wanted an organization free of religious bias which would implement "more practical" rights of codetermination (*Mitbestimmung*) somewhat similar to those which exist in West Germany today. One of the goals of this study is to promote an understanding of the reasons behind the divisions in the German labor movement, a question which is largely uninvestigated in the literature. This topic is highly important, for the incessant squabbling among German proletarians weakened trade unionism and inhibited the progress toward social betterment which all three groups desired. As the following chapters show, the main problem lay in the essentially false picture that the various movements had of one another, blinded as they were by ideology and religion.

These warped perspectives have largely dominated the literature on the Christian labor movement since the turn of the century. According to authors like August Erdmann, an S.P.D. deputy of the Wilhelmian era, and Otto Hue, a free trade unionist, Christian trade unionists were the well-behaved children of the paternalistic order, or, in other words, politically unconscious proletarians who had been duped by the industrial bourgeoisie into undermining the necessary unity of the working class.[1] Christian proponents projected an altogether different image. In numerous studies published before 1933 by the headquarters of the People's Association for Catholic Germany (*Volksverein für das katholische Deutschland*) and other pro-Christian groups, the Christian labor movement was defended as an independent, progressive, aggressive representative of the workers' interests.[2]

The legacy of these essentially political viewpoints has been two equally biased schools of thought in the more recent literature. For various reasons—deficient archival research, a narrow focus of analysis, and also, undoubtedly, strong political and religious prejudice—most authors are drawn toward one pole or the other. Since 1952, for instance, five narrow and rather apologetic biographies of Christian labor leaders have appeared.[3] The pre-war arguments of the People's Association (*Volksverein*) were also propagated by surviving members of the movement like Emil Ritter and Joseph Joos.[4] On the other side one finds highly negative assessments like those of Michael Berger, Klaus Saul, and Mary Nolan[5] or inaccurate criticism from East German scholars.

1. August Erdmann, *Die christliche Arbeiterbewegung in Deutschland* (Stuttgart: J. W. H. Dietz, 1908); August Erdmann, *Die christlichen Gewerkschaften insbesondere ihr Verhältnis zu Zentrum and Kirche* (Stuttgart: J. H. W. Dietz, 1914); Otto Hue, *Die Bergarbeiter: Eine historische Darstellung der Bergarbeiterverhältnisse von der ältesten bis in die neueste Zeit* (Stuttgart: J. H. W. Dietz, 1910–13), 2 volumes.

2. Otto Müller, *Die christliche Gewerkschaftsbewegung Deutschlands* (Karlsruhe: Druck und Verlag der Braunschen Hofbuchdruckerei, 1905); Michael Gasteiger, *Die christliche Gewerkschaften in Süddeutschland* (Munich: Verlag des "Arbeiter," 1908); Albert Franz, *Der soziale Katholizismus in Deutschland bis zum Tode Kettelers* (Mönchen-Gladbach: Volksvereins Verlag GmbH, 1914); Heinrich Imbusch, *25 Jahre Gewerkverein christlicher Bergarbeiter* (Essen: Verlag des Gewerkvereins christlicher Bergarbeiter Deutschlands, 1919); *25 Jahre christliche Gewerkschaftsbewegung Deutschlands 1899–1924* (Berlin: Christlicher Gewerkschaftsverlag, 1924); Franz Müller, *Franz Hitze und sein Werk* (Hamburg: Hanseatische Verlagsanstalt, 1928); Theodor Böhme, *Die christlichnationale Gewerkschaft* (Stuttgart: Verlag von W. Kohlhammer, 1930); Ludwig Frey, *Die Stellung der christlichen Gewerkschaften zu den politischen Parteien* (Berlin: Christlicher Gewerkschaftsverlag, 1931).

3. Joseph Deutz, *Adam Stegerwald* (Cologne: Bund-Verlag GmbH, 1952); Helmut J. Schorr, *Adam Stegerwald—Gewerkschaftler und Politiker der ersten deutschen Republik* (Recklinghausen: Kommunal Verlag, 1966); Erich Kosthorst, *Jakob Kaiser: Der Arbeiterführer* (Stuttgart: W. Kohlhammer Verlag, 1967); Oswald Wachtling, *Joseph Joos—Journalist, Arbeiterführer, Zentrumspolitiker* (Mainz: Matthias Grünewald–Verlag, 1974); Herbert Mockenhaupt, *Heinrich Brauns 1868–1939* (Mainz: Matthias Grünewald–Verlag, 1976).

4. Emil Ritter, *Die katholisch-soziale Bewegung und der Volksverein* (Cologne: Verlag J. P. Bachem, 1954); Joseph Joos, *So Sah Ich Sie* (Augsburg: Verlag Winfried-Werk GmbH, 1958); *idem, Am Räderwerk der Zeit* (Augsburg: Verlag Winfried-Werk GmbH, 1951).

5. Michael Berger, *Arbeiterbewegung und Demokratisierung: Die wirtschaftliche, politische und gesellschaftliche Gleichberechtigung des Arbeiters im Verständnis der katholischen Arbeiterbewegung im Wilhelminischen Deutschland zwischen 1890 und 1914* (Freiburg i. Br.: Dissertationsdruck Johannes Kraus, 1970); Klaus Saul, *Staat, Industrie, und Arbeiterbewegung im Kaiserreich* (Düsseldorf: Bertelsmann Universitätsverlag, 1974); Mary Nolan, *Social Democracy and Society: Working Class Radicalism in Düsseldorf* (New York: Cambridge University Press, 1982).

Thus Herbert Gottwald labels the *Gesamtverband* of Christian trade unions "an organ of the bourgeois *Reaktion*,"[6] while Dieter Fricke observes in Christian labor "a criticism of social abuses radical in appearance only."[7] Sometimes leftist authors do not even deign to mention Christian labor in their studies, thereby refusing to admit Christian workers to the ranks of "German labor."[8]

In the last five years, a truer picture of the Christian labor movement has begun to appear in the works of Klaus Tenfelde, Rudolf Brack, Hans Dieter Denk, and others.[9] But a history of the movement based on the rich archival materials available in Germany, and focused squarely on the movement, not its periphery or one of its parts, is still absent from the monographical literature on Imperial Germany. It is this gap which the present study will attempt to fill.

Perception of the nature and character of the Christian labor movement is impossible without an investigation of the medieval teachings of St. Thomas Aquinas on property rights. Aquinas believed, in short, that God wanted the benefits of property shared very widely in the community. A special "transitionary" chapter of the present study traces the troubled process whereby Aquinas's writings were rediscovered during the mid-nineteenth century, then translated into social and political actions by Catholic priests and eventually the Christian workers themselves. The far-reaching implications of Neo-Thomism, including the concept of codetermination, were never accepted by a majority of German theologians before 1918, but this did not stop Christian labor leaders from using these philosophies as the basis for their criticism of *laissez-faire* industrialism and rejection of existing economic institutions. This fervent desire for change made acceptance of these unions by employers, conservative prelates, and the state very difficult.

6. Herbert Gottwald, "Der Gesamtverband christlicher Gewerkschaften Deutschlands 1899–1933," in Dieter Fricke *et al.*, *Die bürgerlichen Parteien in Deutschland* (Berlin: Das europäische Buch, 1968), vol. 2, p. 114.
7. Dieter Fricke, "Bürgerliche Sozialreformer und die Zerspitterung der antisozialistischen Arbeiterorganisationen vor 1914." *Zeitschrift für Geschichtswissenschaft*, Heft 10 (1975), p. 1177.
8. Hedwig Wachenheim, *Die deutsche Arbeiterbewegung 1844–1914* (Opladen: Westdeutscher Verlag, 1967).
9. Klaus Tenfelde, *Sozialgeschichte der Bergarbeiterschaft an der Ruhr im 19. Jahrhundert* (Bonn: Verlag Neue Gesellschaft GmbH, 1977); Rudolf Brack, *Deutscher Episkopat und Gewerkschaftsstreit* (Cologne: Böhlau Verlag, 1976); Hans Dieter Denk, *Die christliche Arbeiterbewegung in Bayern bis zum Ersten Weltkrieg* (Mainz: Matthias Grünewald–Verlag, 1980). Other works based wholly on secondary sources are Karl Heinz Schürmann, *Zur Vorgeschichte der christlichen Gewerkschaften* (Freiburg: Verlag Herder, 1958); Albrecht Hartmann, "Zentrum und christliche Gewerkschaften 1900–1914," Ph.D. dissertation, Freie Universität Berlin, 1952; and Franz-Maria Censarek, "Die christlichen Gewerkschaften in Deutschland," Ph.D. dissertation, Karl-Franzens-Universität zu Graz, 1967. N.B.: Michael Schneider's work, *Die christlichen Gewerkschaften 1894–1933* (Bonn: Verlag Neue Gesellschaft, 1982), which appeared as the present book was going to press, certainly qualifies as a history of the movement, but the pre-1918 portions of the book are not based on significant archival research.

One begins to appreciate the radical potential of Aquinas's writings by examining some of the specific demands made in the name of Christian natural law. Thus in 1887 the Haid Committee, a caucus of Catholic social critics from Germany and Austria, recommended a living wage, a maximum work day, health, accident, old age, widows' and orphans', and unemployment insurance, and far-reaching labor codetermination in industry.

> With the prudent encouragement of the state, employees' unions can join factory owners to form associations of a higher authority. These associations would not merely protect the interests of workers and employers, but in accordance with the principles of the corporative system, would also strive for the regulation of production so crucial to the maintenance of stable labor relations.[10]

After the turn of the century, Fanny Imle, a social activist close to the People's Association in Mönchen-Gladbach, argued that the workers' struggle for the vote in earlier decades should now be extended to industry with "the demand for codetermination [*Mitbestimmung*]."[11]

The Christian trade unions continued the tradition. The movement placed heavy emphasis on the creation of workers' committees at the factory level and management-labor chambers for each branch of industry, especially the latter, which were to bring together representatives of labor and management to settle matters of mutual interest. Christian labor leaders wanted eventually to include problems like production, pricing, and marketing, heretofore the exclusive concern of management. After World War I, demands for codetermination were made more overtly. Profit-sharing, possession of stock in the company, and worker representatives on the board of directors were added to the pre-war program. Reflecting on the history of his movement in 1952, ex–Christian trade unionist Johann Becker referred to the essentially theological origins of this and other Christian labor demands:

> The realization of Catholic social teaching gives the workers everything that we ever fought for: humane working conditions, appropriate wages, family mutual funds, private housing and acquisition of additional private property, clear and far-reaching guarantees of a job, care in times of sickness, invalidity, old age and legitimate unemployment, and in the case of accidents, sufficient health care. The worker should not be merely an object, but also a subject in the firm. Therefore a right by law to share in decisions [*gesetzlich geregeltes Mitsprache-Recht*].[12]

10. *Protokolle über die Sitzungen der freien Vereinigung katholischen Sozialpolitiker gehalten zu Mainz vom 12. bis 15. August* 1887, p. 144, Sammlung Fechenbach, Hauptabt. 7, Abt. 15, BA Koblenz.

11. Fanny Imle, *Gewerbliche Friedensdokumente* (Jena: Verlag von Gustav Fischer, 1905), p. 1.

12. Johannes Becker to W. Ziebach, 1 November 1952, W. Ziebach Papers 2, KAB Haus Köln.

The ideology of the Christian labor movement was from the beginning quite radical, therefore, and it is inaccurate to maintain that Christian organizations either possessed no separate and distinct ideology,[13] had simply "plagiarized"[14] their ideas from the Social Democrats, or were merely anti-Socialist in nature.[15]

If, however, one leaves ideological and philosophical considerations aside and concentrates on the union tactics and practical politics of Christian labor, the movement truly left much to be desired. It never developed support programs that could compete with the free trade unions, its relationship with the church was never more than a quasi-independent one, and the Christians were often manipulated by the government into highly embarrassing positions. All too often Christian labor supped at the devil's table with a short spoon and it is not surprising, therefore, that the movement was so controversial. Thus the radical ideology and moderate, usually unsuccessful tactics of the Christian labor movement must *both* be placed in the historical balance if we are ever to achieve an objective measurement, devoid of a Socialist or anti-Socialist bias which tips the scales toward overly critical or unjustifiably positive conclusions.

* * * *

The Christian labor movement has also been labeled, erroneously, a purely Catholic and/or Center Party phenomenon.[16] To be sure, the intellectual foundations were Catholic, and for the first two decades of the Imperial period contacts with Protestants were rare. With the founding of the Christian miners' *Gewerkverein* in the 1890s, however, emphasis was placed on the nondenominational nature of Christian trade unionism. At a time when historians of the Wilhelmian era are becoming more and more interested in bourgeois interest-group politics,[17] an analysis of Christian labor's Evangelical wing and

13. Berger, *Arbeiterbewegung und Demokratisierung*, pp. 228–31, argues that Neo-Thomism was formulated by bourgeois Catholics to prevent the Christian workers from asserting independent labor demands and thereby undermining the harmony of the community; the ideology of Christian labor was the ideology of the Center Party. As this study will show, however, nothing could be farther from the truth.

14. Hermann Molkenbuhr, S.P.D. deputy before 1914, to his son Arthur, 15 November 1907, Molkenbuhr Papers II, no. 46, AdSoz Bonn.

15. Mary Nolan, *Social Democracy and Society*, pp. 44, 72, 148–49, 151–52. Also see Ralph René Mendershausen, "German Political Catholicism 1912–1919," Ph.D. dissertation, University of California, San Diego, 1972, pp. 17, 34, 36–37, 80, 144, 175–76, 315, 350.

16. Berger, *Arbeiterbewegung und Demokratisierung*; Johannes Horstmann, *Katholizismus und moderne Welt: Katholikentage, Wirtschaft, Wissenschaft—1848 bis 1914* (Munich: Verlag Ferdinand Schoningh, 1976). This holds true for many other works as well.

17. James C. Hunt, "The Bourgeois Middle in German Politics, 1871–1933: Recent Literature," *Central European History*, vol. 11, no. 1 (March 1978), pp. 83–106.

the opposition it encountered among Protestants in the National Liberal and Conservative parties is particularly significant. The *broader* significance of these contacts will be discussed later in this section.

The present study will not slight, however, the important relationship between Christian labor and the Center Party. Ignored for decades after the appearance of Karl Bachem's semi-official history in the late 1920s,[18] the Center Party of the Imperial period has turned into the site of a prodigious amount of historical digging over the last twenty years. Thomas Nipperdey, Ursula Mittmann, and Horstwalter Heitzer have excavated the party organization, Reichstag *Fraktion*, and the *Volksverein*, respectively,[19] while the spadework of John K. Zeender, Herbert Gottwald, Ronald J. Ross, and Wilfried Loth has produced histories or partial histories of the party under the empire.[20] Other researchers have burrowed deeper into the dig site to turn up finds on specific interest groups, regional interests, and personalities. Thus David Hendon, Ian Farr, and Robert Moeller have probed the relationship between the Center and Christian agrarian groups;[21] Jonathan Sperber, David Blackbourn, and Adalbert Knapp have concentrated on Catholics in Rhineland-Westphalia, Württemberg, and Bavaria, respectively;[22] while further excavation by Klaus Epstein, Margaret Anderson, and Winfried Becker has led to biographies of Matthias Erzberger, Ludwig Windthorst, and Georg Hertling.[23] The present work will add to the mound of Center Party research by clarifying the relationship between labor and the rest of the party.

18. Karl Bachem, *Vorgeschichte Geschichte und Politik der deutschen Zentrumspartei* (Cologne: Verlag J. P. Bachem, 1927–32), 9 vols.

19. Thomas Nipperdey, *Die Organisation der Parteien vor 1918* (Düsseldorf: Droste Verlag, 1961); Ursula Mittmann, *Fraktion und Partei: Ein Vergleich von Zentrum und Sozialdemokratie im Kaiserreich* (Düsseldorf: Droste Verlag, 1976); Horstwalter Heitzer, *Der Volksverein für das katholische Deutschland im Kaiserreich* (Mainz: Kommission für Zeitgeschichte, 1979).

20. John K. Zeender, *The German Center Party 1890–1906* (Philadelphia: American Philosophical Society, 1976); Herbert Gottwald, *Zentrum und Imperialismus*, Ph.D. dissertation, Jena University, 1966; Ronald J. Ross, *Beleaguered Tower: The Dilemma of Political Catholicism in Wilhelmine Germany* (Notre Dame, Indiana: University of Notre Dame Press, 1976); Wilfried Loth, *Katholiken im Kaiserreich* (Düsseldorf: Droste Verlag, 1984).

21. David W. Hendon, "The Center Party and Agrarian Interest in Germany 1890–1914," Ph.D. dissertation, Emory University, 1976; Ian Farr, "The Bavarian Peasants' League," in Richard Evans (ed.), *Society and Politics in Wilhelmine Germany* (London: Croom Helm, 1978); Robert Moeller,"German Peasants and Conservative Agrarian Politics 1914–1924: The Rhineland and Westphalia in War and in Inflation," manuscript under consideration for publication.

22. Jonathan Sperber, *Popular Catholicism in Nineteenth Century Germany* (Princeton, New Jersey: Princeton University Press, 1984); David Blackbourn, *Class Religion and Local Politics in Wilhelmine Germany: The Centre Party in Württemberg before 1914* (Wiesbaden: Franz Steiner Verlag GmbH, 1980); Adalbert Knapp, "Das Zentrum im Bayern 1893–1913," Ph.D. dissertation, University of Munich, 1973.

23. Klaus Epstein, *Matthais Erzberger and the Dilemma of German Democracy* (Princeton, New Jersey: Princeton University Press, 1959); Margaret Lavinia Anderson, *Windthorst: A Political*

Four different "models" of the Center have been recreated in the literature on the basis of what is known from the archival remains. Ronald Ross, whose blueprint is one of the most distinctive, depicts the party as essentially a religious lobby preoccupied with its attempt to overcome barriers of confessional inequality and anti-Catholic prejudice within German society. The denominational, sectarian branch of the party, which was based in the dioceses of Breslau and Trier, argued that these religious goals could be achieved most effectively by a rigid reliance on Catholic strength. The bonds of Catholicism would prevent class tensions from undermining the necessary unity of Catholics, and, so united, the Center could exact concessions from an unwilling, hostile government. This strategy was rejected by an influential group of middle-class Catholics headquartered in Cologne and Mönchen-Gladbach. This faction was convinced that the opposition of Protestant Germany would remain insurmountable until Catholics and Protestants began to cooperate on a wide range of secular issues, eroding four centuries of bias and prejudice in the process by teaching each side to work with and trust the other. Only by shedding the mantle of ultramontanism and becoming a less religious-oriented party could the Catholic cause advance in the long run. By eschewing the Social Democrats and Left Liberals for religious reasons, the western Centrists were forced into a partnership with more tolerant Protestants in the Conservative Party and on the right wing of the National Liberal Party. In the interests of eventually achieving religious parity, Cologne and Mönchen-Gladbach supported the authoritarian establishment and aided Conservative efforts to block badly needed financial and electoral reforms. The Christian trade unions were backed as well, argues Ross, because they avoided partisan political quarrels and allegedly were dedicated advocates of the status quo. The western strategy of cooperation eventually prevailed within the Center, and in this way the Catholics' preoccupation with parity became part of the larger German dilemma of illiberalism.

David Blackbourn constructs a model of the Center Party which is different in many important respects. He does not deny that the quest for equality with Protestants was a motive force for many Center actions, but he believes that the rural, small-town constituency of the party holds the key to an explanation of Center behavior. The Center's alliance with the Conservatives, significant as this was for the political history of Germany, was based on the mutual economic interests of the vast majority of voters behind the two parties. The

Biography (New York: Oxford University Press, 1981); Winfried Becker, *Georg Hertling 1843–1919*, vol. I: *Jugend und Selbstfindung zwischen Romantik und Kulturkampf* (Mainz: Matthias Grünewald–Verlag, 1981). Also see Ellen Lovell Evans, *The German Center Party 1870–1933: A Study in Political Catholicism* (Carbondale: Southern Illinois University Press, 1981).

pro-agrarian policies of the party accelerated the movement of Catholic workers into the Socialist camp and this trend, in turn, made it easier for the leadership to choose between Catholic labor and the other economic groups in the party. The Party's leaders resigned themselves to the inevitable, Blackbourn suggests, and for all intents and purposes abandoned the workers.

The Ross and Blackbourn models are very helpful, but neither is entirely accurate. The major defect in each case, in fact, is a false reconstruction of Christian labor's role in the party. Blackbourn's emphasis on the rural, parochial nature of the Center is quite useful in understanding intra-party relations from 1870 to 1900. However he exaggerates the importance of evidence from rural Württemberg after 1900, and in so doing, overlooks the party's fairly extensive efforts *to prevent* a secession of its Rhenish-Westphalian working-class voters during these years. Ross's work makes a great contribution to our knowledge of the mentality of Center leaders and the hostile political environment in which they operated, but his handling of the Christian-social wing of the party is also deficient. The *Volksverein* was not merely opportunistic in its promotion of Christian labor, for Mönchen-Gladbach was the intellectual and political center of Neo-Thomism after the late 1870s. Nor were Christian trade unionists as inactive and submissive as Ross would have us believe. The Christian unions and their political associates in the *Volksverein* should be viewed as an active intra-party lobby for social reform, and knowledge of this relationship sheds a great deal of light on Center affairs.

The third distinctive model of the party, that of Ursula Mittmann, is superior to the others primarily because it is complex enough to explain the rather complicated grouping of interests represented in the Center. The pressure from overbearing church leaders, the sincere desire for parity, the strong agrarian constituency, and the persistent, though not always strenuous, prodding from Mönchen-Gladbach for social reform are all dealt with in their turn. But, once again, it is Christian labor which does not receive its due. Mittmann argues that the Christian trade unions were largely unpolitical and thus caused little intra-party tension. As the following chapters make quite clear, this was hardly the case.

The final construct, that of Wilfried Loth, is the most ambitious of all. Loth believes that the Center should be seen as essentially four parties in one—the Catholic aristocracy, bourgeoisie, "populist" *Mittelstand*, and workers. The various alliances and ruptures between these groups were the motive force behind the Center's democratization and evolution toward the Weimar coalition. The twenty-year reign of the aristocracy ended in the 1890s when the bourgeoisie, backed by the *Mittelstand* and yet-unmobilized workers, captured party control. The aristocracy briefly resumed its position at the helm in 1907 after bourgeois leadership had been eroded by the challenges of the allied populists and workers. With the collapse of this alliance due to disputes over trade unionism (*Gewerkschaftsstreit*), the bourgeoisie took over again, and, supported by the aristocracy and populists, frustrated the *political* demands of the now isolated working classes. Only the pressures of the war forced these groups to cooperate, albeit grudgingly, with Catholic workers. The emergence of the Center as a bourgeois party, argues Loth, paralleled and was an essential part of the parliamentarization of the empire.

Although it is an impressive scholarly accomplishment, Loth's reconstruction of the Center is flawed in many important respects. The so-called Catholic bourgeoisie, far from being monolithic, was itself divided into numerous factions. And it was with one of these, the Rhenish Christian-social wing of the bourgeoisie, not the *Mittelstand*, that the Catholic workers allied themselves after 1900. This was part of an ambitious political campaign, largely overlooked and otherwise misinterpreted by Loth, to build a broad nondenominational social reform coalition in the Reichstag. The Conservatives and National Liberals, it was hoped, would embrace the concept of a parliamentary *Block* with the Center to further "Christian" labor candidates and labor legislation. The impetus from this direction added momentum to the forces which Ross and Blackbourn have mentioned in attempting to explain the prevailing *rightist* alignment of the Center before 1918, for Christian labor's nondenominationalism and fervent desire for cooperation across confessional lines in pursuit of social reform took Mönchen-Gladbach, and to a great extent the Center Party, in tow during the last two decades of the Imperial period. The party also illustrated a continued willingness to accommodate the *social* reform demands of Christian labor during these years. These facts shed an adverse light on Loth's depiction of an isolated, impotent labor wing of the Center from 1907 to 1917.

The present study, therefore, will clarify many previously misunderstood or ignored Center Party developments. More specifically, it will examine the socio-political disagreements surrounding the founding of the party in 1870/71, the class tensions in the Catholic community during the *Kulturkampf*, the gradual and reluctant acceptance of Christian labor by 1900, the disputes over tariff, financial, social and electoral reform in the late Wilhelmine years, and the whole issue of interconfessionalism or modernism in the Catholic camp, especially from 1903 through the First World War.

This latter topic is particularly important. The Christian trade unions and their bourgeois allies were active at the interface of the various parties. Coalition-building, in short, was the Christian strategy, and every effort was made to bridge the class, religious, and particularistic gaps that separated the political factions of the empire. Christian labor was not entirely unsuccessful in building its *Block*, but the tremendous difficulties and frustrations that were encountered offer a unique glimpse of the nation's division-ridden party system—divisions which certainly militated against the process of parliamentarization that Loth and others claim to have discovered in pre-war Germany. It was not until after World War II, in fact, that many Germans were ready for larger, broader-based political groupings. Nor was it a coincidence that Christian labor leaders like Adam Stegerwald and Jakob Kaiser were very influential in effecting these changes after 1945. For both were veterans of decades of nondenominational politics and represented an interconfessional tradition which in the long run could not be contained within the narrow confines of the political parties of Imperial and Weimar Germany. The CDU/CSU, one of only two major parties occupying the political scene in West Germany today, was the eventual result.

* * * *

Beyond clarifying the nature and character of the Christian labor movement and analyzing its relationship with the bourgeois parties, especially the Center, this study addresses the crucial question of continuity and discontinuity in recent German history. The thesis which emerges here is, first, that ruling church, state, and social elites were too rigid and authoritarian in their outlook toward social and political change before 1918 to agree to meaningful institutional reform. Second, and equally important, the established forces of the Second Reich were quite successful in blocking groups of the left and the right from undermining the establishment's base of power. Some historians, admittedly, will find little unique in this thesis. That the constitutional structure of Imperial Germany was "frozen,"[24] permitting no evolution either to more democratic or to modern totalitarian forms until the Great War shattered these institutions and propelled Germany into a more turbulent and tragic era, will come as no surprise. But it is becoming increasingly common among historians of Imperial Germany, whether they accept or reject the existence of strong links between the Germany of William II and that of Adolf Hitler, to conclude that the Bismarckian edifice was in an advanced state of deterioration by 1914. Before proceeding to exposit in more detail the position taken by the present work and how it fits into what has become one of the most interesting and controversial scholarly debates in recent decades, it will be necessary to describe the broad outlines of those schools of thought wholly or partially objectionable to this author.

According to one viewpoint, the constitutional monarchy established by the Iron Chancellor in 1871 evolved steadily toward parliamentarism under William II. Associated with historians like Fritz Hartung and Werner Frauendienst in the 1950s, this argument received added credence in the following decade from the writings of Eberhard Pikart, E. R. Huber, Udo Bermbach,

24. Epstein, *Matthias Erzberger*, p. 86.

and Dieter Grosser. More recently, Beverly Heckart, Geoff Eley, Thomas Nipperdey, Wilfried Loth, and especially Manfred Rauh have picked up this historiographical cudgel.[25] These authors believe the federal structure of the Reich was weakening before the onslaught of Imperial institutions like the Reich Chancellery, the Imperial ministries (Navy, Finance, etc.), and above all the Reichstag. The Bundesrat allegedly lost an increasing number of political battles with the chancellor, who was in turn pressed forward by the Imperial Parliament on a wide range of issues from democratic financial reform to ministerial responsibility. By 1914 even the sacrosanct rights of the Prussian Army were under intense attack by democratic elements in the Reichstag. The political parties, furthermore, were beginning to expand their popular bases, cooperate more consistently with neighboring parties, moderate religious and ideological differences, and generally adopt procedures conducive to party rule. By 1914 a half-parliamentary regime had been reached, and if the war had not interrupted this healthy development, democratic institutions would eventually have taken complete hold. The strains of war, the post-war political and economic dislocation, the confusion and suffering of the Depression, and the evil genius of Hitler altered all this and paved the way for the tragic events of the 1930s and 1940s. National Socialism had very shallow roots in German society, in other words, and should be interpreted as a deviation from historical patterns.[26]

Fritz Fischer's controversial work, *Germany's Aims in the First World War*, and a sequel, *War of Illusions*, were the seeds of a new school of historical interpretation largely antithetical to that described above.[27] Fischer argued that the leaders of the German Empire had launched the First World War in a

25. Fritz Hartung, *Deutsche Verfassungsgeschichte* (Stuttgart: K. F. Koehler Verlag, 1950); Werner Frauendienst, "Demokratisierung des deutschen Konstitutionalismus in der Zeit Wilhelms II," *Zeitschrift für die gesamte Staatswissenschaft,* vol. 113 (1957), pp. 721–46; Eberhard Pikart, "Die Rolle der Parteien im deutschen konstitutionellen System vor 1914," *Zeitschrift für Politik*, n.f., vol. 9 (1962), pp. 12–32; Udo Bermbach, *Vorformen parlamentarischer Kabinettsbildung in Deutschland* (Cologne: Westdeutscher Verlag, 1967); Ernst Rudolf Huber, *Deutsche Verfassungsgeschichte seit 1789* (Stuttgart: W. Kohlhammer-Verlag, 1969), vol. 4, pp. 318, 346–47, 518–20; Dieter Grosser, *Vom monarchischen Konstitutionalismus zur parlamentarischen Demokratie* (The Hague: Martinus Nijhoff, 1970); Manfred Rauh, *Föderalismus und Parlamentarismus im Wilhelminischen Reich* (Düsseldorf: Droste Verlag, 1973); Beverly Heckart, *From Bassermann to Bebel* (New Haven: Yale University Press, 1974); Manfred Rauh, *Die Parlamentarisierung des Deutschen Reiches* (Düsseldorf: Droste Verlag, 1977); Geoff Eley, *Reshaping the German Right* (New Haven: Yale University Press, 1980); Thomas Nipperdey, "Organisierter Kapitalismus, Verbände und die Krise des Kaiserreiches," *Geschichte und Gesellschaft,* vol. 5 (1979), pp. 418–33; Loth, *Katholiken im Kaiserreich*.

26. See especially Gerhard Ritter's article in Maurice Beaumont, John Fried, and Edmond Vermeil (eds.), *The Third Reich* (New York: Praeger, 1955).

27. Fritz Fischer, *Griff nach der Weltmacht* (Düsseldorf: Droste Verlag, 1961); *idem, Krieg der Illusionen* (Düsseldorf: Droste Verlag, 1969).

daring gamble to establish European hegemony. The implications for the historiography of World War I were radical enough, but the real controversy centered around the obvious parallels to Germany's aggressive acts of World War II, for it now appeared that the genesis of Hitlerian foreign policy was more deeply embedded in time than previous historians had been willing to admit. And it did not take long, as British historian Richard Evans explains, before a younger generation of West German historians discovered even more-far-reaching implications in Fischer's works.

> If there really were some similarities between Hitler's foreign policy and that of Wilhelm II, then might there not also be some similarities in the *internal* political structure of Germany under Hitler and under the last Kaiser? Indeed could not some of the longer-term origins of the Third Reich—origins whose existence the older generation of historians had largely denied, attributing the rise of Nazism solely to the demonic genius of Hitler—be precisely in the developments that took place in Wilhelmine or even Bismarckian Germany? Furthermore, if Germany really did launch the First World War, then must there not have been powerful internal social and economic influences prompting her to do so—influences more profound than the mere incompetence of her diplomacy or the blinkered technical rigidity of her military men?[28]

By 1975, a fully articulated antithesis to the "evolution-to-parliamentarism" thesis described in the preceding paragraph had emerged. The leadership of this younger group reads today like a partial "Who's Who" of prominent Wilhelmine historians: Hans Ulrich Wehler, Volker Berghahn, Dieter Groh, Hans Jürgen Puhle, Wolfgang Mommsen, Dirk Stegmann, Peter-Christian Witt, and Klaus Saul.[29] The latter three, not coincidentally, had done their doctoral work under Fischer.

28. Richard J. Evans, "Wilhelm II's Germany and the Historians," in Evans, *Society and Politics*, pp. 10–11.

29. Hans Ulrich Wehler, *Das deutsche Kaiserreich 1871–1918* (Göttingen: Vanderhoeck and Ruprecht, 1975); Volker Berghahn, *Der Tirpitz Plan* (Düsseldorf: Droste Verlag, 1971); Dieter Groh, *Negative Integration und revolutionärer Attentismus* (Frankfurt: Verlag Ullstein GmbH, 1974); Hans Jürgen Puhle, *Agrarische Interessenpolitik und preussischer Konservatismus im Wilhelminischen Reich (1893–1914)* (Hanover: Verlag für Literature und Zeitgeschehen, 1967); *idem*, "Parlament, Parteien und Interessenverbände 1890–1914," in Michael Stürmer (ed.), *Das kaiserliche Deutschland* (Düsseldorf: Droste Verlag, 1970), pp. 340–77; *idem*, *Von der Agarkrise zum Präfaschismus* (Wiesbaden: F. Steiner, 1972); Wolfgang Mommsen, "Die latente Krise des Deutschen Reiches 1909–1914," in Otto Brandt, Oskar Meyer, and Leo Just (eds.), *Handbuch der deutschen Geschichte* (Frankfurt a. M.: Akademische Verlagsgesellschaft Athenaion, 1973), vol. 4, part 2; Dirk Stegmann, *Die Erben Bismarcks* (Cologne: Kiepenheuer und Witsch, 1970); Peter-Christian Witt, *Die Finanzpolitik des deutschen Reiches von 1903 bis 1913* (Lübeck: Matthiesen, 1970); Klaus Saul, *Staat, Industrie, und Arbeiterbewegung im Kaiserreich* (Düsseldorf: Bertelsmann Universitätsverlag, 1973).

The original power structure of the Reich began to disintegrate, argue Wehler *et al.*, shortly after Bismarck's dismissal. With neither the young Kaiser nor any of his chancellors able to control the country as effectively as the nation's first chancellor, an "authoritarian polycracy" comprised of intra- and extra-governmental elites emerged to administer the bastion of privilege. The repressive side of Bismarck's policies was not completely abandoned, witness the maintenance of rigid laws of assembly, strict censorship, and an intimidating system of class justice, but in the absence of any willingness to risk force against the increasingly restive democratic elements in the land, a more subtle system of manipulation was employed to mobilize non-democratic, non-Socialist elements behind the status quo. Thus aristocratic landowners in the Farmers' League (*Bund der Landwirte*) played on the anti-Semitic prejudices of small farmers to attract mass support for an organization which essentially represented the interests of the eastern nobility, while heavy industrialists enticed a growing number of middle-aged workers into innocuous, yet well-provided-for, company unions. State-run schools and universities served to indoctrinate the masses to traditional monarchical values, and the churches, too, preached the divinely ordained nature of the terrestrial order. The political parties were quieted with occasional economic concessions, while the middle classes in general were encouraged to adopt feudal attitudes through dueling societies, fraternities, and reserve army units. The ultimate method of manipulation was a militaristic social imperialism. Veterans' associations, colonial societies, navy clubs, and Pan-German organizations were used to whip up national enthusiasm and distract society from its growing preoccupation with issues of reform. Even the Social Democrats, the most energetic advocates of progress toward equality, were tamed somewhat by the repressive, intimidating society surrounding them and the diversions their subculture offered.

Considering the rapid pace of industrialization and social change in Imperial Germany, these methods succeeded amazingly well in perpetuating the old power structure. But not without a price. In fact, the growing social and political disparities unleashed "forces of parliamentarization and democratization"[30] which could not be completely dammed. Some writers in the so-called critical school, though they are certainly in a minority, go so far as to argue that there was actually an institutional shift of power underway between the old order and the Reichstag.[31] All agree, however, that as domestic crises became increasingly difficult to solve through intimidation and manipulation,

30. Wehler, *Das deutsche Kaiserreich*, p. 177.
31. Mommsen, "Latente Krise," in Brandt et al., *Handbuch*, vol. 4, part 2; Puhle, "Parlament, Parteien und Interessenverbände," in Stürmer, *Kaiserliche Deutschland*.

the old regime was given *added* incentive to launch a European war. Had not Bismarck's wars of the 1860s rallied the nation and destroyed the momentum of the liberals and progressives? Germany fled from its domestic problems into the trenches of the Great War.

The collapse of the Second Reich in 1918 cannot be interpreted, therefore, as the result of exogenous, war-related factors which interrupted the pattern of pre-war development. The nature of the regime, the war, and the fall of the empire were all inextricably linked. What is more, the problematic historical role of pre-war elite groups did not end with the death of the institutions these elites had so long sought to defend. Manipulation of the masses, anti-Socialist *Sammlung*, and anti-democratic machinations continued throughout the 1920s and were partly responsible for the Nazis' rise to power. The Hitler government was eventually able to outwit, outmaneuver, and dominate the aristocrats, generals, and industrialists, but National Socialist rule itself was characterized by many of the same manipulative techniques—and succeeded where others had failed. The case for continuity in recent German history, concludes Wehler, could not be stronger:

> The fatal success of the imperial power elites, aided by older historical traditions and new experiences, continued to make itself felt until 1945, indeed in some areas beyond: in the susceptibility to authoritarian politics; the hostility to democracy in education and party politics; the influence of pre-industrial leadership groups, norms and ideals; the perseverance of the German ideology of the state; the mystique of the bureaucracy; the superimposition of corporatist structures and class tensions; the manipulation of political Anti-Semitism—so begins a long catalogue of historical burdens. Knowledge of the history of the German Empire from 1871 to 1918 remains, therefore, an indispensable prerequisite for an understanding of German history in the last fifty years.[32]

So much, then, for what one American historian has termed "the new orthodoxy"[33] in German historiography.

Many of the authors discussed thus far, it seems to this writer, err jointly in one important respect. That Imperial Germany's authoritarian institutions were eroding in the current of democratization and parliamentarization is a point made on both sides of the debate. There can be no doubt that radical popular pressure for reform was beginning to grow in Germany, particularly on the eve of the war, but this is not to say that a process of parliamentarization was actually underway. Indeed this argument simply does not stand the test of close historical scrutiny. One must ask, first of all, whether the bourgeois

32. Wehler, *Das deutsche Kaiserreich*, pp. 238–39.
33. James Sheehan, *Journal of Modern History*, no. 3 (September 1976), p. 567.

parties of the empire actually desired parliamentarization. It is not enough to cite isolated pro-reform statements by Ernst Bassermann or Matthias Erzberger, for evidence of this sort pales in significance when the record of these parties' opposition to a liberalization of the Prussian suffrage is considered. Although it has been stated before, it bears repeating that most bourgeois politicians feared Socialist control more than they desired political liberalization. Secondly, it is doubtful that the political parties had developed the degree of compatibility and coalition-mindedness that would have been required to force parliamentarization on an unwilling government. As explained earlier, an examination of Christian labor's political campaigns brings the researcher very close to inter-party relations, and the final impression is that the potential for significant cooperation among the Reich's feuding parties was very slight. Finally, it is distorting to view the ruling establishment of the empire as if it were in a process of disintegration, for there were numerous revealing signs of institutional resilience in the decade before World War I. Thus the ruling elites were no more susceptible to Socialist demonstrations over the Prussian suffrage issue in 1910 than they were to criticism over the impact of high tariffs on meat prices in 1912. Neither the right of interpellation won by the Reichstag in 1913 nor two no-confidence votes that year over Zabern and the expropriation of Polish lands had much effect on a remote Imperial government. All discussion of the question of ministerial responsibility to the Reichstag was rigidly rejected, while the army, despite the increasing curiosity of parliament, remained surrounded by a bastion of constitutional privilege. It is perhaps all too often forgotten by those who argue that German liberals had achieved a "half-parliamentary" system by 1913/14 that the empire had possessed such a system from the beginning. Hostile Reichstags, budget battles, and parliamentary cow trading were nothing new to Germany on the eve; indeed the Iron Chancellor had dealt with many of the same problems. To argue that Germany had *progressed* half way to parliamentarism by 1913/14 is thus self-defeating, for it merely confirms the fact that precious little had changed.

The present study directs its attention to other telltale indications of a persistent old regime. The frustrating experiences of Christian labor, from the difficulties of founding a movement in the first years of the Reich until the final disappointments of the war period, are a good yardstick for measuring the extent to which the imperial establishment was able and willing to reform itself. Christian labor did not suffer from the stigma of atheism and revolutionary radicalism that plagued Socialist reform efforts, and after the turn of the century the emergence of an Evangelical contingent within the Christian trade unions allayed fears of ultramontanist influence and lent an additional aura of respectability to the movement. Christian labor leaders could also use the existence of a stronger Socialist organization to their own advantage by expressing the fear that refusal to pursue social reform would only weaken the patriotic workers and strengthen the enemies of the state. But all of Christian labor's well-designed political initiatives failed. Despite the fact that the Reichstag, which had resisted Christian labor for decades, finally accepted bills favoring corporative rights for trade unions, collective bargaining, co-determinational management-labor chambers, and the eight-hour day, these bills faltered because the Bundesrat unceremoniously refused to budge on the issue of radical social reforms. Most Reich and Prussian officials opposed these bills because it was assumed that greater freedoms for labor would weaken the state in its fight against an allegedly revolutionary S.P.D. Thus the line was consistently drawn at this point, quite unlike the case of progressive financial bills which occasionally were accepted if the monies were earmarked for military expenditure (e.g., 1913). The Bundesrat was hardly a good example, therefore, of institutional entropy before 1914. On the contrary, this and other signs of institutional life suggest that the degree of pressure from below in Germany was not great *in relation to the ability to resist it from above*.

If so, we must begin to reassess the whole phenomenon of manipulative rule, for it would appear that the veritable arsenal of control techniques described by the "critical school" was employed more successfully than most of these authors believe. One of the major problems with this body of thought, in fact, has been a preoccupation with developments at the top to the exclusion of local, grass-roots affairs, thereby preventing any examination of the effects wrought by these manipulative techniques on the masses or on mass organizations. Influenced on the one side by the preoccupation of many sociologists and political scientists with the theoretical aspects of rule by elites, and on the other side, it would seem, by untested Marxist assumptions about the inevitability of the rising tide, it is understandable that Wehler, Berghahn, and the others would not choose to focus their attention downwards. The current work seeks to redress this imbalance somewhat by analyzing the manipulative techniques used on the Christian labor movement from 1870 to 1918. These techniques were sometimes crude, witness the intimidating effect of the anti-Socialist laws on the untargeted Christian associations in 1878; or quite subtle, witness business/governmental efforts to redraft the statutes of the Christian miners' union in 1894, church/governmental intervention in the debate over unifying the labor movement in 1900/1901, and subsequent efforts to play the various union organizations off one another. But in all cases one observes a definite measure of success. Parallel studies are now needed to examine the full extent of manipulation on the Hirsch-Duncker unions, the Polish organizations, and the much-excavated free trade unions, particularly during World War I. The unorganized proletariat will be more difficult, though no less important, to analyze.

Shifting focus downward has the added advantage of refining our knowledge about the social and political climate in which manipulation occurred. A number of British historians, in fact, have done some very significant work in this area during the past few years. A collection of essays edited and introduced by Richard Evans in 1976 argues that the ruling establishment did not manipulate the nation as if it were a puppet theater, "with Junkers and industrialists pulling the strings, and middle and lower classes dancing jerkily across the stage of history."[34] Rather, the patricians were often passive observers at first, pressed strenuously from below by independent movements of both left *and* right. Mobilization of the non-Socialist elements of German society was not initiated from above; on the contrary, ruling elites were forced to gain control of movements already underway.

Two recent monographs by David Blackbourn and Geoff Eley make additional contributions to the debate. "Demagogic manipulation of popular sentiment," observes Blackbourn, "was by no means the exclusive preserve of the government, the traditional elite and their agencies. It had a place in the repertoire of a much wider range of political leaders."[35] He demonstrates this, as noted earlier, by analyzing Center Party politics in rural Württemberg. Hard-pressed by outspoken farmers and artisans, the middle-class party leadership in Stuttgart was forced to resort to a combination of *quid pro quo* concessions and religious appeals to maintain control. Eley concentrates on the so-called national or patriotic associations (*nationale Verbände*), arguing that these groups (Navy League, Pan-German League, etc.), although founded quite independently of the government and often opposed to the moderation of men like Bethmann Hollweg, were nevertheless led by middle-class scholars, lower-level bureaucrats, and professional organizers who managed fairly successfully to mobilize the petite bourgeoisie for radical nationalistic goals. "Wilhelmine politics," Eley elaborates, "was in general increasingly dominated by men of this type—Hahn in the Agrarian League, Erzberger in the Center, and Stresemann in the regenerate National Liberals."[36]

The present work will build on the spadework of Evans, Blackbourn, and Eley. It is true that Christian labor had to contend with the machinations of the traditional elites, but "a wider range of leaders" including various party politicians and clergymen at the local and national levels also sought to mold the non-Socialist proletariat to their own designs. These efforts, like those of the government, were often in response to social and political initiatives waged by the Christian workers themselves. And, although Christian labor eventually asserted its independence in the late 1890s and drifted in a radical

34. Evans, "Wilhelm II's Germany and the Historians," in Evans, *Society and Politics*, p. 23.
35. Blackbourn, *Class Religion and Local Politics*, p. 240.
36. Eley, *Reshaping the German Right*, p. 358.

direction after 1912, the long pattern of intervention "from above" was not without effect. Thus a few far-reaching concessions and an appeal to Catholicism by the Center Party in late 1918 preserved the *Zentrumsturm* and foiled the plans of Adam Stegerwald, general secretary of the Christian trade unions, who had ambitious designs for a new party which would bridge class and confession and finally implement the political goals of the movement. It was not the first time that Christian labor had been unable to prevail against established forces which were solidly entrenched at all levels of German society.

This thesis of institutional resilience and persistence does not stand in contradiction to the idea of continuity in recent German history. Thus it is quite probable that Germany's nervous leaders exaggerated the degree of leftward institutional slippage and fled in panic to the presumed salvation of a short European war. The "inner spring" of the nation's general crisis, writes Arno Mayer, "was the overreaction of old elites to overperceived dangers to their overprivileged positions. In their siege mentality," he continues, "they exaggerated the pace of capitalist modernization, the revolt of the plebs, the frailty of the state apparatus, and the breakaway of the industrial and professional bourgeoisie."[37] The war which these besieged groups triggered in turn shattered the Reich and forced the nation's divided, inexperienced political parties into power. The vast gulf which separated the social classes of Imperial Germany was extended even more in the process, thereby contributing to social conditions which demagogues found easy to exploit in the 1920s and 1930s.

The continuity argument, however, should not be taken too far.[38] For the idea that the systematic barbarity of National Socialist rule was somehow an outgrowth of pre-war society is not credible. Germany's leaders may have risked a war in August 1914, but they did so with far more naiveté concerning the length and nature of war in the technological age than their counterparts of 1939. Various manipulative techniques were employed by patrician and "auxiliary" elites before the Great War, but there was a world of difference between these policies and approaches and the sinister, cynical brutality of the fascists. The fact that pre-war society ostracized a young Adolf Hitler and almost completely ignored the anti-Semitical political parties in Germany goes a long way toward illustrating the relative gentility of this earlier period. Hitler's movement grew out of the trenches on the western front, the seem-

37. Arno Mayer, *The Persistence of the Old Regime* (New York: Pantheon Books, 1981), p. 304.
38. Although the present writer agrees on this point with David Blackbourn and Geoff Eley, *Mythen deutscher Geschichtsschreibung: Die gescheiterte bürgerliche Revolution* (Frankfurt am Main, 1980), he wishes to dissociate himself from their views on the gradual liberalization of the Reich.

ingly inexplicable defeat, the exacerbation of social divisions, and the destruction of the economic fabric of the country. If it is true, as Gottfried Leibniz has written, that the present is pregnant with the future, then the Nazi child should not be laid at the doorstep of antebellum Germany. The terrible infant was conceived at a later date.

* * * *

In summary, this study possesses three plateaus or levels of investigation: an analysis of the authoritarian, persistent nature of the ruling establishment; an analysis of Christian labor's relationship with the bourgeois parties, especially the Center Party; and an analysis of the nature and character of Christian labor itself. It is to this last topic, and in particular to the radical ideological origins of the movement, that we now turn.

Transition: Kolping, Ketteler, and the Origins of Christian Social Thought and Action

No social group in Germany was economically more hard pressed in the second third of the nineteenth century than the old estate of artisans and handicraftsmen.[1] Already threatened by industrial competition from abroad, their situation was made all the worse by the coming of commercial freedom and the attendant onslaught of industry and mechanization at home. Unable to compete without effective tariff or guild protection, handicraftsmen were forced to reduce wages, lay off journeymen, or else join the landless peasants and unemployed journeymen in seeking factory employment. Journeymen in turn found it increasingly difficult to establish their own shops and were consequently locked into a marginal existence of low pay and periodic unemployment. Some sought an outlet in factory employment, while others began to drink, engage in petty crime, or turn against their masters. Strikes and boycotts increased tensions in the workshop, and even more alarming to conservative observers, the young workers began forming secret societies to further "republican" aims. The normally inactive Diet of the German Confederation thought the situation serious enough in 1840 to warrant a series of stern measures outlawing the societies and restricting journeymen in their trade-union-like actions against masters.[2] The latter's frustration with the ad-

1. The classic work on the subject remains Gustav Schmoller's *Zur Geschichte des deutschen Kleingewerbe im 19. Jahrhundert* (Halle: Verlag der Buchhandlung des Waisenhauses, 1870). See also: Heinrich Bechtel, *Wirtschafts- und Sozialgeschichte Deutschlands* (Munich: Verlag Georg D. W. Gallweg, 1967), pp. 337–43.
2. Albert Franz, *Der soziale Katholizismus in Deutschland bis zum Tode Kettelers* (München-Gladbach: Volksvereinsverlag GmbH, 1914), p. 113.

vance of industry and technology and the growing alienation of journeymen faced with bleak prospects at every turn played a significant role in the revolutionary disturbances which shook Germany in 1848–49. A boon to some, industrialism brought only ruin, anger, and despair to many artisans.

Those few Catholics of conservative persuasion who were able to transcend the complacent indifference which most of the upper classes felt for labor questions reacted to this systematic unraveling of the old social and economic order by advocating a return to the estate or corporate institutions which in their eyes had created social stability and harmony in centuries past.[3] To some extent this was a pragmatic retaliation against the forces of social and political modernity which were undermining the position of Catholic noblemen. But there was also a great deal of concern for the lower classes here. The great mass of the people in medieval times had been protected from insecurities and misfortunes, it was felt, by the benevolence of the landlord, the material benefits of the guild, the charity of the church, and the selflessness and magnanimity of the family and local community. There now arose in place of this organic, natural society an artificial commercial system which put the individual at the mercy of capricious market forces, reducing once-proud masters, journeymen, and small landed proprietors to a state of industrial servitude. Among the minority of concerned Catholics, sensitivity to these problems was deepened by the rebirth of interest in the writings of St. Thomas Aquinas which was underway at mid-century.[4] Due to the potentially radical implications of Neo-Thomism and its significance for the history of the Christian labor movement, the social teachings of this medieval scholar should be analyzed in some detail at this point.

St. Thomas and his followers, it must be emphasized initially, were not opposed to the institution of private property.[5] On the contrary, they felt that it was necessary and objected to collective ownership as a system of property holding which was not in conformity with human nature.

> Every man is more careful to procure for himself alone rather than for that which is common to many or all since each one would shirk the labor and leave to another that which concerns the community. Human affairs are also conducted in more orderly fashion if each man is charged with taking care of

3. This paragraph is based on Franz Josef Stegmann, "Geschichte der sozialen Ideen im deutschen Katholizismus," in Helga Grebing (ed.), *Geschichte der sozialen Ideen in Deutschland* (Munich-Vienna: Guenter Olzog Verlag, 1969), pp. 337–38, 361–62; Edgar Alexander, "Church and Society in Germany," in Joseph N. Moody (ed.), *Catholic Social and Political Movements* (New York: Arts, Inc., 1953), pp. 377–81; and Ralph H. Bowen, *German Theories of the Corporative State* (New York: McGraw-Hill, 1947), pp. 31–38.

4. For Catholic social ideas in general, the reader should consult Wilhelm Schwer, *Katholische Gesellschaftslehre* (Paderborn: Ferdinand Schöningh, 1938).

5. For the views of St. Thomas, see the *New Catholic Encyclopedia*, vol. 11, pp. 850–52.

> some particular thing himself, whereas there would be confusion if everyone had to look after one thing forever. A more peaceful state is assured to man, moreover, if each one is contented with his own. Hence it is to be observed that quarrels arise more frequently where there is no division of things possessed.[6]

The institution of private property was therefore a natural order of things which reflected the wisdom of God. Collective ownership was unworkable and could only result in chaos. Aquinas was no advocate, however, of *complete and unattenuated* private property rights. He believed that every man had a God-given right to share the fruits of the land. Only through ownership of or access to material things would he be able to care for his family, develop his potentialities, and achieve his destiny. It followed from this that no individual or social class could abuse or monopolize the right of property ownership at the expense of others in the community. Thus the social function of property limited not only the use of property, but the right of property itself. Such an approach was obviously not shared by most modern entrepreneurs.

Social harmony and responsibility were thus the hallmarks of an ideal "Thomistic" society. These virtues would be perpetuated by autonomous social corporations which would be the foundation of the social structure. Noblemen and peasants, master and apprentice, and the church would possess their own self-regulatory bodies. There would be no monopoly of either the ownership or use of property, and disharmony between the estates (*Stände*) of society would be no more possible than conflict between the limbs of the human organism. Writing at a time when social relationships such as these were to some extent reality, not a romantic dream, St. Thomas felt that the religio-corporate order was based on "natural laws" determined by God. To some devout Catholics of the mid-nineteenth century, therefore, the accumulation of capital by a relatively small number of entrepreneurs and the accompanying social misery of early industrialization were signs of spiritual decay.

The Catholic romanticist Adam Heinrich Müller was probably the first to respond to industrialization in this way. Writing in the 1820s, he recommended that craftsmen be allowed to enjoy their old corporate honors and that industry be "reduced to its proper sphere and brought into balance with the other estates."[7] The Bavarian engineer-turned-philosopher Franz von Baader also saw the root cause of social ills in the dissolution of those social and economic ties which had existed under the religio-corporate system. In the 1830s he advocated the reimplementation of guild privileges and the creation of special "chambers of labor" where priests would represent the interests of

6. Quoted in *ibid.*, p. 850.
7. Quoted in Bowen, *Corporative State*, p. 37.

the downtrodden workers before the state.[8] The circle of Catholic corporatists had grown by the late 1840s and 1850s. The Bavarian publicist Joseph Jörg, editor of the monthly *Historisch-politische Blätter*, felt that society had been "de-Christianized" by liberalism and, as Baader before him, argued for the cooptation of the proletariat into a corporate state (*Ständestaat*) more in keeping with the tenets of Christian faith.[9] Similar views were represented by Dr. Christoph Moufang, editor of *Der Katholik* and head of the large Catholic seminary in Mainz.

These two journals soon gathered about them a moderate following of aristocrats and clergymen in Bavaria, Baden, and the Rhineland. But it was the Catholic nobility of Westphalia which responded most enthusiastically to the estatist program. Led by Wilderich von Ketteler, Prussian Landtag deputy from Thüle, they rejected liberal constitutionalism in Prussia and longed for a return to the medieval concept of rule by monarch, church, and *Stände*, each with its own privileges and prerogatives.[10] The new corporate order, it seemed to them, could be built on the foundations of the conservative provincial diets which had arisen in Prussia in the 1820s. Opposed by the brothers Peter and August Reichensperger, who led the predominant "liberal Catholic" wing of the Catholic *Fraktion* in the Prussian diet, Ketteler and his followers bolted the party in 1853 and returned to their estates. At the end of the decade, corporatism remained what it had been since the 1820s—a topic for journal articles and salon discussions.

The call for a corporate reorganization of state and society would be heard recurringly throughout the century and was a concept never to lose completely its attraction for Catholic conservatives. But many at mid-century who took for granted the superiority of estatist political institutions were content to limit their activity to less ambitious reform efforts designed to bolster the moral, social, or legal positions of the individual estates. These endeavors were seen not only as prerequisites for the more far-reaching plans of Müller, Baader, and the Westphalians, but also as more immediate solutions to the mounting problems facing artisans, factory workers, uprooted peasants, and others. The attempt made in Switzerland and southern Germany to form "Christian factories" where work was performed in church and interrupted by frequent prayer sessions was characteristic of these efforts.[11] In Westphalia, too, small farmers

8. For works on Baader, see Stegmann, "Soziale Ideen," pp. 337–39, 361–63; Alexander, "Church and Society in Germany," pp. 401–6; and Bowen, *Corporative State*, pp. 46–53.
9. Stegmann, "Soziale Ideen," pp. 351–52.
10. On Ketteler and the Westphalians, see Bachem, *Zentrumspartei*, vol. 2, p. 214; and Ferdinand Jacobs, *Von Schorlemer zur Grünen Front* (Düsseldorf: Verlag Haus Altenberg, 1957), p. 12. Ketteler's brother Wilhelm Emmanuel was the bishop of Mainz.
11. Stegman, "Soziale Ideen," pp. 357–58.

led by the ex–cavalry officer Burghard von Schorlemer-Alst vainly sought to thwart the flight of the peasantry to the cities and factories by creating "Christian peasant associations."[12] The first and perhaps most famous of these initiatives, however, was that of the "social priest" Adolf Kolping, who in 1847 moved beyond the realm of charity, *Sozialkritik*, and vague political planning to found the first Christian labor organization.

Kolping was himself of working-class origin, having learned the shoemaking trade as a youth in Cologne.[13] Intelligent, sensitive, and deeply religious, he had trouble adapting to what seemed to him the slovenliness, intemperance, brutality, and immorality of the workshop of the 1830s. In 1836, therefore, he started back to school with the aim of becoming a priest, determined perhaps already then that his would be a social ministry. While studying theology in Munich in the early 1840s, he became enthused with the idea of forming canonical brotherhoods for journeymen to combat the spirit of individualism, materialism, and religious cynicism which he held responsible for the social disintegration of the day. But on the advice of one of his colleagues, the future bishop of Mainz Wilhelm Emmanuel von Ketteler, Kolping abandoned this church-oriented approach. As Ketteler rightly pointed out, given the turbulent atmosphere of the day, the canonical fraternity would never appeal to the hard-pressed journeymen, nor would it attract those already hostile to the church. His associations should not ignore the important role of Catholicism in solving the social question, but they had to be socially active organizations only loosely affiliated with the church.[14]

The journeymen's unions (*Gesellenvereine*) which Kolping later founded, beginning with the first in Elberfeld in 1847, performed the essentially social function which Ketteler had advocated and were able to attract over 60,000 young workers throughout Europe by the time of Kolping's death in 1865.[15]

12. On the founding of the peasant associations, see Schlorlemer-Alst to Bishop W. E. von Ketteler, 15 February 1862, reprinted in Otto Pfülf, S.J., *Bischof von Ketteler: Eine geschichtliche Darstellung* (Mainz: Verlag von Franz Kirchheim, 1899), vol. 2, pp. 179–80; and Jacobs, *Schlorlemer*, pp. 7–16. Pfülf's work is invaluable to the historian of the early Christian labor movement because it is based on Ketteler's private correspondence, only part of which appears in Dr. J. M. Raich's *Briefe von und an Wilhelm Emmanuel Freiherr von Ketteler* (Mainz: Verlag von Franz Kirchheim, 1879). (Hereafter cited as Raich, *Ketteler's Briefe.)*

13. For general discussions on Kolping, see Franz, *Der soziale Katholizismus*, pp. 111–45; Wilhelm Dockhorn, *Die christliche-soziale Bewegung in Deutschland* (Halle: Buchdruckerei des Waisenhauses, 1928), pp. 28–31; and Emil Ritter, *Die katholisch-soziale Bewegung und der Volksverein* (Cologne: Verlag J. P. Bachem, 1954), pp. 88–91.

14. Ketteler described his conversations with Kolping to one Father Engelhardt from Bingen in 1876. Franz, *Der soziale Katholizismus*, p. 120, n. 2.

15. Arnold Brügmann, *Sozialer Katholizismus im 19. Jahrhundert* (Frankfurt am Main: Deutsche Kunst-und Verlagsanstalt, 1943), p. 101; Alfons Gornik, *Die Entwicklung der nicht-sozialdemokratischen Arbeiterbewegung in Deutschland* (Halle: Hofbuchdruckerei von C. A. Kaemmerer and Co., 1909), p. 10.

Perhaps most important to the young artisans themselves was the net of hostels which spread from the Rhineland to southern Germany, Switzerland, and Austria as the movement gained momentum in the 1850s. Here journeymen could find good company and inexpensive room and board; they were encouraged to use the money thus saved to establish savings accounts which could help in times of need or later when they established independent shops. The Kolping *Vereine* also provided the wandering craftsmen with an opportunity to improve their education. Classes in reading and writing were offered along with more advanced subjects such as French.[16] Furthermore, the club reading room gave union members access to general reading material as well as more specific trade-oriented literature. Religion, of course, was not forgotten. Three or four times a year the parish priests and master craftsmen who supervised the unions accompanied the Catholic members to communion. In addition to historical and semi-political themes, weekly lectures also discussed the teachings of the church on marriage, the family, and the Christian community.[17]

With this combination of social, educational, and religious services, Kolping hoped to create a cadre of devout, industrious journeymen, proud of their craft and unsusceptible to radical, anti-Christian ideas. As masters they would also be prepared to reestablish in their shops that patriarchal, familial relationship between master and journeymen which Kolping had found so sorely lacking in the days of his youth. Kolping realized, however, that his efforts to create social harmony would be unsuccessful unless the state, too, came to the aid of the artisans. He had witnessed the short-lived uprising of handicraftsmen in Elberfeld in 1849, and it seemed all too clear to him that the alternative to the maintenance of a viable *Handwerkerstand* was social chaos and revolution. The political movement which developed among German artisans in the two decades after the founding of the first *Gesellenverein* thus had Kolping's fullest sympathy and he did not shrink from openly chastising the government on more than one occasion in the columns of the *Gesellenverein* newsletter for "unsatisfactory legislative protection of the handicraft trades."[18] The reading rooms of union hostels were also stocked with conservative Catholic newspapers which, along with the union's weekly lectures and discussions, propagated the same critical views.[19] Because of this bias, the very cautious Prussian government classified the unions as political organiza-

16. August Bebel, *My Life* (Chicago: University of Chicago Press, 1912), p. 37. The future leader of the German Socialists describes a visit to the *Gesellenverein* in Freiburg in 1858. He became an inactive member at that time.

17. Dockhorn, *Christlich-soziale Bewegung*, p. 30; Franz, *Der Soziale Katholizismus*, pp. 133–34.

18. Quoted in Franz, *Der soziale Katholizismus*, p. 134.

19. Bebel, *My Life*, p. 37.

tions under the *Vereinsgesetz* of 1850.[20] But an objective observer like the popular writer W. H. Riehl also detected in the movement a nascent political activism.[21] There is evidence, moreover, to suggest that the success of the movement among journeymen was a direct result of the fact that the *Gesellenvereine* did not ignore the political nature of the social question like so many other clubs in the "reactionary fifties."[22] By the late 1850s, in fact, those union members who had been able to establish their own shops were founding more overtly political masters' organizations with the aid of *Gesellenverein* priests and other Catholics sympathetic to the artisans' cause.[23]

Indeed, the rapid rise of the *Gesellenverein* in the 1850s and 1860s occurred at a time when labor questions had attained a much broader political significance for German Catholics. Nothing intensified Catholic interest in these matters more than the rapid expansion of the Liberal cooperative movement under the Saxon Landtag deputy, Hermann Schulze-Delitzsch. From modest beginnings in the late 1850s, Schulze's loose organization of consumer, credit, and raw materials–purchase cooperatives had spread throughout Germany and could boast a membership of over 125,000 small businessmen, artisans, and factory workers by late 1863.[24] Schulze's purely economic approach was upsetting to Catholic clergymen who felt that religion was the only solution to the social question, but his efforts would not have been cause for such great alarm had Catholics not interpreted the movement with some measure of justification as a front for the political designs of the north German Liberals. Indeed Schulze, Rudolf von Bennigsen, and others in the *Nationalverein* realized that their goal of progressive reform in Prussia and a Prussian-led unification of Germany could not be realized unless the economic success of the côoperatives could be translated into political support at the polls. The "educational clubs" which sprang up after 1861 in close association with the cooperatives were promoted with this result in mind and help to explain the parliamentary success which the Liberals had obtained throughout Germany by 1863.[25] Catholics opposed to the abolition of the denominational school and the exclusion of Catholic Austria from German unification were beginning

20. Franz, *Der soziale Katholizismus*, p. 137.
21. Brügmann, *Sozialer Katholizismus im 19. Jahrhundert*, p. 99.
22. Bebel recalls that the reading rooms helped satisfy his interest in politics. "For clubs of a purely social nature I had neither money nor inclination." Bebel, *My Life*, pp. 36–37.
23. Franz, *Der soziale Katholizismus*, pp. 134–45.
24. Hamerow, *Social Foundations*, vol. 1, p. 176.
25. Kasimir Eichler to Bismarck, 19 Nov. 1880, Brauweiler Papers 15/13, Portfolio 30 (Reichsarchiv Berlin), StA MG; Werner Conze, *Möglichkeiten und Grenzen der liberalen Arbeiterbewegung in Deutschland: Das Beispiel Schulze-Delitschs* (Heidelberg: Carl Winter, Universitätsverlag, 1965), p. 20; Bebel, *My Life*, pp. 44–58.

to realize that the rights and interests of the church could not be adequately defended unless Catholics attracted more working-class support.

The pressure on Catholics to confront the social problem increased in early 1863 because of the appearance of Ferdinand Lassalle on the German political scene.[26] The Socialist author, philosopher, and self-styled attorney from Breslau rejected Schulze's view that *laissez-faire* economics and "self-help" cooperatives could improve the position of the artisan or factory worker, and called upon the state to take the lead in financing small cooperative workshops. These, he felt, would eliminate the laborers' dependence on the "iron law" of wages, according to which the worker's pay would not rise above his subsistence needs in the long run. To assure state aid in this and other areas, he urged the workers to organize their own political party and push for universal manhood suffrage. Thus in February 1863, after a Saxon labor delegation had come to Berlin, asked for Liberal support of an independent workers' congress, and was flatly refused, the Saxon workers took their appeal to Lassalle.[27] By June 1863, the new labor party which he created had already commenced agitation and was beginning to win adherents among the artisans, journeymen, and factory operatives of Protestant Saxony as well as in the western cities of Elberfeld, Düsseldorf, Cologne, and Mainz.

The growing strength of Lassalle in many of the Catholic strongholds of the Rhineland made the need for a counterprogram of Catholic social action even more urgent. The emerging champions of such activism were not merely acting out of political expediency, however, for they were deeply involved with the Neo-Thomist revival of mid-century. Such a man was Kolping's old acquaintance, Wilhelm Ketteler, bishop of Mainz since 1850, who was hard at work on his own social manifesto by late 1863. Appearing in March 1864 under the title *The Labor Question and Christianity*, his work was designed to provide Catholics with clear guidelines for social action. In the last chapter, Ketteler offered a number of specific ideas.[28] A more complete development of the *Gesellenvereine* and widespread, energetic backing and support for the German *Handwerkerbund* would help in creating a viable corporative life for the workers, but the efforts of these organizations alone would not suffice. Clearly impressed with the Liberal and Socialist labor programs, the bishop encouraged Christian reformers to expand their activity in this direction as

26. For works on Lassalle, see Hermann Oncken, *Lassalle: Eine politische Biographie* (Stuttgart: Deutsche Verlagsanstalt, 1923); and George Brandes, *Ferdinand Lassalle* (New York, 1925).
27. Hermann Oncken, "Der Nationalverein und die Anfänge der deutschen Arbeiterbewegung 1862–1863," in *Archiv fuer die Geschichte des Sozialismus und der Arbeiterbewegung*, vol. 2 (1912), p. 121.
28. W. E. von Ketteler, *Die Arbeiterfrage und das Christenthum* (Mainz: Verlag von Franz Kirchheim, 1864), pp. 115–16, 119–48.

well. *Christian* educational clubs should take the place of their Liberal counterparts and, once the workers were united in the bond of Christianity, *true cooperatives* could be created. The consumer cooperative could provide cheap bread; the credit union a low-interest loan; and the raw materials–purchase cooperative inexpensive wood, bricks, etc. However, without the humbling influence of church teaching, selfishness would soon come to the fore and ruin these operations. "The future of the entire cooperative movement belongs therefore to Christianity."[29]

Ketteler may have been influenced in his plans for a Christian cooperative movement by a similar development already underway in the Rhineland by 1864. Two clubs for Catholic artisans and factory workers (*Arbeitervereine*) had been founded in the Ruhr in the early 1860s, while six similar organizations had been founded exclusively for miners (*Knappenvereine*).[30] Dominated, if not always founded, by socially conscious parish priests,[31] the *Arbeiter-* and *Knappenvereine* were of a largely educational nature, designed to foster religiosity among workers subjected to the tough, sometimes dehumanizing work experience of those days.

The club statutes and protocol books which have survived provide a rare opportunity to analyze this early experiment in Christian social action for proletarians.[32] To avoid the perceived evils and temptations of modern industrial life, members were encouraged to abandon vulgar habits such as swearing, drinking, and card playing, attend mass after work and communion on Sundays, and perform vigils at the bedside of sick or injured comrades. The workers were also told to say prayers regularly, especially to the Virgin Mary and the patron saint of the *Verein*, "in order to attain, through their intercession, the conversion of sins, protection from danger, and blissfulness in the hour of death."[33] Club meetings were given over to the collection of dues, a few songs from the club choir, a short talk from the local priest, and perhaps an opportunity for the workers themselves to ask a few questions or express their opinions. The workers were obliged to do so, however, in "a moderate, orderly fashion."[34] In accordance with this regimentation, members also had to pledge their obedience to the club's executive committee, which usually

29. *Ibid.*, p. 136.
30. Ritter, *Volksverein*, p. 76; Klaus Tenfelde, *Sozialgeschichte der Bergarbeiterschaft an der Ruhr im 19. Jahrhundert* (Bonn: Verlag Neue Gesellschaft GmbH, 1977), p. 364.
31. *Königliches Oberbergamt* Dortmund to *Abteilung des Innern* Arnsberg, 27 March 1873, Reg. Düsseldorf Präsidialbüro 835-1, HSA Düsseldorf.
32. See the *Protokollbuch des katholischen Knappenvereins Essen-Ruhr*, 11 Rep. 103, El, Nr. 25, and the *Protokollbuch des Bergmanns-verein zu Überruhr*, 2 vols., 10 Rep. 103, El, Nr. 23, StA Essen.
33. *Protokollbuch des Bergmanns-verein zu Überruhr*, vol. 1, June 1861.
34. *Ibid.*

consisted of clergymen, prosperous shopowners, and small businessmen from the surrounding area.

One detects, therefore, no *overt* attempt to instill in the miners and factory hands a sense of the unfairness or sinfulness of the very uneven distribution of wealth and property in the early industrial community. Much more emphasis was placed on toleration of these conditions and preparation for the hereafter. This is not to say, however, that the *Arbeiter-* and *Knappenvereine* of the Ruhr performed no critical social function. Although club leaders wanted to keep the membership docile and under control, they combined this with frequent visits to the homes of factory owners and entrepreneurs for the purpose of educating the capitalists to *their* social responsibilities. Once established, furthermore, these clubs emulated the Schulze-Delitzsch cooperatives by providing material benefits such as small loans and mutual sickness and burial funds.[35] Oftentimes, moreover, sporadic club activities like the customary funeral procession for a fallen comrade exuded a certain air of resentment against present social relations. "One is reminded here," writes Klaus Tenfelde, "of the powerful demonstrations of the suppressed workers during the years of the Anti-Socialist laws when. . . the burial of some [Social Democratic] party leaders and friends was used for the expression of silent protest."[36] Thus the *Arbeiter-* and *Knappenvereine* were certainly not devoid of the religiously motivated anti-liberal spirit which dominated the thinking of many Catholic conservatives in the 1860s.

Because of this critical spirit, and the fact that Ketteler was so well informed about new developments in the labor world, he may well have seen these organizations as the nucleus for his own cooperative schemes to aid factory workers. He must have been pleased, therefore, by the stimulus which his book, *The Labor Question and Christianity*, gave this young movement. Five new *Arbeitervereine* were joined by an equal number of newly founded *Knappenvereine* in the mid-1860s. Ketteler's 1864 publication, which ran through three editions in as many months, also contributed to the proliferation throughout the west of the St. Joseph's Savings and Loan Associations (*Spar- und Darlehnsvereine*). The latter catered almost completely to small shopowners and established handicraftsmen and were formed in cities like Münster, Recklinghausen, or Elberfeld, where miners and factory workers were not yet in the majority.[37] The *Arbeiter-*, *Knappen-*, and St. Joseph's

35. See Dr. August Pieper's unpublished manuscript, "Die Geschichte des Volksverein für das katholische Deutschland," vol. 1, pp. 57–58, 78 (hereafter cited as the Pieper Manuscript), StA MG.
36. Tenfelde, *Sozialgeschichte*, p. 392.
37. Rudolf Meyer, *Der Emancipationskamp des vierten Standes* (Berlin: Verlag von August Schindler, 1874), vol. 1, pp. 333, 335.

Vereine may have attracted as many as 5,000 backers by 1869.[38] Though only a fraction of the Liberal cooperative movement, this was nevertheless a respectable beginning.

Interestingly enough, Ketteler was quite interested in yet another labor institution in the mid-1860s—the trade union. He had observed the development of the trade union in England and knew that it was already a form of organization popular among the workers. Private notes made at the time indicate that he was thinking in terms of merging the trade union concept with the religious cooperative approach of the Catholic *Arbeitervereine*.[39] Trade associations should be formed, he noted, for *all* workers of each branch of industry. The basic function of the organization would be that of the trade union, but the association had to "afford its members material and moral protection in the sense of cooperative self-help."[40] Further notes show that far from sowing seeds of bitterness and opposition in society, these "Christian trade unions" were to be systematically and harmoniously integrated into it. District federations could be formed to serve as courts of appeal for the member unions, administer common funds, and represent the workers in negotiations with other estates and corporations. With the backing, significantly enough, of the church, the unions could then work to secure state recognition of the district federations as legally competent bodies with legislative authority to regulate the affairs of labor. The rest of Ketteler's scheme reflected the corporatist political thinking of his brother Wilderich. Nobles, peasants, merchants, artisans, and the church would enjoy similar autonomous positions, and to insure a minimum of social and political friction, Ketteler hoped that an organization comprising all estates and corporate bodies could be created. The mechanism and institutional structure of the new Christian order now appeared clear to the social activist from Mainz.

A number of developments after 1865 induced Ketteler to move beyond the planning state and press for the realization of these goals. For one, the death of Lassalle in 1864 brought J. B. Schweitzer to the head of the General German Workers' Alliance, Lassalle's labor organization. The new leader, however, had none of Lassalle's moderation and tolerance in questions of religion. The Catholicism of the Hapsburgs, wrote Schweitzer in May 1866, was the "curse" which had directed the Austrian imperial family against "every movement to improve conditions in Europe."[41] Anti-Catholic remarks such as

38. No complete statistics exist, but Meyer, *ibid.*, pp. 338–42, provides some isolated figures, and Tenfelde, *Sozialgeschichte*, p. 381, notes that the *Knappenvereine* in Essen alone numbered 1,700 members. Evidence taken from Meyer and Tenfelde permits the above approximation.
39. Ketteler Papers, C Abteil 8, Faszikel 3, Nr. 3, DDA Mainz.
40. *Ibid.*
41. Ketteler to three Catholic members of the Lassallean branch in Dünwald, 25 May 1866, Ketteler Papers, C Abteil 8, Faszikel 3, Nr. 1, DDA Mainz.

this, and reported instances of pro-Protestant agitation by Alliance speakers, prompted Ketteler to question whether Catholic workers could continue to belong to such an organization.

The defeat of Austria in July 1866 was even more jolting to Ketteler. By early 1867, Prussia had forged a confederation of North German states which left Rhenish and other Catholics distinctly in the minority. The feeling of vulnerability was heightened by the system of universal manhood suffrage which Bismarck instituted for the new North German Reichstag. Not only were Catholics exposed to the anti-clerical attacks of the numerically superior Liberals, but now the Socialists could begin to mount an assault on the Catholic masses. Three general elections in 1867/68 brought intense political agitation to Germany, especially in the populous industrial centers of Rhineland-Westphalia, where nearly 20,000 workers and artisans voted "red."[42] The age of mass politics had dawned in Germany.

Ketteler was no more in favor of Bismarck's experiment with a universally elected parliament than he had been with Lassalle's plans four years earlier. The *Ständestaat*, the bishop wrote in February 1867, was the truest and most genuine form of popular representation.[43] A corporate chamber would be more useful than an assembly "where a few party leaders come together with a great number of blind comrades."[44] Ketteler realized that an "estatist constitution" was unrealistic, for it would be impossible "with one leap"[45] to formulate a code of laws capable of establishing such an organic order. But if an enduring political establishment were to be created, gradual steps in the direction of corporatism had to be taken. Foremost among these would be legislation to strengthen the associational ties of the old estates and to create new bonds of union for groups such as industrial workers. On this sound basis, progress could be made toward the ultimate goal of the *Ständestaat*.[46]

In keeping with his private notes of the mid-1860s, Ketteler next sought to enlist the aid of the church hierarchy for his Neo-Thomist political program. Pope Pius IX had announced that deliberations for the forthcoming Vatican Council would commence in December 1869.[47] Ketteler hoped to convince his fellow bishops of the need for a more active church involvement in the

42. Dieter Dowe, "Organisatorische Anfänge der Arbeiterbewegung in der Rheinprovinz und in Westfalen bis zum Sozialistengesetz von 1878," in Juergen Reulecke (ed.), *Arbeiterbewegung an Rhein und Ruhr* (Wuppertal: Peter Hammer Verlag GmbH, 1974), pp. 69–73.
43. W. E. von Ketteler, *Deutschland nach dem Kriege von 1866* (Mainz: Verlag von Franz Kirchheim, 1867), p. 106.
44. *Ibid.*, p. 106.
45. *Ibid.*, p. 106.
46. *Ibid.*, p. 106.
47. Pfülf, *Bischof von Ketteler*, vol. 2, p. 380.

social reform movement and, with their support, win the backing of the Vatican Council and the pope for similar resolutions.[48] The idea was bold, but in 1867 the church must have appeared as the most likely engine for his political designs. The *Katholikentag*, an annual semi-political convention of prominent Catholic laymen and clergymen, had potential for political influence but had thus far proved ineffective as a means of taking meaningful action. Too, the various Catholic *Fraktionen* were everywhere weak and on the wane. Ketteler must have been somewhat relieved, therefore, when the bishops agreed in October 1867 to place the social question on the agenda of the next conference in September 1869, three months before their departure for Rome.[49]

Trade unionism, meanwhile, was beginning to take root in Germany. In July 1868, the Reichstag passed bills legalizing the trade union and the strike. The Liberals and Socialists wasted no time in founding their own trade union movements. Schweitzer's organization broke first ground in this field at a special congress in Berlin in late September 1868, followed only days later by the formation of another association under the tutelage of two Prussian Liberals, Max Hirsch and Franz Duncker. The Hirsch-Duncker unions claimed 30,000 members in May 1869, while the Lassalleans boasted a following of about 50,000 at this time. Dwarfing both organizations, it should not be forgotten, were Schulze's cooperatives which had risen meteorically to a membership of 304,000 by 1869.[50] The time for Ketteler's trade union schcmcs sccmcd as ripc now as it would cvcr bc.

By July Ketteler had finished his address for the Fulda bishops' conference.[51] The social question, he wrote with an eye on the forthcoming Vatican Council, was one that affected all the countries of Europe. Private entrepreneurs and the state had a great responsibility to improve the condition of the working masses, but the church, too, should become involved, for in their present impoverished state, proletarians were no longer affected by tradi-

48. See Ketteler's draft memorandum to his fellow bishops, n.d., Ketteler Papers, C Abteil 8, Faszikel 1, Nr. 1b, DDA Mainz. In this memo the bishop urged his colleagues to ready positions for the Council on crucial issues such as the relationship between church and state. The church, he felt, should be granted its ancient privilege of autonomy. As stated earlier in this study, Ketteler's efforts to attain church freedom were inextricably entwined with his plans for the workers. Also see Moufang's journal, *Katholik*, 1868, II, 3. Heft, pp. 319–51, and 1869, II, 6. Heft, pp. 715, 719, 721, StBib MG. Both articles urge greater participation of the church in organizing workers, and specifically, that the Vatican Council take up this task.
49. Pfülf, *Bischof von Ketteler*, vol. 2, pp. 380–81.
50. For the above statistics, see *ibid.*, p. 685, and Hamerow, *Social Foundations*, vol. 1, pp. 176, 254.
51. The final draft, dated 26 July 1869, is reproduced in Johannes Mumbauer (ed.), *Wilhelm Emmanuel von Kettelers Schriften* (Munich: Verlag der Jos. Kosel'schen Buchhandlung, 1911), vol. 3, pp. 145–66.

tional religious teachings. Unless bold new programs were adopted, he warned, the workers would be lost to anti-Christian parties such as the Liberals and Socialists. Seminaries should adjust their curricula to include courses in labor relations, church stipends should provide certain priests with the opportunity to study political economy in the universities, excursions could be sponsored to study industrial conditions in France and England, and special care should be taken in the selection of priests for industrial parishes. Ketteler felt confident that such programs would produce at least one priest who could do for the workers what Kolping had done for the journeymen. He could help found new labor organizations, inform members of their rights and obligations, and instill in the workers trust and faith in God. The "new Kolping" would also encourage entrepreneurs to construct workers' housing, improve shop conditions, raise wages, initiate profit-sharing plans, and establish other welfare institutions. He was to be the "apostle of peace between capital and labor."[52]

Ketteler stopped short of advocating a centralized, church-controlled union movement. Such an organization, he noted, would be weak, artificial, and unable to adapt to local circumstances. Obviously the bishop feared that a church movement would fail to catch on in areas like the Ruhr where Catholics and Protestants were mixed and preferred, instead, that the unions organize on a local or regional basis and remain independent of the bishops. The hierarchy could stay in touch with the movement through its priests and by way of special lay representatives who would report regularly to each bishop on the physical, intellectual, moral, and religious condition of the workers in that diocese. These diocesan representatives could then meet annually to consider further ways and means for the church to aid the laborers. Between these diocesan gatherings and the already established bishops' conferences, Ketteler would have the political mechanism he needed to work jointly with the unions for corporate freedoms.[53] Labor reforms could then be formulated and administered by the workers themselves. By fostering and encouraging the labor movement, the church would thus make an important contribution to the realization of the new social order which he envisioned.

The actual presentation was made on September 5, 1869, but was largely unsuccessful in achieving its purpose. Some of the bishops agreed to act on his

52. *Ibid.*, p. 163.

53. The church should "encourage, recognize, instruct, and give assistance to trade unions." *Ibid.*, p. 162. In 1865 Ketteler wrote that the church should examine the statutes of new labor organizations, encourage unions "to make proposals, and later, to formulate a constitution for the working class." Other notes called for "autonomous legislation within the unions' proper sphere of interest." Ketteler Papers, C Abteil 8, Faszikel 3, Nr. 3, DDA Mainz. Although Ketteler did not elaborate on the political role of the diocesan and bishops' conferences at Fulda, it seems clear that these institutions were designed to implement the plans outlined privately four years earlier.

recommendations, and Archbishop Melchers of Cologne actually established a commission to investigate industrial conditions.[54] But most bishops were not moved to action. To a generation of clergymen unaccustomed to social and political activism on the part of the church, Ketteler's ideas were too radical. The employer's superior position in society was regarded as given; the workers should accept their lowly position and direct their attention to a better life in the hereafter. The conference disposed of the matter in a single afternoon, resolving that it would be extremely difficult to frame any detailed questions regarding the church's social activities which could serve as a basis for discussion by the Vatican Council. It was decided nevertheless that Ketteler's program should be kept in mind and "an effort made to renew the interest of the coming Council in the duty of the church to take care of the poor."[55] But the clerics who gathered in Rome were no more inclined toward a greater social activism than the Fulda conference had been. The Council, whose deliberations ended in July 1870, failed to give to social Catholicism that spark which Ketteler had hoped it would.

Social Catholicism had captured neither Fulda nor Rome. This was not surprising, however, considering the novel nature of the proposals and the embryonic stage of the movement. Indeed Catholic socialists were just beginning to plant into action the ideas and philosophies which had germinated over the last forty years. The intellectual heritage which the activists carried with them would prove to be a source both of strength and of weakness. Ketteler's growing sense of social realism and penchant to look beyond medieval precedents or religion alone as solutions to society's ills would, when combined with the passion for social justice embodied in Neo-Thomism, serve the reformers well. But there was also a weak side. It was questionable whether the potentially conflicting goals of social justice and *social harmony* would be easily reconcilable in a more rapidly industrializing economy. Nor was it certain that the paternalism of a movement which emanated from the church and church teachings could be made compatible with the inevitable demand of the workers for independence from church tutelage. The strengths and weaknesses of Catholic socialism would receive their first real test in 1869/70 as German Catholics formed their own political party to defend Catholic interests.

54. Hogan, *Ketteler's Interpretation of the Social Problem*, p. 173.
55. Pfülf, *Bischof von Ketteler*, vol. 2, p. 436, quotes from the protocol of the bishops' conference.

1

The Center Party, the *Kulturkampf*, and the Collapse of the First Christian-Social Movement

It was in the late 1920s that Karl Bachem drafted his monumental, nine-volume history of the Center Party.[1] The work, which left few areas of the party's public affairs untouched, was made all the more valuable by the inclusion of many documents from private collections which were lost during the war. Bachem's study has not precluded further research, however, for it was written by an insider whose near-religious devotion to the party usually prevented him from allowing the reader to peer within the *Zentrumsturm* and observe the often-troubled relations therein. The founding of the Center in 1870/71 and the internal affairs of the party during the "struggle of cultures" which Bismarck unleashed on German Catholics in the 1870s and 1880s are two of many cases in point. As the present chapter makes clear, the picture of a united, harmonious Catholic community resisting the threat to its existence from without—a picture which modern researchers have accepted as accurate for the *Kulturkampf* period[2]—does not do justice to the real situation. The

1. Karl Bachem, *Vorgeschichte Geschichte und Politik der deutschen Zentrumspartei* (Cologne: Verlag J. P. Bachem, 1927–32), 9 vols.
2. G. C. Windell, *The Catholics and German Unity 1866–71* (Minneapolis: University of Minnesota Press, 1954), pp. 276–95; Ross, *Beleaguered Tower*, xiii–xiv; David Blackbourn, "The Problem of Democratization: German Catholics and the Role of the Centre Party," in Evans (ed.), *Society and Politics*, pp. 164–65; also see Ralph René Mendershausen, "German Political Catholicism 1912–1919," Ph.D. dissertation, University of California, San Diego, 1972, pp. xi, 26. The most recent interpretations are by Anderson, *Windthorst*, pp. 141–42, 194, and Sperber,

party and the Catholic Church were forced on the defensive by the followers of Ketteler, and only a crude manipulation of the challengers restored order. The Center Party was not as socially progressive, obviously, as Carl Bachem and, occasionally, more recent historians of the era would have us believe. In fact, genuine social progressivism never characterized the Center during the days of the empire, a fact which the very latest historical investigations are beginning to bear out.[3] The social conservatism of the Center described here and in subsequent chapters is thus another departure from the traditional view. The history of the Christian-Social movement which finally emerged in 1869 is inextricably related to these points of revision, and it is to this topic that we now turn.

* * * *

While Bishop Ketteler tried to salvage as much as possible of his social program in Rome, his followers in the Rhineland were initiating political action. Led by Father Joseph Schings, a Ketteler enthusiast from Aachen, and Johann Breuer, a schoolteacher from Elberfeld who had worked with Kolping, Christian socialists in western Germany had formulated plans for a Christian-Social Party. A new journal, the *Christlich-soziale Blätter*, was founded to support this venture. The *Katholikentag* in Düsseldorf was the logical focus of their activity. During the winter of 1868/69, a provisional committee of the *Katholikentag* had drawn up plans for a permanent central committee consisting of one to three representatives from each diocese. The task of the central committee would be to prepare the *Katholikentag*'s agenda, execute its resolutions, and promote the various *Vereine*. As September 1869 approached, Schings, Breuer, and the executive board of the St. Joseph's *Verein* of Elberfeld urged the provisional committee to scrap its plan and establish instead a Christian-social party similar to Schweitzer's General German Workers' Alliance.[4] Catholic labor associations, the *Gesellenvereine*, and all other organizations associated with the *Katholikentag* would provide the new party with the broad base necessary for political effectiveness.

These plans came to naught. The Düsseldorf *Katholikentag* of 1869 paid lip

Popular Catholicism, passim. Although they advance opposite opinions concerning the solidarity of the Catholic community, or milieu, before the *Kulturkampf*—Anderson emphasizes the tenuousness of social and religious ties among German Catholics before 1872—both believe that the Catholic subculture exhibited great cohesiveness during the *Kulturkampf*.

3. For the traditional view, see Bachem, *Zentrumspartei*, vol. 9, p. 125; Franziska Vincke, *Die Arbeitnehmer-Sozialpolitik des Zentrums* (Münster: Wirtschafts- und Sozialwissenschaftlicher-Verlag, 1933), *passim*; Koppel Pinson, *Modern Germany* (New York: Macmillan Co., 1966), pp. 184–85; Hajo Halborn, *A History of Modern Germany 1840–1945* (New York: Alfred A. Knopf, 1969). pp. 290–91. For more recent findings, see Ross, *Beleaguered Tower, passim*; Blackbourn, *Class Religion and Local Politics, passim*; and Zeender, *German Center Party, passim*.

4. *Christlich-soziale Blätter*, no. 8, 12 July 1874.

service to the program of the *Christlich-soziale Blätter*, but rejected the idea of politicizing the Catholics' national caucus. *Katholikentag* leaders feared that a party formed mainly to pursue social reforms would alienate middle- and upper-class Catholics and suggested instead that a special "social section" be formed under the direction of the central committee to promote Catholic labor associations and unify their activity. This resolution differed very little from a resolution passed in 1868. And, far from forming the basis for a new party, the associations were to remain essentially economic and educational in nature. Furthermore, neither Schings nor Breuer were granted seats on the special commission. In their places were Professor Schulte of Paderborne and Vicar Gronheid, head of a Catholic "people's bank" in Münster. Chairman of the social section charged with furthering the workers' cause was Burghard von Schorlemer-Alst, a Westphalian agrarian.[5]

The emergence of a large landowner like Schorlemer was highly significant. Though very paternalistic in his political views, Schorlemer was not a one-sided proponent of agrarianism. He realized that liberalism was making the workers' and artisans' struggle for independence just as difficult as that of the small farmer.[6] Consistent with these views, Schorlemer had participated in a series of conferences which Wilderich von Ketteler, Hermann von Mallinckrodt, and other Westphalian noblemen had convened in Soest almost without interruption since late 1863.[7] The Soest conferences were seen as a means of encouraging the Catholic *Fraktion* to adopt a program more in keeping with the anti-liberalism of the Westphalians. But the virtual disappearance of the Prussian *Fraktion* in 1867, and the approaching state and national elections of 1870, gave rise in Soest to talk of forming a new party altogether. By summer 1869, Mallinckrodt had formulated the first draft of a party program and was ready to present it to other Catholic deputies in Berlin for their perusal. Hoping to avoid the intra-party conflicts of the 1850s and attract as many adherents as possible, even among Protestants, the Westphalians did not wish to press their own corporatist views too emphatically. The party would champion all that was "genuinely progressive," but would be "deeply Christian and truly conservative."[8] The outmaneuvering of Schings and his followers at Düsseldorf must thus be interpreted as an attempt to incorporate the Catholic labor associations into the broader, more compre-

5. This paragraph is based on Filthaut, *Deutsche Katholikentage*, pp. 57–59; Kissling, *Geschichte der Katholikentage*, vol. 1, pp. 440–42; Naujoks, *Katholische Arbeiterbewegung und der Sozialismus*, pp. 83–84.

6. Meyer, *Emancipationskampf*, vol. 1, pp. 328–29.

7. For information on the Soest conferences, see Bachem, *Zentrumspartei*, vol. 3, pp. 97–100.

8. Dr. Huelskamp, member of the *Katholikentag* central committee, to Landtag deputy Joseph Krebs, 14 June 1870, Bachem Papers 848, Portfolio 5, HA Köln.

hensive political movement developing in Westphalia. This became even more evident in the months between Düsseldorf and the completion of the Westphalian statutes in June 1870.

Under the mistaken impression that the new Social Section was to found "a specific Christian-Social Party,"[9] Breuer and the St. Joseph's *Verein* of Elberfeld entered into negotiations with Schorlemer and urged that preparations be made for a convention of peasant and labor associations to perform this task. The Social Section agreed to hold a convention in Elberfeld, but, for reasons mentioned earlier, flatly refused to sponsor a socio-political party. Rather, the Elberfeld caucus would simply facilitate the social and educational mission of the various *Vereine*. Breuer *et al.* accepted the Social Section's verdict for the time being, hoping privately that the Vatican Council would give impetus to their organizational plans in the near future. Party or no party, however, the Christian socialists insisted that some legislative steps be taken to implement the new social order. The righteousness of this cause, they claimed, was recognized by the church. To strengthen their hand, Ketteler printed the heretofore-unpublished Fulda address in the November number of the *Christlich-soziale Blätter*.[10]

Ketteler's move gave great impetus to the Christian-social cause among those aristocratic Catholics who were already somewhat well-disposed to consider social questions seriously, but had not done so out of concern for the alleged "democratic and revolutionary" nature of Schings and Breuer, whose ideas were rejected without much thought as the "bubbling-over of younger minds."[11] With the sanction of an influential nobleman like the bishop of Mainz, things began to change. The circulation of the *Christlich-soziale Blätter* rose to two thousand and highly placed Catholics like Prince Karl von Löwenstein, the chairman of the *Katholikentag* Central Committee, chastised himself and others for their social inactivity. "He who knows no need also does nothing to ameliorate it; he who does not know his duty does not fulfill it."[12] The *Katholikentag*'s Social Section also responded favorably. In a statement issued in late November 1869, Schorlemer, Schulte and Gronheid announced their support of Ketteler's Fulda program.[13] The Social Section was now committed to a fairly ambitious program of social action.

9. Joseph Schings, *Die christlich-soziale Partei in ihren Bestrebungen: Bericht über die erste General-Versammlung der christlich-socialen Vereine Rheinlands und Westfalens zu Elberfeld am 6. 7. und 8. März 1870* (Aachen: Selbstverlag des Herausgebers, 1870), p. 10.

10. *Christlich-soziale Blätter*, nos. 1–2, 15 January and 17 February 1970, and no. 8, 12 July 1874.

11. *Christlich-soziale Blätter*, no. 11, 27 December 1870.

12. Löwenstein to Felix von Loë, 3 November 1869, quoted in Paul Siebertz, *Karl Fürst zu Löwenstein* (Kempten: Verlag Josef Kosel and Friedrich Dusetet, 1924), p. 210.

13. Printed in Schings, *Die christlich-sociale Partei*, pp. 11–12.

The rest of the Section's statement, however, was a thinly veiled warning to the activists from Aachen and Elberfeld that the Section would brook no opposition to its authority. "A single Christian-social association"—referring no doubt to the St. Joseph's *Verein* of Elberfeld—should not speak with "messianic pretension."[14] The associations were economic, not political, organizations whose only task was to stimulate interest for their work "in broader circles"[15] so that gradually a central union could be created. Nor should the associations think that they were appointed to direct the church in its efforts to solve the social question. "At the given hour the Lord of the church can and will arouse those in whose hands this task will be placed."[16] The statement was a hint, even to Bishop Ketteler, that "the given hour" for far-reaching reforms had not yet arrived and that the backing of Pius IX would probably be necessary to lend the bishop's social program the measure of respectability needed to obtain widespread backing among German Catholics. Considering the pope's preoccupation with questions of papal infallibility, the "given hour," as Schorlemer *et al.* were doubtless well aware, might never arrive.

Mindful of the political importance of the Christian socialists, nevertheless, Schorlemer and his associates came to the Elberfeld Conference in March 1870 prepared to make certain concessions to the impatient faction around Schings and Breuer. The Social Section agreed, for instance, to conduct an elaborate two-year investigation of social conditions in Germany to enhance social reform efforts. It also recommended the founding of cooperative construction societies and even committed itself to lobby in the Prussian Landtag for labor legislation. Other results of the conference, however, reflected Schorlemer's obvious desire to integrate the Catholic labor movement into the political apparatus which he, Mallinckrodt and others were building. A central office was created to coordinate the activities of the St. Joseph's *Vereine*, not in Breuer's hometown of Elberfeld, but rather in Münster under the direction of Gronheid. A special committee including Schings, Breuer, and Father Heggen, founder of one of the early *Arbeitervereine*, was formed to found "Christian" labor clubs, but this promotional assignment was to be shared with the *Casinos* and *Bürgergesellschaften*. These local and regional campaign organizations, moreover, were instructed to open their ranks to "all estates," taking special care to "honor the interests of the artisans and workers"[17] in preparation for the upcoming election battle. The same organizations should establish ties with one another as well as with the Social Section of the *Katholikentag*.

14. *Ibid.*
15. *Ibid.*
16. *Ibid.*
17. *Ibid.*

A "Christian party" should take the field in defense against the "materialistic, atheistic and thoroughly unchristian attacks"[18] of the Liberals and Socialists.

Work on the program of the new Christian party was also progressing. After the closing of the Landtag in mid-February 1870, Mallinckrodt made arrangements for a meeting in Ahlen to continue deliberation on the statutes. This was followed by a final conference in Münster in early June.[19] Along with paragraphs defending the church, the denominational school, and a closer union with Austria, the program finally adopted at Münster included social planks which reflected the compromises worked out the previous fall and winter. The workers could not expect the state to solve all their problems, indeed the best aid would come from private charity. "But one thing must be demanded of the government: that it give free reign to all attempts to solve the social question which do not overstep legal grounds, and in particular, *that it greet all efforts which the church originates to heal the social and moral wounds of our time*, and also, that consideration be taken of legislative means to remove abuses which threaten the working class with moral and bodily ruin."[20] Once complete, the Münster program was distributed to editors, local politicians, and other influential Catholics in Prussia. Public assemblies were planned to initiate electoral agitation on the basis of these principles.[21]

The Westphalian landed aristocracy did not, however, represent the views of most German Catholics. This became very clear in early June 1870 when the *Kölnische Volkszeitung* printed a program which made no mention of social reform. Author of the program was the Westphalians' old nemesis, the leader of the liberal Catholics, Peter Reichensperger, who claimed to speak for "Catholic men from the different parts of the country."[22] Though Reichensperger and the staff of the business-oriented *Kölnische Volkszeitung* did not oppose the principle of moderate social reform, they were certainly aware that many middle-class Catholics considered such legislation unnecessary to say the least. The editors of the *Christlich-soziale Blätter* summarized an attitude typical of their most outspoken "philistine" detractors in June 1870.

18. Quoted in Herbert Gottwald and Gunther Hildebrant, "Christlich-soziale Vereine 1868–1878," in Dieter Fricke et al., *Bürgerliche Parteien*, vol. 1, p. 265.
19. For the Ahlen and Münster conferences, see Count Landsberg's remembrances at the fortieth anniversary of the Center Party, *Kölnische Volkszeitung*, no. 246, 22 March 1911, Carl Bachem to Count Praschma, 19 June 1911, and Bachem's notes of a conversation with Landsberg, 6 April 1911, Bachem Papers 848, Portfolio 5, HA Köln.
20. The original Münster program is located in the Bachem Papers 848, Portfolio 5, HA Köln.
21. Dr. Hulskamp to Joseph Krebs, 14 June 1870, Bachem Papers 848, Portfolio 5, HA Köln.
22. *Kölnische Volkszeitung*, no. 159, 11 June 1870.

> I am afraid that the whole affair just smells too much like democracy. My flesh crawls when I think about the rabble in control, mob rule . . . For a long time now the people have been led astray by so-called popular tribunes who promise the proletariat mountains of gold; now the workers are coddled from above by the clergy and nobility. Where will this all lead? The poor employers must soon be done away with. Today there's a strike here, tomorrow there; instead of working, they're drinking in the tavern. Just look at the workers. Aren't they dressed better than before? Don't they eat better than before? Isn't their situation continually better? Things are just too good![23]

That the *Kölnische Volkszeitung* printed the exclusively church-oriented Reichensperger program would seem to indicate, therefore, that Rhenish middle-class forces regarded the social clauses of the Münster program as too controversial to include in a public election proclamation designed to rally all Catholics at the polls. For the time being at least, Catholics should concern themselves with the need to protect the confessional school and the church's priestly orders from the onslaught of the Liberals.[24]

The delicate balance established at the Elberfeld Conference in March between Schorlemer and the Christian socialists was now upset. Not surprisingly, the forces represented at Elberfeld retaliated. Only days after the appearance of the Cologne program, Schorlemer answered with the publication of another program which urged "support for the efforts of the Christian-social labor associations."[25] On June 22, the annual conference of *Gesellenverein* priests declared that they wanted "to see the factory workers protected with all legal means from the difficult circumstances in which they now find themselves."[26] On June 29, Schorlemer presided over a huge rally for workers in Essen organized by Westphalian political leaders and local priests active in the *Arbeiter-* and *Knappenvereine*.[27] Among other things demanded of Reichstag and Landtag candidates were a more equal tax distribution, elimination of social abuses, and "advancement of all the interests of the workers with a healthy program of Christian legislation."[28] One excited Christian socialist clergyman pointed with pride to a new coalition of forces which he felt would surely further the cause of social reform:

> 15,000 Christian peasants have united in Bavaria. 15,000 peasants—that is a solid base. There will soon be just as many in Rhineland-Westphalia.

23. *Christlich-soziale Blätter*, no. 6, 30 June 1870.
24. See the *Kölnische Volkszeitung*, nos. 150 and 174, 1 and 26 June 1870.
25. Quoted in Bachem, *Zentrumspartei*, vol. 3, p. 108.
26. Quoted in Meyer, *Emancipationskampf*, vol. 1, p. 334.
27. Decon Büssem to Carl Bachem, 7 April 1911, Bachem Papers 848, Portfolio 6, HA Köln.
28. Quoted in Huesgen, *Ludwig Windthorst*, p. 84.

> 100,000 German handicraftsmen stand at our side. 80,000 loyal journeymen from Father Kolping's unions extend us a brotherly hand. The Christian-social labor associations will soon count their numbers by the hundreds of thousands. A respectable army! I see a bright future before us. 30,000 German priests will put their hands to the work.[29]

The workers at Essen wanted bourgeois politicians like Bachem and Reichensperger to act on the promises made at Düsseldorf and Elberfeld. There was even talk of electing 40 to 50 deputies of Christian social persuasion.[30]

The social alliance, as Schings referred to it, was never to experience the bright future predicted for it at Essen. To be sure, the June protests were not without some effect. The *Kölnische Volkszeitung* responded positively to the Essen rally and Catholic political leaders paid much lip service to the idea of social reform as the election campaign gained momentum later that summer.[31] But when the newly elected deputies of what came to be known as the Prussian Center Party gathered in Berlin to formulate a definite program in mid-December 1870, there was no mention made of labor legislation. The 50-man *Fraktion* had been formed, the program made clear, exclusively to defend "the freedom and independence of the church and its institutions."[32] As in 1853, the Westphalians had been unable to prevail upon the more numerous and socially indifferent faction around Reichensperger.

Even more damaging setbacks occurred in 1871 despite the fact that Ketteler himself made every effort to revive the faltering movement. The bishop had returned from Rome the previous summer disillusioned with the social ambivalence of the church, but determined "to solve the social problem in a Christian sense."[33] The elections to the new all-German Reichstag in March 1871 seemed to provide him with such an opportunity. He ran successfully as an independent, but hoped to win the support of the other Catholic deputies for a new program which he had formulated in late 1870.[34] Among other things, the draft advanced the now-familiar idea of semi-autonomous labor organizations—a point defended openly by Moufang and Schings during the

29. Quoted in the *Christlich-soziale Blätter*, no. 7, 4 August 1870.
30. *Christlich-soziale Blätter*, no. 11, 27 December 1870.
31. *Kölnische Volkszeitung*, no. 179, 1 July 1870.
32. Quoted in Bachem, *Zentrumspartei*, vol. 3, p. 128. Also see the electoral declaration of the Rhenish Electoral Committee in Cologne, *Kölnische Volkszeitung*, no. 299, 29 October 1870, which made no mention of social reform. This committee, interestingly enough, had been formed in the aftermath of the Westphalians' Essen rally in June and had supposedly accepted the Essen resolutions (*Kölnische Volkszeitung*, no. 179, 1 July 1870).
33. Ketteler to Canon Haffner, 6 May 1870, printed in Raich, *Kettelers Briefe*, p. 410.
34. Pfülf, *Bischof von Ketteler*, vol. 3, p. 265. Ketteler's program was published over two years later under the title *Die Katholiken im deutschen Reich: Entwurf zu einem politischen Program* (Mainz: Verlag von Franz Kirchheim, 1873), 150 pp.

campaign.[35] Showing greater political realism than earlier proposals, the new program also suggested formation of a "corporate Senate" to deliberate jointly with the Reichstag.[36] When Ketteler arrived in Berlin, however, he discovered that the party leadership had already agreed on a program without consulting him.[37] Like the Prussian *Fraktion*, the Reichstag deputies were primarily concerned with the threat of anti-Catholic legislation and would go no farther on the social question than expressing their intention to further "the moral and material welfare of all classes."[38] Feeling that Socialist or Liberal domination of the labor movement presented the greatest threat to the church in the long run, Ketteler formulated a parliamentary resolution under the heading "The Further Development of the Rights of German Labor" and prepared to introduce it in the Reichstag.[39] But he abandoned this attempt too after learning that the Center would not support him.[40]

These results, so very disheartening for the bishop and his closest associates, cannot be truly appreciated without an understanding of the generally rural composition of the Center, and, equally important, the yet embryonic nature of industrialism in Germany. Industry and construction represented only twenty-eight percent of the gross national product in 1871, while industrial production was only a third of the absolute level which would be reached by 1900 and a mere fifth of the 1913 figure. Industrialization, moreover, is always an uneven, regional phenomenon, especially in its early stages. Thus there were vast stretches of the new Reich as yet untouched by the spreading tentacles of the industrial system. And it was primarily from these relatively quiet, out-of-the-way regions that the Center drew its support. Thus David Blackbourn writes of Württemberg, which usually sent four or five Center deputies to the Reichstag, that

> Catholics took almost no part in [the] movement into towns and factories: in the 1860's, after the first wave of internal migration [in Württemberg], none of the six towns over 10,000 was Catholic, only two of the ten of 5–10,000, and only three of the twenty-four of 3–5,000. Catholics made up scarcely one-tenth of the total urban population, but four-fifths of those living in scattered farms and hamlets.[41]

35. Meyer, *Emancipationskampf*, vol. 1, pp. 71–77. Moufang developed these ideas in a speech in Mainz on 27 February 1871. Schings went into even greater detail in the March number of the *Christlich-soziale Blätter*, elaborating a "Christian-social program."
36. Ketteler, *Die Katholiken im Deutschen Reich*, pp. 62–65.
37. Pfülf, *Bischof von Ketteler*, vol. 3, p. 257.
38. The program of the Reichstag Center is printed in Bachem, *Zentrumspartei*, vol. 3, pp. 137–38.
39. Pfülf, *Bischof von Ketteler*, vol. 3, p. 257.
40. Fritz Vigener, *Ein deutsches Bischofsleben des 19. Jahrhundert* (Berlin: R. Oldenbourg, 1924), p. 711.
41. Blackbourn, *Centre Party in Württemberg*, p. 81.

The same was true of other Center-supporting Catholic regions like Silesia (two seats), Bavaria (nineteen seats), and most of Rhineland-Westphalia (twenty-nine seats). Of the Center's sixty-three seats in 1871, in fact, only thirteen were urban, and of these only seven—Aachen, Crefeld, Cologne, Düsseldorf, Essen, Mainz, and Munich—had populations larger than 50,000.[42] Even the larger urban districts, moreover, bore more resemblance to their early nineteenth-century predecessors than the sprawling metropolises they would soon become. For these reasons it was not surprising that many a Centrist did not "know his duty," as Löwenstein put it. Most possessed at best a passing familiarity with the social problems of Germany's pocketed industrial centers.

Like Ketteler's Fulda initiative of 1869, therefore, the program of 1871 was simply too ambitious for the times. It is highly doubtful that the majority of middle-class Centrists shared the strong anti-social feelings of Dr. Johann Sepp of Munich, who lambasted Schings for perpetrating a hoax designed to sow seeds of discontent among otherwise satisfied laborers.[43] However, such views were so widespread, especially among Catholic employers, as to warrant caution on the part of the Center leaders. Reichensperger and *Fraktion* leader Ludwig Windthorst were also concerned that labor legislation, though justified in principle, might arouse the government and the business-oriented Liberals, thus jeopardizing the Center's defense of the church. With the beginning of the so-called *Kulturkampf* in July 1871 the last chance that these leaders would offer immediate support to the Christian socialists disappeared. "We must first win liberty for the church," said Windthorst, "and then we can throw ourselves into the social reform movement."[44]

The Westphalian noblemen in the party were more prone to social action, but as members of the upper class they were sufficiently removed from the labor world to place a lower priority on social legislation than Ketteler and the workers preferred. Schorlemer and his followers, moreover, were preoccupied themselves with the escalating *Kulturkampf* and by 1872 had postponed all plans to aid the proletariat. Demoralized by the exclusive attention paid to church-related issues, little was heard after the early 1870s from Ketteler and the other Neo-Thomists who only years earlier had had such great expectations for their plans.

By this time, however, a younger generation of radical priests and working-class followers was beginning to take matters into its own hands. The situation

42. *Statistisches Jahrbuch für das Deutsche Reich*, vol. 1 (1880), p. 7, vol. 2 (1881). p. 3.

43. Filthaut, *Deutsche Katholikentage*, pp. 57–59; Kissling, *Geschichte der Katholikentage*, vol. 1, pp. 440–42.

44. Quoted in George Metlake (Laux), *Christian Social Reform Program Outlined by Its Pioneer Wilhelm Emmanuel von Ketteler* (Philadelphia: Dolphin Press, 1912), p. 184.

became particularly acute in Aachen. In the wake of Ketteler's Fulda address, the young chaplain Eduard Cronenberg founded a Catholic *Arbeiterverein* and began to urge immediate social and political action.[45] During the Reichstag campaign in February 1871, Cronenberg chastised his fellow Catholics for their philistine attitudes toward the workers. He also spoke out against the hesitation of conservative churchmen. "The interests of the Catholic people extend farther than the interests of the Catholic church."[46] The insubordinate tone of this latter remark moved church, professional, and entrepreneurial circles in Aachen to lodge complaints with Archbishop Melchers in Cologne. Cronenberg's appeals to the workers, it was charged, contradicted Christian principles, were too democratic, and generated unrealistic wishes and hopes among the workers. Church authorities in Cologne agreed and warned Cronenberg to moderate his political activities or face transfer.

These political differences were followed by economic disagreements in the following year. In mid-May 1872, the weavers of a large plant in Eupen struck when the owner refused to raise wages. Catholic textile manufacturers in the Eupen area responded by locking out their employees until the original strikers resumed work. Cronenberg reacted in the characteristic paternal fashion of the Catholic labor associations by telling the strikers to remain calm and avoid any unrest or unseemly behavior while *he* formulated a note of protest against the employers' lockout.[47] Like so many members of the upper classes, Cronenberg believed that workers were incapable of conducting their own affairs in a responsible way. In a statement published in the *Eupener Zeitung*, however, he minced no words with his co-religionists among the bourgeoisie. If the owners continued to mistreat their employees, the pronouncements of the Socialists concerning "the hardheartedness, cruelty, and brutality of the middle class"[48] would be confirmed.

As a result of these accusations of employer injustice, Cronenberg was brought to trial by local Prussian officials for inciting one class against another and thereby endangering the public peace. The young priest did not see it that way. "According to the eternal precepts of [Aquinian] natural law, it is, in my opinion, unfair when an employer wants to force the worker [by a lockout] from taking advantage of wages the way the worker wishes . . . I wanted to speak to the consciences of the factory owners."[49] Undeterred by his acquittal,

45. This paragraph is based on Herbert Lepper, "Kaplan Franz Eduard Cronenberg und die christlich-soziale Bewegung in Aachen 1868–1878," *Zeitschrift des Aachener Geschichtsvereins*, vol. 79 (1968), pp. 57–148. (Hereafter cited as Lepper, "Kaplan Cronenberg.")

46. Quoted in *ibid.*, p. 71.

47. See the testimony of one of the disciplined weavers, *Landgericht* Aachen 97, HSA Düsseldorf.

48. *Eupener Zeitung*, 19 June 1872 (clipping: *Landgericht* Aachen 97, HSA Düsseldorf).

49. Quoted in *Landgericht* Aachen 97, HSA Düsseldorf.

Prussian authorities appealed for aid in silencing Cronenberg to archdiocesan officials in Cologne. The archbishop's office argued that Cronenberg's action had been incorrect, serving only to excite the workers. Cronenberg, who probably believed he was acting as a "new Kolping," again was told to conduct himself more prudently in the future. The fact that by 1872 his *Arbeiterverein* had attracted over 3,000 workers and artisans who otherwise might have joined Socialist organizations probably saved him from transfer.[50]

One witnesses the beginning of similarly assertive tendencies in the *Arbeiter-* and *Knappenvereine* of the Ruhr. The Catholic miners of Überruhr demanded in April 1872, for instance, that the executive board of their club update the backward, deficient statutes of the organization and try to meet the economic needs of the times.[51] Prussian officials reported with alarm the following year that the thirty-odd Catholic labor associations of the district pursued socialistic, revolutionary goals.[52] These observations were surely colored by the anti-Catholic prejudices of Prussian officialdom. Nevertheless, it was true that the Catholic *Vereine* of the Ruhr were paying more attention to worldly matters. Along with religious songs and church-related questions, many clubs had begun to hold discussions of trade unionism. Some may even have used sickness and burial funds to support striking and/or locked-out comrades.[53]

During the fall of 1872, in fact, these pro-union feelings led to the formation of a miners' trade union. Founded by Chaplain Laaf, leader of the huge Christian-social *Arbeiterverein* of Essen, and Lassallean Socialists in the area, the organization was immediately assailed by older priests who were worried that Laaf was leading Catholic workers into the revolutionary camp. Years later, one of these clergymen went as far as to characterize Laff himself as "a hard-working Social Democrat."[54] More serious altercations among Catholics were prevented in the end by the Prussian Ministry of the Interior, which dissolved the new union in early 1873. Alarmed by the rash of strikes coinciding with the economic upswing of 1871–72, the government had begun to question the wisdom of legalizing the trade union. Officials therefore adopted the strictest possible interpretation of the industrial code of 1869 in an attempt

50. Lepper, "Kaplan Cronenberg," pp. 76–77.

51. *Protokollbuch des Bergmanns-verein zu Überruhr*, 7 April 1872, 10 Rep. 103, El, Nr. 23, StA Essen.

52. *Königliches Oberbergamt* Dortmund to *Abteilung des Innern* Arnsberg, 27 March 1873, and the decree of *Oberpräsident* Kühlwetter of Westphalia, 30 June 1873, Reg. D. Präsidialibüro 835 (1), HSA Düsseldorf.

53. Domvikar Otman Vieth, "Die katholischen Knappenvereine im Bereich des heutigen Bistums Essen," 1975, unpublished seminar manuscript presented to the present writer by the author; Tenfelde, *Sozialgeschichte*, p. 389.

54. Dechant Büssem to Carl Bachem, 7 April 1911, Bachem Papers 848, Portfolio 6, HA Köln.

to impose peace on the warring economic parties.[55] That this was an employers' peace goes without saying.

1873 witnessed the spread of this more radical strain of Christian socialism.[56] In an effort to further the economic and political aims of the *Arbeitervereine*, Cronenberg convened a special congress in Aachen in December 1873. Representing 60,000 Catholic workers and artisans, the delegates passed resolutions demanding the enactment of a 10-hour day for factory workers, an 8-hour day for miners, banning of all female labor, and elimination of Sunday work. Other resolutions illustrated the drift toward trade unionism. The *Vereine* should strive for unlimited coalition rights, the right to codetermine factory work rules and the right to participate on an equal footing with employers in the arbitration of wage disputes by commercial courts. To facilitate these efforts, district labor federations should be formed as a step toward a union of all Christian workers in the Reich.

To the demands of the Aachen Congress, the Center leadership replied that any social effort by the party would be labeled demagogic by the Liberals, thus rendering more difficult its main task of protecting the church and the faith. Such logic failed to impress Cronenberg and his followers. The young priest challenged the official Center candidate for Aachen during the Reichstag elections of January 1874, and ran again after the death of his victorious opponent necessitated a by-election in January 1875.[57]

Similar revolts appeared likely in Essen after Laaf's demands for a worker candidacy in 1874 were totally ignored. Anton Rosenkranz, a young miner who had helped found the short-lived union in 1872, recalled later that some of the more outspoken members of the *Arbeiterverein* were incensed by the brusk treatment of Laaf and decided "then and there that things would turn out differently next time."[58] In the meantime, Laaf maintained constant pressure on the Center deputy from Essen, Forcade de Biaix, by holding protest rallies together with the Socialists. A joint rally in October 1874 demanded that Forcade oppose government legislation designed to prosecute workers for breach of labor contracts, and another in November demanded firm guarantees of coalition rights.[59]

With two key Reichstag seats in jeopardy, local Center officials urged Melchers to put an end to these challenges by transferring the two Christian

55. Report of the *Regierungspräsident* in Düsseldorf to the Prussian minister of the interior, 27 July 1878, RD 30428, HSA Düsseldorf; Naujoks, *Katholische Arbeiterbewegung und der Sozialismus*, p. 118; Kirchhoff, *Staatliche Sozialpolitik im Ruhrbergbau*, pp. 24–27.
56. For the Aachen Congress of 1873, see Lepper, "Kaplan Cronenberg," pp. 77–81.
57. Huesgen, *Ludwig Windthorst*, pp. 316–17; Lepper, "Kaplan Cronenberg," pp. 88, 95.
58. Quoted in Kalis, "Die christlich-soziale Arbeiterbewegung in Essen," p. 62.
59. Najoks, *Katholische Arbeiterbewegung und der Sozialismus*, pp. 121–22.

socialists.[60] That these complaints once again failed to dislodge Laaf and Cronenberg was not due, however, to any principled support for their efforts on the part of the archbishop. Indeed, high church circles in Cologne feared that the two labor priests might arouse the workers' passions to the point where the Marxists and atheists would be the only beneficiaries.[61] But the 10,000 laborers amassed by the two *Arbeitervereine* by 1875 still represented potential electoral support for the defenders of the church's religio-political interests in Berlin—provided the Center represented the workers' interests as well.

This placed the church and the Center, as Windthorst well knew, on the horns of a dilemma. Bold Catholic moves to solve the social question in the Reichstag would probably bring retaliation from the business-oriented Liberals or the government. Labor reforms, moreover, were still regarded with outright hostility, or at best insouciance, by most Center deputies.[62] Future Reichskanzler Georg Hertling, who had been selected by Windthorst in 1874 as Center spokesman for social questions, complained of these circumstances in a letter to a friend. "There is practically nothing to do here, and thus far I have not found any encouragement from fellow Centrists; each goes his own way."[63] Without social initiatives in parliament, on the other hand, the Christian-socialists could present grave problems to the Center. This predicament became even more evident as the months drew on toward the scheduled Reichstag election in January 1877. A second Christian-social congress met in Aachen in November 1875, repeated the demands of 1873, and resolved to nominate its own candidates for the coming elections.[64] The revolt had already begun.

Under this growing pressure, Center leaders looked desperately for some indication that the parliamentary risks of socio-political action were decreasing.[65] The hostile mood of the strong liberal element in parliament continued to prevent any serious consideration of such action during the 1874–76 Reichstag period. But after a reconstituted Conservative Party came forward in July 1876 in support of agricultural tariffs, aid to the *Mittelstand*, and maintenance of the confessional schools, the Center's executive committee started to

60. Lepper, "Kaplan Cronenberg," pp. 97–98; Naujoks, *Katholische Arbeiterbewegung und der Sozialismus*, p. 122.

61. Report of the *Regierungspräsident* in Düsseldorf to the Prussian minister of the interior, 12 September 1878, RD 30429, HSA Düsseldorf.

62. The *Christlich-soziale Blätter*, no. 7, 7 July 1874, and no. 25, 23 June 1875, complain about the anti-social views of most Catholics.

63. Hertling to Hermann Cardauns, 29 October 1875, Kl. Erw. 478, BA Koblenz.

64. Lepper, "Kaplan Cronenberg," p. 81.

65. For the reasoning of the Reichstag Center leadership discussed in this paragraph, see Bachem, *Zentrumspartei*, vol. 3, pp. 330–33; and Huesgen, *Ludwig Windthorst*, pp. 319–20.

think in terms of a Center-Conservative alliance. If the Conservatives emerged from the election in 1877 somewhat stronger than they had been in 1871, this alliance would have a working majority in the Reichstag. As a *quid pro quo* for Center backing in other areas, it was not inconceivable that the Conservatives, who had cooperated with the Center on a number of minor social bills in 1874 and 1875, would support a moderate program of social reform legislation for factory workers. Along with the traditional demand of church freedom, the Center's electoral proclamation in December 1876 therefore included support for the legal demands of industrial workers.

This maneuver saved the Center from a major collision with the Christian socialists. Most of the Aachen delegations which had voted in 1875 to oppose the Center were satisfied with the December announcement and supported the party. But in Aachen and Essen, the two longstanding centers of opposition, such last-minute tactics failed. Cronenberg withheld his support and went ahead with a Christian socialist candidacy.[66] In Essen, events took a similar course. After the party renominated Forcade, Rosenkranz protested: "Forcade hasn't tended to the workers' interests and has no feeling for the common people. A man of the fourth estate has to enter the Center *Fraktion* this time so that the party learns something about the woeful state of the workers."[67] With only a week remaining before the election, Laaf attempted to prevent a split with a compromise measure. The workers would back Forcade if, among other things, the party nominated a worker in Essen in 1880. When this point proved too much for the Essen Centrists, the Christian socialists nominated Gerhardt Stötzel, a former metalworker, who defeated Forcade in the crucial run-off election with the aid of the Socialists, who gladly gave their votes to a fellow laborer. Laaf was less fortunate in Aachen, and the official Centrist won a convincing victory. Thus Stötzel became the first non-Socialist worker to enter the Reichstag. Once in Berlin, he joined the Center *Fraktion* in the hope that his presence would facilitate implementation of the Christian-social program.[68]

The Conservatives and the forces grouped around the Center returned to Berlin greatly strengthened after the January elections, but still about thirty seats short of a majority. This naturally caused trepidation among the more cautious Center leaders. When the Reichstag convened in late February 1877, it seemed that Windthorst and Reichensperger still had no intention of acting on the December promises. The Westphalians therefore seized the initiative.

66. Lepper, "Kaplan Cronenberg," pp. 102–9.
67. Quoted in Otto Hue, *Die Bergarbeiter: Historische Darstellung der Bergarbeiterverhältnisse von der ältesten bis in die neueste Zeit* (Stuttgart: J. H. W. Dietz, 1910–13), vol. 2, pp. 317–18.
68. Paul Moellers, "Die politischen Strömungen im Reichstagswahlkreis Essen 1867 bis 1879" (Ph.D. diss., Bonn., 1956), pp. 296–312.

As one deputy later explained, Schorlemer appeared in party caucus in early March and proceeded to read a social resolution.[69] "In order to make good a grave injustice, to avert a great peril, to restore labor, the source of all well-being, to its rightful honor, it is necessary to reverse the [*laissez-faire*] direction followed thus far."[70] Freedom of enterprise should be curbed, master-apprentice relations regulated, Sunday factory work banned, female and adolescent labor curtailed, factory work rules standardized, and commercial courts created in which freely elected worker representatives could participate. Schorlemer's proposal also called for "promotion of corporate associations."[71] A heated discussion ensued "which Schorlemer brought rather forcefully to an end by ordering all participants to discuss the matter with him privately."[72]

Schorlemer's action resulted in what came to be known as the Galen Bill, named after Ketteler's nephew, Count Ferdinand von Galen, who defended the motion in parliament.[73] Galen used Ketteler's gradualist approach to corporate social reform, but for the first time made no mention of abolishing or altering Germany's political structure in the least. Economic institutions, however, were to be changed drastically. The government should introduce legislation creating local and district associations for artisans and workers. Artisans could work within their corporations to establish clearly defined "borders" between industry and handicraft, while factory operatives would be provided with legal status to negotiate and bargain with employers.

As Windthorst had feared in 1874, the Center's proposal was singled out for special criticism.[74] Liberal speakers labeled the bill a throwback to the Middle Ages, the negation of modern economic development, even outright folly. The Conservatives, from whom aid had been expected, also refused to defend the Center's motion, not wishing, perhaps, to be associated with a bill so clearly influenced by the bishop of Mainz. After the Galen Bill was badly defeated, Windthorst was forced to conclude that "we were somewhat too doctrinaire."[75]

69. Georg von Hertling, *Erinnerungen aus meinem Leben* (Munich: Verlag der Jos. Koesel'schen Buchhandlung, 1919), vol. 1, p. 314.
70. Quoted from Proposal No. 74, Anlagen zu den Verhandlungen des Reichstags, Period 3, Session 1 (1877), vol. 46, p. 274. (Hereafter cited as *Reichstag-Anlagen*.)
71. *Ibid.*, p. 274.
72. Quoted in Hertling, *Erinnerungen*, pp. 314–15.
73. *Stenographische Bericht über die Verhandlungen des deutschen Reichstags*, Period 3, Session 1 (16 April 1877), vol. 44, pp. 501–4. (Hereafter cited as Reichstag Debates.)
74. Reichstag Debates, Period 3, Session 1 (16, 17, 18 April 1877), pp. 495–519, 529–52, 555–77.
75. Windthorst to Moufang, 15 May 1877, Moufang Papers D Abteil 7, Faszikel 1, Nr. 8c, DDA Mainz.

Despite these parliamentary setbacks, the pro-labor agitation of the activist chaplains guaranteed the young movement an impressive degree of popularity. Christian-social *Arbeitervereine* claimed at least 60,000 members in Prussia's western provinces in the mid-1870s and had largely rid these districts of Socialist trade union competition.[76] The Socialists' failure to attract union members in the west was accompanied by equally disappointing political developments there. The united Social Democratic Party of Germany (S.P.D.), for instance, numbered only 2,300 in all of Westphalia in 1875.[77] "The priests are the most dangerous enemy of our cause," admitted an embittered, frustrated Lassallean. "They come forward at the decisive moment with our program and say: 'We want the same thing, but religion must be guaranteed.'"[78] Most Socialists were simply unable to recognize anything unique about the theological *Sozialkritik* of the Christian socialists. The red priests were only shrewd opportunists with a copy of "our program". Although such opinions were clearly inaccurate, the Socialists were convinced otherwise and redoubled their efforts to expose the so-called "labor fraud" of the "Christians."

By mid-decade the Socialists were not alone, however, in their growing hostility toward labor opponents. The "Christians," too, were becoming increasingly suspicious and intolerant. Already uneasy with Lassalle and the irreverent Schweitzer in the 1860s, many Christian socialists stiffened their opposition to the Social Democrats after the Lassalleans united with the Marxists at Gotha in May 1875. This was seen as an invitation to godlessness, revolution, and chaotic mass rule. After this the Christian-social *Vereine* were no longer seen as instruments to Christianize the entire labor movement, but rather as bulwarks against the spread of Marxism to the Catholic parts of western Germany. Trade unions, similarly, had to be exclusively Christian organizations to guard against Socialist attempts to exploit the union movement for political purposes. Thus, as talk of trade unionism increased among the workers of the Ruhr in 1874, 1875, and 1876, some Christian-social leaders departed from Ketteler's original idea of a unified trade union movement espousing Christian principles and laid plans for separate, anti-Socialist trade unions. The Center's only labor deputy, Gerhardt Stötzel, founded one such organization for wood workers, stonemasons, and metal workers in 1875, but resistance from employers limited the success of the experiment.

76. Lepper, "Kaplan Cronenberg," p. 81, notes that only half of the existing Christian-social *Vereine* sent delegates to the first Christian-social congress in December 1873. These delegates, nevertheless, represented 61,000 workers and artisans.

77. *Ibid.*, p. 73.

78. Quoted in Ritter, *Volksverein*, p. 68.

The new Reichstag deputy was planning another union for the area's most important group of workers, the miners, in 1877.[79]

His efforts were cut short in the spring of 1877 by the attempt of Ludwig Schröder, a Lassallean miner from Dortmund, to found a trade union for *all* miners in the Ruhr.[80] He began agitation near Dortmund in April, urging workers to stand up for their rights and fight the wage decreases, overtime, and layoffs imposed by the mine owners. Although Schröder's initiative shocked many Catholics, it was received enthusiastically in Essen by Laaf and Rosenkranz.[81] The two had cooperated with the Lassalleans on a number of occasions in the early 1870s, coming to trust them, despite other signs to the contrary, as faithful Christians and opponents of Marxism. The fact that Lassalleans outnumbered Marxists five to one in the Ruhr after the Gotha union contributed to the willingness of Laaf and Rosenkranz to continue this cooperation.

In mid-1877, therefore, Rosenkranz presented a rather ambitious plan to the mastercraftsmen, priests, and fellow workers who sat on the executive board of the Christian *Arbeiterverein* in Essen. The miners and metal workers of Rhineland-Westphalia should first form a trade union to push for demands such as Sunday rest, the eight-hour day, etc. All discussion of party politics and religion would be forbidden so that workers of all faiths and political persuasions could be attracted. Agitation would then spread to the coal and

79. August Erdmann, *Die christliche Arbeiterbewegung*, p. 383; Franz Wieber, "Franz Wieber," in *25 Jahre christliche Gewerkschaftsbewegung* 1899–1924 (Berlin: Christlicher Gewerkschaftsverlag, 1924), pp. 169–70.

80. The Ruhr miners' movement of 1877/78 gave rise to a number of partisan historical accounts. August Erdmann, *Die christliche Arbeiterbewegung*, pp. 381–89, and Otto Hue, *Die Bergarbeiter*, vol. 2, pp. 313–30, are written from the Socialist Party viewpoint of the early twentieth century, while the "Christian" or Center Party interpretation appears in Otto Müller, *Die christliche Gewerkschaftsbewegung Deutschlands mit besonderer Berucksichtigung der Bergarbeiter und Textilarbeiter-Organisationen* (Karlsruhe: Druck and Verlag der Braunschen Hofbuchdruckerei, 1905), pp. 32–34, and Heinrich Imbusch, *Arbeitsverhältnis und Arbeiterorganisationen im deutschen Bergbau* (Essen: Verlag des Gewerkvereins christlicher Bergarbeiter, 1908), pp. 252–58. The former works concentrate on criticism of the cautious, halting attitude of church and Center circles toward the participation of Catholic workers in trade unions, while the latter works chiefly blame the Socialists for attempting to exploit the miners' movement for party purposes. The later account of Naujoks, *Katholische Arbeiterbewegung und der Sozialismus*, pp. 124–29, is based on a somewhat unreliable source—the *Essener Volkszeitung*, organ of the Essen Center Party. Klaus Tenfelde, *Sozialgeschichte*, pp. 514–22, is more objective. An interesting addition to the body of information on the Ruhr miners' movement of the 1870s is a lengthy letter which Anton Rosenkranz and his son sent years later to Müller in response to the latter's work. Dated 27 September 1915, it seems highly likely that the letter was actually written in 1905, when Müller's book first appeared. See Pastor Rosenkranz to Otto Müller, 27 September 1915, *Archiv der katholischen Arbeitnehmerbewegung Westdeutschlands*, vol. 5, KfZG Bonn. (Hereafter cited as Rosenkranz to Müller, 27 September 1915, KfZG Bonn.)

81. The remainder of this paragraph, and the following paragraph, are based on Rosenkranz to Müller, 27 September 1915, KfZG Bonn.

steel areas of the Saar, the Harz, and Silesia. These district associations could later unite in a national federation so powerful that strikes would no longer be required to obtain concessions from employers. With the critical backing of Father Laaf, a skeptical executive board agreed to the plan. After Schröder gave his consent, a joint rally was scheduled in Essen on November 18, 1877, to assure the backing of other suspicious Catholics. Laaf was to deliver the main address.

The Essen rally was only a marginal success. As Rosenkranz later explained, "opponents of the cause"[82] intervened at the last minute to prevent Laaf from appearing. This opposing faction was led by Matthias Wiese, owner of a textile factory in Werden and leader of the Essen Center Party. Wiese was more socially conscious than most employers in western Germany, having promoted the idea of factory safety and the labor welfare programs throughout the Ruhr. But he was afraid that a national union led by the workers might quickly become "too great a power"[83] for local employers to resist. In order to prevent Laaf from speaking at Essen, Wiese presumably obtained firm support from Archbishop Melchers in Cologne, for Laaf was obviously not one to follow orders from the Center.

Stötzel further complicated matters by energetically opposing the plan in favor of a "Christian-social" union. Devout Catholics would never back Rosenkranz, he reasoned, "out of fear for the Socialists."[84] In Stötzel's case the wish was father of the thought. One of the most radical Lassallean deputies in Berlin, Wilhelm Hasselmann, was present at the rally to support the union, thereby giving many the impression that the Socialists intended to exploit the organization for political purposes. Rosenkranz was finally able to secure a slim majority of the nearly 5,000 workers present for his proposal, but without the moral support of Laaf, only a few hundred workers actually registered as members.[85]

Systematic agitation in late November 1877 soon compensated for the setback at Essen. Assemblies held throughout the Ruhr succeeded in attracting a few thousand bold *Arbeiter-* and *Knappenverein* members who were ready for unionism.[86] The success of the movement was so rapid, in fact, that Center officials in the Ruhr convened a meeting in Steele in early December to discuss the party's stance toward the new union.[87] Invited were local party

82. *Ibid.*
83. *Ibid.*
84. *Christlich-soziale Blätter*, no. 2, 14 January 1878.
85. Hue, *Die Bergarbeiter*, p. 320.
86. Rosenkranz to Müller, 27 September 1915, KfZG Bonn.
87. On the Steele conference, see *ibid.*

officials from all Reichstag districts in the Ruhr, the editors of all party newspapers in the area, and representatives of the largest Christian-social labor organizations. According to Rosenkranz's account, the conference agreed to support his plan.

To his surprise, however, many of the editors who had been present at Steele did just the opposite. One of the journalists, the new editor of the *Christlich-soziale Blätter*, Father Arnold Bongartz, confessed shortly after the Steele conference to Laaf and Rosenkranz that he feared the union "would steer a Socialist course as soon as you turn your back."[88] Editor Rittweger of the large Dortmund paper, *Tremonia*, admitted sheepishly that the hostile articles had come "from journalists I could not turn down."[89] It was soon made public that "the journalists" were from the powerful Center newspaper in Berlin, *Germania*. The Berlin Center faction had organized two conferences in Dortmund in mid-December, attended by Catholics opposing Rosenkranz from Essen, Bochum, and Dortmund. Their plan was to found a separate Christian-social union as Stötzel had suggested in November.[90] Like Wiese, Center officials wanted to prevent the growth of "too great a power."

In the meantime, this opposing faction attempted to undermine the growing popularity of Rosenkranz. The following note, which appeared first in *Germania*, and was then circulated throughout the Ruhr, exemplifies the tone of this campaign:

> Participating Social Democratic agitators here in Berlin have explained that Herr Rosenkranz's entire bearing is closer to the S.P.D. than the Christian socialists. [They say] he is, to be sure, outwardly a practicing Catholic, but he acts—"perhaps unconsciously"—genuinely Social Democratic. The [S.P.D.] agitators concerned bore the best testimony to the childish naivete of Herr Rosenkranz and made no bones about the fact that Hasselmann is still chuckling up his sleeve about this.[91]

These comments were obviously printed to discredit Rosenkranz among Catholic workers, but the alleged statements were most likely actually made. For, although they were willing to cooperate with Christian workers, most Socialists felt only contempt for Christian-socialist leaders and were convinced, as stated earlier, that there was nothing originally or truly progressive in the enemy camp.

Before Christmas 1877, *Germania*'s smear tactics began to have effect. Reflecting his own doubts, and perhaps further pressure from the archbishop

88. *Ibid.*
89. *Ibid.*
90. *Christlich-soziale Blätter*, no. 2, 14 January 1878.
91. *Christlich-soziale Blätter*, no. 5, 25 February 1878.

of Cologne, Laaf too began to criticize Rosenkranz's original plan, singling out the fact that Hasselmann, not Schröder, had assumed most of the burden of agitation since November. As the weeks drew on toward the union's constituent assembly in early February 1878, Catholic members either balked from joining or actually withdrew their support from the new union.

Rosenkranz did all in his power during the founding assembly to reverse this trend, but to no avail. When Laaf rose to speak it was not to support Rosenkranz, but rather to encourage those Catholics present to form a union of their own.[92] He was seconded by Rittweger of *Tremonia*, who read a letter which Bishop Ketteler had sent to an important personage in Essen—probably Matthias Wiese—in early 1874.

> The moment of decision has now come for Christian workers. Since some labor party leaders have dragged religion into the labor question and openly preached atheism and hatred of Christianity and the Catholic Church, Christian workers can no longer follow. I deplore this departure from the program of Lassalle, who kept religion out of the labor question and protected the religious beliefs of the workers.[93]

A "hushed silence"[94] fell over the assembly when Rittweger had finished. Few Catholics would follow Rosenkranz after such a negative verdict from the highly regarded bishop of Mainz.

The statutes of the proposed Christian-social trade union appeared in late February 1878.[95] They appear to have been the joint work of Laaf, Stötzel, Rittweger, Bongartz, Wiese, and others who had attended the Dortmund conferences to oppose Rosenkranz in December. Unlike the Hasselmann-Rosenkranz union, which was designed merely "to curb the might of the capitalists,"[96] Bongartz, Wiese, and the sponsors of the Christian union intended to maintain harmonious relations between capital and labor by intermediating between employers, workers, and state mine officials. Demands could be exchanged, compared, compromised, and a fair solution reached. Owners were also asked to contribute to a workers' support fund which would not be used for strike purposes unless all peaceful methods of negotiation and arbitration had been exhausted.

The latter clause proved singularly naive. In late February 1878, the Association of Ruhr Mining Interests announced curtly that workers joining either

92. Rosenkranz to Müller, 27 September 1915, KfZG Bonn; Erdmann, *Die christliche Arbeiterbewegung*, p. 385.
93. *Christlich-soziale Blätter*, no. 5, 25 February 1878.
94. *Ibid.*
95. *Christlich-soziale Blätter*, no. 7, 24 March 1878.
96. *Ibid.*

the Christian or the Rosenkranz-Hasselmann union would be summarily dismissed. Rosenkranz and others were fired and blacklisted, and their union, which had managed to attract 17,000 miners, was crushed. The employers' move also led to the immediate retreat of Bongartz and Wiese. Neither was prepared to engage in a struggle against the owners which they felt could not be won. They emphasized, however, that the idea of a Christian trade union had not been given up for good. "A time [of economic boom] will come when employers need their workers, when owners will be very, very cautious about threatening dismissal. Then we can return to our plan."[97] Not content with this reasoning, Laaf decided to push on with the idea in early April, but could find no workers to back him.[98] Fearing the loss of their jobs, the boldest Catholic miners of the Ruhr had postponed their plans too.

The Schröder-Rosenkranz initiative had thus exposed a fault in the Christian-social structure. The lines of fissure reflected the inherent contradictions of Catholic *Sozialkritik* itself. Since the pre-1848 days of Müller and Baader, Catholic social activists had defended the concept of harmony between the various parts of the social "organism"—a concept epitomized by the union of master, journeyman, and apprentice in the workshop—while simultaneously propagating an anti-capitalistic attitude which presupposed a certain amount of disharmony between capital and labor. With the growth of a militant Socialist movement in the 1860s and 1870s, Christian socialists began gravitating toward one concept or the other. Middle-class conservatives like Wiese, Bongartz, and the *Germania* faction continued to castigate liberal industrialism, but leaned much closer to the patriarchal "guild concept" of labor relations. Close supervision of the workers by priests and other patrons was favored, the strike all but rejected, and cooperation with the atheistic Socialists ruled out completely. Rosenkranz moved in the other direction. The prerequisite for social harmony was a far-reaching reduction in the property rights of the entrepreneur. Strikes were regrettable, but justified under prevailing social conditions, as was economic cooperation with Socialists in "politically neutral" trade unions.

Significantly enough, the majority of Catholic workers followed the more conservative Christian social leaders in refusing to cooperate economically with Socialists. The manipulative influence of priests in the *Arbeiter-* and *Knappenvereine* was responsible for this unwillingness to join ranks with other workers. Despite their eagerness to solve the social question, many of the so-called red chaplains were sure that wildness and radicalism would prevail within any organization of mixed Christian and Marxist membership.

97. Quoted in Müller, *Die christliche Gewerkschaftsbewegung*, p. 34.
98. Rosenkranz to Müller, 27 September 1915, KfZG Bonn.

Thus the moral authority and discipline of the church were used to prevent the corrosion of the workers' religious *Weltanschauung*. Many workers never questioned these instructions, fearing loss of salvation in heaven; others conformed for fear of losing the respect of fellow Catholic laborers, but continued to long for some form of trade unionism, either Christian, Socialist, or neutral; those recalcitrants who had supported Rosenkranz unwaveringly were probably among the first Catholic workers to secede from the *Vereine* and affiliate with the S.P.D.[99]

The activity of the majority of *Arbeiterverein* priests, who were operating quite independently of any suggestion or control from the ruling elites in Berlin, is a good illustration of the stabilizing influence which "auxiliary elites," as they were termed in the introduction to this study, could have. Manipulation was not a technique monopolized by the government, therefore, nor were such methods employed on a *completely* inactive Catholic proletariat, for throughout the 1870s men like Rosenkranz had forced Center leaders and even close bourgeois associates like Laaf on the defensive over the question of political reform and trade unionism.

The rifts within the Catholic camp over the labor question grew worse in the remaining decades before the turn of the century, then burst forth in a bitter "trade union controversy" (*Gewerkschaftsstreit*) which neither the German bishops nor the Vatican proved able to silence (see Chapters 5, 8 and 10). For the time being, however, further tension over the labor question among Catholics was postponed by the passage of the anti-Socialist laws. Alarmed by the steady increase in Social Democratic votes, Bismarck decided in October 1878 to reverse the trend with force. Socialist party organizations were closely regulated and Socialist party adjuncts such as trade unions completely suppressed. Against the advice of employers and Prussian officials in western Germany, who were convinced the Christian organizations were an equally serious threat to the established order, the government decided to exempt Christian *Vereine* from this legislation. The anti-Socialist potential of the *Arbeiter-* and *Knappenvereine* was considered too valuable to waste.[100] This was one of the earliest examples of the state's policy of playing Christian and Socialist workers off against one another. The attempt at manipulation was only halfhearted and not thoroughly planned, however, for the mere threat of government suppression sufficed to weaken the Christian labor movement and

99. For the influence of peer pressure, see the report of the Landrat Essen to the *Regierungspräsident* Düsseldorf, 18 August 1894, Reg. D. 24724, HSA Düsseldorf. For the passive role of most Christian workers, even in an otherwise radical club like the Christian-social *Arbeiterverein* of Essen, the reader should peruse excerpts from the protocols of this association, located in a report to the *Königliche Staatsanwaltschaft*, 7 April 1875, Reg. D. 306, HSA Düsseldorf.
100. Tenfelde, *Sozialgeschichte*, p. 530.

reduce its ability to reach the masses. Many clubs dissolved themselves voluntarily, while others rewrote statutes and eliminated all controversial political and economic activities. Further undermining the government's efforts, moreover, those auxiliary elites whose advice concerning the need to suppress Christian labor had not been heeded in Berlin pushed forward with their own draconian measures. Anton Rosenkranz was eventually forced by his employers to leave the Essen area, while other labor leaders like Stötzel, who was briefly imprisoned for insulting the Reichskanzler, were cowed into submission. To make matters worse, Cronenberg was finally removed from his post by church authorities in Cologne. All these setbacks, together with the economic recession of the 1870s, had a devastating effect on membership. Bongartz reported in 1879 that *Arbeiter-*, *Knappen-*, and St. Joseph's *Vereine* had only about 12,000 members in western Prussia.[101] Rebuffed by employers, the government, the Reichstag majority, and many within the church and Center Party, the Christian labor movement, as indeed the German labor movement, lay in shambles at the end of the decade.

101. Rosenkranz to Müller, 27 September 1915, KfZG Bonn; *Oberbürgermeister* Essen to the *Innenministerium* Düsseldorf, 5 August 1878, Reg. D. 8841, HSA Düsseldorf; Lepper, "Kaplan Cronenberg," pp. 145–46; Arnold Bongartz, *Das katholisch-soziale Vereinswesen in Deutschland* (Würzburg: Verlag von Leo Woerl, 1879), pp. 102–5.

2

Mönchen-Gladbach, *Rerum Novarum*, and Further Disputes over Christian Trade Unionism

From 1878 to 1894 the idea of trade unionism for Christian workers was blocked from realization. The repressive socio-economic climate which existed after passage of the anti-Socialist laws worked against the Christian workers, but this factor was less important than others, for by the mid-1880s the state had relaxed its hold on labor unions, and in 1890 the anti-Socialist laws were dropped altogether. The real barriers to Christian unionism during these years, in fact, were within the Catholic camp itself. Assuming that Christian labor organizations independent of the bishops would radicalize politically, as the Cronenberg experience in Aachen proved (or worse, be "hoodwinked" by the Socialists), Catholic clergymen, employers and other representatives of the middle and upper classes either resisted the idea of labor organization, or molded these ideas to suit the Catholic cause. This pattern of opposition and manipulation becomes highly significant when the historical alternatives are considered, for if Catholic leaders had promoted unionism in the 1880s it would have been much more difficult for the emerging Socialist unions to establish the organizational and financial lead which they in fact possessed by the 1890s. The shortsightedness of Catholic leaders seems even more unfortunate—and ironic—from their point of view if one remembers that Christian workers took matters into their own hands in the mid-1890s and that the Christian trade union movement which eventually established itself came to be regarded by many, though not all, Church and Center Party leaders as the most effective form of resistance against the increasingly powerful Socialist labor unions.

Nor did the Center "throw itself into the social reform movement," as Windthorst had promised in the 1870s. The views of the "Mainz School" were "still much too Socialistic"[1] for the party which had reluctantly introduced the Galen Bill in 1877. Like the Galen Bill, in fact, those social measures which were eventually advocated by this agrarian, small-town, church-oriented party had to be forced on it from within by Christian-social groups which emerged in the 1880s and 1890s to carry on the tradition of the previous generation. It will be the task of the present chapter to explain and further analyze these developments.

* * * *

After Ketteler's death in 1877, the intellectual center of the Christian labor movement shifted from Mainz to the growing textile town of Mönchen-Gladbach. It was here during the 1870s that Franz Brandts, a factory owner dedicated to the social teachings of the Catholic Church, adopted enlightened management practices that would have pleased Ketteler, or even St. Thomas himself. Brandts eliminated Sunday and nighttime work, curtailed child and female labor, shortened working hours for men, introduced health insurance, improved safety conditions, and founded a factory committee so that workers could voice their grievances and help to administer the plant's welfare institutions. With these committees, Brandts hoped to lay the groundwork for a new industrial order in which capital and labor would jointly supervise certain limited aspects of factory operations, unhampered to any great extent by the state, which Brandts, as many Catholics during the *Kulturkampf*, did not trust.[2]

Such institutions appeared even more necessary after passage of the anti-Socialist laws. Suppression of the labor movement would bring "social war"[3] to the Catholic regions of Germany and the resultant chaos, feared Brandts, could only play into the hands of the Marxists. During the winter of 1878/79, therefore, he contacted fellow employers and other "friends of labor" concerning the establishment of a new organization that would enable workers to share some of the benefits of modern industrialism. An article in the *Christlich-soziale Blätter* in June 1879 was followed by further discussion at the Aachen *Katholikentag* in August, and by May 1880 the Catholic employ-

1. Ernst Lieber to Lujo Brentano, 24 September 1881, Brentano Papers 32a, BA Koblenz.
2. *Ibid.* The most informative biographical material on Brandts is found in parts 2 and 3 of Emil Ritter's unpublished work, *Die Männer aus Mönchen-Gladbach*, Ritter Papers ER/D-16, KfZG Bonn. Ritter's sketches are extremely valuable, for they are based to a great extent on non-extant private materials. For this paragraph, see part 2, pp. 6, 11–19, part 3, p. 13.
3. *Arbeiterwohl*, no. 1, 1881, pp. 19–20.

ers' association *Arbeiterwohl* had been founded.[4] "Based on the firm belief," began the by-laws,

> that an effective struggle against the abuses which often result from modern industry and are a dangerous threat to bourgeois society can only be solved by Christian principles, Catholic industrialists and other friends of labor have united in an association to improve the status of the working class in Germany without pursuing ulterior political motives.[5]

Joining Brandts on the executive committee were Dr. Christoph Moufang of Mainz, Father Arnold Bongartz of Rellinghausen, Matthias Wiese of Essen, Dr. Georg Hertling of Bonn, and four of Brandts's fellow Catholic employers from western Germany.[6] Bongartz served as administrative secretary of the organization until the fall of 1880, when ill health caused him to surrender his duties to a young theologian from the Sauerland, Franz Hitze.[7]

By the mid-1880s, Brandts, Hitze and other *Arbeiterwohl* leaders had reached agreement, not without considerable internal tensions,[8] on a threefold program. First of all, in order to allay the fears of church and government officials, Catholic workers would be systematically educated for their future role as trade unionists in *Arbeitervereine* led by priests appointed by the bishops. But this was not merely a sacrifice to the established powers. The paternalistic Brandts rejected the Christian-social movement of the 1870s as so much "radical twaddle,"[9] nor was he alone in these feelings. Many Catholic employers in western Germany were in an angry mood, especially entrepreneurs in Aachen, "who had been burned"[10] by the union-like activities of Cronenberg. Politics would be left exclusively to the Catholic press, moreover, for the workers' clubs were not to raise another generation of "tub-thumping, pot-house politicians."[11] As Hitze explained to a colleague in Munich, "as soon as you pursue politics you'll have the government and the

4. Ritter, *Die Männer aus Mönchen-Gladbach*, part 3, p. 11, Ritter Papers ER/D-16, KfZG Bonn; Franz Müller, *Franz Hitze und sein Werk* (Hamburg: Hanseatisch Verlagsanstalt, 1928), p. 56; Ritter, *Volksverein*, pp. 129–31. The Müller biography of Brandt's associate Franz Hitze is also invaluable to the historian, for it too is based on solid research in pre–WW II Mönchen-Gladbach.
5. *Arbeiterwohl*, no. 1, 1881, pp. 19–20.
6. *Ibid.*
7. Ritter, *Die Männer aus Mönchen-Gladbach*, part 3, p. 11, Ritter Papers ER/D-16, KfZG Bonn.
8. For the details see this author's dissertation, "Christian Labor and the Politics of Frustration in Imperial Germany," Ohio State University, 1978, pp. 72–74.
9. Hitze to Father Otto Müller, 6 November 1918, *Archiv der katholischen Arbeitnehmerbewegung Westdeutschlands*, vol. 5, KfZG Bonn.
10. *Ibid.*
11. *Arbeiterwohl*, December 1881.

employers against you, and, what is even worse, the workers will press you farther and farther forward with your program to the point where you won't be able to go along. Then you'll have your own workers against you."[12] This unpolitical approach, it was felt, would also shield the untrustworthy laborers from Socialist agitation which, despite the anti-Socialist laws of 1878, had never completely disappeared.[13] The education of the workers was thus going to be a cautious, gradual, manipulative process.

Secondly, *Arbeiterwohl* and its journal of the same name would attempt to persuade employers to establish factory committees and welfare institutions.[14] These bodies were seen as the foundation of a new corporative economic order. After workers had gained experience in local factory committees like that established by Brandts, special "chambers of labor" could be formed uniting these committees on a regional level. These regional bodies would present the workers' demands to chambers of commerce, municipal and state governments, or the Reichstag.[15]

And thirdly, Brandts's employers' organization would mollify opposition to *Arbeiterwohl*'s social reform proposals in government and parliamentary circles. This could be accomplished by articles in *Arbeiterwohl*, in-depth statistical studies (*Gutachten*), and generally, by establishing Mönchen-Gladbach as a national center for the study of social problems and their solution.[16]

Brandts and Hitze were able to achieve only moderate success with their second goal of influencing the private business sector. Nearly 200 Catholic employers had joined *Arbeiterwohl* by 1890 and the association's journal, edited by Hitze, had attracted 1,800 subscribers.[17] Only two owners had emulated Brandts' factory committee by 1888,[18] but in the fall of that year an influential convert was made. Very impressed with Mönchen-Gladbach's program, Baron Hans von Berlepsch, *Regierungspräsident* in Düsseldorf, joined Brandts in founding the Public Welfare Association of Left-Bank Rhineland (*Linksrheinischer Verein für Gemeinwohl*). By January 1889 a set of model statutes for factory committees had been formulated, and by spring of the

12. Quoted in Denk, *Christliche Arbeiterbewegung in Bayern*, p. 160, from a letter of the 1880s.
13. Hitze to Father Otto Müller, 6 November 1818, *Archiv der katholischen Arbeitnehmerbewegung Westdeutschlands*, KfZG Bonn; Ritter, *Männer aus Mönchen-Gladbach*, part 3, pp. 22–23, 25–26, 30, Ritter Papers ER/D-16, KfZG Bonn.
14. Ritter, *Volksverein*, p. 134.
15. Pieper Manuscript, part 2, p. 226, StA MG.
16. See Ritter, *Männer aus Mönchen-Gladbach*, part 3, pp. 30ff., Ritter Papers ER/D-16, KfZG Bonn.
17. Ritter, *Volksverein*, p. 135.
18. Max Hering, *Arbeiterausschüsse in der deutschen Industrie* (Leipzig: Verlag von Duncker und Humbolt, 1880), pp. 58–101.

same year the idea of minimal codetermination was beginning to spread slowly among the textile manufacturers of the lower Rhine.[19]

* * * *

In the first area of educating the Catholic proletariat, Mönchen-Gladbach registered much less progress. Catholic *Arbeitervereine* claimed about 35,000 members in July 1889 and *Knappenvereine* added another 9,000.[20] Yet these unimpressive figures did not reflect actual worker membership. Artisans, small businessmen, and civil servants often joined these associations, so they claimed, "as a good cause,"[21] and well-to-do Catholics were frequently included on membership lists as honorary members.[22] In relatively few cases, however, did this ostensible concern for the lower classes reflect a progressive social consciousness. Some joined to make a favorable impression on the parish priest, others for philistine advertising purposes, or sometimes *to prevent* the workers from organizing some day.[23] "[The upper classes] fear the reigning dissatisfaction among the masses and hope that the *Arbeitervereine* will have a pacifying effect,"[24] noted one informed observer from Cologne.

Nor did the local clergy prove equal to the task of educating the workers for future activity in trade unions. Few priests sprang from working-class backgrounds and none received training in social organization at the seminary.[25]

19. *Ibid.*, pp. 13, 58–101, 167; Ritter, *Männer aus Mönchen-Gladbach*, part 3, p. 29, Ritter Papers ER/D-16, KfZG Bonn; Hans von Berlepsch, *Sozialpolitische Erfahrungen und Erinnerungen* (Mönchen-Gladbach: Volksverein-Verlag, 1925), pp. 23–25. Significantly enough, Berlepsch notes that he knew almost nothing about the social question before coming to western Germany in the late 1880s. His relationship with Brandts must therefore have been an educational one at first. It is also interesting to note that the "armchair socialists" in the *Verein für Sozialpolitik* did not become involved with the question of workers' codetermination until 1890. Brandts must therefore have been alone as Berlepsch's instructor. First on the agenda of the initial meeting of Berlepsch's Public Welfare Association, for example, was a discussion of Brandt's factory institutions. See the executive committee minutes of the Association, Reg. D. Präsidialbüro 1055, HSA Düsseldorf.

20. *Arbeiterwohl*, Heft 7, July 1889. See also the unpublished manuscript of church labor leader Dr. Otto Müller, *Eine Geschichte der katholischen Arbeitervereine*, p. 4, KAB Haus Köln. (Hereafter cited as: Müller Manuscript.)

21. Müller Manuscript, p. 4, KAB Haus Köln.

22. Non-worker membership may have been very high indeed. Nikolaus Osterroth, *Vom Beter zum Kämpfer* (Berlin: Buchhandlung Vorwärts, 1920), p. 78, notes that his *Arbeiterverein* near Mannheim included 116 honorary members out of a total membership of 261, or 44 percent. The *Arbeitervereine* in Munich averaged 50 percent during the 1890s. See Denk, *Christliche Arbeiterbewegung in Bayern*, p. 134.

23. Denk, *Christliche Arbeiterbewegung in Bayern*, p. 135.

24. See the remarks of Father Peter Oberdörffer, *Bericht über eine Versammlung von geistlichen Herren der Erzdiöcese welche sich mit Arbeitervereine befassen*, 4 July 1892, Nr. 641. Münsterarchiv Essen.

25. Denk, *Christliche Arbeiterbewegung in Bayern*, pp. 133–34, 372–74.

With the disappearance of overt Socialist activity in 1878, moreover, most parish priests lapsed into a false sense of security. Their approach to the labor question was, as one historian puts it, "primitive enough to make you think."[26] The workers were not instructed in labor relations or social politics, but instead were offered morality plays, travelogues, beer evenings, and sing-alongs. In one case a workers' glee club simply changed its name to *Arbeiterverein* and then continued to enjoy the same function as before.[27]

For most priests and lay leaders, in fact, the *Arbeitervereine* were important only as a means of attracting followers for the church and Center Party. Education in class or estate consciousness, reasoned many, would only benefit the Socialists. "I still remember vividly," recalled a Christian labor leader, "how one chaplain in Duisburg shuddered when a Catholic worker said 'we workers' at a political rally."[28] For the clergyman this had been the "storm-warning signal of the revolution."[29] Small wonder, then, that relations within these clubs were sometimes tense,[30] that membership turnover was high, or that many Catholic workers simply refused to join.

Nor is it really surprising that the S.P.D. was able to gain from these circumstances. Nikolaus Osterroth, a Catholic miner active in the Socialist unions after the turn of the century, leaves us a useful description of his experience with the paternalistic denigration of workers that was so common in the Catholic labor movement of the 1880s and 1890s.[31] Osterroth was the product of a strict Catholic upbringing in a small town near the industrial center of Mannheim. As a young man he attended church and communion regularly, and, though not particularly pious or devout, accepted the social, political, and religious teachings of the church. Because the local *Arbeiterverein* offered him a rare opportunity to socialize in the restrictive atmosphere of the 1880s, Osterroth gladly became a member. In short, he was not a worker who was originally inclined to join the Socialists.

Osterroth became a convert to the S.P.D., however, during the first serious labor dispute in the area. The parish priest and leader of the local *Arbeiterverein* played a central role in this conversion, interestingly enough, by imme-

26. M. P. Fogarty, *Christian Democracy in Western Europe* (Notre Dame, Indiana: University of Notre Dame Press), p. 30.
27. Müller Manuscript, p. 4, KAB Haus Köln.
28. Quoted in the unpublished memoirs of *Volksverein* official Anton Heinen, *Mein Leben als Volksbildner: Worum es mir ging*, p. 8, Box 15/1/6, StA MG. (Hereafter cited as: Heinen Manuscript.)
29. *Ibid.*, p. 8.
30. See the *Protokollbuch des katholischen Knappenvereins Essen-Ruhr*, February and September 1885, 11 Rep. 103, El, Nr. 25, and the *Protokollbuch des Bergmannsverein zu Überruhr*, 26 August 1883, 10 Rep. 103, El, Nr. 23, vol. 2, StA Essen.
31. Osterroth, *Vom Better zum Kämpfer*, *passim*.

diately siding with the owners and sermonizing about the God-given position of authority granted to employers. There had always been lords and servants, he declared from the pulpit, and God had bestowed upon lords the right to instruct their social inferiors. Osterroth was confused by this stance, for it seemed to him that priests should instruct *all* members of the community, not just the workers, in the church's social teachings. As his feeling of dismay grew, Osterroth wrote a lengthy letter to his priest, mistakenly assuming that the next sermon would give justice to the workers' outlook.

> My disappointment was immeasurable. Not one word did I hear in the sermon that would have vindicated my burning hopes. Instead, I got a pathetic litany about the snares and traps of the devil "who stalks those he can eat up like a roaring lion." Then some more racket about the anti-church newspapers which awaken the spirit of opposition and dissatisfaction and separate the flock from the shepherds. I went home spiritless and desolate. I was unable to think, and after dinner I ran to the pub, where I drank myself into a stupor. For an entire week I was in a mood of hopelessness.[32]

In this state of emotional distress, Osterroth came into contact with a group of young workers agitating for the S.P.D. He was astonished to discover that the Social Democrats, far from the picture of revolutionary anarchism and nihilistic destructiveness painted by his priest, actually advocated practical social reforms and trade unionism. Not particularly bothered by now with the atheism of the S.P.D. like some of his more devout Catholic comrades, Osterroth switched allegiance to the S.P.D. that very day.

And he was not alone in joining non-Catholic labor groups. Indeed events in the labor world were rapidly overtaking the Christian-socialists in Mönchen-Gladbach. The relaxation of the anti-Socialist laws in 1881 and the introduction in 1883 and 1884 of compulsory health and accident insurance partially supervised by labor organizations once again created an atmosphere conducive to the growth of trade unions. The Hirsch-Duncker unions, which had survived the government's crackdown in 1878, almost tripled in size after 1882 to a membership of 62,600 in 1889.[33] The Liberal unions recruited most of their members from Berlin, Hamburg, and the industrial centers of Saxony, but had also made significant inroads among the Catholic miners and metal workers of the Ruhr.[34] The Socialist "craft associations" (*Fachvereine*) began to revive in 1882 and 1883 and quickly expanded to a level of 135,000 by

32. *Ibid.*, p. 133.
33. Schröder and Hafterstroh, "Verband der deutschen Gewerkvereine," in Fricke (ed.), *Die bürgerlichen Parteien*, vol. 2, p. 685.
34. Max J. Koch, *Die Bergarbeiterbewegung im Ruhrgebiet zur Zeit Wilhelm II* (Düsseldorf: Droste-Verlag, 1954), p. 32.

early 1889.[35] Like the Hirsch-Duncker organizations, the Socialist unions were based mainly in northern and eastern Germany.

This changed quickly, however, during the great miners' strike of May 1889. The walkout began as a spontaneous protest of younger, poorly paid coal truck haulers near Bochum and Gelsenkirchen, but spread quickly as the older, somewhat better-off hewers, who resented long hours of work and many of the unfair practices in the mines, joined in. As the strike gained momentum and nearly 10,000 miners had walked off the job, two factions emerged in the leadership role. On the Catholic side was a cadre of miners led by Johannes Fussangel, the radical middle-class editor of a Center newspaper in Bochum, and Lambert Lensing, owner of *Tremonia* in Dortmund. Both had been avid supporters of the workers' cause for years. On the other side were Social Democratic labor leaders like Ludwig Schröder, active as an organizer since the 1870s. The Catholic *Arbeiter-* and *Knappenvereine* of the Ruhr tried initially to prevent the strike from spreading, and only when this proved impossible did they agree to participate. Some *Knappenverein* leaders attempted to gain control of the negotiations, but were eclipsed in influence by Fussangel, Schröder, and the confessionally-mixed strike committees. Other religious leaders contented themselves with the distribution of food or perhaps the special presentation of a morality play. The *Knappenvereine*, in short, were unable to wield any great influence over the strikers despite a belated attempt to stay abreast of events. Given the patriarchal nature of these associations, described above, this outcome is not very surprising.[36]

Perhaps the only lasting effect of this, the greatest German strike of the nineteenth century, was the formation of a miners' union in August 1889. The Association for Maintenance and Promotion of Miners' Interests in Rhineland and Westphalia, as the new organization was called, was at first politically well balanced. Of the sixteen workers who came to the fore, seven were supporters of Fussangel and/or the Center Party. Six were Socialist, and three neutral. By early 1890, however, a number of interesting conversions had taken place. Three of the "*Fussangelianer*" and one of the neutral workers, Heinrich Möller, had proclaimed themselves Social Democrats. There is some evidence to suggest that the three objectors from Fussangel's camp were, like

35. Statistics and comments on the Socialist unions are based on Vernon L. Lidtke, *The Outlawed Party: Social Democracy in Germany 1878–1890* (Princeton, New Jersey: Princeton University Press, 1966), pp. 180–82, 292–93.

36. Domvikar Otmar Vieth, "Die Katholischen Knappenvereine," pp. 22, 24, 26; Tenflede, *Sozialgeschichte*, pp. 582–97; Imbusch, *Arbeitsverhältnis und Arbeiterorganisationen*, pp. 277–316; Stephen Hickey, "The Shaping of the German Labour Movement: Miners in the Ruhr," in Evans (ed.), *Society and Politics*, pp. 230, 233–34; Klaus Tenfelde, "Linksradikale Strömungen in der Ruhrbergarbeiterschraft 1905 bis 1919," in Hans Mommsen and Ulrich Borsdorf, *Glückauf, Kameraden!* (Cologne: Bund-Verlag GmbH, 1979), p. 201.

the disillusioned Osterroth, already "ripe inside"[37] for the S.P.D., needing only a brief exposure to the Socialists before severing their tenuous ties with the Catholic cause.

Fussangel and Lensing, not surprisingly, began to reassess their support for the union. When three executive committee members of the new organization ran as Socialist candidates for the Reichstag in February 1890, the two withdrew their backing and, along with Center Reichstag deputy Gerhardt Stötzel, formed the Christian miners' association *Glückauf*. Though nominally interconfessional, *Glückauf* was really an attempt to split the large Catholic minority away from the Socialist union, thereby preserving the Center's constituency in the large Reichstag districts of Dortmund, Bochum, Gelsenkirchen, and Essen.

The first Christian miners' association, however, was a fiasco. On the one hand, Catholic *Knappenverein* leaders in the Ruhr showed a complete lack of enthusiasm for the new union, claiming that they had no time for such matters.[38] In reality, the labor priests of the Ruhr, fearful of the radical consequences of any organization outside *their* control, were busy organizing a Catholic *Knappenbund* which certainly reduced the number of recruits for *Glückauf*.[39] But Christian miners outside the *Knappenbund* were also unmoved. Clearly an attempt to sabotage the older union for political purposes, *Glückauf* attracted few workers of either faith and soon collapsed.[40] The *Alter Verband*, as the Socialist union was now dubbed, continued to expand in the meantime, reaching a level of 36,800 by December 1891—about 28 percent of all miners in the Ruhr.[41] With these developments, the Socialist trade unions had established a foothold in Western Germany. Soon Socialist organizers appeared in other parts of the Rhineland, hoping to capitalize on the excitement generated by the great miners' strike. The westward expansion of the Socialist union movement after 1889 and, more importantly, the general economic upswing which began at the end of the decade boosted overall membership in Socialist unions to over 320,000 by late 1890. If the Christian socialists were to avoid permanent loss of the organizational advantage they

37. Imbusch, *Arbeitsverhältnis und Arbeiterorganisationen*, p. 313, discussed the inner feelings of the objectors with a number of participants from the time.

38. August Brust, "August Brust," in Bernhard Cwiklinski (ed.), *August Brust: Gründer und Vorkämpfer der christlichen Gewerkschaftsbewegung in Deutschland* (Essen, n.p., n.d.), p. 10. This pamphlet is located in the private library of Dr. Bernard Koch, general secretary of the Christian Trade Union Alliance in Bonn.

39. Landrat Essen to the *Regierungspräsident* Düsseldorf, 20 October 1892, Reg. D. 24723, HSA Düsseldorf; *Bericht über eine Versammlung von geistlichen Herren der Erzdiöcese welche sich mit Arbeitervereinen befassen*, no. 641, Münsterarchiv Essen.

40. Koch, *Die Bergarbeiter im Ruhrgebiet*, p. 55.

41. *Alter Verband* statistics are found in the files of the provincial governor of Westphalia, Oberpräsidium, 2830, vol. 2, StA Münster.

had once possessed in the Catholic districts of the west, immediate action was necessary.

The alarming effect which these Socialist trade union advances had in bourgeois circles was heightened by the meteoric rise of the Social Democratic Party itself. Indeed neither suppression nor social insurance had halted the Center's great rival on the left. After setbacks in 1878 and 1881, the S.P.D. garnered over 500,000 votes in 1884, and over 750,000 in 1887. The Reichstag's refusal to renew the anti-Socialist laws in January 1890 led to even greater electoral victories in the following month. Though still trailing the Center, Conservatives, Progressives, National Liberals, and the *Reichspartei* in terms of deputies, the S.P.D. nevertheless surpassed all other parties in popular strength with nearly 1,500,000 votes. With the *Zentrumsturm* in peril, party leaders met in a series of conferences after the elections to discuss methods to strengthen the organizational base of the party.

These meetings resulted in the formation of the People's Association of Catholic Germany (*Volksverein für das katholische Deutschland*) in October 1890.[42] The 20-man directing board included Brandts as chairman and Karl Trimborn, a Progressive lawyer from Cologne, as vice-chairman, as well as Hitze, Galen, Stötzel, and other Center deputies, editors, and priests. By creating a network of local offices or *Volksbüros* whose purpose would be to distribute literature, organize rallies, and win new members, the *Volksverein* hoped to attract a mass following loyal to church and Center and unsusceptible to the Socialists' doctrine of class struggle and revolution. The success of the new organizations was immediate. During its first two years, the *Volksverein* attracted nearly 125,000 members from all classes, founded 16 *Volksbüros*, and established a general secretariat in Mönchen-Gladbach under the able management of Dr. August Pieper, one of the few socially conscious priests from the Ruhr. Together with the *Katholikentag* and Center *Fraktionen*, the institutional structure of political Catholicism in Germany was complete.

The *Volksverein*, however, was no substitute for a thriving trade union organization. By the early 1890s it had become painfully evident that the effectiveness of any political organization would depend to a very great extent on the political leanings of the trade unions. Lensing and Fussangel had realized this well enough, but their clumsy attempt to prevent Socialist domination of the union movement in the Ruhr had resulted in just that.

In early 1890, therefore, Franz Brandts, chairman of *Arbeiterwohl* and the *Volksverein*, responded to the challenge by establishing a trade union for his workers. Others among the 200 *Arbeiterwohl* employers were invited to fol-

42. For the *Volksverein*, see Hüsgen, *Ludwig Windthorst*, pp. 390–92; and Ritter, *Volksverein*, pp. 139–51, 181.

low suit,[43] but all evidence would suggest that none did so. Joseph Broix, a factory owner who had taken over the editorship of the *Christlich-soziale Blätter* after Bongartz's death in 1883, probably spoke for the overwhelming majority of his Catholic colleagues when he wrote in late 1890 that it would be a mistake to found Christian-social unions. This was tantamount to fighting the Socialists with socialism and could therefore only further the cause of revolution. Christian forces should employ religion to combat the false Socialist notion of utopia on earth.[44] Broix's article only underscores what has been said thus far concerning the strong psychological aversion in the Christian camp to anything that smacked of Marxism *or merely labor independence*. Socialism was more than a threat to the *"Herr im Haus"* position of the entrepreneur; it would also lead to unruliness and disorder after uneducated workers came into possession of means of production they were unable to manage. Worker control of the state, one can well imagine, was even more frightening to men like Broix.

* * * *

By 1890, therefore, Mönchen-Gladbach had made little progress with its three-part program of educating the masses, the employers, and the state. Catholic workers were showing signs of unruliness, with probably as many belonging to Socialist unions as the inadequate religious *Vereine*; and the *Volksverein*, for all its political usefulness, could not be seen as an alternative to trade unionism. Catholic employers, moreover, were turning a deaf ear to Mönchen-Gladbach, founding neither factory committees nor Christian trade unions. The conversion of *Regierungspräsident* Hans von Berlepsch to ideas of minimal codetermination was some consolation to Brandts and Hitze, but for the most part the state, too, remained outside Mönchen-Gladbach's sphere of influence in the 1880s. *Arbeiterwohl* had no trouble convincing the Center Party that Bismarck's social insurance program should be amended to reduce the degree of Reich, or as Catholics saw it, thinly veiled Prussian control, but with the exception of the health insurance bill of 1883, the pathbreaking reforms of the 1880s (workmen's compensation, 1884; old-age pensions, 1889) were administered to a great extent from Berlin.[45]

Not until the aftermath of the miners' strike did Mönchen-Gladbach's political fortunes take a radical turn for the better. For one thing, Berlepsch was promoted to Prussian Minister of Commerce and Industry, and in him the

43. Ritter, *Volksverein*, p. 135.
44. *Christlich-soziale Blätter*, no. 12, December 1890, pp. 697–98.
45. Ritter, *Männer aus Mönchen-Gladbach,* part 3, pp. 30ff., Ritter Papers ER/D-16, KfZG Bonn.

arguments of Hitze and Brandts concerning labor codetermination had an influential advocate in Berlin. Dr. Georg Hinzpeter, the privy councilor and former tutor of Wilhelm II from Westphalia, also appears to have been impressed with Mönchen-Gladbach's idea of checking the economic power of the entrepreneur. The *"Herr im Haus"* concept of labor relations was not only unfair to the worker, they reasoned, but as the root cause of labor disturbances was also detrimental to the state. Berlepsch and Hinzpeter approached the young Kaiser with these arguments in late 1899/early 1890 and were able to convince him of the need for new social legislation.[46] The Imperial Manifesto of 9 February 1890 expressed the monarch's desire to extend the safety and insurance legislation initiated by his grandfather. More importantly, the manifesto also stated that the workers' "claim to equality of rights"[47] would be observed:

> For the furtherance of peace between employers and employed the legal determination will be considered of the manner in which workers, through representatives who enjoy their confidence, may share in the settlement of joint affairs, and be authorized to protect their interests by negotiation with the employers and the organs of My government. Through such an arrangement the free and peaceful expression of the worker's desires and grievances will be made possible, and the governmental authorities will be given an opportunity to inform themselves uninterruptedly of the conditions of the workers, and to keep in touch with them . . . For the preliminary consideration of these questions I intend to summon the State Council under My presidency, to be assisted by experts whom I shall call together for the purpose.[48]

Shortly before the manifesto was made public, Hinzpeter visited Mönchen-Gladbach under orders from William to request that Hitze and Brandts help draft the new bills and assure the support of the wary Center Party.[49] Mönchen-Gladbach's efforts were successful, and by spring 1891, the Re-

46. Ritter, *Männer aus Mönchen-Gladbach*, part 2, pp. 20–21, part 3, p. 29, Ritter Papers ER/D-16, KfZG; Mueller, *Franz Hitze*, pp. 101–2; Wilhelm II, *The Kaiser's Memoirs*, (New York: Harper and Brothers Publishers, 1922), pp. 37–38; Berlepsch to the Prussian minister of the interior, 23 January 1890, reprinted in Born and Rassow, *Akten zur staatlichen Sozialpolitik*, pp. 34–38; Diary entry of Count Alfred Waldersee for 3 February 1890, in Otto Meissner (ed.), *Denkwürdigkeiten des General-Feldmarschalls Alfred Grafen von Waldersee* (Berlin: Deutsche Verlags-Anstalt, 1923), vol. 2, pp. 99–100; Otto von Bismarck, *Kaiser vs. Bismarck* (New York: Macmillan Company, 1930), p. 155; Kirchhoff, *Staatliche Sozialpolitik im Ruhrbergbau*, p. 104.
47. Quoted in Bismarck, *Kaiser vs. Bismarck*, p. 80.
48. Quoted in *ibid.*, pp. 80–81.
49. Father Kirchesch to Eduard Schopen, 20 December 1909, Nr. B III 15.9, Bd. 1, pp. 36–39, BisA Trier; Ritter, *Männer aus Mönchen-Gladbach*, part 2, pp. 20–21, Ritter Papers ER/D-16, KfZG Bonn.

ichstag had passed legislation creating optional arbitration tribunals for every district and optional factory committees for every firm with more than 50 employees. If this experiment were successful, William planned to create regional labor chambers (*Oberausschüsse*) that would negotiate with employers and the state concerning work conditions and termination of strikes.[50]

Circulated in May 1891, Pope Leo XIII's famous encyclical *Rerum Novarum* promised to sustain the social and political momentum which Brandts and Hitze had attained by the spring of that year. The document[51] was basically an attempt to apply Thomistic philosophy to the manifest social problems facing the modern world. Thus, while the institution of private property was defended at length as part of a natural order, the pope also urged European Catholics, and the states governing them, to intensify efforts to relieve the plight of the proletariat.

> The poor are members of the national community equally with the rich; they are real component living members which constitute, through the family, the living body, and it need hardly be said that they are in every state very largely in the majority. It would be irrational to neglect one portion of the citizens and favor another; and therefore the public administration must duly and solicitously provide for the welfare and comfort of the working classes; otherwise, the law of justice will be violated which ordains that each man shall have his due. To cite the wise words of St. Thomas of Aquinas: 'As the part and the whole are in a certain sense identical, the part may in some sense claim what belongs to the whole.'[52]

Such efforts to aid the poor would include social legislation as well as promotion of labor organizations genuinely committed to the task of improving the workers' economic situation. For, like Ketteler before him, the pope felt that man possessed a natural tendency, and hence a natural right, to form bonds with other men in private associations designed to promote the well-being of the members. This right had been described by St. Thomas, and references to this effect could also be found in the Holy Scriptures. "Woe to him that is alone," Leo reminded Catholics, "for when he falleth he hath none to lift him up."[53] The state was obligated, therefore, to create a favorable environment for associations to grow. "The state is bound to protect natural rights, not to destroy them."[54]

50. Karl Erich Born, *Staat und Sozialpolitik seit Bismarcks Sturz* (Weisbaden: Franz Steiner Verlag GmbH, 1957), p. 12.
51. Pope Leo XIII, *On the Condition of the Working Classes* (Pittsburgh: The Pittsburgh Observer, 1891.)
52. *Ibid.*, p. 16.
53. *Ibid.*, p. 24.
54. *Ibid.*, p. 25.

Leo was worried, however, that Socialists and anarchists would monopolize the European labor movement and exploit it for political, anti-religious purposes. Coinciding with the formation of the Second Socialist International in 1889, the German miners' strike and the London longshoremen's strike seemed to confirm these fears. Under these circumstances Christian workingmen could do one of two things:

> Either join associations in which their religion will be exposed to peril, or form associations among themselves—unite their forces and shake off courageously the yoke of so unrighteous and intolerable an oppression. No one who does not wish to expose man's chief good to extreme risk will for a moment hesitate to say that the second alternative should by all means be adopted.[55]

Other passages from the encyclical make it clear that the pope preferred exclusive Catholic associations which would bring workers and employers together in the same organization. These "mutual associations" would consider the rights and duties of both capital and labor an appoint committees to settle disputes "should it happen that either a master or workman believe himself injured."[56] Strikes were a dubious phenomenon to be eradicated by eliminating the root cause.

> When work-people have recourse to a strike, it is frequently because the hours of labor are too long, or the work too hard, or because they consider their wages insufficient. The grave inconvenience of this not uncommon occurrence should be obviated by public remedial measures; for such paralyzing of labor not only affects the masters and their workpeople alike, but is extremely injurious to trade and to the general interests of the public; moreover, on such occasions, violence and disorder are generally not far distant, and thus it frequently happens that the public peace is imperiled. The law should forestall and prevent such troubles from arising . . . But if by a strike or other combination of workingmen there should be imminent danger of disturbance to the public peace . . . it would be right to invoke the aid and authority of the law.[57]

The pope did not insist, however, that all Christian labor organizations follow the pattern he had set down in *Rerum Novarum*. The particulars of organization would have to depend on national character, practical difficulties encountered, and "other circumstances of fact and of time."[58] Thus the document included no categorical rejection of strikes or interconfessional associa-

55. *Ibid.*, p. 26.
56. *Ibid.*, p. 29.
57. *Ibid.*, pp. 18–19.
58. *Ibid.*, p. 28.

tions for workers alone. The general, non-definitive nature of the encyclical had its obvious merits. But after the turn of the century, zealous factions in disagreement over the morality of the strike, cooperation with Protestants, or independence from church control would turn to *Rerum Novarum* and find justification for their opposing views. In the long run the encyclical probably did more to hinder the Christian labor movement than to further it. For the time being, however, the document was a promising weapon in the hands of Christian-social activists.

The publication of *Rerum Novarum* in May 1891 stimulated an intense debate among German Catholics concerning the pros and cons of trade unionism for Catholic workers. The most emphatic advocate of social action in the wake of the encyclical, interestingly enough, was not from the Rhineland or Westphalia, as one might expect, but from southern Germany. Shortly after the publication of *Rerum Novarum*, the leader of the Catholic workers of Munich, Father Lorenz Huber, formed an association of *Arbeitervereine* and began agitation for members. Like Hitze, Huber hoped that his efforts would eventually lead to the Christianization of the labor movement. He soon realized, however, that the labor movement would remain in Socialist hands unless churchmen could promise the workers an equally bold course of sociopolitical action. After numerous consultations with Catholic workers,[59] Huber therefore formulated a political program for the Catholic *Arbeitervereine* of Germany. It is significant that the program called upon the state to establish centralized trade unions for every branch of industry. These unions would then work within existing political institutions for social reforms.

Huber presented this program to a small gathering of church and *Arbeiterverein* officials at Mainz in late August 1892. Hitze was also present as spokesman for *Arbeiterwohl* and the *Volksverein*. Huber first emphasized the need for agreement in Catholic labor circles over basic goals and warned that only by "presentation and energetic implementation"[60] of a common program could the *Arbeitervereine* hope to play a decisive role in the German labor movement. He recommended, therefore, that a commission be established during the coming winter to examine his program, or perhaps formulate a new one. The final program should include specific demands upon the state and provide for "entry of the *Arbeitervereine* into the trade union movement."[61]

59. Karl Schirmer, future Christian trade union leader, recalled that Huber first consulted the workers. Karl Schirmer, *50 Jahre Arbeiter* (Duisburg: Echo Verlag, 1924), p. 31. Huber's program of 1892 was published years later in M. Gastegier, *Geschichte der christlichen Gewerkschaften in Süddeutschland* (Munich: Buchhandlung der Verbandes sudd. kath. Arbeitervereine, 1908), pp. 82–85.
60. Quoted in Gasteiger, *Christliche Gewerkschaften in Süddeutschland*, p. 84.
61. *Ibid.*, p. 183.

With an eye on the Reichstag elections scheduled for June 1893, he asked that the commission's work be published before April 1.

Huber had only partial success. Most of those present felt it "out of place"[62] to transform the labor associations *per se* into political organizations, but agreed that labor priests should have a "political guidepost"[63] to enable them to clarify the issue of social reform for their workers. It was decided in the end that those present should form a commission to consider three program proposals: the program already submitted by Huber; a second to be written by Father Peter Oberdörffer of Cologne; and a third by Hitze.

It quickly became evident that Oberdörffer's plans were just as far-reaching as Huber's. The former elaborated his ideas at a "practical-social course" held by the *Volksverein* in late September 1892.[64] "Modern society," Oberdörffer began, "is disordered and fatally ill. It threatens to collapse."[65] As the only cure for these ills, he recommended a corporate reconstruction of state and society, including a plan for a corporate parliament, and a proposal that all new and existing industrial undertakings be transformed into mutual ventures controlled by workers and managers. Wages would be regulated by joint committees and profits fairly divided. This was necessary, he continued, "in order to make the employer's factory also the worker's factory."[66] By altering existing property rights in this way, Oberdörffer hoped to Christianize big business, "the bearer of guilt for our social misery."[67] This program, he concluded, was merely a more precise formulation of the Thomistic principles set down in the encyclical *Rerum Novarum*.

Hitze, whose task it was to write a third socio-political program for the *Arbeitervereine*, was greatly worried by the Huber-Oberdörffer initiatives.[68] In principle he had no major disagreements with either man. The *Volksverein* leader had his doubts concerning the practicality of abolishing existing political institutions, but the concept of labor codetermination in industry was a proposal he had favored for years. Both Huber and Oberdörffer, however, put forward their ideas in the name of Catholicism, especially the latter, who declared he was acting in accordance with Rome. Hitze felt the economic

62. *Ibid.*, p. 183.
63. *Ibid.*, p. 184.
64. Oberdörffer's talk is printed in the *Kölner Correspondenz*, no. 1, 1893, pp. 1–34, StBib MG
65. *Ibid.*, p. 1.
66. *Ibid.*, p. 30.
67. *Ibid.*, p. 25.
68. The following discussion of Hitze is based on: Ernst Lieber to Lujo Brentano, 17 May 1892, Brentano Papers 32a, and August Pieper to Lujo Brentano, 18 June 1929, Brentano Papers 48, BA Koblenz; August Pieper to August Brust, 25 January 1924, *Führer-Korrespondenz*, Heft 2, April/June 1924, pp. 89–91; Pieper Manuscript, vol. 2, pp. 498–99, StA MG.

system needed drastic revision, but not in the name of the pope. In predominantly Protestant Germany such an approach would not only be counterproductive, it could possibly result in new anti-Catholic outbursts.

Indeed, attitudes in ruling circles were a source of great concern for Hitze. The dream of a nationwide system of factory committees crowned by chambers of labor was threatened by the Kaiser's change of heart toward social legislation. Influenced by heavy industrialists from the Ruhr (Krupp) and Saar (Stumm), William II was beginning to doubt the advisability of curbing the power of the entrepreneur. Thus Hitze, fearful of provoking a rollback of *existing* social bills, had been forced into a rather reluctant silence in the Reichstag by 1892. His position as social spokesman in the Center Party, where opposition to labor legislation was still very strong, had suffered as a result. For these additional reasons, the proposals of Huber and Oberdörffer were regarded as tactically unsound in Mönchen-Gladbach.

Nor did Hitze feel the time was ripe for promoting trade unions. Ideally, factory committees, chambers of labor, and other conciliatory institutions should precede trade unions to insure that worker organizations would reject the Socialist precept of class struggle and revolution. In practice, he agreed that a "Christianization" of the union movement might avoid these social dangers without the aid of moderating institutions, but Hitze shrank from this option too, partly due to his own doubts that Catholic workers were ready to participate responsibly in unions, primarily because of the severe opposition to trade unionism in other circles. The Catholic hierarchy and the Center Party feared a radicalization of the Catholic masses, and the government, too, was very sensitive to proposals for strengthening the labor movement and opening the Socialist floodgate. Huber's call for a rapid acceleration of unionism, therefore, might exacerbate relations within the Catholic camp, and more alarmingly, provoke the wrath of the state. By actively promoting unions in 1892, observed Hitze, "I could have done the [reactionary] Stumm and his friends, also in government, no better turn."[69]

There were thus many reasons why Mönchen-Gladbach opposed the proposals of Huber and Oberdörffer. Hitze's probable course of action would have been to prevent publication of the *Arbeiterverein* program suggested by Huber, or delay it as long as possible. Such reasoning may explain the fact that a "draft proposal" appeared in July 1893 without the signature of Hitze and the *Volksverein*.[70]

Signed by socially conscious *Arbeiterverein* officials from Cologne, Mainz,

69. August Pieper to August Brust, 25 January 1924, *Führer-Korrespondenz*, Heft 2, April/June 1924, p. 91.
70. The draft appeared in the *Kölner Correspondenz*, no. 9–11, 1893, pp. 169–72, StBib MG.

Munich, Breslau, and other smaller bishoprics, the program was a very conservative combination of the proposals of Huber and Oberdörffer. Huber, it seems, was thoroughly intimidated, refusing to publish his own, more far-reaching program in Munich for fear of conservative reprisals. Only his minor requests were included in the new draft program, while the demand for gradual dissolution of large landholdings and the scheme for national trade unions were set aside to make the program more appealing to conservative agrarians in the Center. The Bavarian's preference for existing political institutions, moreover, was replaced by a general statement in favor of the corporative state. This, too, would hopefully appeal to conservatives fed up with the Reichstag suffrage and particularists who considered corporatism a step away from Prussian supremacy. The only remaining demand which betrayed the radical origins of the program was Oberdörffer's call for codeterminational factories. To make the program more enticing, the signers claimed papal authority for their proposal and entitled it "The *Catholic* Social Program." After further negotiation with *Volksverein* officials in August 1893 had produced nothing but the old disagreements,[71] Oberdörffer and the commission majority attempted to force their views on the party leadership.

The lack of support in key places proved Oberdörffer's undoing in the end. Pressured from Oberdörffer on the one side and the Center leadership on the other, the central committee of the *Katholikentag* placed the social question on the agenda for August 1894. A closed, stormy session of the Social Section ensued, but the Center leadership eventually prevailed.[72] It had become clear that the ambitious labor chaplain from Cologne was shrewdly opening the door to Center agrarians, especially conservative aristocrats like Rhenish peasant leader Baron Felix von Löe, and this the party could not tolerate. The rumbling of rural unrest over Chancellor Caprivi's liberal commercial treaties was well underway by summer 1894, and the Center, which had backed the government bills, could ill afford to strengthen Löe's hand by yielding to Oberdörffer.[73] Thus the Huber-Oberdörffer program was reduced to one sentence demanding "legal guarantees [for] and promotion of vocational corporations as the main [social] task of the state."[74] As would occur time and again after 1894, the radical thrusts of the minority had been effectively parried in the interests of party unity.

Volksverein officials reassessed their position on the trade union question on the basis of the same rationale. However anxious Oberdörffer and his fol-

71. *Ibid.*, pp. 176–77; Denk, *Christliche Arbeiterbewegung in Bayern*, p. 80.
72. Kissling, *Geschichte der Katholikentage*, vol. 2, pp. 267–68.
73. Zeender, *German Center Party*, pp. 42, 43.
74. Quoted in Filthaut, *Deutsche Katholikentage*, p. 135.

lowers had been to present an ambitious political program, it was obvious to observers in Mönchen-Gladbach that the workers themselves had been almost totally excluded from this action. Huber's plans for national trade unions and unionist parliamentary representation had both been rejected to make the program appealing to agrarians. Labor codetermination in "mutual associations" now seemed quite patriarchal. Nor was there any support for the trade union movement in other Catholic circles. The Cologne *Katholikentag* in 1894 would go no further than recommending the idea of educational trade sections with *Arbeiter-* and *Gesellenvereine*,[75] a resolution which reflected the fact that the leaders of both these organizations preferred the educational trade section to the trade union. Although the encyclical *Rerum Novarum* had produced a change in clerical views toward organizing workers, the majority of parish priests and diocesan officials interpreted the document as no more than a sanction for the acceleration of the Catholic *Arbeiterverein* movement. Independent trade unions were still seen as the first step toward a radicalization and, eventually, a de-Christianization of the Catholic proletariat.

The Center *Fraktion*, moreover, was still not committed to Mönchen-Gladbach's long-range goals. Thus Hitze criticized the government's refusal to legislate chambers of labor, supposedly part of the Center's program, only to see the *Fraktion* willing to support the Kaiser's anti-labor "*Umsturzvolage*" in return for certain religious concessions.[76] William's oft-described desire to stiffen Germany's laws of association in the wake of S.P.D. Reichstag gains in 1893 had further weakened Hitze's position in the Center. For many reasons, therefore, the time was still not ripe to promote trade unions.

Rather, *Fachabteilungen* (trade sections) could be formed within the *Arbeitervereine* in the hope that Catholic workers thus trained might some day found their own trade unions, or gain control of already existing Socialist and Liberal unions.[77] Of the two ideas, the latter was deemed superior. This was Bishop Ketteler's preference, it will be recalled, and his policy of avoiding unnecessary division of the workers' movement was respected by Brandts and Hitze. Mönchen-Gladbach's thinking was further influenced by ongoing developments in the Socialist trade union camp. In March 1892, delegates of the so-called General Commission of German ("free") Trade Unions gathered at Halberstadt for their first nationwide congress. For shrewd observers like

75. *Ibid.*, p. 135.

76. For the Center and the *Umsturzvolange*, see Otto von Bülow, Prussian ambassador to the Vatican, to Chancellor Hohenlohe, 2 March 1895, Deutschland 125, Nr. 1, 6, AA Bonn; and Count Lerchenfeld, Bavarian envoy in Berlin, to Minister-präsident Crailsheim, 11 May 1895, reprinted in Born and Rassow, *Akten zur staatlichen Sozialpolitik*, pp. 60–61.

77. Pieper to Brust, 25 January 1924, *Führer-Korrespondenz*, Heft 2 April/June 1924, StBib MG; Imbusch, *Arbeitsverhältnis und Arbeiterorganisationen*, pp. 393–99. Also see below, Chapter 3.

Hitze, the Halberstadt Congress was a sign that the free trade unions were beginning to assert their organizational independence from the S.P.D. The motions of the local trade union faction, which envisioned the unions as adjuncts of the party, had been overwhelmingly defeated by the more trade union–oriented, centralist majority around General Secretary Karl Legien. The latter had no intention of politically damaging the party, however, and was therefore careful to point out that the free trade unions would work hand in hand with the party to prepare the masses for the class struggle. As far as Hitze was concerned, Catholic "trade sections" had to be formed on a large scale to train leaders who would encourage *further* independence of the free trade unions from the S.P.D.[78]

The decline in Socialist trade union membership gave Mönchen-Gladbach an added incentive to pursue this strategy. From a level of 320,000 in 1890, membership had fallen to 225,000 in 1892 and remained at this point during 1893 and 1894. The younger unions in western Germany were hit the hardest. Low wages and an abortive strike led to the collapse of a Socialist miners' union in the Saar in early 1893, and the Socialist miners' union of the Ruhr, the so-called *Alter Verband*, was also on the wane. The educational trade section was therefore a rather expedient compromise for Christian socialists in Mönchen-Gladbach. With the Socialist trade unions faltering, Hitze and Brandts were given extra time to school Catholic labor leaders whose moderate attitudes would win support for independent trade unionism in the Catholic camp. When the economy turned upwards again, Catholic workers would hopefully encounter less opposition from church and Center and could bring their influence to bear on the Socialist and Hirsch-Duncker unions. The increasing tensions between S.P.D. and General Commission after 1892/93 brightened the prospects of such an infiltration and strengthened the *Volksverein* in its resolve to refrain from promoting separate unions.

By 1894, however, Christian workers were beginning to resist such efforts to manipulate them. In April of that year, plans were laid for a Christian miners' union by August Brust, a Catholic miner active in the Christian-social *Arbeiterverein* of Altenessen. Angered by the outspoken socialism and atheism of the *Alter Verband*, and further by the fact that middle-class Catholics and Protestants had tried to divide the miners for religious or political reasons for the last decade, Brust wanted to unite Ruhr workers in a powerful non-Socialist union capable of exacting demands like factory committees, manage-

78. For the Halberstadt Congress, see Varain, *Freie Gewerkschaften*, pp. 12–13; for Hitze's views, see Pieper to Brust, 25 January 1924, printed in *Führer-Korrespondenz*, Heft 2, April/June 1924, StBib MG. For the views of the majority at Mainz, see August Erdmann, *Die christlichen Gewerkschaften insbesondere ihr Verhältnis zu Zentrum and Kirche* (Stuttgart: J. H. W. Dietz, GmbH, 1914), p. 44.

ment-labor chambers, and collective bargaining from both the mine owners and the state.[79] Naively, perhaps, the miner felt sure the government would back these efforts as soon as the proletariat was organized along Christian, non-Socialist lines. He explained these feelings to a fellow miner after the founding of the union.

> Today's entire economic system is false, and that comes from the power of a few capitalists. As much as the state would like to help, it can't if the workers, and especially the miners . . . don't stand united behind it. All we have to do now is organize, the rest will happen on its own. It won't be possible to implement my program for the workers right away, for unfortunately only a few miners know anything about real *Sozialpolitik*, that is, about Christian *Sozialpolitik*. They would rather follow the dumbest and stupidest cries of the Social Democrats. Once we have the people organized, things will start to be clearer to them.[80]

By the turn of the century, Brust's union would form the backbone of a national federation of Christian trade unions eager to carry on the social struggle which Kolping, Ketteler, and others had initiated a generation earlier. Before Christian workers could reorganize big business, however, they had to overcome substantial opposition to their movement. From this struggle Christian labor would eventually emerge independent in name, but not completely in fact, for Mönchen-Gladbach and the Church continued to exert a fair measure of subtle, indirect control over the movement.

79. Karl Kühne, "Kampf um die christliche Gewerkschaftsidee," in Cwiklinski (ed.), *August Brust*, p. 45; *Tremonia*, no. 10 (1), 10 January 1895.
80. Brust to an unnamed colleague, 29 August 1894, printed in Erdmann, *Die christliche Arbeiterbewegung*, pp. 407–8. Erdmann probably obtained the letter from one of the many Christian unionists who later joined the *Alter Verband*.

3

The Emergence of Christian Labor

The founding of the Christian miners' *Gewerkverein*, as it came to be known, is one of the most interesting, yet largely uninvestigated, chapters in the history of the German labor movement. For years Socialist enemies of the union castigated it as the product of opportunistic bourgeois elements within the church and Center Party. More recently, East German historian Herbert Gottwald has claimed that the *Gewerkverein* "was inspired by representatives of the Catholic bourgeoisie and clergy, even if the Catholic miner August Brust was shoved to the forefront at the founding assembly."[1] In the West, interestingly enough, John K. Zeender has argued that the founding of the first successful trade union for Christian workers might have been the work of Julius Bachem, the gifted political helmsman of the Rhenish Center Party.[2] Ronald Ross makes much the same point, moreover, in asserting that "it was not by chance that the first interconfessional labor organizations emerged in the Rhenish and Westphalian industrial areas immediately after the impressive victories scored there by the Social Democrats in the general elections of 1893."[3] *Post hoc ergo propter hoc*.

As the present chapter documents, the *Gewerkverein* was initiated and inspired by the workers themselves. Unlike the more radical Socialist laborers, whose only effective opponents when forming a union were the

1. Herbert Gottwald, "Der Gesamtverband der christlichen Gewerkschaften Deutschlands 1901–1933," in Fricke *et al.*, *Bürgerlichen Parteien*, vol. 2, p. 114.
2. Zeender, *German Center Party*, p. 77.
3. Ross, *Beleaguered Tower*, p. 95. Ralph René Mendershausen, "German Political Catholicism," pp. 36–37, makes similar remarks.

owners and the state, Brust and his Christian proletarians had to contend with the fierce resistance of employers, government officials, parish priests and pastors, bourgeois party leaders, and, not surprisingly, the Socialist workers themselves. Given these barriers, it is really remarkable that a Christian union was ever founded. Even before the final founding assembly, in fact, the union was shackled by political and religious leaders, Bachem not among them, who feared the consequences of labor independence. It is true, therefore, that the Christian miners' union was manipulated to serve the ends of other groups in 1894, but it is inaccurate to view the entire movement that year as if it were created from above. This initial effort to control the *Gewerkverein* was short-lived, moreover, for by 1898 the workers had asserted themselves and new manipulative efforts were necessary.

As recent research has shown, patterns of resistance and protest like those of the Christian miners were by no means unique during the 1890s. Stimulated by various economic grievances, improved communications, and the effects of decades of expanding public and private education, a plethora of grass-roots movements emerged outside the framework of existing party, church, and governmental structures. These movements presented a serious challenge to the social and political establishment during this turbulent decade.[4] Rural politics was radicalized by the appearance of the *Bund der Landwirte* and the recalcitrant Bavarian Peasants' League in 1893, while Theodor Wacker mobilized peasants and small townsmen in the southwest with his new "People's Party." Petty-bourgeois thinking was whipped up by officially unsanctioned pressure groups like the Navy League and the Pan-German League, while further unrest was caused by numerous anti-Semitical splinter parties outside the pale of respectability. The industrial proletariat, of course, was organized by the gradually solidifying free trade unions, much to the dismay of many S.P.D. hard-liners. The founding of the Christian miners' *Gewerkverein* in 1894, its eventual "revolt" from bourgeois stewardship in 1898, and the recurring question of merger between Christian and Socialist unions should thus be viewed as part of a larger process of political and social awakening in Germany. The reader should not advance to the conclusion, however, that this was simultaneously a process of democratization, for although many of the political parties, above all the Center, eventually scurried to make room for these new groups, both the workers and the political parties above them

4. See the articles by Ian Farr, David Blackbourn, Stephen Hickey, and Geoff Eley in Evans (ed.), *Society and Politics*; Richard S. Levy, *The Downfall of the Anti-Semitic Political Parties in Imperial Germany* (New Haven: Yale University Press, 1975); Hans Joachim Steinberg, "Die Entwicklung des Verhältnisses von Gewerkschaften und Sozialdemokratie bis zum Ausbruch des Ersten Weltkrieges," in Heinz Oskar Vetter, *Vom Sozialistengesetz zur Mitbestimmung* (Cologne: Bund Verlag, GmbH, 1975), pp. 125–33.

proved susceptible to additional manipulation by high church and governmental leaders who were eager to channel the nation's democratic forces into fairly manageable confines. This fact became most evident during the great merger debate of 1900/1902 (Chapter 5), the climactic development of the following three chapters.

* * * *

After the collapse of *Glückauf* in July 1892, Brust and fellow Catholics Hermann Köster and Johann Müller decided to establish an independent Christian organization as soon as the first opportunity presented itself.[5] The Socialist miners' *Alter Verband* was already beginning to experience serious problems. Historians have given many explanations for the precipitous decline of this union in the early 1890s, but have overlooked the fact that wages in the Ruhr sank 12.3 percent from late 1891 to mid-1893. Employers increased pressure on the union during these months, and, as more and more members found themselves unable to withstand the harassment or shoulder the burden of dues, a large-scale exodus from the organization began. The *Alter Verband* lost about two-thirds of its backing in 1892 and 1893, slipping to a membership of 12,400 by March 1894.[6] Sensing that the recession was almost over, Brust felt the time was ripe to draw up plans for his own Christian organization, force wages back to a higher level, and overtake the faltering *Alter Verband*.[7]

Brust's inclination to seize the initiative grew stronger in the spring of 1894 when the *Alter Verband* nominated five members as delegates to an international miners' congress in Berlin and Father Driessen, leader of the Christian-social *Arbeiterverein* of Essen, convoked a rally to make clear to everyone that

5. See Brust's recollections in Cwiklinski, *August Brust*, p. 10.
6. Müller, *Die christliche Gewerkschaftsbewegung*, p. 41, Imbusch, *Arbeitsverhältnis und Arbeiterorganisationen*, pp. 348–59; Koch, *Die Bergarbeiter im Ruhrgebiet*, pp. 53–56, and Hue, *Neutrale oder parteiische Gewerkschaften* (Bochum: Druck von H. Möller, 1900), pp. 67–69, emphasize political and economic factors before or after the period of wage decline beginning in October 1891 and leveling off in January 1893. (See the wage statistics for Ruhr miners appended to Koch, p. 148.) Statistics in StA Münster, Oberpräsidium 2830, vol. 2, clearly indicate, however, that *Alter Verband* membership in the Ruhr peaked in January 1892 at 36,965 and plummeted to 16,625 by December 1892. Members continued to trickle away thereafter as a result of the continuing stagnation of wages.

The *Alter Verband* merged with other Socialist miners' unions at Halle in September 1890. With the rise of Christian miners' groups in the 1890s, this union, too, came to be called the *Alter Verband*. Statistics in this chapter, however, refer *exclusively* to *Alter Verband* membership in the Ruhr. The reader may want to keep the following overall membership figures for the union in mind: 1890: 58,000; 1891: 58,000; 1892: 34,126; 1893: 16,126; 1894: 16,019; 1895: 5,332; 1896: 5,551; 1897: 11,968; 1898: 17,887; 1899: 20,478.
7. *Bergknappe*, no. 27, 7 July 1900.

his workers saw no value in the "unattainable, unpatriotic goals"[8] of the international labor movement.[9] Brust, who was unable to attend the rally himself, wrote an angry letter to Köster a week later concerning the purely negative, anti-Socialist tone of the final resolution to be submitted to the other Catholic *Vereine* of the Essen area in early May.

> [The Resolution] protests the initiative of [the *Alter Verband*] without announcing any action from the Christian associations to improve our economic position. If all that's going to happen, however, is to fight against the Social Democrats, then count me out. The Christian associations are always supposed to batter away against the Socialists, but when it comes to representing the miners' interests, the dear Christians hold back, that is, our leaders, with the exception of a few, don't concern themselves with such things. All right, if they won't help us economically, then I'll not let myself . . . be used as a battering ram. Let those who reared the Socialists fight them too.[10]

Brust then outlined what he felt should be done. He wanted to transform the Catholic and Evangelical *Knappenvereine* into a local trade union led by the workers themselves. Once established on an interconfessional basis in Essen, the union would spread to other parts of the Ruhr. Brust realized, however, that the transformation from *Arbeitervereine* to trade union could not occur overnight. He therefore suggested that the *Vereine* elect two or three members each to a general committee (*Gesamtausschuss*) so that it could look after their economic interests. To speed up the transition from *Arbeiterverein* general committee in Essen to Ruhr-wide trade union, Brust wanted the Center's *Volksverein* to help finance a new labor weekly. It was assumed that Father Driessen, too, would help. In early May a commission of seven miners led by Brust was selected to draft the statutes and economic program for a *Gesamtausschuss* of the confessional labor associations of Essen.[11]

Unknown to Brust and his colleagues, however, Church and Center leaders in Essen were making rapid preparations for another labor union. The idea originated with Driessen, who quickly obtained the support of Essen Center

8. Quoted in *Tremonia*, no. 76 (1), 5 April 1894.

9. For the remainder of the paragraph, see Hue, *Neutrale oder parteiische Gewerkschaften*, pp. 76–77; and Imbusch, *Arbeitsverhältnis und Arbeiterorganisationen*, p. 422.

10. Brust to Köster, 8 April 1894, printed in Imbusch, *Arbeitsverhältnis und Arbeiterorganisationen*, p. 423. One of the leaders of the Christian miners in 1908, Imbusch had access to much material in private hands.

11. *Tremonia*, no. 102 (2), 7 May 1894; *Bergknappe*, no. 27, 7 July 1900; and Imbusch, *Arbeitsverhältnis und Arbeiterorganisationen*, pp. 424–25.

leader Matthias Wiese and Rektor Steinbusch, chairman of the Catholic *Knappenbund* in Essen.[12] Close analysis of the remarks made by Wiese, Steinbusch, and Center deputy Gerhard Stötzel at the annual festival of the Catholic *Knappenvereine* of Essen, where the new plans were announced, indicate that all were leaning toward the idea of forming educational "trade sections" within the church-run labor associations of the area.[13] Such a "union" could be used to support the Center Party and would avert the socialistic demands which were expected from Brust's independent *Gesamtausschuss.*

The members of the preparatory commission were "flabbergasted"[14] by the attempt to outmaneuver them, but soon regained enough composure to inform Wiese that they would stand firm.[15] Brust claimed six years later that this ultimatum "thwarted [Wiese's] unhealthy plan."[16] And yet, this could hardly have been the case. Wiese's willingness to join church leaders in founding confessional unions was ample indication that he had no fear of the miners' commission. For Wiese to have backed down, therefore, Brust must have made significant concessions of his own. Such reasoning explains Wiese's insistence later that summer that Brust be kept as chairman of the union.[17] It would also explain the fact that Brust's opponents in the union were already beginning to grumble that he was kowtowing to influential personages just to stay at the head of the movement.[18]

By late June 1894 Brust's willingness to cooperate with the Catholic power structure of the Ruhr was even more evident. Once Wiese and Steinbusch had been assuaged, he approached the large and influential Catholic *Volksbüro* in Bochum. The bureau chief, Friedrich Becker, had worked closely with Lensing and Fussangel, the founders of *Glückauf,* before joining the *Volksverein* organization in 1893 and was highly regarded by many Catholic workingmen. At Brust's request, the capable and experienced Becker assumed the task of drafting the by-laws for the busy miners on the preparatory commission.[19] Evidence would also suggest that Becker consulted both Fussangel and Lens-

12. For the origins of the plan to counter Brust, see *Bergknappe*, no. 27, 7 July 1900; Müller, *Die christliche Gewerkschaftsbewegung*, p. 42; and *Tremonia*, no. 132 (2), 13 June 1894.
13. *Essener Volkszeitung*, no. 131, 12 June 1894.
14. *Bergknappe*, no. 27, 7 July 1900.
15. See Heinrich Imbusch, *25 Jahre Gewerkverein christlicher Bergarbeiter*, (Essen: Verlag des Gewerkvereins christlicher Bergarbeiter Deutschlands, 1919), p. 30.
16. *Bergknappe*, no. 27, 7 July 1900.
17. *Tremonia*, no. 195 (1), 27 August 1894.
18. Erdmann, *Die christliche Arbeiterbewegung*, p. 476. Erdmann's source was Franz Wieber, leader of the Christian metal workers in Duisburg.
19. *Oberbürgermeister* of Bochum to *Regierungspräsident* in Arnsberg, 31 August 1894, and to the *Oberpräsident* in Münster, 7 November 1894, Oberpräsidium 6442, StA Münster.

ing sometime in July.[20] Before work on the statutes was completed, however, Becker drafted a short declaration which was signed by Brust and mailed to over 200 confessional labor associations in the Ruhr.[21]

A break had to be made, the declaration began, "with the uncertain and unpredictable system of wage suppression,"[22] but expropriation and socialization of property was rejected as a solution. Rather factory committees, collective bargaining, a minimum wage, labor participation in safety investigations, a voice for the workers in the administration of miners' support funds, reform of the state-regulated *Knappschaftsvereine*,[23] and the eight-hour day were favored. Becker also made some interesting revelations concerning the new union that would strive for these changes. The transitional *Gesamtausschuss* was dropped and a separate trade union proposed in its place. The organization would still rest temporarily on the foundations of the *Arbeiter-* and *Knappenvereine*, which were to function as locals for a few months, but was to begin agitation all over the Ruhr, not just in the district of Essen. Thus Brust's timetable had been considerably advanced. That Becker, Wiese, and others had political motives for doing so will soon become evident.

As might have been expected, the *Alter Verband* tried to foil these plans. Before Becker completed his July declaration, in fact, union headquarters in Bochum had received word of Brust's preparations and taken immediate preventive action. The desperate unionists hoped to stack Brust's constituent assembly with delegates pledged to the *Alter Verband* and opposed to the creation of another miners' union in the Ruhr. The *Knappenvereine* of the Ruhr were contacted in late June and an assembly scheduled for 29 July in Witten. Once Brust had been checked, a national miners' congress would be held in Berlin or Hanover to attain the unity of all German miners.

20. *Alter Verband* sympathizers somehow gained access to the files of the old *Rechtsschutzverein* in Bochum, where draft statutes written by Fussangel were found. See Hue, *Die Bergarbeiter*, vol. 2, p. 456; too, *Tremonia*, no. 153 (1), 9 July 1894, printed a notice concerning the work of the miners' commission. Editor Lensing probably received the information from Becker or Fussangel.

21. Hue, *Die Bergarbeiter*, vol. 2, p. 456.

22. The declaration also appeared in *Tremonia*, no. 161 (1), 18 July 1894, and other Ruhr newspapers.

23. The *Knappschaftsvereine* of the Ruhr had evolved in the eighteenth century, coming under state regulation as a result of legislation passed in 1854 and 1865. Basically, they provided the same social services that Bismarck was attempting to develop on a national level—health, accident, widows', and orphans' insurance. These minimal programs were financed by equal contributions from employers and employees and were supposedly administered jointly by representatives of the owners and the so-called miners' elders (*Knappschaftsältesten*). In practice, however, the workers' voice was not always heard. The state also required that employers channel all funds obtained from disciplinary fines into a special account to be used for social purposes. The arbitrary administration of these "miners' support funds" (*Unterstützungskassen*) also led to frequent complaints. See Kirchhoff, *Die staatliche Sozialpolitik im Ruhrbergbau*, pp. 45–47.

Neither of these moves was very successful. The Witten rally was well-attended, but only by the so-called free *Knappenvereine* which already sympathized with the *Alter Verband*. The delegates elected by these associations were denied admission to the Christian assembly in August—a move that succeeded despite numerous Socialist attempts to force an entry. As a result of this setback, the national miners' congress was postponed until December, but it too was unable to reverse the backward slide of the *Alter Verband*. Twelve hundred more members had drifted away by the end of the year, leaving only 11,200 to combat the emerging Christian movement.[24]

Indeed it was not the *Alter Verband*, but socially conservative Protestants who posed the greatest threat to the realization of Brust's plans in 1894. Fully aware that his dream of a large, interconfessional miners' union depended on Evangelical as well as Catholic backing, Brust had attempted from the beginning to popularize his cause with the Protestant *Arbeitervereine* of Essen.[25] This task was rendered more difficult by the fact that most Evangelical *Arbeiter-* and *Knappenvereine* in the Ruhr were controlled by National Liberal parliamentarians, Conservative Party pastors, and lower-level mine functionaries (*Zechenbeamten*) as apprehensive about the aims of Germany's emerging trade union movement as they were about anything proposed by Catholics.[26] Evangelical reaction to the July declaration was thus quite negative. Protestant mine owners were alarmed by the document, drawing the exaggerated conclusion that the Christian organization would employ Socialist tactics such as the general strike. There was a strong suspicion, moreover, that Brust was really just a front for the religious and political interests of the "the ultramontanes." The Center "was trying to take Protestant miners in tow by organizing a 'Christian' trade union."[27]

To be sure, this concern was not altogether unjustified. Lensing had political reasons for backing Brust after the loss of Dortmund to the Liberals in 1893, and Wiese, too, had hopes of attracting Protestant labor votes for Stötzel. In fact, both Becker and Heinrich Bringewald, a Catholic miner with close contacts to Fussangel, were urging Brust to deemphasize the anti-Socialist politics which had failed with *Glückauf* and direct his union mainly against the business-oriented National Liberals. Brust may have sympathized with this anti-Liberal stratagem, but he realized that such overt politicking

24. For the *Alter Verband*'s plans in 1894, see *Tremonia*, no. 153 (1), 9 July 1894 and no. 171 (1), 30 July 1894; Imbusch, *25 Jahre Gewerkverein*, p. 31; and *Regierungspräsident* in Arnsberg to Prussian minister of the interior, 16 April 1895, Reg. D. 9039, HSA. Düsseldorf.

25. See Reisenstein's remarks in *Tremonia*, no. 183 (1), 13 August 1894; see also: Imbusch, *Arbeitsverhältnis und Arbeiterorganisationen*, p. 425.

26. Imbusch, *Arbeitsverhältnis und Arbeiterorganisationen*, p. 435.

27. *Rheinisch-Westfälische Zeitung*, no. 205, 27 July 1894.

would ruin his chances with the Evangelical *Arbeitervereine*. The Center's advice was therefore rejected. Unfortunately for Brust, the Protestants were not aware of this. Observing his contacts with the Center press and *Volksverein*, Evangelical leaders simply assumed the miner was part of a Catholic political maneuver.[28]

Faced with mounting charges that the union was merely a Center power play, the miners' commission took steps to redeem itself in the eyes of Protestants. Five more miners, four of them Evangelical, were asked to join the commission to establish parity between the confessions. In addition, Becker was apparently asked to stop working on the statutes, for he broke off relations with the commission shortly after the first Liberal press attacks in late July. Simultaneously, Brust was approached by Pastor Ludwig Weber of Mönchen-Gladbach, who wielded considerable influence in Protestant labor circles as an executive committee member of the National Association of Evangelical *Arbeitervereine* and a close associate of former court pastor Adolf Stöcker, leader of the Conservative Party's Christian-Social wing.[29] Of considerable importance to the history of Christian labor before and after 1894, this Conservative reform faction should be examined more thoroughly at this point.

Stöcker's Christian-Social movement was organized in 1878 out of the religiously motivated desire to save the workers of Berlin from the grasp of the Socialists. At first as an independent party, and after 1881 as an autonomous organization within the Conservative Party, the Christian-Socials strove for protective legislation for artisans and factory workers, anti-capitalistic tax laws, mild anti-Semitic measures and, perhaps most important of all, increased social activity on the part of the Prussian Evangelical Church. Stöcker seems also to have envisioned transforming the Conservative Party into a large Protestant *Volkspartei* which would control the Reichstag jointly with the Center.[30]

After a decade of moderate success in the Reich capital, the movement began to crumble. Stöcker's unwillingness to further radical anti-Semitic designs led to the secession of most of his petty-bourgeois followers, while the Christian workers of Berlin deserted him as a result of his insufficient interest in promoting trade unions. The so-called young Christian-Socials led by

28. *Rheinisch-Westfälische Zeitung*, no. 224, 15 August 1894; Erdmann, *Die christliche Arbeiterbewegung*, pp. 396–97; *Bergknappe*, no. 11, 15 July 1897, no. 2, 15 January 1898, and no. 36, 21 October 1899; Hue, *Die Bergarbeiter*, vol. 2, p. 456; also see the remarks of the National Liberal editor from Bochum, Rudolf Quandel, in *Tremonia*, no. 183 (1), 13 August 1894.

29. See Brust's speech at Essen on 26 August, printed in *Tremonia*, no. 195 (1), 27 August 1894; *Oberbürgermeister* of Bochum to the *Oberpräsident* in Münster, 7 November 1894, Oberpräsidium 6442, StA Münster; and Erdmann, *Die christliche Arbeiterbewegung*, p. 413.

30. For Stöcker's early career, see Walter Frank, *Hofprediger Adolf Stöcker und die christlich-soziale Bewegung* (Berlin: Verlag von Reimar Hobbing, 1928), pp. 39– 131.

Stöcker's protégé Friedrich Naumann were also dissatisfied. As far as Naumann was concerned, good Christians should fight the materialistic philosophy of the S.P.D., but accept the party's goal of socializing the means of production. The moderate, palliative means advocated by the court pastor did not enthuse them. On the other extreme, the Conservatives adamantly opposed the idea of opening the party to the lower classes. By 1893/94, in fact, Conservative leaders were encouraging the Kaiser and the Prussian minister-president, Count Botho von Eulenburg, to discontinue social reform plans, introduce new anti-Socialist laws, and sweep away the Reichstag suffrage.[31]

Faced with the reactionary drift of the Conservatives, a loss in Christian-Social voting strength, and the growing dissatisfaction of the younger members of the party, Stöcker and his "older" followers attempted to strengthen their hand by catering to the organizational needs of the proletariat.[32] Weber, who had played the largest single role in forming the National Association of Evangelical *Arbeitervereine* in August 1890, drafted a new social program for the *Vereine* in May 1893, which advocated a nationwide system of trade unions linked institutionally to employers' groups. Such a scheme would advance the economic position of the workers, while also eliminating strikes, boycotts, industrial sabotage, and other perceived evils of the Socialist labor movement. During the fall and winter of 1893 and 1894, Stöcker and his associate in the Conservative *Fraktion*, Dr. Georg Hüpeden, urged that these "trade unions" be granted corporate political rights.[33] Significantly enough, Stöcker also spoke in May 1894 for Chaplain Oberdörffer's Catholic Social Program.[34] The pastor's desire for a Catholic-Protestant reform coalition had clearly not waned.

It is not surprising, therefore, that Weber approached Brust, for here was a promising opportunity to bridge confessional differences, progress toward well-ordered labor relations, and encourage the Right to take up the cudgel for social reform. To be sure, Weber had no more intention of playing into ultramontane hands than the National Liberals. His conversation with Brust in early August 1894 was thus frank and to the point.[35] Weber wanted to know if Center Party leaders or priests were the real founders of the union and if it would tolerate all political views of its members. Brust managed to convince

31. *Ibid.*, p. 322; Theodore Heuss, *Friedrich Naumann* (Stuttgart: Rainer Wunderlich Verlag Hermann Leins, 1937), pp. 64–91; Dietrich von Oertzen, *Erinnerungen aus meinem Leben* (Berlin: Verlag von Edwin Runge, 1915), p. 123.

32. Frank, *Hofprediger Adolf Stöcker*, pp. 320–23.

33. *Ibid.*, p. 322; Heuss, *Friedrich Naumann*, pp. 87–88; Wilhelm Kulemann, *Die Berufsvereine* (Jena: Verlag von Gustav Fischer, 1908), vol. 2, pp. 110, 122–23.

34. *Tremonia*, no. 120 (2), 30 May 1894.

35. For the conversation see Weber's memoirs, as quoted by Erdmann, *Die christliche Arbeiterbewegung*, p. 413.

the Conservative pastor that his union was not being manipulated by ultramontanes, whereupon Weber agreed to help sell the plan to other Protestants.

Weber first broached the topic to his sympathetic Christian-Social colleague, Pastor Werth, chairman of the National Association of Evangelical *Arbeitervereine*. Together the two were able to convince other Evangelical labor leaders to meet with Brust's commission a few days later in Essen to review the July declaration and by-laws of the new union.[36] This second meeting resulted in increased Protestant support for Brust, but it is highly doubtful whether it actually furthered his cause, for little by little the principles were revised to suit the suspicious Liberals within the National Association.[37] The corporatist criticism of the wage system was stricken and a statement inserted advocating maintenance of fair wages. All mention of the eight-hour shift was similarly erased, in favor of "reduction in shift time when it is deemed necessary for the protection of health and life."[38] With Weber's backing, the commission succeeded in retaining its already limited demands of codetermination, but to insure that Socialist purposes could not be pursued, all discussion of politics was banned from union meetings. The union would promote "the spiritual, material, and industrial interests of its members with legal means according to Christian principles."[39]

The structure of the union was also altered. Reflecting employer opposition to the mine-by-mine locals, the Liberals insisted that all organizational functions be permanently transferred to the confessional labor associations. New members had to either belong to a Protestant or Catholic labor association or else obtain certification from police headquarters that they were not followers of the S.P.D. The individual associations would send representatives to a general assembly which in turn would elect the union's central executive committee. Protestants were guaranteed equal representation on this committee because it was felt that Catholics would always have a majority of the members. The executive committee was also required to submit all decisions to an "honorary council" (*Ehrenrat*) controlled by middle- and upper-class dignitaries, who would then "advise" the workers.

This elaborate system of checks and guarantees virtually ruled out the type of anti-capitalistic endeavors that Brust had had in mind for the long run. He

36. See Weber's letter in *Tremonia*, no. 188 (1), 18 August 1894. The protocols of the meeting are printed in *Tremonia*, no. 183 (1), 13 August 1894.
37. Brief descriptions of the meetings are contained in Karl Kühne, "Kampf um die christliche Gewerkschaftsidee," p. 45; Imbusch, *Arbeitsverhältnis und Arbeiterorganisationen*, pp. 430–31; and *Westfälischer Merkur*, 14 August 1894 (clipping in: Oberpräsidium 6442, StA Münster). Parts of the revised statutes are printed in Imbusch, *25 Jahre Gewerkverein*, pp. 32–38; and *Tremonia*, no. 212 (2), 15 September 1894.
38. Imbusch, *25 Jahre Gewerkverein*, p. 33.
39. *Ibid.*, p. 33.

had come close to creating another anti-Socialist "battering ram," exactly what he said he would not do in April. Brust nevertheless agreed to these revisions because he realized that the 15–20,000 Protestant *Arbeiterverein* members of the Ruhr would not join a union without the support of their middle-class leaders. Once in the union, the intimidated, submissive types would gain class consciousness and be ready to assume more control. As Brust explained to a colleague later that month, "all we have to do now is organize; the rest will happen on its own."[40]

The personal diplomacy and tactical maneuvering which had absorbed Brust's time and energy since June seemed to have succeeded as the delegates gathered in Essen for the constituent assembly. Spokesmen for 100 Catholic, 58 Evangelical, and 25 Christian-Social *Arbeiter-* and *Knappenvereine* were present, representing about 20 percent of all miners in the Ruhr. This impressive showing could not hide the fact, however, that Christian labor unity was still quite fragile. Most Protestant associations had sent delegates with instructions to observe the proceedings and participate in debates, but not to vote for any resolutions. The elections to the union's executive committee had therefore been scheduled for a later assembly to give Protestant delegates time to report to *Arbeiterverein* superiors concerning Catholic reaction to the union's new program.[41]

Brust chaired the assembly with the obvious intention of preserving the crucial compromise worked out two weeks earlier.[42] He pledged, for instance, that Christian miners would never participate in a general strike or cooperate with the *Alter Verband* as long as it stood under Socialist leadership. Unfortunately the closing remarks were delivered by Peter Oberdörffer, whom Weber and the Christian-Socials may have asked to attend. Oberdörffer's campaign to restructure Germany's economic institutions was in full swing at the time and the chaplain probably considered the Essen meeting a good opportunity to promote his plans. As explained earlier, Oberdörffer wanted capital and labor to manage a firm as equals. The first step in this direction would be the creation of Christian labor organizations equal in strength to employer groups already in existence. Once parity were obtained, the groundwork would be laid for the desired "mutual association." In the meantime, the workers and their priest-overseers would face one struggle after another with big busi-

40. Brust to an unnamed colleague, 29 August 1894, printed in Erdmann, *Die christliche Arbeiterbewegung*, pp. 407–8.
41. *Tremonia*, no. 195 (1), 27 August 1894; Mayor Vossmann of Gelsenkirchen to Landrat Gelsenkirchen, 5 August 1894, LA Gelsenkirchen 45, StA Münster; *Dortmunder Zeitung*, no. 228 (1), 20 August 1894; *Tremonia*, no. 194 (2), 25 August 1894.
42. *Tremonia*, no. 195 (1), 27 August 1894.

ness.[43] Oberdörffer therefore advised the delegates to avoid bitter polemics with the Social Democrats. He also urged the workers to prepare for strike action.

> Given the workers' many enemies you will not be able to avoid waging war against your adversaries, but to do this you'll need money, money, and more money! The union may have to support blacklisted members and will also be in need of funds if a great strike [*eine grosse Aktion*] becomes necessary for economic reasons that do not violate Christian principles. In this sense I recommend that you proceed with your work in the spirit of unity, courage, and perseverance and you will not fail.[44]

Coming from one of the most renowned labor leaders in the expansive archdiocese of Cologne, such encouragement was very significant. But the chaplain's anti-capitalistic views were hardly appropriate at a time when confessional unity rested so precariously on the brink.

Oberdörffer, in fact, was not really interested in the success of Brust's interconfessional experiment. To facilitate supervision by Catholic priests, he favored the creation of separate organizations for Catholic and Protestant miners and may have overstated his views at Essen to drive a wedge between the two faiths.[45]

Meanwhile the debate over the nature of the organization had been complicated by the employers' desire to introduce still more conservative statute changes. Like other industrialist organizations, the powerful Association of Ruhr Mining Interests had been alarmed by Oberdörffer's speech. Brust's refusal to cooperate with the *Alter Verband*, however, was considered more significant.[46] The mine owners had not attacked the new organization since the increase of Evangelical influence in mid-August[47] and were still hopeful that Brust could be used to protect business interests against Socialist attacks.[48] The employer association therefore urged state mining officials in Dortmund to guide the writing of the statutes in such a way that the union would remain

43. *Tremonia*, no. 249 (1), 29 October 1894.
44. Quoted in Erdmann, *Die christliche Arbeiterbewegung*, p. 402.
45. *Kölner Correspondenz an die geistlichen Präsides*, no. 9–10, 12 August 1890, and no. 5–6, 1895, StBib MG. In the latter issue, Oberdörffer asserted "that even for the miners, with their unique circumstances, it would have been better to establish two confessional organizations with the same statutes." For Schmitz's speech, see *Tremonia*, nos. 246 (2) and 247 (1), 25–26 October 1894. He refutes Oberdörffer's ideas on confessional unions here. That Schmitz felt a need to do so suggests that Oberdörffer was working against Brust in Cologne.
46. *Rheinische-Westfälische Zeitung*, no. 237, 28 August 1894.
47. The last attack had occurred in no. 220 of the *Rheinisch-Westfälische Zeitung* on 11 August 1894.
48. Imbusch, *25 Jahre Gewerkverein*, p. 38, notes that the entrepreneurs were only interested in "anti-Socialist attack troops."

largely innocuous. Otherwise, the programmatic demands which had survived the Protestant revisions might result in the type of economic warfare that Oberdörffer was advocating.

Usually sympathetic to the owners' concerns, officials in Dortmund insisted that the commission make its intention to steer a peaceful course much more explicit. The miners responded submissively in early September by once again rewording the statutes. The demands of August were left unchanged, but the purpose of the organization was redefined as "the improvement of miners' moral and social position and the establishment and maintenance of peaceful relations between capital and labor."[49] There was no longer any mention of the "material and industrial interests" of the workers, and the function of the organization now bore a striking resemblance to the "yellow," anti-union associations formed by employers after the turn of the century.

For reasons that are not clear, the peace clause was removed from the statutes in late September, perhaps because Oberdörffer had intervened or, more likely, due to second thoughts on Brust's part.[50] But the renewal of open opposition from the mine owners and additional pressure from Weber and Werth was enough to force the readoption of the new wording in mid-October.[51] Again the evidence is sparse, but it would appear that Brust considered resigning at this point.[52] With encouragement from progressive *Volksverein*

49. Evidence for the employers' initiative has been pieced together from a number of different sources. The statute was reworded at the commission's session of 2 September and printed in *Tremonia*, no. 212 (2), 15 September 1894. Brust had stated at the Essen assembly in late August that the State Mining Office should be included in the final deliberations, and Werth confirmed on 7 October that mine officials, had indeed been consulted (*Rheinisch-Westfälisch Zeitung*, no. 278, 8 October 1894). Imbusch mentions in his official history of the union that the Mine Office at this time sympathized with the views of the Association of Ruhr Mining Interests (Imbusch, *25 Jahre Gewerkverein*, pp. 39–40). And finally, mine officials, entrepreneurial circles, and business-oriented journalists all claimed in 1913 that the mine owners had been involved with the founding of the union in 1894 (*Königliches Oberbergamt* Dortmund to the *Regierungspräsident* in Arnsberg, 15 October 1913, and to the Prussian minister of trade and industry, 19 November 1913, Reg. Arnsberg I 1476, StA Münster). I have assumed that the owners used their close relationship with the Mining Office to exert influence on the union, rather than direct negotiations, which would have been counterproductive.

50. Müller, *Franz Hitze*, p. 131, notes that the weeks after the assembly of 26 August had witnessed a "spirited dispute" over the wording of the statutes. The peace clause was removed . . . between 15 September 1894—its first appearance in *Tremonia*—and 1 October, when the Evangelical *Arbeiterverein* of Langendreer discussed the statutes (*Rheinisch-Westfälische Zeitung*, no. 279 (2), 9 October 1894). See also Brust's remarks at Essen on 28 October in *Tremonia*, no. 249 (1), 29 October 1894.

51. *Rheinisch-Westfälische Zeitung*, no. 279 (2), 9 October 1894; *Tremonia*, no. 249 (1), 29 October 1894.

52. Brust insisted four years later that he had been very reluctant to accept a position with the union in 1894 (*Bergknappe*, no. 19, 1 October 1898). Similarly, August Pieper wrote Archbishop Simar in 1901 that Brust "had been pressed" into service in 1894. Pieper to Simar, 27 October 1901. Generalia 23.2, vol. 3, Erzb. Registratur Köln.

leader Franz Hitze, who emboldened Brust by promising to accept a seat on the proposed *Ehrenrat*, the miner decided to stay on as union leader.[53]

The owners' decision to tolerate trustworthy unions in the Ruhr did not enhance Brust's prospects with the Evangelical *Arbeitervereine*. Led by Rudolf Quandel, editor of a National Liberal newspaper in Bochum, and Hermann Francken, National Liberal Landtag deputy from Gelsenkirchen, the most adamantly anti-Catholic labor leaders had never shared Weber's confidence in Brust's political neutrality. Quandel had only agreed to participate at Essen, in fact, because he felt confident that church and Center would desert the organization as a result of the Protestant by-law revisions. The impressive Catholic showing at Essen and, above all, Oberdörffer's "advice" to the delegates illustrated the fallacy in this reasoning and induced Quandel and Francken to beat a hasty retreat. Agents were sent to other parts of the Ruhr to dissuade Protestants from joining the union. These efforts proved successful in September when the executive committee of the Rhenish-Westphalian Association of Evangelical *Arbeitervereine* decided to adopt a completely "neutral" stance to the Christian miners' union. The Association would not support the organization publicly, and each *Arbeiterverein* could decide for itself whether to attend the union's constituent assembly in October 1894.[54]

Such "neutrality" was hardly designed to encourage the individual associations. Weber therefore convened a rally at Gelsenkirchen on 7 October to counteract the growing skepticism among Protestant *Verein* leaders. He and Werth spoke persuasively on Brust's behalf and were able to elicit support for the main points of the completed statutes.[55] But appearances could be deceptive. Religious prejudices and memories of *Glückauf* lingered, causing many Protestants to question the sincerity of Catholics like Brust, Köster, and Müller. By the end of October, in fact, it was clear that many Evangelical labor leaders had been unable to resist the anti-Catholic demagoguery of Quandel and Francken. The rank and file for its part was either afraid to speak up or else easily swayed by the prejudicial arguments of *Arbeiterverein* sponsors. District associations (*Kreisverbände*) in Recklinghausen and Witten-Hagen boycotted the constituent assembly on 28 October, while only scattered support was found in Essen, Gelsenkirchen, Dortmund, and Iserlohn. The sole *Kreisverband* fully represented was Bochum, and a motion advocating attendance passed there with a slim, one-vote margin. Of the 57 Evangelical

53. Müller, *Franz Hitze*, pp. 131–32, places the date of the conversation "a few weeks" after Hitze's speech before Catholic *Arbeiterverein* leaders in Cologne on 24 September, but before the constituent assembly of 28 October.
54. *Rheinisch-Westfälische Zeitung*, no. 224, 15 August 1894; *Westfälischer Merkur*, 18 October 1894 (clipping in: *Oberpräsidium* 6442, StA Münster); Landrat in Gelsenkirchen to *Regierungspräsident* in Arnsberg, 15 October 1894, LA Gelsenkirchen 45, StA Münster.
55. *Ibid.*

Vereine present at Essen in August, perhaps 20 to 30 had returned in October.[56]

The final gathering did nothing to bridge the widening gap between Catholic and Protestant labor. Oberdörffer was the main culprit once again.[57] Indirectly criticizing the statutes, the chaplain advocated energetic representation of material interests and defended his earlier statement about *ad hoc* cooperation with the *Alter Verband*. These remarks brought Werth to his feet. It was always difficult to found an organization, he noted, but even harder to maintain it. He warned the delegates not to violate the statutes and to elect responsible officials to the executive committee. Weber seconded Werth. The Protestants in the union would never cooperate with Socialists. "I consider the Social Democrats the greatest evil of our time . . . Let me make it quite clear: Our union is no *Kampfverein*!"[58]

Oberdörffer received more applause from the floor, but the miners on the commission cautiously avoided seconding him.[59] The statutes as revised in August and September had already been accepted by the delegates, and Brust wanted to avoid creating "unnecessary difficulties for the young movement."[60] Thus the Trade Association (*Gewerkverein*) of Christian Miners for the Mining District of Dortmund, as the new union was called, came to life without further delay.

Little remained, however, of the *bona fide* trade union which Brust and Becker had envisioned in July. Strikes were all but ruled out by statute, leaving grievance petitions to employers and chambers of commerce as the only means to express the miners' "moral and social" interests. Little material aid could be offered the members otherwise, for dues were set at 25 pfennige a quarter—less than one-third of what the *Alter Verband* asked. The *Gewerkverein* also depended on the confessional associations for tasks such as recruiting, dues collection, etc., and until the founding of the union newspaper *Bergknappe* in November 1895, Lensing's *Tremonia* performed this service.[61] Decision-making authority, moreover, was divided between the executive committee and an *Ehrenrat* consisting of bourgeois labor leaders.

56. Mayor of Gelsenkirchen to Landrat in Gelsenkirchen, 9 October 1894, LA Gelsenkirchen 45, StA Münster; *National Zeitung*, 24 October 1894 (clipping in: *Oberpräsidium* 6442, StA Münster); *Rheinisch-Westfälische Zeitung*, no. 298 (2), 28 October 1894; police commissioner in Dortmund to *Regierungspräsident* in Arnsberg, 18 February 1895, Bestand 3, StA Dortmund; *Tremonia*, no. 36 (2), 6 February 1895.

57. A stenographic report of the assembly appeared in *Tremonia*, no. 249 (1), 29 October 1894.

58. *Ibid.*

59. Imbusch, *25 Jahre Gewerkverein*, p. 37.

60. *Ibid.*, p. 37.

61. The union statutes were printed in entirety in *Bergknappe*, no. 45, 23 December 1899; also see *Bergknappe*, no. 9, 24 August 1896; Müller, *Die christliche Gewerkschaftsbewegung*, p. 45; and *Tremonia*, no. 90 (1), 2 April 1895.

Representing the Catholics were Oberdörffer, Wiese, and Hitze. Weber, Werth, and Karl Legewitt, chairman of an Evangelical *Arbeiterverein* in Essen, represented the Protestants.[62] It was no slip of tongue, therefore, when Hitze referred to the union in October 1895 as a *"Fachabteilung."*[63] With its clerical advisers and *"Nichtkampfverein"* statutes, the Christian association was designed to function as an educational trade section.

The distinction between trade union and confessional trade section was blurred still further by the continued exodus of Protestants from the new organization. Meeting at Langendreer in mid-November 1894, the general commission of the Rhenish-Westphalian Association of Evangelical *Arbeitervereine* decided to uphold the policy of neutrality established by the executive committee in October. Weber had exerted all his influence to convince the commission that Christian trade unionism was the only effective means to combat the S.P.D., but had run headlong into Francken. The National Liberal parliamentarian charged that Weber had been duped by "hotspurs" like Oberdörffer into making "short-sighted concessions to demagogic ultramontanism."[64] These personal invectives were so devastating that only 27 of the 65 *Verein* agents backed the pastor's motion of active support for the new Christian union.[65]

Francken and Quandel acquired an influential ally that winter in the person of Baron von Stumm, the patriarchal iron and steel magnate of the Saar. Stumm had observed the activity of Brust and Weber in the Ruhr and was determined to thwart similar attempts in his mines. Like the workers under Diederich, title character in Heinrich Mann's *The Loyal Subject*, Stumm's employees could count on "fatherly benevolence." Any challenge to his paternal authority, on the other hand, would be "shattered against an unbending will."[66] Thus in January 1895, when Evangelical *Arbeiterverein* leaders sought to establish a legal-aid bureau, Stumm and his fellow owners blocked

62. Imbusch, *25 Jahre Gewerkverein*, p. 37; Erdmann, *Die christliche Arbeiterbewegung*, pp. 413–14; Ritter, *Volksverein*, p. 295; and *Der Arbeiter* (organ of the Catholic *Arbeitervereine* of southern Germany), no. 15, 12 April 1895. Oberdörffer was unable to cooperate with Weber and soon resigned. A *Knappschaftsverein* elder took his place. By 1895 or 1896, Wiese had also stepped down, interestingly enough, in favor of Heinrich Brauns. The future Weimar labor minister was then a parish priest in Essen-Borbeck. Werth died in 1896 and was replaced by another *Knappschaftsverein* elder. With Hitze attending to political duties in Berlin much of the year, the *Ehrenrat* was controlled, for the most part, by Weber and Brauns.

63. *Tremonia*, no. 279 (1), 11 October 1895.

64. *Kölnische Zeitung*, no. 152, 16 February 1898.

65. *National-Zeitung*, 20 November 1894 (clipping in: *Oberpräsidium* 6442, StA Münster).

66. Quoted in Barbara W. Tuchman, *The Proud Tower* (New York: Macmillan Company, 1966), p. 307. The reader should also consult Fritz Hellwig, *Carl Ferdinand Freiherr von Stumm-Halberg 1836–1901* (Heidelberg: Westmark-Verlag GmbH, 1936), pp. 506–56.

the idea until local pastors agreed that the agency would not be transformed into another *Gewerkverein*.[67] Not content with this victory, Stumm, an influential spokesman of the *Reichspartei*, carried his struggle against Christian socialism to the nation's parliament in Berlin. In two highly controversial speeches, Stumm blasted Weber as a dangerous agitator and Friedrich Naumann as an S.P.D. collaborator.[68] Stöcker defended his lieutenants in the Prussian Landtag in March but, in so doing, worsened the Christian-Social position. For the *Kreuzzeitung*, Stöcker's sole supporter in the Conservative press, turned on the court pastor, demanding that he dissociate himself from the young radicals.[69] Far from promoting the cause of the Christian-Socials, support for the *Gewerkverein* had led to a number of humiliating setbacks for Stöcker and his followers.

Stumm's campaign, together with the decision of Rhenish-Westphalian *Arbeiterverein* leaders in November, encouraged all but a few of the Protestant associations which had voted to join the *Gewerkverein* to abandon Brust's cause.[70] Brust's following in Bochum dwindled to almost nothing, and an assembly convened in early March to reverse this trend was so poorly attended that nothing could be accomplished. A similar situation existed in Iserlohn, and in Dortmund only three Protestant workers had joined the union by February. Making matters worse, the Rhenish-Westphalian commission refused to reverse its November decision during a meeting in mid-February. With this setback all prospects for a rapid increase in Protestant backing disappeared. The *Regierungspräsident* in Arnsberg reported in October 1895 that Protestant workers were still refusing to join the *Gewerkverein* because middle-class *Arbeiterverein* leaders had convinced them it was merely a well-disguised ultramontane plot.[71] Brust's plans for interconfessional labor unity had fallen victim to a cynical mixture of religious bigotry and manipulation by political parties, business, and the government.

* * * *

67. See Naumann's *Hilfe* article of January 1895, printed in Theodor Schieder (ed.), *Friedrich Naumann Werke* (Cologne: Westdeutscher Verlag, 1964), vol. 5, pp. 185, 745.
68. Reichstag Debates, Period 11, Session 3 (12 December 1894; 9 January 1895), pp. 77, 211.
69. Heuss, *Friedrich Naumann*, 93; Frank, *Hofprediger Adolf Stöcker*, pp. 324–45.
70. For the turnaround, see *Tremonia*, nos. 36 (2), 49 (1), 62 (1), and 90 (1), for 6 and 19 February, 4 March, and 2 April 1895; Franz Ulrich, *Gewerkverein* leader in Dortmund, to Dortmund Police Department, 22 January and 3 February 1895, Bestand 3, StA Dortmund; and Imbusch, *25 Jahre Gewerkverein*, p. 34.
71. *Regierungspräsident* in Arnsberg to Prussian minister of the interior, 26 October 1895, Reg. D. 9039, HSA Düsseldorf.

The ongoing recession added to Brust's membership problems.[72] Reflecting the low demand for labor, the average miner's pay in the Ruhr had not advanced one pfennig from late 1893 to mid-1895. The succeeding twelve months brought only a sluggish 4 percent increase. With little hiring activity and a constant flow of workers into the Ruhr from eastern Germany, few miners of either faith took the risk, albeit slight, of joining the *Gewerkverein* and losing their jobs. Four thousand workers, mainly Catholic, flocked to the recruiting stations from January to March 1895; then the pace slowed considerably. The next six months brought less than 900 new recruits, and by March 1896, membership stood at only 6,200, or about 4 percent of all Ruhr miners.[73]

Understandably enough, the more impetuous among those who had joined favored energetic action to improve their position. Union radicals had been pressuring the leadership to strike since February 1895, and by spring 1896, Brust, too, was growing impatient to force a wage hike.[74] The passive economic activity of the *Gewerkverein* was a clear indication, however, that the *Ehrenrat* had no intention of giving in to the radical wing. In a joint meeting of executive committee and *Ehrenrat* in mid-June 1895, the union decided to collect information from 88 mines concerning the administration of miners' support funds. A petition based on this time-consuming effort was submitted to the Association of Ruhr Mining Interests in March 1896. To combat the arbitrariness of lower-level mine functionaries, the *Gewerkverein* requested that workers' committees be allowed to share management responsibilities in the administration of these funds. Beginning to wonder, perhaps, if the *Gewerkverein* had forgotten why it had been created, the owners' association did not deign to reply. Late in 1896, *Bergknappe* had to admit that the support fund petition had been a disappointing failure.[75] The union's request for wage increases fell on the same deaf ears. A series of articles running in *Bergknappe* from February to May 1896 admitted that the owners had done a lot for their employees, but charged that workers with large families were not

72. Unless otherwise noted, membership figures for the *Gewerkverein* and *Alter Verband* in the remainder of this chapter are based on the statistics submitted by the union to Prussian officials in the Ruhr. See LA Duisburg-Mühlheim 481–482, HSA Düsseldorf; Oberpräsidium 2830 (2) and 2833, StA Münster; and *Regierungspräsident* in Arnsberg to Prussian minister of the interior, 28 April 1896, Reg. D. 9039, HSA Düsseldorf.

73. Koch, *Die Bergarbeiter im Ruhrgebiet*, p. 148; *Tremonia*, no. 90 (1), 2 April 1895.

74. *Regierungspräsident* Arnsberg to Prussian minister of the interior, 16 April 1895, Reg. D. 9039, HSA Düsseldorf; *Bergknappe*, no. 6, May 1896.

75. For the support fund petition, see Müller, *Die christliche Gewerkschaftsbewegung*, pp. 47–48; *Tremonia*, no. 166 (1), 19 June 1895; and *Bergknappe*, nos. 4, 5, 7, and 13, for April–May, July, and December 1896.

receiving adequate wages.[76] The paper, which was mainly the responsibility of Heinrich Brauns at this time,[77] appealed to the owners as Christians to grant a 20 percent wage increase. Pay rose less than 2 percent during the winter and spring of 1896.[78] Mainly concerned with the demand for coal and the amount of labor required for the desired level of production, owners were unmoved by the *Ehrenrat*'s concept of "Christian moral duty." The *Gewerkverein* rank and file, meanwhile, grew more and more restless.

A crisis of a different sort was developing within the *Alter Verband*. In February 1895, the leaders of the union, among them S.P.D. members Johann Meyer and Ludwig Schröder, were arrested on false charges and sentenced to three years' imprisonment. Fearful of further suppression, 6,000 miners deserted the organization immediately, and by April 1896, a shrunken following of 3,600 was all that remained of the once-impressive *Alter Verband*. Under these circumstances it was only natural that many of the remaining and recently departed members began to blame not only the government but also the S.P.D. for their troubles. Leader of this dissident faction was the former metal worker and editor of the union newspaper, Otto Hue. Only by dissociating the union from Marxist politics and emphasizing purely trade union goals could the *Alter Verband* hope to regain the 33,000 members it had lost since 1891. Such a "neutral" stance would also facilitate joint strike activity with the more successful *Gewerkverein*, whose leader, Brust, had always made the exclusion of Socialist politics on the union level the *sine qua non* for any such cooperation.[79] Thus internal pressures seemed to be forcing the two rival unions closer together in the mid-1890s.

Heinrich Möller, *Alter Verband* chairman and S.P.D. deputy, opposed Hue's strategy. Möller liked to consult Bebel and other party leaders before embarking on trade union actions and, as an outspoken Marxist, was not about to "creep into a hiding place"[80] with his views. Nor did cooperation with the Christian miners appeal to him. Brust was a marionette in the hands of priests and employers, while the *Gewerkverein* was little more than a glorified *Knap-*

76. *Bergknappe*, nos. 1–5, January–May, 1896.
77. Brust was still working full time in the mines in 1896. It thus seems highly unlikely that he could have composed such a lengthy article series. *Alter Verband* charges that Brauns did most of the editorial work were probably true. See *Bergknappe*, no. 6, 1 May 1897. For more evidence that Brauns often assisted Brust with editorial work, see Ritter, *Die Männer aus Mönchen-Gladbach*, part 6, pp. 3–4, Ritter Papers ER/D-16, KfZG Bonn.
78. Koch, *Die Bergarbeiter im Ruhrgebiet*, p. 148.
79. *Ibid.*, pp. 56–57; *Regierungspräsident* Arnsberg to Prussian minister of the interior, 2 November 1896, Reg. D. 9039, HSA Düsseldorf; also see Brust's remarks at Essen cited in *Tremonia*, no. 195 (1), 27 August 1894.
80. Möller to Hue, 14 March 1897, printed in *Bergknappe*, no. 18, 1 November 1897.

penverein with no interest in the miners of Silesia and the Saar, let alone the international labor movement. Hue should concentrate on luring Christians into the Socialist camp, not on deals with leaders who flirted with the workers' enemies.

Hue's ideas began to seem less humiliating, however, after the *Gewerkverein* campaigned for "oppositionist" candidates in the *Knappschaftsverein* elections of June 1896. If another, more radical wind were blowing in the Christian organization, common action against the bourgeoisie was possible. These new developments, and the popularity of Hue's views with the rank and file, induced Möller to offer Brust peace terms.[81] The two feuding unions would cease all politically biased agitation and pursue only trade union goals. Möller left the exact form of cooperation in the Ruhr open, but proposed another German Miners' Congress for the national level.

Brust rejected Möller's proposals. The Christian leader suspected that Möller would somehow attempt to exploit the alliance for party purposes.[82] Besides, Brust was dealing from a position of strength. With more than twice as many members as the *Alter Verband*, it was highly likely that a continuation of hostilities would lead to the collapse of his once-great rival. For months, in fact, Brust and *Ehrenrat* member Heinrich Brauns had planned to intensify competition between the two unions. All Christian *Knappenvereine* in the empire would be invited to a special congress at Bochum, seat of the *Alter Verband*, in early 1897. The delegates would formulate a program of labor legislation and discuss a plan to extend *Gewerkverein* influence to other mining districts in Prussia. Renowned Protestants like the "armchair socialist" Adolf Wagner and the labor historian and former National Liberal deputy Wilhelm Kulemann would join Hitze on the speakers' platform, lending an aura of respectability to the whole affair. With its newly won prestige, the *Gewerkverein* would be able to recruit tens of thousands of non-organized Catholic and Protestant miners.[83]

Brust and Brauns had equally ambitious plans for other branches of industry. The two wanted Christian labor leaders in every corner of the Reich to follow the *Gewerkverein's* lead and challenge the supremacy of the free trade unions. Neither put any faith in the ability of *Fachabteilungen* to temper the religious and political intolerance of "the frees" (*die Freien*), nor did they feel there was any time to lose before founding a network of more viable, non-Socialist organizations. To be sure, the first signs of a Christian countermove-

81. Möller to Brust, 13 June 1896, printed in *Bergknappe*, no. 8, 1 August 1896.
82. Brust to Möller, 15 June 1896, printed in *Bergknappe*, no. 8, 1 August 1896.
83. *Bergknappe*, nos. 7, 10–11, and 13, for 1 July, 24 September, 24 October, and 24 December 1896; and Müller, *Die christliche Gewerkschaftsbewegung*, p. 51.

ment among non-miners were already in evidence by 1896. Christian railwaymen and tileworkers in Trier and Lippe-Detmold, respectively, had founded separate unions, and in Munich, too, the groundwork for several more Christian unions had been laid by Father Huber and the mechanic Karl Schirmer. With 259,000 unionists in the General Commission, however, Herculean efforts were needed if "the Christians" (*die Christlichen*) were to catch up. The Bochum Congress would initiate the struggle.[84]

These developments could not have occurred at a more propitious moment for Ludwig Weber and the Christian-Social Party. The attacks of Baron Stumm and the *Kreuzzeitung* in early 1895 had been followed by far more devastating reversals in the winter of 1895/96. The Kaiser, the *Oberkirchenrat*, and the Conservative Party had denounced the Christian-Socials after Stöcker had proven unable to curb the social and political radicalism of Friedrich Naumann. The drama ended in February 1896 when the aging pastor split from both the Conservatives and Naumann to form a separate party. Naumann, in turn, founded his own "National-Social Union," an organization which he hoped would eclipse all parties on the left and center. To further these ambitious goals, the young vicar advocated, among other things, a merger of the Evangelical *Arbeitervereine*, the free trade unions, and the emerging Christian organizations. His first step was to back Hue in urging the *Gewerkverein* to abandon its independent existence.[85] Such a scheme was clearly designed to capture supporters for his new association at the expense of Center and S.P.D., but it was also threatening to fledgling parties like the Christian-Socials, who were dependent now more than ever on the political aid of the Christian proletariat. Considerations such as this explain Weber's wholehearted support for the Bochum Congress and the planned spread of the movement.

Hitze's feelings were mixed. Given the Kaiser's feelings against the S.P.D., a demonstration of patriotic workers in favor of labor reforms was by no means unappealing. Nor was Hitze opposed to a nationwide organization of Christian miners. The *Alter Verband* could no longer represent the workers effectively,

84. Huber to Schirmer, n.d. (1895), quoted in Ritter, *Volksverein*, p. 296; *Bergknappe*, no. 15, 1 August 1898; *Der Arbeiter* (Munich), no. 47, 22 November 1895, and no. 5, 31 January 1896; Kulemann, *Die Gewerkschaftsbewegung* (Jena: Gustav Fischer Verlag, 1900), pp. 335–36; Gasteiger, *Christliche Gewerkschaften in Süddeutschland*, pp. 224–26; Karl Schirmer, "Karl Schirmer," in *25 Jahre christliche Gewerkschaftsbewegung*, p. 208.

85. As early as 1895 Naumann advocated a unified trade union movement. Separate Christian trade unions were necessary in certain areas, he admitted, but should not be promoted as an end in themselves. See his *Gedanken zum christlich-sozialen Program*, in Schieder (ed.), *Friedrich Naumann Werke*, vol. 5, p. 71. By late 1896 with the founding of his own party, however, Naumann had moved a step farther and advocated merger. *Regierungspräsident* of Arnsberg to the Prussian minister of the interior, 13 May 1897, Reg. D. 9039, HSA Düsseldorf.

and Hitze appreciated the greater degree of class consciousness among the miners. He stopped short, however, of advocating a general movement of Christian trade unions. Although very few trade sections had been founded since 1892, the *Volksverein*'s co-founder clung to the hope that Catholic workers so trained could exert a salutary influence on the Socialist unions, which had still not advanced past the membership peak reached in late 1890 (320,000). Hitze was also worried that German trade unions would develop in a radical direction unless the proper socio-institutional framework were created for them. Until unions were granted corporate status, given their own vocational chambers, etc., the growth of unionism had to be viewed with certain misgivings. Furthermore, the church could be expected to balk at the plans of Brust and Brauns, and Center Party leaders still feared that labor independence would lead to Christian-social revolts like those of the 1870s.[86]

These tactical differences emerged at the forty-third *Katholikentag* in Dortmund in late August 1896. Brust had been selected by the Dortmund organizing committee as one of the main speakers on the social question. In his speech, the miner spoke out strongly in favor of Christian trade unions. A resolution to this effect was introduced by Brust, but the *Katholikentag*'s social commission, largely under Hitze's direction, rejected the motion in favor of confessional trade sections (*Fachabteilungen*).[87] The Center Party leadership considered it doubly important to suppress any stirrings of labor independence given the challenge to party unity from agrarian circles. Indeed the attacks of Rhenish and Bavarian peasant leaders against the alleged indifference of the Center to agricultural interests were a matter of grave concern to Center leaders in the mid-1890s and trouble from other fronts was simply intolerable.[88] According to the conservative logic of Center helmsmen, the best method of preventing labor trouble was to foil plans for trade unions. The workers, of course, saw things differently, and more clearly, but the older, more cautious Hitze could not bring himself to see the illogic of the party leadership.

Without *Katholikentag* sanction, Brust's recommendations were robbed of the effect they might otherwise have had on the German Catholic community. As far as can be determined, in fact, there were only two new unions in

86. For Hitze's views in the mid-1890s, see Reichstag Debates, Period 11, Session 3 (6 February 1895), p. 692; Pieper to Brust, 25 January 1924, *Führer-Korrespondenz*, no. 3, March 1924; Ritter, *Volksverein*, p. 297. Horstwalter Heitzer, *Georg Kardinal Kopp und der Gewerkschaftsstreit* (Cologne: Böhlau Verlag, 1983), p. 25, confuses Hitze's support of the *Gewerkverein* with support for Christian trade unionism in general.

87. *Verhandlungen der 43. Generalversammlung der Katholiken Deutschlands zu Dortmund vom 23. bis 27. August 1896*, pp. 254–55, 375. Heitzer, *Kardinal Kopp*, pp. 25–26, incorrectly describes the motion as advocacy of Christian trade unionism.

88. Zeender, *German Center Party*, pp. 77–78.

Aachen and Eupen toward the end of the year—some consolation, but hardly what Brust and Brauns had had in mind.[89]

The Bochum Congress (31 January–2 February 1897) was equally disappointing in terms of spreading the movement. Brust intended to establish recruiting stations for his union in the Saar, the Siegerland, and Silesia. With the exception of the Saar, where the patriarchal Catholic *Knappenbund* (8,000 members) refused to cooperate, *Knappenvereine* from all these areas sent delegates. A joint commission was formed to settle the details of the plan, but due to the complexities of the Prussian *Vereinsgesetz*, which prohibited "political" organizations from maintaining statewide ties, merger with the *Gewerkverein* was rejected. Though greatly disappointed, Brust found some satisfaction in the fact that his promotional efforts in the east-bank areas of Rhenish Prussia had at least succeeded in popularizing trade unions there. With additional encouragement from Adolf Stöcker and Heinrich Brauns, the Christian miners and metal workers of the Siegerland formed their own union in May 1897.[90]

The Bochum Congress, however, did improve the *Gewerkverein*'s position in the Ruhr. With encouragement from Brauns and Weber, the delegates readopted Friedrich Becker's 1894 program of eight-hour shifts, minimum wages, obligatory factory committees, permanent collective bargaining commissions, and limited codetermination. The impact of the assembly was increased by pro-labor remarks from Hitze, Wagner, and Kulemann, while the *Gewerkverein* general assembly, which was meeting simultaneously in Bochum, added further impetus to the Congress's resolutions by empowering union leaders to negotiate with employers for a ten percent wage increase. A petition to this effect was submitted to the Association of Ruhr Mining Interests on 21 February.[91]

The reaction of miners in the Ruhr was immediate. Membership, which had climbed slowly from 6,200 in March 1896 to 8,250 in early February 1897,[92] began to accelerate after the Bochum assemblies, and by March, Brust could boast a following of nearly 11,000. Convinced now that the *Gewerkverein* was not pursuing religious goals, Protestant workers were also beginning to join in

89. *Regierunsgspräsident* of Aachen to the Prussian minister of the interior, 7 April 1897, Reg. D. 9039, HSA Düsseldorf; *Bergknappe*, no. 6, 1 May 1897; Müller, *Christliche Gewerkschaftsbewegung*, pp. 58–59.

90. *Bergknappe*, no. 6, June 1896, and subsequent numbers that summer, no. 2, 26 February 1897, and no. 19, 24 June 1899; Kulemann, *Die Berufsvereine*, vol. 2, pp. 346–48; Müller, *Christliche Gewerkschaftsbewegung*, p. 26.

91. For the Bochum Congress, see *Bergknappe*, no. 2, 26 February 1897; and Imbusch, *Arbeitsverhältnis und Arbeiterorganisationen*, pp. 483–85.

92. *Bergknappe*, no. 10, 2 July 1897.

greater numbers. As the Landrat in Gelsenkirchen reported, the Christian organization seemed to be "the rising sun"[93] for the miners of the Ruhr.

Counsels in the *Alter Verband* were mixed as to the proper course of action. Möller was incensed by Brust's rejection the previous year and, together with S.P.D. leaders, wanted to hold a counter-demonstration to neutralize the effect of the Christian congress. Hue, on the other hand, was convinced that the *Alter Verband*'s days as an independent organization were numbered. Membership in the Ruhr had still not risen above the 1896 low of 3,400 and the *Gewerkverein* was gaining in popularity. The only way to influence future developments in the miners' movement, he felt, was close cooperation and eventual merger with the Christians.[94]

Hue therefore presented his party opponents with a *fait accompli* by greeting the arriving Christian delegates in the columns of his newspaper on 30 January. He bemoaned the ongoing struggle between the two organizations, emphatically denied the Marxist orientation of the *Alter Verband*, and regretted that Socialist organizers had bitterly attacked Brust in the past.[95] Another article on 20 February found no difference between the political demands of the two unions, and asserted that the Bochum Congress had heralded the "beginning of the end of disunity among German miners."[96] The *Ehrenrat* would attempt to perpetuate present divisions, but to no avail. For when it came to championing the miners' rights, clear reason would gain the upper hand, and "those who want to sever a natural bond [between workers]"[97] would be deposed and forced to flee. There would be no room for Weber, Hitze, and Brauns in Hue's "neutral" union.

Brust was too confident in the continued growth of the *Gewerkverein* and too suspicious of the *Alter Verband* to contemplate merger. Thus the executive committee issued a declaration rejecting the idea of merger with the *Alter Verband*. The statement ended, however, on a positive note. The continued existence of two unions did not preclude the maintenance of friendly relations. "*Schiedlich-Friedlich*" would be the policy of the *Gewerkverein* in the future.[98]

Coming on 21 February—the day of the *Gewerkverein*'s wage petition—the

93. Landrat Gelsenkirchen to *Regierungspräsident* Arnsberg, 1 March 1897, Reg. Arnsberg I 93, StA Münster.

94. See the observations of the *Gewerkverein* executive committee in *Bergknappe*, no. 2, 26 February 1897; and the report of the *Regierungspräsident* Arnsberg to the Prussian minister of the interior, 13 May 1897, Reg. D. 9039, HSA Düsseldorf.

95. See the report of the *Regierungspräsident* Arnsberg, cited above in note 94.

96. Quoted in Hue, *Neutrale oder parteiische Gewerkschaften*, p. 84.

97. *Ibid.*, p. 84.

98. *Bergknappe*, no. 2, 26 February 1897.

new stance toward the *Alter Verband* takes on added significance. For it appeared that Brust was attempting to force the mine owners to the bargaining table by raising the specter of a general strike.[99] Brust added to this impression on 28 February by warning the employers that refusal to negotiate could lead to "a struggle."[100] Although Brust was clearly bluffing—the union treasury could not endure a strike for more than a day or two—he went even further two weeks later, warning that the union would continue to press its demands "in accord with all the miners of the district."[101] Not surprisingly, the employers refused to be cowed into submission by a paper tiger. The Ruhr Association claimed it had no authority in wage matters, then advised individual mines to avoid all dealings with "third parties"[102] attempting to interfere with the writing of wage contracts. Brust's brashness and inexperience had created a very awkward situation for the young organization.

Hue had no intention of allowing the Christians to retreat. He felt a general action of some sort would improve relations between the unions still further, weaken the *Ehrenrat*, and lead, perhaps, to the desired merger. He therefore drew up plans for a joint protest rally at Bochum on 28 March. The owners' refusal to recognize trade unions as representatives of the employees would be singled out for special criticism and the Reichstag requested to grant unions corporate status. The workers would also reiterate the *Gewerkverein*'s wage demands, and if the owners still refused to negotiate, an attempt would be made to elicit a binding arbitration settlement from the newly created (1891) industrial courts. In the event of a strike, Hue wanted Möller to convince the French, Belgian, and British miners to refuse overtime work. In this way German markets—and the strikers' jobs—would be preserved.

Hue's wage initiative was obviously designed to appeal to the Christians' sense of legality and due process. On 27 March, however, *Gewerkverein* officials published a note in the bourgeois press dissociating themselves from the Bochum rally and advising members not to attend.[103] Nor would the union strike for higher wages. Rather, a petition would be submitted to the Reichstag demanding obligatory worker committees, more powerful arbitration tribunals, and corporate status for trade unions. For the months ahead the organization should concentrate on strengthening its financial base to be able to cope more effectively with employer intransigence in the future. The *Ehrenrat* had prevailed again.

99. See the report of the *Regierungspräsident* Arnsberg cited above in note 94.
100. *Bergknappe*, no. 7, 15 May 1897.
101. *Bergknappe*, no. 3, 15 March 1897.
102. *Ibid.*
103. The note was published in *Bergknappe* a few weeks later (no. 4, 1 April 1897).

The *Gewerkverein*'s refusal to join the Socialists at Bochum, even in a joint arbitration effort, weakened Hue's position and allowed Möller to regain control of the union. The Socialist deputy had disapproved of the merger strategy all along, sensing therein a threat to S.P.D. interests. He cooperated with Hue, nevertheless, to prevent the more popular editor from usurping the chairmanship and blocking an important avenue of party influence.[104] The failure of Hue's conciliation efforts with Brust, however, caused a considerable shift of opinion within the union in Möller's favor. This shift probably explains Möller's unexpected victory over Hue's candidate (Thiemann) in the balloting for union chairman that Easter.[105] With Möller in charge again, plans for cooperation with the *Gewerkverein* were discontinued, and, by May 1897, relations between the two unions were as bad as ever.[106] Ironically, it was not just the bourgeoisie that was perpetuating working-class divisions. For orthodox Marxists like Möller obviously differed little from Center leaders in viewing trade unions primarily as recruiting stations for a party. Proletarians would unite behind the S.P.D. or not at all.

The embarrassing circumstances surrounding the *Gewerkverein*'s change of course in March gave Möller no opportunity to realize his ideal of Marxist hegemony in the Ruhr, strange though it may seem. Christian membership topped 13,000 in April and reached 15,000 by early July. This recruiting success can only be explained by the fact that wages had risen 5.5 percent since the Bochum Congress in February. With wages increasing and hiring on the rise, union membership was less risky and less burdensome financially. The Christian union, moreover, was perceived by the workers as the more viable organization, with momentum behind it. For each new member of the *Alter Verband* from February to June, 23 joined the *Gewerkverein*.[107]

Emboldened by this success, the Christian miners' union made yet another attempt to accelerate the growth of Christian trade unionism. The occasion was the third annual convention of *Arbeiterverein* members from the archdiocese of Cologne in June 1897. Oberdörffer had opposed creation of this convention on the grounds that it would weaken the authority of *Arbeiterverein* priests, but had been overridden by Archbishop Krementz, who agreed

104. The *Regierungspräsident* Arnsberg discusses Möller's tactical cooperation in the report cited above, note 94. The friction between Möller and Hue surfaced in the former's letter of 14 March, printed in *Bergknappe*, no. 18, 1 November 1897.

105. *Regierungspräsident* Arnsberg to Prussian minister of the interior, 9 November 1897, Reg. D. 9039, HSA Düsseldorf.

106. See Brust's remarks at Aachen in January 1898, *Bergknappe*, nos. 5–6, for 1 and 15 March 1898. Thiemann had continued to oppose Möller after the *Alter Verband* congress in April 1897 and had been ousted from the executive committee as a result.

107. Koch, *Die Bergarbeiter im Ruhrgebiet*, p. 148; *Der Arbeiter* (Munich), no. 24, 11 June 1897.

with Hitze and Brauns that the workers should at least be allowed to express themselves. This setback did not deter Oberdörffer, however, from continuing his opposition to labor independence. In a series of articles and speeches after 1894, he propagated the idea of Catholic confessional unions controlled by the church—an approach which was readily accepted by a considerable number of *Arbeiterverein* priests in the diocese. These circumstances prompted Brust's supporters in 1897 to use the annual workers' convention, whose motions were not binding on parish priests, as a psychological lever against Oberdörffer's more conservative faction. A resolution called for acknowledgment of the *Gewerkverein*'s success in the Ruhr and stressed the necessity of founding similar organizations without delay.[108] Theodor Berse, one of Brust's colleagues, delivered the main address in favor of the motion and was backed emphatically by a still-active Anton Rosenkranz. Brauns was there to defend the motion too. Failure to organize the yet-loyal masses, he warned, would result in their lapse into absolute indifference or capture by the S.P.D. The motion was only partially successful. Significantly, it was Hitze who played the inhibiting role once again. Unlike the previous summer at Dortmund, the Center's social expert was no longer confident that educational trade sections within Catholic *Arbeitervereine* could effectively infiltrate and Christianize the free trade unions. The continuation of anti-Christian, pro-Socialist articles in the union press had apparently changed his mind on this point. The Socialist metal workers' organ, for instance, had criticized Christianity as a "poor imitation of Buddhism" and the story of Moses as a "crude hoax."[109] But opposition in church and Center circles to independent trade unions remained, and there was still no sign that the unions would be granted corporate rights or chambers of labor. Hitze therefore recommended a more gradual strategy:

> At the annual conference of *Verein* chairmen yesterday a resolution was passed that trade commissions be formed within every labor association. These will be the nucleus for trade unions to be founded later . . . Today, where specific interests are in special need of representation, we should dedicate ourselves again to the goal of trying to found *Fachabteilungen* that we can greet as the bearers of a great Christian trade union organization.

108. Ritter, *Die Männer aus Mönchen-Gladbach*, part 3, p. 52, Ritter Papers ER/D-16, KfZG, Bonn; Ritter, *Volksverein*, p. 205; Müller, *Die christliche Gewerkschaftsbewegung*; *Kölner Correspondenz an die geistlichen Präsides*, nos. 1–2, 5–6 for January–February and May–June 1895 and nos. 5–6, May–June 1897, StBib MG; and *Offizieller Bericht über den 3. Delegierten-Tag der katholischen Arbeitervereinigungen der Erzdiözese Köln zu Köln am 13. Juni 1897*, pp. 15–19, StBib MG.
109. Quoted in Franz Wieber, "Franz Wieber," in *25 Jahre christliche Gewerkschaftsbewegung*, pp. 172–73.

Hitze's remarks led to a compromise wording of the *Gewerkverein*'s proposal. Similar unions should be founded for other branches of industry where "the state of industrial relations"[110] warranted such organizations. This version, which allowed local priests to continue on as before, was accepted without further debate.[111] Though disappointed, the delegates did not attempt to challenge their social and religious superiors.

Interconfessional unions had not been formally sanctioned by the church. Most of Oberdörffer's following was therefore unmoved by the convention's motion. But a few important converts were made in Aachen, Düren, Cologne, and Düsseldorf during the fall and winter of 1897/98.[112] Despite the hostile attitude of many in church circles, 50,000 workers were organized in Christian trade unions in western Germany by spring 1898.

Developments within the *Gewerkverein*, meanwhile, were beginning to assume added significance. It is no mean task to determine trends and tendencies among the rank and file of the Christian miners' union, but fortunately the sources allow some comment, for the feelings of the members were becoming an increasingly important factor in *Gewerkverein* decision making by 1897/98. At the time the union was founded the majority of initiates seem to have been "genuine Christian comrades who stuck to their principles and were true to their [Catholic] *Weltanschauung*,"[113] as one source describes them. Brust had reckoned on a submissive group of followers in 1894, it will be recalled, but assumed that time would produce a more energetic breed. The emerging spokesman of this dominant moderate faction, accordingly, was not Brust, but most probably Theodor Berse, who was wont to chastise younger workers for desiring too much too soon. The miner's lot was and would always be a tough one, and he simply had to be satisified with what little he had. "One can't get everything at once. Things come bit by bit as circumstances and, above all, the law permits."[114]

110. *Offizieller Bericht uber den 3. Delegiertentag . . . zu Köln*, pp. 18–19.
111. *Ibid.*, p. 19.
112. *Oberbürgermeister* of Crefeld to *Regierungspräsident* in Düsseldorf, 14 March 1898 and report of the Crefeld Police Department, 3 April 1898, Reg. D. 9047, HSA Düsseldorf; Müller, *Die christliche Gewerkschaftsbewegung*, pp. 67–68; Heinrich Kurtscheid, "Heinrich Kurtscheid," in *25 Jahre christliche Gewerkschaftsbewegung 1899–1924* (Berlin: Christlicher Gewerkschaftsverlag, 1924), pp. 219–20; *Regierungspräsident* in Cologne to King Wilhelm, 24 January 1899, Reg. D. 403/9045, LHA Koblenz; Kulemann, *Die Gewerkschaftsbewegung*, pp. 373–74, 389, 399–400, 405–7; and Immelen to the editor of *Der Arbeiter* (Munich), 8 December 1897, printed in Gasteiger, *Christliche Gewerkschaften in Süddeutschland*, p. 250.
113. "100 Jahre Recklinghäuser Zeitung 1831–1931," Zeitungsarchiv Nr. XII/7, StA Recklinghausen.
114. Officer Schwinderlauf to *Polizei-Verwaltung* Oberhausen, 24 December 1900, Landratsamt Duisburg-Mulheim 473, HSA Düsseldorf.

Even in 1894, however, a younger, more impetuous faction was in existence. Father Oberdörffer, for instance, had received considerable applause from the delegates for his advice about strikes and cooperation with the *Alter Verband*, and government reports from the early months note the presence of discontented members near Bochum.[115] One gets the definite impression that Brust sympathized with this radical faction, but refused for obvious tactical reasons to defy the *Ehrenrat*, the *Knappenvereine*, and the older members. Thus Brust gave every impression of readying the union for strike action in the spring of 1897, only to retreat in the end.

The great influx of new members that year, which saw the union swell to over 20,000 by December, changed the tactical situation within the union. There is every indication, in fact, that Berse and the older miners were forced rather suddenly into the minority. Already by the summer of 1897, for example, a more activist group of German Catholic miners around Johann Effert began calling for strike action against the owners.[116]

Significantly enough, the *Gewerkverein* also began to make headway with the Polish miners streaming into the Ruhr. For years after the founding of the union the thousands of Polish-speaking miners in the area (34,361 in 1897, or 18.6 percent of all miners) stood aloof from the organization, most unable to understand the German-speaking agitators and therefore highly suspicious and mistrustful of the union. Beginning in 1897, however, a Polish paper in Bochum, *Wiarus Polski*, started to edit a special number for Polish miners, and, because of the *Gewerkverein*'s largely Catholic composition, advocated membership in the Christian union. Within a year, 5,000–6,000 Polish miners, representing 25–30 percent of *Gewerkverein* membership, had joined. The pressure on Brust to take the offensive probably mounted as a result of this turnaround, for, as recent social research has shown, the Polish miners tended to be young, single, and aggressive.[117]

Merger with the Socialists was quite a different matter from strike action, but beginning in the summer of 1897 Brust began to experience additional difficulties in this area. An outspoken faction within the *Gewerkverein* led by Johann Wahl, the Protestant vice-chairman of the union, opposed the *Gewerkverein*'s ongoing feud with the *Alter Verband* and was attracted by the

115. *Regierungspräsident* Arnsberg to the Prussian minister of the interior, 16 April 1895, Reg. D. 9039, HSA Düsseldorf.

116. *Bergknappe*, nos. 10 and 11, 2 and 15 July 1897.

117. Imbusch, *Arbeitsverhältnis und Arbeiterorganisationen*, pp. 504–5; Richard C. Murphy, "Polnische Bergarbeiter im Ruhrgebiet: Das Beispiel Bottrop," and Christoph Klessmann, "Polnische Bergarbeiter im Ruhrgebiet: Soziale Lage und gewerkschaftliche Organisation," in Mommsen and Borsdorf (eds.), *Glückauf, Kameraden!* pp. 96, 113; Christoph Klessmann, *Polnische Bergarbeiter im Ruhrgebiet 1870–1945* (Göttingen, 1978), p. 61; Stephen Hickey, "The Shaping of the German Labour Movement," in Evans (ed.), *Society and Politics*, p. 230.

idea of merger propagated by Father Naumann and Hue. Wahl was supported by many of the *Gewerkverein*'s Protestant members in Bochum and most certainly by the radical Catholics around Effert. There may have been some sympathy among the rank and file Poles, but none from *Wiarus Polski*. On New Year's Day 1898, Wahl openly repudiated Brust and the *Ehrenrat* by encouraging Christian workers to pay more attention to Hue's articles and speeches and, if non-organized, to join either union.

Within two weeks Wahl had been denounced by the *Gewerkverein* general assembly and *Ehrenrat* and removed from his post.[118] Brauns and Weber had initiated the disciplinary action with the emphatic approval of Brust, who sensed an opportunity to tighten his grip on the union leadership. This goal seemed assured in mid-January 1898 when the *Arbeiter-* and *Knappenverein* representatives in the assembly granted him a handsome salary to edit *Bergknappe,* thereby enabling the miner to devote his full attention to union affairs. It was not long, however, before Brust began to criticize the *Ehrenrat* in an attempt to mend his fences with radicals in the union affronted by the ouster of Wahl. Speaking at Aachen in late January, for instance, Brust defended the right of the chairman and executive committee to make all union decisions. In February and March, he grew even more assertive. As police reports from the time indicate, Brust's temperament seemed to have changed since the previous year. Able to quit the mines for the first time since his teens and afford a few of the luxuries of life previously denied him, Brust was far less willing now to take advice from middle- and upper-class notables. As if to bolster his courage for the coming struggle with those who had manipulated him for so long, the ex-miner began to drink quite heavily.[119] The "love-child" had become *l'enfant terrible*.

Brust's revolt against the authority of the *Ehrenrat* was triggered by events in the mines near Osnabrück in April 1898.[120] Trouble between labor and management had first arisen there as a result of the owners' decision to continue operations on a religious holiday in early January (Twelfth Night). Similar disregard for church holidays in February prompted the miners to ask the *Gewerkverein* to expand its activity north to protect them during the clash that was considered inevitable on all sides. When over 300 miners were fired

118. For the dispute with Wahl, see *Bergknappe*, nos. 2–4 for 15 January, 1 and 15 February 1898; and *Regierungspräsident* Arnsberg to Prussian minister of the interior, 13 April 1898, Reg. D. 9039, HSA Düsseldorf.

119. *Bergknappe*, nos. 5–6, 1 and 15 March 1898; police commissioner in Essen to *Regierungspräsident* Arnsberg, 14 September 1898 and Landrat Essen to *Regierungspräsident* Arnsberg, 21 September 1898, Reg. D. 9048, HSA Düsseldorf.

120. For the details, see *Tremonia*, nos. 154 (1), 157 (3), 160 (1), 163 (2), 166 (1), 174 (1), 175 (2), 176 (1), and 180 (1), for 6, 7, 10, 13, 15, 20, 21, and 23 April 1898.

for honoring a Catholic holiday in late March, *Gewerkverein* agitators flocked to the area, recruiting nearly 1,500 new members, who promptly announced their intention to strike if the disciplined miners were not rehired.

Incensed by Brust's violation of the union's pledge to maintain peaceful relations between capital and labor, Weber convened the *Ehrenrat* in an effort to bring a halt to the whole action.[121] The union's patriarchs recommended that he open negotiations with the owners, appeal to the Prussian minister of trade and industry, and warn the miners not to strike. Brust cooperated with the *Ehrenrat* on the first two points, but refused to take its "advice" on the third. Rather, he urged the workers not to yield to management force and assured them that the *Gewerkverein* would not desert their cause.

This time Brust was not bluffing. Shortly after miners in Piesberg walked off the job on 12 April, the executive committee voted to support them. Weber had telegraphed union headquarters that he would tolerate no insubordination, and his colleague Legewitt, too, had reminded union officials that "the *Ehrenrat* comes first, then the executive committee."[122] Brust's defiance was contagious, however, and Weber and Legewitt were simply ignored. Aware that the proud miners could not be treated like children, Hitze backed down and participated in no more *Gewerkverein* meetings. Angered by Hitze's passivity, Weber and Legewitt resigned in disgust, much to the dismay of Stöcker, who, mindful of the upcoming Reichstag elections, had supported striking workers in Siegen only months before the Piesberg walkout. Not until 1904 would the Christian-Socials be able to reestablish ties to the *Gewerkverein*. Brauns, who had always been on good terms with Brust, continued to take part in union affairs from the proximity of his Borbeck parish, as did many of the more progressive-thinking *Knappenverein* leaders who were not as shocked by the strike.[123] The power of the *Ehrenrat* had been crushed, but otherwise, it should be stressed, the decentralized organizational structure created in 1894 remained unaltered.

Brust's decision to back the Piesberg workers had all the earmarks of a desperate gamble to stay at the helm of the union and maintain its impressive growth. The ouster of Johann Wahl was not popular with the radical members, and Brust, as explained earlier, was already under considerable pressure from this direction to do something for the workers. The Piesberg strike could now be offered as definitive proof that the Christian union was not just a "glorified *Knappenverein*." The action had the additional advantage of being marginally

121. An accurate documentation of Weber's efforts was printed by Brust in *Bergknappe*, no. 9, 1 May 1898.
122. *Ibid.*
123. Joseph Joos, *Am Räderwerk der Zeit* (Augsburg: Verlag Winfried-Werk GmbH, n. d.), p. 32.

popular with some conservative Catholics. The union had struck, after all, in defense of a church holiday and easily won the support of the Center press and otherwise-suspicious peasants and small tradesmen in the area.[124] It is doubtful that the strike led to great membership gains, for the action did not budge the owners from their hard-line position, and Weber, it must be assumed, took a number of conservative workers *of both confessions* with him when he exited the union.[125] For Brust, however, the gamble was worthwhile, even if not totally successful. He had overthrown the *Ehrenrat* and finally given the radical members cause to cheer.

Alter Verband Chairman Heinrich Möller was impressed. When the *Gewerkverein* continued its radical policies in June 1898 by assaulting moderate *Knappschaftsverein* elders as "toadies and bootlickers,"[126] therefore, he proposed that the two unions form an alliance for the elders' elections in November 1898. The Christian organization was asked to vote for *Alter Verband* candidates if they were "tried members,"[127] or if they merely had a good chance to win.

Although he felt that Möller was asking too much, Brust was eager to reach an agreement. Internal pressure to alter his stance to the other union had not subsided, and, equally important from his point of view, neutral forces were once again gaining strength within the *Alter Verband*. Ludwig Schröder had returned from prison in April, eager to break off relations with the S.P.D. He was immediately elected vice-chairman of the union. Another new member of the executive committee, Eberhard Pokorni, had gone against the party in Bochum and voted for the Center during run-off elections to the Reichstag in June. Furthermore, Johann Meyer, who was known to support Schröder and Pokorni, was due for release from prison later that year.[128]

Wishing to strengthen the neutral faction gathering around Hue, Brust decided to make a compromise offer. Both unions would unite around the

124. See the articles in *Tremonia* cited above in note 120.
125. Irmgard Steinisch, "Der Gewerkverein christlicher Bergarbeiter," in Mommsen and Borsdorff (eds.), *Glückauf, Kameraden!* pp. 275–77, argues that the growth of the *Gewerkverein* from 1894 to 1898 depended on the support of the church and Center Party, and that the Piesberg strike alienated these circles and led to a levelling-off of growth until almost the end of the decade. Steinisch's statistics are correct, but her explanation is faulty. As the present study has shown, membership trends during the early years reflected the weakness of the *Alter Verband* and the prevailing wage rates, while the church and Center were not as supportive as Steinisch thinks. The Piesberg strike certainly led to problems with *some* conservative Catholics, but this was nothing new. The failure of the strike and the exodus of Wahl and Weber that year hurt the union much more in Protestant circles.
126. *Bergknappe*, no. 11, 1 June 1898.
127. Möller to Brust, 22 June 1898, printed in *Bergknappe*, no. 20, 15 October 1898.
128. *Regierungspräsident* to Prussian minister of the interior, 13 April and 13 November 1898, Reg. D. 9039 and 9042, HSA Düsseldorf; Hue, *Neutrale oder parteiische Gewerkschaften*, pp. 104–5.

candidate from the strongest organization in each district. The *Gewerkverein*'s numerical superiority would thus receive consideration. Brust also insisted that the *Alter Verband* nominate neither fanatical opponents of the *Gewerkverein* nor outspoken Socialists. Sensing that Brust's proposal was aimed directly at him, Möller broke off negotiations and began running separate *Alter Verband* candidates. Möller's decision returned inter-union relations to their former state of feud in the weeks before the elections, and by the winter of 1898/99, bitter press polemics had led to libel suits on both sides.[129]

Rank and file pressure finally brought an end to the five-year feud that spring. Government reports indicate that the neutral challenge to Möller gained momentum after the elections, reducing his influence within the union. Conditions in the *Gewerkverein* were even more unstable. In February 1899 a number of general assembly members met to plot Brust's overthrow if he did not improve relations with the *Alter Verband* before the *Knappschaftsverein* replacement elections in July.[130] Pressed in a direction he had already considered seriously the summer before, Brust met with Hue on 26 June 1899 and agreed to cooperate with the *Alter Verband* in the future "on all labor-related matters."[131] Brust had finally left the job of fighting the *Alter Verband* to others.

The agreement ended a period of Socialist-Christian infighting dating back to the great miners' strike of 1889. At that time the bold miners of the Ruhr saw the *Alter Verband* as their salvation and flocked to it in great numbers. By 1897 the Socialist union had waned in strength and the *Gewerkverein* possessed numerical superiority. Despite this seeming vacillation of the rank and file, their behavior was really quite consistent, for what was wanted by that minority of workers who could not be intimidated was an organization that could stand up to the might of capital. The apparent pressure within both unions for cooperation or perhaps merger by 1898/99 is evidence in support of this point. Indeed it was becoming increasingly clear to organized miners in the late 1890s that the vast majority of workers, being either too submissive or too radical, could never be won over to unionism by two feuding organizations which together claimed only 15 percent of the mining force in the Ruhr. And if forced to choose between *Gewerkverein* and *Alter Verband* in the long run, there was good reason to conclude in 1899 that the latter would prevail, the

129. See Brust's description of negotiations with the *Alter Verband* at Bochum in late June and his letters to Möller of 14 and 16 July 1898, printed in *Bergknappe*, no. 20, 15 October 1898; also see *Bergknappe*, no. 17, 1 September 1898.

130. *Regierungspräsident* Arnsberg to Prussian min. of the interior, 13 November 1898 and 27 November 1899, Reg. D. 9042, HSA Düsseldorf; police commissioner in Gelsenkirchen to *Regierungspräsident* Arnsberg, 20 March 1899, Reg. Arnsberg I 74, StA Münster.

131. Quoted in Hue, *Neutrale oder parteiische Gewerkschaften*, p. 88. See also *Bergknappe*, no. 20, 1 July 1899.

former's membership lead notwithstanding. The Socialist union was financially sounder, offered a few more benefits, and possessed more salaried functionaries. Most important of all, perhaps, was the fact that it belonged to a central federation of trade unions which greatly enhanced the strength and bargaining power of the individual organizations. It is not surprising, therefore, that the question of centralization was an issue of increasing concern to Christian workers at the end of the century.

This topic will be discussed in the following chapter. For now it is important to conclude that Christian labor had finally emerged as an independent force. That this had not occurred earlier can be attributed to the still-nascent social and political consciousness of Christian workers and the manipulative and intimidating tactics of middle- and upper-class circles. As an independent movement which had increasingly resented these techniques of domination, however, the Christian trade unions would not be as easily controlled by the Catholic church, the Center Party, and other auxiliary elites in Germany. The task of controlling them increased in importance and difficulty as a centralized, equally independent federation of Christian labor unions emerged at the turn of the century.

4

Centralization Efforts and the Question of Trade Union Politics

The Christian trade unions had made significant progress since Brust began to carve out a niche for himself in 1894. By 1898 approximately 65,000 laborers belonged to the movement. Joining the *Gewerkverein* and other western unions were numerous organizations for textile workers, railwaymen, and glass workers in southern Germany promoted by Father Lorenz Huber of Munich and working-class leaders like Karl Schirmer, Hans Braun, and Moritz Schmidt. In Berlin unions for construction workers, tailors, and butchers' journeymen had been founded by Paul Weigel, the impatient leader of Catholic workers in the capital.[1] As the Christian trade union movement grew stronger, however, the need for a common program and central directorate became increasingly clear to Christian leaders. The various groups had little or no contact with one another and differed on many important issues.

Some of the Christian trade unions in southern Germany, for instance, were local organizations comprising several trades, unlike the *Gewerkverein*, which was striving to organize one trade nationwide. Furthermore, the tileworkers' union in Detmold forbade strikes and included employers on the executive committee, while the Christian railwaymen of Trier were pledged to harmonious relations with state railroad authorities as well as open opposition to internal enemies of the state. Moreover, the unions in Aachen and Eupen had

1. See the present author's Ph.D. dissertation, "Christian Labor and the Politics of Frustration in Imperial Germany," Ohio State University, 1978, pp. 140-41; and Denk, *Christliche Arbeiterbewegung in Bayern*, pp. 250–62.

included clauses in their by-laws that could be construed as advocacy of electoral support for the Center Party. To the *Gewerkverein* as well as the overwhelmingly Protestant unions in Siegen and Detmold, such clauses were highly objectionable. These divergencies did not augur well for centralization efforts, but an attempt had to be made if the highly centralized free trade unions were to be overtaken.

Indeed, by the turn of the century the 58 unions affiliated with the General Commission had a great deal to offer their rank and file. Heading the list, perhaps, was the enhanced ability to wield the strike as an effective weapon against employers. Whereas Socialist unions waged only 179 of 544 (32.9 percent) successful strikes during the lean years from 1890 to 1894, this figure increased to 1,865 of 3,225 (57.8 percent) during the economic upswing from 1895 to 1899. This record is explained not only by the greater bargaining power and economic security which the workers possessed due to the booming economy, but also by the improved financial stability of the unions themselves. Average dues had increased from 9.4 marks in 1892 to 13.9 in 1900, and when this did not suffice, General Commission subsidies made up the difference. The percentage of strike costs borne by national headquarters fluctuated between 22 and 76 from 1895 to 1899. But victorious strikes were not all the free trade unions had to offer. By the end of the 1890s, 269 full-time secretaries edited union newspapers, handled recruiting, and administered support programs such as the 21 unemployment funds, 10 health funds, and 44 travel funds the affiliated unions boasted at this time.[2] In short, the roughly half-million workers belonging to Socialist unions were beginning to reap the benefits of over a decade of difficult organizational work. If Christian workers were to compete successfully on a separate basis at the union level, there was no time to lose.

The issue was first discussed by a small group of Christian workers attending an international social conference at Zurich in late August 1897. Impressed by the highly structured trade union organizations of Germany, Switzerland, and Britain, and embarrassed by the dearth of Christian labor delegates at Zurich, the Christian workers met on the eve of their departure for Germany to discuss what action could be taken to right the situation after their return home. Present at the caucus were Karl Schirmer and Hans Braun of Munich, Paul Weigel of Berlin, the Cologne metal worker Johannes Giesberts, and the secretary of the Catholic *Arbeitervereine* of Württemberg,

2. Gerhard A. Ritter and Klaus Tenfelde, "Der Durchbruch der freien Gewerkschaften Deutschlands zur Massenbewegung im letzten Viertel des 19. Jahrhunderts," in Vetter (ed.), *Vom Sozialistengesetz zur Mitbestimmung*, pp. 89, 92, 96–97; Gerhard A. Ritter, *Die Arbeiterbewegung im Wilhelminischen Reich: Die Sozialdemokratische Partei und die freien Gewerkschaften 1890–1900* (Berlin-Dahlem: Colloquium Verlag 1959), pp. 161, 170.

Matthias Erzberger. All promised to promote Christian trade unionism, and more, to establish closer ties with one another in the process. A national congress was judged the best means to initiate such cooperation. The small gathering also decided that Schirmer should encourage Huber and other leaders in the prestigious South German Association of Catholic *Arbeitervereine* to make the necessary preparations. The decision, just as Brust's in 1894, was based on a realistic appraisal of the need to cooperate with church and bourgeois circles in the early stages of an endeavor that promised to be highly controversial.[3]

Schirmer made his request after returning to Munich.[4] Unfortunately, there is little indication of the type of response he received. Moritz Schmidt's editorials in *Der Arbeiter* provide the only clues. On two occasions after the Zurich meeting he hinted that the proper time for a national conference had not yet come.[5] Bavarians should first found more trade unions in order to avoid being overrun by the Rhinelanders. Bavarian particularism seemed to have prevented rapid realization of the plans drawn up in Zurich.

With the Bavarians dragging their feet, the initiative in preparing the congress passed from Munich to Christian labor circles in Aachen. Several Christian trade unions had been founded there, it will be recalled, in the wake of Brust's *Katholikentag* address in 1896. Hubert Immelen, an ambitious Catholic journalist, was largely responsible for these foundings and, interestingly enough, had ulterior political motives for doing so. Anxious to rise quickly into a position of leadership in the Catholic political community, he hoped to forge a political lobby strong enough to prod the Center in the direction of social reform. At a special assembly in late September 1897, the Aachen association formulated a Reichstag petition demanding Sunday rest, the ten-hour day, unemployment insurance, and other labor reforms. Plans were then announced for a national conference in January 1898 to discuss the question of politicizing the embryonic Christian labor movement. It was high time, felt Immelen, that Christian trade unionists go beyond the usual well-meaning talk and begin in earnest with the honorable work of social reform.[6]

3. *Der Arbeiter* (Munich), no. 29, 22 July 1898; "Der internationale Arbeiterschutz-Kongress in Zurich und sein Einfluss auf die christliche Arbeiterbewegung in Deutschland," in *Jahrbuch der christlichen Gewerkschaften für 1909*, pp. 26–42; Gasteiger, *Christliche Gewerkschaften in Süddeutschland*, p. 249.
4. *Der Arbeiter* (Munich), no. 29, 22 July 1898.
5. *Der Arbeiter* (Munich), no. 43, 22 October 1897, and no. 1, 7 January 1898.
6. *Regierungspräsident* in Aachen to Prussian minister of the interior, 31 March and 3 October 1898, Reg. D. 9039 and 9042, HSA Düsseldorf; Gasteiger, *Christliche Gewerkschaften in Süddeutschland*, pp. 249–50; Schirmer, "Karl Schirmer," pp. 209–10; Immelen to editor of *Der Arbeiter* (Munich), n. d. (1897), printed in Gasteiger, *Christliche Gewerkschaften in Süddeutschland*, pp. 41.

Immelen's plans for a national conference were ready by early July 1898. The first Christian labor congress would meet at Mainz in mid-August and include discussion of the "social, economic, and political situation" of the working class. All resolutions passed at Mainz would be submitted as petitions to the Reichstag. Significantly, Immelen had scheduled his congress two weeks before the *Katholikentag*. He had not mentioned the Center by name, but there can be little doubt that he was still trying to take the party in tow.[7]

Brust had the most objections to the proposed format. In his opinion, the congress should formulate a trade union program, not initiate a political campaign. He admitted that Immelen's political agenda was worthy of brief consideration, but felt that a more thorough handling should be postponed until clarity was established on the matter of trade union goals. To make positively sure that the gathering in Mainz would not be awkward for the *Gewerkverein*, Brust wanted to delay the congress until representatives from the major Christian unions could meet and agree on a shorter, less political agenda.[8]

Determined not to lose the crucial backing of the *Gewerkverein*, Immelen conceded to Brust's demands. The congress was postponed until early September, and a debate over the nature of the new national organization was placed at the top of the agenda. Brust was given the privilege of delivering the main address; Immelen and Schirmer would present opposing arguments (*Koreferate*). Immelen also wanted to meet with Brust and other trade union leaders during the Crefeld *Katholikentag* in late August to discuss the matter further. Assuming that the congress agenda would be altered to suit *Gewerkverein* wishes, Brust and the executive committee agreed on 14 August to send a delegation of four to Mainz in early September. Schirmer and his colleagues in Munich had agreed to Immelen's plans in late July.[9] Evidence on the response of other Christian organizations is lacking, but it can be assumed that all, with the probable exception of the Bavarian and Prussian railroad unions, followed the lead of Essen and Munich.

The Crefeld meeting was held on 26 August 1898. It was hurriedly arranged by Brust almost certainly after consultation with Heinrich Brauns and other Catholic labor leaders in Mönchen-Gladbach. Present were Pieper of the *Volksverein*, Matthias Erzberger, Chaplain Hessdörffer, Peter Michels of the

7. Immelen's circular to the other Christian trade unions in Germany, dated simply "early July 1898," is printed in Gasteiger, *Christliche Gewerkschaften in Süddeutschland*, pp. 254–55.
8. The various replies to Immelen are quoted or printed in *ibid.*, pp. 256–58. See especially that of the *Gewerkverein* executive committee, dated 22 July 1898.
9. Immelen to Huber and Schirmer, 24 July 1898, quoted in *ibid.*, pp. 258–59; Immelen to Brust, n.d. (probably early August 1898), quoted in *ibid.*, p. 260; *Bergknappe*, no. 17, 1 September 1898; *Der Arbeiter* (Munich), nos. 31–32, 5 and 12 August 1898.

Crefeld textile union, and Brust. After a cursory search for Immelen, who could not be found, the meeting was begun without him.[10] Brust opened by recommending that the delegates first justify the need for Christian trade unions. The *Gewerkverein* leader was well aware of the need to counter Socialist charges that the Christians were undermining proletarian unity. The congress should then determine whether these unions would be local or national, confessional or interconfessional, partisan or politically neutral, and further define the goals and tactics of the movement. Other questions such as the union press and bureaucracy could also be handled.[11]

Erzberger, at this point, made a daring suggestion. The Mainz Congress should not be held in September, but postponed indefinitely. He was not in disagreement with Brust's agenda; rather, he wanted time to popularize the idea of a national organization among the highly particularistic South Germans. He proposed, therefore, that separate North and South German preconferences be held in the course of the upcoming year to settle the issues raised by Brust. Pieper, Brust, and Michels consented to these arrangements, and Hitze, who had missed the meeting too, also agreed when informed later that day.[12] A circular was formulated and sent to the Christian labor organizations which had planned to attend in September, notifying them of the postponement. When Immelen learned about the meeting the next day he objected bitterly to the "one-sided, arbitrary, and unjust"[13] nature of this decision. But with less than 5,000 workers to back him in Aachen, and no support from the *Volksverein*, Immelen's protests were ineffective.

The *Volksverein*'s support for the idea of nationwide Christian trade unions led by men like Brust and Erzberger was consistent with efforts underway in

10. Gasteiger, *Christliche Gewerkschaften in Süddeutschland*, pp. 259–60.

11. No minutes to the conference exist. It has already been established, however, that Brust intended to hammer out an agenda at Crefeld in time for the Mainz Congress in September. Gasteiger (p. 259) also notes that the Crefeld meeting was the agenda-setting conference demanded by Brust in July. A comparison of the *Gewerkverein*'s note to Immelen of 22 July (Gasteiger, pp. 256–57) and the communiqué signed by the participants after the Crefeld session (Gasteiger, pp. 260–61) supplies ample material to reconstruct Brust's presentation.

12. Once again, the details of the meeting must be reconstructed. Michels was a newcomer to the movement and could not have turned the meeting around in this fashion. Hessdörfer was in league with Immelen (*Bergknappe*, no. 5, 1 March 1898) and must also be ruled out. As explained earlier, Brust was prepared to bring the matter to a close at Crefeld. Hitze's *post hoc* approval (Gasteiger, p. 259) indicates that the *Volksverein* had not proposed the change either. And finally, the idea of a separate conference for southern Germany has all the earmarks of south German origin. For the fact that Erzberger was in basic agreement with Brust's ideas on the trade union question, see the former's speech at Munich in February 1898, printed in *Der Arbeiter* (Munich), no. 5, 4 February 1898; and Klaus Epstein, *Matthias Erzberger and the Dilemma of German Democracy* (Princeton, New Jersey: Princeton University Press, 1959), pp. 401–4.

13. See Immelen's circular of 29 August to the other Christian unions quoted in Gasteiger, *Christliche Gewerkschaften in Süddeutschland*, p. 263.

Mönchen-Gladbach since early 1898. The economic upswing had been underway for almost two years, yet only two or three trade sections had been founded in western Germany. In the meantime, membership in Socialist unions had risen to 491,000, while Christian trade unions had tripled in size. After Brust's revolt against the *Ehrenrat*, moreover, it was apparent that Christian workers had gained too much class consciousness to tolerate further "schooling" from priests and social betters. Thus Christian trade unionism was accepted as a *fait accompli*.[14] Hitze and Pieper could not stand idly by, however, and allow political schemers like Immelen to gain control of the movement and transform it into a narrow, confessional pressure group. The *Volksverein*, in fact, had designs of its own for the Christian trade unions. A broad-based social reform coalition was taking shape in 1898, and Mönchen-Gladbach intended for the Christian unions to play an important role. Highly significant, these developments deserve more attention at this point in the analysis.

Shortly after his resignation as Prussian minister of commerce and industry in June 1896, Hans von Berlepsch approached Adolf Stöcker, *Volksverein* Chairman Franz Brandts, and other progressive industrialists, university professors, and bourgeois labor leaders with ambitious plans. Realizing that his energies were being expended uselessly in Berlin, where he no longer had the ear of the King or the Prussian Cabinet of Ministers, Berlepsch had decided to work outside government to promote his ideas of social reform. A new journal would be founded for the explicit purpose of raising the social awareness of Germany's highly conservative bureaucracy.[15] Next, steps would be taken to encourage other governments in Europe to initiate social legislation. As a former minister, Berlepsch was well aware that William's unwillingness to proceed with social reforms was based to a considerable extent on the arguments of German businessmen concerning the need to protect German industry from cheaper foreign competition. Once international progress had been registered, reform coalitions could be formed in each country to promote further progress. For Germany, Berlepsch hoped that unrelenting Reichstag

14. Hitze lent his crucial support to pro-union resolutions at *Arbeiterverein* conventions in Cologne and Münster, respectively, in June and December 1897. Pieper spoke out for the young movement repeatedly at the end of the year and also joined Schirmer in encouraging the efforts of Chaplain Küpper in Düren in January 1898. See *Der Arbeiter* (Munich), no. 48, 26 November 1897; Ritter, *Volksverein*, p. 292; and Kulemann, *Die Gewerkschaftsbewegung*, p. 399. Heitzer, *Kardinal Kopp*, p. 25, errs in stating that the *Volksverein* had furthered Christian trade unionism since at least 1895. This statement also contradicts his later, more accurate assertion (p. 40) that the *Volksverein* advocated *Fachabteilungen* as a means to attain a neutral trade union movement.

15. Ritter, *Männer aus Mönchen-Gladbach*, part 2, pp. 21–22, Ritter Papers ER/D-16, KfZG Bonn; Berlepsch to Rottenburg, 4 August 1896, cited in Herbert Schwab, "Gesellschaft für Soziale Reform," in Fricke *et al.*, *Bürgerlichen Parteien*, vol. 2, p. 169.

pressure on the federal states would weaken Bundesrat resistance to reform, while the bourgeois labor movement, in turn, would pressure parliament as well as impress the Kaiser with the loyalty and patriotism of the working class.[16]

By October 1897, the first issue of *Soziale Praxis*, edited by the former progressive journalist Ernst Francke, had appeared.[17] A committee was also formed in Brussels that fall in order to draft statutes for an international society of social reformers.[18] Throughout the winter of 1897/98, then, debate began in Germany concerning the necessity of greater cooperation to further social legislation at home. Very little is known about this debate, except that one faction, led no doubt by Friedrich Naumann and the more radical wing of the Society for Social Politics around Lujo Brentano and Heinrich Herkner, insisted that social progress in Germany could not be postponed until other countries such as France and Belgium caught up with Germany.[19]

It is significant that *Volksverein* general secretary August Pieper was very heavily influenced by Naumann, Brentano, and Herkner during the discussions that fall and winter.[20] By the Crefeld *Katholikentag* of 1898, in fact, Pieper had already advanced past the ideas of his more cautious mentor Hitze. He wanted to support the emerging Christian trade union movement in the hope, not unjustified at the time, that successful competition with the free unions would eventually force the latter to negotiate a merger on the basis of political and religious neutrality. To facilitate such a merger, Pieper was probably already urging union leaders like Brust to consider discarding the word "Christian" from the name of the new national organization. He feared that its inclusion would encourage Catholic Church authorities to intervene in union affairs, thereby alienating non-Catholic workers, complicating inter-union relations, and dooming the Christian organization to a permanent existence of peripheral importance like the Hirsch-Duncker unions. Once the General Commission had been "neutralized," already existing tensions between the free trade unions and S.P.D. would increase. With outspoken Socialist depu-

16. For the Kaiser's views and Berlepsch's appreciation of them, see Wilhelm's proclamation of 9 February 1890, printed in Bismarck, *Kaiser vs. Bismarck*, p. 79, and Berlepsch to Hohenlohe, 29 May 1895, quoted in Born, *Staat und Sozialpolitik*, pp. 120–21.

17. Franz Brandts was one of the main financial backers of the journal. Dieter Lindenlaub, *Richtungskämpfe im Verein für Sozialpolitik* (Wiesbaden: Franz Steiner Verlag GmbH, 1967), vol. 1, p. 189.

18. *Bergknappe*, no. 32, 11 August 1900.

19. *Bergknappe*, no. 3, 19 January 1901.

20. Ritter, *Männer aus Mönchen-Gladbach*, part 4, p. 11, Ritter Papers ER/D-16, KfZG Bonn. Hitze, on the other hand, oriented himself with Berlepsch and Schmoller, who wanted to proceed slowly. See Hitze's remarks in *Schmollers Jahrbuch*, 1898, Heft 2, p. 375; and Lindenlaub, *Richtungskämpfe*, vol. 1, p. 189.

ties removed from their posts as union editors and chairmen, Pieper felt the "natural" desire of the proletariat to improve its lot within the existing framework of government and society would be greatly enhanced, and the trade union movement would become the major impetus for progressive, "evolutionary" social change. The S.P.D. would either become a reform party or lose mass support.[21] Pieper hoped for the latter.

To many observers in Berlepsch's coalition, the process of dissolution within the Socialist camp seemed far advanced by 1898. The growing controversy over trade union goals and tactics was the most widely cited example. The recession of the early 1890s had convinced many Socialists that the ultimate collapse of capitalistic society was drawing near.[22] To be sure, even the dominant radical wing around *Fraktion* chief August Bebel had no intention of taking to the streets or rejecting the parliamentary role of the party. When underlying social and economic conditions had advanced to the right stage and society was permeated with Socialist ideas, Socialism could be legislated into existence "without the application of any means of force."[23] In this crucial, final stage, however, it was mandatory that all forces be concentrated in the hands of the party. The primary role of a trade union, therefore, was an auxiliary, political one.[24] Small wage increases, shortening of worktime, and improvement in job conditions were "Sysiphus labors"[25] at best, a retardation at worst, of the spread of Socialist consciousness among the masses.

Not all trade unionists were prepared to follow the advice of the true believers, however, especially after 1896, as the economic upswing increased the chances of successful trade union action. Otto Hue was probably the first to challenge the party openly, but in 1897, the prestigious, long-established printers' union joined the revolt. Contemptuously disregarding the attitudes

21. Pieper to Brust, 25 April 1923, Pieper Papers 35, and Pieper to Otte, 29 November 1932, Pieper Papers 36, StA Münster; Pieper Manuscript, part 3, pp. 775, 777, StA MG; Hitze's speech in Reichstag Debates, Period 9, Session 5 (9 March 1898), p. 1438; and Heitzer, *Kardinal Kopp*, pp. 40–42. Heitzer believes that Pieper meant the Mainz Congress of the spring of 1899 when he noted in 1937 that he had advised Christian unionists from the beginning to drop the word "Christian." The Crefeld *Katholikentag* of 1898 seems more likely.

22. Heinrich Brauns, *Die "freien" und die Hirsch-Dunckerschen Gewerkschaften bis 1907* (Mönchen-Gladbach: Verlag der Westdeutschen Arbeiter-Zeitung GmbH. 1907), p. 40; Gerhard A. Ritter, *Die Arbeiterbewegung im Wilhelminischen Reich: Die Sozialdemokratische Partei und die freien Gewerkschaften 1890–1900*, pp. 106, 125.

23. See Bebel's remarks, as quoted in Vernon Lidtke, *The Outlawed Party: Social Democracy in Germany 1878–1900* (Princeton, New Jersey: Princeton University Press, 1966), p. 288.

24. See Bebel's remarks at the 1893 and 1896 party congresses, quoted in Brauns, *Die "freien" und die Hirsch-Dunckerschen Gewerkschaften*, p. 40; and Ritter, *Sozialdemokratische Partei und die freien Gewerkschaften*, p. 154. See also Varain, *Freie Gewerkschaften*, p. 13.

25. Hue, *Neutrale oder parteiische Gewerkschaften*, pp. 126, 129.

toward trade unionism described above, the union initiated a campaign for permanent collective bargaining commissions (*Tarifgemeinschaften*) which brought forth howls of "treason"[26] from party purists. The controversy ended with the expulsion of the Marxist faction from the union and severance of relations with the S.P.D. in September 1897.[27] The lithographers followed suit in 1898, calling for opposition to the Social Democrats.[28] The dissident faction in the General Commission was still a small minority[29] at the time but Christian labor leaders like Pieper were confident that the quickening pace of the economy would drive more and more unions into the neutral camp.

Pieper, Naumann, and others were also cognizant of subtle, yet significant, shifts in the attitude of S.P.D. leaders toward the role of a Socialist party in a bourgeois society. Even during "the heroic period" of the 1880s, radicals like Bebel, who expected the death knell of capitalism to sound in the near future, had devoted considerable time and energy to the promotion of social legislation.[30] This paradox was explained to a certain extent by the fact that party moderates and fellow travelers expected the S.P.D. to take seriously its claim to represent the interests of the working class,[31] but there were theoretical reasons, too. As time moved on toward the inevitable downfall of capitalism, the party could promote reforms which would embody these ongoing changes. At some time in the future, as Vernon Lidtke explains, "it would be possible for the Social Democrats to introduce a fully Socialistic program at the appropriate moment. When the moment would come, no one knew, but when it came there would no longer be an effective resistance to a Socialist society."[32]

It is significant that these gradual reforms were considered acceptable only if proposed by the S.P.D. or occasionally by another party such as the Center. The party drew the line at reforms proposed by the government, which were opposed as paltry measures designed not to aid the proletariat, but to lure it away from the S.P.D. Bismarck's social reform legislation was rejected on these grounds, as was that of the young Kaiser in the early 1890s.[33] As the decade wore on, however, the party came under increasing pressure to aban-

26. *Ibid.*, p. 141.
27. *Der Arbeiter* (Munich), no. 37, 10 September 1897.
28. *Westdeutsche Arbeiter-Zeitung*, no. 28, 14 July 1900.
29. The miners, printers, and lithographers claimed 62,500 members in late 1899; the General Commission contained 580,000. See *Mitteilungen des Gesamtverbandes der christlichen Gewerkschaften Deutschlands*, no. 11, 2 September 1901, p. 91.
30. Lidtke, *The Outlawed Party*, pp. 233, 286.
31. *Ibid.*, p. 160, 164–71.
32. *Ibid.*, p. 287.
33. *Ibid.*, pp. 160, 275; Stegmann, *Mitbestimmung*, pp. 105–6.

don this obstructionist practice. South German Socialists around the ex–civil servant Georg von Vollmar began to urge the leadership to adopt a more positive parliamentary approach in 1891, and by the mid-1890s, free trade union leaders were complaining that the party's preoccupation with future developments had led to a disinterest in social reform.[34] After the renewed growth of the S.P.D. Reichstag *Fraktion* (44 to 56 seats) in June 1898 and the subsequent "revisionistic" campaign of the Socialist journalist Eduard Bernstein, party leaders undertook a reassessment of their oppositionist tactics.[35] As far as men like Pieper were concerned, the formation of a Christian trade union federation committed to the task of neutralizing the free trade unions could only accelerate the revisionistic tendencies in the Socialist camp. The idea, of course, was not unique. Naumann and the National-Socials had been pushing for a "neutral" trade union movement since the founding of the new party in November 1896.

Anti-Socialist considerations such as this explain Pieper's behavior at the Crefeld *Katholikentag*. Put most simply, Brust and Erzberger could be counted on to support Pieper's goals. In the South, Erzberger was considered a definite ally. He had already impressed superiors in Stuttgart as a skilled political leader and was therefore well suited to promote national unions in a highly particularistic corner of the Reich. Moreover, his advocacy of interconfessionalism, the prerequisite for neutral trade unions, was rare among South German Catholics.[36] In the North Brust, an advocate of interconfessionalism and political neutrality, was attempting to use the trade union movement to promote Christian *Sozialpolitik* and, in so doing, "stop the S.P.D. cold."[37] The *Gewerkverein*'s flirtation with the neutral faction in the *Alter Verband* during the summer of 1898 was a promising step in this direction. Thus Brust, too, was seen as an ally. What little evidence there is suggests that Hitze was not ill disposed to Pieper's ideas either, but that he probably advised extreme caution.[38]

Pieper's influence in the labor world, and hence his ability to implement

34. Beverly Heckart, *From Bassermann to Bebel* (New Haven: Yale University Press, 1974), p. 19; Ritter, *Sozialdemokratische Partei und die freien Gewerkschaften*, p. 154.

35. On Bernstein see Ritter, *Sozialdemokratische Partei und die freien Gewerkschaften*, pp. 198–204; and Sidney Hook's introduction to the English translation of Bernstein's *Die Voraussetzungen des Sozialismus und die Aufgaben der Sozialdemokratie* (New York: Schocken Books, 1961).

36. See Epstein, *Matthias Erzberger*, pp. 9, 404; and Erzberger's 1898 pamphlet *Christliche oder sozialdemokratische Gewerkschaften?* discussed in Epstein, pp. 401–2.

37. See Brust's speech at Aachen in January 1898, printed in *Bergknappe*, nos. 5–6, 1 and 15 March 1898.

38. Ritter, *Männer aus Mönchen-Gladbach*, part 3, pp. 61–62, Ritter Papers ER/D-16, KfZG Bonn.

these neutral strategies, was greatly increased by another series of events in 1898. In July of that year, Archbishop Krementz sanctioned the creation of a centralized association for the Catholic *Arbeitervereine* of his diocese. He called upon Pieper to serve as chairman and on Father Otto Müller, Pieper's young protégé in Mönchen-Gladbach, to be the secretary general.[39] The restructuring was an attempt to strengthen the church's position with the workers in the wake of recent S.P.D. and free union advances in the West. But Pieper and Müller did not limit themselves to purely defensive measures. The two employed the controversial *Arbeiterverein* convention, described earlier, as an instrument for the promotion of interconfessional trade unionism. The fourth convention at Essen in late October 1898 passed a resolution in favor of interconfessional trade unions on a Christian basis, then defined a Christian organization as one which openly professed a belief in God, obeyed the Ten Commandments, recognized the necessity of a natural order,[40] and strove to eliminate social ills with legal, peaceful means. To lend weight to the convention's resolution on the trade union question, Müller, Brauns, Giesberts, and other Christian trade unionists were commissioned to supervise the founding of Christian unions.[41] As Pieper wrote a few months later, "Experience has shown that [execution of the convention's] resolutions cannot be left to the initiative of the individual *Arbeitervereine*, and more, that if anything noteworthy is to be accomplished, permanent stimulation and guidance is necessary."[42] The work of the Essen commission would be facilitated by a new *Arbeiterverein* newspaper, the *Westdeutsche Arbeiter-Zeitung*, which Pieper placed in the hands of Johannes Giesberts, himself an advocate of eventual merger with the free unions.[43]

The rise of Pieper and Müller within the church labor movement was highly significant because for the first time since Ketteler, Christian trade unionism had found the sanction of a powerful bishop (Krementz of Cologne). It is true that clerical opposition to Christian labor had begun to weaken before 1898 as a result of free trade union gains, but the Catholic Church had still not become the promoter of unionism that Ketteler had envisioned a generation earlier. Like Ketteler before them, in fact, Christian organizers in the 1890s had had

39. Pieper Manuscript, part 3, pp. 787, 805ff., StA MG.
40. This refers to the necessity of private property as explicated by St. Thomas Aquinas.
41. Otto Müller, Johannes Giesberts, and August Pieper, *Christliche Gewerkvereine, Ihre Notwendigkeit, Aufgabe und Thätigkeit: Auszug aus den Verhandlungen des 4. Delegiertentages der katholischen Arbeitervereine der Erzdiözese Köln zu Essen am 23. Oktober 1898* (Krefeld: M. Buscher, 1898), pp. 2, 14, StBib MG; *Kölnische Volkszeitung*, no. 932, 24 October 1898.
42. *Mitteilungen an die Präsides der katholischen Arbeitervereine der Erzdiözese Köln*, no. 1, 24 June 1899, p. 2, StBib MG.
43. *Ibid.*, p. 2; Ritter, *Volksverein*, p. 292; Joos, *Am Räderwerk der Zeit*, p. 37; and Johannes Giesberts, "Aus der Gründungszeit," in *Westdeutsche Arbeiter-Zeitung*, no. 14, 6 April 1929.

August Pieper

Franz Hitze

Johann Giesberts

Franz Brandts

to contend with those who argued that social misery was not a violation of God's divine plans, rather a reflection of them. The idea of emancipating labor from the tutelage of the church was unthinkable to prelates who assumed that the workers would be won over easily by clever Marxists and atheists. Brust's break with the *Ehrenrat* and his penchant for tough, crude rhetoric only increased the pessimism of conservative parish priests. These views were still widespread among Catholic clergymen in 1898, but with the hand of the bishop over their heads, Pieper and Müller could circumvent this opposition. Such were the benefits of a rigid hierarchy. Once Christian unions had grown in numbers, a propitious moment could be found to obtain the endorsement of the bishop for "neutral" trade unions as well.

While the *Volksverein* was strengthening its hold on the Catholic labor movement in the West, preparations for the first National Congress of Christian trade unions were brought to a close. After a brief, relatively frictionless period of negotiation and correspondence between Essen, Mönchen-Gladbach, and Stuttgart, a trade union program was finalized in early November 1898.[44] Undoubtedly the most important aspect of the program was its acceptance of interconfessionalism. Without an explicit recognition that members of both Christian confessions were welcome, the *Gewerkverein*, the Lippe tileworkers, the Siegen miners and metal workers, and others would never have participated in the new national federation. Discussion of specifically Protestant or Catholic points of religion was therefore strictly forbidden. It was stipulated, however, that the unions would stand "squarely upon Christian principles."[45] Thus, the draft program had not departed from the concept of "positive Christianity" adopted by the Fourth *Arbeiterverein* Convention at Essen two weeks earlier: "Christian" was broadly defined, but some *profession* of Christian belief was required of the organization. The minimal demand that Christian unions merely *tolerate* the political and religious views of all members—a concept which was dubbed "negative Christianity"—was not deemed adequate at Mainz.[46]

44. See Brust's circular to other Christian trade union leaders, 10 October 1898, quoted in Gasteiger, *Christliche Gewerkschaften in Süddeutschland*, p. 263. See also Gasteiger, p. 264; Epstein, *Matthias Erzberger*, p. 404; and Müller, *Die christliche Gewerkschaftsbewegung*, p. 103. The main participants in the negotiations were Erzberger, Giesberts, Brust, and the *Gewerkverein* Executive Committee. Similarities between the November program and the protocols of the *Arbeiterverein* convention at Essen (see above, notes 41–42) indicate that Pieper, Müller, and Brauns also took part. Gasteiger (pp. 267–70) prints only the program agreed on at the South German preconference. Reports in *Der Arbeiter* (Munich), nos. 48 and 50, for 2 and 16 December 1898, indicate, however, that the November program survived with no revision. Gasteiger's version can thus be accepted as the original.

45. Quoted in Gasteiger, *Christliche Gewerkschaften in Süddeutschland*, p. 267.

46. For a more detailed discussion of positive and negative Christianity, see Heinrich Brauns, *Die christlichen Gewerkschaften* (Mönchen-Gladbach: Verlag der Westdeutschen Arbeiter-Zeitung

Other points in the program reflect Brust's desire to concentrate at first on purely trade union goals. In the absence of state labor exchanges, unemployment insurance, and *adequate* protection against sickness, accidents, and invalidity, the trade union would have to supply many of these services itself. It should also supervise safety procedures on the job, provide members with legal advice, and work for the establishment of worker committees, industrial courts, and other arbitration institutions. Petitions to entrepreneurs, chambers of commerce, and the authorities were acceptable means to employ, but the unions would not hesitate to strike if necessary. Just as the capitalist had a right to the "largest possible" return on his investment, so too could the worker expect the "largest possible"[47] return from his labor. Because workers and employers threatened to be constantly at odds with one another in advancing such conflicting claims, however, the program recommended that Christian trade unions moderate their demands and conduct their operations "in the spirit of conciliation."[48] The authors wanted to dissociate themselves from the theory and practice of the class struggle and propagate instead the idea of harmony between the "limbs" of the social body. Thus the corporatist doctrines of St. Thomas Aquinas, which had been the theological justification for Mönchen-Gladbach's programs since the 1880s, were now incorporated into the charter of the Christian trade unions. That the strike had not been rejected altogether, however, would later lead to altercations with clergymen who preferred a more conservative interpretation of Thomistic philosophy.

Though largely self-help in nature, the program did not ignore politics. Thus, "discussion of reforms to be achieved by constitutional means within the existing framework of society"[49] was mentioned in the first paragraph as an additional facet of trade union activity. This clause of the program provided the unions with the opportunity to pursue those far-reaching social reforms desired by Christian socialists in Essen, Mönchen-Gladbach, and elsewhere. The authors were quick to point out, however, that discussion of party questions was forbidden. "The trade unions shall be politically neutral, that is, they shall not attach themselves to any political party." This statement was the necessary corollary of interconfessionalism and the exclusion of confessional matters. It was also part of Mönchen-Gladbach's overall plan. The Christian unions could not advance the principle of neutralism unless they practiced neutrality themselves.[50]

GmbH, 1908), p. 49; and Augustin Wiebbelt, *Keine Neutralisierung der christlichen Gewerkschaften* (Duisburg: Verlag der "Echo vom Niederrhein," n.d.), pp. 10–13.

47. Quoted in Gasteiger, *Christliche Gewerkschaften in Süddeutschland*, p. 270.

48. Quoted in *ibid.*, p. 270.

49. Quoted in *ibid.*, p. 267.

50. Müller, *Die christliche Gewerkschaftsbewegung*, pp. 108–9, who based his work to a great extent on discussions with Christian labor leaders, mentions this concern.

The paragraphs on trade union tactics, interconfessionalism, and party-political neutrality were accepted verbatim by trade union and *Arbeiterverein* representatives at two preconferences in December 1898. So, too, were clauses favoring nationwide unions for each branch of industry and workers as editors of union newspapers.[51] The question of labor independence, however, had not been completely settled as the delegates gathered for the National Congress at Mainz in mid-May 1899. Out of deference to the lingering preference for trade sections among Catholic clergymen of the South and parts of the North, the November draft program had included a passage recommending that *Ehrenräte* be established for all Christian unions. Brust, who for obvious reasons was a bitter opponent of the clause, managed with the backing of Schirmer to rally the Mainz Congress against the provision. A last-ditch attempt by Immelen to block labor independence by requiring that trade union editors have academic degrees was similarly defeated.[52] Not only were the unions to be interconfessional and neutral, they were also to be free of outside control.

The crowning accomplishment of the Mainz Congress was the establishment of a national federation of Christian trade unions (*Gesamtverband*). Heading the organization was a twelve-member central commission led by Brust, Erzberger, Weigel, Schirmer, and Braun. The commission would gather statistics, edit a new union newspaper, execute the resolutions of future congresses, and promote Christian trade unions of the variety outlined in the Mainz program (*Mainzer Leitsätze*).[53] Fulfillment of this last task had been made easier during the fall and winter of 1898/99 by the establishment of numerous new organizations throughout the West, South, and East, and by the continued growth of the older unions. As a result, there were now 108,000 Christian trade unionists in Germany, 65,000 of whom had joined the national organization at Mainz. And, in certain areas of Germany like the Rhineland, Christian unions had managed to regain much of the ground lost to the free unions since the late 1870s. Within a decade, Christian laborers felt sure they could extend their influence to the Socialist strongholds of northern and eastern Germany as well.[54]

51. See Gasteiger, *Christliche Gewerkschaften in Süddeutschland*, pp. 268, 270.

52. *Kölnische Volkszeitung*, nos. 473 and 477 for 23 and 24 May 1899; Epstein, *Matthias Erzberger*, p. 404.

53. Gasteiger, *Christliche Gewerkschaften in Süddeutschland*, pp. 273–74.

54. *Westdeutsche Arbeiter-Zeitung*, nos. 8 and 28 for 20 May and 7 October 1899, and no. 33, 18 August 1900.

5

The Great Merger Controversy

The years 1899–1903 were disastrous ones for the *Gesamtverband* of Christian trade unions. Hopeful in 1899 of competing with the General Commission *at the union level,* prodding both free trade unions and S.P.D. into Hans von Berlepsch's reform coalition, and moving the government, in turn, to adopt a slate of progressive labor laws, the Christians would see all these goals foiled by mid-1903. As in earlier decades, the combination of church and state opposition to the labor movement was partially responsible for these setbacks. This was especially the case with the controversial debate over merger of the Socialist and Christian unions. Fearful of the radical consequences which might result from a unification of labor forces, conservative churchmen and government leaders successfully manipulated the Christian labor movement into a highly embarrassing about-face. Simultaneously the youthful *Gesamtverband* became embroiled in a bitter dispute over the tariff question. The merger and tariff controversies were compounded, moreover, by serious mistakes made by the movement at the trade union level. These various developments form the basis of analysis in the following two chapters, which, taken together, are crucial to an understanding of the ultimate triumph of the Socialist trade unions. The present chapter uncovers the details surrounding the first of these issues, the great merger debate.

* * * *

Mönchen-Gladbach's merger schemes had thus far been kept very private. Publicly, the *Volksverein* maintained that union with the General Commission was forever out of the question.[1] For those well-to-do Catholics, villagers, and

1. Müller, Giesberts, and Pieper, *Auszug aus den Verhandlungen des 4. Delegiertentages . . . zu Essen am 23 Oktober 1898,* p. 17, StBib MG.

small-townsmen who had never come face to face with a Socialist or discussed issues with one in the cloakroom of the Reichstag, even the slighest hint of cooperation with Marxists conjured up images of Jacobin radicalism, mob rule, atheism, and urban decadence. For this reason, openness was considered too risky at first. Shortly before the Mainz Congress of 1899, however, Mönchen-Gladbach began to publicize its views. By the winter of 1899/1900, the *Volksverein*'s neutrality campaign was in full swing.[2]

The explanation for this turnabout is no simple one. With the creation of a national federation modeled after the General Commission in late May 1899, one prerequisite for merger had been established. But there were other, more compelling reasons for the decision. For one thing, free and Christian workers were already drifting closer to one another as a result of the crescendoing strike movement.[3] So strong was the feeling of proletarian unity in Crefeld, for instance, that labor priests encouraged Christian silk weavers to join a Socialist strike in January 1899 for fear the church would lose all contact with the workers if more prudent counsel were given.[4] Events in the Crefeld wool industry that month took a more peaceful course, but here too, Christian and Socialist workers cooperated by forming a "social commission" to negotiate with employers.[5] From Crefeld, the idea spread to Aachen and Mönchen-Gladbach, where similar commissions were formed for textile workers in August and September 1899 respectively.[6] Quarrels between Christian and free unions were also set aside in the Ruhr. *Gewerkverein* and *Alter Verband* drafted a joint program for reform of the state-regulated *Knappschaftsvereine* in August 1899 and formed alliances for miners' elections in July and November.[7] The numerous examples of economic cooperation between political opponents in western Germany gave Mönchen-Gladbach a definite incentive to stay abreast of events and forge ahead with its plans for neutrality.[8]

2. *Westdeutsche Arbeiter-Zeitung*, nos. 6, 8, and 28, for 6 May, 20 May and 7 October 1899; Otto Müller, *Christliche Gewerkvereine: Ihre Aufgabe und Thätigkeit* (Mönchen-Gladbach: Verlag der Westdeutschen Arbeiter-Zeitung, 1899); *Die Notwendigkeit und Aufgaben der christlichen Gewerkvereine* (Mönchen-Gladbach: Volksverein Flugblatt Nr. 15, 1899); *Christliche Gewerkvereine* (Mönchen-Gladbach: Arbeiter-Bibliothek, 1/2 Heft, 1900). The three brochures cited here were essentially the same manuscript, issued under various titles by *Volksverein* or *Arbeiterverein* presses in Mönchen-Gladbach from November 1899 to February 1900. Müller was largely responsible for the *Westdeutsche Arbeiter-Zeitung* at this time. See Giesberts, "Aus der Gründungszeit," *Westdeutsche Arbeiter-Zeitung*, no. 14, 6 April 1929.

3. There were 483 strikes in Germany in 1896, 578 in 1897, 985 in 1898 and 1,162 in 1899. *Bergknappe*, no. 31, 4 August 1900.

4. *Oberbürgermeister* of Crefeld to the *Regierungspräsident* in Düsseldorf, 14 March 1899, Reg. D. 9049, HSA Düsseldorf.

5. Kulemann, *Die Berufsvereine*, vol. 2, p. 374.

6. *Ibid.*, p. 375; *Regierungspräsident* in Aachen to the Prussian minister of the interior, 3 October 1899, Reg. D. 9042, HSA Düsseldorf.

7. *Regierungspräsident* in Arnsberg to the Prussian minister of the interior, 27 November 1899, Reg. D. 9042, HSA Düsseldorf; Hue, *Neutrale oder Parteiische Gewerkschaften*, p. 100.

8. Müller, *Christliche Gewerkvereine: Ihre Aufgabe und Thätigkeit*, p. 38.

Volksverein circles were further motivated by developments within the Socialist camp. In February 1899 Bernstein's tract *Evolutionary Socialism* appeared and was received favorably by a considerable number of free trade unionists.[9] At the third congress of the Socialist unions in mid-May, moreover, two resolutions were submitted that advocated formation of a "German trade union *Bund*"[10] that would unite all existing trade union organizations in Germany. Neither resolution was debated, but the congress did put social legislative issues on the agenda for the very first time.[11] As a result of these revisionistic trends, an S.P.D. spokesman announced in June 1899 that his Reichstag colleagues would support a minor piece of labor legislation *proposed by the government*. Hitze, who followed the S.P.D. speaker, welcomed the pathbreaking decision and expressed hope that the Socialists would continue to cooperate with the bourgeois parties in the future. Beneath Mönchen-Gladbach's surface optimism, however, lay worries about the enhanced popularity of a more reform-oriented S.P.D. The emergence of a neutral trade union movement was thus a soothing scenario worthy of realization, for the divisive issue of political neutrality could become the wedge which drove the S.P.D. asunder.[12]

The unity of all workers seemed even more important to Mönchen-Gladbach as a result of the developing social *Reaktion* in Berlin. As explained earlier, William II attached great significance to the loyalty of his working-class subjects. Strongly patriarchal, he had always insisted that reforms such as labor chambers and corporate rights for trade unions were impossible as long as the workers supported the S.P.D. Consistently with these views, William responded in true Bismarckian fashion to the Socialist electoral advances of 1893 and 1898. On the one hand, Germany's social insurance schemes were expanded and improved, albeit at a much slower pace than in the early 1890s. Earlier plans to improve the legal status of trade unions, however, were postponed indefinitely.

The spiraling stike movement in the late 1890s only increased these anti-union tendencies. Far from recognizing trade unions, William was now prepared to take draconian measures against them. During a speech at Bad Oeynhausen in September 1898 the Kaiser warned trade unionists that severe punishments would be meted out for workers who barred the access of non-strikers (*Arbeitswilligen*) to the job. Further details were announced during the

9. *Westdeutsche Arbeiter-Zeitung*, no. 6, 6 May 1899.

10. *Protokoll der Verhandlungen des dritten Kongresses der Gewerkschaften Deutschlands abgehalten zu Frankfurt a. M. vom 8. bis 13. Mai 1899* (Hamburg: Verlag der General Commission der Gewerkschaften Deutschlands, 1899), p. 202.

11. *Ibid.*, pp. 104, 161, 171. Resolutions concerning coalition rights and factory inspection were passed.

12. Reichstag Debates, Period 10, Session 1 (13 June 1899), p. 2514; Heitzer, *Volksverein*, p. 186.

Crown Speech in December, and the so-called Prison Bill (*Zuchthausvorlage*) was laid before parliament in March.[13]

In response to William, the social reform faction gathering around Berlepsch introduced its own measures in late April 1899. The National Liberals, who had been drifting away from the *Herr im Haus* standpoint under pressure from the reform-minded Young Liberals, demanded a Reich Labor Office, while the Center and Progressives called for chambers of labor that would counterbalance the strength of employers' groups.[14] A week later on 3 May, Berlepsch invited party and trade union leaders to a conference in Berlin to debate the recently completed statutes of an international society for the promotion of labor legislation. The participants, who included Hitze, Stöcker, Naumann, Ernst Bassermann of the National Liberals, Richard Rösicke and Max Hirsch of the Progressives, and August Brust and Paul Weigel of the Christian trade unions, approved the by-laws and nominated a committee to pave the way for a special department of the International to push for social reforms at home.[15]

Hitze, Brust, and the others delayed the actual founding of the German section, significantly enough, to give the committee time to recruit the free trade unions and S.P.D.[16] Bebel informed the bourgeois leaders on 11 May, however, that his party had no faith in the effectiveness of a society composed of such "heterogeneous elements."[17] In a letter to Victor Adler, leader of the Austrian Social Democrats, Bebel explained why. Because Berlepsch's coalition included many so-called social conservatives, the party feared that there would be too many compromises with the Socialist program for the sake of holding together this coalition. Such a softening of Social Democratic principles was intolerable. "After one sees how people like Hitze and his consorts work in the Reichstag, one does not yearn for more contact with them in a voluntary association[18] . . . At the bottom of my heart I'm happy that the *Fraktion* didn't let itself in for this, because Bernstein and the Bernsteinians would have used it as a triumph for his views [concerning the need for social reform in cooperation with the bourgeois parties]."[19]

13. On the Prison Resolution, see *Bergknappe,* no. 24, 15 December 1898; and Born and Rassow, *Akten zur staatlichen Sozialpolitik,* pp. 107–8. See also the remarks of the *Volksverein* newsletter, *Volksverein,* printed in *Bergknappe,* no. 6, 1900. The short article warned of reactionary tendencies, emphasized the importance of trade unions, and recommended the two *Volksverein* brochures cited in note 2 above.

14. *Preussische Jahrbücher,* vol. 96, Heft 3, June 1899, pp. 546–48.

15. *Ibid.,* pp. 548–49; *Bergknappe,* no. 32, 11 August 1900.

16. *Westdeutsche Arbeiter-Zeitung,* no. 4, 26 January 1901; *Bergknappe,* no. 3, 19 January 1901.

17. Bebel to Professor Werner Sombart, 11 May 1899, quoted in Lindenlaub, *Richtungskämpfe,* vol. 2, p. 420.

18. Bebel was referring to Hitze's usual willingness to agree to almost any compromise, even if it meant only a very minimal improvement for the workers.

19. Bebel to Adler, 11 May 1899, printed in Friedrich Adler, *Victor Adler Briefwechsel mit August Bebel und Karl Kautsky* (Vienna: Verlag der Wiener Volksbuchhandlung, 1954), p. 317.

Undaunted by this, renewed attempts were made to soften the S.P.D. and expand the anti-Prison Bill front that summer and fall. "Armchair socialists" Gustav Schmoller, Hans Delbrück, and Adolf Wagner appealed publicly to the patriotic feelings of rank and file Socialists, for instance, while Naumann and Brentano made preparations for a series of mass rallies against the new piece of anti-labor legislation. By intensifying its campaign for a neutral trade union movement, Mönchen-Gladbach felt it could aid these efforts. A powerful trade union commission would surely drive formerly recalcitrant bourgeois deputies and the S.P.D., or part of it, into the new coalition.[20]

As explained earlier, Pieper was convinced that the impetus for neutralizing the frees would have to come from the Christian trade unions. The unions were independent of the *Volksverein,* however, and, with the exception of Brust and Giesberts, showed no inclination to pursue such an overtly political strategy. Anxious lest the *Gesamtverband* fail to fulfill its mission, Mönchen-Gladbach issued a series of neutralist brochures in the winter of 1899/1900. Unfortunately for Pieper and Müller, who authored the pamphlets, ambiguities and contradictions limited the effectiveness of this propaganda campaign. The most troublesome aspect of the booklets was their seeming rejection of overt "positive-Christian" goals for the movement.

> There is no longer religious unity among the masses. There are also workers who are really Christians, as well as workers who call themselves Christian but know very little about Christianity. *For a thoroughgoing cure of our economic wrongs, however, the greatest possible union of all workers is necessary.* We should, therefore, not exclude those from the labor organization who no longer possess positive Christianity in its true form but still adhere to those just and moral laws of nature that God has placed in the hearts of all men, even heathens.[21]

With no religious or confessional training, that is, even most non-believers could be counted upon to possess a sense of common decency and morality and a respect for religious fundamentals such as education of children, maintenance of the family, etc.[22] Mönchen-Gladbach was placing its trust in natural laws or, as it was defined elsewhere, "the dictates of reason"[23] to moderate union affairs. Running throughout the whole pamphlet, moreover, was the implicit claim that the workers had a "natural right" to come together in neutral unions. That Leo XIII felt otherwise goes practically without saying.

20. Lindenlaub, *Richtungskämpfe,* vol. 1, p. 74, and vol. 2, p. 426; Pieper Manuscript, part 3, pp. 775, 777, StA MG; *Westdeutsche Arbeiter-Zeitung,* no. 35, 1 September 1900.
21. *Christliche Gewerkvereine,* Arbeiter-Bibliothek, 1/2 Heft, p. 29.
22. *Ibid.*, p. 15.
23. See the final resolution of the sixth *Arbeiterverein* convention at Cologne in May 1900, quoted in the protocols of the Prussian Bishops' Conference at Fulda, 21 August 1900, Appendix 7, p. 31, Bertram Papers, I-A25-b7, AA Wrocławiu.

Clearly, Pieper and Müller wanted to remove as many barriers as possible to a free-Christian merger. In fact, the authors placed only one demand upon the free trade unions: the denunciation of Marxism. In raising this demand, however, Mönchen-Gladbach seemed to abandon its new-found trust in natural law. Here was one religious fundament—the God-ordained institution of private property—respect for which would not come naturally. Christian trade unions would have to purge the labor movement of all enemies of the natural order.

> A Christian organization has to work toward driving the Social-Democratic spirit out of the so-called "free" trade unions. [The Christian unions] have to try to bring the free trade unions closer and closer to the point where the frees denounce the S.P.D. [*sich von der Partei lossagen*]. [The Christian trade unions] have to drive a wedge between the free trade unions and Social Democrats until the former are completely out from under the influence of the latter.[24]

The point was quite clear. Inviting controversy and misunderstanding, however, the brochure concluded "that the word 'Christian' shall thus have no other meaning than anti-Socialist."[25] Once the Socialist unions stood squarely on the basis of existing society and rejected the idea of socialized production, the Christian unions should abandon their independent existence, merge with the free unions, and rely on natural laws to dictate reasonable trade union policies. The name "Christian" would be dropped at this time, for it would no longer be necessary to distinguish between Socialist and anti-Socialist trade unions, "just as today no one speaks of Christian guilds, but simply of guilds."[26]

Pieper and Müller did not want to divorce the unions from all overt association with Christian principles. On the contrary, the authors made it quite clear that neutral trade unions would be pledged to the preservation of natural (i.e., private) economic institutions sanctioned by God. Thus, although ambiguously phrased, the brochures could still qualify as "positive Christianity."

Well over 25,000 copies of Mönchen-Gladbach's brochures were sold by mid-1900.[27] The idea of a neutral trade union movement was accepted wholeheartedly by most Christian trade union leaders and used as material for

24. Müller, *Christliche Gewerkvereine: Ihre Aufgabe und Thätigkeit,* p. 37.
25. *Ibid.,* pp. 28–29; *Christliche Gewerkvereine,* Arbeiter-Bibliothek, 1/2 Heft, p. 29.
26. Müller, *Christliche Gewerkvereine: Ihre Aufgabe und Thätigkeit,* p. 38.
27. Müller Manuscript, p. 49, KAB Haus Köln. The brochure printed by the *Westdeutsche Arbeiter-Zeitung* press (see note 2 above) sold 25,000 copies, then a second edition was issued in mid-1900. The *Volksverein* versions must have sold thousands more. The total number of pamphlets and brochures issued by the *Volksverein* in 1900, for instance, was 1,000,042. See Brugmann, *Sozialer Katholizismus,* p. 323.

agitation by Christian unions throughout the Reich.[28] In most cases the workers interpreted the booklet as a justification for the cooperation of Center, Liberal, or Marxist workers in the same union as long as party-political issues were excluded from union affairs.[29] The unity of the workers was all-important.[30] By interpreting the brochures as a call for the union of workers of all political persuasions, Christian unionists had already advanced one step beyond Pieper and Müller, who had not been so tolerant of S.P.D. voters. Manipulation was sometimes very difficult to control.

Despite the angry mood of Christian laborers following the Prison Bill, however, most did not feel that merger *per se* would occur for years. The exclusion of religious and political propaganda from the free trade unions was still not a reality. Giesberts, Brust, and Schirmer were hopeful, nevertheless, that German workers could at least make a start toward unity by forming a loose cartel of Socialist, Liberal, and Christian workers along the lines of the Swiss Labor Alliance. The Swiss experiment, begun in 1889, had advanced to the stage of merger negotiations in the spring of 1899.[31]

Not all Christian leaders were enthusiastic about the brochure. Franz Wieber of the metal workers led a faction of proletarians opposed to neutralism, but generally speaking, such opposition was more typical in those unions where Christian workers were not yet in full control. Hubert Immelen of Aachen scoffed at the idea of a "poisoned, nondenominational, Social Democratic mish-mash,"[32] while Eugen Roth, Matthias Erzberger's successor as leader of the Christian workers in Württemberg, was incensed at Mönchen-Gladbach's alleged disregard for the concept of positive Christianity recognized at Mainz.[33] Father Driessen of Cologne was perhaps the most active

28. Müller, *Die christliche Gewerkschaftsbewegung*, p. 116; Heinrich Brauns, *Die christlichen Gewerkschaften* (Mönchen-Gladbach: Verlag der Westdeutschen Arbeiter-Zeitung GmbH, 1908), p. 46; Hue, *Neutrale oder parteiische Gewerkschaften*, pp. 138–39; Erdmann, *Die christliche Arbeiterbewegung*, pp. 454, 456; *Bergknappe*, no. 44, 3 November 1900.

29. The organ of the Lippe tile workers, *Gut Brand*, wrote on numerous occasions in 1900 that it had been a mistake to call the unions "Christian." On the suggestion of Giesberts, the union struck the clause forbidding Social Democrats to join in early 1901. See Hue, *Neutrale oder parteiische Gewerkschaften*, p. 138; and *Westdeutsche Arbeiter-Zeitung*, no. 8, 23 February 1901. Similarly, the Aachen textile union was forced "by the other Christian trade unions" in 1900 to strike the clause advocating *Sozialpolitik* in the spirit of the Center Party. See Kulemann, *Die Berufsvereine*, p. 368. See also the remarks of Giesberts and Brust in June 1900 quoted below.

30. *Westdeutsche Arbeiter-Zeitung*, no. 33, 18 August 1900. Giesberts noted years later that the paper became his responsibility not long after its founding. Giesberts, "Aus der Gründungszeit," *Westdeutsche Arbeiter-Zeitung*, no. 14, 6 April 1929.

31. Erdmann, *Die christliche Arbeiterbewegung*, p. 469; *Westdeutsche Arbeiter-Zeitung*, no. 28, 7 October 1899; Kulemann, *Die Gewerkschaftsbewegung*, p. 134; and *Bergknappe*, no. 35, 1 September 1900.

32. Quoted in Erdmann, *Die christliche Arbeiterbewegung*, pp. 524–25.

33. *Ibid.*, p. 454.

opponent of neutrality. Such a tactic, one of his followers wrote to Brust in May 1900, was irresponsible and naive. The attempt would result in the secession of the Christian workers or perhaps their capture by the S.P.D. The Christian trade unions, moreover, had more than a temporary mission to fulfill. They had to propagate "Christian justice, freedom, and brotherly love"[34] among workers and employers for all time. A Christian union should proclaim its adherence to Christian principles in all economic activities.

It was this lack of "positive Christianity," then, which united all opponents of the brochure in the Christian camp. To be sure, there was a difference between professing a belief in God and the Ten Commandments and merely forbidding union members to ridicule these concepts. But the brochure's defense of a natural order more than qualified as positive Christianity. Mönchen-Gladbach was no less opposed, moreover, to the cooperation of Marxist and Christian workers in the same trade union. By interpreting "neutral" literally, most proponents and opponents of the brochure had misunderstood the *Volksverein*'s strategy, which was anything but neutral. Considering the importance Pieper and Müller placed on the brochures, this confusion must have been very frustrating.

The negative reaction of most free trade unionists to the booklets was no doubt less surprising. Hans Bömelburg, national executive committee member and leader of the 83,000-strong stonemasons' union, agreed that discussion of religion should be excluded from union meetings and newspapers. Merger with the Christians, however, would never work. Along with social insurance legislation and political reforms to insure safety on the job, the union would also have to strive for elimination of problems like unemployment. But unemployment would continue to plague workers until the capitalist system itself were abolished. Unless Christian workers could accept this political reality, cooperation in the same trade union was impossible. The stonemasons' organ *Grundstein* was even more blunt. Workers of all religions and political persuasions were welcome to join the free unions, but neutrality should not be be carried further than this. Discontinuation of agitation for the ultimate goal of socialism could never be permitted. The wood workers (74,000) spoke out for the S.P.D. in similar fashion, as did the chairman of the General Commission, Karl Legien, who probably represented the vast majority of those free unionists (408,000) who remained silent on the issue. Membership in the free trade unions was open to all workers, regardless of political or religious beliefs. Union activity, however, would enhance the workers' awareness of the ongoing class struggle, and these feelings would naturally be translated into support for that party which believed in the

34. Hans Becker to Brust, 25 May 1900, printed in *Bergknappe*, no. 27, 7 July 1900.

Klassenkampf. Such definitions of neutrality were as one-sided as that proposed by the *Volksverein.*[35]

The response of the slowly growing neutral faction in the General Commission (14 percent of membership in 1900) constituted a problem of equal dimension from Mönchen-Gladbach's point of view. Christian Tischendörfer of the lithographers' union (6,000), for instance, was urging Christian workers to abandon the Christian trade unions and work against the S.P.D. from within the free unions. Philipp Rexhäuser of the printers (29,000) proposed that the united trade unions form a parliamentary block independent of all parties, while the chairman of the tobacco workers' union (18,500), Adolph von Elm, recommended creation of an extraparliamentary trade union congress to pressure the Reichstag parties into greater socio-political activity. The end result of this pressure politicking, he hoped, would be the socialization of the means of production by a decision of parliament.[36]

The most emphatic proponent of neutralism remained Otto Hue, whose union had expanded to an *overall* level of 36,000 by mid-1900. Hue was convinced that the General Commission had no recourse but to merge with the competing Christian federation, for otherwise key industrial regions like the Ruhr, the lower Rhine, the Saar, Lorraine, and Silesia would be lost to the free unions.[37] As a preliminary step toward amalgamation of the two national federations, Hue wanted to effect an *Alter Verband-Gewerkverein* merger in the Ruhr. The *Alter Verband* general assembly laid the groundwork for Hue's long-sought goal in April 1900 by ousting Möller as chairman and proclaiming the party-political independence of the union. The organization would also promote economic cooperation between free, Christian, and Hirsch-Duncker unions and seek to arbitrate labor disputes before striking.[38] Later that summer, Hue published a 157-page book entitled *Neutral or Party Trade Unions?* The tract attempted to prove the necessity of a unified labor movement by illustrating the counterproductive nature of the miners' feud in the Ruhr. This nationwide alliance might not occur "in the near future," but it would certainly take place before "the recalcitrants" thought it would: "What is a decade in the course of human history?"[39] As the sales of the editor's book

35. For the free union response, see *Westdeutsche Arbeiter-Zeitung,* nos. 28, 32, and 35, for 14 July, 11 August, and 1 September 1900; and Hue, *Neutrale oder parteiische Gewerkschaften,* p. 125. Free trade union statistics for 1900 are found in *Mitteilungen des Gesamtverbandes,* no. 11, 2 September 1901.

36. *Bergknappe,* nos. 14 and 15, for 7 and 15 April 1900; Ritter, *Sozialdemokratische Partei und die freien Gewerkschaften,* pp. 171–74.

37. Police commissioner of Bochum to the *Regierungspräsident* in Arnsberg, 30 August 1900, Reg. Arnsberg I 95, StA Münster.

38. Hue, *Neutrale oder parteiische Gewerkschaften,* p. 108; *Regierungspräsident* in Arnsberg to the Prussian minister of the interior, 24 November 1900, Reg. D. 9042, HSA Düsseldorf.

39. Hue, *Neutrale oder parteiische Gewerkschaften,* p. 156.

began to mount that fall, Hue joined Pastor Friedrich Naumann, founder of the struggling National Social Party, in an effort to negotiate a merger with the *Gewerkverein*.[40]

A much more prominent participant in the neutrality debate that year was August Bebel, head of the S.P.D. national executive committee and Reichstag *Fraktion*. Insistent in the early 1890s that the free trade unions subordinate themselves to the political dictates of the S.P.D.,[41] Bebel had, however, changed his mind by 1900. Although he outwardly blamed the bourgeois parties, not the Socialists, for the divisions in the trade union movement,[42] he must have been aware that the party's attempt to dominate the unions had been a serious mistake. The move had driven thousands of religiously devout, non-Socialist workers into the hands of rival organizations and created numerous enemies for the S.P.D. within the General Commission itself. The party press was also feuding over the issue. The S.P.D.'s theoretical journal, *Neue Zeit*, and a number of leading party dailies including *Vorwärts* insisted that the free unions agitate openly for the Socialists, while the influential *Rheinische Zeitung*, party organ for Aachen, Cologne, and Bonn, was calling for a merger of the various union organizations along neutral lines.[43] With *Reaktion* threatening in Berlin and the controversy over revisionism far from settled, the party could not afford additional divisiveness. Thus Bebel took steps to end the debate. A public lecture on this issue in Weissensee near Berlin in February failed to attract sufficient attention, so on 31 May 1900 the S.P.D. leader agreed to speak at an assembly convened by the neutral lithographers in the large *Gewerkschaftshaus* in Berlin.[44]

The speech contained three basic arguments. First, trade unions had to be politically and religiously neutral. In every factory or mine there worked laborers of differing political views, religious beliefs, and national origins. In order to present a strong front against employers, who were well-organized themselves, a union had to attract as many of these workers as possible and could not be concerned with the political or religious views of its members. Second, a union had to pursue *Klassenkampfpolitik*. Religious and party-political questions should be excluded, but reforms such as improved rights of

40. *Kölnische Volkszeitung*, no. 62, 19 January 1901. The *Regierungspräsident* in Düsseldorf reported to the king on 31 January 1901 (Reg. D. 403/9048, LHA Koblenz) that the two unions seemed to have come closer to one another since October.

41. See Chapter 4, notes 23 and 24.

42. August Bebel, *Gewerkschaftsbewegung und politische Parteien* (Stuttgart: Verlag von J. W. H. Dietz, GmbH, 1900), p. 24.

43. Hue, *Neutrale oder parteiische Gewerkschaften*, p. 125; *Westdeutsche Arbeiter-Zeitung*, no. 28, 7 October 1899.

44. The speech was printed that year in brochure form. See Bebel, *Gewerkschaftsbewegung und politische Parteien*, p. 24.

coalition and assembly; elimination of Sunday and evening work; protection for working women and children; implementation of commercial courts, industrial inspectorates, labor chambers, and a Reich labor office; improvements for state workers; and legislation concerning tariffs and the cost of living were well within the sphere of trade union politics. Other political issues could be decided by each union member as he or she saw fit. And third, to be successful politically or economically, existing divisions in the labor movement had to cease. Bebel recommended a merger into one organization, but realized this would not occur overnight. A cartel of the various unions would have to suffice for the moment.

With its emphasis on religious and political neutrality, trade union unity, and practical social reform, Bebel's speech was cause for considerable enthusiasm among Christian unionists.[45] This excitement was tempered, however, by the sobering realities of yet-existing inter-union differences. The complete socialization of the means of production advocated by many free unions and the persistence of anti-religious tendencies in free union speeches and articles could not be ignored. Moreover, with confusion over the nature of neutral unions in the Christian camp, Christian leaders were not eager to rush to the negotiating table. Before any such move could be considered, time was needed to clarify the issues raised by the brochures. A full-fledged debate over the neutrality issue was therefore omitted from the agenda of the second Congress of the Christian trade unions at Frankfurt in June 1900.[46]

But Brust, who chaired the Congress, was unable to avoid the debate. The issue was raised by one of Driessen's followers, who railed against the alleged abandonment of the *Mainzer Leitsätze*.[47] Giesberts countered with arguments favoring merger that echoed Bebel's arguments of the previous week.

> The goal of our efforts remains the general, neutral organization. We Christian workers are together with workers of other beliefs in the factory, we live in the same house, we come across one another all the time, so why shouldn't we be in the same labor organization striving jointly for the raising of our living conditions? We can't ignore the 600,000 workers organized in free trade unions, nor can we hope to make believers out of the non-devout, even in fifty years. So let's take things as they are and try to get along with each other. If we can cooperate with other organizations on economic mat-

45. *Westdeutsche Arbeiter-Zeitung*, no. 23, 9 June 1900; Erdmann, *Die christliche Arbeiterbewegung*, p. 454.
46. *Bergknappe*, no. 28, 14 July 1900.
47. No protocols of the first two congresses at Mainz and Frankfurt were published. The following discussion is based on Erdmann, *Die christliche Arbeiterbewegung*, pp. 450–56. The Socialist journalist and Reichstag deputy was present at the proceedings. The reader should also consult the *Kölnische Volkszeitung*, nos. 511–512, 5 June 1900; and Müller, *Die christliche Gewerkschaftsbewegung*, pp. 110–18.

> ters, I don't see why we can't merge completely if the organizations would just leave politics and religion out of the picture and be purely economic interest groups.[48]

Brust seconded Giesberts and included a controversial thought of his own.

> As I see it, we can calmly strike the word "Christian" from the trade union movement. The belief [in Christianity] and the will to be unshaken in this belief has nothing to do with names . . . Neither the Christian nor the Socialist *Weltanschauung* belongs in the union; if both sides would recognize this and practice this, all reason for further divisions would disappear and the neutral trade union would come into its own.[49]

The debate deteriorated quickly after these remarks. Brust charged that the anti-neutral workers in attendance were dupes of Driessen, which was vehemently denied by the Cologne delegation. Giesberts was finally able to unite the delegates behind a motion entrusting the newly formed executive committee[50] with the task of establishing clarity on the issue before the third Congress in spring 1901.

The Frankfurt debate proved to be a source of great embarrassment for the Christian trade unions. Observing the altercations at Frankfurt, Karl Legien proclaimed in the General Commission's weekly newsletter that the Congress had heralded the disintegration of the Christian trade unions. S.P.D. papers ran similar articles, as did Progressive organs.[51] To make matters worse, Immelen, Driessen, and other former allies like Lambert Lensing of *Tremonia* intensified their attacks against "the Mönchen-Gladbach faction" within the national federation.[52] Both *Bergknappe* and the *Westdeutsche Arbeiter-Zeitung* swung over to the defensive in response to these criticisms, claiming that the brochure had been purely theoretical, and that merger with the free unions might not occur for twenty or thirty years.[53] But Brust was too much the polemicist to ignore his enemies completely. When the time came, Brust

48. Quoted in Erdmann, *Die christliche Arbeiterbewegung,* p. 455.
49. Quoted in *ibid.,* p. 456.
50. Due to the widely separated residences of the members of the national commission established at Mainz, this initial steering committee accomplished few of its assigned tasks. The national executive committee was a more manageable body, the majority of members living in Rhineland-Westphalia.
51. *Bergknappe,* nos. 37–39, for 15, 22, and 29 September 1900; *Frankfurter Zeitung,* no. 155 (5), 7 June 1900; see also the protocols of the Prussian Bishops' Conference at Fulda, 21 August 1900, Appendix 7, pp. 32–33, Bertram Papers, I-A25-67, AA Wrocławiu; and the *Regierungspräsident* in Arnsberg to the Prussian minister of the interior, 24 November 1900, Reg. D. 9042, HSA Düsseldorf.
52. *Bergknappe,* nos. 39–40, 29 September and 6 October 1900.
53. *Bergknappe,* no. 27, 7 July 1900; *Westdeutsche Arbeiter-Zeitung,* nos. 28, 31–33, for 14 July, 4, 11, and 18 August 1900.

wrote defiantly, the Christian unions would not hesitate to merge with the free unions. The opposition of "half-dead old men"[54] like Driessen would not be able to prevent this. If the free trade unions wanted to begin by *immediately* forming a cartel, the Christians would not stand in the way.[55]

As the neutrality debate raged that summer, Berlepsch's ideas for international social cooperation came to fruition. The International League for the Protection of Labor was founded in Paris in late July 1900, and shortly afterwards in Germany the Society for Social Reform was begun. By early January 1901, enough organizations and prominent personages had expressed interest in the Society to permit a formal constituent assembly in Berlin. The entire bourgeois reform movement was represented—Berlepsch, Francke, Schmoller, Brentano, Naumann, Hirsch, Stöcker, Hitze, Pieper, Giesberts, and Brust. The Catholic and Evangelical *Arbeitervereine,* the Christian and Hirsch-Duncker unions, and other bourgeois labor groups joined as corporate members. Still wary of such close cooperation with the bourgeois enemy, the free unions and S.P.D. remained aloof.[56]

The major goal of the new organization was to create unity on social reform issues in the Reichstag.[57] Once parliament was united behind specific proposals, Kaiser and Bundesrat would surely yield. The Christian trade unions, who were represented by Giesberts on the executive committee of the Society, did not question the practicality of this approach, but were skeptical about the degree of commitment to social reform that could be expected from the bourgeois leaders of the organization.[58] To impress Berlepsch and the others with the need for far-reaching reform, Christian labor leaders began to discuss plans for a "German Workers' Congress" of all non-Socialist labor groups. The Congress would speak out on certain pieces of legislation and generally make the demands of the member organizations known. As a dramatic demonstration of bourgeois labor strength, the Congress would also force the free trade unions to the negotiating table, or at least accelerate the revisionistic course of the S.P.D.[59]

54. *Bergknappe,* no. 27, 7 July 1900.

55. *Bergknappe,* no. 35, 1 September 1900. Neither did Giesberts fall completely silent. See his remarks of 1900/1901, notes 29–30 above.

56. *Bergknappe,* no. 3, 19 January 1901; Schwab, "Gesellschaft für Soziale Reform," in Fricke *et al., Bürgerliche Parteien,* vol. 1, p. 169.

57. *Westdeutsche Arbeiter-Zeitung,* nos. 3–4 for 12 and 26 January 1901.

58. *Westdeutsche Arbeiter-Zeitung,* no. 4, 26 January 1901.

59. Two sources from fall 1903 (*Mitteilungen des Gesamtverbandes,* no. 19, 21 September 1903; and Ernst Francke's statement in the *Kölnische Volkszeitung,* no. 1012, 3 December 1903) indicate that the idea of holding such a congress had been discussed by Christian labor leaders of the Society for Social Reform for several years at committee meetings. Giesberts's bold remarks in the *Westdeutsche Arbeiter-Zeitung,* no. 4, 26 January 1901, offer some proof that the first such discussions took place during the winter of 1900/1901.

The first major test of the Society for Social Reform illustrated the fallacy of the parliamentary strategy described above. The National Liberal, Progressive, and Center resolutions of spring 1899 emerged from commission to their second reading before the full house on 16 January 1901. Bills calling for a Reich Labor Office and management-labor chambers connected to the already existing industrial tribunals—a compromise designed to cater to staunch conservatives on the Bundesrat—were passed by an overwhelming majority.[60] At first the federal councilors seemed amenable to the idea of chambers that would bring workers and employers together for the peaceful settlement of disputes.[61] Only the Württembergians and Saxons felt the institutions would exacerbate already existing tensions and "be used by the Socialists for the purpose of achieving their goals more quickly."[62] In the end, however, both bills were rejected. In the absence of documentation, it can only be surmised that William, still desirous of stern measures against unions, squelched the plan. The Reichstag, at any rate, was not even informed that the wishes of the majority parties had been denied. Such was the "power" of parliament in Imperial Germany.

As far as Christian labor leaders were concerned, the humiliating defeat merely underscored the need to rid the labor movement of Marxist influence. Only when the entire working class was united in a reform-minded, patriotic organization would William become more amenable to improvements in the rights of labor. Long before 1901, however, the growing assertiveness of the Christians had prompted the government to bring an end to all talk of "neutral" trade unions. Provincial and subprovincial officials had welcomed the emergence of Christian trade unions at first, since they saw in these organizations a potential dam against the free unions and the S.P.D. But the overthrow of the *Ehrenrat* in 1898, the cooperation of Christian and Socialist miners and textile workers in 1899, and the Frankfurt Congress of 1900 changed all this. The specter of a radical, united proletariat now took the place of earlier, more sanguine visions.[63]

60. Reichstag Debates, Period 10, Session 2 (16 January 1901), pp. 725–43.
61. See Reich minister of the interior Posadowsky's inquiry to the various state governments, 10 January 1901, and their replies, in Reichsministerium des Innern, Nr. 6765, ZStA Potsdam.
62. Saxon minister of foreign affairs to the Reich Ministry of the Interior, 24 January 1901, Reichsministerium des Innern, Nr. 6765, ZStA Potsdam.
63. For the early years, see the *Regierungspräsident* in Aachen to the king, 16 April 1894, Reg. Aachen 403/9037, LHA Koblenz; *Regierungspräsident* in Arnsberg to the Prussian minister of the interior, 16 April 1895, Reg. D. 9039, HSA Düsseldorf; and the *Regierungspräsident* in Düsseldorf to the king, 31 January 1897, Reg. D. 403/9048, LHA Koblenz. For the turnaround, see the *Regierungspräsident* in Arnsberg to the Prussian minister of the interior, 30 September 1898, Reg. D. 9042, HSA Düsseldorf; Landrat in Mönchen-Gladbach to *Regierungspräsident* in Düsseldorf, 2 March 1899, Reg. D. 9049, HSA Düsseldorf; *Oberbürgermeister* Krefeld to *Regierungspräsident* in Düsseldorf, 14 March 1899, Reg. D. 9049, HSA Düsseldorf; and *Regierungspräsident* in Düsseldorf to the king, 31 October 1899, Reg. D. 403/9048, LHA Koblenz.

Suspecting that the church could do more to control the situation, the *Regierungspräsident* in Düsseldorf, the *Oberpräsident* of the Rhineland in Coblence, and the Prussian minister of the interior undertook a joint investigation of the matter which resulted in two significant steps. First, Archbishop Simar of Cologne was encouraged to exert his influence in Mönchen-Gladbach to prevent priests under his control from promoting cooperation with Socialist workers. Second, Archbishop Kopp of Breslau, who had been chairman of the Prussian Bishops' Conference since the death of Krementz in 1899, was urged to take disciplinary action against the neutral faction within the Christian trade unions.[64]

Simar was no opponent of the labor movement. He held the view, common in church circles since *Rerum Novarum,* that the workers had a natural, God-given right to organize. He was duly alarmed, however, by the apparently well-founded charges of the Prussian authorities against labor priests in his diocese. There was a great difference between organizing *per se* and marching hand in hand with the Socialists. Simar therefore asked Pieper if there were any truth to the allegations. Pieper's answer was well reasoned and convincing. The *Arbeiterverein* priests of the lower Rhine had sanctioned the social commissions formed in 1899, but had always sought to cooperate with employers. Furthermore, they had never promoted socialistic tendencies among the workers. Greatly relieved, Simar informed Coblence that he had full confidence in the peaceful, constructive activity of his subordinates.[65]

The government's initiative in Breslau was much more effective, for it coincided with a growing opposition to the Christian trade unions among *Arbeiterverein* officials in Kopp's sprawling archdiocese. Led by Franz von Savigny, executive committee member of the Berlin-based Association of Catholic *Arbeitervereine* of Northeastern Germany, this minority faction had always regarded independent organizations like Weigel's as an affront to church authority and a violation of the principles set down in *Rerum Novarum.* Savigny's views received nationwide attention in an article series which appeared in the *Märkisches Kirchenblatt* shortly before the Mainz Congress in 1899. The articles accepted the natural right of workers to organize, but refused to admit that Leo XIII had intended to sanction independent, intercon-

64. *Oberpräsident* of the Rhineland to Archbishop Simar of Cologne, 19 June 1900, Generalia 23.2., Vol. 3, Erzb. Registratur Köln; Carl Bachem notation of 7 November 1900, Bachem Papers 386, HA Köln. Brust claimed in 1902 that the *Kölnische Zeitung,* National Liberal organ of the Rhineland, played a significant role in alarming government circles to the radicalization of the Christian unions in 1899/1900 and had first emphasized the need for Church-government intervention. *Bergknappe,* no. 12, 22 March 1902.

65. Pieper to Simar, 23 July 1900, and Simar to the *Oberpräsident* of the Rhineland in Coblence, 3 October 1900, Generalia 23.2, vol. 3, Erzb. Registratur Köln. The contents of Simar's letter to Pieper can be gleaned from Pieper's reply.

fessional trade unions. The main weapon of the union, the strike, was morally objectionable in too many cases, especially in industries like mining, iron and steel, and transportation, whose continued operation was indispensable to the community as a whole. The workers, moreover, were incapable of applying Christian principles of morality to economic life. Only the church could perform this task; hence, the necessity of priest-led, confessional labor associations.[66]

The article series was revised and printed as a brochure in the wake of Mönchen-Gladbach's neutral offensive of 1899/1900. With the aid of conservative Centrists grouped around the prestigious party organ *Germania,* the brochure was then distributed throughout the German Catholic community. One of the recipients, Church canon Franz in Breslau, was impressed by Savigny's arguments and brought them to the archbishop's attention. At approximately the same time (May–June 1900), pressure to oppose the Christian trade unions was being applied by the Prussian Ministry of the Interior. A social conservative himself, Kopp needed little encouragement to speak out against neutralism. After further consultation with Franz and the archconservative Bishop Korum of Trier, Kopp left for Fulda to deliver the main address on the labor question.[67]

Unlike other opponents of neutralism, Kopp understood that Mönchen-Gladbach's trade union program was based on an acceptance of a moral and just set of natural laws, including private property rights.[68] Much more pessimistic in his assessment of human nature, however, he refused to accept these minimum requirements as adequate. Would the neutral union, he asked the bishops, be able to convince heathen strike picketers that it contradicted natural law to prevent non-strikers from continuing to work? Kopp did not think so. The only natural law at work in such a situation would be that which allowed "the most boisterous and unscrupulous"[69] to prevail. In order to prevent "unsuitable elements"[70] from dictating union policy, the reliability, firmness, and authority of the parish priest was necessary. Kopp recommended, therefore, that Catholic priests abandon the Christian trade unions

66. On Savigny, see Müller, *Die christliche Gewerkschaftsbewegung,* pp. 199–200; and Erdmann, *Die christliche Arbeiterbewegung,* pp. 458–60.

67. Kopp to Korum, 9 July 1900, Korum Papers 331, BisA Trier; Carl Bachem notation of 7 November 1900, Bachem Papers 386, HA Köln; Carl Bachem, "Bericht über die Vor- und Nachgeschichte des Fuldaer Pastorale vom 22. August, 1900," sent to Papal Nuncio Frühwirth in Munich on 28 July 1912, in Bachem Papers 321, HA Stadt Köln (hereafter cited as Bachem, "Bericht," 28 July 1912); Carl Bachem notation of 13 February 1914, Bachem papers 981, HA Köln; Erdmann, *Die christliche Arbeiterbewegung,* p. 460.

68. Kopp's speech was appended to the protocols of the Prussian Bishops' Conference at Fulda, 21 August 1900, Appendix 7, pp. 29–34, Bertram Papers, I-A25-67, AA Wrocławiu.

69. *Ibid.,* p. 32.

70. *Ibid.,* p. 32.

and revert to the concept of confessional "trade sections" first proposed by Hitze in 1892. Kopp's intentions would shortly be the source of great controversy, so the concluding passage of his speech should be quoted at length.

> There is no obvious reason why *Arbeitervereine* cannot be divided into sections for each branch of industry, the sections discussing their special concerns, the *Vereine* those matters of general interest, but always under the direction of the clerical chairman. Agreements with neighboring *Vereine* and, from time to time, with non-Catholics, as well as a centralization [of the sections] for all Germany would also be possible. With this organization there are guarantees that moral laws will be obeyed in labor relations, that the associations will remain untouched by corrupting agitation, that they will guard against one-sided emphasis of the material element, and avoid a dangerous isolation from other classes of society. Such an organization, built on strictly Catholic foundations, would be capable of winning the trust of all circles, employers and the authorities included. If it were pursued seriously, bringing together the entire Catholic working class, it would represent, given the fact that the other labor groups are disunified, the greatest social power in Germany. It could save the workers and society from the grasp of the Socialists and make a much deeper impression on non-Catholics than organizations based on indifference [like the] interconfessional *Gewerkvereine* . . . The barriers which block the realization of these plans lie in the hesitation of a great, albeit well-intentioned, part of the clergy [which] holds back for want of an authoritative stimulus . . . The excellent teachings of the pope's Labor Encyclical are not known or understood, for otherwise it would not be possible for basic questions of organization, as the above, to arise. The encyclical acknowledged the religious element as the basis for the entire organization . . . and did not intend that two organizations be constructed side by side, one half-religious, the other exclusively materialistic. It is time, therefore, that a new decree is directed to the clergy [urging] energetic support for the social tasks of the present.[71]

The pastoral letter *(Hirtenbrief)* to the parish priests, which had been written by Franz on the basis of Savigny's brochure, was even more explicitly directed against the Christian trade unions.

> We are asking that *Arbeiterverein* leaders pay special attention to this matter . . . The *Fachabteilungen* within the *Arbeitervereine* will supply proof as they develop on a wide scale that no new, religious-neutral creations are required to defend and promote the material interests of Christian workers, rather that the Catholic *Arbeitervereine* are capable, and strong enough, to represent the material, class interests as well as the spiritual well-being of their members.[72]

71. *Ibid.*, pp. 33–34.
72. The *Pastorale* appeared in the *Kölnische Volkszeitung*, no. 893, 3 October 1900.

The conference protocols recorded that the letter was read to the bishops by Kopp, approved unanimously, and sent to the printing offices for distribution to the various parishes, and the press, in October.[73]

Center circles in the West reacted quickly. Karl Trimborn, leader of the Rhenish Center Party, hurried to Simar to inquire if the letter should be interpreted as a condemnation of the Christian trade unions. Trimborn was afraid that such a move would lead to an explosive increase in free union membership, which, in turn, would injure the Catholic cause in the political arena. Simar replied that the bishops had only intended to warn *Arbeiterverein* priests about certain dangerous tendencies within the unions, but did not wish to outlaw the whole movement. The archbishop was under the impression that the phrase "religious-neutral" in the pastoral letter referred to the free trade unions, not the Christians. Obviously relieved, Trimborn relayed the good news to Julius Bachem, who printed the interpretation in the *Kölnische Volkszeitung,* hinting that Simar approved.[74] The crisis seemed to have passed.

It soon became evident, however, that this was not the case. On 11 October, Archbishop Nörber of Freiburg forwarded the Prussian *Hirtenbrief* to church canons in his diocese with an accompanying decree (*Erlass*) of his own. Unlike Bachem's articles, the decree reflected the true spirit of Kopp's letter. The Christian trade unions, he asserted, were moving ineluctably down the path to socialism, and in so doing, were preparing the yet-numerous masses of loyal workers for capture by the atheistic S.P.D. To call an organization performing such a dubious task "Christian" was a mockery of the true meaning of the word. Taken in conjunction with the *Hirtenbrief*, Nörber's decree could have only one meaning: the exodus of Catholic workers from "Christian" organizations should begin at once.[75]

Nörber's decree jolted Christian labor leaders to their senses. As usual, Brust was the most pointed in his comments. He scoffed at Bachem's attempt to interpret the *Hirtenbrief* in a favorable light. The letter, proclaimed Brust, was clearly directed against the unions. The enemies of the movement were mistaken, however, if they thought the unions would be weakened by "the accursed, unfortunate step."[76] On the contrary, it would only strengthen

73. Protocols of the Prussian Bishops' Conference at Fulda, 21 August 1900, p. 3 (as cited in note 68 above).

74. *Kölnische Volkszeitung,* nos. 896 and 915, for 4 and 10 October 1900. Carl Bachem noted on 7 November 1900 (Bachem Papers 38b, HA Köln) that Trimborn's conversation with Simar was the basis for his cousin's articles. The above description of the talk is based on the articles and a subsequent conversation between Carl Bachem and Simar. See Bachem's notation of 5 January 1901, Bachem Papers, 38b, HA Köln.

75. For Nörber's *Erlass,* see Bachem, "Bericht," 28 July 1912; and *Kölnische Volkszeitung,* no. 915, 10 October 1900.

76. *Bergknappe,* no. 41, 13 October 1900.

Christian workers in their resolve to reject the guardianship of the church. "The Christian proletariat has outgrown its children's shoes."[77]

Brust's outburst earned him a stern reprimand from Hitze, but the unanimity of assent among Christian workers had an altogether different effect on Simar. Fearing that some Christian unionists might flock to the S.P.D. in protest, he contacted *Gewerkverein* leaders in Essen and sought to clarify misunderstandings about the *Hirtenbrief.* He also stated publicly in Bonn that the bishops had been asked to vote at Fulda before they could thoroughly examine Kopp's proposals. Simar's remarks emboldened Bishop Schneider of Paderborn, who now claimed that he had voted for the *Hirtenbrief* against his will, not wishing as the youngest bishop to oppose all the others.[78] Kopp, not surprisingly, was furious. "In the future," he complained to Korum, "we will have to ask every voter: Is this your free, unforced will?"[79] Simar's actions evoked a similar comment. "I think he's weak and confused; he made a helpless impression at the conference, not knowing what to answer, which explains this talk of 'surprise' in Bonn."[80] But unwilling to risk further embarrassing publicity, and a bit shaken himself by the workers' protest,[81] Kopp made no attempt to rebuke Simar or force him to retract his statements.

Nörber's *volte-face* in late October must have been equally irritating to Kopp. Pressure had been building for Nörber ever since he issued the decree. Several of his church canons had politely refused to forward the pastoral letter and decree to parish priests, and the Christian workers, too, were quite upset about the obvious exaggerations contained in the *Erlass*. Sensing that Savigny had painted too dark a picture of the unions, Nörber met with Catholic workers in Mannheim on 24 October and in Freiburg on 2 November, assuring them that he would not oppose the spread of Christian trade unions in his diocese. He warned the delegations, however, to operate on the basis of positive Christianity and forget about merger with the free unions.[82]

With Simar, Nörber, and Schneider publicly opposed to the Fulda *Hirtenbrief*, the moment seemed ripe for conciliatory action on the part of the unions to allay the worst fears of the bishops concerning neutralism. The Christian trade union national executive committee met in Cologne on 8

77. *Ibid.*
78. Carl Bachem to Simar, 26 January 1901, Bachem Papers 38b, HA Köln; *Trierische Länder-Zeitung,* 23 January 1901 (clipping in Hohn Papers, Ergänzungsband 2, StA MG); Kopp to Korum, 3 November 1900, Korum Papers 331, BisA Trier; Kopp to Korum, 19 December 1900, Korum Papers 378, BisA Trier.
79. *Ibid.*
80. Kopp to Korum, 3 November 1900, Korum Papers 331, BisA Trier.
81. Kulemann, *Die Berufsvereine,* vol. 2, p. 175, received this information from Catholic *Arbeiterverein* sources in Berlin.
82. For Nörber's reversal, see Bachem, "Bericht," 28 July 1912.

November to discuss the matter. The leaders of all major unions except the anti-neutralist metal workers in Duisburg, led by Franz Wieber, were finally able to agree on the following compromise arranged beforehand by Giesberts and Brust:[83]

> We declare emphatically what is self-evident: that now, as before, [the Christian trade unions] recognize Christian principles *as the guiding principles* in the execution of trade union goals. A federation of all workers of the various industries in unified organizations is, to be sure, the goal we strive for, but we must insist that the activities of such associations never violate Christian principles. Due to the fact that such trade unions seem impossible under the prevailing conditions in the foreseeable future, we will hold to the program drawn up at the first Congress of Christian trade unions at Mainz, according to which our unions are to rest on an interconfessional, politically non-partisan basis.[84]

Some ambiguities remained as to positive and negative Christianity, and the neutral union had not been denounced; but for the most part, the statement was a cleverly disguised retreat from previous positions.

It remained to be seen whether the concessions were great enough to please the bishops. Center and union forces in the West were especially worried that Savigny, who was considered the instigator of the whole affair, would engineer another *coup de main* against the unions. A number of steps were taken, therefore, to prevent this from occurring. At the behest of the *Kölnische Volkszeitung,* the *Augustinusverein* executive committe asked that all Center papers cease discussing the trade union controversy until the press association's general assembly could meet in late November. Futher polemics and flare-ups had to be avoided at all costs. On 26 November, the assembly listened attentively to Pieper's defense of the unions, then passed a motion advocating press support for interconfessional, politically non-partisan (*politisch-unparteiisch*) trade unions established on a basis of authoritative Christian principles. The word "neutral" was scrupulously avoided.[85]

Three days later, Julius Bachem asked his cousin Carl Bachem, Reichstag and Prussian Landtag deputy from Crefeld, to join Hitze and Trimborn in obtaining a similar vote of confidence from the executive committee of the Reichstag Center Party. The leader of the *Fraktion*, Ernst Lieber, had spoken

83. Giesberts, *Protokoll des III. Kongresses zu Krefeld,* p. 40; *Bergknappe,* no. 49, 8 December 1900. Giesberts did not become a member of the executive committee until spring 1901. It can thus be assumed that Pieper and Müller were also involved in the compromise.
84. Quoted in the *Kölnische Volkszeitung,* no. 1013, 9 November 1900.
85. Carl Bachem notation of 7 November 1900, Bachem Papers 38b, HA Köln; *Augustinus-Blatt,* no. 12, December 1900, pp. 83–85, StBib MG.

out against the Christian trade unions in the Reichstag on 24 November, adopting many of Nörber's criticisms of mid-October. Arguing, no doubt, that the Christian laborers were indispensable for the political survival of the Center in the West, Bachem won the support of all the leading Centrists except Lieber, who had been called away from Berlin.[86] Finally on 17 December, Bachem received the grudging support of Lieber too. The party's leader considered Brust "a dubious element,"[87] and was still convinced that the Christian trade unions would merge with the frees, mainly because the church was not up to the task of preventing a further radicalization of the Catholic labor movement. But, outnumbered by the others on the executive committee, and soothed to a certain extent by Bachem, Lieber agreed that Hitze should defend the unions on the first suitable occasion in the Reichstag. This occurred in late January 1901.[88]

All that remained was to secure the support of the 11 of 14 Prussian bishops who had not spoken out since Fulda. Accordingly, a lengthy memorandum (*Denkschrift*) attacking Savigny's position was prepared in Cologne by Julius Bachem. It was decided at the last minute, however, not to send the memorandum. Hitze felt the matter was already decided in the unions' favor. If the *Denkschrift* were sent, "the bishops' feeling of defeat would be strengthened, and it could seem as if that had indeed been the purpose."[89] Carl Bachem had also learned that Kopp was still smoldering over the *Kölnische Volkszeitung*'s "insolent, unprecedented jostling of the entire episcopate."[90] Kopp and Korum would remain resentful in years to come, unable to forget the fact that Cologne and Mönchen-Gladbach had managed to circumvent the directives of the hierarchy. The position of the other bishops is not known, but it seems reasonably certain that they continued to look askance at the independence of the Christian trade unions, though unwilling to condemn the organization after the complicated developments that fall.[91]

The anger of Korum and Kopp could not hide the fact, however, that the "infected West,"[92] as Kopp referred to it in 1910, had won no more than a Pyrrhic victory. Mönchen-Gladbach's plans to forge a unified labor movement

86. Julius Bachem to Carl Bachem, 29 November 1900 and Carl Bachem notation of 11 December 1900, Bachem Papers 38b, HA Köln; and Reichstag Debates, Period 10, Session 2 (24 November 1900), p. 144.
87. Carl Bachem to Hitze, 17 December 1900, Bachem Papers 38b, HA Köln.
88. Reichstag Debates, Period 10, Session 2 (21 January 1901), p. 774.
89. Carl Bachem notation of 12 January 1901, Bachem Papers 38b, HA Köln.
90. Carl Bachem to Hitze, 17 December 1900, Bachem Papers 38b, HA Köln.
91. See Simar to Carl Bachem, 29 January 1901, Bachem Papers 38b, HA Köln. Simar noted here that his task of defending the Christian trade unions before the other bishops could well be a difficult one.
92. Kopp to Frl. Schalscha, 12 January 1910, printed in the *Frankfurter Zeitung*, no. 279, 9 October 1910.

had been completely scrapped,[93] and with this, Pieper's scenario of existence on the periphery of the labor world nudged closer to reality. In fact, the only politically important Catholic or Christian organization in Western Germany still advocating a neutral trade union movement, however meekly, was the national executive committee of the Christian trade unions. And by spring of 1901, this body had weakened its already tenuous commitment still further.

One factor contributing to the continued erosion of support for neutralism among Christian trade unionists was the admonishments from Archbishop Simar. The archbishop was determined to shield the Christian trade unions from the wrath of Kopp and Korum and felt the *Volksverein* should facilitate this effort by rewriting its controversial brochures. Carl Bachem agreed, but was unable to convince Hitze, who wanted to avoid the controversy and confusion that yet another statement of tasks and goals would create.[94] Less overt methods were adopted instead. Giesberts was apparently forced to avoid all mention of neutralism in the *Westdeutsche Arbeiter-Zeitung* after January 1901,[95] and Brust was urged to adopt "a calmer, more correct"[96] approach to labor relations. It was hardly a coincidence, therefore, that the *Gewerkverein* not only rejected Hue's advances that winter but also broke the two-year alliance with the *Alter Verband* that spring.[97] As the anti-neutralist Franz Wieber put it, the "hotheads" had taken "a cold water cure."[98]

The process of burying neutrality was taken one more step at the Crefeld Congress in May 1901. In order to outmaneuver Wieber, Driessen, *et al.* and block Savigny's machinations, union leaders felt compelled to attenuate their already weakened position on neutralism. There was always a danger, however, that such a move would alienate the thousands of Christian workers who stood squarely behind Mönchen-Gladbach's original brochures. A resolution was submitted to the Congress, therefore, which expressed support for the November declaration, but reiterated that the question of a united organization

93. In addition to the evidence already presented to support this statement, see Bachem, "Bericht," 28 July 1912. Here he writes that the plan had been "dropped immediately." See also Müller's warning that *Arbeiterverein* priests follow Nörber's advice with regard to neutralism, in *Präsides-Korrespondenz,* nos. 5–6, 1901, pp. 120–21, StBib MG.

94. Simar to Carl Bachem, 29 January 1901 and Carl Bachem to Pieper, 3 February 1901, Bachem Papers 38b, HA Köln.

95. The last mentioning of neutralism came on 12 January 1901. Wieber claimed that a letter from the bishop of Münster, which was circulated in his diocese and also received in Mönchen-Gladbach, effected the change in policy. See the *Deutsche Metallarbeiterzeitung,* no. 45, 9 November 1901.

96. Carl Bachem to Simar, 26 January 1901. Bachem Papers 38b, HA Köln.

97. *Regierungspräsident* in Arnsberg to the Prussian minister of the interior, 11 December 1902, and *Regierungspräsident* in Münster to the Prussian minister of the interior, 31 December 1902, Reg. D. 9042, HSA Düsseldorf.

98. Quoted in *Deutsche Metallarbeiterzeitung,* no. 45, 9 November 1901.

of German workers had no practical significance in the foreseeable future.[99] More importantly, the leadership announced that it would allow unions with a dissenting opinion to belong to the national federation. This latter statement all but ruled out a merger, for Moritz Schmidt, Peter Molz, and the leaders of other state railway unions would never consider joining the Christian federation if it meant that their workers would soon be immersed in a "Socialist" organization. Wieber understood this well enough and agreed to retract the metal workers' charge that the November declaration had contradicted Christian principles.[100] Given his previous views on the matter, Wieber's return to the fold was evidence enough for any careful observer that merger with the free unions was no longer official policy in the Christian camp.[101]

The rationale for Christian labor's submission to the Catholic hierarchy in the question of neutralism should be examined in more detail at this point, for the explanation hinges on the significant, though often obscure, rank and file. Put succinctly, church condemnation would probably have destroyed the movement by forcing some workers to the frees, others to the *Fachabteilungen* advocated by Kopp and Korum, and still others out of the ranks of organized labor altogether. The roughly 120,000 workers who had joined a Christian union by 1901 had done so in part to protect and promote their economic interests, in part to eschew the perceived religious abuses of the Socialist unions. Condemnation would have forced the rank and file to choose which meant more to them. For some, the fear of excommunication which condemnation implied was sufficient stimulus to flock to church-controlled "unions." The impression which church pronouncements made on those workers, still probably in the majority, who were fully immersed in the religio-cultural milieu of the Catholic community cannot be underestimated. Others had already found in the workplace, and in their relatively democratic Christian union, a haven from the omnipresent, authoritarian church. They had grown more independent and secular in their thinking, cherishing private religious feelings and beliefs but alienated from the organization of the church. Some were perhaps to the stage of questioning not only the sincerity of the church but even the factualness of its teachings. Everyday contact with free-thinking Socialist workers had undoubtedly furthered this trend, bringing more than a few to the point of crossing over to the stronger Socialist unions. Indeed the

99. The resolution is printed in Giesberts, *Protokoll des III. Kongresses zu Krefeld*, p. 34.
100. *Ibid.*, pp. 80–81.
101. See, for instance, the optimistic report of the *Regierungspräsident* in Düsseldorf to the king, 31 July 1901, Reg. D. 403/9048, LHA Koblenz. Opposition to the free unions was also emphasized repeatedly in the Christians' national organ, *Mitteilungen des Gesamtverbandes*, nos. 8, 12–14, and 16, for 22 July, 16 and 30 September, 14 October, and 11 November 1901 and no. 2, 27 January 1902. Johannes Giesberts was editor of the *Mitteilungen*, thus earning a seat on the national executive committee.

tendency of the Christian trade unions to function, however involuntarily, as a consciousness-raising sojourn for some workers along the way toward the frees was already evident. Thus to preserve the future of the organization, Christian labor leaders had to steer a course through the narrows created by the bishops. To cut membership losses to a minimum, both moderates and radicals had to be given good reason to remain in the Christian camp. The Crefeld Congress of 1901 was designed to do just this.

Contrary to all expectation in the West, the Crefeld resolution played right into Savigny's hands. The young, impetuous nobleman had continued his intrigues against the Christian trade unions after the Fulda conference of 1900, but both *Katholikentag* and *Augustinusverein* had sided with his opponents. Savigny won what seemed to be a major victory in the fall of 1900 when Kopp removed Dr. Phillip Hille, pro-union general secretary of the eastern *Arbeiterverein* association, and replaced him with the anti-unionist *Licenziat* Fournelle, but by spring 1901, Savigny and Fournelle were still not in complete control. The association's annual convention rejected their proposal for trade sections in May, backing the less conservative resolution of the Hille faction. The delegates agreed to encourage *Arbeiterverein* members to join Christian trade unions as long as the unions offered guarantees that positive Christian principles would be observed. A commission was established to work out the details of union-*Arbeiterverein* cooperation before the next convention in May 1902.[102]

News of the Crefeld Congress, however, eroded Hille's support on the executive committee. Savigny used the Congress's confirmation of the November declaration and the apparent defeat of Wieber to convince his fellow committeemen that merger schemes had not been rejected in the West. Already skeptical since fall, the executive committee now agreed to begin work on draft statutes for separate Catholic trade unions.[103]

The work dragged on through the fall and winter. On 10 April 1902, with the statutes completed, the trade union commission established by the *Arbeiterverein* convention the previous spring met for the first time. Fournelle, who sat on this body as well, opened the meeting by presenting the completed statutes for the commission's consideration. "Leading representatives"[104] of the Christian trade unions who had been invited by the commission to take

102. Kulemann, *Die Berufsvereine*, vol. 2, p. 177; Gornik, *Entwicklung der nichtsozialdemokratischen Arbeiterbewegung*, p. 83; *Protokoll über die Verhandlungen des IV. Kongresses der christlichen Gewerkschaften*, pp. 25–26; *Bergknappe*, no. 40, 6 October 1900.
103. Gornik, *Entwicklung der nichtsozialdemokratischen Arbeiterbewegung*, p. 102.
104. *Ibid.*, pp. 83–84. Gornik was probably referring to the leader of the Christian construction workers, Josef Wiedeberg, who had replaced Weigel on the national executive committee of the Christian trade unions. Wiedeberg resided in Berlin.

part in the deliberations rejected these proposals outright, whereupon Fournelle made a compromise offer. His suggestion is illustrative of the basic disagreement that was driving the two Christian labor factions farther and farther apart. Would the Christian trade unions consent to the appointment of clerical representatives to decide union policy when moral and religious questions arose? After union leaders refused to compromise on the matter of independence, the commission decided to back Fournelle and the executive committee. A split in Christian ranks appeared unavoidable.

By summer 1902, the break was complete. Despite the protests of the Christian labor press in the West and South and considerable opposition within the eastern association, the delegates to the poorly attended *Arbeiterverein* convention at Berlin in mid-May 1902 approved the statutes for trade sections, or *Fachabteilungen*, as they came to be known.[105] The new splinter movement was sanctioned by Kopp, and Korum quickly added his support by leading the *Arbeitervereine* of his diocese into the East German association. The Christian trade unions had escaped formal condemnation in 1900 only to find another equally serious challenge facing them in 1902.

Damage was unavoidable this time. Attempts to spread the Christian trade unions to the crucial industrial districts of Berlin, Silesia, parts of Saxony, and the Saar faltered on the determined opposition of parish priests forwarned by their bishops about the dangers of Christian trade unionism. Devout Catholics in these areas joined *Fachabteilungen* or, as was more often the case, remained non-organized. Those workers that had already formed Christian unions, such as the 44,000 railwaymen in Trier, steered clear of the national federation and formed an alliance with the confessional trade sections. Many Catholics, of course, joined the free trade unions. Most disappointing of all, perhaps, was the indefinite postponement of the German Workers' Congress. Plagued by the threat from "Berlin" and other internal problems described in the next chapter, all plans of increasing the political influence of the *Gesamtverband* had to be delayed. With powerful enemies in Trier and Breslau and eight times as many workers in the General Commission as in the Christian federation (681,000 vs. 84,600), the likelihood that Christian trade unionism would prevail in Germany seemed slight indeed.

* * * *

The collapse of the movement toward merger of the Christian and Socialist trade unions, which ended for the former in the highly damaging secession of the *Fachabteilungen*, is a very instructive example of the phenomenon of manipulation in Imperial Germany. The state did not act out of a desire to

105. Kulemann, *Die Berufsvereine*, vol. 2, p. 177.

mobilize mass support for the old regime; it *re*acted to a spontaneous development which had begun with the radicalization of the Christian rank and file at the end of the 1890s. Nor did the state act alone; rather, it made very clever use of an "auxiliary elite," in this case the Catholic bishops. The church placed pressure on the Center Party and *Volksverein*, which in their turn managed to convince Christian labor leaders of the folly of merger by placing the whole issue in the context of excommunication. Realizing that a significant portion of the membership of the Christian federation would not risk this, Christian labor leaders retreated. It is debatable whether the church, Center, and *Volksverein* gained anything from their efforts, for the crisis had certainly exacerbated relations in the Catholic community. The state, on the other hand, emerged the real gainer, for it had prevented the birth of a united federation of trade unions. Such a union would certainly have increased the pressure on the established order to reform and considerably raised the cost of continued opposition to change. Now, however, the state could fall back on its policy of playing one movement off against the other. In such ways the old regime perpetuated itself.

6

Tariffs, "Center Party Unions," and Grass-Roots Stagnation

The reemergence of the old dispute over clerical supervision of the labor movement created considerable recruiting problems for the *Gesamtverband* and distracted Mönchen-Gladbach and the Christian trade unions from their socio-political plans. In the midst of the merger controversy, however, the unions were hurled into another critical situation which exacerbated membership problems and further delayed a workers' demonstration in favor of social reform. The crisis was precipitated by one of the most hotly contested political debates in Germany at the turn of the century—the question of tariff reform. Although the organization never officially sanctioned a tariff hike, appearances were to the contrary, and the federation almost collapsed over the issue. These controversies combined with other tactical errors made by Christian trade union leaders to delay the construction of strike and support funds, the *sine qua non* of success at the grass-roots level. These local setbacks were most obvious in the Ruhr, where the Christian miners' *Gewerkverein* lost its lead over the *Alter Verband* and slipped far behind the Socialist union by the time of the great miners' strike of 1905. All three issues—merger, tariffs, and grass-roots mistakes—are important aspects of the internal history of Christian trade unionism and must be appreciated, in addition, if we are to gain a proper perspective on the victory of the Socialist unions over their Christian challengers. The question of grass-roots stagnation will be dealt with secondly in this chapter. Our first task is an analysis of the effects of the great tariff debate.

* * * *

For such a debate, the Christian trade unions were sorely unprepared. The *Mainzer Leitsätze* called for "discussion of reforms to be achieved by constitutional means within the existing framework of society," and in the first two years of its existence, the *Gesamtverband* publicly advocated corporate status for trade unions, compulsory arbitration, chambers of labor, unemployment insurance, improved health insurance, increased freedom of assembly, and the eight-hour day.[1] The organization had also issued a public protest against the Prison Bill.[2] With the possible exception of their participation in the Society for Social Reform, however, the Christian trade unions had not become involved in pressure politics and had no immediate plans to influence the general course of political events. The consensus at Mainz in May 1899 had been that political influence on issues such as tax, tariff, or suffrage reform would come by itself as the numerical strength of the unions grew.[3] Thus the *Mainzer Leitsätze* were vague as to which methods the organization should employ in attempting to influence legislation and did not specify, as Bebel had in 1900, which issues, if any, lay outside the sphere of trade union politics. Further complicating matters, the guidelines forbade alignment of the federation with any one party, or presumably any one group of parties (S.P.D. and Progressives, Center and Conservatives, etc.). The rationale for this neutralist clause had been clear enough in 1899, but if the unions were to pursue politics, how could this be done without choosing sides? The tariff debate of 1900/1902 illustrated the inadequacy of the *Mainzer Leitsätze* and generated tensions that came very close to creating a second permanent split in the Christian labor movement.

Franz Wieber was the first in the Christian trade union camp to discuss the tariff question. When the Bundesrat began deliberations over the issue in the fall of 1900, he wrote in *Der deutsche Metallarbeiter,* the organ of the Christian metal workers, that tariff increases worked against the proletariat by raising prices and negating the gains of hard-fought wage struggles. Tariffs seemed doubly threatening in 1900 with the economy showing signs of slowing down. It was the duty of the Christian trade unions, therefore, to block such legislation, "in other words, to get involved in politics."[4] His article gave rise to widespread criticism among Christian unionists who were angry that Wieber, the self-professed crusader against Socialism, had contradicted

1. *Mitteilungen des Gesamtverbandes*, no. 2, 29 April 1901, no. 6, 24 June 1900, and nos. 2, 3, 5, and 6 for 27 January, 10 February, 10 March, and 24 March 1902; *Kölnische Volkszeitung*, no. 477, 24 May 1899.
2. *Kölnische Volkszeitung*, no. 477, 24 May 1899.
3. *Mitteillungen des Gesamtverbandes*, no. 16, 11 August 1902.
4. Wieber's article is quoted in the Socialist *Deutsche Metallarbeiterzeitung*, no. 35, 31 August 1901.

himself by advocating the Socialist and left-liberal position on tariffs.[5] Not wishing, perhaps, to jeopardize his anti-neutralist campaign against Mönchen-Gladbach, Wieber did not pursue the matter further.

Johannes Giesberts and August Brust were also quite opinionated with regard to tariffs. During the winter of 1900/1901, the two advocated higher duties to protect agriculture, industry, and the jobs of German workers. Brust and Giesberts also suggested that the increased revenues be used to finance social insurance programs like widows' and orphans' insurance, one of Hitze's old demands.[6] Though clearly in the material interests of the workers, the tariff-social insurance compromise also reflected ideological concerns. Well-schooled in Catholic social teaching, Christian labor leaders insisted that attention be paid to the material interests of all the estates that made up the social body. "Christian justice" demanded that farmers, artisans, industrialists, and factory workers enjoy some measure of material prosperity. Convinced of the righteousness of these views, neither Brust nor Giesberts had any qualms about expressing them in *Bergknappe,* organ of the Christian miners, and the *Westdeutsche Arbeiter-Zeitung*, which served as the official organ of numerous Christian trade unions.

With other Catholic unionists discussing the tariff issue, Wieber saw no reason why he should remain silent.[7] As the metal worker had feared in 1900, the economic boom of the late 1890s had given way to a deepening recession, especially in the iron and steel industry, which had already laid off workers and lowered wages about 25 percent. Wieber found it impossible to understand, therefore, how his colleagues could contemplate action that would raise the workers' cost of living. "As things stand, the workers, not the agrarians, are the ones who will have to fight against hunger and misery in the near future."[8] With such thoughts in mind, he urged the *Gesamtverband* central committee to speak out against Bülow's tariff package.[9]

The central committee met in Cologne on 17 August 1901.[10] Because the overwhelming majority favored the new tariff bill, backing for Wieber was rejected outright. So too was the idea of a pro-tariff stance. If the central committee openly advocated agricultural protection, reasoned the majority at Cologne, the *Gesamtverband* would surely be labeled a pro-agrarian, or what was worse, a Center pary organization by the S.P.D. and Progressives. Con-

5. *Ibid.*
6. *Westdeutsche Arbeiter-Zeitung*, no. 45, 10 November 1900; and no. 15, 13 April 1901; *Bergknappe*, nos. 9 and 13, 2 and 30 March 1901.
7. Wieber's views are discussed in *Deutsche Metallarbeiterzeitung*, no. 35, 31 August 1901.
8. Quoted in *ibid.*
9. Müller, *Christliche Gewerkschaftsbewegung*, p. 141.
10. For the meeting see *ibid.*, p. 141; *Bergknappe*, no. 45, 9 November 1901; and *Mitteilungen des Gesamtverbandes*, nos. 11–12, 2 and 16 September 1901.

fessional prejudices would come to the fore, Protestant and Catholic members would turn against one another, and the organization might fall apart. Thus the assembly censured Brust, Wieber, and the other union editors who had discussed the tariff question, urging them to adopt a stricter interpretation of the *Mainzer Leitsätze*. *Gesamtverband* resolutions concerning labor legislation and social insurance should be acted upon by individual union members within the party of their choice. "But political issues [such as the tariff] which set parties passionately against each other and are resolved exclusively from the vantage point of party doctrine should be kept out of the unions, if only to preserve the unity and solidarity of the movement."[11]

Wieber refused to obey. One week after the central committee meeting he ran an article in *Der deutsche Metallarbeiter*[12] which mocked the idea common in Christian labor circles that workers should support the tariff out of a sense of Christian justice for the farmers. The article drew rebukes from Giesberts and other union editors in September 1901,[13] but Wieber would not be silenced. Far from it, he accused Giesbert and other union leaders of playing "love child"[14] with Center Party agrarians, then took his case to the union rank and file. A tour through rural southern Germany in October won few converts, but Christian workers along the lower Rhine and Ruhr were more interested. Assembly after assembly in Crefeld, Cologne, Duisburg, Mülheim a. Rh., Düsseldorf, and Essen spoke out against the new tariff proposal and called on the Christian trade unions to fight it.[15] Christian leaders scoffed at the threat publicly,[16] but privately they expressed shock at the susceptibility of a growing number of their followers to the arguments of Wieber and other anti-tariff agitators.[17]

The free trade unions were naturally delighted by all this. An emerging threat in 1899, the Christian counter-organization showed signs of serious internal dissension, perhaps collapse, in 1901. Thus Wieber's revolt was covered at length in the Socialist and free union press and the tariff issue exploited to the hilt.[18] This propaganda was not without effect, especially in

11. *Mitteilungen des Gesamtverbandes*, no 12, 16 September 1901.
12. The article is reprinted in *Deutsche Metallarbeiterzeitung*, no. 35, 31 August 1901.
13. *Protokoll über Verhandlungen des IV Congresses . . . zu München*, p. 70; *Mitteilungen des Gesamtverbandes*, no. 12, 16 September 1901.
14. For Wieber's accusations, see *Deutsche Metallarbeiterzeitung*, no. 45, 9 November 1901.
15. *Ibid.*, nos. 45 and 49, 9 November and 7 December 1901.
16. *Westdeutsche Arbeiter-Zeitung*, nos. 43–45, 26 October, 2 November, and 9 November 1901.
17. Rhenish Center leader Karl Trimborn described Giesberts's remarks to this effect at a caucus of the Reichstag *Fraktion* on 27 November 1901. See Carl Bachem's notes in the Bachem Papers 172, HA Köln.
18. *Deutsche Metallarbeiterzeitung*, nos. 35, 45, 49, and 51 for 31 August, 9 November, 7 December, and 21 December 1901; Landrat in Essen to the *Regierungspräsident*, 3 September 1901, Reg. D. 9052, HSA Düsseldorf.

the Ruhr, where the *Alter Verband* began to gain considerable ground on the *Gewerkverein*. The frees were not alone, however, in seeking to exploit the *Gesamtverband*'s growing troubles. The rallying call of free trade had led to the formation of a wealthy new interest group, the Commercial Treaty Association (*Handelsvertragsverein*), which also hoped to reap advantage from the anti-tariff upsurge in the Christian camp.[19] Unexplored by previous historians, this latter threat should be examined in some detail.

The Commercial Treaty Association was founded in November 1900 by leaders of the Progressive Alliance *(Freisinnige Vereinigung)*, a small left-wing party of bankers, light industrialists, and *laissez-faire* intellectuals. The most important goal of the organization was to commit the National Liberal Party to the cause of free trade. With additional backing from the S.P.D., the radical South German People's Party, and the moderate Progressive People's Party *(Freisinnige Volkspartei), the Handelsvertragsverein* would command 151 seats in the Reichstag—48 short of a majority when all deputies were present.[20] Given the pro-tariff position of the Conservatives, the *Reichspartei,* and most of the right-wing splinter parties in the Reichstag, the Commercial Treaty Association had no choice but to approach the Center for the necessary votes. The protectionist bent of Center agrarians further narrowed the list of possible recruits to those Center deputies representing working-class or largely urban constituencies. The *Gesamtverband's* position on the tariff question suddenly loomed very large in significance.

For help in winning over the Christian trade unions, the *Handelsvertragsverein* approached Pastor Hermann Kötschke, leader of the Düsseldorf branch of Naumann's National Social Party.[21] The Evangelical minister had close ties to the workers of the lower Rhine, was a good speaker, and was apparently well liked. He was joined by Pastor Wohlleben of Cologne, another Protestant active in the labor movement. With funds made available by the *Handelsvertragsverein,* the two founded the *Westdeutsches Volksblatt*, which began to print articles against tariffs in the name of the Christian trade unions. The wealthy "pocket-book association" (*Portmon-*

19. For a general discussion of the *Handelsvertragsverein,* see Ludwig Elm, *Zwischen Fortschritt und Reaktion* (Berlin: Akademie-Verlag, 1968), pp. 84–95.

20. In reality, the association needed far fewer than 48 seats, for absenteeism was a problem in the Reichstag at this time. During the vote over the tariff bill in December 1902, for instance, only 302 of 397 deputies showed up. Bachem, *Zentrumspartei*, vol. 6, p. 161; Hertling to his wife, Anna, 18 October 1902, Hertling Papers 15, BA Koblenz.

21. This paragraph is based on the report of the police commissioner of Düsseldorf to the *Regierungspräsident*, 1 October 1902, Reg. D. 9053, HSA Düsseldorf; *Bergknappe*, no. 46, 16 November 1901; *Westdeutsche Arbeiter-Zeitung*, no. 42, 19 October 1901; and *Mitteilungen des Gesamtverbandes*, no. 17, 25 November 1901.

naieverein), as Brust referred derisively to the left-liberal pressure group,[22] also distributed a pamphlet through Kötschke urging Christian unionists to force the *Gesamtverband* to adopt an anti-tariff position. The authors of the pamphlet felt confident that the Center would not impose voting discipline on the *Fraktion* if it were clear that by supporting the tariff, labor backing would be lost. Hard-pressed deputies from the West and parts of the South would thus be free to vote against the unpopular duties, while agrarians could satisfy their constituents by accepting the tariff hike. The booklets were printed in great number and offered to the various Christian unions of the West without charge.

These efforts met with very limited success. The metal workers and wood workers of Cologne, Düsseldorf, and Duisburg welcomed Kötschke's aid and agitated for *Westdeutsches Volksblatt*, as did the leftist organ of the Christian tile workers, *Gut Brand*. Established forces within the *Gesamtverband*, however, soon took steps to halt the spread of Wieber's revolt. Brust blocked distribution of the pamphlet among *Gewerkverein* functionaries, and Giesberts swung over to the offensive with articles against the Commercial Treaty Association in the *Westdeutsche Arbeiter-Zeitung*. A special session of the *Gesamtverband* central committee on 16 November further undermined the Progressives' campaign against tariffs. Wieber was given six weeks to apologize for maligning Christian labor leaders in October, the *Westdeutsches Volksblatt* was condemned, and individual unions were forbidden to discuss the tariff, which, as a controversial party-political issue, lay outside the sphere of labor politics permitted by the program of the Christian trade unions. As individuals, members could take any stance to the bill they desired.[23]

The decision conformed with the practical interpretation of the *Mainzer Leitsätze* formulated in August. But, as the Socialist *Deutsche Metallarbeiterzeitung* observed, there was more to it than this.

> The resolution places the *Westdeutsche Arbeiter-Zeitung* in an especially privileged position. Although it is designated as the union organ by a number of Christian trade unions, the paper is not formally a union organ, rather that of the Catholic *Arbeitervereine;* but as such it can continue to make propaganda for the raising of grain duties . . . while the opponents of tariffs in the Christian trade union camp are, at least in the press, muzzled [*mundtodt gemacht*] by the resolution.[24]

22. *Bergknappe*, no. 46, 16 November 1901.
23. *Ibid.*, nos. 46 and 50 for 16 November and 14 December 1901, and no. 12, 22 March 1902; *Westdeutsche Arbeiter-Zeitung*, nos. 43–44 for 26 October and 2 November 1901; *Mitteilungen des Gesamtverbandes*, no. 17, 25 November 1901.
24. *Deutsche Metallarbeiterzeitung*, no. 49, 7 December 1901.

With no outlet to express their views other than the union newspaper, most Christian unionists had indeed been silenced.

Wieber and his associates once again refused to cooperate. Caucusing on 20 November 1901 in Duisburg, the executive board of the metal workers' union gave Wieber a complete vote of confidence and refused to countenance any apology.[25] One of the board members, Peter Schlack of Mülheim a. Rh., summarized the views of his colleagues two days before the board met.

> The protest movement against higher tariffs will not be halted. Are we to believe that a duty on groceries, a matter that concerns all trade unions, is not a trade union question? Is there anything which cuts deeper into the existence of the worker than tariffs? I can't understand how trade union leaders who have risen from the midst of the workers and have come to know the misery of working-class circles can speak out for higher tariffs—What good is it if wages rise 10 percent, but food prices rise 20 percent? I'm a Center man, but I must say that great pressure is being exerted by the party on the unions so that they will serve Center Party needs.[26]

The last charge, which may have referred to the fact that Wieber had been expelled from the executive committee of the Duisburg Center Party,[27] was pounced on by the leftist press, especially the *Korrespondenz des Handelsvertragsvereins*.

> The opposition of Catholic workers to the Center's position in the tariff debate has already been expressed in numerous public rallies. Because the Center pays no heed, the workers have mobilized their union against it. The Christian metal workers continue to work calmly and energetically against the threatening rise in the cost of living. Yes, the movement against tariffs is growing. The Christian tile workers' union has written and spoken against tariffs with a fiery zeal. There is also a stir in the Christian wood workers' union. If the Center still does not hear, the formation of an independent Christian Labor Party is inevitable.[28]

Having failed to capture the *Gesamtverband*, the left-liberals appeared to have another ambitious plan.

Faced with this threat, Christian leaders felt compelled to take much more drastic action. The Munich Congress of the Christian Trade Unions (June 1902) expelled the rebellious metal workers and founded a new metal workers' union. The vote to eject the Duisburg faction was a good indication, however,

25. *Westdeutsche Arbeiter-Zeitung*, no. 49, 7 December 1901.
26. Quoted in *Deutsche Metallarbeiterzeitung*, no. 49, 7 December 1901.
27. Report of the police commissioner of Düsseldorf, 1 October 1902, as cited above in note 21.
28. The article is quoted in *Mitteilungen des Gesamtverbandes*, no. 19, 23 December 1901.

that Wieber's cause was not dead among the rank and file. Twenty-six delegates had voted yes, 9 no, and 18 had abstained.[29]

Gambling on Wieber's grass-roots strength, the *Handelsvertragsverein* decided to forge ahead with the creation of a new party. Kötschke was once again asked for assistance. His mission was to intensify opposition to tariffs among Catholic workers, artisans, grocery store owners, and small businessmen of the West. He should then nominate lower-class Catholics for election to the Reichstag in every district where incumbent Centrists refused to sign statements opposing the tariff bill. Such pressure would hopefully force the Center to lift voting discipline in the *Fraktion* or encourage a revolt from the voting authority of parliamentary leaders.[30] Realizing that many Catholics had been reluctant to follow him in the fall for fear of betraying the Center to the allegedly Jewish *Handelsvertragsverein*, Kötschke remained in the background this time and let a disaffected Catholic journalist from Düsseldorf, Albert Minjon, initiate the campaign. Inspired by Leo XIII's Encyclical on Christian Democracy (*Graves de Communi;* January 1901), Minjon was only too willing to engage in charitable Christian action for the people, as the document had prescribed. By fall 1902, a well-financed "Christian Democratic People's Party" was threatening Center deputies in the West with electoral defeat should they support Bülow during the second reading of the tariff bill scheduled to begin in October.[31]

The scheme failed. The sensitive urban deputies in the Center had required that two basic conditions be met before supporting the bill. First, that the new revenues be used for a social purpose such as widows' and orphans' insurance, and second, that the overwhelming majority of the Reichstag oppose the S.P.D. and left-liberals. In this way Centrists from urban or proletarian constituencies could argue that the party had acted in a socially responsible manner and that the leftists represented only a radical, unpatriotic, obstructionist fringe.[32]

The course of events in the fall of 1902 was greatly relieving to this wing of the party. The *Volksverein* managed to convince Center leaders that the wid-

29. *Protokoll über die Verhandlungen des IV. Congresses . . . zu München*, pp. 72–73, 75.
30. *Westdeutsche Arbeiter-Zeitung*, no. 46, 15 November 1902.
31. Police commissioner of Düsseldorf to the *Regierungspräsident*, 1 September 1903, Reg. D. 9054, HSA Düsseldorf; Hubert Jedin (ed.), *Handbuch der Kirchengeschichte* (Freiburg: Herder Verlag KG, 1973), vol. 6, part 2, p. 251; report of the Police Department of Rheydt, 3 November 1902, Reg. D. 9054, HSA Düsseldorf.
32. Carl Bachem to Dr. Urfry, of the Crefeld Center Party, 2 July 1901, Bachem Papers 340, HA Köln; Carl Bachem to Heinrich Otto of the *Niederheinische Volkszeitung*, 12 November 1901, Carl Bachem to Franz Bachem, 14 November 1901, and Carl Bachem to Hitze, 23 November 1901, Bachem Papers 172, HA Köln; Carl Bachem to Catholic factory owner Hoeveler, 31 January 1902, Bachem Papers 174, HA Köln.

ows' and orphans' insurance was necessary for election purposes, and the government, mindful of the Center's parliamentary influence, went along. The pro-tariff majority was also quite large, thereby satisfying another prerequisite of left-wing Centrists. Under pressure from the government and, it would seem, the Church, Center Party agrarians abandoned the struggle for a much higher tariff rate and supported the government's proposals. So too did most Conservatives and Free Conservatives. The National Liberals and the moderate Progressive People's Party also backed the bill. Both parties were under tremendous psychological pressure to join the respectable, "bourgeois" (*bürgerlich*) majority and fight the excessive obstructionist tactics of the left. The right-liberals were also impressed by the willingness of the agrarians to compromise. In the final vote on 14 December 1902, two-thirds of the Reichstag (202 to 100) backed the government.[33]

Easing the pressure on left-wing Centrists even more was the fact that Wieber did not join forces with Minjon and Kötschke that fall. Wieber's refusal to do so resulted largely from the fact that the fight against tariffs looked hopeless. Wieber took a large delegation of metal workers to Cologne to sway the *Katholikentag* in August 1902 to his anti-tariff views, but the assembly was unmoved. For all these reasons, Wieber decided that it was foolish to perpetuate the feud. Thus, in September 1902, he dropped the tariff issue and sued for peace with Giesberts and Brust. All of Minjon's advances were rejected and the Christian Democratic People's Party publicly denounced. A grateful *Gesamtverband* invited Wieber and his followers back to the fold in mid-1903.[34]

* * * *

For the Christian trade unions, however, the tariff controversy had not ended. As the months drew on to the Reichstag elections of June 1903, the *Gesamtverband* was attacked furiously by the free trade unions and left-liberals for its alleged partisan, pro-Center Party orientation. The accusations were particularly embarrassing, for not only was the organization's political neutrality called into question, but also its stature as a labor organization. Despite the fact that tariffs would certainly protect the jobs of German work-

33. Archbishop Kopp to Bülow, 25 February 1902, and Bülow's reply, 1 March 1902, Deutschland 125 Nr. 1 secr., AA Bonn; Carl Bachem to Heinrich Otto, 25 November 1902, Bachem Papers 345, HA Köln; Elm, *Zwischen Fortschritt und Reaktion*, p. 93; Bachem, *Zentrumspartei*, vol. 6, pp. 156–61.

34. For this paragraph, see the "Biographische Sammlung Franz Wieber," StA Duisburg; report of the police commissioner of Düsseldorf, 1 September 1903, as cited above in note 31; *Verhandlungen der 49. Generalversammlung der Katholiken Deutschlands in Mannheim vom 24. bis 28. August 1902* (Mannheim: Druck und Verlag von Jean Gremm, 1902), pp. 447–56; *Westdeutsche Arbeiter-Zeitung*, nos. 12, 13 and 17 for 21 March, 28 March, and 25 April 1903.

ers, most laborers focused on the apparently more controversial issue of higher prices for food and consumer goods. Support for Bülow's tariffs was easily portrayed as a betrayal of the working class.

The Christian federation, of course, had not openly advocated tariff increases or pressured the Reichstag parties to do so. The central committee sessions of August and November 1901 had made this abundantly clear. But to many workers, including a large percentage of Christian unionists, the central committee's insistence on neutrality was nothing but a shrewd maneuver to defeat Wieber and protect the Center. Nor did it seem fair or impartial for the central committee to condemn the *Westdeutsches Volksblatt* but say nothing about the *Westdeutsche Arbeiter-Zeitung* which had run articles by Giesberts against Minjon, Kötschke, and the Commercial Treaty Association. And who could deny that Giesberts and Brust had intensified their attacks against the free unions and S.P.D. during the fall of 1901, just as the tariff bill was laid before parliament? To be sure, the executive council, central committee, general assembly, congress, and press of the *Gesamtverband* were entirely independent of the Center. But in the midst of a volatile controversy like that over tariffs, the seeming unity of purpose between the Center and the Christian trade unions was all the proof needed by most workers to conclude that the *Gesamtverband* was a Center Party organization. Many, of course, had made up their minds on this issue years earlier and needed no additional proof whatsoever.

Those already convinced could point, for instance, to the growing *rapprochement* between the Center Party and "its" unions. In August 1899 the *Katholikentag* passed a resolution introduced by August Pieper of the *Volksverein* favoring the growth of Christian trade unions. This represented a significant departure from past years. Mönchen-Gladbach's unwillingness to promote unionism in the 1880s and 1890s resulted partly from the fact that most in Center circles still responded to the idea of Christian unions with a hostility born of rural and small-town provincialism. "Class consciousness" was seen as evidence of a disintegrating social fabric which could only harm the nation and the Center. Once organized, Christian workers might run their own candidates, as had occurred in 1877, or else vote for the S.P.D.

By the turn of the century, however, the working class had grown more important politically, even for a traditionally rural-based party like the Center. The non-agricultural labor force in Germany was rapidly approaching the agricultural in absolute numbers by this time and the proletariat was the fastest-growing non-rural class. The trend was most noticeable in some of the Center's traditional *Hochburgen* of western Germany. From 1870 to 1900, for example, the population of Cologne grew meteorically from 135,371 to 372,229, while Düsseldorf rose rapidly from 80,695 to 213,767. The Center possessed 12 overwhelmingly urban Reichstag seats like these in 1900, and although this represented only 11.8 percent of the party's total seats (12 of 102), the Center was too proud of the *"ausschlaggebende"* position it had enjoyed in parliament since 1898 to risk losing any one of them. That this could happen as a result of ignoring organized labor was painfully evident in Catholic Munich, where the Social Democrats were already in possession of both of the Center's former seats. The growth of the working class in towns located in largely rural districts was just as ominous for the Center. Münster, Osnabrück, and Bonn, to cite but three examples, nearly doubled in size after 1871, while the surrounding countryside remained fairly stable. Thus even the rural deputies in the Center found it increasingly difficult to shun the workers. These trends, together with the spectacular overall growth of the S.P.D. from 11 to 56 Reichstag seats in the decade after 1887, combined to convince most Centrists that Christian trade unions, far from harming the party, might be its salvation. Others, not suprisingly, continued to harbor the older, more conservative views. For this reason, perhaps, the *Katholikentag* of 1899 allowed no open discussion of the trade union resolution.[35] To the public, Christian trade unions and Center Party were to seem one.

Adding credence to the charge of "Center Party unions" was the growing dependence of the Christian trade unions on a variety of services provided by the party. It was no secret, for instance, that the emerging cadre of *Gesamtverband* secretaries was trained systematically by the *Volksverein* at an impressive array of courses, seminars, and workshops offered in Mönchen-Gladbach every year.[36] After Hitze's defense of the Christian trade unions in the Reichstag in January 1901, moreover, the Center *Fraktion* was probably regarded by the public as the protector of the workers against the conservative bishops. It was also widely known that Adam Stegerwald had established a close working relationship with the *Kölnische Volkszeitung* after he took over the *Gesamtverband*'s general secretariat at Cologne in January 1903.[37] It should be reiterated that the unions did not enjoy a cooperative relationship with all elements of the party. A significant number of Center deputies from the Saar, the Mosel, and Silesia continued to oppose the movement.[38] Nor did

35. Carl Bachem to Richard Müller (Fulda), 27 May 1898, Bachem Papers 86d, HA Köln; Johannes Giesberts, "Johannes Giesberts," in *25 Jahre christliche Gewerkschaftsbewegung 1899–1924*, pp. 180–81; *Augustinus-Blatt*, nos. 6 and 8, for June and August 1899, StBib MG; *Verhandlungen der 46. Generalversammlung der Katholiken Deutschlands vom 27. bis 31. August 1899*, pp. 294–95, StBib MG; Koppel Pinson, *Modern Germany*, p. 221.

36. For the dependence of the unions on the educational facilities at Mönchen-Gladbach, see August Pieper to Vicar General Kreutzwald at Cologne, 5 November 1901, Generalia 23.2, vol. 3, Erzb. Registratur Köln. See also Brust's remarks in the Socialist *Bergarbeiter-Zeitung*, 3 December 1904 (clipping in Reg. D. 9055, HSA Düsseldorf).

37. See the Socialist *Arbeiter-Zeitung*, 21 August 1906 (clipping in: Reg. D. 9058, HSA Düsseldorf).

38. Carl Bachem to Julius Bachem, 17 November 1905, Bachem Papers 229, HA Köln.

all Catholic employers in western Germany follow the lead of *Volksverein* chairman Franz Brandts. Yet, when differences over the party's stance to the Christian trade unions emerged from closed caucuses, the new-found pro-union position of the Center leadership, and the political expediency of this stance, became clear.

In October 1902, for example, the Catholic entrepreneurs of Coesfeld locked out all employees in an attempt to break Carl Schiffer's textile union. The Landrat in Coesfeld, the local Center Party press, the organ of the Christian Peasants' Association, and a few Catholic *Arbeiterverein* priests of the area supported the move. With the help of leading Rhenish Centrists like Karl Trimborn, Franz Hitze, Franz Brandts, the Bachem cousins, and Karl Herold, the agrarian leader and head of the Westphalian Center Party, Schiffer was eventually able to bring the disputed lock-out to arbitration. Angered over the Center's acceptance of trade unionism, a few of the most influential Coesfeld owners withdrew their support from the official Center candidate during the elections of 1903, but without the workers' votes, the employers' bid was unsuccessful.[39]

Trimborn's reorganization of the Rhenish Center Party that winter was another indication of the growing importance of Christian labor within the party. The progressive-minded lawyer who headed the Rhenish Center Party and held the prestigious Reichstag seat for Cologne created a hierarchy of local and district secretariats controlled by a commission in Cologne on which laborers were given many seats.[40] But it was the district nomination committee, heretofore the autonomous decision-making body in selecting Reichstag candidates, which Trimborn wanted most to reform.

> The social and political articulation of the electoral body [*Wahlkörper*] should find the fullest possible expression in the district committee. One important consideration is the *representation of the working class in the committee,* as for example, the Crefeld nominating committee has already done. Present leaders and their close associates frequently raise the objection that the local apparatus will become top-heavy and hard to handle, that one has to avoid [class] friction, that the interests of the workers and the small man have been sufficiently cared for by the committees as they are, etc. There may be much truth in this—but the signs of the times cannot be ignored. Our people are not satisfied when something is done *for* them; rather, it must be done *with* them. They want to participate, not merely say thanks. The circumstances which can follow from the expansion of the

39. Schiffer to Carl Bachem, 25 October 1902, Carl Bachem to Schiffer, 27 October 1902, Carl Bachem to Franz Brandts, 30 October 1902, Carl Bachem to Schiffer, 30 October 1902, Bachem Papers 169, HA Köln; *Augustinus-Blatt*, no. 11, November 1902, StBib MG; Lipphaus to Herald, 8 June 1903, Stocht to Herald, 10 June 1903, Herald Papers 1, BA Koblenz.
40. The statutes of the Rhenish Center are located in the Bachem Papers 190, HA Köln.

> electoral committee are a *much smaller* evil than the anger which will follow from the exclusion [of the workers]. The electoral committees must be lubricated with a large drop of democratic oil, namely, before the upcoming election campaign, which [will bring] a shrewd stirring-up of dissatisfaction and particular interests [by the S.P.D.].[41]

Trimborn was clearly trying to stave off disaster at the polls.

The effects of his appeal were negligible in the Rhineland. Local committees supported Richard Breidebach, leader of the Christian miners of Siegen, in Wetzlar-Altenkirchen, while the Duisburg party nominated Franz Wieber's colleague Christian Kloft. Hard-pressed committees in Westphalia were somewhat more accommodating. Joining an aging Gerhard Stötzel in Essen as Center candidates were Schiffer in Alten-Iserlohn and Brust's colleague, Theodor Berse, in Bochum-Gelsenkirchen. Some progress was also registered in Bavaria, seat of the second largest concentration of Christian unionists in Germany, where a significant number of labor delegates were nominated to the annual convention of the Bavarian Center in January 1903.[42]

In return, Carl Schirmer and his Christian working-class followers in southern Germany issued a statement praising the legislative work of the Reich and Bavarian Center *Fraktionen*, but urging continued progress in the area of labor representation.[43] The Center was also repaid handsomely for its consideration of the unions in western Germany. In addition to the four Christian unionists running for the Reichstag, Giesberts, Brust, and union secretaries from every "local" of the *Gesamtverband* campaigned energetically for the Center. As a result of these efforts, the Center was able to reduce the effect of the S.P.D.'s anti-tariff propaganda among Catholic workers. Catholic *Arbeiterverein* members and the *Westdeutsche Arbeiter-Zeitung* campaigned for the Center too, but, as Pieper explained to parish priests in western Germany after the elections, no one should doubt who had performed the real yeoman's service:

> During the recent Reichstag elections the Catholic members of the Christian trade unions were the most vigorous and sacrificing agitators for the Center Party, even if, naturally, outside of the unions as such . . . All political work for the Center will be without effect, therefore, if we don't provide for a powerful development of the Christian trade unions . . . The Center Party, in those areas where its mandates depend on labor votes, will lose these seats in every case in the near future if the Christian trade unions do not keep the Catholic workers away from the Social Democrats.

41. Karl Trimborn, "An uns selbst," undated clipping (November 1902) from the *Niederrheinische Volkszeitung*, in *ibid*.
42. *Kölnische Volkszeitung*, no. 91, 29 January 1903.
43. *Ibid*.

The threat from the S.P.D. in these areas, Pieper concluded, was "the Achilles' heel of the Center Party."[44]

The growing importance of the Christian trade unions to the Center also caused a noticeable shift in the party's stance to social reform. The Center's record in this area had been quite sporadic since the 1870s. Not until 1877 did Windthorst and Reichensperger yield to the Christian-socialists and introduce the ill-fated Galen bill. Preoccupation with the *Kulturkampf* and the continued opposition of Catholic employers had delayed the action for seven years. Paradoxically, the government's initiatives in the 1880s encouraged the Center to return to its oppositionist stance. The centralized nature of Bismarck's reforms caused fears of enhanced Prussian or, as many Centrists saw it, anti-Catholic tendencies in Germany. The 1890s witnessed little improvement. In 1895 the Center very nearly supported the Kaiser's anti-labor *"Umsturzvorlage"* in return for religious concessions, and in 1899 the party once again came close to accepting William's Prison Bill. Only the protests of the Bavarian deputies, who faced a tough electoral battle against the S.P.D. that summer, prevented the party from accepting one of the most reactionary pieces of legislation ever presented to the Reichstag.[45] However, with the rise of an *organized* Christian proletariat in the early 1900s, and the continued growth of the Center's great rival on the left, the workers could not be treated in such a cavalier fashion. Thus the party's national executive committee was careful to consult the Christian trade unions in preparing the party's election proclamation (*Wahlaufruf*) in 1903, and most of the workers' demands were incorporated in the document.[46] Later that year the Center followed through with an impressive social legislative initiative (see Chapter 7) and in the succeeding years became a fairly reliable sponsor of Christian labor's social programs in parliament. The party would take many steps in the years to come that were not in the interests of the workers, but it could no longer afford to leave its "Achilles' heel" so completely unshielded. This pro-labor imperative has been ignored, it must be said, by some historians who focus too exclusively on local, south German Center politics during the mid-Wilhelmine period.[47]

By the elections of 1903, therefore, the Christian trade unions had gained an influential political ally in the Center Party. But in the process rival organizations were supplied with even more "proof" of the *Gesamtverband*'s affilia-

44. *Präsides-Korrespondenz*, nos. 9–10, October–November 1903, pp. 266–68, StBib MG.
45. Count Lerchenfeld, Bavarian Envoy in Berlin, to Minister-President Crailsheim, 8 August 1899, Ges. Berlin, Pol. Schriftwechsel 1070, GStA München.
46. August Pieper to Adolf Gröber, 30 March 1903, Bachem Papers 193, HA Köln; Bachem, *Zentrumspartei*, vol. 7, pp. 457-60.
47. See Blackbourn, *Centre Party in Württemberg*, pp. 52–54, 193–95; and Denk, *Christliche Arbeiterbewegung in Bayern*, pp. 381–83.

tion with the Center. The effect on membership was devastating. The old nemesis of confessional hatred kept thousands of Protestant workers from joining, while many others were alienated by the unions' association with higher tariffs. The *Gesamtverband*'s loss, of course, was the General Commission's gain. From mid-1902 to mid-1904, a period of economic upswing dominated by the tariff debate and numerous state and national elections, the Christian federation grew slowly from 86,400 to about 100,000. The free trade unions, on the other hand rose meteorically from 681,100 to slightly over 1,000,000.[48]

* * * *

Reinforcing the negative impact which the merger and tariff controversies had on Christian membership growth was the debilitating effect of underdeveloped support programs at the union level. The unions affiliated with the *Gesamtverband* appear to have held their own in funds paid to striking or locked-out members,[49] although one finds no evidence that Christian national headquarters in Cologne disbursed last-resort aid like its Socialist counterpart in Hamburg. Thus in 1900 Hans Braun, a leading Christian trade unionist from Munich, advocated a central strike fund because, as he put it, "not Christianity, rather the guarantee of material advantages"[50] would hold the movement together. But nothing came of the idea and the Christian unions had to fend for themselves in the years after 1900. Not surprisingly, the Socialists, not the Christians, initiated most wage actions. The free trade unions "exploit all the advantages of the offensive," observed the police commissioner in Essen, "while their opponents are allotted the defensive. The Social Democratic union leaders understand better how to win the great masses of the people."[51] Further explanation for the ability of the free trade unions to mobilize the masses can be found in the area of supplementary unemployment, health, legal aid, travel, and funeral funds. By 1904 *Gesamtverband* unions had very little if anything to offer the worker here,[52] whereas the free trade unions administered programs which had grown sounder financially with every passing year after the mid-1890s.

48. *Protokoll der Verhandlungen des V. Kongresses der christlichen Gewerkschaften Deutschlands* (Cologne, 1904), p. 34; Varain, *Freie Gewerkschaften*, p. 36. For the political and confessional reasons behind Christian membership stagnation, see police commissioner of Düsseldorf to the *Regierungspräsident*, 1 September 1904, police commissioner of Essen to the *Regierungspräsident*, 7 September 1903, 29 August 1904, and 21 September 1904, in Reg. D. 9054–55, and the *Regierungspräsident* in Düsseldorf to the minister of the interior, 15 November 1904, Reg. D. 9041, HSA Düsseldorf.

49. Berger, *Arbeiterbewegung und Demokratisierung*, p. 86.

50. Quoted in Denk, *Christliche Arbeiterbewegung in Bayern*, p. 332.

51. Police commissioner of Essen to the *Regierungspräsident*, 29 August 1904, Reg. D. 9055, HSA Düsseldorf.

52. Berger, *Arbeiterbewegung und Demokratisierung*, pp. 47, 287.

The deficient strike and benefit programs of the Christian unions can be explained by the youth of the movement and the enervating effect of the various controversies which have been discussed in the last two chapters. But union leaders were also at fault. Influenced by their experience in confessional labor associations, where dues were kept low, Christian trade unionists like August Brust, Carl Schiffer, Carl Shirmer, and Adam Stegerwald hesitated to ask the rank and file to make heavy contributions each month.[53] Lower dues, it was felt, would attract workers away from the costlier Socialist unions. For even a few pennies a month, however, workers expected something in return, and by 1903/4 the free trade unions were seen by most potential recruits as the best bargain for the money. Only those workers who valued their "Christianity" far in excess of their "material advantages," therefore, were likely to join and remain members of a Christian trade union. Not until 1904/5 did Christian leaders realize their mistake and begin a forced-draft program to expand support funds. By this time, unfortunately, there was only a slight chance of closing the gap, for the frees were far ahead and growing at a rapid pace. Thus religious, political and *economic* factors must be appreciated in explaining the growing lead which the General Commission had opened up by the early years of the century.

The problems experienced at this time by the Christian miners' *Gewerkverein* are a good illustration of how numerous factors could converge to frustrate promotional efforts. The union was recognized by friend and foe alike as the backbone of the entire Christian labor movement, and yet in Brust the *Gewerkverein* did not possess a leader with talent equal to the position. During the great merger debate, it will be recalled, Brust had been among the loudest in calling for the formation of a cartel with the free trade unions, only to reverse himself awkwardly as a result of stern warnings from Mönchen-Gladbach about the imminent danger of church intervention. This turnaround did not enhance the image of the *Gewerkverein* in the eyes of radical workers, nor did it ward off problems in the Saar and Silesia, where the *Gewerkverein* lost tens of thousands of more conservative potential recruits to the machinations of bishops Kopp and Korum. It was also Brust who spoke out for tariffs in the columns of *Bergknappe*. In so doing, he not only associated his union with a bill which was very unpopular with most workers, but he also gave credence to the charge of "Center Party unions." The former miner compromised the political neutrality of his union still more by mobilizing the *Gewerkverein* for his own candidacy as a Center deputy during the Prussian Landtag elections of 1903.[54]

53. See the figures in *ibid.*, pp. 284, 287; and Denk, *Christliche Arbeiterbewegung in Bayern*, pp. 153, 258, 276, 331–32.

54. Police commissioner of Düsseldorf to the *Regierungspräsident*, 1 September 1904, Reg. D. 9055, HSA Düsseldorf.

At the union level, moreover, Brust was even less effective as a leader. He was most emphatic in his advocacy of low dues as a method of undermining the *Alter Verband*, and his stubborn, proprietary nature led to the hiring of few additional functionaries. This made the continued support of religious *Knappenvereine* necessary and, along with the lower dues, etc., enhanced the attractiveness of the *Alter Verband* for new recruits.[55] But Brust's greatest blunder was undoubtedly his mishandling of the significant Polish-Catholic minority in the *Gewerkverein*. Poles were not represented on the executive committee, did not receive fair consideration as candidates during *Knappschaftsverein* elections, and were frustrated in their desire for a Polish edition of *Bergknappe*. Finally, after years of neglect and prejudicial treatment, they formed their own union. Thus the Christian union lost thousands of Catholic members, a great deal of potential growth, and another opportunity to maintain its lead over the *Alter Verband*, which had never attracted as large a Polish following.

1902 was the turning point in the competition between the two unions in the Ruhr. The *Gewerkverein* slipped from 35,100 to 32,800, while the *Alter Verband* expanded from 15,000 to 20,000. Not coincidentally, the merger controversy climaxed with the founding of "Catholic trade unions" in May 1902, the Poles seceded from the *Gewerkverein* in November 1902, and Bülow's tariff bill passed in December 1902. That year, moreover, the *Alter Verband* spent seven times as much for strike support and generally possessed a more impressive benefit program. By 1903 the Social Democratic union had passed 30,000 and in mid-1904 boasted over 48,000 members in the Ruhr. The *Gewerkverein* stood embarrassingly at 36,700 in June 1904. The Christian union claimed about 6,000 members elsewhere in Germany at this time, far behind the *Alter Verband*, which had recruited 32,000 members from other mining districts.[56] The backbone of the Christian labor movement had definitely weakened.

Mindful of this, the executive committee of the *Gewerkverein* forced Brust to resign in late October 1904. The founder of the union threatened to fight his colleagues, but was dissuaded from doing so in early January 1905 by Father Heinrich Brauns and the members of the *Gesamtverband* executive committee, who knew the Christian labor movement could ill afford another embarrassing squabble.[57] Brust's ouster was a definite victory for the radical faction

55. *Regierungspräsident* Münster to the Prussian minister of the interior, 31 December 1902, HSA Düsseldorf; Imbusch, *Arbeitsverhältnis und Arbeiterorganisationen*, pp. 603–4.

56. Landratsamt Duisburg-Mühlheim 481–82, HSA Düsseldorf; police commissioner of Essen to the *Regierungsprasident*, 31 August 1902, September 1903, and 29 August 1904, Reg. D. 9053–55, HSA Düsseldorf.

57. *Zentralblatt der christlichen Gewerkschaften Deutschlands* (hereafter cited as *Zentralblatt*), no. 2, 29 January 1906; police commissioner of Düsseldorf to the *Regierungspräsident*, 1 September 1904, police commissioner of Essen to the *Regierungspräsident*, 21 and 27 September

around Johann Effert which had forced Brust to cooperate with the *Alter Verband* in 1899 and had been trying to do so again ever since Brust broke off relations with the other union in 1901. Police reports to the contrary,[58] however, Effert's faction did not reign completely supreme now in the *Gewerkverein*, for moderate leaders like Theodor Berse, Hermann Köster, the Imbusch brothers, and Father Brauns still possessed influence. The real gainers were probably the thousands of Protestant miners who had vowed never to join the union unless Brust were unhorsed.[59] Signifying the new spirit of confessional parity in the *Gewerkverein* was the appointment of Karl Kühne, one of the Evangelical *Alte Kämpfer* from the 1890s, to Brust's old position.

The Christian union had no chance to consolidate itself, however, for in the midst of this internal crisis, wildcat strikes in the mines near Bochum and Oberhausen threatened to spill over into a general strike of the Ruhr miners. By mid-January 1905 about 20 percent of the work force in *Gewerkverein*-controlled areas like Essen, Recklinghausen, and Oberhausen had struck and the Catholic masses were in an ugly mood.[60] "What do I care about *Rerum Novarum*," went one ditty, "I snap my fingers at Kopp and Korum!"[61] The pressure on Christian leaders to strike was increased by the fact that the *Gewerkverein* had earned a reputation under Brust as a spineless union due to its unwillingness to participate in many of the smaller strikes which had broken out since 1900.[62] A decision to strike, therefore, might prove once and for all that the Christian union was a real *Kampfverein*.

But other factors cautioned restraint. For one thing, the *Gewerkverein* lacked "punching-power" (*Schlagkraft*),[63] as Heinrich Imbusch put it a few years later. Thus in December 1904 the union had 271,102 marks in savings, compared to 734,901 marks for the *Alter Verband*. The Social Democratic union, moreover, could always count on additional support from the General Commission in Hamburg, while *Gesamtverband* headquarters in Cologne was much less reliable. If the Socialists decided to strike, therefore, a danger existed that the *Gewerkverein* would collapse as the angry, desperate miners flocked to the strongest union.[64]

1904, and 5 November 1904, Reg. D. 9055, HSA Düsseldorf; police commissioner of Bochum to the *Regierungspräsident*, 1 November 1904 and 16 February 1905, Arnsberg I 82, StA Münster.

58. District police commissioner Essen to the *Regierungspräsident*, 2 July 1905, Reg. Arnsberg I 82, StA Münster.

59. *Regierungspräsident* Düsseldorf to the minister of the interior, 20 December 1904, Reg. D. 9042, HSA Düsseldorf.

60. Imbusch, *Arbeitsverhältnis und Arbeiterorganisationen*, p. 603.

61. Quoted in Ross, *Beleaguered Tower*, p. 108.

62. Steinisch, "Der Gewerkverein christlicher Bergarbeiter," in Mommsen and Borsdorf (eds.), *Glückauf, Kameraden!* p. 278.

63. Imbusch, *Arbeitsverhältnis und Arbeiterorganisationen*, pp. 603–4.

64. The executive committee of the *Gewerkverein* had decided *not* to strike in December 1904.

Fortunately, a majority of *Alter Verband* leaders was also against a strike, fearing that the effects of winter, the unity of the owners, and large stockpiles of coal would spell disaster for the union. A minority faction was urging action, strongly believing that a strike would lead to a great influx of new members and perhaps crush the Christians. The rank and file had less strategic considerations in mind, but their behavior was playing into the hands of union radicals, for in *Alter Verband*-controlled areas like Dortmund, Bochum and Gelsenkirchen, 70 percent of the work force was already off the job. The lesser evil for the *Gewerkverein* would have been to ignore wildcatting Christian miners and call for state intervention on behalf of the workers, and in this way strengthen the hand of moderates in the *Alter Verband*. Hermann Köster, Heinrich Imbusch, and even the "hotspur" Johann Effert, argued along these lines at an assembly of the various miners' unions on 12 January. To save face before the ranks, it was agreed to strike on the sixteenth if state mediation produced no results.[65]

The *Gewerkverein*'s strategy failed to save the union from the dreaded general strike. Pressure on union leaders to strike increased tremendously during the four-day "truce" as the ranks of striking workers swelled uncontrollably from 64,000 to 108,000, or about 39 percent of the total force of Ruhr miners. By the sixteenth, moreover, state mediators had made no impression whatsoever on the confident mine owners. Thus the Socialist, Christian, Polish, and Hirsch-Duncker unions finally joined the wildcatters, and the number of strikers grew quickly to 218,000 or 78 percent of the miners. As Imbusch, Effert, *et al.* had feared, the *Alter Verband* was the main beneficiary of this action, despite the fact that the strike was only a marginal success. Able to disburse nearly five times as much in strike benefits, the Socialist union won 80,000 new recruits. The *Gewerkverein* claimed about 38,000 new members, but had clearly fallen further behind its competition.[66]

As a result, valiant efforts were made to restructure the union and make it more *schlagkräftig*. Recruiting stations were finally removed from the *Arbeiter-* and *Knappenvereine*, regular union locals established, and the number of functionaries increased from 13 to 26. Dues were raised to bolster the treasury, and the executive committee was streamlined and made more effi-

See the district police commissioner of Essen to the *Regierungspräsident*, 21 December 1904, 403/7030 LHA Koblenz.

65. See *ibid.*, and also: *Regierungspräsident* Düsseldorf to the *Oberpräsident* of the Rhineland, 6 January 1905, 403/7030, and *Bericht über die am 12. Januar 1905 in Essen abgehaltene Delegiertenversamlung der an der Ausstandsbewegung der Bergarbeiter im Ruhrgebiet beteiligten Organisationen*, pp. 5–6, 10, 403/7031, LHA Koblenz; Imbusch, *Arbeitsverhältnis und Arbeiterorganisationen*, p. 603.

66. Police commissioner of Essen to the *Regierungspräsident*, 1 September 1906, Reg. D. 9058, HSA Düsseldorf; Imbusch, *Arbeitsverhältnis und Arbeiterorganisationen*, p. 590.

cient, while the *Ehrenrat*, which had not played a great role since 1898, was finally abolished. In order to attract Protestants, furthermore, parity between the confessions was guaranteed on the executive committee; thus Karl Kühne, the Evangelical chairman of the union, was joined by Franz Behrens, a well-known Protestant labor organizer from Berlin, who was appointed to the new post of secretary general.

The *Gewerkverein* also participated actively in the factory-level management-labor committees which had been established by the Prussian government after the miners' strike. These committees proved successful in raising wages, and, because the institution had been part of Christian labor's platform for decades, credit for this redounded upon Kühne, Behrens, and the *Gewerkverein*.[67]

These developments had an interesting effect upon relations with the Social Democrats. Before the strike of 1905 the Christian union had experienced four years of recruiting losses to the more dynamic *Alter Verband*. So much so, in fact, that Socialist labor leaders expected the *Gewerkverein* to collapse during the great wage action of that year. When this did not occur, the Social Democrats continued to push for the defeat of their rival, urging members to desert and boycotting the elections to the local factory committees, which were castigated as an attempt to manipulate the proletariat. The *Alter Verband* also tried to transform the newly founded *Siebenerkommission*, a committee of union leaders representing the interests of all four organizations which had struck, into a roof organization controlled by the Socialists. The revitalization of the *Gewerkverein*, however, effected a change of tactics. Sensing that the committees were a source of increased Christian strength, the *Alter Verband* began to place more emphasis on working through them and in general became much more conciliatory toward a foe whose resilience had been underestimated. Thus the Christian union was able to ward off the threat to its existence and force a more moderate strategy upon its arch-rival.[68]

But none of these efforts succeeded in reversing the momentum which the *Alter Verband* had gained by 1905. The ever-perceptive police commissioner of Essen has left us a very concise explanation for this.

> In spite of everything, the growth of the Christian trade unions lags behind that of the Social Democratic unions. Social life in the various local branches

67. Police commissioner Dortmund to *Regierungspräsident* Arnsberg, 10 October 1905, Reg. Arnsberg I 97, StA Münster; police commissioner Essen to *Regierungspräsident* Düsseldorf, 30 September 1907, Reg. D. 9059, HSA Düsseldorf.

68. *Regierungspräsident* Düsseldorf to the minister of the interior, 26 September 1905, Reg. D. 9041, *Regierungspräsident* Arnsberg to the minister of the interior, 22 December 1905, Reg. D. 9041, *Düsseldorfer Volkszeitung* (clipping in: Reg. D. 9057), police commissioner Düsseldorf to the *Regierungspräsident* Düsseldorf, 1 September 1906, Reg. D. 9058, and *Oberbürgermeister* Essen to the *Regierungspräsident* Düsseldorf, 28 August 1907, Reg. D. 9059, HSA Düsseldorf.

> of the Christian unions is not as brisk as in the Social Democratic, and everywhere assemblies are poorly attended. Only on special occasions is it possible to mobilize members for the good of the union. But also the leaders of the union locals of both directions exhibit noticeable differences in their knowledge of social affairs and tact in leading a labor organization. This results quite frequently in a situation where the speeches of the Social Democratic unionists during joint assemblies of the two unions, given a more skillful approach and a more radical political stance, are more effective, and the Christian trade unionists are forced into the role of mere hangers-on. The consequence of this, however, is that Christian workers believe their interests are better represented in the Social Democratic trade unions, and gradually, after the organizational thinking of Christian workers has been awakened in a Christian trade union, they cross over to a Social Democratic organization.[69]

The *Gewerkverein* had introduced numerous reforms and championed the popular management-labor committees, but a few months' work could not erase the accumulated effect of a decade of clerical opposition, involuntary compromises, and tactical mistakes. In this sense the *Gewerkverein* mirrored the problems facing the entire Christian labor movement in 1904/5.

* * * *

The jolting experience of the merger controversy, the bitter infighting over tariffs, the mixed blessing of the Reichstag campaign of 1903, the failure of the *Gesamtverband* to construct a sound system of support programs, and other problems had changed the complexion of the Christian labor movement. From dreams of dominating the trade union world and forging a strong new political coalition, the unions now found themselves torn internally, weak financially, bobbing ineffectually in the wake of the Center Party, and far behind their rival in the labor world. Given these unfavorable circumstances it is understandable that Christian labor leaders and their bourgeois allies began to look increasingly to the political arena for the desired victory over the Socialist labor movement. If the Christian trade unions could wrest significant socio-political concessions from the stingy Reich government, surely the rank and file workers would abandon the negativism of the Socialists and flock to the movement responsible for these improvements. Indeed the instrument for revitalizing the overall position of Christian labor had already been formed by the fall of 1903. These efforts will be the subject of the next chapter.

69. Police commissioner of Essen to the *Regierungspräsident*, 1 September 1906, Reg. D. 9058, HSA Düsseldorf.

7

The Frankfurt Workers' Congress of 1903

"Since the 1870s we've had the so-called *Kulturkampf*," noted August Brust, Catholic founder of the *Gewerkverein*, to a Protestant colleague in 1894.

> Both Christian confessions [he continued] have bitterly struggled against one another—at the workers' expense. With the establishment of a Christian miners' union, we must once again progress to the point where the two religious communities get along with one another peacefully. This would also serve the interests of the working class.[1]

At the time the statement was made, Brust had primarily trade union cooperation in mind. But the relevance of his observation for labor *politics* was certainly not lost on the tough-minded miner; in the years to come, as the Christian unions struggled unsuccessfully against the economic and *political* might of capital, the spirit of nondenominationalism was carried over necessarily into the legislative arena.

The first manifestation of this interconfessional political strategy was the German Workers' Congress. Under discussion since 1900/1901, it was finally held at Frankfurt a. M. in late October 1903. By demonstrating their loyalty to the Kaiser and dissociating themselves from the S.P.D., the 620,000 workers represented there hoped to facilitate reform of Germany's rigid laws of assembly and association, obtain legal, corporate status for trade unions, and promote establishment of management-labor chambers. The non-Socialist parties of the Reichstag, so often divided along religious lines, would be driven

1. Quoted in Karl Kühne, "Kampf," in Cwiklinski, *August Brust*, p. 10.

together into a united coalition which the Kaiser, already impressed with the loyalty and patriotism of "his" German laborers, would not ignore.

The Christian trade unions had taken part in most of the preparations for the Congress and were undoubtedly the most prestigious organization in attendance. The *Gesamtverband*, however, was not responsible for initiating the 1903 demonstration. Hard-pressed by serious internal and external difficulties, Christian leaders had postponed their socio-political plans indefinitely by 1902.[2] The prime mover behind the Frankfurt Congress, in fact, was Adolf Stöcker's Christian-Social Party.

As explained earlier, the Christian-Socials turned increasingly to the workers for political support after the early 1890s. By the turn of the century, these efforts were beginning to bear fruit. The *Kölnische Volkszeitung* spoke for all progressive Catholic circles when it welcomed the pro-labor position of Stöcker's Evangelical faction in June 1900, and in a few overwhelmingly Protestant areas like Detmold, Siegen, and Dillenburg, this friendly relationship resulted in close ties between union locals and Christian-Social Party cells (*Ortsgruppen*).[3] Nowhere were these links closer than in Berlin, heart of Protestant Germany and home of Stöcker's original movement. The *Freie Kirchlich-soziale Konferenz*, a Christian-Social version of the *Volksverein*, established its first *Volksbüro* there in October 1899, recruiting Franz Behrens, an Evangelical unionist and Stöcker devotee, as bureau chief. The new agency was instrumental in forming the Berlin Cartel of Christian Trade Unions in July 1900, and actually performed the administrative functions of that body for the first few months.[4] In November 1901, moreover, Behrens and *Konferenz* general secretary Lic. Reinhardt Mumm united the Berlin Cartel, the Protestant and Catholic *Arbeitervereine*, the local branches of the Hamburg-based Association of Patriotic Retail Clerks, and a few lesser worker groups in a political organization designed to exert influence on city councils and elect Christian workers to industrial courts, health insurance committees (*Krankenkassenvorstände*), and other social institutions. The Committee for Labor Elections and Social Affairs, as the Christian-Socials' new group was called, expanded its activities to the national level in October 1902 by estab-

2. *Mitteilungen des Gesamtverbandes*, no. 19, 21 September 1903.

3. *Kölnische Volkszeitung*, no. 512, 5 June 1900; Dietrich von Oertzen, *Erinnerungen aus meinem Leben* (Berlin: Verlag von Edwin Runge, 1915), pp. 129-33; *Protokoll des 7. Christlich-Socialen Parteitages in Mülheim a. d. Ruhr am 23. September 1903*, p. 5, StBibMG (hereafter cited as: CS Protocol 1903).

4. Dietrich von Oertzen and Franz Behrens, *Patriarchalische Verhältnisse und modernes Arbeitsrecht: Mit dem Geschäftsbericht des Generalsekretariats und einem Überblick über die 10. Hauptversammlung der kirchlich-sozialen Konferenz* (Berlin: Verlag der vaterländischen Verlags-und Kunstanstalt, 1905), pp. 9, 11 (hereafter cited as: *Kirchlich-soziale Konferenz: Geschäftsbericht 1905*); Franz Behrens, "Franz Behrens," in *25 Jahre christliche Gewerkschaftsbewegung*, pp. 155-57.

lishing a secretariat in Berlin to represent the views of Christian workers before the Reich Insurance Office.[5]

As Stöcker observed in 1903, however, the party had much more work ahead of it. The Christian-Socials would never achieve dramatic success at the polls until they established a much closer relationship with the Christian trade unions in western Germany and promoted a program of "energetic, organized, sustained social action"[6] throughout the Reich.

The decision to push ahead with the German Workers' Congress must be viewed as part of this overall effort. The idea originated with Mumm and Behrens and was quickly seconded by Francke and Berlepsch of the Society for Social Reform.[7] As Mumm explained later, however, only workers were to play an overt role during the proceedings.

> The genuine proletarian nature of the rally was to be represented plainly for all those who spoke so readily of [the Christian workers as] "a gang of puppets" [*Gängelband*]. Also, if rights were to be demanded for the workers, it seemed morally correct that the workers themselves should offer public proof of their readiness to attain these new rights.[8]

Preparations for the Congress were therefore placed solely in the hands of Behrens, who took up the matter with the executive board of the Committee for Labor Elections and Social Affairs on 14 January 1903.[9] The board accepted Behrens's proposals and agreed that he should approach Max Hirsch, leader of the Hirsch-Duncker unions, and Ludwig Weber, chairman of the National Association of Evangelical *Arbeitervereine*. The Berlin representatives of the Patriotic Retail Clerks and Catholic *Arbeitervereine* would speak with their respective leaders, Wilhelm Schack and Lic. Fournelle, while Ernst Francke, who was also present at the meeting, was chosen to formulate a public proclamation (*Aufruf*) and draw up a tentative agenda. The National Social Christian Tischendöffer had already taken the liberty of informing Giesberts about the Congress. To heighten the impact of the Congress, it was scheduled for late May or early June 1903, shortly before the Reichstag elections.[10]

5. For the Committee for Labor Elections and Social Affairs, see Franz Behrens, "Franz Behrens," p. 158; and *Mitteilungen des Gesamtverbandes*, no. 16, 11 August 1902, and nos. 24–25 for 31 November and 14 December 1903.
6. CS Protocol 1903, p. 4.
7. Francke to Berlepsch, 15 January 1903, Berlepsch Papers 36, ZStA Merseburg. See also the *Kölnische Volkszeitung*, no. 1012, 30 December 1903, for Francke's denial that the Society for Social Reform was the prime mover behind the Congress.
8. Reinhard Mumm, "Ausbildungskurse," *Die Arbeit*, no. 34, 20 August 1910.
9. Francke to Berlepsch, 15 January 1903, Berlepsch Papers 36, ZStA Merseburg.
10. *Ibid.*

But the Congress was to be much more than a one-time electoral demonstration. In keeping, no doubt, with earlier talks between Catholic and Protestant labor leaders, Mumm and Behrens hoped that permanent ties could be established once non-Socialist laborers had assembled in the same hall. Just as Protestants, Catholics, trade unionists, and *Arbeitervereinler* had come together in Berlin, so should the national organizations cooperate to attain common political goals.[11] At the helm of the Congress, exhorting the non-Socialist proletariat to push for goals that for years had eluded the Society for Social Reform, would be the Christian-Socials' own Franz Behrens. Here was "energetic, organized, sustained social action" *par excellence*.

The decision of the Christian trade unions to join the other organizations at Frankfurt can probably be attributed to the forcefulness and new-found influence of the *Gesamtverband's* general secretary, Adam Stegerwald. The enthusiasm of the former cabinet-maker's apprentice for the Christian-Social initiative stemmed from a deep-seated hatred of the free trade unions, whose backers had always insulted him, as well as from a strongly felt aversion to the S.P.D., which he felt would lead the working class to ruin by provoking the wrath of the Kaiser.[12] Stegerwald was also pleased with the thoroughly secular nature of the demonstration. "When Leo XIII let Christian democracy fall in 1901," he recalled years later, "I spoke no more of the church's social teachings as a creative system of thought . . . Rather, I promoted all-German social politics, hoping that here creative energies could be found and developed."[13] The idea of a German Workers' Congress, furthermore, was in keeping with the general secretary's dislike for the narrow, provincial *Kirchturmspolitik* of many Catholic and Evangelical religious leaders.[14] And perhaps most important of all, Stegerwald, as the chief administrator of the Christian trade unions, was quite familiar with the *Gesamtverband*'s organizational and financial disadvantages vis-à-vis the free trade unions. The idea of a bold *political* stroke to win the masses must therefore have appealed to him. Thus Stegerwald

11. See Behrens's remarks at Frankfurt, *Protokoll der Verhandlungen des Deutschen Arbeiterkongresses* (Hagen: Verlag von Otto Rippel, 1903), pp. 71-72.

12. Adam Stegerwald, "Adam Stegerwald," in *25 Jahre christliche Gewerkschaftsbewegung*, pp. 134-35, 137.

13. Stegerwald to Thomas Esser, 5 June 1940, Kl. Erw. 471–72, BA Koblenz. The encyclical *Graves de Communi*, issued on 18 January 1901, was interpreted by many, Stegerwald included, as a reversal of the support for social reform announced by the pope in *Rerum Novarum*. This was not the case, but Leo's warning that "Christian democracy" was incompatible with the concept of a *Volksstaat* where all citizens possessed equal social and political rights was well suited to disillusion social reformers like Stegerwald. The fact that Stegerwald was auditing Lujo Brentano's courses in economics and political science at the University of Münich that winter must have further influenced the young unionist to think solely in terms of a secular approach to politics. See Adam Stegerwald, "Adam Stegerwald," p. 135. For *Graves de Communi*, see Hubert Jedin (ed.), *Handbuch der Kirchengeschichte*, vol. 6, part 2, pp. 243, 250-52.

14. *Der deutsche Holzarbeiter*, no. 10, 1900, cited in Gasteiger, *Christliche Gewerkschaften in Süddeutschland*, p. 277.

defended Behrens's plan and soon established a close working relationship with the Stöcker advocate. The politics of nondenominationalism had found two determined champions.

After the positive response from western Germany, Behrens arranged a caucus between representatives of the Hirsch-Duncker unions (110,000), the *Gesamtverband* (93,000), the Evangelical *Arbeitervereine* (71,000), and the Catholic *Arbeitervereine* of southern (66,000), western (63,000), and eastern Germany (45,000). The Christian organizations had united beforehand on an agenda for the Congress proposed by Francke and Berlepsch, and were hopeful that the liberal unions would follow suit. The liberal spokesman, Hirsch's second-in-command, Carl Goldschmidt, had no objections to an agenda that included coalition and assembly rights, recognition of the corporate status of trade unions, and management-labor chambers. He therefore announced that his organization would also participate. A provisional committee led by Behrens and Stegerwald was formed to make final arrangements.[15]

Unfortunately for the Christian organizations, Goldschmidt was not the real power in the Hirsch-Duncker organization. Until his death in 1905, Max Hirsch was the only decisive voice on the central committee (*Zentralrat*), and the aging founder of the liberal unions had nothing but contempt for those who had dragged Christianity into the labor movement. Hirsch had no desire to send a representative to the caucus in Berlin in March 1903 and did so only because he could not avoid the meeting. Representatives of the various labor groups were already in the capital for the general commission session of the Society for Social Reform.[16] Nor did Hirsch feel afterwards, like Goldschmidt, that all barriers to participation at Frankfurt had been removed. The union patriarch saw no reason why he should cooperate with labor organizations "that are not really neutral and neglect or even fight against other goals which are highly important to the workers"[17]—a thinly veiled reference to the tariff issue. He also considered management-labor chambers a "dubious"[18] institution which could easily be turned against trade unions. Despite repeated entreaties by Berlepsch,[19] therefore, Hirsch refused to join the other organizations. The Hirsch-Duncker steering committee seconded him at a session in late spring 1903.[20]

15. *Zentralblatt*, no. 22, 4 November 1907; Paul Umbreit, *Die gegnerischen Gewerkschaften in Deutschland* (Berlin: Verlag der Generalkommission der Gewerkschaften Deutschlands, 1907), p. 125; *Bericht über die Verhandlungen des zweiten Deutschen Arbeiter-Congresses* (Cologne: Christlicher Gewerkschaftsverlag [Adam Stegerwald], 1907), p. 66.
16. *Zentralblatt*, no. 22, 4 November 1907; *Mitteilungen des Gesamtverbandes*, no. 6, 23 March 1903.
17. Hirsch's explanation is printed in the *Zentralblatt*, no. 22, 4 November 1907.
18. *Ibid.*
19. Francke to Berlepsch, 20 and 30 September 1903, Berlepsch Papers 36, ZStA Merseburg.
20. No rationale for the refusal was given to the provisional committee of the congress at this time. *Protokoll der Verhandlungen des Deutschen Arbeiterkongresses*, p. 13.

The members of the provisional committee were greatly shaken by the *Zentralrat*'s refusal and momentarily considered canceling their plans. Without the Hirsch-Duncker unions, the largest single organization in the bourgeois labor movement, the demonstrative effect of the Congress would be greatly reduced. In mid-June, however, it was decided to proceed without the liberals in the fall. Emotion played a great role in the decision. The initial feeling of disappointment soon turned to anger at the Hirsch-Duncker *Zentralrat*, stiffening Christian leaders in their resolve to go it alone. Confidence increased during the summer as more and more enthusiasm for the venture was evidenced in other sectors of the non-Socialist labor world. The Provisional Committee received positive replies to its inquiries from the Catholic *Gesellenvereine* (60,000), Schack's white-collar employees (47,000), the Trier Railwaymen (54,000), Württembergian and Bavarian transport workers (30,000), and a vast array of independent *Arbeitervereine* and factory clubs totaling about 75,000. With this additional support, the Provisional Committee could feel confident that the Congress would have a significant impact on public, and hopefully official, opinion. A show of non-Socialist labor strength seemed particularly crucial, moreover, after the Socialist electoral victories that June. With rumors circulating that social reforms would be discontinued and universal suffrage abrogated to punish the "ungrateful" workers, it seemed high time to advertise the fact that hundreds of thousands of German proletarians, though upset by the lack of certain social reforms, were nevertheless loyal to Kaiser and Reich.[21]

Tact was indeed the best policy in the summer of 1903. For, significantly enough, the Reich chancellor had begun to take a greater interest in social reform than heretofore. Bülow's change of heart, as so many of his decisions, was based largely on opportunistic considerations. To survive politically, Bülow had to achieve success on those issues most important to the Kaiser. These, in 1902/3, were the Midland Canal, passage of tariff and commercial treaty bills, and, most important of all, completion of the fleet. William was not satisfied with the level of naval construction in 1903 and was already demanding a third naval bill financed from increased taxation of tobacco, beer, and brandy. Bülow knew full well that passage of tariff, naval, and tax bills in the Reichstag would require a series of *quid pro quo* agreements with the various parties, especially the Center, which occupied the pivotal position in parliament. Center demands for repeal of the anti-Jesuit laws, payment of Reichstag deputies, and new social legislation, however, would meet considerable opposition in the Bundesrat. Flirtation with the Catholics would also infuriate the reactionary clique of courtiers surrounding the Kaiser. Bülow had

21. *Ibid.*, pp. 5-10. 13-14; *Zentralblatt*, no. 22, 4 November 1907.

never been popular in these circles and was greatly concerned that their intrigues would someday spell disaster for him.[22]

With powerful adversaries in government and the Kaiser's entourage, Bülow had no recourse but to convince William of the need for parliamentary concessions. If it were clear that the emperor favored passage of certain bills, reactionaries at court would be foiled and opposition in the Bundesrat mollified. The chancellor took every opportunity in the winter of 1902/3, therefore, to persuade the Kaiser to support repeal of the anti-Jesuit laws. And, to bolster the monarch's sagging confidence in the efficacy of social reform, Bülow arranged a number of audiences for Dr. Adolf Harnack, Stöcker's activist counterpart among the liberal theologians. It was surely no coincidence, moreover, that Georg Hinzpeter began to correspond with William again on a regular basis.[23] In a system which bred intrigue, Bülow could play with the best.

These efforts were not without effect. In early 1903 the chancellor expressed confidence that the Kaiser's antipathy toward the Jesuits was yielding to the dictates of political reason.[24] Bülow also won imperial approval for payment of Reichstag deputies.[25] Furthermore, there were positive signs concerning social reform. At the traditional reception of the *Oberpräsidenten* in Berlin on New Year's Day 1903, William advocated some form of state-recognized vocational representation for the workers[26] and predicted that they could be won away from the S.P.D. if treated "in a benevolent fashion."[27] During a Reichstag speech on 20 January 1903, Bülow informed the startled deputies that the Kaiser was firm in his belief that German laborers should have equal rights. Significantly, these rights "would find their expression in the law."[28] So confident was William that the workers would not desert the monarchy, in fact, that he treated the election results of June very nonchalantly. Bülow's archrival, Field Marshal Alfred Waldersee, noted shortly before the run-off elections (*Stichwahlen*) that William placed too much store

22. This paragraph is based on the diary entries of the reactionary Count Alfred von Waldersee for 11 January, 19 January, 8 December, and 13 December 1903. Heinrich Otto Meisner (ed.), *Denkwürdigkeiten des General-Feldmarschalls Alfred Grafen von Waldersee* (Berlin: Deutsche Verlags-Anstalt, 1923), vol. 3, pp. 200–202, 222–23.

23. See Waldersee's entries for 11 January, 19 January, 2 February, and 8 February 1903, in *ibid.*, vol. 3, pp. 200–202, 205, 207.

24. Waldersee entry for 19 January 1903, in *ibid.*, p. 201.

25. Waldersee entry for 4 February 1903, in *ibid.*, p. 206.

26. See the remarks of Reich secretary of the interior Posadowsky before the Prussian Ministry of State on 26 January 1904, Reichskanzlei, Nr. 532, Bl. 38–45, ZStA Potsdam. The Kaiser promised the workers "eine geordnete Vertretung ihrer Fachinteressen," which was a clear reference to management-labor chambers.

27. Waldersee entry for 11 January 1903, in Meissner (ed.), *Alfred Grafen von Waldersee*, vol. 3, p. 200.

28. Reichstag Debates, Period 10, Session 2 (20 January 1903), p. 7430.

in the hurrahs of the masses and "believes he has the recipe to win the workers."[29] The Kaiser seemed to have revived the *Volksmonarchie* which had given rise to such great hopes at the outset of his reign.

By mid-summer, however, this positive state of mind had begun to yield to the pessimistic, gloomy arguments of those in court, military, and Conservative Party circles.[30] During a cruise in the North Sea in early August, the recitation of a recent article concerning the political events of 1848 sent William into a fit of "pathological violence"[31] over the coming revolution and the need to suppress it brutally. Far from deserving equal rights, the masses were now described as "beasts that can only be controlled and directed by very definite orders."[32] The Kaiser soon returned to a more optimistic point of view, but, as Bülow learned from the courtier Count Eulenburg, a relapse was not unlikely. "You will—with a certain amount of justice—answer the question, 'How is H.M.?' with 'Going strong! The trip has done him good!. . . But when you are in bed at night. . .you will probably torment yourself and wonder how much longer you will be able to say that."[33]

Bülow must have had doubts of his own that year concerning the firmness of William's commitment to the cause of social reform, for the chancellor made no legislative initiative along these lines in the session of 1902/3. To the inquiries of subordinates concerning Trimborn's demand for management-labor chambers in March, Reich secretary of the interior Posadowsky replied that action would have to be postponed "indefinitely" (*bis auf weiteres*).[34] A Reichstag resolution that same month concerning introduction of a bill in the 1903/4 session guaranteeing trade unions corporate status met with the same negative results.[35] The government's disposition began to change, however, with the news on 7 September that a congress of non-Socialist workers would be held in late October.[36] As Francke learned from an informant in the Reich Chancellery, the *Aufruf* bolstered Bülow's confidence at a critical moment. By pointing to hundreds of thousands of loyal workers, he would reduce the

29. Waldersee entry for 21 June 1903, in Meissner (ed.), *Alfred Grafen von Waldersee*, vol. 3, p. 217.
30. The mood at court is described well by Count Robert Zedlitz-Trützschler, *Twelve Years at the Imperial German Court* (New York: George H. Doran Co., 1924), pp. 50–53.
31. Bernhard von Bülow, *Memoirs of Prince von Bülow* (Boston: Little, Brown and Company, 1931), vol. 1, p. 707.
32. *Ibid.*, p. 707.
33. Eulenburg to Bülow, 9 August 1903, reprinted in Johannes Haller, *Philip Eulenburg: The Kaiser's Friend* (New York: Alfred A. Knopf, 1930), pp. 160–61.
34. Posadowsky's directive of March 1903 was cited by *Regierungsrat* Spielhagen in a report of 15 November 1903, in Reichsministerium des Innern, Nr. 6765, Bl. 239, ZStA Potsdam.
35. Klaus Saul, *Staat, Industrie, und Arbeiterbewegung im Kaiserreich* (Düsseldorf: Bertelsmann Universitätsverlag, 1974), p. 37.
36. See Posadowsky's circular to the Prussian Ministry of State, 29 October 1906, Reichskanzlei, Nr. 533, Bl. 71, ZStA Potsdam.

influence of reactionary anti-labor elements at court.[37] The news about the Congress coincided with related developments that increased the pressure on Bülow to act. Although the evidence is not conclusive, it seems that Center leader Peter Spahn told Bülow during their talk at Norderney in early September that the Center would introduce a resolution reflecting the Congress's demands in December.[38] Not to be outdone by the Christians, moreover, Hirsch-Duncker leaders decided to submit a separate petition at the opening of the fall session of the Reichstag.[39] Sufficiently impressed, Bülow informed Posadowsky in mid-October 1903 that he could begin preliminary work on a bill granting trade unions corporate status.[40]

The chancellor also received Francke for a confidential discussion a few days before the delegates assembled at Frankfurt.[41] The Chancellor sympathized with most of the workers' demands and had no objections to receiving a delegation after the completion of the proceedings. Bülow asked only that Francke inform him what the workers would say so that he could discuss his reply beforehand with the Kaiser. Largely as a result of Bülow's change of course and the success of intrigues at court, the German Workers' Congress had achieved a certain measure of success before it ever convened.

The debates at Frankfurt did nothing to detract from this auspicious beginning. A telegram was sent to the Kaiser proclaiming the patriotism of the participating organizations, and William, always moved by such testaments of loyalty, returned an encouraging reply. The proceedings were also evidence enough that the workers were "ready" to take on new rights and responsibilities. The three addresses by Giesberts (Management-Labor Chambers), Schiffer (Rights of Assembly and Association), and Schack (Corporate Status of Trade Unions) were well reasoned pleas for reform. And, under the able management of Behrens and Stegerwald, all resolutions passed without the friction and dissent one might have expected from such a wide assortment of organizations. Equally impressive was the fact that Behrens found adequate backing for his proposal of permanent political cooperation between the various groups present. The Provisional Committee was transformed into a per-

37. Francke to Berlepsch, 30 September 1903, Berlepsch Papers 36, ZStA Merseburg.

38. For evidence on Spahn's annual meetings with Bülow, see Dr. Martin Spahn, "Das Jahr 1906," in *Das deutsche Volk*, no. 29, 15 July 1928 (clipping in: Bachem Papers 923, HA Köln). The main purpose of these talks was to inform the chancellor of party plans for the upcoming session. It seems highly likely, therefore, that the Center's resolution of December 1903 was discussed.

39. *Kölnische Zeitung*, no. 983, 21 October 1903. The meeting of the Hirsch-Duncker *Zentralrat* took place on 1 October 1903.

40. Francke to Berlepsch, 21 October 1903, Berlepsch Papers 36, ZStA Potsdam.

41. Francke describes the conversation in *ibid*.

manent executive board which would strive for the execution of the Congress's resolutions. The delegates would gather again before fall 1906.[42]

The response of parties and press reflected the fact that a political force of considerable importance had emerged. Socialist papers continued to speak of "puppets" and "well-behaved children,"[43] but privately, party leaders were worried. In April Karl Kautsky, a prominent theoretician in the S.P.D., expressed concern that the government might be able to split the party by pursuing an opportunistic policy of social legislation. "But that is not probable. Neither the Kaiser, the Junkers, nor big business is clever enough to introduce these policies which are so dangerous to us, policies which Bülow would certainly like to make."[44] In the long run Kautsky would be proven correct, but one can imagine the anxiety felt in Socialist circles that October when it appeared the Bülow, having strengthened his position, was evidently prepared to cooperate with the new Congress. Thus the derision which Socialists heaped upon the gathering of Christian workers in 1903 must have masked a very grudging respect for a serious rival in the labor world. The General Commission of free trade unions, interestingly enough, was less anxious to mock the Congress, fearing no doubt that such attacks might backfire.[45]

Progressive organs were also less critical than heretofore. The *Frankfurter Zeitung* regarded the independence shown by the Christian workers as a great step forward, while the *Berliner Tageblatt*, though pessimistic concerning chances for legislative success, was nevertheless full of praise for the effort.[46] This positive reaction carried over into National Liberal circles as well. Most party papers echoed the supportive stance of Bassermann and the majority of the Reichstag *Fraktion*, while the normally conservative *Kölnische Zeitung*, not wishing to swim against the current of liberalism's "frank approval" (*rundes Einverständnis*)[47] of the Congress, expressed a cautious acceptance, too. Center and Christian-Social journalists added their plaudits to those of the Liberals, as did academic and government-oriented papers like *Soziale Praxis*, *Preussische Jahrbücher*, and the *Norddeutsche Allgemeine Zeitung*. *Reichsbote*, an organ representing Stöcker's sympathizers within the Conservative Party,[48] was equally complimentary.

42. *Protokoll der Verhandlungen des Deutschen Arbeiterkongresses*, pp. 16, 71–82.
43. Quoted in the *Neue Preussische Kreuzzeitung*, no. 503, 27 October 1903.
44. Kautsky to Adler, 4 April 1903, printed in Adler, *Victor Adler Briefwechsel*, p. 416.
45. For the free trade union response, see *Bergknappe*, no. 49, 5 December 1903; and *Mitteilungen des Gesamtverbandes*, no. 21, 29 October 1903.
46. *Frankfurter Zeitung*, no. 298, 27 October 1903; *Berliner Tageblatt*, no. 551, 29 October 1903.
47. *Kölnische Zeitung*, no. 1013, 29 October 1903.
48. For the response of these papers and others, see the *Kölnische Volkszeitung*, nos. 908, 918, and 927, for 29 October, 1 November, and 4 November 1903.

Generally speaking, however, the German Right regarded the new phalanx of non-Socialist proletarians as a highly dubious phenomenon. Iron and steel magnates in the Ruhr and Saar were alarmed by the "radical" nature of the Frankfurt resolutions, as was Henry A. Bueck, Chairman of the Central Association of German Industrialists. The nationalist workers might think they were opposing the Socialists, but if unlimited coalition rights were obtained, the class struggle would only be intensified. Then both owners and loyal workers would be overpowered by the S.P.D.[49] The Conservatives came to much the same conclusion. Too much emphasis had been placed on rights and not enough on duties at Frankfurt. Freer coalition laws would strengthen the Socialists in the cities and, what was worse, spread their cause to the country. The concept of codetermination embodied in management-labor chambers was also objectionable to Conservatives. The working class, they assumed, was too alienated to work harmoniously with employers.[50] Like the industrialists, the agrarians had accepted Marx's basic premise: the inevitability of the class struggle. From this vantage point it was only logical to conclude that a more liberal political course would not only hasten the coming clash, but also weaken the state's capability to defend itself.

Bülow could not afford to indulge in such views.[51] By late 1903, in fact, pressure on him to introduce social reforms became even greater. A tax reform bill had been presented to the Reichstag in December 1903 which, for passage, would require careful consideration of Center Party demands.[52] Too, the obstinate behavior of the *Bund der Landwirte* had worsened the prospects of Conservative support for the chancellor's commercial treaties.[53] Thus Center backing in this area had also become more crucial. With the Kaiser still hesitant on the Jesuit issue, moreover, social reform was the only concession which Bülow could offer Catholics in parliament.[54] National Liberals and

49. *Deutsche Industrie-Zeitung*, nos. 44–45, 30 October and 6 November 1903. For the negative response of other business-oriented papers such as *Post*, the *Rheinisch- Westfälische Tageblatt*, and the *Anti-sozialdemokratische Korrespondenz*, see *Bergknappe*, no. 47, 21 November 1903.
50. *Neue Preussische Zeitung (Kreuzzeitung)*, nos. 503 and 513, 27 October and 1 November 1903. For the negative response of other Conservative papers such as the *Deutsche Tageszeitung* and *Konservative Korrespondenz*, see *Bergknappe*, no. 47, 21 November 1903, and the *Kölnische Zeitung*, no. 1013, 29 October 1903.
51. On 27 December 1903 the Conservative deputy Stolberg urged Bülow to strike against the Socialists (Bülow Papers 107, BA Koblenz). Bülow replied on 7 January 1904 that such an initiative would set the bourgeois parties against one another, ruining his efforts at creating a solid majority for his programs (Reichskanzlei, Nr. 1391-5, Bl. 41, ZStA Potsdam).
52. For Bülow's attempts to moderate Center demands, see Bülow to Count Ballestrem, 7 April 1904, Bülow Papers 107, BA Koblenz; and Bülow to Archbishop Kopp, 13 March 1904, Bachem Papers 218, HA Köln.
53. Posadowsky before the Prussian Ministry of State, 26 January 1904, Reichskanzlei, Nr. 532, Bl. 38–45, ZStA Potsdam. Posadowsky was speaking, it must be noted, under authorization (*im Auftrag*) of Bülow.
54. *Ibid.*

Progressives, it was hoped, would also be beholden. Posadowsky was therefore instructed to urge the various ministries of state within the empire to consider an obliging response to the Frankfurt Congress.

Posadowsky's remarks before the Bundesrat and Prussian Ministry of State in January 1904 were well suited for the conservative noblemen and patricians on these bodies. The day had passed, began the secretary, when the S.P.D. could be treated with force. Such policies had only helped the party along the way to its present strength. The only recourse was to promote the *embourgeoisement* of the radical Socialist movement, and the program of the Frankfurt Workers' Congress offered the best chance of doing so. By recognizing trade unions and creating a freer environment for their activities, the government could win the masses from the S.P.D. and force it to adopt moderate views. The price, moreover, would be minimal, for the authorities would maintain adequate controls over the labor movement and could more easily justify action to halt radical activity that violated the workers' new rights and responsibilities. Should the Reichstag demand elimination of too many controls, the Federal Council would stand firm.[55]

Not everyone agreed. Convinced that the Bundesrat did not have the backbone to resist parliamentary pressure for extensive revisions, Saxony refused to consider any reforms and urged Posadowsky to make a blunt reply to the Center's petition.[56] But, with the promise of certain anti-Socialist safeguards (*Kautelen*), Prussian, Bavarian, Badenese, and Hessian ministers joined the other states and bowed to Reich needs.[57] Trade unions would no longer be required to submit information to the police every three months concerning members and use of funds, but the authorities would still have the right to obtain this information on demand—clearly an attempt to intervene against Socialist or any radical activity. The granting of legal personality to trade unions would facilitate the accumulation of greater financial resources, but the state reserved the right to sue unions in the event of illegal activity during strikes. And finally, all state laws requiring the presence of police at trade union rallies and demonstrations would remain in effect, as would restrictive practices against state employees and rural laborers.[58] On the basis of this tentative agreement, Posadowsky was instructed to draft a Reichstag statement.

55. *Ibid.*

56. Report of the Württembergian Bundesrat plenipotentiary Schicker to the minister-president, 21 January 1904, reprinted in Peter Rassow and Karl Erich Born, *Akten zur staatlichen Sozialpolitik in Deutschland* (Wiesbaden: Franz Steiner Verlag GmbH, 1959), p. 177.

57. *Ibid.*, p. 178; minutes of the Prussian Ministry of State, 26 January 1904, Reichskanzlei, Nr. 532, ZStA Potsdam.

58. Posadowsky before the Prussian Ministry of State, 26 January 1904, Reichskanzlei, Nr. 532, Bl. 38–45, ZStA Potsdam.

Simultaneously, Posadowsky's staff moved past preliminary work and began in earnest to draft a bill on the corporate rights of trade unions (*Rechtsfähigkeit der Berufsvereine*). Once this bill was enacted, another on management-labor chambers would follow.[59] The federal states had completely reversed their previous (1901) position on this issue in their January session with Posadowsky, undoubtedly because the Kaiser had expressed so clearly his support for some institution joining capital and labor the year before. Considerable opposition was expected from entrepreneurial circles, however, and the secretary did not want to endanger his *Rechtsfähigkeit* bill by introducing it simultaneously with management-labor chambers.[60] No imperial law governing rights of assembly (*Reichvereinsgesetz*) was possible after the promises made to the federal states, but Posadowsky hoped to incorporate a few minor improvements in his trade union bill.[61] By spring 1904, the third period of social reform in the history of the Second Reich had begun. The reactionary Waldersee reflected the change of course in his last diary entry on 5 March: "I pray to God that I don't have to live through that which I see coming."[62]

The Christian workers responsible for these developments were not as well informed about the social-legislative changes underway in Berlin. Corresponding to Bülow's wishes, Francke had mailed the chancellor a copy of the address Behrens would deliver during the reception of the Frankfurt delegation at the Reich Chancellery in December.[63] Francke took the opportunity to urge Bülow to strengthen his Reichstag statement of January 1903 by promising that the demands of the Congress would receive "the most serious appreciation in decision-making circles."[64] Otherwise, "great masses of monarchical laborers"[65] would be disappointed and the attempt to create a patriotic labor movement would fail. Bülow followed this advice during his meeting with Christian labor leaders on 13 December 1903. The chancellor showed himself surprisingly well informed on matters of social legislation and

59. See the report of *Regierungsrat* Speilhagen, one of Posadowsky's staff members, on 15 February 1904, Reichsministerium des Innern, Nr. 6766, Bl. 42, ZStA Potsdam. Saul, *Staat, Industrie, Arbeiterbewegung*, pp. 36–42, 49, errs in concluding that Posadowsky was only concerned with the corporate status of trade unions.
60. *Ibid.*
61. See the draft of the bill sent to Bülow on 24 June 1904, Reichskanzlei, Nr. 532, Bl. 100–162, and the accompanying guidelines (*Gründzuge*), Bl. 90–99. These documents further underscore the fact that Posadowsky planned a more obliging response to the Congress than Saul believes to have been the case.
62. Waldersee entry for 5 March 1904, in Meissner (ed.), *Alfred Grafen von Waldersee*, vol. 3, p. 232.
63. Francke to Bülow, 3 November 1903, Reichskanzlei, Nr. 532, Bl. 13, ZStA Potsdam.
64. *Ibid.*
65. *Ibid.*

informed his guests that he "appreciated"[66] the Frankfurt demands and would consider them carefully.

Not wishing to commit the federal states before they had been consulted, however, Bülow made no further promises.[67] Posadowsky's Reichstag statement on 30 January 1904 was also rather uninformative.[68] All that was important was that the Center know its demands were being acted on. Once the legislation were presented to parliament, Bülow was fairly confident that the Reichstag support could be purchased "cheaply."[69] He had clearly given the Frankfurt delegation a false impression of his intentions.

Christian labor leaders were somewhat suspicious after their reception in Berlin,[70] but became even more so when Posadowsky, not Bülow, replied to the Center interpellation in January. Was this an indication of Bülow's appreciation for the demands of Christian workers? Posadowsky's unwillingness to commit himself was all the more reason for skepticism concerning the future of social reform.[71] The work of the German Workers' Congress, it appeared, was much further from completion than the participating organizations had been led to believe.[72] Even more extraparliamentary pressure had to be maintained on the bourgeois parties, and through them, on the government.[73] To acquire a greater measure of direct influence on party decisions, moreover, Christian workers planned to obtain as many Reichstag seats as possible during the next elections. With a united parliamentary front behind the Frankfurt program, the government would be more inclined to make concessions. Future congresses could then continue the work begun in 1903. As Giesberts put it, the Christian-national proletariat had "to keep the iron hot for striking."[74]

66. Bülow's response is quoted in *Mitteilungen des Gesamtverbandes*, no. 26, 28 December 1903.

67. *Ibid.*

68. Reichstag Debates, Period 11, Session 1 (30 January 1904), p. 610.

69. Posadowsky before the Prussian Ministry of State, 26 January 1904, Reichskanzlei, Nr. 532, Bl. 38–45, ZStA Potsdam.

70. *Mitteilungen des Gesamtverbandes*, no. 26, 28 December 1903.

71. *Mitteilungen des Gesamtverbandes*, no. 4, 22 February 1904.

72. The Kaiser's telegram in October, for instance, had given rise to "the best of hopes." See *Bergknappe*, no. 46, 14 November 1903. For the less optimistic mood after Posadowsky's speech, see the Congress Executive Committee Declaration of 26 February 1904, *Bericht über die Verhandlungen des zweiten Deutschen Arbeiter-Kongresses*, pp. 33-35.

73. The remainder of this paragraph is based on *Mitteilungen des Gesamtverbandes*, nos. 25–26 for 14 and 28 December 1903.

74. *Mitteilungen des Gesamtverbandes*, no. 25, 14 December 1903.

8

Christian-National *Blockpolitik*

From 1903 to late 1906, Christian labor leaders attempted to forge a bloc in parliament which would be responsive to the social and electoral demands of the movement. Unlike the mood of optimism which reigned in Christian circles at the turn of the century, one detects during these years a definite sense of desperation. The free trade unions offered the worker much more at the union level: a larger strike fund, a greater staff, and the numerical strength to force demands upon employers. To regain the momentum and make the Christian trade unions attractive to the working masses, Christian leaders bargained for a dramatic political success that would bring quick, visible benefits to the skeptical workers. The goal of winning the masses primarily through political programs was fraught, however, with great risks. For if the government did not respond to the proposals of the "patriotic" workers, the Social Democrats would make a mockery of the Christians' legalistic approach. Christian laborers therefore went to great lengths to increase their presence in parliament and gain influence with the bourgeois parties, a policy which was seen as an effective means of impressing the Kaiser and Bundesrat.

The quest for parliamentary representation was more difficult for Protestants within the Christian labor movement than for their Catholic counterparts. Organized Catholic workers were some 350,000 strong by 1903[1] and could concentrate these forces on one political party. Catholic proletarians also possessed valuable allies at Rhenish Center headquarters in Cologne who could bring pressure to bear on local electoral committees. In contrast, the

1. This figure includes Catholic *Arbeiterverein* members, Catholic *Gesellenverein* members, and Catholic members of the Christian trade unions.

National Association of Evangelical *Arbeitervereine* was a weak organization sorely divided between quarreling Hirsch-Duncker and Christian factions. These divisions, and the persistent confessional prejudices, contributed to the unimportance of the Protestant wing of the Christian trade unions,[2] and lessened its chance of acquiring political representation. Schack's white-collar union boasted a larger following, but was hampered in its search for Reichstag seats by the extreme anti-Semitic views of its chairman. Complicating matters further, the Evangelicals had far fewer qualified labor leaders than the Catholics and lacked a well-developed facility such as the *Volksverein* to train more. No bourgeois party could be expected to nominate a worker who had never spoken publicly or held office at least at the local level.

Worse still, in order to achieve victory in critical industrial areas like Saxony, the Ruhr, and the Saar, this relatively small, untrained force had to unite the conservative, unsympathetic parties of the Right around a lower-class candidate, or else seek Catholic support. The Center, however, had rejected all electoral alliances for the primary elections (*Hauptwahl*) in 1903 and had only agreed to run-off (*Stichwahl*) cooperation under intense pressure from Posadowsky.[3] The party seemed content to rely on its own strength for parliamentary seats. Evangelical *Schwarzseher* could be forgiven for seeing only black.

Driven by Stöcker's unbounded optimism, Christian-Social leaders were confident that the Evangelical labor movement could overcome these barriers. Party plans were announced at the Christian-Social convention in late September 1903.[4] The elections three months earlier had witnessed a significant political realignment in the western industrial districts. The S.P.D. had defended its seat in Elberfeld-Barmen and seized Solingen, Lennep-Mettmann, Bochum, and Dortmund from the National Liberals and Progressives. In other districts such as Duisburg and Essen the non-Socialist margin of victory had been greatly reduced. The only bourgeois party that actually gained ground was the Christian-Socials. The party won two seats in the Siegerland and garnered nearly 24,000 new votes in the Ruhr—only 3,000 short of the left-liberal *Freisinnige Volkspartei*.

With continued growth in party membership Christian-Social leaders were sure their voters would represent the margin of victory in many western districts during the next Reichstag elections. From this position of strength, the party could bargain more successfully with the other bourgeois parties. Christian-Social backing for National Liberal, Center, or Conservative candi-

2. Of the 95–100,000 unionists in the *Gesamtverband* in early 1904, about 20,000 were Protestant. August Pieper to Franz Brandts, 23 February 1904, Bachem Papers 215, HA Köln.
3. See Carl Bachem's notation of 19 June 1903, Bachem Papers 198, HA Köln.
4. For this paragraph, see CS Protocol 1903, StBib MG.

dates in one district would be traded for support from these parties in other areas. Once these alliances had been formed, Stöcker and his followers planned to nominate numerous Evangelical trade unionists. "Not until the Christian-Social Party marches hand in hand with the Christian trade unions," Stöcker proclaimed, "will many labor votes be cast for [us]."[5] The Christian-Socials were also ready to prevail upon the other Protestant parties to run Evangelical unionists. In areas such as the Ruhr, Sieg, and Saar this goal could be accomplished by threatening to run independently unless "suitable, social-oriented candidates"[6] were nominated by other parties.

Before the Christian-Socials could run Protestant trade unionists, however, promising workers had to be found, educated, and indoctrinated to the party's views. The problem had first become apparent during the preparations for the German Workers' Congress. Aside from Behrens, only Wilhelm Schack of the related German-Socials was ready to play a major role at Frankfurt. In order to right this situation, Ludwig Weber solicited a number of charitable organizations for aid in establishing a new agency to begin the task of "educating" Evangelical laborers. These efforts were not without success, but it soon became apparent that the bulk of the operating costs would have to come from other sources. Thus Weber turned to the Prussian Evangelical Church. A petition signed by the Evangelical *Arbeitervereine*, the Christian-Social *Konferenz*, and the other social and religious groups Weber had contacted was submitted to the General Synod in mid-October 1903. The Evangelical *Arbeitervereine* at the Frankfurt Workers' Congress sent a petition of their own a week later.[7]

In what was apparently a coordinated effort, Stöcker also approached the General Synod. Together with a group of socially conscious noblemen, the sixty-eight-year-old evangelist requested Church funding for a variety of new programs designed to halt the exodus of workers from the Church into the S.P.D. Stöcker and his associates also encouraged the Synod to lend moral support to all Evangelical social groups that were trying to create "a Christian-national-monarchical countermovement against the Socialists."[8] The underlying political motivations for the proposal need little comment. As he had for decades, Stöcker assumed that *his* party would be the sole political beneficiary of any major church effort by Protestants to solve the social problem.

5. *Ibid.*, p. 4.
6. *Ibid.*, p. 6.
7. Reinhard Mumm, "Ausbildungskurse," *Die Arbeit*, no. 34, 20 August 1910; *Verhandlungen der fünften ordentlichen Generalsynode der evangelischen Landeskirche Preussens* (15 October–4 November 1903), EZA Berlin, pp. 860–61 (hereafter cited as: *Generalsynode* 1903). *Reichsbote* article of late October 1903, reprinted in the *Kölnische Volkszeitung*, no. 918, 1 November 1903.
8. *Generalsynode* 1903, pp. 136–37, EZA Berlin.

The petition was not wholly successful. Reflecting William II's more generous attitude toward the workers, the *Oberkirchenrat* and the executive committee of the General Synod pledged 220,000 marks annually for lecture tours in industrial areas, social awareness programs for seminary students, more urban missions (*Stadtmissionen*), and increased spiritual efforts directed at proletarians. However, the church flatly refused to promote the Christian labor movement so as not to become involved in matters of a purely economic or political nature outside the sphere of church responsibility.[9] It was for reasons such as this that Stöcker and Weber had fought since the 1870s to free the Evangelical Church from the domination of the Prussian Ministry of State.

Weber's efforts to aid Evangelical laborers met with even less success. The Synod's social commission decided not to debate his controversial proposals, opting instead to pass them on to government officials in Berlin for consideration. The commission's spokesman made it quite clear, however, that neither Synod nor *Oberkirchenrat* were in favor of a special educational agency outside their control. In defiance of these wishes, Weber circulated a declaration among the Synod delegates calling for public contributions. The document was signed by the overwhelming majority of the churchmen and printed in over 100 newspapers.[10] Much to the dismay of the Christian-Socials, the appeal netted less than 4,000 marks, not enough to fund operations for one year. As Mumm observed, the good intentions of the Synod delegates could not hide the fact that social lethargy was still widespread in Evangelical Church circles. Only after Ernst Francke promised a subsidy from the Society for Social Reform could the *Soziale Geschäftsstelle* for Evangelical Germany begin work.[11]

During its first year in operation,[12] the *Geschäftsstelle* established a library, a legal-aid service, and a publishing facility and sponsored numerous "agitation tours" for Behrens, Mumm, and others. The new agency also took over the Reich insurance secretariat established by the Christian-Social *Konferenz* in 1902. The most significant contribution to the elevation of the Evangelical proletariat, however, was the six-week training course (*Ausbildungskurs*) held in Berlin during the summer of 1904. After intense schooling in public speaking, church history, labor relations, the intricacies of Germany's social insurance system, and other subjects, the most capable participants were given charge of newly established Christian-Social *Volksbüros* in Hagen, Mülheim-

9. *Ibid.*, pp. 855–56, 875–76.

10. *Ibid.*, pp. 865, 867; *Kirchlich-soziale Konferenz: Geschäftsbericht 1905*, p. 16.

11. *Ibid.*, p. 16; Mumm, "Ausbildungskurse."

12. For this paragraph, see *Kirchlich-soziale Konferenz: Geschäftsbericht 1905*, pp. 4–17; and the archive of the organization, *Akten der Sozialen Geschäftsstelle für das Evangelische Deutschland*, EZA Berlin.

Ruhr, Duisburg, Kassel, Bromberg, Berlin, and Breslau. Ten others obtained positions as trade union, co-op, *Arbeiterverein*, or *Stadtmission* secretaries. These educational workshops, of course, did not always transform former workers into competent leaders. The archive of the *Geschäftsstelle* in Berlin, for instance, contains the story of one unfortunate *Volksbüro* chief from Duisburg who had to be dismissed for lack of "talents."[13] But with two additional training courses planned for 1905, Christian-Social leaders felt that a cadre of reliable Christian-Social laborites would be ready for campaigning in 1908.

Despite feverish promotional efforts on the part of party, *Konferenz*, and *Geschäftsstelle*, however, Stöcker and his associates still lacked the necessary *mass* backing in 1904 to execute their new political strategy. They were, as the Socialists observed derisively, generals without an army. This situation began to change in early 1905 as a result of developments within the Christian miners' *Gewerkverein*. Aware that Brust's rough character, overbearing personality, and pro-Center political views had alienated thousands of potential members in Protestant circles, especially after he ran for the Prussian Landtag as a Center candidate in November 1903, the executive committee of the union proclaimed suddenly in late fall of 1904 that he would have to step down. A Protestant miner took over the chairmanship, and in a widely publicized move, Franz Behrens was offered the post of secretary general. As leaders of the largest Christian trade union, both were also given seats on the executive committee of the *Gesamtverband*.[14]

Almost overnight the Protestant wing of the movement became a force of respectable magnitude. In mid-March 1905 the Rhenish-Westphalian Association of Evangelical *Arbeitervereine* (30,000) abandoned its ten-year-old policy of neutrality toward trade unions and encouraged all non-organized association members to join Christian trade unions. This decision, and the general excitement in western mining districts following the great miners' strike of January 1905, explain the fact that 30–40,000 Protestants had joined the *Gewerkverein*. Exact statistics are lacking, but it seems safe to assume that thousands more flocked to other Christian unions in the following months. From the summer of 1905 to the fall of 1906, for instance, the Evangelical Associations of Brandenburg, Saxony, Thuringia, Hanover, and Bochum

13. *Akten der Sozialen Geschäftsstelle*, E2/45, EZA Berlin.

14. *Zentralblatt*, no. 2, 29 January 1906; police commissioner of Düsseldorf to the *Regierungspräsident*, 1 September 1904, police commissioner of Essen to the *Regierungspräsident*, 21 and 27 September 1904, and 5 November 1904, Reg. D. 9055, HSA Düsseldorf; police commissioner of Bochum to the *Regierungspräsident*, 1 November 1904 and 16 February 1905, Arnsberg I 82, StA Münster.

(Ruhr) urged their members, which jointly numbered 25,000, to join unions affiliated with the *Gesamtverband*.[15]

All that remained for Stöcker, Mumm, and Behrens to do was to recruit this emerging force for the Christian-Social Party. The prospects of success were good. Veteran observers of the labor scene in the Ruhr and northern Sauerland pointed out that the miners' strike had generated so much distrust among Evangelical miners and non-miners alike that National Liberal labor voters were threatening to vote Christian-Social unless their party ran labor candidates at the next election.[16] Anxious to exploit this angry mood, Stöcker's followers announced in early 1906 that the party would run independently in Mülheim-Duisburg, Essen, Bochum-Gelsenkirchen, Dortmund-Hörde, Hatingen-Witten, and Hamm-Soest. To the south in Altenkirchen-Wetzlar, a coalition of Evangelical and Catholic workers, anti-Semites (German-Socials), and Conservative Party pastors had agreed to support Behrens against the National Liberals in 1908.[17] Victory there would give the Christian-Socials possession of three adjacent Reichstag districts in the Sieg and Lahn valleys. Favorable developments were underway in the Saar too. The region's Chamber of Commerce informed the *Regierungspräsident* in the fall of 1905 that "the Christian trade unions"[18] had urged the Evangelical *Arbeitervereine* to join them in backing a Christian-Social candidate in Saarbrücken or Ottweiler–St. Wendel. The idea was categorically rejected by *Arbeiterverein* chairman Father Nold, who was convinced that the Christian trade unions would merely "deliver the whole region to the Center."[19] Like other districts in western Germany, nevertheless, the two National Liberal bastions of the Saar were under siege. A confrontation of major proportions was in the making.

* * * *

15. *Kölnische Volkszeitung*, no. 471, 8 June 1905; *Regierungspräsident* of Arnsberg to the minister of the interior, 22 December 1905, Reg. D. 9041, HSA Düsseldorf; *Westdeutsche Arbeiter-Zeitung*, no. 29, 22 July 1906 (clipping in: Reg. Arnsberg I 106, StA Münster); *Die Arbeit*, no. 15, 14 April 1907; J. Windolph, *Der deutsche Protestantimus und die christlichen Gewerkschaften* (Berlin: Kommissionsverlag des "Arbeiter," 1909), pp. 18–19.

16. See Julius Bachem's comments before the *Augustinusverein*, 21 February 1905, in the *Augustinus-Blatt*, no. 2 (February 1905), StBib MG; letter from National Liberal labor circles printed in the *Kölnische Volkszeitung*, no. 670, 5 August 1906; *Kölnische Volkszeitung*, nos. 38, 171, and 673, for 15 January, 28 February, and 6 August 1907; Landrat Altenkirchen to *Regierungspräsident* Koblenz, 14 September 1905, 403/8448, and Landrat Wetzlar to the *Regierungspräsident* Koblenz, 441/25553, LHA Koblenz.

17. *Kölnische Volkszeitung*, nos. 38, 171, and 673 for 15 January, 28 February, and 6 August 1906. Landrat of Altenkirchen to the *Regierungspräsident*, 14 September 1905, 403/8448, LHA Koblenz; Landrat of Wetzlar to the *Regierungspräsident*, 441/25553, LHA Koblenz.

18. Quoted in no. 5819 (15 January 1906) of the *Gewerkschaftliche Nachrichten*, a confidential information sheet sent by Saar Chamber of Commerce circles to the *Regierungspräsident* in Trier, 442/3792, LHA Koblenz.

19. *Ibid.*

While the Christian-Socials mobilized Evangelical labor for the elections of 1908, Catholic unionists waged an intense struggle to democratize the Center. Thus General Secretary Stegerwald complained bitterly to Julius Bachem that, after years of waiting for nominations to safe Reichstag seats, the Christian trade unions were beginning "to doubt the honorable intentions of leading Centrists."[20] In Bavaria Carl Schirmer organized a Christian workers' lobby in the Center "for the purpose of achieving representation in the parliaments and, generally, an influence in political life corresponding to our great numbers."[21] There is a great deal of evidence, moreover, that Catholic trade unionists were also quite impressed with the rise of the Christian-Socials and wanted the Center to accommodate the emerging party by forming the type of electoral pacts described at the Christian-Social convention of 1903.[22] Bachem and Trimborn, who also looked favorably upon the advancing "Christian-Social colors"[23] and were themselves in favor of a stronger labor wing in the Center,[24] had little trouble convincing Stegerwald and other union leaders that their political future lay with the Center.[25] But rank and file laborers were harder to reach. By early 1906, in fact, there was already talk among some Christian trade union secretaries in western Germany of emulating the British example and forming an interconfessional, non-Socialist labor party. In Bavaria, too, Christian workers were threatening to abandon the Center and nominate their own labor representatives.[26]

That Christian trade union national leaders turned their backs on unruly elements amidst the rank and file and refused to countenance an independent

20. Carl Bachem refers to Stegerwald's letter of mid-1904 in a letter to Julius Bachem, 31 December 1904, Bachem Papers 349, HA Köln.
21. Quoted in Denk, *Christliche Arbeiterbewegung in Bayern*, p. 162. Also see p. 164.
22. As mentioned above (see notes 17 and 18), Christian unionists in the Saar and Siegerland had warmed to the idea of Christian-Social labor candidacies. Also see Stegerwald's letters of 15 and 20 August 1906, in nos. 701 and 717 (16 and 21 August 1906) of the *Kölnische Volkszeitung*. Behrens stated on two occasions (*Die Arbeit*, no. 48, 28 November 1907, and no. 12, 21 March 1908), moreover, that the politics of interconfessionalism had sprung from the workers. The same claim, significantly enough, was made by the *Kölnische Volkszeitung* (no. 669, 5 August 1906).
23. Trimborn made the statement to Dietrich von Oertzen, manager of the Christian-Social *Geschäftsstelle*, in 1904 or 1905. Oertzen to Mumm, 3 June 1916, Mumm Papers 1056, Bl. 84, ZStA Potsdam.
24. Julius Bachem to Carl Bachem, undated (but before 1 July 1904), Bachem Papers 349, HA Köln.
25. At the general assembly of *Arbeiterwohl* on 10 January 1906, for example, Julius Bachem opposed the patriarchal views of Catholic employers and backed the demands of Stegerwald, Giesberts, and Schiffer for the social, economic, and political emancipation of labor. *Kölnische Volkszeitung*, no. 27, 11 January 1906; *Zentralblatt*, no. 4, 26 February 1906. In general for the soothing influence which Bachem had on Stegerwald and other union leaders, see Martin Spahn, "Julius Bachem," *Hochland*, April 1918, pp. 17–21.
26. *Protokoll der Verhandlungen des VI. Congresses der christlichen Gewerkschaften Deutschlands (22–24 Juli 1906)* (Cologne: Verlag des Generalsekretariats, 1906), p. 103; Denk, *Christliche Arbeiterbewegung in Bayern*, p. 379.

political stance may have been costly from the standpoint of preventing membership drain to the Socialist unions. But even if the Catholic unionists had wanted to leave the Center—and generally, despite all the pressure they put on it, they did not—the fact remains that the *Gesamtverband* needed the Center at this time. Indeed the party appeared to be the only hope of a solution to the worsening *Gewerkschaftsstreit* which had prevented the Christian trade unions from recruiting gains in the conservative dioceses. Also related to Christian labor *politics* after 1906, these developments deserve more attention at this point in the analysis.

The leaders of the countermovement of *Arbeiterverein* craft sections (*Fachabteilungen*) in Berlin, Breslau, and Trier opposed the concept of the strike, it will be recalled, rejected cooperation with Protestants, and generally feared what would happen if Catholic workers led their own interconfessional unions. Hoping to avoid the inevitable labor violence and political radicalization which they felt would surely come from independent unions, the "Berliners'" prejudices and presumptions led them naturally to the plan of innocuous, church-controlled organizations. Founded in 1902, the craft sections had fought the Christian trade unions for a year before agreeing to join their adversaries in the German Workers' Congress of 1903. By the end of the year, however, both sides had resumed the feud and had begun to place pressure on Center Party leaders and the German bishops for moral and political support. By and large the Center and the western bishops championed the cause of the Christian trade unions for fear of losing an effective bulwark against the S.P.D., while Kopp, Korum, and a few anti-labor deputies supported the *Fachabteilungen*. As the polemics grew in intensity through 1904 and 1905 the Christian trade unions and the craft sections extended their search for patrons to Rome.[27]

When, in late January 1906, the Vatican finally expressed its desire for a termination of all polemics,[28] the Christian trade unions had lost yet another chance to win broader support among the masses. For radically inclined Catholic workers turned away from the Christian unions as organizations limited in effectiveness by the church, while the more submissive types refused to join unions which had been described in such pessimistic language by conservative clergymen. Stegerwald estimated that the trade union controversy had cost the *Gesamtverband* at least 100,000 members in the Saar alone. A recruitment drive in Silesia in 1904 was a complete failure. In Berlin 30–35,000 Catholic workers remained aloof, while in Dortmund, *Fachab-*

27. See the present author's dissertation, "Christian Labor and the Politics of Frustration in Imperial Germany," Ohio State University, 1978, pp. 249–54, for greater detail.

28. Brack, *Deutscher Episcopat und Gewerkschaftsstreit*, pp. 106–12. Each bishop was to decide which organization was best suited for conditions in his diocese.

teilungen kept Christian trade union membership at the low level of 3,000. Further losses were registered in the Siegerland, the Eichsfeld, and the surrounding cities of Hanover, Hildesheim, and Magdeburg. Indeed, during the twenty-seven months of industrial boom which preceded the pope's warning (October 1903–January 1906), only 105,000 workers, many of whom were Protestant, had joined the Christian national federation.[29] As Stegerwald and other union secretaries were quick to point out, it was not just the union that suffered: the political potential of Catholic labor also was hurt.[30]

The trade union controversy, in fact, had given rise to worries in union and Center circles that went well beyond the concerns described in the preceding paragraph. The Christian trade union *Zentralblatt* hinted at the nature of the problem in late February 1906:

> The trade union question is pressing more and more to a definite decision, not so much for us in the Christian trade unions as for Catholic workers and Catholics in general. The controversy is drawing more interest in wider Catholic circles than was at first the case. Socially and politically progressive Catholics are just as uncomfortable with the Berliners' narrow-minded politics of isolationism [*Ausschliessungspolitik*] as the workers and likewise see these developments as dangerous. For in the last analysis, this narrow-minded confessionalism, even if it stays within the bounds of the moral laws of Christianity, means the abrogation of civil, political, and socio-political freedom of action . . . This has to lead to a confrontation, even a split, in the Catholic camp. To forestall such an eventuality, responsible Catholic circles will finally have to intervene with all decisiveness.[31]

August Pieper shed more light on the dangers perceived by union patrons in Mönchen-Gladbach and Cologne:

> I can attest to the fact that our work in the economic and socio-political area was the first to lead to untroubled, friendly cooperation with serious non-Catholics and arouse in these quarters an unqualified trust . . . With regard to the *Gewerkschaftsstreit* I've always emphasized that the maintenance of the non-denominational character of the Christian trade unions was impor-

29. *Protokoll der Verhandlungen des VII. Kongresses der christlichen Gewerkschaften Deutschlands (18–21 July 1909)* (Cologne: Christlicher Gewerkschaftsverlag, 1902), p. 22; petition of the Catholic labor association "St. Martin" to Kopp, September 1905, *Archiv der katholischen Arbeitnehmerbewegung*, vol. 5, KfZG Bonn; August Pieper to Canon Kemper of Warburg, 16 May 1906, *Archiv der katholischen Arbeitnehmerbewegung*, vol. 5, KfZG Bonn; Brack, *Deutscher Episkopat und Gewerkschaftsstreit*, pp. 100–105; *Kölnische Volkszeitung*, no. 49, 18 January 1906; mayor of Gebhardsheim to the Landrat of Altenkirchen, 20 September 1906, and Landrat of Altenkirchen to the *Regierungspräsident*, 3 June 1907, 441/25554, LHA Koblenz.
30. Stegerwald before the *Augustinusverein* on 13 May 1905, *Augustinus-Blatt*, no. 5, May 1905, StBib MG; also see the remarks of union secretary Inkermann at Dortmund on 20 October 1905, report of Dortmund Police Department, 20 October 1905, *Bestand* 3, StA Dortmund.
31. *Zentralblatt*, no. 4, 26 February 1906.

> tant mainly because the consequence was the maintenance of the political, nondenominational character of the Center Party . . . If Catholic workers are forbidden to cooperate with Protestant workers, that means that joint political ventures with non-Catholics also cannot be permitted.[32]

Indeed by early 1906 the Berliners had already begun to draw the logical *political* conclusion from their views on the labor question. In Hanover, for instance, *Fachabteilung* sympathizers were threatening to withdraw electoral support from Protestant Guelphs and form an independent "Catholic Peoples' Party."[33] Trends such as this did not augur well for successful electoral cooperation with the Christian-Socials in Rhineland-Westphalia, threatened to undercut the overall political strategy of the German Workers' Congress, and, as Pieper hinted, endangered far-reaching socio-political efforts such as those of Hans von Berlepsch's Society for Social Reform.

Even more discomforting was the fact that the Berliners' isolationist tendencies played right into the hands of anti-Catholic demagogues whose campaign against the Center had gained in ferocity since Chancellor Bülow had succeeded in effecting a partial repeal of the Jesuit Laws in spring 1904. The dangers of *Ausschliessungspolitik,* many Centrists argued, could be seen in Baden, where National Liberals, Progressives, and Socialists had cooperated to defeat Center candidates in the state run-off elections of late October 1905. Too, when the Center Reichstag *Fraktion* entered its usual bill demanding religious tolerance in January 1906, Protestant criticism was angrier and more passionate than ever before. If in the midst of this growing wave of bigotry and religious prejudice even a small number of Centrists succumbed to the Berliners' brand of fervent Catholicism, confessional relations would deteriorate further, Bülow and other leading statesmen would not be able to resist the advice of the demagogic Evangelical League, and a Badenese-like coalition in Berlin, or perhaps even a new *Kulturkampf*, might result. All Catholics would suffer if things came to this.[34]

It was in this atmosphere of rising confessional tension outside the *Zentrumsturm*, and crescendoing class tension within, that Julius Bachem published his controversial article "We Must Get Out of the Tower" (*Wir müssen aus dem Turme heraus!*).[35] The Center's leading strategist did not intend to transform the Center into a broad-based, interconfessional party of

32. Pieper to Carl Bachem, 8 November 1932, Pieper Papers 36, StA Münster.
33. Carl Bachem to Father Joseph Dahlmann, 1 June 1906, Bachem Papers 254b, HA Köln.
34. Heckart, *From Bassermann to Bebel*, pp. 91ff.; Carl Bachem to Joseph Dahlmann, 1 June 1906, Bachem Papers 254b, HA Köln; *Kölnische Volkszeitung*, no. 567, 2 July 1906; Julius Bachem to Felix Porsch, 2 December 1910, Bachem Papers 308, HA Köln.
35. *Kölnische Volkszeitung*, no. 193, 8 March 1906. The article was originally published in the March number of the *Historisch-politische Blätter*.

the center-right, as one historian has claimed.[36] The idea was appealing to Bachem, but he considered it beyond the realm of possibility.[37] In 1906 his major concern was to avert the danger to the party stemming from the trade union controversy by presenting to Protestant Germany the image of a purely political, nondenominational party concerned more with solving the social question than pursuing narrow, religious goals.[38] One of the best ways to demonstrate the party's real nature and overcome the deep-seated, seemingly insurmountable prejudice of German Protestants would be a series of generous electoral pacts during the Reichstag and Landtag elections of 1908. Local committees were urged to lend primary election support to suitable candidates from Protestant parties, even in districts where the Center stood a chance to win on its own.

> It would be truly impossible to underestimate the advantage [to Catholics] if in this way the various parties of the Reichstag gained more men who were experienced in socio-political affairs and tolerant, far-sighted, and without prejudice with regard to religion. One thinks about men like Professor Adolf Wagner, Evangelical leaders of the Christian trade unions like Behrens, of the artisans' movement like Jakobskötter . . . and practitioners of the cooperative movement like *Geheimrat* Kaas, among others. As the last name illustrates, we don't want to exclude liberal candidates as a matter of principle.[39]

Clearly, Bachem's electoral strategy was not unlike that announced by the Christian-Socials at Mülheim in 1903.[40] In fact, in response to a public challenge from Behrens that the Center should back Evangelical laborers in 1908 if it were serious about the *"Turm"* article,[41] Bachem asserted that the party would not only nominate labor candidates itself in suitable districts, "but will also gladly support labor nominees of other parties put up against the S.P.D.

36. Karl Buchheim, *Die Geschichte der christlichen Parteien in Deutschland* (Munich: Kösel-Verlag, 1953), p. 135.
37. *Kölnische Volkszeitung*, no. 1060, 18 December 1903, no. 1057, 20 December 1905, and no. 627, 22 July 1906.
38. See the sources cited above in note 34 for evidence that the article was directed at the "confessionalists" within the Center. That his concerns had grown out of the *Gewerkschaftsstreit*, see the *Zentralblatt*, no. 20, 2 October 1905, and no. 4, 26 February 1906.
39. This quote is taken from a follow-up article in the *Kölnische Volkszeitung*, no. 669, 5 August 1906.
40. The conclusion reached by Ronald J. Ross, *Beleaguered Tower: The Dilemma of Political Catholicism in Wilhelmine Germany* (Notre Dame: University of Notre Dame Press, 1976), p. 38, that Bachem, though concerned primarily with tactical objectives, had "as a symbolic gesture" advocated "the large-scale influx of Protestants into the Centrum's ranks," is inaccurate. The *Turm* article itself called merely for electoral aid for tolerant Protestants, while the April sequel, *"Nochmals: Wir müssen aus dem Turme heraus!"* went no farther. After election, the Protestants supported by the Center would cooperate closely with Catholics, but "the external form of this relationship" was not seen as "decisive." *Kölnische Volkszeitung*, no. 280, 3 April 1906.
41. *Kölnische Zeitung*, no. 840, 7 August 1906.

in areas where the Center, as a minority party, cannot prevail."[42] The party was especially willing to lend aid to Evangelical unionists "because they have learned to appreciate the advantage of peaceful cooperation between confessions in the Christian trade unions."[43] It seems clear, then, that the idea of numerous labor candidacies was an integral part of Bachem's new strategy. The loyalty of the Christian trade unions would be assured and the danger posed by angry rank and file secessionists averted. And in the long run, Bachem's strategy of compromise would also shield the church and Center from another period of discrimination and persecution.

Bachem's article was soon the topic of heated debate within the Center Party. *Fraktion* leaders in Berlin were sharply divided. A majority around Carl Bachem was eager to employ the new strategy, especially in Hanover, but Georg Hertling, Silesian party chief Felix Porsch, and others were afraid the new emphasis on nondenominationalism would not only anger the pope, but might also weaken religious bonds between Catholics to the point where the party would splinter into socio-economic and national (Polish) groups.[44] The Center press was also split over the issue. So much so, in fact, that the executive board of the *Augustinusverein* felt it wise to postpone indefinitely any discussion of the *Turm* article.[45] Nor were local electoral committees in confessionally mixed areas like the Ruhr of one opinion concerning the need to leave the *Zentrumsturm*. Lambert Lensing, editor of *Tremonia* in Dortmund, for instance, argued that a sacrifice of Center votes was "absolutely imperative"[46] for tactical reasons, while Wilhelm Hankamer of the *Essener Volkszeitung* stubbornly refused to see the logic of abandoning the struggle for domination of the industrial districts.[47]

The idea that potential seats should be sacrificed encountered even greater resistance in Silesia, the Saar, and other strongholds of the Catholic craft section movement. Along with tactical concerns such as the need to rally Polish Catholics, labor priests and politically active clergymen in these areas pointed out first of all that Bachem's strategy would never work. Far from aiding the Catholic cause, electoral agreements with Protestants would only jeopardize the church's position, for Lutherans would never willingly abandon their crusade against ultramontanism. Rather, the Center should strive to

42. *Kölnische Volkszeitung*, no. 693, 13 August 1906.

43. *Ibid.*

44. Carl Bachem to Joseph Dahlmann, 1 June 1906, Bachem Papers 254b, HA Köln; Georg Hertling to Julius Bachem, 6 April and 10 April 1906, Hertling Papers 56, BA Koblenz; John K. Zeender, "German Catholics and the Concept of an Interconfessional Party 1900–1922," *Journal of Central European Affairs*, January 1964, p. 428.

45. *Augustinus-Blatt*, no. 8, August 1906, StBib MG.

46. Lensing to Herold, Herold Papers 2, 22 November 1906, BA Koblenz.

47. *Augustinus-Blatt*, no. 7, July 1906, StBib MG.

increase its strength, thereby enhancing the bargaining position of church officials in negotiations with the Kaiser and Reich chancellor.[48]

These considerations, however, do not explain the bitter response to Bachem's views in the "confessionalist" camp. The determining factor behind this highly negative reaction was the fact that *Wir müssen aus dem Turme heraus!* was seen quite correctly as the logical outcome of Bachem's association with and fervent support for the nondenominational labor movement.[49] In addition to the accusation that Christian trade union leaders propagated dangerous, "unnatural" economic philosophies, the Berliners could now add the charge of religious indifference. Preoccupied with selfish interest group politics, the Christians had forgotten their church. Thus the trade union controversy and the so-called Center controversy *(Zentrumsstreit)* which began with Bachem's article should not be seen as parallel or related issues. The latter was merely a deeper, more complicated phase of the former.[50]

The ire of craft section supporters increased during 1906 as the *Gesamtverband* unleashed its own interconfessional political campaign. After an open discussion of political tactics that winter and spring,[51] union plans for 1908 were announced by Giesberts at the organization's sixth Congress at Breslau in July. The idea of an interconfessional labor party currently advocated by some members of the Christian organization had to be rejected, he noted, because this approach would alienate the bourgeois parties and put stones in the path of social reform. It would be foolish, moreover, for angry unionists to cast votes for the S.P.D. merely because bourgeois candidates seemed unsuitable. Chris-

48. Transcript of a conversation between Kopp and Count Oppersdorf, 16 January 1914, Benigni Materials 4, in the Brauweiler Papers 15/13/40, StA MG; *Trierische Landeszeitung*, 27 May 1909 (clipping in: Hohn Papers 15/2, StA MG); *Germania*, no. 272, 27 November 1909; Ross, *Beleaguered Tower*.

49. Herman Cardauns, *Julius Bachem*, p. 11, undated pamphlet in the Ritter Papers 14-3, KfZG Bonn; Athanasius (Adolf ten Hompel), *Das Cölner Osterdienstags-Protokoll* (Bonn: Universitäts-Buchdruckerei und Verlag, 1909), p. 6.

50. Zeender, "Interconfessional Party," pp. 424–39, Rudolf Morsey, *Die deutsche Zentrumspartei 1917–1923* (Düsseldorf: Droste-Verlag, 1966), pp. 36–42, and Ross, *Beleaguered Tower*, pp. 33–79, overlooked the fact that the *Gewerkschaftsstreit* and the politics of Christian labor after 1903 led directly to the *Zentrumsstreit* after 1906.

51. In early November 1905, the executive committee of the German Workers' Congress called upon all member organizations to increase pressure on the bourgeois parties for political representation. *Bericht über die Verhandlungen des zweiten Deutschen Arbeiter-Kongresses*, pp. 38–39. During the first months of 1906, then, the *Gesamtverband* drew up plans to debate the matter at its upcoming congress. *Kölnische Volkszeitung*, no. 346, 25 April 1906. A preliminary discussion of political stratagems was conducted in the *Zentralblatt* that spring; see nos. 6–7 and 9 for 26 March, 9 April, and 7 May 1906. These developments, the *Zentralblatt* statement of February 1906 (quoted above, note 31), and the pro–Christian-Social orientation of Catholic unionists in the *Gesamtverband* seem to support the speculation of Ernst Deuerlein, *CDU/CSU 1945–47* (Cologne: Verlag J. P. Bachem, 1957), pp. 28–29, that Bachem wrote the *Turm* article at the behest of Stegerwald and the General Secretariat.

tian labor influence could be enhanced only by obtaining seats in the bourgeois parties. To accomplish this,

> the cooperation [*Zusammengehen*] of the bourgeois parties will be absolutely necessary in certain areas. Our task is to facilitate this [cooperation] and exert influence such that agreements are reached, above all by the selection of [common] candidates.[52]

Once elected, Christian trade unionists sitting in different *Fraktionen* would cooperate closely to insure that party caucuses were presented with uniform social demands. Success with these reforms would discredit the Marxists, fill the sails of the Christian labor movement, and speed it past the free trade unions.

But political influence, especially within three or four different parties, could not be achieved without a mass following. One way around this delemma, noted Stegerwald in his annual report of June 1906, was to effect "a closing of the ranks" (*engerer Zusammenschluss*)[53] within the German Workers' Congress. In accordance with these needs, an ambitious effort was announced in early October.[54] The *Gesamtverband* urged its members to join confessional labor associations if they had not already done so, while the National Association of Evangelical *Arbeitervereine* of western and southern Germany urged their members, likewise, to join Christian trade unions. The proclamation was highly significant, for it was the first time that national leaders of the Evangelical *Arbeitervereine* had come out in favor of Christian trade unionism. It was also at this time, the reader will recall, that steps were taken to bolster the financial strength and benefit programs of the Christian organizations. The goal of all these measures was to elevate *Gesamtverband* membership from the mid-1906 level of 245,000 to a total nearer the Congress's backing of 900,000.

While the new membership drive got underway, Christian unionists pressed the bourgeois parties for a commitment to "Christian-national *Blockpolitik*," as friends and foes alike dubbed it. For the time being politics, not trade unionism, would have to provide the momentum necessary to overcome the Social Democrats. Stegerwald, Giesberts, Schiffer, and other labor leaders on the central committee of the Rhenish Center Party had no trouble recruiting that body for the Breslau program in August. Nominating committees throughout the Rhineland were urged to comply with the committee's recommendations. "Where that has not happened," stated Giesberts in early Sep-

52. *Protokoll der Verhandlungen des VI. Kongresses der christlichen Gewerkschaften*, p. 104.
53. Quoted in the *Kölnische Volkszeitung*, no. 590, 10 July 1906.
54. *Westdeutsche Arbeiter-Zeitung*, no. 41, 13 October 1906.

tember, "the local leadership is responsible."[55] The Westphalian party organization was also amenable to the unions' demands for electoral agreements with other parties, but resistance at the local level persisted in this province too. Hankamer of Essen, for instance, was highly critical of the Christian trade unions, referring to them as "outsiders"[56] who knew relatively little about the exigencies of politics in the Ruhr. As it had since the 1850s, the Essen organization would "count its votes"[57] in the primary election of 1908.

Hankamer's remarks elicited a rather interesting reply from Stegerwald. The *Gesamtverband*'s general secretary pointed out angrily that Hankamer's *"Kirchturmspolitik"*[58] was not in keeping with the times and would only benefit the Socialists. The unions were also familiar with the Ruhr and would "know how to treat the situation there at the next elections."[59] Stegerwald challenged Center circles in Essen to another exchange of views on election tactics, but asked that *the whole Reich*, not just the Ruhr, be considered. "Then the 'outsider' will show that perhaps he knows more about affairs in the German fatherland, and also in the Center Party, than those in Essen seem willing to admit."[60] Stegerwald's zeal was apparently too great for Julius Bachem and the chief editor of the *Kölnische Volkszeitung*, Hermann Cardauns. Already anxious to avoid polemics in the *Augustinusverein*, the two had no desire to unleash the fiery general secretary on the Essen Center Party. They knew it would take years, not months, before Centrists would leave their "tower" and take up a position before the walls, as Bachem's metaphor ran. The cooperative strategy, moreover, had originated with the unions and the Christian-Socials, not Bachem and Cardauns. Thus the differences between Hankamer and the unions were quietly buried toward the end of August, and Stegerwald's proposed debate did not take place. That it did not was the first sign that a rift was developing between the Rhenish party and the unions over the pace of advance.

The Evangelical wing of the Christian labor movement was also pushing for realization of the demands raised at Breslau. With Behrens at the helm, of course, this effort was largely indistinguishable from regular Christian-Social politics. The party's plans for the Ruhr, described above, were given final expression in late October 1906. Local committees in the eight largest Reichstag districts of the area were united into a central nominating association under Behrens's chairmanship in Essen. Evangelical laborers would be run in

55. *Kölnische Volkszeitung*, no. 821, 3 September 1906.
56. Hankamer's remarks are quoted in the *Kölnische Volkszeitung*, no. 717, 21 August 1906.
57. *Ibid.*
58. *Ibid.*
59. *Ibid.*
60. *Ibid.*

these districts if the National Liberals, Conservatives, and Center did not nominate suitable candidates of their own. Final preparations were also being made for an extension of this strategy to other parts of Germany. A "Committee for the Election of Patriotic Workers" (*Nationalarbeiterwahlausschuss*) had been formed that August, once again under Behrens's leadership. Besides electing Evangelical trade unionists to parliament, the new committee planned to reconcile differences between bourgeois parties and fuse these organizations into an effective anti-Socialist coalition (*Zusammenfassung der bürgerlichen Parteien*). With the aid of Stöcker, who had approached wealthy friends for financial contributions, the Committee began agitation in Saarbrücken, Frankfurt a. M., Eisenach, Erfurt, Dresden, and Berlin in November. Efforts in other cities were to follow shortly.[61]

By early December the Committee had already registered a few victories. Behrens's election in Altenkirchen-Wetzlar seemed assured when the Center promised to cast its votes for him on the first ballot. In Hagen-Schwelm, Reinhard Mumm was able to unite Center, Conservative, National Liberal, and Progressive voters around the candidacy of Ernst Francke. The German Socials, the German Reform Party, and the *Bund der Landwirte*, organizations which possessed thirteen seats in central and eastern Germany, also approached Behrens with promises of support for Evangelical social candidacies.[62] The most impressive success came in the "red kingdom" of Saxony. Desperate for electoral aid after the Socialist onslaught of 1903,[63] the Conservative *Landesverein* incorporated the Dresden branch of the Committee for the Election of Patriotic Workers into the party structure. Implicit in the action was a commitment to run Evangelical unionists for Reichstag and Landtag seats, although no specific arrangements to do so had been made by early November.[64]

The widely observed move of the Saxon Conservatives climaxed a debate raging in the Conservative camp over the merits of Christian-national *Blockpolitik*.[65] Conservative leaders had no trouble appreciating the necessity of an anti-Socialist coalition.[66] That the bourgeois parties should rally around Chris-

61. *Kölnische Zeitung*, no. 1152, 29 October 1906; *Rheinisch-Westfälische Zeitung*, no. 755, 6 August 1906; *Kölnische Volkszeitung*, nos. 693 and 950 for 13 August and 6 November 1906.
62. *Regierungspräsident* of Arnsberg to the Prussian minister of the interior, 10 December 1906, Reg. D. 9041, HSA Düsseldorf; Professor Otto Kraus to Francke, 11 December 1906, Francke Papers 4, BA Koblenz.
63. The S.P.D. had seized 22 of the 23 Saxon Reichstag seats.
64. *Neue Preussische Zeitung (Kreuzzeitung)*, no. 475, 10 October 1906; *Zentralblatt*, no. 22, 5 November 1906.
65. *Conservative Correspondenz*, 23 April, 10 May, and 25 June 1906 (clippings in: 61 Re 1 Reichslandbund [Pressearchiv], ZStA Potsdam); *Deutsche Tageszeitung*, no. 350, 29 July 1906; *Neue Preussische Zeitung (Kreuzzeitung)*, no. 350, 29 July 1906.
66. *Neue Preussische Zeitung (Kreuzzeitung)*, no. 486, 17 October 1906.

tian trade union candidates, however, was a completely different matter. The membership of workers in the Conservative *Fraktion* was viewed by party leaders as an unworkable situation. If a laborer tried to further the political goals of his union, he would be a source of constant friction within a truly conservative party. But if the unionist agreed to compromise and cooperate with other members of the *Fraktion*, he would be hounded mercilessly by angry comrades.[67] Despite the fact, therefore, that numerous speakers at the party's national convention in late November praised the expediency of the Saxon experiment, the spokesman for the party's autocratic steering board gave the following die-hard response:

> We have to convince the workers that promises like those made by a Herr Trimborn are unknown to us. We can't fulfill them and therefore the workers can't vote for us. I would have no objections if Christian workers came into the Reichstag. But you'll have to ask yourselves will such a deputy illustrate objectivity and independence toward the Social Democrats, then staunchly cooperate with the Conservatives? Does he really give us a guarantee that he'll mount the rostrum as a Conservative Reichstag Deputy? Otherwise, not much is gained with such people, even if we have 70 or 80 Conservatives in the Reichstag. I'd rather have 20 that can document their conservatism with their speeches and actions.[68]

With no sympathy from Conservative leaders, the Christian trade unions could not hope to sway local committees which were equally unmoved by the political logic of the Saxons.

Developments within the National Liberal Party were even less promising. Though largely supportive of the political program of the German Workers' Congress, the Liberals were never warm to the idea of a political alliance with the Christian trade unions. The *Gesamtverband* was regarded as far too Catholic and anti-capitalist for a Protestant, business-oriented party. Behrens and his anti-Semitic associates were viewed with an even greater degree of skepticism. It was not too surprising, therefore, that Bassermann made no effort to contact the Committee for the Election of Patriotic Workers, whose letter he left unanswered. This is not to say, however, that the prospect of Hirsch-Duncker or Evangelical *Arbeiterverein* deputies was looked upon more favorably. Like other bourgeois politicians, Bassermann and the National Liberals feared the consequences of one-sided interest group representation from workers of all political shades.[69]

67. *Neue Preussische Zeitung (Kreuzzeitung)*, no. 350, 29 July 1906.

68. *Neue Preussische Zeitung (Kreuzzeitung)*, no. 580, Beilage 2, 12 December 1906.

69. *Kölnische Zeitung*, no. 805, 28 July 1906; *Die Arbeit*, organ of the Committee for the Election of Patriotic Workers, no. 16, 21 April 1907; Bassermann to Stresemann, 31 August 1908, Stresemann Papers 137, H126510, BA Koblenz; Bassermann to Stresemann, 7 September 1908, Schiffer Papers 9, BA Koblenz.

Only in the Ruhr was there cause for optimism. Under heavy pressure from working-class voters, National Liberal committees in Duisburg, Recklinghausen, Bochum, and Dortmund had promised to nominate laborers in 1908. Worried by the rise of the S.P.D., Ruhr Liberals were also responsive to the demands of Christian unionists for interconfessional alliances during the primary elections. Thus an "old National Liberal politician"—probably Hermann Francken of Bochum—proposed in a newspaper article that pacts be made in Duisburg, Essen, Bochum, Dortmund, Elberfeld, Saarbrücken, and Ottweiler. The Bochum delegation to the National Liberal national convention at Goslar in October 1906 went one step further and actually urged the party to debate the idea of *Hauptwahl* agreements with Catholics.[70]

Weeks before Goslar, however, the Bochum initiative had been undermined in the left-liberal press. Fearful that such alliances would isolate Progressive candidates, the *Frankfurter Zeitung* ran a number of articles which were designed to break up the emerging coalition. The Center had reached the limits of its growth in western Germany, the reports claimed, and was therefore using the Christian trade unions as a lever to obtain the aid of Liberal voters. The paper expressed incredulity at the naiveté of the National Liberals for falling into the ultramontane trap. Assuming that electoral deals had already been made, outraged Liberals from other parts of the empire complained bitterly that a "national" party had no business cooperating with *Reichsfeinde* like the Center. The storm of protest was so great that party leaders like Bassermann, who sympathized with the tactic proposed by the Westphalians, felt compelled to table all debate over the issue at the national convention. The party's official newsletter, *Nationalliberale Correspondenz,* categorically rejected the idea of *Hauptwahl* pacts with Catholics a few days later. These were ominous signs for the future of interconfessional politics in Germany.[71]

The vision of a bourgeois *Block* working harmoniously in and out of parliament to defeat radical Socialism and further the cause of evolutionary social reform was thus a long way from realization. It must be emphasized, however, that great strides had been taken since the Frankfurt Workers' Congress of 1903. The idea of collusion during primary elections appealed to Conservatives, Centrists, Christian-Socials, and other right-wing politicians, while Bassermann and the Westphalian Liberals, though unable to force their party into such pacts, were nevertheless valuable allies. By late 1906, moreover,

70. *Kölnische Volkszeitung*, no. 703, 16 August 1906; *Neue Preussische Zeitung (Kreuzzeitung)*, no. 486, 17 October 1906, *Frankfurter Zeitung*, no. 305, 4 November 1906.

71. *Kölnische Volkszeitung*, no. 127, 14 February 1906; Bassermann to Francke, 22 December 1906, Francke Papers 4, BA Koblenz; *Neue Preussische Zeitung (Kreuzzeitung)*, no. 486, 17 October 1906; *Kölnische Volkszeitung*, no. 995, 21 December 1906.

Christian laborers had been promised numerous Reichstag candidacies from the Center and other parties. *Gesamtverband* leaders felt sure that the membership drive begun that fall would force other nominating committees to pay attention to the electoral demands of Christian workers.[72]

Political developments in Berlin gave Christian labor leaders all the more reason for optimism. After numerous delays, Posadowsky was finally given permission to enter his trade union bill in late October 1906. *Gesamtverband* agitators attempted to exploit the situation by holding mass rallies in Berlin and Bochum on the twenty-fifth anniversary of the government's first social law (21 November 1906). The new piece of legislation was presented at these rallies not as entirely adequate, but only as proof that Reich leaders intended to ignore the "disloyalty" of Socialist workers and proceed with the task of establishing equal rights for all classes. To accelerate this process, Christian leaders announced in late November that a second Workers' Congress would be held at Berlin in late January 1907. The demonstration would enhance efforts to "close ranks" within the Congress, create pressure in parliament to remove objectionable provisions of the trade union bill, and encourage Bülow to exert pressure on the Bundesrat to accept Reichstag amendments. The likelihood that these ambitious goals would be achieved was increased in early December 1906 when the Hirsch-Duncker unions, no longer under the control of Max Hirsch, informed Hans von Berlepsch of the Society for Social Reform that they would join the other non-Socialist labor groups at Berlin.[73] The demands of over a million patriotic workers, assumed Congress leaders, would be difficult to ignore.

72. For the political motivation behind the membership drive, see the *Zentralblatt*, no. 23, 19 November 1906, and no. 4, 25 February 1907; and *Westdeutsche Arbeiter-Zeitung*, nos. 43 and 46 for 27 October and 17 November 1906.

73. See the minutes of the Prussian Ministry of State, 30 October 1906, Reichskanzlei, Nr. 533, Bl. 59, ZStA Potsdam; *Tremonia*, no. 373 (2), 23 November 1906; *Kölnische Volkszeitung*, no. 989, 19 November 1906; *Zentralblatt*, no. 23, 19 November 1906; *Bericht über die Verhandlungen des zweiten Deutschen Arbeiter-Kongresses*, p. 67.

9

The Collapse of the Frankfurt Initiative and Trade Union Tactics 1907–1913

On 12 December 1906 Bülow convened special sessions of the Bundesrat and Prussian *Staatsministerium*. In the Reichstag budget committee two days earlier the Center Party had criticized the 29.2 million marks requested by the government for suppression of the Hottentots in Southwest Africa. The party felt that 20.2 million would suffice if regular troops who were not fighting the natives were replaced by less expensive police units. Charging that the Center had encroached on the jurisdiction of the army, Bülow informed the Prussian and federal councilors that he intended to dissolve the Reichstag. His arguments were opposed by the Prussian minister of finance (Rheinbaben) and the Reich secretaries of the navy (Tirpitz), finance (Stengel), and interior (Posadowsky), who wanted to avoid a conflict with the Center to insure parliamentary support for the needs of their departments. Armed with the written authorization of the Kaiser, however, Bülow prevailed. When a majority of Catholics and Socialists rejected the government's bill on its second plenary reading the next day, the chancellor announced to the applause of Conservatives, National Liberals, and Progressives that new elections would be held.[1]

As will be seen below, the premature dissolution of the Reichstag, the "Hottentot elections" of January 1907, and the subsequent period of the "Bülow Bloc" were disastrous for Christian labor. Not only was the political strength of Christian labor groups tested before the interconfessional ini-

1. Bachem, *Zentrumspartei*, vol. 6, pp. 330–71; Theodor Eschenburg, *Das Kaiserreich am Scheideweg* (Berlin: Verlag für Kulturpolitik, 1929), pp. 39–44.

tiatives of 1906 could gain momentum, but the atmosphere of exacerbated denominational suspicion and hatred engendered by the elections led to extremely counterproductive bickering within the ranks of non-Socialist labor itself.

This atmosphere also brought to an abrupt halt all progress which had been made toward a broad-based *Block* to pursue social reform. The chancellor's break with the Center exacerbated the divisiveness and factionalism which had long characterized relations in the German parliament, and added to the barriers which stood in the path of any evolution to western-style parliamentarism. A brief analysis of the origins of Bülow's feud with the Catholics, therefore, is of particular significance to this study. The relatively backward governmental system of Imperial Germany had worked to the advantage of Christian labor and the German Workers' Congress in 1903. Then, it will be recalled, the demands of the Congress had been convenient for Bülow. Now, in the most capricious fashion, the tables were turned.

Bülow's policy of cooperating with the Center became increasingly unpopular with Protestants after the partial repeal of anti-Jesuit legislation in March 1904. How was it possible, wondered many, that the Catholic Church could exert so much pressure on the head of government of the strongest Protestant state in Europe? The devout could only conclude that Bülow would have to go. To the normal intrigues against the chancellor, therefore, were added those of court pastors, the *Kaiserin*, and north German leaders like King Albert of Saxony and Prince Frederick Charles of Meiningen, who were outraged that Saxony, the cradle of the Reformation, should have to tolerate a Catholic society whose members vowed obedience to the pope alone. Religious indignation in central Germany was compounded by an intense opposition to the social reforms demanded by the Center in the name of the German Workers' Congress. As the nervous rulers of "red Saxony" saw it, the party's social programs were merely paving the way for Socialist domination of the Reich. Thus Albert and his fellow rulers in the Thuringian principalities took every opportunity to urge William II to strengthen the position of the Bundesrat and terminate the dangerous practice of making concession after concession to the Center.[2]

The Kaiser had no use for *Schwarzseher*, and does not seem to have harbored a great deal of animosity toward Catholics in general.[3] The Center Party,

2. Count Lerchenfeld to Bavarian minister-president Podewils, 31 December 1906, MA 76140, and 9 March 1907, Ges. Berlin, Pol. Schiftwechsel 1079, GStA München; report of the Württembergian Bundesrat plenipotentiary Schicker to the minister-president, 21 January 1904, reprinted in Rassow and Born, *Akten*, p. 177; Bülow, *Memoirs*, vol. 2, pp. 12–13; Zedlitz-Trützschler, *Twelve Years*, p. 90.
3. Bachem, *Zentrumspartei*, vol. 6, pp. 262–69.

on the other hand, was a different matter. Convinced as he was that the party took orders from the pope, William was highly suspicious of its every move, referring to the party usually as "a gang" or "pack of dogs."[4] For the same reason Jesuits were railed against in marginal comments as "the devil's brood" or "sons of hell."[5] In return for even the smallest concessions to the Center on the Jesuit issue, therefore, the Kaiser expected outright passivity from Centrists on other matters.

This was something which Bülow could not deliver. Eager to maintain an image of national reliability, the Center was usually prepared to accommodate most of the government's needs. But with Bavarian peasants, Swabian artisans, and Rhenish trade unionists demanding relief from mounting tax burdens, party leaders could hardly vote credits or revenues for every extra cruiser or cavalry regiment requested by the military. Complicating matters further, Centrists were anxious to defend the budget rights of the Reichstag against encroachment from the federal states, especially Prussia. Most Catholics took this cause very seriously, for the Reichstag was seen as the only effective bulwark against "the wrath of East Elbian Protestantism" (*Furor Protestanticus Ostelbianus*), as Karl Bachem usually described it in Latin. Thus, despite Bülow's warnings to Center leaders that such manifestations of parliamentarism were undermining his position at court,[6] the party continued to use its pivotal position throughout 1904 and 1905 to insure at least a modicum of frugality.

The situation became acute in 1906. The revelations of former Christian unionist Matthias Erzberger that spring concerning the mismanagement and corruption of Germany's colonial administration, though accurate, were nevertheless handled in a clumsy, tactless manner that angered the Kaiser. When the Center refused to vote funds for the construction of a railway in Southwest Africa in June, William flew into a rage at both the Center and Bülow. It was probably at this time that the ailing chancellor was ordered "to settle his accounts with the Center and break with it,"[7] as the Controller of the Imperial Household, Count Zedlitz-Trützschler, recalled later. Bülow urged an intermediary at court to explain to William that the Center's intransigence was far less problematic than Conservative opposition had been to the Midland Canal, and that "one must never let oneself be influenced by ignorant and irresponsible prattlers."[8] If it was given at all, however, such advice had little effect on

4. Quoted in Bülow's private manuscript over the Daily Telegraph affair, pp. 315–16, Bülow Papers 34, BA Koblenz.
5. Bülow, *Memoirs*, vol. 2, p. 12.
6. Bülow to Count Ballestrem, 7 April 1904, Bülow Papers 107, BA Koblenz; Bülow to Kopp, 13 March 1904, Bachem Papers 218, HA Köln.
7. Zedlitz-Trützschler, *Twelve Years*, p. 215.
8. Bülow to Count Tschirschky, n.d. (early June 1906), printed in Bülow, *Memoirs*, vol. 2, p. 283.

the angry monarch. In July he wired Bülow that there had to be a way "to protect our civil servants and officers from that slanderer, calumniator, and professional [*gewerbsmässig*] backstairs skulker Erzberger."[9]

All available evidence leads to the conclusion that by fall 1906 Bülow was prepared to call for new elections should the Center again place him in an embarrassing situation. Through such a maneuver Bülow hoped to reduce the Center's Reichstag strength and force the party to abandon all pretense to parliamentary power. Erzberger would be discredited, the air at court cleared, and the chancellor's eroded prestige with the Kaiser restored. Shortly after a Center speaker criticized the new colonial director on 3 December, therefore, Bülow requested and received William's consent to dissolve parliament. Rather than risk political ruin through "lack of energy," the chancellor hurled the country into one of the most bitter, hard-fought election campaigns in the nation's history.[10]

The well-laid political plans of the Christian trade unions crumbled overnight. In Saxony, for instance, Conservative Party leaders ostracized the Committee for the Election of Patriotic Workers and nominated a slate composed exclusively of upper- and middle-class candidates. Although solid evidence is lacking, it seems that the Conservatives did so in order to exploit fully the colonial vote of 13 December. The pro-Center leanings of Behrens and his followers would in any event inhibit the type of tub-thumping campaign the Conservatives had in mind.[11] Left in the lurch, Christian workers ran independently. Georg Hartmann, leader of the "patriotic workers" in Saxony, campaigned in Schneeberg-Aue, and a colleague ran in Zwickau- Crimmitschau.[12] Both candidacies collapsed, however, when neither the Conservatives nor the National Liberals offered assistance. The bourgeois Right was content to beat the nationalist drum, and for good reasons: the technique unseated fifteen of twenty-two incumbent Socialists in Saxony that year.

Developments in the Saar were no less problematic for the Christian trade unions. Unable to unite Christian workers around labor candidates in 1905, Evangelical and Catholic unionists were suddenly thrust into the midst of an intense Center–National Liberal struggle for control of the area. The example of Saarbrücken will suffice. The Center nominated Franz Wernerus, a Christian metal worker who promised to draw Evangelical laborers away from the

9. Quoted in Bülow's manuscript cited above in note 4, pp. 315–16.

10. For Bülow's motivation, see the Lerchenfeld reports cited in note 2; Bülow to General von Liebert, 31 January 1906, printed in the *Norddeutsche Allgemeine Zeitung*, no. 2, 3 January 1907; Bülow, *Memoirs*, vol. 2, pp. 287–88; Bachem, *Zentrumspartei*, vol. 6, pp. 378, 391–92.

11. For the campaign strategy of the Conservatives and National Liberals in Saxony, see the report of the Bavarian envoy Count Montgelas, 16 January 1907, MA 1936 Deutsches Reich 95484, GStA München.

12. *Frankfurter Zeitung*, no. 6, 6 January 1907.

National Liberals. The unionist was unacceptable to local "Berlinist" clergymen, however, and by early January 1907 they had managed to rally enough support for another candidate. The coup presented Catholic members of the *Gesamtverband* with a difficult choice. Out of a sense of party loyalty, Wernerus and the majority of Catholic workers backed the new Centrist, but a minority of Catholic unionists were so incensed by Wernerus's fate that they voted National Liberal. When Protestant *Gewerkverein* leader Wilhelm Gutsche joined their campaign against the Center, relations within the union deteriorated to the lowest point in years.[13]

Christian laborers experienced further setbacks in the industrial northwest. One positive development during the fall of 1906, it will be recalled, was the willingness of Westphalian National Liberals to consider *Hauptwahl* agreements with the Center. With Centrists branded as enemies of the state, however, the idea of interconfessional cooperation was quickly cast aside. In retaliation, Rhenish Center leaders also insisted that new strategies be adopted. Speaking at the general assembly of the *Augustinusverein* on 29 December, Julius Bachem, Hermann Cardauns, and Carl Trimborn refused to consider either primary or run-off support for the National Liberals—the party which stood most solidly behind Bülow's disciplinary action against the Center. So suspicious were Centrists of the National Liberals, in fact, that most lent credence to far-fetched rumors that the Reichstag suffrage was in danger. How better to deal a blow to Catholic strength?[14]

Stegerwald, who had not experienced the *Kulturkampf* and had relatively little interest in religio-political affairs, protested that the anti-Liberal stratagem advanced by Bachem *et al.* might easily allow the S.P.D. to seize every industrial district in western Germany. But Bachem was unmoved. Only if the Liberals were so crippled in the *Hauptwahl* that they could clearly not usurp the Center's pivotal Reichstag position should Centrists back a National Liberal in a run-off. The sight of his political mentor strongly hinting at Center support for the S.P.D. must have dumbfounded Stegerwald, for he did not reply.[15]

The Christian-Socials encountered similar problems in the Ruhr. Because Behrens's plan to form one nominating committee for the area had not been implemented by 13 December, each district decided on its own candidate for the elections in January. Swayed by the jingoism and demagoguery of the campaign, many committees forgot the "party line" and refused to run independently against the National Liberals and Conservatives. So strong was the

13. *Regierungspräsident* of Trier to the Prussian minister of the interior. 9 January 1907, 403/8464, LHA Koblenz; *Bergknappe*, no. 7, 16 February 1907.
14. *Augustinus-Blatt*, no. 1, January 1907, StBib MG.
15. *Ibid.*

pull of nationalism and Protestantism, in fact, that Evangelical workers in Duisburg, Bochum, and Dortmund turned their backs on Behrens and released National Liberal leaders from pledges made earlier to nominate workers. Bourgeois candidates, it was argued, would facilitate the cooperation of all "national" parties. The few Christian-Social committees that remained loyal to Behrens attempted to regain lost momentum by nominating Evangelical unionists as planned, but this backfired when National Liberal leaders threatened to run a Protestant worker in Siegen against Stöcker unless Christian-Social pressure in the Ruhr was terminated. Rather than jeopardize the seat of their leader, all committees complied.[16]

Further problems arose for Christian labor during the *Stichwahlen*. In the area stretching from Cologne to Osnabrück, twelve Socialists faced certain victory in run-offs if the Center, National Liberals, and Progressives could not resolve their differences. Worried that a Socialist sweep would give added impetus to the free trade unions in these districts, Stegerwald repeated his warnings to Center Leaders in Cologne throughout January. *Gewerkverein* leaders in Essen were also placing a great deal of pressure on Westphalian party boss Karl Herold. The miners were particularly interested in defeating *Alter Verband* chief Otto Hue, who faced a National Liberal candidate in Bochum-Gelsenkirchen. This campaign culminated with a mass rally of Catholic unionists in Düsseldorf on 28 January 1907. The workers "recommended" that the Center back National Liberal candidates if the Liberals reciprocated in Essen, Düsseldorf, and Cologne.[17]

Fortunately for the *Gesamtverband*, Karl Herold was also disturbed by the scenario of Socialist victory, free trade union advance, and collapse of the Center in the Ruhr. Therefore, at the first session of a new central committee which had been created to coordinate Center voting in the run-offs,[18] Herold argued for a pro–National Liberal *Stichwahl* policy. This would enable him to form the series of pacts desired by the Christian trade unions and "give a great uplift to their movement by completely defeating the S.P.D."[19] Most of those

16. *Frankfurter Zeitung*, no. 352, 21 December 1906, no. 356, 25 December 1906, no. 358, 28 December 1906, no. 9, 9 January 1907, no. 11, 11 January 1907, no. 26, 26 January 1907; *Tremonia*, no. 397, 18 December 1906, no. 401, 22 December 1906, no. 407, 30 December 1906, no. 2, 2 January 1907, no. 7, 7 January 1907, no. 14, 14 January 1907; *Kölnische Zeitung*, no. 1345, 17 December 1906, no. 1361, 20 December 1906, no. 1371, 23 December 1906, no. 1, 1 January 1907, no. 4, 2 January 1907, no. 36, 11 January 1907, no. 51, 15 January 1907, no. 54, 16 January 1907, no. 70, 20 January 1907, no. 292, 18 March 1907, no. 647, 20 June 1907.
17. Karl Bachem notation of 29 January 1907, Bachem Papers 259, HA Köln; *Kölnische Volkszeitung*, no. 93, 31 January 1907.
18. The official minutes of this session of 29 January 1907 are in the Herold Papers 2, BA Koblenz. What follows below is based primarily on Karl Bachem's more detailed notes, Bachem Papers 259, HA Köln.
19. *Ibid*. (Bachem notes).

present were unmoved. Backing for the "capitalistic *Kulturkampfspartei*" would be "suicide," they reasoned, while support for the "subversive *Revolutionspartei,*"[20] though also highly dubious and bound to demoralize the Christian trade unions, was probably the better of the two evils. With the majority leaning away from Herold and the Christian trade unions, Karl Bachem suggested a more flexible, face-saving set of run-off guidelines. Any candidate willing to defend the Reichstag suffrage and existing coalition rights and political freedoms, as well as promote social reform and religious tolerance, would qualify for Center support. According to Bachem's record of the meeting, the guidelines were acceptable to all, "even though it is clear that most National Liberals will reject them, while the Social Democrats will not."[21] Local committees in the Ruhr had at least some leeway for compromise with the National Liberals and "appearances are thoroughly preserved, which is necessary out of consideration for the Christian trade unions."[22]

Two days later the unions' hopes for a broad, anti-Socialist coalition in the northwest were brought closer to realization. Having bent somewhat to the demands of Christian labor on the twenty-ninth, Center leaders were now subjected to pressure from the Catholic *Oberpräsident* of the Rhineland and Archbishop Fischer of Cologne, both of whom considered the S.P.D. a far greater threat to church and state than the National Liberals. On 31 January, therefore, Trimborn offered to back the Liberals, but insisted on mutual support in Essen, Düsseldorf, and Cologne. Prussian officials passed the offer on to National Liberal leaders in Cologne later that day.[23]

The National Liberals flatly refused. Far from envisioning an authoritative turn to the Right under Bülow, as Center leaders feared, National Liberals in Cologne sensed a great opportunity to fulfill long-frustrated liberal demands like secular education, progressive tax laws, and the appointment of Liberals to ministerial posts. Rhenish party leaders were thus thoroughly against any *Stichwahl* policy that would preserve a "clerical-conservative majority." Not surprisingly, Trimborn announced in early February 1907 that Centrists should abstain in any district where Socialists and National Liberals faced one another. The deal was off. During the run-offs on 5 February, not surprisingly, the S.P.D. won five seats in the industrial West and remained just as strong as it had been in 1903.[24]

20. *Ibid.*
21. *Ibid.*
22. *Ibid.*
23. *Oberpräsident* Schorlemer-Lieser to Archbishop Fischer, 26 January 1907, *Regierungspräsident* Düsseldorf to Schorlemer-Lieser, 29 January 1907, 403/8465, LHA Koblenz; *Kölnische Volkszeitung*, no. 205, 8 March 1907.
24. Schorlemer-Lieser to the Prussian minister of the interior, 6 February 1907, 403/8465, LHA Koblenz; *Kölnische Volkszeitung*, no. 205, 8 March 1907; *Regierungspräsident* Düsseldorf to

The German Workers' Congress did not retire empty-handed from the elections of 1907. Thirteen representatives of affiliated organizations took their seats in a Reichstag whose Socialist delegation had been cut from eighty-one to forty-three. The political losses to non-Socialist labor, however, greatly outweighed the numerical gains. Far from driving the bourgeois parties together, Christian labor leaders had watched helplessly as these parties were driven apart. The ambitious campaign to "close ranks" within the Congress, moreover, was completely undermined. Angered by the presence of Catholic unionists at Center Party rallies, pro-Center articles run by union newspapers, and other alleged violations of political neutrality, many Evangelical *Arbeitervereine* reversed decisions made in 1905/6 and urged members to get out of Christian trade unions. The latter had their own list of grievances, pointing to the fact, for instance, that the Rhenish-Westphalian Association of Evangelical *Arbeitervereine* had urged all members to vote "national." The Hirsch-Duncker unions, which also succumbed to the nationalist hysteria of the campaign, were singled out for particular criticism by Catholic unionists. The attacks of the *Westdeutsche Arbeiter-Zeitung*, the *Zentralblatt*, and Behrens's newspaper, *Die Arbeit*, were so severe, in fact, that Hans Berlepsch, the founder of the Society for Social Reform, was unable to achieve a reconciliation between the two union camps. The second German Workers' Congress, in the meantime, had been canceled—yet another victim of the Hottentot elections.[25]

The campaigning that year also disturbed the internal harmony of the *Gesamtverband*. Squabbles like those in the Saar were not easily put to rest, nor did once-friendly Catholic priests quickly forget the pro–National Liberal stance adopted by the unions. Not until late 1907 could Stegerwald assert that his organization had recuperated from the divisiveness caused by the elections. A year of reprimands to local union leaders and numerous public statements reiterating the political neutrality of the Christian trade unions lay behind the weary general secretary.[26]

Setbacks such as these were not, however, the worst to befall Christian labor

---

Schorlemer-Lieser, 3 February 1907, 403/8465, LHA Koblenz; *Die Arbeit*, nos. 16 and 25, 21 April and 23 June 1907; *Kölnische Zeitung*, nos. 109 and 125, 30 January and 4 February 1907.

25. *Bericht über die Verhandlungen des zweiten Deutschen Arbeiter-Kongresses*, pp. 65–69, 87, 122–23; *Zentralblatt*, no. 24, 3 December 1906, no. 25, 17 December 1906, no. 2, 28 January 1907, no. 4, 24 January 1908; *Westdeutsche Arbeiter-Zeitung*, no. 51, 22 December 1906, no. 52, 29 December 1906, no. 13, 30 March 1907, no. 14, 6 April 1907, no. 20, 18 May 1907, no. 22, 1 June 1907, no. 24, 15 June 1907, no. 25, 22 June 1907; *Die Arbeit*, nos. 16–20, 21 April, 28 April, 5, 12, 18 May 1907, no. 12, 21 March 1908; *Kölnische Zeitung*, no. 1361, 20 December 1906, no. 460, 1 May 1907, no. 563, 29 May 1907; *Jungliberal-Blatt*, no. 5, 10 May 1907.

26. *Zentralblatt*, no. 23, 18 November 1907, no. 4, 24 February 1908.

as a result of the Bülow Bloc. Far more devastating were the blows dealt to the Frankfurt initiatives of 1903. No sooner had Posadowsky entered his trade union bill *(Rechtsfähigkeit der Berufsvereine)* in October 1906 than, according to plans made in 1904, a management-labor chambers bill was sent on its way through the cumbersome legislative machinery of state.[27] Encountering no opposition in the Prussian *Staatsministerium* with this bill in December and January, Posadowsky pressed Bülow for permission to formulate an Imperial *Vereinsgesetz*. Simultaneously, the aggressive Reich secretary announced in the Reichstag that his trade union bill, which according to constitutional procedure had been withdrawn after the dissolution, would be reintroduced during the next session. Posadowsky was pushing for a complete accommodation of the German Workers' Congress. The chancellor expressed interest in these ideas through an intermediary in March 1907.[28]

That Bülow had not replied directly, however, was a good sign that Posadowsky's days were already numbered. Every passing week during the election campaign made it clearer that Bülow's hopes for pacifying the Center were illusory. The party had only become more indignant and ungrateful, as Bülow saw it. Thus the chancellor prepared to continue his *Blockpolitik* until the Catholics came to heel.[29]

For such a policy Posadowsky was highly unsuited. The Progressives resented his parliamentary lobbying for the tariff bill of 1902 and, though not opposed to the secretary's social programs, were suspicious of his close working relationship with Trimborn and other Catholics. The Conservatives, on the other hand, considered Posadowsky a state socialist and lukewarm agrarian. As the Württembergian ambassador in Berlin wrote at the time, Posadowsky's social program was particularly upsetting to the Conservatives, "working on them like the bloody shirt."[30] It was no secret, moreover, that Posadowsky had attempted to dissuade Bülow from breaking with the Center and chafed at the thought of working with the new cartel for any length of time. In short, Posadowsky's presence was increasingly embarrassing to Bülow, and this the

27. Posadowsky to the Prussian Ministry of State, 29 October 1906, Reichskanzlei, Nr. 533, Bl. 71, ZStA Potsdam. The replies of the various Prussian ministers are located in Reichskanzlei, Nr. 533, Bl. 145–55, 169, ZStA Potsdam.
28. Posadowsky to Bülow, 18 March 1907, Reichskanzlei, Nr. 2241, Bl. 3, ZStA Potsdam; Reichstag Debates, Period 12, Session 1 (9 March 1907), vol. 277, pp. 344–47; note from one of Bülow's aids in the Chancellery to Posadowsky, 26 March 1907, Reichskanzlei, Nr. 2241, Bl. 4, ZStA Potsdam.
29. See Bülow's response to a *Reichskanzlei* report of 13 March 1907 that many Centrists favored a *rapprochement* with him, Reichskanzlei, Nr. 1391/2, Bl. 53–53a, ZStA Potsdam.
30. Württembergian Bundesrat plenipotentiary Varnbüler to Foreign Minister Weizsäcker, 23 June 1907, Kgl. Min, d. auswärtigen Angelegenheiten E73a, verz. 12e, HSA Stuttgart.

chancellor could not permit. He had risked too much for appearances already.[31]

Matters came to a head over the new *Vereinsgesetz* in the spring of 1907. Posadowsky advocated a progressive bill that would enhance the prestige of the German Workers' Congress, allowing its members to catch and overtake the Socialists. But Bülow, mindful of the need to maintain some degree of harmony in his polarized coalition, was more interested in a plan suggested by the Prussian minister of the interior, Bethmann Hollweg, whereby an "exceptional law" banning the use of foreign languages at public assemblies would be welded onto the *Vereinsgesetz*. The language clauses would appease Prussian Conservatives worried by the growing national Polish movement in the eastern provinces of the empire, while the Progressives and National Liberals, it was hoped, would accept the bill as an improvement over the existing legislation. Posadowsky's concern for the Christian and Hirsch-Duncker unions, both of which were competing for Polish workers in Silesia and the Ruhr, had simply been ignored. Aware that Bethmann's proposals would only add impetus to Socialist and radical Polish agitation, the affronted Reich secretary attempted to impose his views on the chancellor. But to no avail. The pull of the Prussian Conservatives from the Right was too great. When it became clear that other conservative clauses would be added to the *Vereinsgesetz*, and that Bülow wanted to decrease the tempo of social reform in general, Germany's most influential advocate of Christian-social reform felt compelled to tender his resignation.[32] In accepting it, Bülow made clear to all what inside observers had known for years—the chancellor had never had more than an opportunistic, tactical interest in labor legislation. As the *Zentralblatt* of the Christian trade unions commented quite accurately, Posadowsky had been "sacrificed to the new political constellation."[33] So too, the paper feared, had the cause of social reform.

The reconvening of the German Workers' Congress seemed imperative. Not long after Posadowsky's resignation, therefore, the decision was made to hold

31. Born, *Sozialpolitik*, p. 208, notes that Posadowsky's Reichstag speech of 19 February 1907, which had omitted the prescribed attacks against the Center, caused high government circles to conclude that the secretary's continued tenure in office was out of the question. In July, *Die Arbeit* (no. 28, 14 July 1907) printed a report emanating from Westphalian industrial sources that William and Bülow had decided in February that Posadowsky was not the right man for the job given his opposition to the Bloc.

32. See Varnbüler's report, cited above in note 30; Bethmann Hollweg to the Prussian Ministry of State (with Bülow's marginal comments), 19 March 1907, Reichskanzlei, Nr. 2241, Bl. 5–9, ZStA Potsdam; Count Lerchenfeld to Bavarian minister-president Podewils, 1 July 1907, Ges. Berlin, Pol. Schriftwechsel 1079, GStA München; see also *Die Arbeit*, no. 27, 6 July 1907, which reprints a report from the Berlin correspondent of the Viennese *Neue Freie Presse*, who claimed to have confidential information from a close friend of Posadowsky.

33. *Zentralblatt*, no. 13, 30 June 1907.

a second demonstration at Berlin in late October 1907. Hoping to maximize the effect of the Congress in parliamentary and governmental circles, the executive committee extended invitations to numerous politicians and ministers and once again requested an audience with the Imperial chancellor.[34]

Bülow was very reluctant to accede to this wish. Any association with "the very far-reaching [social] resolutions"[35] which officials in the Reich Chancellery expected of the Congress might alienate the Conservatives and right-wing National Liberals. Too, the issue of Prussian suffrage reform had been discussed widely that summer in the left-liberal and Socialist press. Should Christian workers add this demand to an already ambitious social program—and there was some reason to think that they might[36]—Bülow would create even more tension within the Bloc by receiving them.

Refusal to meet with the workers, on the other hand, could be equally embarrassing after the much-publicized reception in 1903.[37] The Socialists would have a field day criticizing the government's treatment of "loyal" workers, while the majority of National Liberals and Progressives, who wanted to maintain cordial relations with the Congress,[38] would be very irritated. In the end Bülow decided to receive the delegation *before* the Congress convened, thereby avoiding any association with specific resolutions. The executive committee was notified of this arrangement in September 1907.[39]

Responding through Ludwig Weber, the leader of the Evangelical *Arbeitervereine*, Christian labor leaders rejected Bülow's suggestion. Such a reception, they argued, would play into the hands of Socialist agitators by creating the impression of a government-controlled organization. Catholic members of the executive committee were particularly opposed to the pre-Congress reception because they would appear to be deserting the Center and joining forces with the anti-Catholic bloc. The predictable response of bourgeois Catholics would create problems in the Christian trade unions at a time when the bitterness of the elections had almost been forgotten.[40] Bülow accepted these arguments, but insisted that copies of all addresses and resolutions be for-

34. The announcement of the Congress is printed in *Die Arbeit*, no. 33, 11 August 1907.
35. Undersecretary of State in the Reich Chancellery Wahnschaffe to Bülow, 29 August 1907, Reichskanzlei, Nr. 533, Bl. 188, ZStA Potsdam. Bülow penciled his approval to Wahnschaffe's suggestions.
36. On 11 August 1907, *Die Arbeit* (no. 33), organ of Behrens's Committee for the Election of Patriotic Workers, advocated the Reichstag suffrage for Prussia. The announcement for the German Workers' Congress appeared in the same issue.
37. See Wahnschaffe's letter to Bülow of 29 August 1907, cited above in note 35.
38. See the letter of Hirsch-Duncker unionist Anton Erkelenz to the "parliamentary committee" of the Hirsch-Dunckers, n.d. (fall 1907), Erkelenz Papers 2, BA Koblenz.
39. *Geheimrat* Martins to von Loebell, head of the Reich Chancellery, 4 October 1907, Reichkanzlei, Nr. 533, Bl. 192, ZStA Potsdam. Bülow's marginal comments are on the document.
40. *Ibid.*

warded to him before the Congress met. If the proceedings were "calm and businesslike,"[41] and Bülow were presented with no "surprises,"[42] a reception afterwards was acceptable.

Stegerwald and Behrens, the "chiefs" (*führende Köpfe*) of the German Workers' Congress, had no desire to add new social demands like unemployment insurance and the eight-hour day to the Frankfurt program. Nor were they interested from a tactical viewpoint in abolishing the Prussian three-class suffrage in 1907.[43] With the original demands of 1903 in jeopardy, it would have been unwise to raise more far-reaching, seemingly unattainable demands. Such an approach would only alarm Bülow and force him into the open arms of the Conservatives. Stegerwald and Behrens were thus more than willing to inform Bülow of their limited plans for Berlin.[44] By committing themselves beforehand, however, the Congress leaders had sacrificed the flexibility needed in any parliamentary situation. This would prove a costly decision.

Convening in Berlin from 20 to 22 October 1907, the second Congress was in many ways more impressive than the first. The choice of Berlin made it easy for government and parliamentary leaders to be on hand in impressive numbers, while also providing more publicity and focusing national attention on the debates. Even without the Hirsch-Duncker unions, moreover, member organizations claimed nearly a million workers. The slightly expanded list of social demands was thus backed by a much larger phalanx of supporters. And, much like the first Congress, speakers were frank, yet undemagogic in presenting their arguments for social reform.

Marring the whole affair from the standpoint of the average German worker was the question of Prussian electoral reform. Stegerwald had no illusions concerning the unpopularity of this plutocratic suffrage, even among Christian workers, and took pains, therefore, to criticize the system in his address. Unfortunately for Stegerwald and the executive committee, a clear majority of the delegates responded enthusiastically to the resolution of Johann Fischer, a Württembergian Evangelical *Arbeiterverein* leader and former National So-

41. *Ibid.*
42. Wahnschaffe to Ludwig Weber, 14 October 1907, Reichkanzlei, Nr. 533, Bl. 194, ZStA Potsdam.
43. The Committee for the Election of Patriotic Workers met on 23 October and accepted Behrens's resolution to work for secret elections in Prussia (*Die Arbeit*, no. 44, 31 October 1907). The day before Stegerwald and Behrens had pigeonholed a resolution from the floor of the Congress demanding a positive stance toward universal, direct, equal, secret voting laws in Prussia.
44. Weber to Wahnschaffe, 16 October 1907, Reichskanzlei, Nr. 533, Bl. 195, ZStA Potsdam. Copies of Franz Wieber's and Adam Stegerwald's speeches, and the address to be made before Bülow, followed the next day (Bl. 197, 200, 219).

cial, who urged the Congress *to go on record* as an advocate of universal, equal, direct, and secret suffrage in Prussia. Unwilling to sever the last ties to Bülow, Congress leaders were forced to cut off the debate over Fischer's resolution in a rather dictatorial fashion, arguing unconvincingly that as a party-political, not a social, question, the Congress could not handle the matter. Christian leaders appeared even more "anti-labor" now than they had in the great tariff debates of 1901/2.[45]

One result of this affair was the undermining of the very grudging respect which Christian workers had earned from their Socialist counterparts after the Frankfurt Congress of 1903 and the strengthening of lingering attitudes concerning the so-called fraud of Christian labor. Thus Hermann Molkenbuhr, a Social Democratic Reichstag deputy, reminded his son that the Christian labor movement had never since the beginning of its history proposed anything truly original, having merely "plagiarized"[46] Socialist programs. As Molkenbuhr's diary entry after the Berlin Congress illustrates, critical outlooks such as this were quite sincere, not just rhetoric for election time. "Bethmann Hollweg," who had spoken to the delegates briefly during the convocation of the Congress,

> received much applause, but as the [supposedly] contented ones began to speak, the real workers' nature came to the fore. Along with the Christian and patriotic spirit a proletarian consciousness has also taken hold, and as the Congress began to formulate its demands, real worker demands which did not originate in the heads of Socialist intellectuals were put forth. Poor ministers. It will be difficult to continue this hypocrisy when even the contented ones begin to demand the eight-hour day, universal suffrage for the Landtag, and similar things.[47]

Molkenbuhr's concluding comment foreshadowed the eventual radicalization of Christian labor during the last years of the empire. His observations were also an excellent indication of the gap which still separated the German labor movements. Although the Christians might win temporary recognition from the Social democrats as cunning political opponents, as in 1903, it was felt the movement was destined to fall behind because it was an artificial creation which contradicted "proletarian consciousness."

In addition to the embarrassment this caused Congress leaders, the unwillingness to push for political reform in Prussia also widened the gap be-

45. *Bericht über die Verhandlungen des zweiten Deutschen Arbeiter-Kongress*, pp. 50–51, 89–93, 227–30.
46. Molkenbuhr to his son Arthur, 15 November 1907, Molkenbuhr Papers II, no. 46, AdSoz Bonn.
47. Diary entry for 23 October 1907, Molkenbuhr Papers, Kassette IV, Tagebücher I, 1905–9, AdSoz Bonn.

tween Christian and left-liberal labor. Despite his inability to soothe *Gesamtverband* and Hirsch-Duncker leaders in the spring of 1907, Hans von Berlepsch continued to work for a reconciliation. The former Prussian minister was especially hopeful that the influential "Düsseldorf faction" around the young Hirsch-Duncker metal worker Anton Erkelenz would be able to sway the union leadership to a pro-Congress standpoint.[48] Ashamed of the slow growth of the Hirsch-Duncker unions in recent years, Erkelenz wanted to boost the political influence of his "humble, peripheral organization"[49] by joining the other non-Socialist labor groups at Berlin.

Confident that he would succeed in this mission in July, Erkelenz watched in frustration that summer as the heavy-handed tactics of Christian leaders, who were still angry over the elections, undermined his position with the offended Hirsch-Duncker executive committee. "Why should we resuscitate an organization in the death throes by tying it to our strengthening organization?" barked Stegerwald. "That's not in the interests of the Christian unions."[50] These setbacks dampened Erkelenz's spirit, but it was not until the dispute over the suffrage at Berlin that Erkelenz's faction also abandoned the idea of political cooperation with the Christians. A sharp attack in the *Frankfurter Zeitung*, written most probably by Erkelenz, was followed in the winter of 1907/8 by an attempt to found a separate "Liberal workers' congress." High on the list of reform priorities, not suprisingly, was the liberalization of Prussia.[51]

Behrens, in the meantime, had led his Workers' Congress associates to the Reich Chancellery for the appointed session with Bülow. Bethmann Hollweg had already informed the Congress that an Imperial *Vereinsgesetz* and a management-labor chambers bill were in the making, but it must have been encouraging to hear from the chancellor himself that these reforms were at last nearing completion.[52] After four years of waiting, Christian labor groups would finally have an opportunity to argue before skeptical audiences that the German Workers' Congress, not the free trade unions or S.P.D., had promoted

48. Berlepsch to Erkelenz, 7 June 1907, 15 June 1907, and 10 July 1907, Erkelenz Papers 2, BA Koblenz.

49. Anton Erkelenz, *Biographische Niederschrift*, n.d. (post–WWI), p. 220, in the Erkelenz Papers 103, BA Koblenz. Erkelenz refers specifically to the summer of 1907.

50. See Stegerwald's remarks as quoted by Berlepsch, whose notes of a *Gesamtverband* executive committee session of 2 April 1907 are printed in Fricke, "Bürgerliche Sozialreformer," *Zeitschrift für Geschichtswissenschaft*, Heft 10 (1975), p. 1186.

51. *Frankfurter Zeitung*, no. 307, 5 November 1907; Otto Thomas to Erkelenz, 17 November 1907, Erkelenz Papers 2, Erkelenz to the Hirsch-Duncker "parliamentary Committee," n.d. (fall 1907), Erkelenz Papers 2, BA Koblenz; police commissioner Essen to *Regierungspräsident* Düsseldorf, 30 September 1908, Reg. D. 42810, HSA Düsseldorf.

52. *Bericht über die Verhandlungen des zweiten Deutschen Arbeiter-Kongresses*, pp. 19–22. The addresses to Bülow, and his reply, appear on pages 231–33.

working-class interests. With the experience of an inadequate trade union bill and Posadowsky's resignation fresh in their minds, Christian workers had no doubts that a tough parliamentary struggle for revisions lay ahead. Should the confessional unity of the Bloc prove weaker than the centripetal pull of individual party programs, however, a situation conducive to the success of Congress lobbying efforts might arise.

The publication of Bethmann's *Vereinsgesetz* in late November 1907 confirmed the suspicions of Christian laborers concerning his social conservatism. "Private rights" (*privatrechtliche*) such as legal personality for trade unions had been omitted from the new law, leaving only the area of "public rights." These provisions were an improvement over the rigid laws of Prussia and Saxony, but there were some crucial defects and retrogressions. Rural laborers, state employees, and domestic servants, for instance, were excluded from the bill. There was also no attempt to reform Germany's authoritarian strike laws (*Koalitionsrecht*). Moreover, the language paragraphs worsened the legal position of Germany's Polish, Danish, and French minorities, while also undermining trade union efforts to recruit members from these communities. Unable to attract foreign workers into the unions, organized labor felt it could be easily undercut by owners with access to cheap, unorganized workers from abroad.[53]

The first reading of the bill on 9–10 December was equally disappointing for non-Socialist labor. A week earlier the Bloc had almost broken apart over the issue of tax reform, but Bülow, threatening that he and Bethmann would resign unless the liberals halted attacks on the government, had managed to restore order to his coalition. The Progressives and National Liberals were therefore unwilling to engage in anything but very reserved criticism of the *Vereinsgesetz*. The specter of Bülow or a more reactionary successor working with the Center again was simply too threatening. The bill went to the committee in early January 1908 with little likelihood of drastic alteration by the Bloc.[54]

The bill that emerged from the second committee reading on 18 March remained unacceptable to Christian labor leaders. There had only been a few changes. Anxious to complete the *Vereinsgesetz* before the Prussian elections that summer, Bethmann gave in to Progressive demands that rural laborers be included. He also accepted a milder version of the language paragraphs. But the Conservatives were duly compensated. A clause was added banning youths under 18 from membership in "political" organizations. All Center, Christian

53. *Die Arbeit*, no. 48, 28 November 1907; *Zentralblatt*, no. 25, 16 December 1907.

54. Count Lerchenfeld to Bavarian minister-president Podewils, 4 December and 4 December 1907 (separate reports), Ges. Berlin, Pol. Schriftwechsel 1079, GStA München.

trade union, and S.P.D. amendments, including one which exempted trade unions from the language paragraphs, were defeated.[55]

With the final plenary reading approaching in early April 1908, Behrens made a final, daring attempt to revise the *Vereinsgesetz* in labor's favor. The Evangelical labor leader obtained an audience with Bethmann-Hollweg and urged him to state in parliament that trade unions would be uninhibited in their agitation by the language paragraphs. Such a statement would set an example for local police officials, Landräte, and *Regierungspräsidenten* subordinate to the minister of the interior. Behrens probably hinted that, as chairman of the German Workers' Congress, he could create trouble for the government on the final reading. Well aware that the voting would be close, Bethmann reversed the position he had taken in committee on a similar amendment and agreed to the proposal. In return, however, he insisted that Behrens vote for the language paragraphs. Both men carried out their ends of the deal on 4 April and the controversial clauses were accepted by a slim 19-vote margin.[56]

For his last-minute handiwork Behrens should have won the acclaim of all Christian workers. In the highly charged atmosphere of the Bloc period, however, such a pragmatic assessment was impossible. Like all Catholics, Giesberts and the Center's labor wing had great hopes that Bülow's coalition would collapse as a result of the *Vereinsgesetz*—the first major piece of legislation it had confronted. When, instead, the Bloc survived, great anger and frustration were felt. Center laborers had extra reason to feel this way, for the *Gesamtverband* had also experienced a great degree of Bloc-engendered frustration since December 1906. That Behrens, a Christian trade unionist, should help preserve the Protestant cartel by accepting the controversial language paragraphs seemed an act of betrayal to the Christian unions and the substantial number of Catholics who had voted for him.

"The Behrens Case" (*Der Fall Behrens*) led very quickly to a crisis within the Christian labor movement. The *Westdeutsche Arbeiter-Zeitung* found it hard to believe that an experienced unionist could place so much trust in Bethmann's oral interpretation of the law, while the Catholic editor of *Bergknappe*, not content to criticize, called for Behrens's resignation as general secretary of the *Gewerkverein*. The Center press of the Ruhr, especially Wilhelm Hankamer's *Essener Volkszeitung*, followed suit. *Die Arbeit*, organ of the Committee for the Election of Patriotic Workers, was quick to defend Behrens against these attacks, but the Christian-Social and Evangelical *Arbeiterverein* press swung over to the offensive, stating in no uncertain terms that further persecution of Behrens would bring an end to existing interconfes-

55. For the major developments in committee, see Rassow and Born, *Akten*, pp. 307–43.
56. *Die Arbeit*, nos. 15–16, 11 and 18 April 1908; *Zentralblatt*, nos. 7 and 9, 20 April and 4 May 1908.

sional ties. Evangelical miners in the Saar lent credence to these articles by threatening to bolt from the union if Behrens were ousted.[57]

Hankamer and other Centrists in the Ruhr were unimpressed by these warnings. Since the *Gesamtverband*'s political initiatives of 1906, these circles, like the "Berliners," had begun to regard the interconfessionalism of the Christian trade unions as a liability for the Center. The pro–National Liberal stance of the unions during the elections, Behrens's stewardship of a largely Catholic delegation to the Reich Chancellery a few months later, and his "betrayal" of the Center on the *Vereinsgesetz* vote strengthened the impression that Christian labor had deserted the Catholic cause. To avoid further problems of this sort, Hankamer and his followers decided to drive a wedge between the Catholic and Evangelical wings of the non-Socialist labor movement. Embarrassing details of the feuding within the *Gewerkverein* were sent anonymously to the *Frankfurter Zeitung* which quickly printed them in the hope that the Hirsch-Dunckers could lure Evangelical unionists away from the *Gesamtverband*. Centrists in the Ruhr also encouraged Heinrich Imbusch, Hermann Vogelsang, and other Catholic workers in control of *Bergknappe* to take steps against Behrens. The *"Bergknappe-clique"* proved amenable to this plan after Imbusch was promised a Reichstag or Landtag nomination, and on 21 April 1908, the miners initiated proceedings against Behrens before the central committee of the *Gesamtverband*.[58]

The plot failed. Stegerwald and the national leadership refused to sabotage the *Gesamtverband* and the German Workers' Congress by making a martyr out of Behrens. The matter was settled with a resolution that urged Christian trade unionists to maintain closer contacts in parliament and put union interests ahead of party ties. A renewed attack on Behrens during the *Gewerkverein*'s executive committee meeting of 24 April was also repulsed when Johann Effert, the highly popular leader of the miners' *Siebenerkommission*, came to the Protestant's defense.[59] Thus ended the greatest threat to the unity of non-Socialist labor since the secession of the Berliners in mid-1902.

There was little cause for rejoicing, however, for Christian laborers had registered nothing but losses since the fall. Far from advancing the cause of non-Socialist labor with a dramatic political success, the German Workers' Congress had suffered ridicule over the Prussian suffrage issue, alienated the Hirsch-Duncker unions, and narrowly averted collapse in the wake of Beth-

57. Police commissioner of Bochum to the *Regierungspräsident*, 30 April 1908, Reg. Arnsberg I 83, StA Münster; *Westdeutsche Arbeiter-Zeitung*, no. 18, 2 May 1908; *Zentralblatt*, no. 9, 4 May 1908; *Die Arbeit*, no. 16, 18 April 1908.

58. The intrigues of Hankamer *et al.* were described in great detail to the *Regierungspräsident* of Arnsberg in August 1908 by the Christian miner Johann Effert. The memorandum is located in Reg. Arnsberg I 83, StA Münster.

59. *Ibid.*; *Zentralblatt*, no. 7, 20 April 1908.

mann's conservative *Vereinsgesetz*. No less demoralizing was the fact that Posadowsky's trade union bill (*Rechtsfähigkeit der Berufsverein*) had been dropped in the meantime. The tempo of social reform was indeed slowing down.

* * * *

Given this situation, it would have been ill advised to ignore other channels through which to obtain gains for the worker. In fact, since the elections Christian labor had been engaged in private efforts to encourage industry to adopt collective bargaining (*Tarifgemeinschaften; Tarifverträge*) as standard practice. The campaign began under the auspices of the Society for Social Reform, which devoted its General Assembly session of December 1906 to an investigation of this issue. The executive committee of the *Gesamtverband* met in the spring of 1907 to discuss means of implementing collective bargaining agreements. By mid-year the individual unions of the federation, particularly the textile, metal, and mine workers, were establishing contacts with entrepreneurs who could be expected to lend a sympathetic ear. Others, it was hoped, would follow the example.[60]

We have a good deal of information about the exploratory meetings held with mine owners in the Ruhr. The *Gewerkverein* preceded its talks with a flurry of public assemblies in March, calling for corporate status for trade unions, legal recognition of trade unions, industrial chambers joining both capital and labor, and, in general, a highly institutionalized form of cooperation between worker and owner.[61] On 7 April, Heinrich Imbusch and other *Gewerkverein* secretaries, joined by Heinrich Brauns of the *Volksverein* and Hans Berlepsch of the Society for Social Reform, met with the director of the Bergwerk Dorstfeld, Friedrich Trippe, and his business manager. The two belonged to the Society and agreed that collective wage contracts for the region were desirable—among other reasons, to prevent job turnover—but that a more cohesive organization of the mine owners themselves was a prerequisite for such bargaining. All present urged Trippe "to disseminate the main ideas raised in the discussion among the circles of mine owners."[62]

Trippe's mission was probably doomed before it began. The majority of mine owners in the Ruhr were rigidly anti-labor and were particularly worried that collective bargaining would severely attenuate their right to be "*Herr im*

60. See Berlepsch's notes from a session of the *Gesamtverband* executive committee held in Cologne on 2 April 1907, printed in Fricke, "Bürgerliche Sozialreformer," *Zeitschrift für Geschichtswissenschaft*, Heft 10 (1975), pp. 1184–85.
61. Police commissioner of Essen to the *Regierungspräsident*, 30 September 1907, Reg. D. 9059, HSA Dusseldorf.
62. See Berlepsch's notes of the meeting, printed in Fricke, "Bürgerliche Sozialreformer," as cited above in note 60.

Haus."[63] Thus the manager of the Association of Ruhr Mining Interests spoke out that May against "the specific demands of the trade unions, namely, those for collective bargaining, whose fulfillment would result in extreme damage to home industry."[64] He then pondered whether a new organization of the mine owners better able to resist the unions should not be founded. The result was the Mines' Association, or *Zechenverband*, which proceeded after its incorporation in early 1908 to blacklist union leaders and generally adopt a much tougher stance toward organized labor.[65]

Their private moves checked, Christian labor leaders turned again to the political arena. Working through the Catholic Center Party, which had been a fairly reliable legislative agent for the Christian trade unions in the sociopolitical sphere since the turn of the century, two bills were introduced in the Reichstag in late 1907. The first stipulated that firms under contract with the Imperial navy must comply with collective bargaining practices.[66] The second requested that the chancellor "propose legal means to regulate the right of wage contracts for workers."[67] Both bills passed the Reichstag in February 1908 with overwhelming support.

Nothing came of either. The Reichstag's request to regulate bargaining was passed from the Bundesrat, to the chancellor, to the Reich Ministry of the Interior, where it remained pigeonholed until the collapse of the empire in 1918.[68] The fate of the first bill was quicker and served to illustrate the nature of the difficulty encountered by such legislation. While the representatives of the ship-building industry howled in protest, the Prussian and Reich ministers agreed in June 1908 that the state "has to guard strenuously against any interference with the independence of the employer" and in October prevented state enterprises from bargaining with labor organizations "out of consideration for the private sector."[69] So much, then, for the "growing influence" of the Reichstag.

* * * *

Not much remained of the demands of the first German Workers' Congress by 1908. The bill guaranteeing unions corporate rights had been abandoned by

63. See ch. 1 of Paul Osthold, *Die Geschichte des Zechenverbandes* (Berlin: Otto Elsner Verlagsgesellschaft, 1934).
64. Quoted in *Bergknappe*, no. 23, 8 June 1907.
65. For these developments, see Saul, *Staat Industrie und Arbeiterbewegung*, pp. 83–93.
66. See Gröber's introduction of the bill and reference to the Christian trade unions, as well as Behrens's defence of the motion, in the Reichstag Debates, 31 January 1908, vol. 230, pp. 2782, 2789–90.
67. Reichstag Debates, 25 February 1908, vol. 230, p. 3392.
68. Saul, *Staat, Industrie, Arbeiterbewegung*, pp. 65, 442.
69. Cited in *ibid.*, p. 64.

the government, while demands for expanded rights of coalition and assembly had been left largely unsatisfied by the new *Vereinsgesetz*. Collective bargaining efforts had gotten nowhere. In fact, of the original Frankfurt demands, only the management-labor chambers bill remained undecided in mid-1908. The draft which Posadowsky passed on to Bethmann the year before was revised in the fall of 1907 and published in tentative form for public scrutiny and debate in February 1908.[70] This unprecedented step—explained no doubt by the government's desire to appear impartial to the demands of both capital and labor—was followed by more debate in the Bundesrat that summer and fall. When, in January 1909, a management-labor chambers bill was finally laid before parliament,[71] five long years had elapsed since Posadowsky's staff had begun preliminary work.

The reform was an extremely cautious one.[72] The chambers would not encompass every branch of industry in a given city or district (*territoriale Gliederung*), as Posadowsky had planned; rather there would be separate chambers for individual industries (*fachliche Gliederung*). Bethmann was convinced that territorial chambers would turn into "political debating clubs"[73] for members of opposing classes, unlike the trade-oriented chambers, which seemed better equipped to promote a harmonious economic partnership. Trade union leaders were barred from election to the chambers for much the same reason. Fearing that union secretaries would easily dominate and radicalize the proceedings, the government required that labor candidates have no record of arrest and be able to offer proof of employment in a factory or mine during the year preceding the election—qualifications few union functionaries could match. In order to minimize further the "terroristic disruption of the populace,"[74] which government officials expected from the free trade unions and S.P.D. during the chamber elections, Bethmann certified the owner-employee accident compensation committees as nominating bodies. Unlike their health insurance counterparts, these committees had remained free of trade union and Socialist influence and were quite popular with employers as a result.

The role of Bethmann's management-labor chamber would also be very

70. See Prussian minister of the interior Bethmann Hollweg to Bülow, 2 November 1907, Bethmann Hollweg to the Prussian Ministry of State, 28 November 1907, Reichskanzlei, Nr. 533, Bl. 227, 233, and the finished proposal of 1 February 1908, Reichskanzlei, Nr. 534, Bl. 10, ZStA Potsdam.

71. See Reichstag *Anlagen*, Period 12, Session 1, no. 1418, vol. 255, pp. 79ff.

72. The following discussion of Bethmann's views is based primarily on his memorandum to the Prussian ministers of 6 July 1908, Reichskanzlei, Nr. 534, Bl. 20, ZStA Potsdam, and to a lesser extent his memorandum to the federal states of 14 July 1908, reprinted in Rassow and Born, *Akten*, pp. 395–97.

73. Bethmann to the Prussian ministers, 6 July 1908, as cited in *ibid*.

74. *Ibid*.

limited. Not all industries, for instance, would have chambers, for each state was given the right to decide which branches of the state economy actually needed such institutions. Nor would the new bodies exert much influence during a strike. They were to function mainly as courts of appeal to the industrial tribunals established in the 1890s and were excluded, therefore, from all cases solved or simply not heard by the lower courts. Aside from these duties, chambers would also submit position papers to the state concerning pending industrial legislation. In this way the government would be able to base its proposals, should it so choose, on the resolutions of the legally recognized spokesmen of the business and laboring communities. This semi-political role made it even more imperative for the government to exclude trade union secretaries, because "otherwise," wrote Bethmann, "organized labor would be elevated to the level of an organ of state."[75]

Despite the obvious drawbacks to his bill, Bethmann was hopeful that non-Socialist workers (as opposed to non-Socialist *union leaders*) would accept the chambers and actively support the struggle against revolutionary Socialism.

> One may look upon the national reliability of the Christian labor movement, the Hirsch-Duncker associations, the yellow trade unions, etc., as yet untested. But it's a fact that these movements drive a wedge into the S.P.D.'s terroristic Bloc and, with any tact by employers in the management-labor chambers, will be able to be used against the Socialists.[76]

With moderate concessions to show for their efforts, perhaps these non-Socialist groups could teach Socialist workers to appreciate the benefits of cooperation. A complete reconciliation between capital and labor would probably never occur, but if only a few agreements could be hammered out, then a slow process of reciprocity and compromise would begin. In the long run, noted Bethmann, "the S.P.D.'s dogmatic, intolerant rule of force"[77] would be broken.

The response of the free trade unions, logically enough, was quite negative. Convinced that management-labor chambers would not permit the workers' views and interests to be represented fairly, the General Commission had spoken out four years earlier for pure labor chambers (*Arbeiterkammer*).[78] Legien's speech in the Reichstag in January 1909 reflected this stance.[79] It

75. *Ibid.*
76. *Ibid.*
77. *Ibid.*
78. *Protokoll der Sitzung des Gewerkschaftsausschusses der Gewerkschaften Deutschlands*, 23 March 1905, DGB Haus Düsseldorf; *Correspondenzblatt der Generalkommission der Gewerkschaften Deutschlands*, nos. 20 and 23, for 20 May and 10 June 1905.
79. Reichstag Debates, Period 12, Session 1 (15 January 1909), vol. 234, p. 6300.

might be possible to attain a certain degree of stability in labor relations when workers reached a position of equal power with employers. But a true harmony of interests between capital and labor was impossible under the capitalist system, and this was the underlying weakness of the government's bill. Only when the workers themselves owned the means of production would harmony between managers and laborers be possible.

Legien found it difficult to understand, therefore, why the Christian trade unions advocated codeterminational chambers. Non-Socialist workers suffered from the same social conditions as the Social Democrats, so why allow employers to manipulate labor within a joint chamber? The Christian trade union leadership, Legien concluded, was probably subordinating itself to Center Party, hence bourgeois, interests.

It was not the Socialist viewpoint, however, which prevailed on the Reichstag committee established to consider the government's bill. Alongside Legien, Bömelburg, and Brandys of the free trade unions were Giesberts, Schirmer, Wiedeberg, and Behrens of the Christian trade unions, Fleischer of the Catholic *Fachabteilungen*,[80] and Schack of the Patriotic Retail Clerks, as well as Hitze, Trimborn, Naumann, and other supporters of non-Socialist labor. Thus the committee draft of April 1909 called for joint chambers, but, importantly, with much more prestige and influence than those envisioned by Bethmann. The Bundesrat, not the individual states, was given the right to decide where chambers were needed, thereby assuring that a somewhat larger number would be created. The jurisdiction of the new bodies was also expanded. Should striking workers appeal first to the chambers for arbitration, not the local industrial tribunals, the legal competence of the latter would be preempted. Along with the semi-political duties included in the government's bill, moreover, the committee wanted management-labor chambers to establish labor exchanges, investigate commercial and industrial relations, and bring quarreling parties together for collective bargaining sessions. The committee also insisted that the functionaries of both trade union and employer associations be eligible for chamber elections.[81]

It would seem that Christian labor placed its hopes for genuine codetermination in the proposed management-labor chambers. In his speech on *Arbeitskammer* at Frankfurt in 1903, for instance, Giesberts observed that it was unwise so early in the political process to comment in detail on the future functions of the chambers, but that a guarantee of "free and equal codeter-

80. Like all the "Berliners," Fleischer opposed strikes. As he admitted years later, however, "the aversion to liberal capitalism was there from the beginning." Notation by Dr. Heinz Brauweiler, editor of the *Düsseldorfer Tageblatt*, concerning a talk with Fleischer on 13 July 1942, Brauweiler Papers 24, StA MG.

81. Reichstag *Anlagen*, Period 12, Session 1, no. 1418, vol. 255, pp. 79ff.

mination [*Mitwirkung*] in all questions that touch on the interests and welfare of workers"[82] was required. In 1905 the *Zentralblatt*, edited by Giesberts, offered more specifics by agreeing that strike tactics were justified "because the workers have no codeterminational [*mitbestimmenden*] influence over the regulation of production, prices, and markets. As soon as such influence is guaranteed," the article continued, "the prerequisites for union tactics pursued thus far will fall by the wayside."[83] Such wording did not exist in the Reichstag's bill of 1909, one must presume, because Christian labor envisioned a very gradual evolution of the functions of these chambers and thought that demands of codetermination in 1909 would only undermine parliamentary support. As it stood, nevertheless, the committee draft, unlike the government's bill, would have greatly strengthened the position of labor vis-à-vis capital and, for all intents and purposes, recognized trade unions as the legal representatives of the entire working class.

With the battle lines drawn between Bundesrat and Reichstag, the executive committee of the German Workers' Congress called a special session in Berlin on 21 April 1909. Stegerwald, Behrens, Schack, and the others gave a strong vote of confidence to the work of the Reichstag committee and urged parliament to stand firm. Congress leaders also warned the government that management-labor chambers without trade union secretaries would never be accepted by the German worker.[84] The session had been preceded, interestingly enough, by eighteen mass rallies throughout Germany which passed similar resolutions. Politicians from all parties had been selected as guest speakers in a shrewd move to win broad support. At Bamberg, for instance, *Kommerzienrat* Manz of the National Liberals "spoke in complete agreement with the position of Christian labor."[85] The Congress seemed to have revived from the debacle of the previous year.

In Wilhelmian Germany, however, the resolutions of mass rallies, worker lobbies, and Reichstag committees were seldom effective in high places. Unwilling to compromise on the eligibility of union secretaries, the Bundesrat withdrew the management-labor chambers bill that spring. Bethmann reentered it in much the same form in February 1910, but when a Reichstag committee packed with trade unionists of every stripe insisted on far-reaching improvements in May and was backed by an overwhelming majority of the full house in December 1910, the government stalled for a year, then allowed the bill to fall automatically with the dissolution of parliament in December 1911.

82. *Protokoll der Verhandlungen des Deutschen Arbeiterkongresses (25–26 Oktober 1903)*, p. 60 ZSg.1 63/6, BA Koblenz.
83. *Zentralblatt*, no. 17, 21 August 1905, pp. 273–75.
84. *Zentralblatt*, no. 9, 3 May 1909.
85. *Ibid*.

Assuming that the Reichstag majority would not compromise on the issue of trade union secretaries, the government made no attept to reintroduce it after the elections of January 1912. So ended the last attempt by the leaders of pre-war Germany to improve the socio-economic *rights* of labor vis-à-vis capital.[86]

This outcome was embarrassing for those who gambled on the willingness of Reich leaders to reform the nation's labor laws. After the setbacks over neutrality and tariffs at the turn of the century, Christian laborers had concluded in desperation that only a rapid, dramatic introduction of Christian-social reforms could slow down the advance of the free trade unions. The quarrel with Berlin from 1903 to early 1906, followed by the collapse of Christian *Blockpolitik* and the slower tempo of reform under the Bülow Bloc, ended this desperate bid for recruits in a most devastating fashion, for the ridicule which resulted from these setbacks exacerbated Christian labor's basic organizational and financial disadvantage at the union level.

Before turning to this struggle of survival in the trade union world, some commentary on the broader historical lessons to be learned from the developments discussed thus far in this chapter is required. Indeed, the years of the Bülow Bloc contain many examples of the phenomenon of manipulation which this study has attempted to clarify. The "Hottentot elections" of 1906/7 are a classic illustration of the techniques which were so often employed by the state to weaken and frustrate oppositionist groups, and on the whole were quite successful. So potent was the nationalist-imperialist hysteria generated by the government that the S.P.D. Reichstag *Fraktion* returned to Berlin with only 53 percent of its former strength. The Center Party had also been taught an object lesson in the *limits* of parliamentary power. The state, however, sometimes lost control of the forces it set in motion. Thus pressure on the Rhenish Center, employed indirectly through the archbishop of Cologne, moved that party to offer truce terms to the National Liberals, but the latter were so incensed with the "unpatriotic" Catholics that no agreement to cooperate against the Socialists was accepted. As a result, the S.P.D. maintained five seats in the Rhine-Ruhr area.

Christian labor's frustration during these years can also be better understood within the context of governmental manipulation. Although the chancellor and his ministers were taking steps to slow the pace of social reform in 1907, Christian labor leaders, who were concerned about this, were given the opposite impression on numerous occasions. In March, for instance, Bülow wrote to the Society for Social Reform thanking it for bringing collective bargaining closer to realization.[87] Christian unionists were also encouraged to

86. Reichstag *Anlagen*, Period 12, Session 2, no. 523, vol. 276, pp. 2669ff.
87. Bülow to the Society for Social Reform, 11 March 1907, printed in *Bergknappe*, no. 13, 30 March 1907.

be optimistic about social reform during the negotiations preceding the Second German Workers' Congress and by Bethmann Hollweg's appearance before the delegates. The state then proceeded to pursue its own interests. Collective bargaining was rejected as a threat to the established order, and management-labor chambers were abandoned when it appeared they would become more than a convenient lever to play Christian and Hirsch-Duncker workers off against their Socialist counterparts.

Such manipulation was highly embarrassing and humiliating for Christian labor leaders, and, because it hastened the radicalization of non-Socialist groups, cannot be seen as particularly successful or clever. Equally true, on the other hand, is that it cannot be seen as a sign of weakness in the face of the advancing "forces of democratization and parliamentarization." All social legislation deemed threatening to the regime was rejected out of hand. There were others, moreover, even more adept at manipulation than the ruling elites. In the case of Christian labor, the church and Center Party played this role fairly successfully. This theme will be pursued below.

* * * *

The collapse of the Frankfurt initiative and the rejection of other pieces of legislation designed to bolster the rights of labor in the workplace magnified the importance of basic trade union strength, for additional gains from most employers would have to be earned by striking, boycotting, and otherwise forcing capital to the bargaining table. And, despite the absence of any legislative support, collective bargaining did indeed become more prevalent after the first years of the century. The number of collective wage contracts in Imperial Germany rose from a very negligible quantity in 1903 to 12,437 by 1912. Roughly 15 percent of the industrial work force was covered by these agreements in the latter year, primarily *organized* workers in the metal-working, construction, and small trades sector. Nearly one-third of these victories had been won in the year 1912 alone, a sign that the trend was accelerating, and 79.5 percent of them without recourse to a strike. Collective bargaining was still in its infancy, but clearly the proletariat was beginning to reap handsome benefits from past struggles, for the mere threat of force often sufficed with those manufacturers too numerous and too small to organize an effective resistance against the unions.[88]

All evidence indicates that Christian labor was unable to stay abreast of these trends. Christian trade unions participated in a mere 35.1 percent of the wage contracts negotiated from 1903 to 1907 and only 67.3 percent of those

88. Hartmut Kaelble and Heinrich Volkmann, "Konjunctur und Streik während des Übergangs zum organisierten Kapitalismus in Deutschlands," *Zeitschrift für Wirtschafts- und Sozialwissenschaften*, vol. 92, no. 5 (1972), pp. 536–37; Saul, *Staat, Industrie, Arbeiterbewegung*, p. 61.

signed from 1908 to 1912.[89] To be sure, Christian trade unions were not represented in many districts of eastern and northern Germany where contracts were signed, and the figures do illustrate great improvement over time. Yet there was no basis for the claim that, as Adam Stegerwald boasted in 1910, Christians unions "participated everywhere, almost without exception, as contracting parties."[90] Privately that year, in fact, *Gesamtverband* leaders expressed grave concern about the exclusion of their members from the bargaining process by Social Democratic unions eager to monopolize the shop floor. Protestant employers in the light industrial sector exacerbated the situation by frequently refusing to deal with a Christian organization. If they had to negotiate with a trade union, noted many leftward-leaning small businessmen, it would not be with "politically biased, religious organizations," as the Christian unions were alleged to be.[91]

The results could be devastating for the excluded party. Having blocked the Christian trade union from participation in talks with the chemigraphic trades in 1903, for instance, free trade union membership rose from 40 percent to 95 percent of the workers in that sector by 1908. Chemigraphic employees literally flocked to the union with exclusive bargaining privileges.[92] Next to the fratricidal *Gewerkschaftsstreit* between "Mönchen-Gladbach" and "Berlin," the Socialist "closed shop" among the small trades weighed most heavily on the minds of Christian labor leaders in the decade before the war.

In order to compensate for these losses the Christian trade unions sought a comparably exclusive and advantageous bargaining position in heavy industry.[93] The major problem with this tactic was that the nation's mining, metallurgical, textile, and large-scale chemical industries were controlled by employers' associations more than willing and powerful enough to resist the collective bargaining demands of even the strongest labor federation. The only feasible way to attain such rights short of legislation, argued *Gesamtverband* leaders, was for big business to grant these rights voluntarily. The Krupps, Stumms, and Kirdorffs had to be convinced that the Christian trade unions were safe, reliable bargaining partners.

With this goal in mind, Stegerwald and his colleagues sought a *rapprochement* with the nation's heavy industrialists. At the *Augustinusverein* session of

89. Berger, *Arbeiterbewegung und Demokratisierung*, p. 286; Saul, *Staat, Industrie, Arbeiterbewegung*, p. 61.

90. Adam Stegerwald, *Wo stehen wir in der Gewerkschaftsbewegung?* (Cologne: Verlag Adam Stegerwald, 1910), p. 14.

91. See Heinrich Brauns to Archbishop Fischer, 5 November 1910, and a *Volksverein* memorandum to diocesan authorities in Cologne, 9 July 1910, Gen. 23.61., vol. 1, Erzb. Registratur Köln. The latter document was based on "detailed discussions with Christian labor leaders."

92. Stegerwald, *Wo stehen wir*, p. 15.

93. See the sources cited above in note 91, plus Ernst Franke to Bethmann Hollweg, 28 September 1910, Reichskanzlei, Nr. 2269, Bl. 31, ZStA Potsdam.

February 1910, Catholic labor leaders urged Center journalists to discontinue polemics against the *Hansabund*, the Manufacturers' League, and the Central Association of German Industrialists.[94] Later that year the *Zentralblatt*, edited a short while by the general secretary, encouraged workers to reject the idea of capitalist exploitation and respect the tremendous economic and technological burden borne by Germany's wealthiest entrepreneurs. "These ideas must be promoted even if we run the risk of coming under suspicion as traitors to labor."[95] During the course of 1911 the bimonthly journal of the movement proceeded to analyze the recent work of "armchair Socialist" Adolf Weber, who argued that trade unions should be more concerned with means to increase worker productivity than methods, like the strike, which merely disrupted production and redistributed wealth. After a series of discussions between Weber, *Zentralblatt* editors, and the executive committee of the *Gesamtverband*, a book authored by Christian trade union ideologue Theodor Brauer appeared in early 1912 arguing for anti-strike strategies quite similar to Weber's.[96] In return for sheathing their daggers, however, Christian laborers wanted to be afforded the degree of bargaining respect due a patriotic labor organization. The *Gesamtverband* was ready to combat the "extremist doctrine of the class struggle,"[97] but had the right to expect big business to facilitate, not hamper, this crusade.

The growth of the national labor associations (*nationale Werkvereine*), also known as "yellow trade unions," was an added incentive for Christian labor to mend fences with big business. For the local, employer-manipulated yellow unions were a clear threat to the *Gesamtverband* at a time it was struggling to appeal to businessmen as a safe, moderate alternative to the unions of the General Commission. Not surprisingly, the *Zentralblatt* complained angrily in 1907 when yellow organizations in Augsburg and northern Bavaria began to stunt Christian trade union growth there. By 1911 the threat had increased as roughly 18,000 workers in Bavaria belonged to yellow unions, about two-thirds of Christian strength in that state. The danger was felt more keenly after the popularity of national labor associations spread to western Germany. From auspicious beginnings in 1909, the movement grew to almost 19,000 in Rhineland-Westphalia by 1911 with a strong center of support in Essen, the home of the largest Christian trade union.[98] Here was all the more reason to emphasize Christian labor's conciliatory philosophies.

94. *Augustinus-Blatt*, no. 2, February 1910, StBib MG.
95. *Zentralblatt*, no. 23, 14 November 1910.
96. Berger, *Arbeiterbewegung und Demokratisierung*, pp. 125–26.
97. *Zentralblatt*, no. 23, 14 November 1910.
98. Denk, *Christliche Arbeiterbewegung in Bayern*, pp. 280, 334–35; Klaus Mattheier, *Die Gelben Nationale Arbeiter zwischen Wirtschaftsfrieden und Streik* (Düsseldorf: Padagogischer Verlag Schwann, 1973), p. 138.

Pressure from the Catholic church greatly increased the need for Christian labor to keep its sword in the scabbard. As the following chapter will illustrate, church criticism of the Christian trade unions intensified after 1907/8, leading *Gesamtverband* circles to conclude quite rightly that the Vatican would condemn the organization if it participated in a new strike wave. The possibility became quite distinct in the summer of 1910 when Pope Pius X outlawed the Sillon, a French organization with a socio-political tradition similar to the *Volksverein* in Mönchen-Gladbach.

A number of factors converged in 1910/11, therefore, to discourage Christian strike activity: exclusion from the bargaining process in light industry; a corresponding need to encourage voluntary acceptance of Christian labor by heavy industry; stiff competition from non-striking national labor associations; and waning tolerance on the part of Catholic clergymen for the economic strife characteristic of the modern body social. As a result of these pressures the number of *Gesamtverband* members on strike declined from 7.6 percent of total membership in 1910 to 5.4 percent in 1911 and 3.7 percent in 1912. In great contrast, 18.3 percent of General Commission membership struck in 1910, 13.9 percent in 1911, and 18.6 percent in 1912.[99] To many laborers the Christian trade unions were indeed "traitors to labor."

There is a great deal of evidence, in fact, that certain elements of the Christian rank and file were growing increasingly restive as the years drew on to 1912. Although the percentage of members participating in strikes declined to very low levels, the absolute number of offensive strikes (*Angriffsstreiks*) increased steadily from 82 in 1908 to 250 in 1912, more than any other year in *Gesamtverband* history with the exception of 1906. Strikes of the offensive variety also represented a consistently higher percentage of total wage actions in the *Gesamtverband* than in the General Commission over these years—an average of 19.3 percent versus 15 percent from 1909 to 1912. There was a definite tendency, moreover, to ignore Cologne and cooperate with Social Democratic and other unions. Thus the percentage of actions waged alone decreased from 55.5 in 1907 to 26.7 in 1910.[100]

These figures suggest that Christian trade union leaders, although firmly in command of the miners, textile workers, and other large organizations, were *beginning* to lose control of many of the smaller unions in the Christian federation. These splinter organizations, and some of the weaker locals of the bigger unions, were faced with the choice of striking alongside the dominant Socialist unions in the area or losing radical factions which, in a union or local

99. Berger, *Arbeiterbewegung und Demokratisierung*, p. 286; Dieter Groh, *Negative Integration and revolutionärer Attentismus: Die deutsche Sozialdemokratie am Vorabend des Ersten Weltkrieges* (Frankfurt: Verlag Ullstein GmbH, 1974), pp. 734–35.

100. Kaelble and Volkmann, "Konjunctur und Streik," pp. 542–44; Berger, *Arbeiterbewegung und Demokratisierung*, p. 286.

of negligible size, were not expendable. The Police Department of Düsseldorf described this process of membership drain as early as 1908:

> One stone after another is crumbling away from the Christian trade union movement. The awareness is spreading that the employers are united and do not organize according to their religious or political convictions. And those Christian trade unionists who grow doubtful lean naturally to that side where they see growth and success, and that, despite scattered setbacks, tactical mistakes, or local decline, is the free trade unions, who impress the worker with their great numbers.[101]

As the economy expanded after 1908, small, wildcat strikes at the periphery of the Christian labor movement increased in frequency. The revolt took on new dimensions in June 1911 when the Christian metal workers, the fourth largest union in the *Gesamtverband*, rejected the anti-strike strategy emanating from Cologne and Essen. "The Christian miners can keep up this fight because they're the same strength," noted Franz Wieber, the leader of the union. "But what about us? What can we possibly do against the half-million Socialist metal workers?"[102] In 1912 Joseph Joos of the *Westdeutsche Arbeiter-Zeitung* also joined the chorus of criticism against the no-strike concept.[103] Thus the peaceful tactics of the *Gesamtverband* were not pursued without an increasing amount of turbulence within the organization.

These developments climaxed in March 1912 with the adamant refusal of the Christian *Gewerkverein* to participate in the Ruhr miners' strike. It has become almost conventional among Wilhelmian historians to attribute the decision to a fear of papal condemnation.[104] Although there is some truth to this conclusion, it is nevertheless much oversimplified and misleading. For one thing, *Gesamtverband* leaders were under the impression that the danger of draconian action against the Christian trade unions had finally passed. Four years of fear and uncertainty over the church's position ended, it seemed, in an agreement negotiated in late February 1912 between Adam Stegerwald and authorized representatives of the Prussian Bishops' Conference—about ten days before the strike. The bishops expressed complete satisfaction with the

101. Police Department of Düsseldorf to the *Regierungspräsident*, 1 September 1908, Reg. D. 42810, HSA Düsseldorf.
102. Fritz Kraus of the executive committee of the Christian metal workers' union to district leader K. E. Weinbrenner, 13 June 1911, Weinbrenner Papers, Bestand 46/3, StA Duisburg. Kraus quotes the union chairman, Franz Wieber.
103. Berger, *Arbeiterbewegung und Demokratisierung*, p. 126.
104. Kirchhoff, *Staatliche Sozialpolitik*, p. 174; Koch, *Die Bergarbeiter im Ruhrgebiet*, p. 132; Saul, *Staat, Industrie, Arbeiterbewegung*, p. 270; Matthier, *Die Gelben*, p. 237; Steinisch, "Der Gewerkverein christlicher Bergarbeiter," in Mommsen and Borsdorff, *Glückauf, Kameraden!* p. 279.

general secretary's explanation that the Christian trade unions had been founded "in order that devout Catholic and Evangelical workers would have an organization . . . in which individual members would not be expected to associate themselves with views or actions in private or public life, especially in the economic sector, which are irreconcilable with the moral and religious teachings of the Catholic or Evangelical Church, according to the manner in which these teachings are formulated by the responsible church authorities."[105] This compromise may help to explain why Stegerwald argued *for* participation in the Ruhr strike at a *Gewerkverein* strategy session in early March.[106] Only a few theologians interpreted the strike as an immoral use of force, which meant under the new agreement with the bishops that striking was now a relatively uncontroversial option. Here was an excellent opportunity, moreover, to prove to the unorganized masses that the Christian trade unions were not controlled and manipulated by the church. And finally, there was a pressing need to impress the Christian rank and file, especially within the *Gewerkverein* itself. Observers in Cologne and Mönchen-Gladbach were afraid the union would lose most of its members to the Socialists if it did not strike.

Leading *Gewerkvereinler* were not convinced. In fact Stegerwald left the meeting himself convinced that Behrens, Köster, Imbusch, *et al.* were much better informed about local and regional affairs than he.[107] They were apparently less sanguine than Stegerwald with respect to the prospects of church tolerance, first of all, for the usually well-informed police chief of Essen lists the *Gewerkschaftsstreit* as one of the major reasons the union held back its cohorts in March 1912.[108] And it is fairly easy to understand why *Gewerkverein* headquarters was particularly worried by the prospects of papal condemnation. Not only were the miners the backbone of the entire Christian labor movement, but, unlike the situation which prevailed within the textile, wood workers', and construction workers' unions of the *Gesamtverband*, the large Catholic wing of the *Gewerkverein* still maintained a strong allegiance to the religious clubs of the region. According to figures from the General Secretariat, 80–90 percent of the Catholic members of the union in the Ruhr

105. Quoted in the *Kölnische Volkszeitung*, no. 195, 4 March 1912. For the negotiations, see Bertram to Porsch, 5 March 1912, and Carl Bachem's notation of 11 March 1912, Bachem Papers 320b, HA Köln, and Brack, *Deutscher Episkopat und Gewerkschaftsstreit*, pp. 226–29, 239–41. For the bishops' approval, see Stegerwald's remarks in *Protokoll der Verhandlungen des ausserordentlichen Kongresses der Christlichen Gewerkschaften Deutschlands* (Cologne: Christlicher Gewerkschaftsverlag, 1912), p. 11.

106. Nieder to Brentano, 28 January 1913, Brentano Papers 46, BA Koblenz.

107. *Ibid.*

108. Police chief Essen to the *Regierungspräsident*, 5 November 1912, Reg. D. 42809, HSA Düsseldorf.

still belonged to Catholic *Knappenvereine*.[109] The high degree of affiliation with the church's own labor organizations underscored the possibility that a not-insignificant portion of the members would be susceptible to manipulation by labor priests who, like many of the miners themselves, would swallow their emotions and place their aspirations for the Christian trade union movement aside if the pope so ordered. Other workers, many others, would openly defy the church and probably drift to the left, but a decision not to strike would hopefully avoid the whole dilemma. It would also demonstrate to Rome the basically peaceful nature of the entire movement.

The leaders of the *Gewerkverein* reckoned that opposition to the strike would also demonstrate a great deal to the *Zechenverband*, the association of Ruhr mine owners. Since the failure of Christian labor to legislate collective bargaining in 1907/8, in fact, the Christian miners had sought to remove any doubts which their employers possessed about the patriotism and reliability of the union. During the summer of 1909 Behrens offered to support entrepreneurial candidates in the Saar at the next election if the owners discontinued their harassment of the *Gewerkverein*. The union's general secretary was less willing to pursue friendlier relations in the Ruhr, but under pressure from Catholic secretaries in late 1910 Christian-Social agitation against employers in the National Liberal Party was toned down considerably and the patriotic intentions of the union emphasized to a much greater degree.[110] And, in the ultimate act of appeasement, the *Gewerkverein* decided in October 1911 to oppose any action "that could arouse the authorities, the mine owners, and the national-minded workers."[111] Thus the *Gewerkschaftsstreit* was only one consideration on the minds of *Gewerkverein* leaders in March 1912; the decision was also a desperate bid for bargaining recognition.[112]

Nor can one overlook the presence of the "national-minded workers." As the above quote indicates, the yellow trade unions were clearly a source of worry for the *Gewerkverein*. The first such organization in western Germany was founded at Krupp in 1909 and by the end of the year had established a foothold among the metal workers of the Ruhr. Thus the elections to the commercial courts of the region in December 1909 resulted in a loss of 1,136

109. Stegerwald to Bishop Bertram, 25 October 1912, Stegerwald Papers 1, Stegerwald Stiftung Köln.

110. *Bergknappe*, no. 33, 14 August 1909; *Die Arbeit*, no. 45, 6 November 1909, and no. 16, 16 April 1910; Behrens to Mumm, 20 August 1909, Mumm Papers, Nr. 1056, ZStA Potsdam; K. E. Weinbrenner to Franz Wieber, 23 January 1911, Weinbrenner Papers, Bestand 46/3, StA Duisburg; police chief Essen to the *Regierungspräsident*, 27 September 1910, Reg. D. 42781, HSA Düsseldorf.

111. Police chief Gelsenkirchen to the *Regierungspräsident*, 7 October 1911, Reg. Münster VII 46, Bd. 1, StA Münster.

112. Steinisch, "Der Gewerkverein christlicher Bergarbeiter," in Mommsen and Borsdorff, *Glückauf, Kameraden!* pp. 289–91.

Christian seats and a very strong yellow showing of 2,763. As the *Zentralblatt* pointed out, the yellows had gained at Christian expense.[113] Making matters worse for the *Gewerkverein* after mid-1911 was the fact that the mine owners, after hesitating for two years to follow the lead of the metal industry in founding company unions, finally abandoned this opposition and energetically promoted national associations among their employees. From seven unions with a scant 131 members in the Ruhr in November, the movement expanded rapidly to twenty-four unions with 3,348 members by early March 1912.[114] Together with the impression *Gewerkverein* leaders wanted to make in Rome and the demonstration of reliability to employers in the *Zechenverband*, refusal to strike would also enable the union to compete with its new anti-strike competitors on the right and undercut employer support for this increasingly popular form of organization.[115]

Finally, the *Gewerkverein*'s controversial action must be viewed within the context of inter-union relations in the two years preceding the strike.[116] The *Alter Verband* and the *Gewerkverein* had resumed a somewhat more cooperative relationship, it will be recalled, after the great strike of 1905. Then, in the intervening five years, each union availed itself of numerous opportunities to assert its independence and undermine its archrival. The final blow to the *Détente* established in 1905 came during two crucial miners' elections in the late summer of 1910. The voting for mine security inspectors (*Sicherheitsmänner*) in August saw the *Alter Verband* win 1,090 representatives, the *Gewerkverein* 436, the Polish association 105, the national association 104, and the Hirsch-Duncker organization only 7. During the miners' elders' election (*Knappschaftsältestenwahl*) in September, the frees won 299 seats, the Christians 88, the Poles 30, and the yellows 2. The latter defeat was so decisive that the *Gewerkverein* lost all representation on the elders' executive committee. The outcome, plus a better than two-to-one membership advantage in the Ruhr, convinced *Alter Verband* leaders that the costs of further cooperation were higher than the potential benefits of conflict, for it now appeared possible to crush the Christian union.[117]

The miners' elections of 1910 also discredited Johann Effert and the more

113. *Zentralblatt*, no. 25, 13 December 1909.

114. Saul, *Staat, Industrie, Arbeiterbewegung*, pp. 155–56; Klaus Mattheier, "Werkvereine und wirtschaftsfriedlich-nationale (gelbe) Arbeiterbewegung im Ruhrgebiet," in Jürgen Reulecke (ed.), *Arbeiterbewegung an Rhein und Ruhr* (Wuppertal: Peter Hammer Verlag GmbH, 1974), p. 188.

115. The report of the Essen police chief, cited above in note 108, lists the yellow competition as another major factor in the *Gewerkverein*'s decision. Also see Mattheier, *Die Gelben*, p. 237, note 20.

116. See the report of the Essen police chief cited above in note 108.

117. Police chief of Essen to the *Regierungspräsident*, 31 January 1911, Reg. D. 846, and Karl Funcke to the *Regierungspräsident*, 7 March 1912, Reg. D. 15939, HSA Düsseldorf.

radical faction of the *Gewerkverein* rank and file. Effert, the highly popular chairman of the *Siebenerkommission*, was an outspoken advocate of interunion cooperation and frequently advised unorganized workers to join any of the four unions. He was also an energetic supporter of strike action to force capital to heel. And, significantly enough, 56 percent of the *Gewerkverein* membership voted to raise an extra levy in the spring of 1910 to prepare for such a showdown.[118] Effert's support within the union dwindled, however, after the election setbacks.

> These defeats, which were widely attributed to the fact that members of the *Gewerkverein* had voted for candidates of the *Alter Verband*, aroused spirited rancor in the Christian union. Opinions were voiced to the effect that such a blurring of the borders between the two organizations should not be permitted again and that in the future differences must be given stronger emphasis.[119]

Such feelings of resentment were reinforced in the following months by the knowledge that the *Alter Verband* intended to exploit wage actions in an attempt to take the smaller *Gewerkverein* in tow. Thus not striking was viewed increasingly in terms of self-defense and organizational independence. As Heinrich Imbusch put it in March 1912, "if the *Gewerkverein* strikes, it's finished. The freedom of the union, and of the miners, will be dead and gone [*für immer dahin*], and the miners will be dominated by Social Democrats and anarchists."[120] This fear, along with the factors analyzed earlier, drove the *Gewerkverein* headlong into a collision with the other three striking unions.

Although an alternate course may have been even costlier, the union's decision was definitely not inexpensive. The strike was broken in a week, to be sure, but in the process the *Gewerkverein* lost over 4,000 members in the Ruhr and another 11,000 in the Saar. Judging from the equally dismal membership situation in the striking unions, it seems safe to conclude that the *Gewerkverein*'s deserters either joined wildcat cliques disillusioned with organized unionism or flocked to the haven of a national association. In the Ruhr alone, for instance, yellow strength among the miners increased from a prestrike level of 3,348 to 17,360 by the end of the year.[121]

The union's opposition to the strike proved valueless, furthermore, as a demonstration of the conciliatory nature of the Christian labor movement.

118. Heinrich Imbusch, "Johann Effert," *Handwörterbuch des Gewerkschaftswesens*, II, p. 407; *Mülheimer-Volkszeitung*, 3 January 1910; police chief Essen to the *Regierungspräsident*, 27 September 1910, Reg. D. 42781, HSA Düsseldorf.
119. See the report of the police chief of Essen, cited above in note 108.
120. Quoted by the police chief Essen, to the *Regierungspräsident*, 6 March 1912, Reg. D. 16939, HSA Düsseldorf.
121. Mattheier, "Werkvereine," in Reulecke, *Arbeiterbewegung an Rhein und Ruhr*, p. 188.

Thus Merry del Val, cardinal secretary of state at the Vatican, scoffed that the *Gewerkverein* had not refused to strike for moralistic considerations, but merely because it was low on funds.[122] During the spring of 1912, in fact, the Vatican completed preparations for an encyclical which, had it not been amended that summer, would have outlawed the Christian trade unions (see Chapter 10).

Nor were the Ruhr mine owners in the least impressed. The *Zechenverband* refused to recognize the *Gewerkverein* as a bargaining partner, and the organ of the owners, the *Rheinisch-Westfälische Zeitung*, published "evidence" of a deal with the Vatican to embarrass the union.[123] There seems every reason to believe that the mine owners still agreed with Emil Kirdorf, a wealthy mining magnate and one of the directors of the Central Association of German Industrialists, who in 1905 had charged that the Christian trade unions were more dangerous than the Social Democratic organizations. This was so, he felt, because the workers would eventually reject the unrealistic revolutionary fantasies of the Socialists and flock to Christian labor with its more feasible, hence more threatening plans of attenuating private property rights.[124] And, admittedly, there was some logic to this point of view. Had not the Christian trade unions spoken publicly about the ultimate goal of codetermination?

After the debacle in the Ruhr, and an equally embarrassing decision not to strike in the Saar in December 1912 (see Chapter 10), *Gesamtverband* unions began to bring their tactics more in line with the progressive ideology Kirdorf feared. The stock conservatism of the church, the intransigence of the government, and capital's decision to promote national *Werkvereine* left Christian labor with no choice but to compete more aggressively for the favor of radical workers. Despite a deepening recession, for instance, another 234 offensive strikes were waged in 1913, a figure which again represented a percentage of total wage actions higher than that of the Socialist unions. More importantly, the number of *Gesamtverband* members on strike rose from 3.7 percent in 1912 to 6.1 percent in 1913, a level which can be more readily appreciated if one remembers that the number of striking General Commission unionists decreased from 18.6 percent to 9.9 percent of total membership during the same period.[125] This was the first time since 1905 that the strike activity of the

122. Ritter to Hertling, 13 July 1912, M Arb. 383, AStA München.
123. Steinisch, "Der Gewerkverein christlicher Bergarbeiter," in Mommsen and Borsdorff, *Glückauf, Kameraden!* pp. 280–81; *Rheinisch-Westfälische Zeitung*, 14 April 1912.
124. For Kirdorf's statements of 1905, see Paul Osthold, *Die Geschichte des Zechenverbandes* (Berlin: Otto Elsner Verlagsgesellschaft, 1934), pp. 17–18.
125. Kaelble and Volkmann, "Konjunktur und Streik," pp. 542, 544; Berger, *Arbeiterbewegung und Demokratisierung*, p. 286.

two federations was of roughly the same order of magnitude. As Chapter 11 demonstrates, finally, these trends coincided with a marked radicalization of the politics of Christian labor.

The Christian trade unions also stood on fairly solid organizational ground by 1912/13. The financial structure of the *Gesamtverband* became much sounder after 1904, for instance, as income growth far outpaced membership gains. These reforms enabled Christian unions to increase average annual expenditure per member from 11.4 marks in 1905 to 17.7 marks in 1913. Even more impressive was the sevenfold increase (52 to 350) in the number of functionaries employed by Christian unions.[126] This development augured well for recruitment, agitation, and expansion in general.

These changes produced tangible results throughout the Reich. In Rhineland-Westphalia, the bastion of Christian trade unionism, *Gesamtverband* membership grew from 72,000 in 1903 to 200,000 in 1912, overtaking the free trade unions, which expanded more slowly from 98,000 to 195,000 in western Germany.[127] "If we had an area of agitation where our strength was as concentrated as that of the Christians in Rhineland-Westphalia," barked a frustrated Karl Legien in 1905, "no other organization would be able to make headway against us either. The Christians will not trample us," he noted more optimistically, "they will disappear very soon".[128] But during the years which followed the *Gesamtverband* became less exclusively a West German phenomenon, with the percentage of members from the southern and eastern provinces increasing from 22 percent to 43 percent. Hoping to further this trend in October 1912, the Christian trade unions convened their eighth congress at Dresden in the heart of "red Saxony." A new union of agricultural workers had been founded two months earlier for the same purpose of encroaching on the hitherto-Socialist monopoly of working-class districts in eastern Germany.[129]

There was a darker side, however, to the Christian *Drang nach Osten*. Just like the German colonizers of the Middle Ages, Christian trade unionists pressed outwards because development possibilities at home were nearly exhausted. Thus a relieved Legien noted in 1911 that "the Christians can't develop past a certain point, even in those districts where the church still has

126. *Statistisches Jahrbuch für das Deutsche Reich*, 1906, 1914; Berger, *Arbeiterbewegung und Demokratisierung*, p. 67.
127. Mattheier, *Die Gelben*, p. 138; Berger, *Arbeiterbewegung und Demokratisierung*, pp. 48, 283, 285.
128. *Protokoll der Verhandlungen des fünften Kongresses der Gewerkschaften Deutschlands* (Berlin: Verlag der General Kommission der Gewerkschaften Deutschlands, 1905), p. 130.
129. For the Christian rural laborers' union, see that organization's *Geschaftsbericht für 1913* (Cologne: Christlicher Gewerkschaftsverlag, 1914), pp. 5–7, 39–41.

decisive influence.[130] The main reason for this was the inability of the *Gesamtverband* to make headway with recruitment in the network of Catholic labor associations. Within the Association of Catholic *Arbeitervereine* of Western Germany, for instance, only 53,364 of the 204,096 members belonged to a Christian union in 1912. The southern association presented an even more dismal picture, with roughly 14,500 of 97,823 members in a Christian trade union. Recruiting within the *Gesellenvereine* and Catholic youth groups was also unsuccessful.[131] The explanation for this weakness is complicated, ranging from opposition by priests who resented the competition of Christian unions to indifference by other clergymen who assessed the Socialist danger in rural and suburban areas as minimal,[132] but the fact remains that Christian leaders could no longer afford to allow eastern and northern Germany, where the *Gesamtverband* had thus far devoted little effort, to go relatively uncontested.

In moving to Social Democratic centers of strength, however, the Christian trade unions carried along comparative structural liabilities. Thus the free trade unions could afford to spend an average of 24.4 marks per member from 1905 to 1913, while the Christian unions managed to distribute only 14.1. Social Democratic organizations also devoted a significantly lower percentage of this expenditure to items which did not directly benefit the members. Administration, press, recruiting, and other "overhead costs" represented only 23 percent of total expenditure in the General Commission from 1905 to 1911, far below the *Gesamtverband* level of 38.4 percent.[133] These figures indicate that the free trade unions, which grew from 1,344,804 members in 1905 to 2,525, 042 members in 1913, may have attained certain economies of scale which the smaller Christian federation (350,930 in 1913) was simply unable to enjoy. The fixed costs of managing labor unions increased, in other words, as the organization grew in size, but slowed after a certain point; beyond that these costs could be spread more easily over an increasing income and reduced in percentage terms. Moreover, a veritable army of 3,108 trade union secretaries practically assured the General Commission of continued advantages of scale, for growth potential, though limited by numerous social, political, and geographical factors, was still to a great degree a function of the

130. *Protokoll der Verhandlungen des achten Kongresses der Gewerkschaften Deutschlands* (Berlin: Verlag der General Kommission der Gewerkschaften Deutschlands, 1911), p. 156.
131. Denk, *Christliche Arbeiterbewegung in Bayern*, pp. 16, 217, 329, 402; Berger, *Arbeiterbewegung und Demokratisierung*, p. 264.
132. Stegerwald to Bertram, 25 October 1912, Stegerwald Papers I, Stegerwald Stiftung Köln; Denk, *Christliche Arbeiterbewegung in Bayern*, pp. 142, 270.
133. *Statistisches Jahrbuch*, 1906–1915.

ability to reach the unorganized masses.[134] Thus the free trade unions had the potential, *ceteris paribus*, to recruit roughly nine times as many members in any given year as the Christian unions—and usually did—due to the fact that the larger organization possessed nine times as many recruiters. There was a definite mathematical certainty to the free trade union lead in 1913, therefore, and the sheer numbers behind the General Commission contributed still more to this almost automatic advantage. Collective bargaining breakthroughs, strike successes, and an increased ability to compete for unorganized workers were the result. This rather frustrating reality continued to plague the Christian trade unions until the outbreak of war in 1914 created new possibilities for the weaker organization.

134. For the inability of the Christian trade unions to reach many thousands of potential recruits, see Johann Karl Vietor to Franz Behrens, 15 February 1907, printed in Dieter Fricke, "Zur Förderung der christlichen Gewerkschaften durch die nichtmonopolistische Bourgeoisie," *Zeitschrift für Geschichtswissenschaft* (Heft 9, 1981), vol. 29, pp. 817–19.

10

Rifts in the Tower: The Conflict over Modernism in the Center, *Volksverein*, and Christian Trade Unions

The *Leitmotiv* of this study has been the vain struggle of Christian labor to supplant the Social Democrats in the union movement. As previous sections of the present work have shown, economic-structural inadequacies made it very difficult to convince the unorganized worker that a Christian union offered the best representation vis-à-vis the centralized interests of capital. Another important element in the failure of Christian labor was the disunity of the movement. Differences over tactics and specific political issues aside, it was the quarrel over the basic purpose of a Christian labor movement which came to plague the efforts of men like Adam Stegerwald and Johannes Giesberts. If it had not been for the barriers placed in the path of the *Gesamtverband* by the countermovement of confessional craft sections founded in 1902 by Bishops Kopp and Korum, the Christian trade unions' efforts in the labor world would—without overstating the point—certainly have been facilitated. It is this intra-Catholic feud which the present chapter will analyze.

* * * *

By 1908 the six-year-old organization of Catholic trade sections, or *Fachabteilungen*, possessed a well-stocked arsenal of articulate objections to trade unionism. As one of the movement's leaders stated years later, the controversy between unions and trade sections revolved around "the question of adherence to Thomistic natural law."[1] To *Fachabteilung* patrons,[2] the idea of a struggle for power (*Machtkampf*) between workers and employers stood in direct contradiction to the natural, divine order of things postulated by St. Thomas Aquinas, for the end result of this struggle would be "either the complete subjection of the economically weak to the domination of international capitalism, or else the forcible toppling of all existing cultural relationships."[3] The employers' freedom of contract, on the one hand, and the workers' right to strike, on the other, "must therefore remain within the confines of those rights and obligations which, independent of all contracts, are founded on natural law and divine commandments."[4] Despite the fact that Christian trade union leaders had abandoned "neutralism" and joined other bourgeois labor groups in an anti-Socialist front, therefore, theological differences continued to separate the two Christian organizations. By advocating the strike and denying the "obvious" connection between economic, moral, and religious issues, the *Gesamtverband* had violated natural law and undermined the stability of state and society. The task of creating an orderly and secure relationship between the various limbs of the social body was primarily the duty of the state, but the church could do its part, argued the Berliners, by instilling in the working class a greater spirit of cooperation and conciliation. This goal would be realized more quickly "if not just individuals *but also free economic organizations* let themselves be guided by a religious and moral consciousness based on clear, viable, Catholic principles."[5] The theological *Sozialkritik* of the Berlin faction was thus irreconcilable with the more radical interpretation which Mönchen-Gladbach gave to the writings of St. Thomas Aquinas. The dispute, of course, was not a new one to the German Catholic community. The reader will recall that Catholic social activists had begun to quarrel over these issues in the 1870s (see Chapter 1).

But the question of strikes and power struggles was not the only issue separating Berlin from Mönchen-Gladbach. For the former was also very uncomfortable with the nondenominationalism of the Christian trade unions. Catholics and Protestants together in a union made it quite awkward for the priest to perform his indispensable supervisory duties, but what was worse, the "Christians" were insisting that nondenominational tactics like those which had helped to undermine the authority of factory owners be carried over

1. See Heinz Brauweiler's notes of a conversation with Dr. Paul Fleischer, former Reichstag deputy and an associate of Franz von Savigny, 13 July 1942, Brauweiler Papers 24, StA MG.
2. The remainder of this paragraph is based on an undated, unsigned (probably *Lic.* Fournelle) position paper sent by the Berliners to church officials in Breslau, Gen. 23.61., vol. 1, Erzb. Registratur Köln.
3. *Ibid.*
4. *Ibid.*
5. *Ibid.*

into the political arena. The Center Party was to be "interconfessionalized" with an electoral strategy designed to enhance the political might of Christian labor. This irritated the Berliners immeasurably, for they were convinced that Protestant suspicions of Catholics would never decrease to the point where mutual sacrifices would be made at the polls. In the last analysis, only the Center would lose. Thus Catholics should concentrate on maximizing the strength of their own party and in this way protect the interests of the church and of Catholics in general.

The Berliners' rejection of nondenominational unionism cut much deeper, however, than disagreements over electoral tactics and strategy. Close cooperation with Protestants would also ruin the faith of Catholic workers, it was felt, for "out of 100 Protestants," as one Berliner put it, "99 are no longer Christians."[6] Such a statement was obviously exaggerated, but the advocates of confessionalism were not just reacting to phantoms, for there were real, discernible trends toward secularism among *Protestant* workers which were quite disturbing. Alleged signs of religiosity such as church attendance and participation in communion were alarmingly low in the decade before 1914 and were lowest in industrial cities. The rate of disaffiliations from Protestant churches, moreover, jumped three- to fivefold from 1906 to 1914.[7] So what could possibly be gained, asked followers of Kopp and Korum, from workers who seemed so anxious to sever their religious ties?

The answer, obviously, was that nothing positive could result. Already there were signs, argued the Berliners, that "atheists" and "revolutionary Social Democrats"[8] rubbed elbows with the devout in the Christian unions, an interesting charge which was also not without some merit. Police reports from Düsseldorf and Essen reveal that an apparently large number of Christian trade unionists had stayed in the *Gesamtverband* only long enough to learn to appreciate the benefits of unionism. Thus enlightened, they deserted for the General Commission, which seemed better equipped to carry the union banner.[9] If one remembers that annual membership turnover in the Christian unions was quite high, fluctuating between 50 and 80 percent,[10] then it is quite possible that Christian organizations, while losing thousands to the ranks of the unorganized, also supplied a not-insignificant number of veteran unionists

6. Quoted in Ross, *Beleaguered Tower*, p. 135.
7. Vernon Lidtke, "Social Class and Secularization in Imperial Germany: The Working Classes," *Publications of the Leo Baeck Institute*, Year Book 25 (1980), pp. 23–26.
8. Quoted in Ross, *Beleaguered Tower*, p. 98.
9. Police commissioner of Essen to the *Regierungspräsident*, 1 September 1906, Reg. D. 9058, and Police Dept. of Düsseldorf to the *Regierungspräsident*, Reg. D. 42810, 1 September 1908, HSA Düsseldorf.
10. Berger, *Arbeiterbewegung und Demokratisierung*, p. 47.

to Socialist unions each year. When it became known in *Fachabteilung* circles that the *Volksverein* in Mönchen-Gladbach recruited two-thirds of its salaried agents (*Vertrauensmänner*) in western Germany from the Christian trade unions, Berlin's anger knew no bounds.[11] For the incredible, intolerable fact remained that a crucial Catholic institution like the *Volksverein* was making financial contributions to members of a labor organization which was itself aiding, however unintentionally and indirectly, the growth of the church's greatest adversary!

Indeed there could be little doubt which religious influences were at work on the free trade unionist. Vernon Lidtke has described the results of one contemporary survey of Socialist workers' religious views:

> [Socialist] workers were unanimous in condemning church and clergy . . . All but a few discounted the Biblical story of creation as an ignorant myth; Darwinist influence manifested itself in their language. While some organized workers denounced the Bible as the worst book on the face of the earth, a far greater number viewed it as a major contribution to cultural history and some even allowed that it might contain kernels of moral truth. A few believed in God; a few were confused by the issue; some were agnostics or pantheists; but the largest number dismissed God as a fiction. Baptism and confirmation were viewed with open disdain, but some believed church weddings were preferable to civil ceremonies. Religious burial came in for intense criticism because pastors received special honoraria for their services. Even organized workers were generally favorable to religious holidays, but not for religious reasons. Religious holidays gave them a few days of rest . . . With one exception, the Socialist workers . . . expressed admiration and respect for Jesus. But here too the explanation is that they offered an essentially secular interpretation of Jesus. They saw him [not as someone supernatural or sacred, but] as a friend of "poor people," a "true workers' friend," and an "ideal human."[12]

Thus the patrons of *Fachabteilungen*, though clearly extreme in their thinking, were not as irrational in their critique of Christian trade unionism as some historians would have us believe.[13] To avoid the dangers of an increasingly secular world, workers should remain within the bonds of a purely Catholic association supervised very closely by the church.

By 1908 the objections of the zealots in the German Catholic community to the economic activism and nondenominationalism of the Christian trade unions had been elevated to a still higher plane. This new plateau of opposition was known as integralism, or anti-modernism. The word "modernism" was a

11. Heinrich Brauns to Kopp, 6 November 1909, Gen. 23.61., Erzb. Registratur Köln.
12. Lidtke, "Social Class and Secularization," pp. 29–30.
13. Ross, *Beleaguered Tower*, *passim*, is too one-sidedly supportive of the "western" (Cologne–Mönchen-Gladbach) point of view.

catchall term used to describe the views of those theologians and lay persons in Europe who desired liberal reforms within the church. Some advocated abandonment of celibacy for priests, others talked of redefining the centuries-old definition of the church as the only legitimate spiritual link between man and God, and still others wanted less episcopal control and supervision of lay organizations. The supporters of the Christian trade unions, who insisted on complete and total independence from the church in pursuit of economic and political gains which would have to be obtained, occasionally, by power struggles fought alongside Protestant comrades, were thus vulnerable to the charge of "modernism." For it seemed to conservative Catholics that Bachem, Stegerwald, and others were defying the authority of the bishops and drifting in the direction of a new "Christian" religion, or worse, contributing to the growth of atheistic Socialism.

The sensitivity of orthodox prelates to the perceived weakening of church authority grew as modernist writings began to proliferate in Europe around the turn of the century. The secularization of the French school system in 1905 added to the atmosphere of confessional suspicion and distrust. After Pope Pius X condemned modernism in his encyclical *Pascendi* in September 1907, more pressure was exerted on secular organizations like the *Gesamtverband* and the *Volksverein* to give up their "heretical" ways.[14] It was no coincidence, therefore, that in the year following the pope's encyclical differing opinions over the allegedly modernistic activities of the Center, the *Volksverein*, and the Christian trade unions precipitated a crisis in the Catholic political community of Germany. This crisis, which lasted until 1912, will be investigated in the remainder of this chapter.

* * * *

The disputes unleashed in the Catholic camp by Julius Bachem's "Tower" article were quieted by the Bloc elections of January 1907 and remained so throughout much of that year. During the winter of 1907/8, however, the fragile unity within the Center began to crumble. Thus in November Bachem scolded the *Bopparder Volkszeitung* for printing a pro-Center statement submitted by six Catholic priests. "Aren't you thereby offending the feelings of Catholics entrusted to you who don't swear allegiance to the Center?"[15] The *Oberschlesische Volkszeitung* was similarly criticized for describing the Center as an exclusively Catholic party. "Just once," noted Bachem, "we would like to see a paper that is also for non-Catholic people."[16] These articles, and others that winter and spring, were written primarily for the tactical purpose of

14. Hubert Jedin (ed.), *Handbuch der Kirchengeschichte*, vol. 6, part 2, pp. 435–500.
15. *Kölnische Volkszeitung*, no. 1274, 1907 (clipping in: Bachem Papers 277, HA Köln).
16. *Ibid.*

facilitating electoral and parliamentary cooperation with "well-intentioned, fair-minded Protestants,"[17] a stance that might also have helped the Christian unions. But to the zealous "confessionalists" within the party and episcopate,[18] chastisings such as these were additional proof that Bachem and his allies in Mönchen-Gladbach and the unions were naive strategists and indifferent Catholics. Indeed the experience of the Bülow Bloc in 1907/8 lent some weight to the charge of naiveté, for the Center was being systematically snubbed and ignored by the chancellor and the Protestant parties.

Fachabteilung patrons had also reopened their feud with the *Volksverein* by this time. In May Mönchen-Gladbach published an "Index of Social Literature" which avoided all mention of works with theological content or confessional bias, especially those recommending specifically Catholic associations for youth, women, retail clerks, and workers. In omitting works that put forth the views of the church and the bishops, declared Korum's *Trierische Landeszeitung*, "the *Volksverein* has turned down a nondenominational path that will lead in the end to the . . . corruption [*Verderben*] of German Catholics."[19] The Christian trade unions had also incurred the wrath of confessionalists. Thus in April the "Behrens Case"[20] was cited by the organ of the eastern Catholic labor associations, *Der Arbeiter*, as an eye-opening lesson in the dubious consequences of interconfessional unionism. The National Liberal candidacy of Evangelical unionist Franz Pfordt in Ottweiler elicited much the same response. When Pfordt's Prussian Landtag campaign was backed by the *Saar Post*, a paper which claimed to speak for both the Center and Christian trade unions, church canon Hansen of Illingen charged that the organ had been duped by the Liberals, who were merely trying to win over the proletariat for their campaign against the confessional school. Hansen went on to deliver one of the most scathing indictments of the Christian trade unions heard thus far in the *Gewerkschaftsstreit*.[21]

Craft section tempers flared even higher in May 1908 when the *Volksverein* and the Christian trade unions attempted to open the Association of Catholic Retail Employees to Protestants. Giesberts, Father Brauns, and other Christian leaders hoped that the association would be able to attract thousands of new members and join the Christian trade unions in a common economic and political front to reform big business. The plan was rejected emphatically by Cardinal Kopp, who not only regarded it as socialistic, but also considered it a

17. Carl Bachem to Bertram, 18 July 1908, Bachem Papers 277, HA Köln.
18. For this faction, see above, Chapters 5 and 8.
19. *Trierische Landeszeitung*, 10 July 1908 (clipping in: Hohn Papers 15/2, 1908, StA MG).
20. See above, Chapter 9.
21. *Saar Post*, 31 July 1908, and *Neunkirchener Zeitung*, 8 August 1908 (clippings in: 442-3790, LHA Koblenz).

slap in the face to the many priests active in the organization. Consequently, Kopp exerted his influence among the clerical delegates at the retail clerks' annual assembly in Trier to defeat the unions' motion.[22]

By mid-summer 1908, therefore, a crisis was developing in the Catholic camp over the allegedly "modernistic" activities of the *Kölnische Volkszeitung*, the *Volksverein*, and the Christian trade unions. Not surprisingly, both sides to the dispute sought to rally support for their cause from the episcopate. In a letter to Bishop Bertram of Hildesheim, for instance, Carl Bachem made a strong case for the numerous articles written by his cousin. As "a born minority party,"[23] he began, the Center could only protect religious and church interests by cooperating with tolerant Protestants. The demagoguery of the Evangelical League had reduced the number of Lutherans willing to do this to the small faction around Stöcker, but even the Christian-Socials would be unable to resist anti-Catholic agitation if the Center were stamped as a denominational, Catholic party. Catholics would then be entirely isolated, for an alliance with the S.P.D. would only further harm the cause. The new *Kulturkampf*, he concluded quite logically, could only be warded off with Protestant help.

The *Volksverein* was also quick to respond to the charges leveled against it. In mid-July 1908 Brandts protested to Archbishop Fischer that the association's interconfessional compaign was merely designed "to help [our] people endure the social and religious struggles of the day and gain more influence in all areas of public life."[24] The chairman trusted that "after so much proof of benevolent goodwill toward the *Volksverein*," the episcopate would vindicate the organization "against such unfair charges, all the more because this type of attack can lead to consequences that are disadvantageous to the necessary peace between Catholics."[25] A few weeks later, however, Pieper hurried to Fischer with the even more alarming news that Korum and the bishops sympathetic to his cause were demanding that the episcopate have a representative on the *Volksverein*'s executive committee[26]—a move designed, among other things, to undercut the organization's support for the Christian trade unions.[27]

22. Kopp to Pieper, 9 September 1910, Bachem Papers 294, HA Köln; *Trierische Landeszeitung*, 10 July 1908 (clipping in: Hohn Papers 15/2, 1908, StA MG); also see Karl Schirmer's remarks in *Zentralblatt*, no. 18, 7 September 1908.

23. Carl Bachem to Bertram, 18 July 1908, Bachem Papers 277, HA Köln.

24. Brandts to Fischer, n.d. (July 1908), Hohn Papers 15/2, 1908, StA MG.

25. *Ibid.*

26. Pieper to Hohn, 6 August 1908, Hohn Papers 15/2, 1908, StA MG.

27. Korum had hoped to gain control of the unions through the *Volksverein* for years. (See Korum to the chairman of the Catholic *Arbeitervereine* of the Diocese of Trier, 28 October 1902, Gen. 23.61., vol. 1, Erzb. Registratur Köln). Aside from the *Volksverein*'s political and agitational support for the unions, a major bone of contention was the alleged financial support of Mönchen-

Despite his own desire for a closer supervision of *Volksverein* activities, the archbishop was not prepared to disgrace the association and undermine its economic and political effectiveness. "You can place full trust in me," he assured Pieper. "And when I stand up for you, I won't stand alone."[28] The upcoming bishops' conference, it appeared, would be a divisive one.

The Christian trade unions were very alarmed by the offensive directed against them too. The criticisms and outbursts mentioned above, especially that of Hansen, gave the unionists good reason to feel this way, but more trouble signs appeared in late July. Through informants in church circles, Christian labor leaders learned that Franz von Savigny was "actively at work"[29] again promoting his trade sections, having visited a number of bishops in western Germany. Assuming that the Berliners would not be content with attacking the *Volksverein* at Fulda, the Catholic members of the *Gesamtverband* executive committee decided to inform the hierarchy "calmly, but firmly,"[30] that no alteration of the basic guidelines established for the federation at Mainz in 1899 was necessary. Opening at Zurich in early August, the first International Congress of Christian Trade Unions offered the unionists a timely opportunity and an appropriate forum to express their views.

The main address at Zurich by Giesberts was a tactful defense of the interconfessional nature and moderate political goals of the Christian trade unions of Germany.[31] As such, it more than adequately accomplished the purpose mentioned above. Problems began, however, during the debate that followed his presentation. Never one to shy away from a fight, Stegerwald barked that as long as the Catholic religion was not endangered, "no pope or bishop can unilaterally forbid the workers to organize [along interconfessional lines] for economic purposes."[32] Franz Wieber seconded Stegerwald, asserting that church control of the union activities would be harmful for both the workers and the bishops. Schiffer was equally blunt.

> There are many Catholics in this hall—I'm also a Catholic—but with all due respect and veneration to our spiritual overlords, namely, our bishops, we

---

Gladbach for the *Gesamtverband*. No direct subsidies were made, but *Volksverein* spokesmen admitted that two of three association agents in western Germany, where the bulk of *Volksverein* members lay, were Catholic members of the Christian trade unions. (Heinrich Brauns to Kopp, 6 November 1909, Gen. 23.61., vol. 1, Erzb. Registratur Köln.)

28. Pieper to Hohn, 6 August 1908, Hohn Papers 15/2, 1908, StA MG.

29. Johann Effert to the *Regierungspräsident* of Arnsberg, 20 August 1908, Reg. Arnsberg I 83, StA Münster.

30. *Ibid.*

31. *Bericht über die Verhandlungen der ersten internationalen Konferenz christlicher Gewerkschaftsführer* (Cologne: Christlicher Gewerkschaftsverlag, 1908), pp. 24–40, ZSg. 1-63/5, BA Koblenz.

32. *Ibid.*, p. 48.

> must still say: This far and no farther! They have the right and the duty to show us the way in religious and unsecular matters, but when it comes to vocational questions, that is, more or less economic matters, a bishop should not want to claim the right to speak authoritatively. We're independent in this area and must be so.[33]

The protocols record that Schiffer's statement was interrupted twice by cheers and loud applause. Clearly the German representatives and the majority of foreign delegates were in a much more belligerent mood than Giesberts.

The Congress at Zurich played into the hands of the confessionalists by rekindling the same fear of labor independence which had led the hierarchy to speak out at Fulda eight years earlier. Because of the modernist trends in Europe since 1900, however, these fears had greatly increased. An emphatic supporter of the Christian trade unions before 1908, Bishop Benzler of Metz was surely not alone when he remarked that the Zurich affair had destroyed his sympathy for the movement.[34] Fischer was not as deeply shaken as many of his colleagues, but was nevertheless greatly disturbed. In a conversation with Pieper shorly before departing for Fulda, he described the unionists' remarks as "crude"[35] and regretted the fact that Berlin would now have more ammunition to use against the unions and their protectors in the *Volksverein*. The bishops at Fulda were not prepared to move as far in the direction of condemning the nondenominational *Gesamtverband* as Kopp and Korum, who disputed the right of the predominantly Catholic organization to make decisions independently of the bishops. It was agreed, however, that in certain areas the bishops could indeed "speak authoritatively," and that Fischer should make a public statement to this effect.[36] As a Catholic association, the *Volksverein* was not let off so easily. The organization which had done so much to promote Christian trade unionism since 1898 was asked to grant the episcopate an executive council seat.[37]

Fischer's statement over Zurich was delivered on 16 August 1908 before a

33. *Ibid.*, p. 42.
34. Brack, *Deutscher Episkopat und Gewerkschaftsstreit*, p. 124.
35. Pieper to Hohn, 6 August 1908, Hohn Papers 15/2, 1908, StA MG.
36. Johann Effert to the *Regierungspräsident*, 20 August 1908, as cited above in note 29.
37. Korum's faction had been pressing the *Volksverein* for years. Finally in June 1908 Brandts and Pieper consented to present an annual statement of finances to the Fulda Conference. Still not satisfied, the conservative bishops around Korum decided in July to demand an executive council seat. (Herbert Gottwald, "Volksverein für das katholische Deutschland," in Dieter Fricke [ed.], *Bürgerliche Parteien*, vol. 2, p. 817; Pieper to Hohn, 6 August 1908, Hohn Papers 15/2, 1908, StA MG.) The protocols to the Fulda Conference of 1908, which are located in the Bertram Papers, IA-25b-15, pt. 2, AA Wroclawie, do not record that the issue was formally discussed. That a decision was made, however, is certain. See the Pieper Manuscript, part 3, pp. 781–82, StA MG; Edmund Schopen, *'Köln' eine innere Gefahr für den Katholizismus* (Berlin: Hermann Walther Verlagsbuchhandlung, GmbH, 1910), p. 84; ten Hompel, *Osterdienstags-Protokoll*, p. 7.

group of Catholic *Arbeiterverein* secretaries who had gathered in Düsseldorf for the opening of the *Katholikentag*.

> In a recent assembly that also handled labor concerns a few hard words were spoken with regard to the bishops that have troubled my heart, a heart which beats warmly for the working people. I want to assume that these remarks were not meant in this way, but I know, and I have experienced it again today, that the *real* working people, the Catholic working people, is true to the bishops and true to the priests that the bishops sent to you.[38]

The archbishop's tolerance for the Christian trade unions had obviously worn very thin. His closing remarks four days later were a veiled warning to the same effect. "The bishops will never interfere with matters that do not fall under their authority, but as true shepherds of the church they will always stand up for the Catholic principles which are valid for private as well as public life in *all* its various forms."[39]

In August 1908, Christian trade union leaders caucused in Düsseldorf to assess the situation and map out further strategy.[40] Convinced that Fischer and the majority of bishops had not deserted them, the unionists concluded that the real danger lay, as before, in Trier and Breslau. Should the episcopate demand full retractions from the unionists who had spoken at Zurich, however, all were agreed that no concessions could be made on the crucial issues at stake. Church control of the unions was unacceptable, and all attempts to sever the Protestants from the movement had to be resisted. If "forced into the ring,"[41] the unions would not hesitate to defend themselves.

These tough words belied the vulnerable situation in which the Christian trade unions found themselves. The organization had experienced tremendous internal difficulties as a result of the Reichstag elections and the Behrens incident. Membership growth was stymied and the free trade union lead appeared almost insurmountable. If the *Gesamtverband* were to grant supervisory rights to the bishops, or establish closer ties with the confessional trade sections, Protestant unionists would surely secede. If, on the other hand, the church declared Christian trade unions a danger to the faith and unfit for good Catholics, tens of thousands of Catholic workers would desert the movement as an act of religious conscience. Despite the bold talk at Zurich and Düs-

38. *Verhandlungen der 55. Generalversammlung der Katholiken Deutschlands zu Düsseldorf vom 16. bis 20. August 1908* (Düsseldorf: Verlag und Druck vom Düsseldorfer Tageblatt, GmbH, 1908), pp. 148–49.
39. *Ibid.*, pp. 469–70.
40. For the meeting, see Effert to the *Regierungspräsident*, 20 August 1908, as cited above in note 29.
41. *Ibid.*

seldorf, therefore, the unions were clearly in no position to defy a *united* episcopate. If the *Gesamtverband* were to maintain its independence, its growth potential, and both confessional wings, it was imperative that Archbishop Fischer preserve his majority on the bishops' conference, thereby obviating the need for defiance.

Thus in late August 1908, as attacks from *Der Arbeiter* (Berlin) mounted in intensity, Giesberts and Stegerwald requested an audience with Fischer to explain their position. Still angered over the workers' brusque treatment of the bishops at Zurich, the archbishop refused them admittance[42] and began to consider means to revitalize "the defective Catholic spirit of social organizations"[43] in his diocese. The rejection startled the two Catholic functionaries, for they had assumed that Fischer's all-important support was incontrovertible. Unwilling to risk a fate similar to that which had already befallen the *Volksverein,* they made immediate efforts through intermediaries in Mönchen-Gladbach to assuage the prelate.[44]

By late October 1908 the dispute had been settled "in a manner thoroughly satisfactory to him,"[45] as Stegerwald *et al.* explained four years later. One of the concessions made was a public apology by Schiffer and Wieber at Munich. Without conceding the crucial issue of labor independence, the two explained that no insult to the episcopate or injury to the church had been intended by the blunt remarks in Zurich. Schiffer, whose statement had also angered the Dutch bishops, traveled to Utrecht to make further amends. Stegerwald stated publicly in Frankfurt, moreover, that the apologies had been made in accordance with the conscience and religous conviction of the unionists involved.[46] Fischer may not have demanded more, but other steps were taken to insure his friendship. In October the *Gewerkverein* severed its three-year tie to the *Siebenerkommission,* and in December the union decided to boycott a miners' congress convened by the *Alter Verband* "in order to prove to the public, and also the episcopate, that the Christian trade unions do not go through thick and thin with the Social Democrats."[47]

As in years past, the price of continued toleration by the church was high,

42. Police commissioner of Essen to the *Regierungspräsident*, 30 September 1908, Reg. D. 42810, HSA Düsseldorf.
43. ten Hompel, *Osterdienstags-Protokoll*, p. 11.
44. Police commissioner of Essen to the *Regierungspräsident*, 30 September 1908, Reg. D. 42810, HSA Düsseldorf.
45. See the "explanation," drafted for unknown purposes in 1912 by Stegerwald, Giesberts, Schiffer, and Wieber, in Stegerwald Papers I, Stegerwald Stiftung Köln.
46. *Ibid.*; *Zentralblatt*, no. 20, 5 October 1908; Brügmann, *Sozialer Katholizismus*, p. 396; *Kölnische Volkszeitung*, no. 942, 2 November 1908.
47. Police commissioner of Essen to the *Regierungspräsident*, 27 September 1909, Reg. D. 9041, HSA Düsseldorf. The commissioner refers to a meeting of the *Gewerkverein* executive committee with *Gesamtverband* representatives present.

for Socialist and Hirsch-Duncker papers quickly exploited the Christians' dilemma. The *Bergarbeiter-Zeitung* greeted the Munich apologies in September with cynical articles describing the alleged "march to the right" and "inglorious retreat"[48] of Christian trade union leaders. The paper also ran damaging reports on the escalating polemics between Berlin and Mönchen-Gladbach. This latter theme was picked up later in the month by the Hirsch-Duncker press, which had originally refrained from comment. Seizing on reports that priests in the Saar had refused to enter confessional booths with Christian trade unionists, *Der Gewerkverein* asked if there were "any better proof of how totally absurd it is to pack religious matters into an economic labor movement."[49]

Supplied with such embarrassing information, free and liberal trade union agitators had no trouble recruiting Protestant workers who might otherwise have joined Christian unions. A letter sent by the liberal unionist Anton Erkelenz to a friend in Sweden was typical of the reaction uncommitted workers must have had to Zurich, for Erkelenz had himself toyed with the idea of crossing over to the *Gesamtverband.*

> I don't know if you have followed the debate in Germany over the Zurich Congress. If so, then you must have noticed that the leaders of Germany's Christian trade unions repentantly abandoned everything that they announced in Zurich. It's a fact, therefore, that in future cooperation at such affairs as Zurich, the foreign organizations that take part will be indirectly dependent on the frowning German Catholic bishops.[50]

If a seasoned observer like Erkelenz had overlooked the fact that Christian leaders had not really compromised on the issue of union independence, the non-unionized masses must have drawn the same conclusion. One report from Christian trade union functionaries about recruiting difficulties in the aftermath of Zurich strengthens this assumption.[51]

With Fischer's faction still tolerant of the *Gesamtverband* nevertheless, the Christian trade unions were able to resist the increasing pressure placed on them by Bishop Korum. Determined to bend the unions to his will, Korum met with Giesberts and Stegerwald in Trier for nearly four hours on 16 October 1908. The primary objective of the negotiations, the bishop noted later, was "to bring about a union of the two parties."[52] Korum's terms for peace

48. *Bergarbeiter-Zeitung*, nos. 36 and 38, for 5 and 19 September 1908.
49. *Der Gewerkverein*, no. 74, 23 September 1908.
50. Erkelenz to Dahborg, n.d. (fall 1908), Erkelenz Papers 3, BA Koblenz.
51. See the *Bericht des Vorstandes [des Christl. Metallarbeiter-Verbandes Deutschlands] für die Zeit vom 1. Januar 1908 bis 1. Januar 1910*, from the private library of Bernhard Koch, currently general secretary of the Christlicher Gewerkschaftsbund, Bonn.
52. Korum before the Fulda Bishops' Conference in December 1910, B III 15.9, vol. 2, BisA Trier.

between union and *Fachabteilung* included a *private* declaration recognizing the right of a bishop to supervise the activities of social and economic organizations in his diocese. This, assumed Korum, would allow the unions to save public face. Stegerwald and Giesberts were dumbfounded, for any such declaration would have produced an immediate exodus of Behrens and the entire Evangelical wing of the movement. And a purely Catholic labor organization, they explained, would be totally ineffective in Germany. But Korum would not listen. Nor would the unionists yield. With no middle ground on the issue of church control, relations soon deteriorated to their former state.[53]

Only the pope, it seemed, would be able to dislodge the Christian trade unions from their independent position. But there were no encouraging signs from this quarter either during the fall and winter of 1908/9. Hard-pressed by *Fachabteilung* headquarters in Berlin to withdraw his protection of the Christian trade unions in the archdiocese of Cologne, Fischer inquired of Pius on 20 October 1908 if the Vatican intended to adhere to its neutrality declaration of January 1906. The pope restated his view that each bishop should decide which organization was best suited for his diocese, and confirmed this position in a letter to Fischer seven weeks later. August Pieper and Peter Spahn, who had been commissioned by the executive committee of the Center Reichstag *Fraktion* to explain the political significance of the unions to Vatican circles, received the same response from Cardinal Secretary of State Merry del Val on 27 December 1908. The pope's position was unaltered, furthermore, when Father Otto Müller, Johannes Giesberts, and Franz Wieber paid homage in Rome in early April 1909.[54] The disgruntled Berliners had nowhere to turn.

The defiant behavior of the *Volksverein* was also quite infuriating to conservative Catholics. Undaunted by the news from Fulda, the organization forged ahead with plans for the "interconfessionalization of the social and economic sector."[55] What was regarded as a major step in this direction was taken at the Düsseldorf *Katholikentag* in mid-August 1908. August Pieper, Heinrich Brauns, and forty-five *Gesamtverband* functionaries were on hand for the proceedings of the social commission to support a controversial motion introduced by the Interconfessional Union of Düsseldorf Artisans. The *Katholikentag* was asked to approve the idea of a "great *Mittelstandsorganisation*"[56] comprising journeyman, artisans, clerks, and other white-collar employees. Unlike the Association of Catholic Retail Employees, whose main function

53. *Ibid.*; Stegerwald to Franz Bachem, 17 October 1908, printed in *Germania*, no. 290, 19 December 1911; Hartrath to Hohn, 10 February 1911, Hohn Papers 15/2, 1913, StA MG.
54. Prussian envoy at the Vatican Mühlberg to Bethmann Hollweg, 4 December 1909, Päpstlicher Stuhl 26 *secr*. 1, AA Bonn; Brack, *Deutscher Episkopat und Gewerkschaftsstreit*, pp. 128–30; Bachem, *Zentrumspartei*, vol. 7, p. 213; Müller Manuscript, p. 61, KAB Haus Köln.
55. Effert to the *Regierungspräsident*, 20 August 1908, as cited in note 29.
56. *Ibid.*

was educational, the new association would cooperate closely with the labor movement to mollify the opposition of employers and exact concessions from the state. Brauns and the workers envisioned an organization 500,000 strong with members from all political parties except the S.P.D. The motion was passed over the vehement objections of the Berliners, who warned that such a union would undermine Catholic beliefs and bring an end to the Center Party.

The *Volksverein* illustrated the same confidence with regard to the episcopate's demand for a codetermining voice on the *Volksverein* executive council. In negotiations which dragged on throughout the late fall and winter, Brandts and Pieper repeatedly refused to accede to the wish of the bishops. Three arguments were offered in defense of this stand. First, the *Volksverein* had always kept the archibishop of Cologne informed about its activities and had even offered to present the bishops with a special annual report about the entire operation of the organization. Mönchen-Gladbach also pointed out that the influence it had been able to exert on interconfessional economic organizations would be reduced if the *Volksverein* were viewed in these circles as a church organization. Finally, it was argued that the hierarchy would be dragged into controversial economic and political struggles which would expose it to attacks by enemies of the church. Kopp and Korum rejected these arguments with the wave of a hand, of course, for neither bishop intended to condone strikes or tolerate the independence of the Christian trade unions. Unable to make headway in these negotiations, the *Volksverein* called upon the papal nuncio in Munich, Dr. Andreas Frühwirth, for help. Greatly elated, Brandts returned from a visit to Münich in May 1909 with the news that it was not necessary to assign the bishops an executive council seat. Permanent contact with the archbishop of Cologne would be sufficient.[57]

That Rome had refused to intervene against the Christian trade unions, the *Volksverein,* and the *Kölnische Volkszeitung* did not mean, however, that Vatican circles were convinced of the righteousness of the western position. In fact, just the opposite was the case. While in Munich, Brandts noted with surprise that Frühwirth considered the strike a violation of moral law. The nuncio, like the pope himself, was also deeply disturbed by the idea that the church had nothing to say in economic matters. "Time and time again," wrote Brandts, "the prelate came back to the International Congress . . . at Zurich because of Schiffer's thoughtless statement that 'the bishops have to be told: This far and no farther.'"[58] Rome was no less opposed to the secularism of the Center and *Volksverein*. Pius stated this privately to the Vatican historian

57. Edmund Schopen, *'Köln' eine innere Gefahr*, p. 84; Bachem, *Zentrumspartei*, vol. 7, pp. 208–9; Gottwald, "Volksverein," in Fricke (ed.), *Bürgerliche Parteien*, vol. 2, pp. 818–19; Ritter, *Die Männer aus Mönchen-Gladbach*, part 2, p. 25, Ritter Papers ER/D-16, KfZG Bonn.
58. *Ibid.* (Ritter).

Ludwig Pastor in 1907 and had also taken action to this effect in Italy. In a series of decrees issued since July 1904, the pope brought the social and political organizations of lay Catholics under episcopal control and excommunicated those who had had the audacity to question these rulings.[59] Pius's reluctance to apply the same "anti-modernistic" principles to Germany was merely an act of expediency, therefore, not one of principle. He realized that Cologne and Mönchen-Gladbach were backed by thousands of German Catholics and did not want to risk weakening the Center at a time when Catholic unity was vital to church interests.[60]

Others in Rome had less concern for these reasonings of state. The powerful undersecretary of state at the Vatican, Umberto Benigni, was the foremost advocate of stringent measures against Christian-social organizations north of the Alps. Like the Berliners, Benigni adhered to a strict interpretation of *Rerum Novarum* which denied to Catholic workers the right to participate in independent, nondenominational trade unions. He was also an active political conservative, having ties to the ultrareactionary *Action Française* in France. In the fall of 1907, furthermore, Benigni created a secret, Europe-wide vigilante organization known as *Sodalitium Pianum,* whose purpose it was to collect information on suspect individuals and organizations and relay these reports to Rome. Through official and semi-official press organs at the Vatican, personal contact with Merry del Val, and private audiences with the pope himself, Benigni hoped to convince his superiors that extra-episcopal associations such as the Christian trade unions, the *Volksverein,* or the "Sillon" in France represented "modernism in practice" and were therefore a greater danger to the church than any consequence which might follow from their condemnation. As he saw it, cooperation with Protestants in independent organizations was the first step toward a break from the church similar to that which had occurred in the sixteenth century.[61] By 1909, the undersecretary had registered no success with these intrigues. But the orthodox, devout Pius, as is often the case with monarchs, was a very malleable individual. "The Holy Father is too good," observed Kopp after a visit to Rome in 1904. "His good heart leads him astray too easily into all kinds of promises and assurances.[62] Thus the pope was liable at any time to give way to his deeply felt antipathy for the struggling Christian-social movement of Imperial Germany.

Incensed by the events of the fall and winter of 1908/9, meanwhile, conser-

59. Wilhelm Wühr (ed.), *Ludwig Freiherr von Pastor 1854–1928: Tagebücher-Briefe-Erinnerungen* (Heidelberg: F. H. Kerle Verlag, 1950), pp. 477–82; Prussian minister of culture Trott zu Solz to William, 21 September 1910, Rom-Vatikan 199-309, 1, AA Bonn.
60. Jedin (ed.), *Handbuch der Kirchengeschichte*, vol. 6, part 2, p. 498.
61. *Ibid.*, pp. 487–93; Bachem, *Zentrumspartei*, vol. 7, pp. 286–328.
62. Kopp to Korum, 26 December 1904, Korum Papers 378, BisA Trier.

vatives in Germany were plotting action of their own. How, they asked, could the Christian trade unions continue to operate freely and independently after they had insulted the bishops and refused on two occasions to deal with Bishop Korum? Had the *Volksverein* grown so powerful that it could go over the head of the Fulda Conference to the pope's representative in Munich? These developments convinced conservatives that the Christian trade unions, the *Volksverein,* and a large body of Centrists influenced by Bachem were trying to "free . . . German Catholics from the influence of the episcopate . . . and weld Catholics and Protestants together in a great Christian-social bloc [which would be active] in all areas of public life and religious practice."[63] Like Benigni, they feared a "Protestantization"[64] of German Catholics that would complete the Reformation. To forestall such an eventuality, influential clerics, intellectuals, journalists, agrarians, and parliamentarians, at least one of whom belonged to *Sodalitium Pianum,* began to establish closer ties during the fall and winter. On Eastern Tuesday (13 April) 1909, they met secretly in Cologne to debate a three-point program: opposition to all attempts to alter the confessional nature of the Center; closer organizational ties between the *Volksverein* and the episcopate; and unification of the *Fachabteilungen* and the Christian trade unions in cartel form. Because experience had shown that practically nothing could be done directly against the *Gesamtverband,* the conferees dropped the third point. A close reading of the conference protocol makes it clear, however, that the participants were confident that points one and two of the program would suffice to avoid the "dubious consequences"[65] (declining respect for the bishops, religious indifference, interconfessionalization of the Center, arrogant interest group politics, etc.) which had resulted from the growth of Christian trade unions in Germany. A petition was sent to the bishops of few weeks later.

The *Osterdienstag* initiative led rather quickly to a resolution of the crisis which had been developing in the Catholic camp over the alleged interconfessionalization of the Center. The opposing factions jockeyed for position in party circles during the summer and fall of 1909 hopeful that their opponents would be silenced by Center leaders in Berlin.[66] The result, Hertling wrote his wife on 29 November, was "a compromise wholly satisfactory to no one, but less pleasing to the *'Kölner Richtung'* than to its antagonist [from Berlin]."[67] At a conference of Reich and Prussian Centrists the day before, a declaration

63. ten Hompel, *Osterdienstags-Protokoll*, p. 7.
64. *Ibid.*, p. 12.
65. *Ibid.*, p. 6.
66. Julius Bachem to Hertling, 24 July 1909, Hertling Papers 37, BA Koblenz; also see Giesberts's remarks at the General Assembly of the *Augustinusverein* on 18 August 1909, *Augustinus-Blatt,* no. 8, August 1909, StBib MG.
67. Hertling to his wife, Anna, 29 November 1909, Hertling Papers 19, BA Koblenz.

was formulated over the nature of the party.[68] The Center was not fundamentally a denominational party, the statement began, for it required its deputies to represent the interests of all Germans in a given district. Nor was it necessary that members adhere to the Catholic faith or, if Protestant, vote in a way that contradicted their religious convictions. What was given to Bachem, Trimborn, and Hitze with one hand, however, was taken away with the other. "This fundamental character is in no way inconsistent with the fact that throughout the years of the *Kulturkampf* the Center Party had to regard the defense of legislative and administrative measures directed against Catholics as its first and most pressing task, or that today one of [the Center's] chief duties is still to guarantee the legal and political rights [*staatsbürgerliche Gleichberechtigung]* of the Catholic minority."[69] It was just such a statement that the Christian-social leaders of the party wanted to avoid, because as they saw it this passage would merely play into the hands of National Liberal and, to a lesser extent, Conservative supporters of the Evangelical League. The result would hamper far-reaching electoral and parliamentary cooperation with these parties. Only after years of interconfessional work to solve social, economic, and national problems would the Center really be able to achieve equality for Catholics, for the Protestant majority would never grant such rights until it had overcome its prejudicial view of Catholics as ultramontane *"Reichsfeinde."*[70] Confirming the mild setback experienced by Cologne and Mönchen-Gladbach, the Center entered a bill in early December demanding repeal of the remaining anti-Jesuit laws. Accompanied by the predictable anti-Catholic outbursts, the motion was defeated in February 1910.[71]

The Easter Tuesday coalition was also moderately successful in its quest to bring the *Volksverein* under closer episcopal supervision. Not long after receiving the *Osterdienstag* protocol, Kopp informed Silesian Center circles that he would initiate another discussion of the *Volksverein*'s independence at the upcoming bishops' conference in Cologne (6 August 1909).[72] The resolution which resulted from this debate was clearly aimed at inhibiting Mönchen-Gladbach's agitation and alleged financial support for the Christian trade unions. The bishops expected the *Volksverein* to conform exactly to the principles set down in its by-laws, inform the archbishop of Cologne concerning all expenditures, and instruct association representatives (*Vertrauensmänner*) in

68. The declaration is printed in Bachem, *Zentrumspartei*, vol. 7, pp. 236–37.
69. *Ibid.*
70. Pieper to Undersecretary of State in the Reich Chancellery Wahnschaffe, 13 April 1913, Reichskanzlei, Nr. 2270, Bl. 114, ZStA Potsdam.
71. Bachem, *Zentrumspartei*, vol. 7, pp. 110–14. Bachem exaggerates the "victory" of Cologne in 1909.
72. Ritter, *Die Männer aus Mönchen-Gladbach*, part 2, p. 25, Ritter Papers ER/D-16, KfZG Bonn.

every diocese to reach an understanding with the responsible bishop before undertaking any important action.[73] Unwilling to test the tolerance of the bishops further, and somewhat relieved that no executive council representation had been requested, the *Volksverein* succumbed to these demands immediately. At a conference in Frankfurt on 19 November, association functionaries were instructed to maintain the closest possible contact with the bishops, informing them of assemblies, rallies, private caucuses, and the status of the organization.[74] Fischer was supplied with a financial report for the fiscal year 1909/1910, and in an apparent attempt to abide by its statutory obligation to promote Catholic interests, the *Volksverein* completely withdrew from all polemics in the trade union controversy.[75]

The anti–trade union nature of the campaign to shackle Mönchen-Gladbach is well illustrated by events in the archdiocese of Breslau during the fall and winter of 1909/10. At the Breslau *Katholikentag* (29 August–2 September) Kopp extended an olive branch to the *Volksverein* by inviting the association to intensify agitation in his diocese. The nature of the terms offered to Franz Brandts later that fall were similar to those which Korum had offered Giesberts and Stegerwald in 1908. Mönchen-Gladbach was to promote unions and trade sections equally, refrain from all polemics, and bar the most outspoken pro-union functionaries from the archdiocese of Breslau. The *Volksverein* chairman answered that his association could not support an organization that opposed trade unionism, but was willing to exclude anti-Berlinist material from *Volksverein* literature. Moreover, instead of veteran labor organizers like Heinrich Brauns, Pieper and executive council member Dr. Carl Sonnenschein would manage Silesian operations. Kopp's counter-offer indicates well the conservative drift of his thinking. Pieper and Sonnenschein were unacceptable; rather, the *Volksverein*'s eastern section should be run by church canon Frank and other clergymen from the archdiocese, while two-thirds of all dues collected would remain behind in Breslau for use as Frank saw fit.[76] As Pieper reported a year later, the negotiations faltered over this point, for Kopp's proposal "envisioned an independent *Volksverein* organization in the diocese of Breslau . . . the consequence of which would have been a dissolution of the entire association."[77] The archbishop felt equally justified in his

73. The resolution is printed in the conference protocols, Bertram Papers IA-25b-16(4), AA Wroclawie.

74. Gottwald, "Volksverein," in Fricke (ed.), *Bürgerliche Parteien*, vol. 2, p. 819.

75. See the minutes to *Volksverein* executive council sessions of 23 August 1910, 5 July 1911, 2 October 1911, and 11 July 1912, in the Hartrath Papers 2, StA MG.

76. Pieper Manuscript, part 3, pp. 572–73, StA MG; Wilhelm Ziebach Diary, entry of 4 December 1910, *Archiv der katholischen Arbeitnehmerbewegung*, KfZG Bonn; Brack, *Deutscher Episkopat und Gewerkschaftsstreit*, pp. 152–55.

77. Minutes to *Volksverein* executive council session of 19 December 1910, in the Hartrath Papers 2, StA MG.

stance: "What was I supposed to say to Silesians who answered [my] recommendation of the *Volksverein* with: 'We don't want our dues sent to Mönchen-Gladbach so that Christian trade union secretaries receive salaries'?"[78]

Kopp's waning tolerance for the "modernistic" Christian-social faction in the Catholic camp was pushed to the limit by two more controversial incidents that winter. On 28 December 1909 the representatives of the Socialist, Christian, Hirsch-Duncker, and Polish miners' unions met in Essen to protest the blacklisting practices of employers in the Ruhr. A few days later Kopp noticed a newspaper interview which the Christian leader Johann Effert had granted to liberal reporters. As soon as a favorable opportunity presented itself, noted Effert, the unions were prepared to initiate a strike that would paralyze the entire industry and lead to the nationalization of the mines. At about the same time, the archbishop received an angry protest resolution from Emilie Hopmann, president of the Catholic Women's League, which criticized Kopp's confessional League of Girl and Women Workers and called for more trust in the *Volksverein*. The archbishop reacted with a bitter note to Amalie Schalscha von Ehrenfeld, chairwoman of his own women's organization. "Doesn't Hopmann ever read the daily newspapers? Hasn't she read what the Christian labor secretary Effert blurted out recently? This openheartedness went too far for even the Socialists."[79] In the spring of 1910, then, Kopp announced in the diocesan gazette that the founding of new branches of the *Volksverein* must be brought to his attention. "In every single case," he wrote Korum, "I will [then] prevent the founding."[80] Events had come full circle since the Breslau *Katholikentag* the previous summer.

These trends did not augur well for the membership drive inaugurated by the Christian trade unions in the wake of the financial reform of 1909. Added to the embarrassment over inheritance taxes (Chapter 11) and the aloofness of the suspicious Evangelical proletariat, Christian organizers had to contend with the increasingly troublesome fact that a significant percentage of the Catholic working class questioned the moral credentials of the *Gesamtverband*. In order to eliminate the source of this problem, the unions took a number of potentially embarrassing steps. In Februrary 1910, the *Zentralblatt* dissociated the movement from Effert's threat of a strike, declaring that it expressed a purely personal view and did not reflect the anti-Socialist, moderately pro-business strategy of the Christian trade unions. Such a disclaimer

78. Quoted in Brack, *Deutscher Episkopat und Gewerkschaftsstreit*, p. 154.
79. Kopp to Schalsche von Ehrenfeld, 12 January 1910, Bachem Papers 294, HA Köln. For other developments discussed here, see *Mülheimer Volkszeitung*, 3 January 1910 (clipping in: Landratsamt Mülheim-Duisburg 842, HSA Düsseldorf); Wilhelm Zieback Diary, entry of 4 December 1910, *Archiv der katholischen Arbeitnehmerbewegung*, KfZG Bonn.
80. Quoted in Brack, *Deutscher Episkopat und Gewerkschaftsstreit*, p. 157.

could hardly have appealed to the miners of the Ruhr. Mönchen-Gladbach and the *Gesamtverband* also attempted to elicit declarations of confidence from the Center *Fraktionen*, the *Katholikentag*, and the *Augustinusverein*. Had these efforts succeeded, the political neutrality of the unions would once again have been called into question. The point is academic, however, for at every turn Christian leaders ran headlong into the uncompromising opposition of Kopp, who foiled these plans by issuing threats of church censure to the leaders of the above-mentioned Catholic organizations. After the Fulda Conference (23–25 August), moreover, Christian trade unionists learned that Kopp and Korum had once again raised the issue of the *Volksverein*, demanding the dismemberment of the association into diocesan units headed by bishops. All efforts at appeasement seemed destined to fail.[81]

The years 1910 and 1911 witnessed renewed disputes within the Catholic community over the alleged modernism of the Center, *Volksverein*, and Christian trade unions.[82] By late 1911 German Catholics had been feuding and struggling almost without interruption for three and a half years. The seemingly interminable feud had resulted in no clear victory for either side, but it must be emphasized before proceeding that the conflict had placed far greater barriers in front of the interconfessionalists than has often been assumed. The attempt to tear down the Center's denominational facade and maneuver the party into a more friendly relationship with other bourgeois parties had not been completely unsuccessful, as the upcoming Reichstag elections would prove. The "compromise" resolution of November 1909, however, was no doubt partially responsible for the dearth of Protestant sacrifices made during the campaign. A harassed *Volksverein*, moreover, had made a number of important concessions to the bishops and was no longer entirely free to make decisions. The Christian trade unions had thus far conceded nothing, but the cost of maintaining their independence had been high. Even the pro-union bishops were not entirely satisfied that the movement was safe for Catholic workers.[83]

Rome, moreover, had only been restrained from letting fall the sword of Damocles by the *démarche* of the Prussian government. In early September 1910 Chancellor Bethmann Hollweg received a worried Franz Behrens. The Evangelical unionist had been commissioned by the Protestant members of the

81. *Ibid.*, pp. 158–59; *Zentralblatt*, no. 3, 7 February 1910; Gottwald, "Volksverein," in Fricke (ed.), *Bürgerliche Parteien*, vol. 2, p. 818; Pieper to Frohberger, 20 September 1910, Bachem Papers 294, HA Köln.
82. For a detailed discussion, see this author's dissertation, "Christian Labor and the Politics of Frustration in Imperial Germany," Ohio State, 1978, pp. 350–55.
83. Both Ross, *Beleaguered Tower*, pp. 128–31, and Brack, *Deutscher Episkopat und Gewerkschaftsstreit*, chapters 12–13, *passim*, underestimate the extent to which "Cologne" had been constrained by "Berlin."

Gesamtverband to solicit the aid of Prussian leaders in shielding the movement from papal condemnation. Behrens was able to convince Bethmann that Christian union efforts to rally the bourgeois parties would reduce S.P.D. voting strength in 1912, whereupon the chancellor promised to instruct the Prussian emissary at the Vatican, Otto von Mühlberg, to take the necessary steps. Mühlberg's action probably took the form of a private warning to Benigni that any interference with the national tasks of Christian labor could result in a severance of diplomatic relations between the Curia and Berlin. Aware that the pope could not afford to lose contact with the rulers of so many Catholics, Benigni postponed his plans.[84]

But only until the elections were over. Spurred on by Benigni,[85] it seems almost certain that Pius intended to lend the authority of canonical law to the *Osterdienstag* demand for separate Catholic and Protestant unions united in cartel form. This solution was apparently seen as one which would permit the Christian proletariat to oppose the Socialists, avoid problems with the Prussian government, and satisfy the Vatican's own demands for supervision and guarantees of religious purity. An interesting series of events in late spring 1912 altered Rome's course. Rome was alarmed by the formation of a cartel which united the Catholic *Arbeitervereine* of western and southern Germany—a move designed, among other things, to promote the economic *and political* program of the Christian trade unions. The Vatican sent a telegram to delegates attending the cartel's first congress in Frankfurt a. M., warning them not to violate the dictates set down in *Rerum Novarum*. Addressed to Giesberts, the note was generally accepted as a sign that the pope would take action against the unions in the near future. The great outcry which went up in western Catholic circles complicated these plans, for, greatly startled, Pius decided to ask the Prussian bishops their opinion of the yet unpublished encyclical. The moderately pro-union response of the episcopate, and the renewed warning from Mühlberg that Christian labor should be left alone, led, then, to revisions in the text that summer. The Vatican pointed out, however, that the dangers represented by the *Gesamtverband* were too great to be completely ignored by the new ruling.[86]

84. Felix Porsch to Wilhelm Marx, 25 September 1910, Marx Papers 221, and Julius Bachem to Carl Bachem, 9 October 1910, and Carl Bachem's notation of 12 October 1910, Bachem Papers 295–96, HA Köln; Ritter to Hertling, 14 June 1912, M. Arb. 383, AStA München.

85. Mülberg to Bethmann Hollweg, 19 March 1912, Päpstlicher Stuhl 26 *secr.* 1, AA Bonn; Benigni to Jonckx (in Belgium), 2 March 1912, Benigni Papers 4, in Brauweiler Papers 15/13/42, StA MG.

86. It is generally assumed that the encyclical was not begun until after the Frankfurt Congress of May 1912. (See, for instance, Brack, *Deutscher Episkopat und Gewerkschaftsstreit*, chapter 14, *passim.*) In December 1913, however, Archbishop Fischer's general vicar, Peter Kreuzwald, testified that Fischer was too ill to travel to Rome at Easter 1912 "and could therefore exert no

Dated 24 September 1912, the encyclical *Singulari Quadam*[87] was outspoken in its theoretical opposition to the Christian trade unions. The *Gewerkschaftsstreit* demanded the Vatican's attention, the document began, because a danger existed that German Catholics would "gradually, unwittingly content themselves with a blurred, undefined sort of Christian religion which is customarily referred to as interconfessionalism."[88] The nondenominational labor movement had also violated the instructions for social action established by Leo XIII.

> Whatever the Christian does . . . he must as the final goal subordinate everything to the greatest good. All his actions, however, insofar as they are good or evil in a moral sense, that is, insofar as they comply or deviate from the natural laws of God, are subjected to the judgment and the offices of the church. All who boast of the Christian name, as individuals or in associations, may not, if they want to do their duty, stir up hostility and feud between the estates of bourgeois society, but must rather promote peace and mutual understanding. The social question and the related controversial questions concerning the character and nature of work, wages, and strikes are not of a purely economic nature and thus not to be counted among those questions that can be solved in the absence of church authority. On the contrary, the social question is beyond a doubt a moral and religous issue and therefore must be solved according to moral law from the religious standpoint.[89]

This reasoning led Pius to the conclusion that Catholic denominational associations were to be preferred above all others. In Catholic areas, "and also in other areas where it can be assumed that these [confessional unions] can adequately meet the various needs of the members,"[90] purely Catholic associations should be founded and promoted. The Vatican could *never* look

---

influence over the drafting of the encyclical" (*Der Kölner Gewerkschaftsprozess* [Cologne: Christlicher Gewerkschaftsverlag, 1913], p. 68). In addition, Bishop Rosentreter of Kulm told Carl Bachem in August 1913 that the Berliners had sought to influence the writing of the document "for months" before the Frankfurt Congress, while the Prussian bishops were not asked until afterwards (Bachem notation of 7 August 1913, Bachem Papers 328, HA Köln). Father Rathscheck, a close associate of Bishop Schulte of Paderborn, told Bachem in February 1913, furthermore, that a special passage had been added to the document after Frankfurt (Bachem notation of 8 February 1913, Bachem Papers 328, HA Köln). And finally, Franz Heiner, a German prelate in Rome who worked closely with Pius and Merry del Val, wrote that the Christian trade unions had been in the "greatest danger" before the Congress (Heiner to an unnamed friend, 10 June 1912, Bachem Papers 320a, HA Köln). For the Vatican's desire to curb "the dangers represented by the *Gesamtverband*" that summer, see Ritter to Hertling, 19 July 1912, M. Arb. 383, AStA München.

87. Printed in *Der Kölner Gewerkschaftsprozess*, pp. 35–39.
88. *Ibid.*, pp. 35–36.
89. *Ibid.*, pp. 36–37.
90. *Ibid.*, p. 37.

favorably upon the founding of interconfessional organizations in the above-mentioned regions, the document continued, for such associations presented a grave threat to the purity of the faith and the authority of the Catholic church. This did not mean that Rome frowned on all socio-economic cooperation between Catholics and Protestants. Rather, "we prefer that Catholic and non-Catholic organizations form ties with one another by way of the new, up-to-date institution called the cartel."[91]

Having made it abundantly clear what he preferred, Pius yielded at this point to the bishops and the Prussian government. In return for papal "toleration" of the Christian trade unions in the areas where they presently existed, however, the pope insisted that certain prerequisites be met. First, Catholic unionists had to join an *Arbeiterverein* so that the clergy could teach them the moral and religious principles pertinent to trade union activity. Second, the pope forbade the unions *per se* to engage in any action which contradicted these teachings. Third, the bishops were instructed "to observe and oversee the behavior of the unions [to see] that no harm comes to Catholics who participate in them."[92] Fourth, all disputes among German Catholics over labor matters should be referred directly to Rome for final arbitration. If these conditions were met, papal toleration of the *Gesamtverband* would continue. In short, the Christian trade unions had been placed on probation.

The Prussian bishops convened at Fulda in early November 1912 to accept the dictates of the Holy Father, translate the encyclical from Latin into German, and send it on to the press. Before publication on 10 November, Vicar General Kreutzwald of the archdiocese of Cologne was instructed by Kopp to meet with Christian labor leaders and inform them of the contents of the document.[93] The archbishop was concerned lest the unionists "give way to first impressions."[94] When Kreutzwald met with Brauns, Giesberts, and Stegerwald on 8 November, however, the three had already read an official version printed in the *Kölnische Zeitung* and were understandably shaken by the news. Most upset was the unions' general secretary, who insisted that his organization might have to speak out publicly against the encyclical.[95] Pressed by the ever-cautious Giesberts, however, Stegerwald agreed to suppress his pessimism and "look at the bright side."[96]

A letter two days later to Joseph Joos, editor of the *Westdeutsche Arbeiter-*

91. *Ibid.*, p. 38.
92. *Ibid.*, p. 38.
93. See the protocols of the Fulda Conference on 5 November 1912, Bertram Papers IA-25b-24 (11), AA Wroclawie.
94. Kopp to Porsch, 10 November 1912, Bachem Papers 329, HA Köln.
95. *Ibid.*; *Der Kölner Gewerkschaftsprozess*, p. 40.
96. *Der Kölner Gewerkschaftsprozess*, p. 80.

Zeitung, indicates that Stegerwald was unable to keep this promise. In order to preserve the independence of the *Gesamtverband,* wrote Stegerwald, a special congress should be convened, the word "Christian" stricken from the statutes, and the Catholic *Arbeitervereine* informed that relations would be terminated as soon as difficulties arose over implementation of the pope's ruling.[97] As for the encyclical itself, Stegerwald intended to protest the unwarranted interference of Rome in matters that did not fall under its authority. The resolution would be phrased forcefully, but would not overstep "the limits of the permissible."[98]

> I am quite conscious of the consequences, the responsibility, and the struggles of salvation that will begin [he wrote to Joos]. Nevertheless, read the sentences of the encyclical that I've marked and ask yourself: (1) whether Protestant members can still belong to our movement under such ignoble conditions, and (2) whether trade union activity as we think of it is still possible within this barbed-wire fence. A positive answer for either question is impossible. Furthermore, our movement sits on a permanent volcano since this encyclical was issued. No trade union group can follow these ideas and develop powerfully in the face of the strong Social Democratic movement. We must now discuss how our movement is to avoid stagnation and slow death. To remain dumb to all this would be the most dangerous and unmanly thing that we could do.[99]

Stegerwald's suggestions were accepted by the union's executive committee on 13 November, and on the fifteenth, Behrens spoke with Bethmann concerning the most effective means of governmental support for the upcoming action. Unlike on previous occasions, the chancellor was encouraged to refrain from applying pressure in Rome. The unionists were afraid that Pius had been pushed far enough and would counterattack if the union protest were combined with another humiliating *démarche.* Naively perhaps, Christian labor leaders felt they could avoid condemnation or excommunication, while still saving face before the skeptical masses.[100]

Stegerwald's plans, meanwhile, had caused great consternation in Center and *Volksverein* circles. Though greatly angered by the encyclical, Brauns wrote Bishop Schulte on the fourteenth that the special congress had been prepared by the unions alone, not Mönchen-Gladbach. The veteran labor organizer obviously wanted to shield the *Volksverein* from any church retalia-

97. Stegerwald to Joos, 10 November 1912, Stegerwald Papers 1, Stegerwald Stiftung Köln.
98. *Der Kölner Gewerkschaftsprozess,* p. 42. Also see Carl Bachem's notation of 18 November 1912, Bachem Papers 328, HA Köln.
99. Stegerwald to Joos, 10 November 1912, Stegerwald Papers 1, Stegerwald Stiftung Köln.
100. Behrens to Stegerwald, 16 November 1912, Stegerwald to Giesberts, 18 November 1912, Stegerwald Papers 1, Stegerwald Stiftung Köln; Bachem notation of 12 December 1912, Bachem Papers 329, HA Köln.

tion that might follow against the Christian trade unions. In Berlin, Hitze, Trimborn, and Porsch tried to convince Giesberts that the congress should be canceled. The three party leaders knew that the "limits of permissible" were narrow and could be easily exceeded by the worked-up unionists. The pope's wrath would then be vented on the politically important unions, and maybe on the Center itself, for by this point, Pius's dislike for the *"Kölner Richtung"* was an open secret.[101] These efforts bore some fruit on the seventeenth when, after a three-hour session, the editorial staff of the *Kölnische Volkszeitung* got Stegerwald to agree "at least to think over the matter."[102]

Bishop Schulte, the most emphatic supporter of the Christian trade unions in the episcopate, was also striving to prevent a collision between church and *Gesamtverband*. Warned separately by Franz Brandts and Center deputy Karl Kuckhoff that Christian labor leaders were in an excitable state, Schulte arranged a meeting with Stegerwald on the fifteenth.[103] The general secretary opened the meeting by producing a bundle of newspaper articles which claimed that the Christian trade unions had finally been shackled by the church. Stegerwald was also worried about rumors from Berlin concerning S.P.D. and Conservative Party interpellations against the pope's interference in the affairs of German labor. Both developments demanded that a special congress be held, for the unions had to show the public that they were perfectly capable of protecting their own interests.

Schulte responded that adverse criticism or no, the pope's decrees could not be treated with disrespect. The bishop coupled this warning, however, with the rather startling observation that the Socialist and Conservative interpretations of the encyclical were entirely false. Neither the pope nor the episcopate wanted to supervise or control the unions' economic activity. All that was intended was a closer scrutiny to insure that no religious or moral dangers arose from membership in the organization. Nor did the encyclical mean that the bishops were forbidden to promote Christian trade unions in Catholic as well as largely non-Catholic areas. These comments were included in the "theoretical part" of the document and did not apply to Germany. Schulte proceeded to tell Stegerwald that a written statement summarizing this "interpretation" would be placed at the unions' disposal for public use. At Stegerwald's request, the bishop promised to ask Kopp for similar assurances.[104]

101. Brack, *Deutscher Episkopat und Gewerkschaftsstreit*, p. 305; Giesberts to Stegerwald, 18 November 1912, Porsch to Giesberts, 22 November 1912, Stegerwald Papers 1, Stegerwald Stiftung Köln; Bachem notation of 18 November 1912, Bachem Papers 328, HA Köln.
102. Frohberger to Carl Bachem, 19 November 1912, Bachem Papers 328, HA Köln.
103. For the meeting, see *Westfälisches Volksblatt*, no. 25, 27 January 1914; and *Der Kölner Gewerkschaftsprozess*, pp. 41–42, 60–61.
104. *Ibid.*

That Stegerwald placed even the slightest hope in Kopp was the result of a letter which the archbishop had sent to Porsch on 10 November. The note—which had come into Stegerwald's hands via Pieper—was drafted after Kopp had learned from Kreutzwald that the unionists were worried about the encyclical. For Kopp, who had expected a much harsher ruling from Rome, this concern was groundless. The pope had not condemned the *Gesamtverband,* he noted, "and the bishops, most of whom stand behind the Christian trade unions, will not claim supervisory rights . . . Everything remains as before . . . the [union] leaders can therefore forget all this mistrust and pessimism."[105]

Thus Kopp and Schulte, who stood poles apart on the trade union question, had reached the same conclusion concerning *Singulari Quadam.* The archbishop's judgment was probably blurred by the disappointment he felt in the aftermath of the encyclical, but he was also determined to keep the peace among the bishops and, perhaps most important of all, prevent the unionists from taking steps that would be disastrous for the German Catholic community. As far as Schulte's lenient interpretation of the papal document is concerned, the wish seems to have been father of the thought. For even a cursory reading of the encyclical leads, as the unionists had realized, to an altogether different conclusion.

It is quite likely, therefore, that Stegerwald left the conference with Schulte somewhat skeptical concerning the likelihood that the entire episcopate, much less Rome, would allow the unions to pursue an independent course. Such a conjecture would explain Stegerwald's grudging behavior during the meeting with Julius Bachem *et al.* two days later, as well as a letter which he sent Giesberts on the eighteenth. At the congress later that month, noted Stegerwald, the unions should not let things come to a conflict with Rome.

> But on the other hand, we want to remain a movement with self-consciousness and backbone. Without these properties no labor movement in Germany can prevail against the Social Democratic giant. Furthermore, we may not choose all-too-diplomatic phrases in the resolution, because we must cater to the psyche of the masses. The Vatican's encyclical with all its crass passages is read in thousands of assemblies by our opponents and held before our people in tens of thousands of factories. Faced with this situation, our people also need something in their hands to sap the strength from the reproaches of the others. Finally, the present [harsh] form has been chosen for the resolution to show Rome, church authorities in Germany, and broad circles of the clergy, that the eternal guardianship of the working class has its limits.[106]

105. Kopp to Porsch, 10 November 1912, Bachem Papers 329, HA Köln.
106. Stegerwald to Giesberts, 18 November 1912, Stegerwald Papers 1, Stegerwald Stiftung Köln.

Such an approach was perfectly suited to precipitate the crisis which Stegerwald said he wanted to avoid.

A catastrophe was averted at the last minute by the continued efforts of Schulte and Kopp. The former wired a written version of his interpretation to Stegerwald on 20 November and followed this up on the twenty-second with the news that Kopp had granted permission to distribute copies of his letter to Porsch among the delegates at the unions' congress—now scheduled for the twenty-sixth in Essen. On both occasions Schulte implored the labor leader not to lay too much emphasis on the independence of the movement, rather to speak cautiously and respect the pope's wish for peace in the *Gewerkschaftsstreit*. Aware by this time that Schulte was in the process of extricating the movement from the entire crisis, Stegerwald assured the bishop that no injurious remarks would be made, but, still not completely satisfied, pressed Schulte for a declaration from Kopp that his name would be linked publicly to the lenient interpretation of the encyclical. When Schulte replied on the twenty-third that Kopp wanted the entire episcopate to be associated with the interpretation and had taken the appropriate steps, Stegerwald swung into line, and with editorial help from Schulte, drafted a much milder resolution. The general secretary also exerted his influence on keynote speaker Karl Schiffer, who proceeded to eliminate two-thirds of the address that he had already prepared.[107]

The Essen Congress of 26 November 1912 was thus a very restrained affair, nothing like the protest assembly which had originally been planned. In fact, the initiative was transformed into an impressive piece of propaganda against the free trade unions, the Hirsch-Dunckers, the Evangelical *Bund,* and others who had proclaimed the end of the Christian trade unions. The congress was also a major setback for the *Fachabteilungen* in Berlin, for Stegerwald was able to declare that the Fulda Conference recognized the right of trade unions to make decisions independently and would not prevent the *Gesamtverband* from expanding into exclusively Catholic areas (i.e., Silesia). Highlighting the day's activity was a telegram from the head of Emperor William's Privy Council relaying the Kaiser's approval of "the patriotic demonstration of the representatives of Christian-National labor."[108] It was not the first time in the history of the movement that a crisis of major proportions had been narrowly averted.

* * * *

107. Schulte to Stegerwald, 20, 22, 23, 24, and 25 November 1912, Stegerwald to Schulte, 25 November 1912 (2 letters), Schiffer to Stegerwald, 23 November 1912, Stegerwald Papers 1, Stegerwald Stiftung Köln; Schulte to Kopp, 23 November 1912, Stegerwald to Schulte, 23 November 1912, quoted in Brack, *Deutscher Episkopat und Gewerkschaftsstreit*, p. 312.

108. *Protokoll der Verhandlungen des ausserordentlichen Kongresses der christlichen Gewerkschaften Deutschlands*, p. 64.

In Cologne a weary Stegerwald found little consolation in his apparent victory. The movement had been able to protect itself from all attacks, but in the process, he lamented, membership had been held to only 350,000. "If through the years the Christian trade unions had been able to develop in accordance with principles agreed on by all, three-quarters of a million members would belong today. Think how different this constellation would be in opposition to the Social Democrats!"[109] With the trade union controversy between Berlin and Cologne finally resolved, Stegerwald felt the path to impressive growth and greater political effectiveness was clear.

But this was a delusion to a very great extent. The *Gewerkschaftsstreit* was only one of many problems plaguing the Christian trade unions, not the least of which were leadership deficiences, tactical errors, misjudgments, and a dubious relationship to the state. The movement which broke out among the Saar miners in November and December 1912 illustrates this point well and therefore warrants discussion at this point. The Saar miners' action also represents an appropriate epilogue to the themes analyzed thus far in this chapter. For the threatened strike by Christian miners took place against the backdrop of the *Gewerkschaftsstreit* and was initiated by labor activists who were conscious of the fact that the "tolerance" of the church would be put to an immediate test. It is thus to these developments that we now turn.

* * * *

The *Gewerkverein* of Christian miners had suffered tremendous losses in the Saar during 1911 and 1912. The main problem was the comparatively low wage rate paid by mines in the Saar and the unions' unwillingness to take corrective action, desirous as it was of maintaining good relations with big business and the National Liberals (see Chapter 9). The situation was exacerbated by confessional squabbles caused by the Reichstag elections of January 1912 and quarrels over the *Gewerkverein's* refusal to join the Ruhr strike in March. From a high of 18,000 members, only 7,000 remained by November.[110] Judging from the reasons for this membership erosion, it is safe to assume that it had been mainly the radical rank and file who had deserted.

The mood of the miners worsened in mid-November when the State Mining Directorate (*Bergverwaltung*) announced new regulations for state mines which paid no attention to the question of wages. Sensing an opportunity to revive the union, the *Saar Post*, an unofficial organ of the *Gewerkverein* edited by an ex-official of the union, seized on the issue with a series of articles

109. *Augsburger Postzeitung*, 5 December 1912 (clipping in: Ges. Päpstl. Stuhl 904, GStA München).
110. *Zentralblatt*, no. 20, 30 September 1912; *Saarbrücker Volkszeitung*, no. 12, 16 January 1913.

highly critical of the new work rules.[111] But the paper shrank from all talk of a strike, interestingly enough, until *after* the Essen Congress had clarified the papal encyclical *Singulari Quadam.* "Now that complete clarity has been created on all sides by the latest statement of the bishops," the *Saar Post* declared, "the work of the trade unions, which is so terribly necessary in the Saar area, can be carried forth with new strength."[112] A strike, the article series concluded, was regrettable, but justified. The *Saar Post* had wasted little time in putting the church's tolerance to the test.

The articles struck a receptive chord among the Christian rank and file. Even before the series, many Christian unionists had been in an angry mood due to the pope's encyclical. "What do we care about *Singulari Quadam,* we stand firm and true behind our Adam,"[113] roared the radicals in support of their general secretary. Now the *Saar Post* had flown in the face of conservative religious principles in calling for a strike, and many Christian workers were ready to follow. By mid-December thousands had returned to the Saar *Gewerkverein,* spoiling for a fight. On 15 December, in fact, the rank and file delegates at an area-wide meeting attended by representatives from union headquarters in Essen and the *Gesamtverband* in Cologne pressed for an immediate strike, despite earlier assurances from mining officials that wages would probably rise if the economy continued to improve. The official *Gewerkverein* account of the meeting makes it quite clear that the union leadership was barely in control of the situation. Appalled by the fact that a mere 14 percent of Saar miners belonged to the *Gewerkverein,* the leadership insisted that "the unorganized be led to the union"[114] before the first day of the strike, which the leaders proposed be pushed back to 2 January. Amid grumbling that the leaders were "applying the brakes,"[115] the postponement was approved.

These developments were not welcomed by the unions' general secretary in Cologne. Earlier that year, to be sure, Stegerwald had looked for a *major* strike by a Christian trade union to demonstrate for the masses the total independence of his organization from the church. Thus in March he traveled to Essen to argue for *Gewerkverein* participation in the Ruhr strike, only to relent to union arguments that the *Gewerkverein* might collapse during a strike under the pressure of competition from the more radical *Alter Verband* on the

111. For the series, see the clippings in LHA Koblenz, 442/3822. For the dissociation of the *Saar Post* from the union itself, see Franz Behrens to Bethmann Hollweg, 17 December 1912, Reichskanzlei 546, ZStA Potsdam.

112. *Saar Post,* no. 276, 28 November 1912 (clipping: 442/3822, LHA Koblenz).

113. Quoted in Ross, *Beleaguered Tower,* p. 109.

114. Heinrich Imbusch, *Die Saarbergarbeiterbewegung 1912/13* (Essen: Verlag des Gewerkvereins christlicher Bergarbeiter Deutschlands, 1913), p. 50.

115. *Ibid.,* p. 50.

left and the anti-strike, yellow organizations on the right. Refusal to strike would be popular with the "national workers," break the strike, and prevent the *Alter Verband* from winning an inter-union power play.[116] Stegerwald's determination to offer public proof of the activism and bona fide nature of his unions continued into the fall, it will be recalled, climaxing with angry private outbursts in the immediate aftermath of the encyclical. But the accommodating "interpretation" of Schulte and Kopp seems to have brought Stegerwald to his senses, so that after the Essen Congress he was willing to quit while he and the *Gesamtverband* were ahead. His disposition while developments unfolded in the Saar, as Giesberts put it, was to counteract "the passionate pushing of the masses."[117]

One method of doing so was to mollify Prussian officialdom and encourage a conciliatory response to *Gewerkverein* wage demands. Thus Stegerwald, Giesberts, and Behrens wrote Reich Chancellor and Prussian Minister-President Bethmann Hollweg on the sixteenth, imploring him to intervene with von Sydow's Ministry of Commerce and Industry to prevent a clash. Wages had historically been lower in the Saar than in other mining regions, the unionists noted, and this situation had only supplied ammunition to the Socialists. Moreover, the Reich secretary of the interior had praised the national, patriotic mission of the Christian trade unions in the Reichstag on the tenth, defending the movement against attacks from Rome and admitting publicly that the Prussian government had intervened on behalf of the unions at the Vatican. "If now, a few days later, a Christian union has to launch a strike against a great state-owned concern, this will be . . . a new, huge agitational weapon for the Social Democrats"; they would "exult in triumph" and "make our patriotic work extremely difficult."[118] Forced themselves to adopt a pace set by the rank and file, not the leadership, Christian leaders were trying to manipulate the government by playing on upper-class fears of Socialist subversion and red revolution. The establishment was not the only side which could play at the game of manipulation.

Unfortunately, Bethmann was not impressed. He agreed with the Mining Directorate that the new work statutes were fair and sympathized with those mining officials who felt a strike would release the Directorate from its prom-

116. Nieder to Brentano, 28 January 1913, Brentano Papers 46, BA Koblenz; police chief Gelsenkirchen to the *Regierungspräsident*, 7 October 1911, Reg. Münster VII 46 Bd. 1, StA Münster; police chief Essen to the *Regierungspräsident*, 6 March 1912, and *Geh. Commerzienrat* Funcke to the *Regierungspräsident*, 7 March 1912, Reg. D. 15939, HSA Düsseldorf; Klaus Mattheier, *Die Gelben*, pp. 225, 237.

117. Quoted in Imbusch, *Die Saarbergarbeiterbewegung*, p. 87.

118. Stegerwald, Giesberts, and Behrens to Bethmann Hollweg, 16 December 1912, Reichskanzlei 546, ZStA Potsdam.

ise of a possible wage increase. Appreciative of the *Gesamtverband's* anti-Socialist services, Bethmann nevertheless instructed Sydow to see if a compromise could be arranged.[119] Yet after hours of haggling with union spokesmen, the state was only willing to concede that the Directorate's hedged wage promise should be made legally binding. Sydow reported with pride to Bethmann that nothing, in essence, had been granted that had not already been conceded before the strike decision, and that "the authority of the state has been thoroughly preserved."[120] With this paltry concession the union leaders returned to the task of warding off the strike, which, as a direct challenge to the state, they viewed with great anxiety.

Indeed the situation in the Saar looked bleak. The *Gewerkverein* had gained 9,000 new members as the new year approached, but this still left 68 percent of Saar miners outside the union. Only a few thousand of the unorganized appeared eager to strike, moreover, and there was still a fairly large non-strike minority within the union itself. It was decided on the twenty-eighth, therefore, to call off the strike and present a corresponding motion to the delegates of the Saar *Gewerkverein* the following day.[121]

On the twenty-ninth, a Sunday, the union leadership received unsolicited help from Bishop Korum of Trier. In a letter to the church canons of the Saar which was read from every pulpit, Korum urged his subalterns to warn "their parish children" from taking such an "ill-considered step,"[122] especially after Sydow's concessions. The letter, which was also published in the *Saarbrücker Volkszeitung,* fell on stone deaf ears, for the overwhelming majority of delegates at the afternoon's meeting of the *Gewerkverein* rejected their leaders' motion to abandon the approaching strike. The meeting was adjourned until the next day when, after a personal appeal from Stegerwald himself, the motion was finally accepted with 100 of 350 delegates still bitterly opposed.[123] The episode illustrated not only the personal unpopularity of Korum in Christian trade union circles but also the waning authority of the church. The secular or "modernist" tendency in the Christian trade unions had proceeded past the point where the bishop could exert a great degree of moral influence over "his children."

But the authority of the Christian trade unions had also been challenged. The Saar wage movement of 1912/13, in fact, ended in a fiasco for the

119. Bethmann to Bassermann, 14 December 1912, and Wahnschaffe to Sydow, 18 December 1912, Reichskanzlei 546, ZStA Potsdam.
120. Sydow to Bethmann, 31 December 1912, Reichskanzlei 546, ZStA Potsdam.
121. *Kölnische Volkszeitung*, no. 1455, 31 December 1912; police chief Saarbrücken to the *Regierungspräsident*, 29 August 1913, 442/3788, LHA Koblenz.
122. Printed in the report of the *Oberpräsident* of the Rhineland to the king, 11 February 1913, 442/3823, LHA Koblenz.
123. *Ibid.*

Gewerkverein. The *Alter Verband* exploited the anger among the Christian rank and file by recruiting 3,000 new members. An exodus also began from that minority faction of the Christian union which had opposed a strike from the beginning. These workers appear to have joined local yellow unions, not *Fachabteilungen*.[124] Making matters even worse, Sydow could not resist gloating over his success in the matter. He ridiculed the Christian trade union leadership privately to Bethmann Hollweg, then spoke in a similarly derogatory vein in the Prussian Landtag.[125] It was now painfully evident to everyone that the government was willing to use the *Gesamtverband* when it served the interests of the state, but was unwilling to offer anything tangible—and in this case offered nothing—in return. Caught between the increasing radicalism of its members and the unbending authoritarianism of the government, Christian labor had no favorable alternative as a moderate organization. Rather than compromise its conciliatory principles and seize the initiative against the state, Stegerwald *et al.* were forced to choose public embarrassment.

* * * *

In 1912/13 the leaders of the *Gesamtverband* had been rather successfully manipulated by first the church, then the state, into *abandoning* actions initially designed to please the angriest elements within the Christian rank and file. In such ways the traditional ruling establishment and its auxiliary elites preserved and protected the old order. As the following chapters illustrate, however, these techniques also contributed to the leftward drift of the movement in the years 1913–1918.

124. Landrat of Ottweiler to the *Regierungspräsident*, 14 February 1913, 442/3793, LHA Koblenz; and Landrat of Saarlouis to the *Regierungspräsident*, 19 August 1913, 442/3788, LHA Koblenz.

125. Sydow to Bethmann, 31 December 1912, Reichskanzlei 546, ZStA Potsdam; Imbusch, *Saarbergarbeiterbewegung*, pp. 63–68.

11

Financial Reform, Bourgeois Solidarity, and the Radicalization of Christian Labor on the Eve of War

As Chapters 9 and 10 have shown, a wide variety of political, religious, and organizational factors contributed to the inability of Christian labor to compete successfully with the free trade unions in the decade before World War I. Certainly by 1912, if not earlier, the struggle had been irreversibly lost. The crushing reality of these setbacks contributed, as in previous years, to an intensification of political activity on the part of the Christian labor movement. A dramatic political victory, it was hoped, would rejuvenate the Christian cause and shift momentum away from the General Commission. Beginning roughly in 1909, therefore, Christian labor forged ahead with its strategy of *Blockpolitik* (Chapter 8), attempting once again to create a broad-based, progressive alliance of non-Socialist parties and social reform groups. The efforts miscarried for all the same reasons they had failed in 1906/7 (Chapter 9). Finally embittered by a hopelessly divided party system and the lack of concern shown for their cause by the government, the church, and broad elements of bourgeois society, Christian workers were drifting rapidly to the left on the eve of the war, despite the best efforts of Stegerwald, Behrens, and others to prevent this. The failure of *Blockpolitik*, or the "*Volk* movement," as it was now termed, will be analyzed in the present chapter.

There is much of historical significance which can be learned from the detailed developments discussed here. An investigation of Christian labor politics on the eve of war sheds new light, for instance, on the ineffectiveness of the nation's party system and the general political course Germany was traveling at this critical juncture in its historical journey. A Christian labor bloc of the bourgeois parties was just as difficult to achieve in a country of such social, political, religious, and federal pluralism as a "Blue-Black Bloc" uniting Center and Conservatives or a "Bloc from Bassermann to Bebel." The Christian labor movement made its own contribution to parliamentary inefficiency, ironically enough, by stirring the waters within the bourgeois parties. The tenuous equilibrium of conservative and progressive forces in the Center Party began to deteriorate on the eve of the war under intense pressure from Christian labor, while similar prodding from non-Socialist workers upset relations within the Conservative and National Liberal parties, all without achieving great success. An analysis of the continuing frustration of Christian *Blockpolitik* is thus an excellent means of measuring the tremendous societal forces which not only drove the various bourgeois parties apart, but undermined the unity of each one of them.

The tattered condition of the parties also says something important about the direction of the nation's political development, for it seems apparent from an analysis of Christian labor's experience that many of the crucial conditions which historical and abstract theoretical studies cite as prerequisites for the growth of parliamentary democracy were absent in Germany. The empire could not have been *evolving* toward western systems of government—as argued by Bermbach, Grosser, Rauh, *et al.*—with political parties that lacked the effective leadership, internal discipline and cohesion, and ideological compatibility with neighboring parties necessary to form stable coalitions which would be capable of maintaining sufficient pressure on an old order desirous of perpetuating itself. Equally important to this line of reasoning is the parallel fact that the nation *did* possess the necessary prerequisites for a *perpetuation* of the existing order in peacetime. Social, economic, political, and cultural institutions to bolster the old regime were firmly implanted, and the guardians of this system did not lack the moral fiber necessary to resist the forces of change. Indeed it was this strength which became such a problem. Overreacting to the radicalization of the lower orders of German society—including a formerly moderate Christian labor movement—many in high places were tempted into an "escape to the front" (*Flucht nach vorn*).[1] World War I was the tragic result.

Christian labor played an interesting and significant role in the fateful

1. For a historical and theoretical discussion of the prerequisites for parliamentary democracy, see Dieter Grosser, *Vom monarchischen Konstitutionalismus zur parlamentarischen Demokratie*, pp. 1–25, 207–19, especially p. 211. A more theoretical approach can be found in Michael Laver, *The Politics of Private Desires* (New York: Penguin Books, 1981), pp. 147–53, and Abram Deswaan, *Coalition Theories and Cabinet Formations* (Amsterdam: Elsevier, 1973), *passim*. For the parallel line of reasoning on the strength of the old order in Germany, see especially Arno Mayer, *The Persistence of the Old Regime*, passim.

course of domestic politics in Germany in the decade before Sarajevo. An issue which aroused tremendous passion during this period, more, perhaps, than the complicated issue of Prussian voting rights, was the question of financial reform. It is thus appropriate to begin our analysis by orienting the reader to this controversial question.

* * * *

During the government's tax reform proposals in 1906, Christian laborers criticized the federal states for refusing to allow the Reich to levy *direct* taxes (income, wealth, etc.). Giesberts, Behrens, and others argued that by relying on beer, wine, tobacco, and other *indirect* revenues to fund Imperial military programs, the worker, the peasant, and the small trader, whose incomes were minimal, were forced to pay a disproportionately large share of the costs. These criticisms resulted in an intra-party amendment, introduced by a sympathetic Center deputy from western Germany (Am Zehnhoff), which called for a direct tax on both large and small inheritances. Within the Center *Fraktion* the Silesian and Westphalian noblemen led the opposition to the amendment, labeling it a "socialistic-communistic type of tax" which would prepare the way for "the Socialist state." The representatives from less affluent rural constituencies agreed, and the Am Zehnhoff amendment, with only seven or eight advocates, was crushed. Catholic labor's vehement protests were totally in vain.[2]

Performing a complete *volte-face* in June 1909, however, Christian trade union deputies joined the Center and Right in voting *against* Reich inheritance taxes. In the years thereafter the move put the Center and Christian trade unions at the mercy of S.P.D. and free trade union agitators who exploited the rejection of the highly popular property tax in preparation for the Reichstag elections of 1912. As will soon become evident, the motives for Christian labor's stand in that crucial year underscored the weaknesses of a movement whose leaders often assigned priority to religio-cultural considerations. The following section can therefore be seen as a variation on the theme of vulnerability to church pressure which was explored in the previous chapter. The movement was far too susceptible to influences of this type to be effective in the environment of Imperial Germany.

* * * *

2. For the laborers' viewpoints, see Carl Bachem to Peter Spahn, 17 November 1905, Richard Müller (Fulda) to Julius Bachem, 19 November 1905, Bachem Papers 239, HA Köln; *Die Arbeit*, no. 4, 23 January 1908; *Westdeutsche Arbeiter-Zeitung*, no. 42, 17 October 1908. For the Am Zehnhoff amendment and Center *Fraktion* discussion, see the *Kölnische Volkszeitung*, nos. 139 and 156, 17 and 23 February 1906, and Carl Bachem's notations of 16, 22, and 23 March 1906, Bachem Papers 241, HA Köln.

By mid-February 1909 Treasury Secretary Sydow's tax proposals, which combined 400 million marks of indirect consumer levies with 100 million marks of estate duties (*Nachlasssteuer*), including a tax on *large* landed inheritances, had run aground in the Reichstag budget committee. Complicating the situation was the position of the Conservatives. The Junker-dominated party had decided the previous fall to block any Reich taxation of income, wealth, or landed inheritances, and to prevent the Bülow Bloc from imposing any specific tax programs on the federal states. The Conservatives opposed the progressively constructed inheritance tax, for one thing, because it was considered socialistic. They also knew that Sydow's inheritance tax alone was not likely to passify their coalition partners, the Liberals and Progressives, who were also eager for reform of Prussia's plutocratic "three-class" suffrage. And this could not be tolerated, for Prussia was the party's base of power. Conservative uneasiness mounted in mid-March 1909 when Bülow seemed to have effected a reconciliation with Kaiser William. The monarch had snubbed his first minister since the Daily Telegraph affair in November, but if William were to be won over by the scheming Bülow into liberalizing the electoral system, all was lost for the all-important cause of conservatism in Germany.[3] Thus on 24 March Conservative leader Oskar von Normann announced that his party would complete the reform with all parties willing to approve 400 million marks of indirect taxes and 100 million marks of state contributions (*Matrikularbeiträge*) levied as the states saw fit and oppose any Reich tax on inheritances, income, or wealth. As Normann told Center leader Georg Hertling, the Right was "fed up with bloc politics" and desirous of pursuing a course "more in keeping with [its] own principles."[4]

But it was by no means certain that the Catholics would comply. The Conservatives knew that most in the *Zentrumsturm* interpreted the chancellor's "punishment" of the party since 1907 as a prelude to another period of discriminatory legislation against the church and that many Centrists were therefore anxious to weaken Bülow in any way possible. Like their counterparts on the right, moreover, noblemen in the Center loathed property taxes. On the other hand there was considerable rank and file Center support for Sydow's inheritance tax because this time it exempted the small man. The southern and western farming elements in the Center liked the proposal, while the Center's labor voters, especially in the Ruhr, were reported in an angry

3. Karl Speck, "Die Reichsfinanzreform in der Commission," *Allgemeine Rundschau*, 6 March 1909 (clipping in: Bachem Papers 282a, HA Köln); Peter-Christian Witt, *Die Finanzpolitik des deutschen Reiches von 1903 bis 1913* (Lübeck and Hamburg; Matthiesen Verlag, 1970), pp. 243–72; Lerchenfeld to Podewils, 12 March and 17 March 1909, Ges. Berlin, Pol. Schrifwechsel 1081, GStA München.

4. Carl Bachem notation of 21 March 1909, Bachem Papers 283, HA Köln.

mood over the prospect of new consumer taxes. Another factor which balked Hertling and the Center leadership was uncertainty over Conservative willingness to bolt the Bloc. In late April, however, Normann informed Hertling that the Conservatives were determined to form a new majority and, importantly, had decided to work for 100 million marks of direct and indirect imperial taxes on business wealth. Eager to embarrass Bülow, and pleased with the anti-liberal, anti-capitalist nature of the new tax proposals, the Center executive committee decided to follow the Right's lead on 22 April 1909.[5]

Four days later Hertling convened a *Fraktion* caucus to unite the party behind the decisions of its leaders. As Hertling well knew, the task would be a difficult one. The party could anticipate intense opposition from Bavarian and Württembergian deputies, who favored a Reich inheritance tax which exempted small landholders. An equally tough fight could be expected from Christian labor. With the exception of the Christian trade union's *Zentralblatt*, which had limited itself to a criticism of the proposed tobacco tax,[6] the Christian labor press had waged an intensive campaign since February in favor of Bülow's inheritance taxes. Wiedeberg's *Die Baugewerkschaft* noted with great displeasure, for instance, that in rejecting the proposed inheritance tax the upper classes "were ready to speak of the plight of widows and orphans, but were in a moment ready to impose hundreds of millions of new taxes on the broad masses of the poor population without even batting an eye—people who earn less than 900 marks a year. They are ready to do this in order to avoid any further burden on themselves."[7] Behrens increased pressure on the parties in April by calling for both inheritance taxes *and* anti-business taxes on mobile wealth. His claim to speak for all non-Socialist workers became more credible in late April when the *Westdeutsche Arbeiter-Zeitung* adopted the same stance.[8] It is highly doubtful, therefore, that the *Fraktion* caucus on the twenty-sixth went smoothly, nor is it likely that succeeding weeks brought any improvement. For, with the backing of *Volksverein* chief August Pieper, the *Westdeutsche Arbeiter-Zeitung* kept up constant pressure on the party until early June.[9]

At this point, however, intrigues at court intervened once again to reduce the effectiveness of Christian labor politics. Since the Daily Telegraph affair of 1908 a clique led by Count Max von Fürstenberg and Eugen Röder, the

5. Karl Zamieden to Lambert Lensing of *Tremonia*, 7 April 1909, Herold Papers 3, BA Koblenz; *"Dürener Anzeiger,"* 8 March 1909 (clipping in: 403/8458, LHA Koblenz); Julius Bachem, "Was Werden wird," *Tag*, no. 83, 8 April 1909; Hertling to his wife, Anna, 23 April 1909, Hertling Papers 19, BA Koblenz.

6. *Zentralblatt*, nos. 3, 4, and 7, 8 February, 22 February, and 5 April 1909.

7. Cited in the Reichstag Debates, Period 12, Session 1 (7 July 1909), vol. 237, p. 9188.

8. *Tag*, no. 91, 20 April 1909; *Westdeutsche Arbeiter-Zeitung*, no. 19, 8 May 1909.

9. *Westdeutsche Arbeiter-Zeitung*, nos 22–24, 29 May, 5 June, 12 June 1909.

emperor's master of ceremonies, had suspected Bülow of pursuing "socialistic" policies which could only be averted by the chancellor's removal.[10] In early June, then, Count Praschma, a Silesian Catholic and leading Centrist in league with the two above named, sent a series of startling messages to Center and Conservative leaders.

> I would have written sooner [he wrote Hertling on 5 June] but I was promised further news after Fürstenberg's visit with the Kaiser . . . What I learned was as follows: The relationship between Kaiser and chancellor is still the same unfriendly one. Just as before the Kaiser wants to let him go . . . It was already being said at that time, however, that the chancellor would cleverly exploit the opposition of stock exchange and industrial circles to the property taxes planned by the Center and Conservatives . . . Just now I received a telegram which states that important decisions from His Highness, perhaps dissolution, are in the offing as a result of machinations by the chancellor. I'm coming through Berlin tonight and have a 1½-hour layover in which I hope to find out more.[11]

Praschma's conversations in Berlin led to the following message which was sent to Herold, Spahn, Gröber, and the Conservative leader Heydebrand:

> Have spoken with said gentlemen and learned that since the day before yesterday the chancellor has definitely decided to initiate a struggle with all means [at his disposal] and dissolve parliament and wage new elections with the utmost governmental pressure at the head of the united liberals. He's hoping for the approval of the Kaiser and the federal states. Liberal leaders and the press are informed, the most far-reaching promises concerning electoral reform in Prussia have been made. The Kaiser can't be counted on. After he said a few days ago that he'd gladly be rid of [Bülow, he reversed himself] the day before yesterday at breakfast, addressing him as "dear Bernhard" for the first time [since November].[12]

It is difficult on the basis of available evidence to determine the accuracy of these reports. That National Liberal leader Ernst Bassermann, shipping magnate Albert Ballin, and other leading industrialists and bankers *wanted* Bülow and William to take such action, there can be no doubt.[13] That Bülow, but much less the Kaiser, had *already agreed* to this course seems less probable. The key fact remains, however, that nervous Catholics in Berlin believed the rumors and acted accordingly. Thus Baron Savigny, of Westphalia, urged his fellow Centrists to caucus at the earliest possible moment. "The position of

10. Bülow, *Memoirs*, vol. 2, pp. 535–38, 553–54.
11. Praschma to Hertling, 5 June 1909, Hertling Papers 37, BA Koblenz.
12. Praschma to Herold, 6 June 1909, Herold Papers 3, BA Koblenz.
13. Eschenburg, *Kaiserreich am Scheidewege*, pp. 207–8, 223–36, 235.

our party, and with it, the fate of all German Catholics, especially those in Prussia, hangs in the balance."[14] Other Centrists were no doubt unconvinced by the rumors, but played along in a cynical attempt to protect vested interests and allow religious emotions to overpower any class tension that might be generated by rejection of the inheritance tax. Manipulative techniques were obviously not the exclusive preserve of the government.

Opposition to Bülow's tax proposals was now elevated to the level of a desperate struggle between the liberal-progressive and the conservative-religious *Weltanschauung* (separation of church and state, elimination of confessional schools, etc.). As a result of the new situation, the attacks of Catholic labor ceased immediately. The *Westdeutsche Arbeiter-Zeitung*, which had criticized the Center as late as 12 June, supported the party and warned of the dangers of liberalism in its next article of 19 June.[15] Within the *Fraktion*, Giesberts, Schiffer, and the other Catholic unionists were won over to the leaders' viewpoint by the same religious arguments and, it would seem, by a promise that the party would accept inheritance taxes in the future.[16] An appeal to Catholic loyalties mollified the opposition of the Bavarians and Württembergians too, and on 24 June 1909 the party stood united against Bülow. The *volte-face* of Catholic labor and the South Germans contributed to the chancellor's undoing, significantly enough, for the inheritance tax was defeated by a scant eight votes.

Stegerwald, who never allowed religious sentiments to interfere with his politics, was greatly disillusioned.[16] It was only a year earlier in the aftermath of the *Vereinsgesetz* debate that the central committee of the *Gesamtverband* had instructed labor deputies to give trade union interests precedence over party matters. The fact that Behrens supported the inheritance taxes after a lengthy, outspoken speech against indirect taxation was all the more embarrassing for Christian labor, for the central committee resolution of 1908 had also called upon union deputies to maintain closer parliamentary contacts and vote in unison on controversial issues. It is not surprising, therefore, that Stegerwald expressed frustration and weariness with politics in the immediate aftermath of the financial reform of 1909. Giesberts and the other "Christians" had placed a greater priority on their religion than on their class, thus lending credence to Social Democrat charges that the church's primary social function was to thwart the development of class-consciousness. To be sure, "Christian" could easily be equated with "anti-labor," for the inheritance taxes that were rejected exempted all persons inheriting less than 20,000

14. Savigny to Herold, 9 June 1909, Herold Papers 3, BA Koblenz.
15. "Aus dem Reichstag (19 June)," *Westdeutsche Arbeiter-Zeitung*, no. 26, 26 June 1909.
16. *Die Arbeit*, nos. 30 and 32, 24 July, 7 August 1909; *Westdeutsche Arbeiter-Zeitung*, nos. 33 and 36, 14 August, 4 September 1909.

marks—in other words, the entire working class. The S.P.D. would obviously have a heyday exploiting the *Gesamtverband*'s alleged "betrayal of labor," especially with reports circulating that many Center workers, suspicious of the sincerity of their leaders' motives in attacking Bülow and the Liberals, were "fed up with the daily Bloc fodder."[17] If one considers the fact that the threat to the Catholic Church in 1909 was more perceived than real, it becomes clear that the Christian trade union deputies in the Center had made a very damaging tactical error.

The best defense against the S.P.D.'s tax agitation, Stegerwald decided, was a bold and ambitious counterattack. In the summer of 1909, however, the Christian trade unions were in a desperate situation. Armed with barbed criticisms of Christian labor's rejection of inheritance taxes, the free trade unions and S.P.D. stood poised to deliver their faltering Christian rivals a *coup de grâce*. The reviving economy and the much stronger battalion of functionaries employed by the General Commission (2,000 vs. 300) enhanced the chances of success in this endeavor.[18] Therefore, if the frees were to be halted and the subsequent floodtide of Socialist electoral victories averted, much more aggressive methods of fighting the Left were needed. Only an "organized folk-movement," as Carl Schiffer put it, could operate effectively against "the well-organized, disciplined army of the Social Democrats."[19] The leaders of all bourgeois parties and social groups had to reeducate (*umbilden*) the German working classes to see through the propaganda of the S.P.D. It was equally important, however, that the rich be reeducated to appreciate the need for sacrifice and reform. Against the united forces of a society willing to eliminate social injustices, the Socialists could never prevail.[20] Moreover, such a "folk-movement" held out the only prospect for healthy political developments in Germany, for if the masses continued to be swayed by the "unpractical doctrines"[21] of socialism instead of the Christians' more positive approach to politics, the government would be reluctant to introduce social reforms, the propertied classes would refuse to pay taxes to support such programs, parliamentary life would be ridden with class tension and division,

17. Karl Zamieden to Lambert Lensing, 7 April 1909, Herold Papers 3, BA Koblenz. For Stegerwald's disillusionment with Reichstag politics, see *Die Arbeit*, no. 24, 17 June 1911.
18. See the *Volksverein*'s memorandum of 9 July 1910 to diocesan authorities in Cologne, Gen. 23.61., vol. 1, Erzb. Registratur Köln. The document was based on "detailed discussions with Christian Labor leaders."
19. *Tag*, no. 109, 10 May 1912.
20. Hertling to his wife, Anna, 20 April 1910, Herling Papers 20, BA Koblenz. Hertling had just spoken with Christian trade union leaders in the Reichstag.
21. Stegerwald before the *Gesamtverband* central commission on 22 September 1909, cited in the *Zentralblatt*, no. 21, 18 October 1909. This paragraph is also based on his speech in Aachen on 17 October 1909, printed in *Westdeutsche Arbeiter-Zeitung*, no. 43, 23 October 1909, and his annual report of 20 June 1910, in *Zentralblatt*, no. 13, 27 June 1910.

and important national tasks such as tax, tariff, and military legislation would be very difficult to accomplish. Thus Stegerwald and his associates in the General Secretariat recommended added emphasis on extra-parliamentary anti-Socialist efforts.

The campaign to emancipate the leftward-leaning working classes from the grip of Marxist dogma was in full swing by late 1909. In the Christian labor press, and at scores of mass rallies held during 1910 and 1911, Christian leaders exposed embarrassing disagreements between the free unions and the S.P.D., discussed the views of the "revisionists," and encouraged Socialist and unorganized workers to oppose a movement that had apparently done nothing for the proletariat but encourage reactionary policies in Berlin. Typical of the rhetoric was a speech by Giesberts before 8,000 followers in Münster. Protestants and Catholics had to unite, he noted, in the common struggle against "a deadly enemy of bourgeois society that wants to introduce complete equality and freedom, undermine Germany's monarchical constitution, and root out Christianity."[22] The German Workers' Congress joined the campaign too, issuing a declaration in September 1911 that damned the S.P.D.'s "unpatriotic behavior" during the second Morocco crisis.[23]

The *Volk* movement, however, was not merely an extraparliamentary phenomenon. It also incorporated with new intensity the earlier strategy of Reichstag *Blockpolitik*—attainment of a parliamentary coalition to impress or intimidate the Kaiser and Reich chancellor. Thus Behrens wrote his colleague Reinhard Mumm in August 1909 that it was "politically and morally imperative"[24] that the Christian-Social Party abandon its independence and merge with the Conservatives. The present position of the Christian-Socials, limited to a few western districts and forced to dilute the views of the Christian labor movement to suit the needs of the Economic Union in the Reichstag, was intolerable. Union with the Conservatives, on the other hand, would gradually extend the party's social progressivism to the second largest *Fraktion* in parliament, enable Protestant unionists to obtain more seats, and allow the new party to attract working-class votes as the Center had done for years. Behrens insisted, therefore, that the party convention that fall discuss merger. Adolf Stöcker's ideas were "too great that they should live on in so small a fashion."[25]

The results of Behrens' initiative at the Christian-Social Darmstadt convention of September 1909 are obscured by the lack of documentary evidence,

22. *Münsterischer Anzeiger*, 19 June 1911 (clipping in: Reg. Münster VIII 47, StA Münster).
23. *Bericht über die Verhandlungen des dritten Deutschen Arbeiter-Kongresses* (Cologne: Christlicher Gewerkschaftsverlag, 1914), pp. 39–40.
24. Behrens to Mumm, 20 August 1909, Mumm Papers, Nr. 1056, ZStA Potsdam.
25. *Ibid.*

but political developments during the following year indicate that the Christian-Socials reached a compromise. In numerous articles appearing in *Die Arbeit* and *Reich*,[26] organ of the Christian-Social *Konferenz*, the Conservatives were urged to refrain from running their own candidates in the Rhineland and certain areas of eastern Germany possessing large concentrations of proletarian and petty-bourgeois voters. The Conservatives, it was argued, relied too heavily on the agitation of the *Bund der Landwirte* to prevail in western Germany and were even perceived by artisans and small farmers in the East as a lobby serving only large landholders. The party should therefore abandon these areas and throw its votes to the Christian-Social "wing" of the German conservative movement. A close reading of the above-mentioned articles leads to the conclusion that most Christian-Socials realized that merger with the Conservatives would mean a complete sacrifice of the smaller party's labor program, not the greater influence which Behrens envisioned. The Christian-Social proposals in 1910 indicate, however, that Behrens prevailed with his plan of broadening the party's social and geographical base.

The Conservatives reached much the same conclusion concerning relations between the two parties. In Baden, Württemberg, and certain districts of Rhineland-Westphalia, Saxony, and eastern Germany, local party and *Bund der Landwirte* leaders recognized that the party had to either nominate Christian laborers or support the Christian-Socials if the conservative movement as a whole were to survive.[27] Not a few Conservatives, moreover, agreed with party journalist Dietrich von Oertzen, who proposed in September 1910 that the executive committees of both parties meet to formulate a formal electoral alliance.[28] When *Reichsbote*, a Conservative organ, and a few individual Conservatives advocated merger, however, the idea was quickly laid to rest by Heydebrand. His Herford speech of 23 November 1910 illustrates well the barriers on the right that stood in the way of a solid, popularly based folk-movement.

> Whether we've come to the point where a complete merger of the two parties should be implemented, is to me somewhat doubtful. I can't help saying that I have the feeling that the Christian-Social Party, in representing the interests of the workers, places the workers' point of view too much in the foreground, that not enough consideration is taken of the fact that there are also employers, that employers must have authority, that employers must be, so to

26. *Die Arbeit*, nos. 13, 18, 24, 32, 34, 39, and 49 for 26 March, 30 April, 11 June, 6 August, 20 August, 29 September, and 3 December 1910; the *Reich* articles are discussed in the *Neue Preussische (Kreuz-) Zeitung*, no. 272, 14 June 1910.
27. *Die Arbeit*, no. 40, 3 October 1907, nos. 24 and 46, 6 August and 12 November 1910; *Neue Preussische (Kreuz-) Zeitung*, no. 272, 14 June 1910.
28. *Die Arbeit*, no. 46, 12 November 1910; *Westfälische Politische Nachrichten* (clipping in: Reichsministerium des Innern, Nr. 1137, Bl. 46, ZStA Potsdam).

> speak, masters of their house. I want to warn the Christian-Social Party to pay more attention to the employer than they do, something which is also in the interests of the worker. In this respect I often have the feeling that the Christian-Social Party, and perhaps we too, have yet to learn this. I think, however, that it is more correct for the two directions, Conservative and Christian-Social, to continue to exist separately.[29]

The crescendoing electoral agitation of the Left had clearly brought the Conservatives and Christian-Socials closer than at any time since their parting of the ways in 1896. This would be proven in 1912 and in the years immediately preceding the war. But demands for fuller coalition rights, codetermination, and social insurance were simply not included in Heydebrand's or the party's definition of true conservatism.

The relationship between Christian labor and the Center Party also underwent significant changes before the elections of 1912. Despite Trimborn's organizational reforms in the Rhineland in 1902 and 1903 and the election of six labor deputies to the Reichstag in 1907 and five to the Prussian Landtag in 1908, demands for a greater voice within the party persisted. Given the interconfessional nature of the Christian trade unions, Catholic workers in western Germany looked upon the confessional *Arbeitervereine* as the logical instrument to express their views.[30] *Arbeiterverein* chiefs August Pieper and Otto Müller resisted the idea, however, because under the new *Vereinsgesetz* the state was empowered to oversee the activities of political associations—and state interference with important pastoral functions of the church was intolerable to most Catholics, especially while Bülow, whom they distrusted, was in power.[31]

A compromise solution was reached in September 1908 with the creation of a special "Workers' Political Committee" for the archdiocese of Cologne. Among other things, the committee would present the views of Catholic labor to party officials at the local, regional, and national level. The organizational structure of the new body would be independent of the *Arbeitervereine* and would respect "the imperatives of [Center] Party discipline."[32] Plans were drawn up to found similar institutions outside Cologne during the winter of 1908/9, but, as Müller recalled later, "the plans were not implemented."[33]

29. *Kölnische Zeitung*, no. 585, 24 May 1911.
30. See the protocol of a meeting of the Diocesan Committee of *Arbeiterverein* Chairmen for the Archdiocese of Cologne, 13 January 1908, *Archiv der katholischen Arbeitnehmerbewegung*, vol. 5, KfZG Bonn.
31. Diocesan Committee meeting of 26 May 1908, protocol in *ibid*.
32. See Otto Müller's discussion of the origins of the new workers' committee before the Diocesan Committee, 25 March 1918, in *ibid*.
33. Müller Manuscript, p. 30, KAB Haus Köln.

Church officials in the other dioceses of the empire apparently felt that greater political independence for Catholic labor would be too risky for the Center and could also undermine the educational programs of the *Arbeitervereine*.

The matter was not resolved, however, for the unpopular financial reform of 1909 brought even greater proletarian pressure for a more formal representation within the structure of the party. At the forefront of the movement stood Stegerwald, who felt Catholic labor should exert greater influence on the Center's tariff and tax policies, thereby preventing further embarrassing situations for the *Gesamtverband*. Furthermore, the general secretary wanted to incorporate the Catholic *Arbeitervereine* into his anti-Socialist folk-movement, and to do this, a greater political role was imperative. After Pieper and Müller proved amenable to these suggestions at a conference held in Duisburg on 21 December 1909, the diocesan Political Committee of Cologne was expanded in February 1910 to the dioceses of Münster and Paderborn. It was also stipulated that *Arbeiterverein* secretaries from the other dioceses as well as Catholic labor deputies, *Gesamtverband* secretaries, and other pro-Center members of the Christian labor movement could join. Reflecting the role he had played in expanding the committee, Stegerwald was selected vice-chairman of the executive board next to Wilhelm Weyer, leading labor secretary of the Association of Catholic *Arbeitervereine* of Western Germany.[34]

While Behrens sought to expand the popular base of the Conservative Party, Stegerwald and the political committee pursued the same goal with the Center. In recently industrialized areas of Westphalia, for instance, efforts were made to reform the outmoded, often non-existent party organization. Karl Herold, the head of the Westphalian organization, was also urged as early as April 1910 to initiate electoral agitation against the Socialists in the above-mentioned areas and coordinate these actions with those of *Arbeiterverein* and *Gewerkverein* secretariates. Catholic labor leaders were also quite active in organizing the new middle class of clerks, technicians, and white-collar workers—groups thought to be imbued with progressive, anti-clerical ideas and hence a threat to the Center. But organizational work did not exhaust the program of the new committee. In private discussions at the annual convention of the western *Arbeitervereine* in May 1910, Catholic political leaders learned of union plans to obtain 20 Reichstag seats for Protestant laborers within the National Liberal, Conservative, Christian-Social, and other rightist parties. More detailed evidence of the talks is not available, but it seems certain that the Center was urged to support these hoped-for candidacies by withdrawing from the *Hauptwahl* in the districts involved. Pieper, Müller, and other church labor leaders were also pressured into forming a national association of Catho-

34. See Stegerwald's speech before the *Gesamtverband* central commission on 22 September 1909, printed in *Zentralblatt*, no. 21, 18 October 1909; Müller Manuscript, p. 30, KAB Haus Köln; and Müller before the Diocesan Committee, 25 March 1918, as cited above in note 32.

lic *Arbeitervereine* including eastern Germany, expanding the activities of the Political Committee to this level, and sponsoring periodic national *Arbeiterverein* rallies that would call on *all* parties to pay more heed to the electoral and program demands of the Christian labor movement. Along with gaining more influence in the Center, therefore, the Political Committee was also determined to support the National Liberal and Conservative Party orientation of Christian labor described above. The Committee was the advocate *par excellence* of political interconfessionalism.[35]

Stegerwald, Giesberts, Weyer, and the others had every reason to be pleased with the response of the Center during the primary elections of 12 January 1912. Not only were a dozen Catholic unionists nominated for the Reichstag, six of whom were elected, but Stegerwald's recommendations concerning the need for far-reaching electoral sacrifices in the interests of anti-Socialist *Sammlung* were followed more frequently than in 1907. Not as worried about the imminent danger to the church as they had been during the previous election, Centrists engaged in *Hauptwahl* support of the Conservatives in 40, the *Reichspartei* in 10, the Christian-Socials, *Bund der Landwirte*, and other rightist splinter groups in 43, and the National Liberals in 6 Reichstag districts. In response to the grant of about 225,000 votes in 109 of Germany's 397 electoral departments, the conservative parties threw approximately 40,000 votes in 33 districts to the Catholics. Embittered over the collapse of the Bülow Bloc, the National Liberals did not reciprocate in the primary elections, but Christian labor took some consolation in the fact that a united front of bourgeois parties including the National Liberals backed Count Posadowsky, one of the most avid supporters of the Christian-national labor movement, in Bielefeld. The National Liberals were also wary of run-off cooperation with the "clericals", except in the hotly tested Ruhr, where Karl Herold, a Catholic agrarian in favor of the unions' pro–National Liberal strategy in 1907, had agreed on a *Stichwahl* alliance with National Liberal leaders as early as December 1910.[36]

35. See the protocol of the Political Committee's meeting in Düsseldorf on 20 October 1910, appended to Wilhelm Weyer to Karl Herold, 11 November 1910, Herold Papers 3, BA Koblenz; Johann Effert to Karl Herold, 20 April 1910, Herold Papers 3, BA Koblenz; Johann Effert to the *Regierungspräsident* of Arnsberg, 20 August 1908, Reg. Arnsberg I 83, StA Münster; August Pieper, "Das Zentrum und die wachsende gewerbtätige Bevölkerung," *Präsides Korrespondenz*, nos. 3–4, March–April 1912, pp. 71–74, StBib MG; Wilhelm Ziebach Diary, vol. 1, entry for 19 July 1910, *Archiv der katholischen Arbeitnehmerbewegung*, KfZG Bonn; *Präsides Korrespondenz*, nos. 6–7, June–July 1910, pp. 217–18, StBib MG; *Mitteilungen an die Präsides der katholischen Arbeitervereine der Erzdiözese Köln*, no. 37, 15 September 1910, pp. 413–19; Adam Stegerwald, "Neue Aufgaben der katholischen Arbeiter- und Jugendvereine," *Soziale Revue*, 1911 (III. Quartalsheft), pp. 346–57.

36. *Frankfurter Zeitung*, no. 10, 11 January 1912; Jürgen Bertram, *Die Wahlen zum Deutschen Reichstag vom Jahre 1912* (Düsseldorf: Droste Verlag, 1964), pp. 46–47; *Tag*, no. 260, 4 November 1911; Center leader Rheinländer of Hagen to Herold, 26 January 1911, Herold Papers 4, BA Koblenz.

It would be an exaggeration, of course, to attribute the Center's generous electoral policies solely to pressure from Catholic labor. So convinced were Julius Bachem and the editorial staff of the *Kölnische Volkszeitung* of the need for bourgeois unity, in fact, that it is often difficult to determine whether Bachem and his cousins or Stegerwald and the General Secretariat led the way. Much the same can be said of Karl Trimborn and the Secretariat of the Rhenish Center Party. Included on the committee to determine the party's run-off strategy in western Germany, for example, were Trimborn and his staff and leading Centrists from the districts involved, plus Julius Bachem, August Pieper, and Adam Stegerwald.[37] One need only review the election campaign of 1906/7, however, to arrive at the conclusion that the workers possessed the deeper, less compromising commitment to nondenominational politics. By 1911/12, moreover, cooperation with parties like the National Liberals not only promised to harm the S.P.D. and free trade unions at the polls, but also fit well into Christian efforts to encourage Liberal employers to come to the bargaining table. The *Gesamtverband*, it will be recalled, had striven to win new members after 1909 by negotiating collective wage agreements in heavy industry (Chapter 9). Trimborn's public appeal for support of the Westphalian National Liberals in January 1912 is yet another indication of which faction was the driving force behind the pro-Liberal strategy:

> I call upon . . . all followers of the Center Party . . . to vote for the right-wing National Liberals in the run-off and assure under all circumstances their victory over the S.P.D. The interests of the fatherland, which must make progress everywhere, demand it of you, and particularly consideration for the Christian-national labor movement . . . whose healthy development must lie close to the hearts of all clear-sighted friends of the fatherland.[38]

Mönchen-Gladbach also believed in the politics of interconfessionalism, as Pieper's talk at the Windthorst League in July 1910 and Heinrich Brauns's presentation before the *Augustinusverein* in December 1910 make quite clear.[39] But once again it is hard to escape the feeling that Brauns, Müller, Pieper, *et al.* were driven on many occasions by their followers. The history of the Political Committee provides many examples in support of this view, as does Stegerwald's remark to Franz Bachem in October 1908 that Mönchen-Gladbach's policies were often dictated by a "sly opportunism."[40] It should

37. Jörg to Herold, 9 January 1912, Herold Papers 5, BA Koblenz.
38. *Kölnische Zeitung*, no. 83, 24 January 1912.
39. *Westdeutsche Arbeiter-Zeitung*, no. 29, 16 July 1910; *Augustinus-Blatt*, no. 12, December 1910, StBib MG
40. Stegerwald to Franz Bachem, 17 October 1908, printed in *Germania*, no. 290, 19 December 1911.

also be mentioned that Martin Spahn, son of Center leader Peter Spahn, wrote that political cooperation between bourgeois parties in 1912 was to a great extent attributable to the "growing influence"[41] of the Christian trade unions. Thus, although the point needs qualification, the primary and run-off agreements formed in the fall and winter of 1911/12 should be seen as one of the crowning accomplishments of the politics of Christian labor.[42]

Unfortunately, the Center's sacrifices did little to enhance the presence of Christian labor in the Reichstag, for, with some notable exceptions, the Protestant parties did not nominate Christian trade unionists. The Conservatives and Free Conservatives established an important precedent by running Hermann Dunkel, co-founder of the Committee for the Election of Patriotic Workers, in Frankfurt a. d. O., Paul Krug, head of the *Gesamtverband*'s Württembergian secretariat, in Reutlingen, and seven non-unionized workers, artisans, and clerks in eastern and northern Germany. This represented a mere fraction of the 224 candidates run by both parties, however, and none of the proletarians were elected. The Economic Union sponsored Christian trade unionists in Lübeck, Berlin, Herford, and Frankfurt a. M., but, with the exception of Herford, where Conservatives briefly considered voting for Behrens's colleague Hermann Wallbaum, these candidacies were hopeless from the start. Christian-Social laborers found consolation in the fact that Conservative, *Bund der Landwirte*, and Center votes had helped elect Reinhard Mumm in Siegen and Franz Behrens in Wetzlar. There was also some satisfaction derived from the more flexible behavior of the National Liberals, who nominated and elected a Christian miner in Bochum (Heckmann), the chairman of a Christian union unaffiliated with the *Gesamtverband* in Göttingen (Ickler), and another non-Socialist labor leader in Eisenach (Marquart).[43] Three seats for Evangelical laborers was a far cry, nevertheless, from the 20 hoped for in 1910.

Equally discouragingly, Christian labor and its bourgeois allies were unable to prevent a leftist landslide in 1912. The S.P.D. amassed 4,250,401 votes and 110 seats, thereby surpassing the Center as the largest *Fraktion* in parliament and robbing the "Blue-Black" coalition of its majority. The causes are not

41. *Tag*, no. 240, 12 October 1912.
42. The labor origins of Center electoral strategy in 1912, like the origins of Bachem's 1906 article "We Must Get Out of the Tower!", have been overlooked by other historians who concentrate solely on Bachem himself. See Ross, *Beleaguered Tower*, pp. 34–39; Bertram, *Wahlen*, pp. 22–28, 34–35; Ralph René Mendershausen, "German Political Catholicism 1912–1919," Ph.D. dissertation, University of California, San Diego, 1972, pp. 104–12.
43. *Neue Preussische (Kreuz-) Zeitung*, no. 608, 29 December 1911, and no. 21, 13 January 1912; Bertram, *Wahlen*, pp. 156–57; *Frankfurter Zeitung*, no. 324, 22 November 1911; also see the extra edition of the *Kölnische Volkszeitung*, March 1912, in the Bachem Papers 317, HA Köln.

hard to find. As a result of indirect tax increases in 1902, 1906, and 1909, the share of Imperial income from these sources had risen from 43 to 57 percent.[44] For the average worker earning only two or three marks a day, such increases were often impossible to tolerate. Added to long-felt resentments over the plutocratic suffrage system in Prussia, Germany's authoritarian laws of assembly and association, and other inequities and injustices of Wilhelmian society, the growing tax burden on the masses was all that was needed to produce a drastic shift to the left in 1912.[45]

In the face of these setbacks, Christian laborers intensified efforts to draw the bourgeois parties together. The *Zentralblatt* initiated the campaign with a clever propaganda piece aimed at the highly imperialistic National Liberals in early February 1912.[46] Germany was the most rapidly developing country in the civilized world, the article began. Her population increased by about 900,000 annually and vast quantities of raw materials were imported every year to meet the requirements of the nation's burgeoning industries. To sustain this growth, the nation had to export vast quantities of finished goods, but in China, Persia, and the Balkans an almost countless number of jealous countries stood in the way. The most recent attempt to block Germany's export trade in Morocco had increased international tension and brought Europe to the brink of war. What Germany needed most, therefore, was the greatest possible degree of internal solidarity, and yet the German people had devoured one another in an electoral struggle that sent to the Reichstag 110 Socialists bent on hindering the government's efforts to protect the country's worldwide economic interests. Had the National Liberals stood united with the Center and Right, as the Christian trade unions had urged, scores of Social Democrats would not have advanced to the run-off elections and those who did could have been easily defeated. The S.P.D.'s victory would soon sober the bourgeois parties to the point of accepting these facts, but before this occurred, sound political development in Germany was out of the question, and the nation would continue to stand divided before a hostile world.

At the time this article appeared, Catholic labor's Political Committee and the *Volksverein* were preparing their most determined attempt thus far to affect an easing of tensions between the Center and National Liberals. Such a *rapprochement* was imperative if the "great bloc from Bassermann to Bebel" were to be foiled. The necessary steps were enumerated by Pieper before the *Augustinusverein* on 26 February 1912.[47] First, all polemics with the National Liberals should be avoided, even if Liberal attacks continued. Second, given

44. *Statistisches Jahrbuch für das Deutsche Reich*, 1901–1912.
45. Bachem, *Zentrumspartei*, vol. 7, pp. 74–75.
46. *Zentralblatt*, no. 3, 5 February 1912.
47. *Augustinus-Blatt*, no. 3, March 1912, StBib MG.

the anti-clerical feelings of the Liberals, the Center should place much less emphasis on efforts to free the church from the remnants of *Kulturkampf* legislation. Third, the party should advocate the interests of commercial, light, and heavy industrial circles more so than in the past. Fourth, the congenial relationship established between local Center and National Liberal nominating committees in certain districts of western Germany had to be maintained and similar run-off and primary election pacts formed in other districts. And finally, the Center should devote most of its time to "national, economic, civic [*staatsbürgerlich*], and social issues, particularly because sharp disagreements between the National Liberals and the Right do not exist here."[48] Giesberts, Stegerwald, and Johann Becker, the unions' social insurance expert, seconded Pieper, adding that the party should not forget the need for direct Reich taxation. Becker hinted that income and wealth taxes should be furthered instead of inheritance taxes because the former stood at least a marginal chance of acceptance by the Conservatives. This solution would also "conciliate the Liberals."[49]

The initiative was only partially successful. Reflecting the Center's reluctance to accept new taxes of any kind, the laborers' tax demands were excluded from the resolutions passed by the assembly. The need to improve relations with the National Liberals was included in the association's recommendations to the Catholic press, but, because no agreement was reached over the means to this end, Pieper's specific proposals were also left unmentioned. The ruffled feathers of Christian labor were smoothed somewhat, however, when the executive committees of the Reich and Prussian Center *Fraktionen* approved the journalists' diluted resolution three weeks later in Berlin. With Catholics and Conservatives already on extremely good terms, observers of the Center-Right focused their attention on the National Liberals to see which way the party would turn.[50]

The crisis within the National Liberal camp during the spring of 1912 has been discussed by other historians and need only be briefly summarized here.[51] Pressed by the Young Liberal Clubs toward the left, and by the Central Association of German Industrialists toward the right, Bassermann steered a moderate political course designed to prevent the disintegration of his party. The idea of a Great Bloc of the Left was politically unrealistic, he wrote in early April 1912, but so too was all talk of anti-Socialist *Sammlungspolitik*. "If the National Liberal Party sails in the wake of Heydebrand and Erzberger,

48. *Ibid.*
49. *Ibid.*
50. *Ibid.*; *Augustinus-Blatt*, no. 4, April 1912, StBib MG.
51. Heckart, *From Bassermann to Bebel*, pp. 211–29; Dirk Stegmann, *Die Erben Bismarcks* (Cologne and Berlin: Verlag Kiepenheuer v. Witsch, 1970), pp. 305–15.

it has lost its significance and future."[52] The liberalization of the Reich and Prussia could be best assured by cooperating primarily with the Progressives. Other than a renewed commitment to social reform, something which Bassermann and the National Liberals had advocated since the late 1890s, there was nothing here to please Mönchen-Gladbach and the Christian trade unions.

Christian circles were greatly relieved, therefore, when the Progressives, Center, and Conservatives agreed to a National Liberal proposal in the Reichstag budget committee on 18 May 1912. To cover the cost of recently announced military increases, the four parties asked the government to introduce a bill before 1 April 1913 that would tax some kind of property.[53] No specific tax was mentioned, reported the Bavarian envoy in Berlin, "because otherwise the compromise would fall apart."[54] The Progressives favored Reich inheritance taxes as revenge for 1909, the National Liberals were prepared to accept either Reich inheritance or wealth taxes, the Center advocated Reich wealth taxes or state contributions based on property taxes, and the Conservatives wanted a Reich stock exchange tax, or else increased matricular contributions from the states. Assuming that the only possible solution was a National Liberal–Center–Conservative–backed wealth tax that would require sacrifices from industry as well as from agriculture, Mönchen-Gladbach and the workers' Political Committee began agitation for the tax during the late summer and fall of 1912.[55] The hope was that parliamentary cooperation in the area of financial reform would act as a stimulus to rightist bourgeois unity on other matters. Christian labor would be one step closer to the coalition that was considered necessary for stable political development in Germany.

Christian laborers had even more cause for optimism that year over developments within the Conservative camp. The *Gewerkverein*'s refusal to participate in the Ruhr miners' strike of March 1912—a move which had been planned for months as a demonstration of Christian labor's patriotism and national reliability—was roundly acclaimed by Conservatives in and out of parliament.[56] The

52. Bassermann to Bülow, 3 April 1912, Bülow Papers 107, BA Koblenz.
53. To smooth relations with the National Liberals, Mönchen-Gladbach and the unions had advocated a Reich wealth tax since the beginning of the year. Martin Spahn saw the tax compromise of May 1912, therefore, as the first positive result of Christian labor's attempt to drive the bourgeois parties together. Martin Spahn, "Das Zentrum als berufsständische organisierte Partei," *Tag*, no. 164, 16 July 1912; *idem, Deutsche Lebensfragen* (Kempten: Kösel Verlag, 1913), pp. 91–92.
54. Lerchenfeld to Hertling, 18 May 1912, MAI 955, GStA München.
55. *Westdeutsche Arbeiter-Zeitung*, no. 35, 31 August 1912; *Augustinus-Blatt*, no. 10, October 1912, StBib MG; Otto Müller before the Diocesan Committee of *Arbeiterverein* Chairmen for the Archdiocese of Cologne, 25 March 1918, as cited above in note 32; *Mitteilungen an die Präsides der katholischen Arbeitervereine der Erzdiözese Köln,* no. 46, September 1912, pp. 554–55, 563–66, 571–73.
56. Police chief Gelsenkirchen to the *Regierungspräsident*, 7 October 1911, Reg. Münster VII 46, Bd. 1, StA Münster; also see Heinrich Imbusch, *Bergarbeiterstreik im Ruhrgebiet im Frühjahr* 1912 (Cologne: Christlicher Gewerkschaftsverlag, 1912), pp. 46–75.

Deutsche Tageszeitung, organ of the *Bund der Landwirte*, was particularly impressed, praising the "emphatic veto" which the Christians had given to the "treasonous behavior of the Social Democrats."[57] The unions were pleasantly surprised, moreover, when the paper continued this policy in April and May after other Conservative and National Liberal organs resumed their traditionally hostile stance to the *Gesamtverband*. A letter from Count Rantzau of the Prussian Conservative Party, calling for support of the Christian labor movement, was featured, as was another, interestingly enough, from a Christian unionist who spoke out against "yellow" trade unions.[58] The agrarians appeared to have reconsidered their opposition to Christian trade unionism.

Anxious to test the seemingly more positive mood in conservative circles, Carl Schiffer, now chairman of the *Gesamtverband*'s central committee, submitted a lengthy article against yellow unionism to the neutral daily *Der Tag*.[59] Right-wing politicians should not place their hopes in the so-called Labor Associations of the Fatherland (*Vaterländische Arbeitervereine*), he argued, for the Socialists could never be defeated with organizations that made no attempt to solve those critical problems that had led to the growth of Socialism in the first place. Low wages, poor working conditions, legal discrimination, and political inequality had fueled the fires of the Social Democrats, and these flames would not be extinguished by organizations created to undermine the basic coalition freedoms of trade unions. S.P.D. agitation was aided further by the growing religious indifference of the masses, Schiffer continued, but the masses would continue to exit the church until the upper classes adopted less hypocritical views concerning Christianity. The workers were tired of sermons about the need for Christians to fight the Socialists when rich landlords and capitalists ignored their own Christian duty to help the poor and downtrodden.

Another factor working in favor of the Socialists, the article pointed out, was the low level of political schooling. Yellow trade unions, however, were in no position to combat demagoguery and reeducate the workers to the necessity of fulfilling important national tasks, for in the yellow union only the workers were asked to sacrifice. The Christian trade unions stood a much better chance of counteracting radical Socialism, Schiffer argued, because they were the only movement that fought simultaneously for the workers, the church, the bourgeois parties, and the fatherland. Schiffer concluded by calling on bourgeois society to help in this endeavor. "The best and most influential leaders from all parties and walks of life must suppress their differences, step to the fore, and work together harmoniously. A just and sound emancipation of the folk on a grand scale—not just at election time—has to start."[60]

57. *Deutsche Tageszeitung*, no. 145, 20 March 1912.
58. *Westdeutsche Arbeiter-Zeitung*, no. 12, 23 March 1912; *Die Arbeit*, no. 19, 11 May 1912.
59. *Tag*, no. 109, 10 May 1912.
60. *Ibid*.

The article struck a responsive chord in *Bund der Landwirte* circles, as the following letter from Gustav Rösicke, co-chairman of the *Bund*'s steering committee, to co-chairman Conrad von Wangenheim indicates:

> The enclosed paper was sent to me. The first article in it impressed me very much. If the Christian trade unions truly possess the spirit expressed in this article, this would mean, in my opinion, a highly encouraging beginning for the healing of the disposition of our industrial masses. Indeed as I see it, one must resign oneself to the viewpoint that the workers will not be won over or held back [from the S.P.D.] no matter what disposition one is able to instill in them unless they're convinced that their interests will also be firmly guaranteed. When I compare today's labor relations with those of the 1870s, it's clear that at that time a great exploitation of the workers took place without any consideration of the just claims and interests of labor. Competition brought this in its wake. The liberal legislation created a ruthless exploitation of the given situation and the assertion of individual rights with no consideration of the other or the general welfare. Since that time relations have changed considerably, and one has to admit—at least this is my opinion—that these changes were justified to a very great extent. That egotistical and individualistic tendencies exist [among industrialists] and will continue to exist is, of course, obvious. I'm writing this to you because I feel that we in the *Bund* will have to concern ourselves more and more with the [social] question. Perhaps even in the next sitting of the steering committee a discussion over these matters can be arranged.[61]

The minutes to this meeting, unfortunately, are not extant. We do know that Wangenheim sympathized with the idea of "drawing in the working population"[62] for the agrarian cause. But the support of the *Bund* was not unqualified: the agrarians would promote both yellow *and* Christian unions so long as the latter eschewed the strike, fought the Socialists, moderated their socio-political demands, and supported tariffs for agriculture.[63] "A change has taken place in the Conservative Party in the direction of Christian-Social

61. Roesicke to Wangenheim, 5 July 1912, printed in Tippelskirch Manuscript, Kl. Erw. 230–3/4, BA Koblenz.

62. Wangenheim to Roesicke, 14 August 1913, quoted in Abraham J. Peck, *Radicals and Reactionaries: The Crisis of Conservatism in Wilhelmine Germany* (Washington, D.C.: University Press of America, 1978), p. 114.

63. *Korrespondenz des Bundes der Landwirte*, no. 59, 27 November 1912; *Deutsche Tageszeitung*, nos. 511 and 602, 8 October and 27 November 1912; *Die Arbeit*, nos. 36 and 42, 7 September and 19 October 1912; *Westdeutsche Arbeiter-Zeitung*, no. 29, 20 July 1912; *Germania*, 12 April 1914 (clipping in: Rom Vatikan 311-199/30, AA Bonn). Both the *Korrespondenz des Bundes der Landwirte* (no. 45, 21 August 1912) and the *Deutsche Tageszeitung* (quoted in *Die Arbeit*, no. 42, 19 October 1912), furthermore, expressed their warm approval of the German Evangelical *Volksbund*, another Christian-Social attempt to emulate the *Volksverein*. The new organization was pledged to work with "devout Catholics" for the solution of "Christian, national, and social problems." (*Die Arbeit*, no. 43, 26 October 1912.)

thinking," observed *Reichsbote*, a pro-labor Conservative organ, but much more work was required "to strengthen the Conservatives' social consciousness."[64] Acting on this advice, Behrens opened negotiations with the agrarians "over the question of labor organizations"[65] in November. At the top of the agenda, no doubt, stood questions such as yellow trade unionism and legal protection of strike breakers (*Arbeitswilligenschutz*).

The *Bund der Landwirte* was also amenable to greater electoral cooperation with Christian labor. The debate over this issue, which had lain dormant since Heydebrand's speech in 1910, was reopened by Behrens in late July 1912. The *Gewerkverein* general secretary charged that the Conservatives had largely ignored the Christian-Socials' appeal for an electoral division of labor between the two parties in January, thereby disrupting the politics of compromise agreed on by the Center and its allies in the Economic Union. Printing an article from "an old politician"—probably Rösicke or Wangenheim—the *Deutsche Tageszeitung* admitted the mistake, adding that in preparation for the next elections the Conservatives and Christian-Socials should avoid counterproductive divisions. The editor of the paper and leading functionary of the *Bund*, Georg Oertel, went even further during a speech in Cologne and predicted that the next Reichstag would see Conservatives, Christian-Socials, and other right-wing parties united in a parliamentary federation or cartel. When Behrens suggested that the electoral campaign of 1918 should also witness Conservative–Christian–Social agreements during *Hauptwahlen*, the agrarians agreed; they suggested that Conservative voters support Christian-Social candidates in all districts where Christian-Social voters outnumbered Conservatives, and vice versa. The concession was highly significant, for only with the combined help of Center and Conservatives would Evangelical unionists obtain increased representation in parliament.[66]

The *rapprochement* between the *Bund der Landwirte* and Christian labor must not be viewed in isolation. In fact, this development was merely part of a larger effort designed to place the *Bund* in the forefront of the movement for bourgeois *Sammlung*. In May 1912, for instance, the Conservative Party introduced a bill in the Reichstag demanding police protection for strike breakers. The resolution was seen in agrarian circles as a means to improve relations with heavy industry, enhance Conservative prospects among petty-bourgeois voters, and, hopefully, drive a wedge between the National Liberals

64. Quoted in *Die Arbeit*, no. 37, 14 September 1912.
65. Behrens to Stegerwald, 16 November 1912, Stegerwald Papers I, Stegerwald Stiftung Köln.
66. *Die Arbeit*, no. 30, 27 July 1912, no. 36, 7 September 1912, and no. 45, 9 November 1912; *Neue Preussische (Kreuz-) Zeitung*, no. 416, 5 September 1912, and nos. 460 and 470, for 1 and 6 October 1912.

and Progressives in the Reichstag.[67] In July, moreover, the League entered into negotiations with the Central Association of German Industrialists concerning a joint grant of 30,000 marks to the German Union of the Middle Class (*Reichsdeutscher Mittelstandsverband*). "It is a very great sum," Wangenheim told an associate, "but at stake is the question of whether we can effectively unite the productive classes and, in so doing, present our opponents with a concentrated force during future elections."[68]

Another conference was planned for September 1912 to arrange permanent cooperation between the three organizations. For reasons which cannot be precisely determined, however, no agreement was reached that fall or winter. Other historians have emphasized the suspicions of heavy industrialists concerning the radical, anti-capitalistic views of many artisans.[69] However, a resolution passed by the general assembly of the *Bund der Landwirte* in February 1913 leads to the conjecture that tariff, tax, and perhaps even social questions created equally troublesome relations between industry and agriculture.

> We exhort the whole agricultural community, the bourgeois middle classes [bürgerliche Mittelstände], and the nationally minded labor force to form a common defense against Socialism in politics and public life. The goal of such cooperation, however, must be: the continuation of patriotic economic policies that protect all German work, just social policies that protect and improve the living conditions of the old middle class just as those of the workers [*genauso wie die der Arbeiterschaft*], and equitable tax policies that draw on the resources of big business [*Grosskapital*] corresponding to its privileges in government today.[70]

If it is remembered that the agrarians were in the process of smoothing relations with Christian labor in the months before this resolution, the conclusion seems justified that Conservative leaders were holding out for a coalition of "national" forces which would include broad elements of the non-Socialist

67. See Saul, *Staat, Industrie, Arbeiterbewegung*, pp. 340–41. The tactical reason behind promoting the issue of strike-breaker protection probably went deeper than Saul thinks. After the Ruhr strike, the question of *Arbeitswilligenschutz* was also felt to be acceptable to Christian labor. Support for the bill from industry and national labor would weld both into the agrarian's emerging coalition. Industry, however, would also have to make compromises. In a pamphlet a few months earlier, for instance, the *Bund* had proclaimed that the parties of the right "will not draw back from the further development of social legislation" (*Rüstzeug zur Reichstagwahl! Eine Aufklärungsschrift für die kommenden Wahlen* [Berlin: Druckerei und Verlag Aktiengesellschaft der "deutschen Tageszeitung," Dec. 1911], pp. 90–91).
68. Wangenheim to Endell, 3 August 1912, printed in Hans-Jürgen Puhle, *Agrarische Interessenpolitik und preussischer Konservatismus im Wilhelminischen Reich (1893–1914)* (Hanover: Verlag für Literatur und Zeitgeschehen, 1966), p. 323.
69. Saul, *Staat, Industrie, Arbeiterbewegung*, p. 538.
70. Quoted in Puhle, *Agrarische Interessenpolitik*, p. 317.

working class, not just the controversial yellow organizations. With industrialists, non-Socialist unions, and agrarians *all* in disagreement over social issues, however, the time for such a coalition was not ripe.

The agrarians were therefore pursuing a strategy tangential to that of Christian labor. The main point of contact was a determination to isolate and destroy the Social Democrats, as witnessed by the debate over electoral alliances. Other areas of cooperation were being negotiated. That the *Bund der Landwirte* had taken the initiative in this respect, moreover, and not the Conservative Party *per se*, is not surprising. For, as Hans-Jürgen Puhle points out, the *Bund der Landwirte* was not only closer to the masses, having agitated among them for nearly twenty years, but was also highly dependent on parliament for fulfillment of agrarian demands.[71] The *Bund* was therefore more appreciative of the need to cooperate with other groups to form successful coalitions. When, after the elections, contacts with economic groups of all sorts appeared to provide the only key to parliamentary success, the agrarians did not hesitate to take this step.

* * * *

The year which began on a pessimistic note had thus produced many positive developments for Christian labor. Far-reaching bourgeois cooperation against the S.P.D. and free trade unions as well as positive work to pass social reforms, tax legislation, etc., finally seemed within grasp. It was hoped that the financial bill drafted by the government during the winter of 1912/13 would add further momentum to the progress made with these efforts. But it depended on Bethmann's ability to choose a tax which would facilitate agreement, not struggle, among the bourgeois parties. And this was not going to be a simple task. The National Liberal–Center–Conservative compromise of May 1912 had called for a "property tax" without specifying any one in particular. All that was certain was that it would not be an inheritance tax, for powerful agrarian lobbies in the Center and Conservative Parties opposed it. And yet this was the only tax for which Saxony, Bavaria, and other South German states in the Bundesrat had shown any enthusiasm.

Hoping to unite these disparate interests, Bethmann proposed a rather complicated compromise resolution. One hundred ten million marks of the required 186 million would be covered by Reich levies on fire insurance policies, legal documents incorporating new firms, and other less controversial taxes. For the remaining sum, each state would raise new income (*Einkommen-*), wealth (*Vermögen-*), or inheritance taxes (*Erbschaftssteuern*), then forward these revenues to Berlin. If by December 1914 the states had not

71. *Ibid.*, pp. 274–78.

acted, they would be required to institute the wealth gains tax at the state level. This compromise won the halting approval of the Bundesrat and was published in late March 1913.[72]

The decision, which the Christian trade unions had no chance to influence, was disappointing to Christian labor. Assuming that the Reich wealth tax would be the only property tax acceptable to a center-right bourgeois majority, the Political Committee of the Catholic *Arbeitervereine* of western Germany had held numerous rallies since the fall of 1912 to promote the tax in Center circles. These efforts were not without success, as witnessed by Karl Herold's advocacy of the *Vermögenssteuer* before the *Augustinusverein* in February. The workers' hope that the Conservatives would agree to the tax was also not entirely misplaced. Thus on two occasions in February Conservative agrarians spoke out for a direct tax that would increase the burden on big business. In late March, furthermore, party leader Count Westarp told Treasury Secretary Kühn, threateningly, that the *Fraktion* would throw itself behind wealth taxes if the government insisted on dictating which taxes should be raised by the federal states. The National Liberals were also in favor of the Imperial wealth tax, though admittedly not as a one-sided levy on capitalists. The Christian labor movevent therefore adopted a wait-and-see attitude toward Bethmann's tax package. If property taxes raised by the states were acceptable to the bourgeois majority, the non-Socialist workers would support this approach. If the Reichstag pressed for the wealth tax, however, Christian workers made it clear they would back this effort too.[73]

Indeed in early April 1913 it looked as if the Center-Right might agree to the tax favored by Christian labor. Center leaders Gröber and Spahn were the first to suggest this. Meeting with Westarp, Count Kanitz, and a few other Conservative deputies on 11 April 1913, the Centrists argued for a straight wealth tax levied by the Reich. The National Liberals would have their direct tax and be severed from the Progressives and Socialists, who were pushing for the objectionable inheritance taxes. The Center, Conservatives, and National Liberals could then use this new cooperative relationship as the foundation for *quid pro quo* compromises on the upcoming tariff debates and other matters

72. Witt, *Finanzpolitik des deutschen Reiches*, pp. 358–65, Rauh, *Parlamentarisierung des deutschen Reiches* pp. 254–71.

73. *Westdeutsche Arbeiter-Zeitung*, no. 35, 31 August 1912 and no. 16, 19 April 1913; also see Otto Müller's remarks before the executive committee of the Cartel Association of Catholic *Arbeitervereine* of Germany, 25 March 1918, *Archiv der katholischen Arbeitnehmerbewegung*, vol. 5, KfZG Bonn; *Augustinus-Blatt*, no. 2, February 1913, StBib MG; Witt, *Finanzpolitik des deutschen Reiches*, p. 363; Puhle, *Agrarische Interessenpolitik*, p. 317; Westarp to Heydebrand, 22 March 1913, reprinted in Kuno Graf von Westarp, *Konservative Politik im letzten Jahrzehnt des Kaiserreiches* (Berlin: Deutsche Verlagsgesellschaft, 1935), vol. 2, pp. 276–77; Undersecretary of State in the Reich Chancellery Wahnschaffe to Bethmann Hollweg, 16 March 1913, Reichskanzlei, Nr. 2270, Bl. 98, ZStA Potsdam; *Die Arbeit*, no. 11, 15 March 1913.

such as social reform.[74] What was not mentioned to the Conservatives was the soothing influence such developments would have on Christian labor. The unions had been pressing for bourgeois *Sammlung* for years and regarded the wealth tax as *a first step* in this direction.[75]

Kanitz was excited about the plan, but Westarp and the others balked. For one thing, the government's proposals could always be amended to give *complete* freedom of decision to the states as to which taxes should be raised. Secondly, there was no guarantee that the Progressives and Socialists would not suddenly champion the wealth tax, thereby raising the dubious specter of democrats and Marxists dictating tax policy to the government, the states, and the upper classes.[76] Early the next day, however, Westarp informed Bethmann's aid Wahnschaffe that the party was not categorically opposed to the Center's idea.

> There is talk of the wealth tax in the air. We don't want this, but there are two motives that could perhaps move us to cooperate [with the Center and National Liberals]. The tax is more bearable for us than the inheritance tax, and furthermore, I don't want to see us in a situation where we'll have to chase the train if the Bundesrat finally decides to unite with the other parties behind the wealth tax. For the degree of decisiveness that I'll show for the government's proposals, therefore . . . there's a double prerequisite: the amount of conviction we gain that the Bundesrat will remain firm against the wealth tax, and further, that chancellor and Bundesrat are decidedly opposed to covering the military bill with the inheritance taxes desired by the leftist majority.[77]

74. Westarp to Heydebrand, 13 April 1913, reprinted in Westarp, *Konservative Politik*, vol. 2, pp. 278–80.

75. For the pro-union orientation of the Center's financial policies in 1913, see Martin Spahn, *Deutsche Lebensfragen* (Kempten: Kösel Verlag, 1913), pp. 91–92; and Ernst Bassermann, "Die politische Bendeutung der Deckung der Heeresvorlage," undated clipping (probably fall 1913) from the *Nationalliberale Blätter* in the Stresemann Papers 135, H126179, BA Koblenz. Witt, *Finanzpolitik des deutschen Reiches*, p. 369, asserts that the Center had tactical reasons for proposing the wealth tax, but does not mention what these reasons were. Rauh, *Parlamentarisierung des deutschen Reiches*, pp. 273–74, claims that the party's proposal was only to serve as an "alibi," and that in reality Gröber and Erzberger wanted to unite the parties around a capital gains tax. This was probably true (see Martin Spahn's testimony after the war, *Die Ursachen des deutschen Zusammenbruches in Jahre 1918: Das Werk des Untersuchungsausschusses der Verfassungsgebendenden Deutschen Nationalversammlung und des Deutschen Reichstages 1919–1928*, vol. 7, part 1, p. 236), but Rauh, as Witt, does not explain that the Center needed this alibi to calm the workers who were pushing for the wealth tax. Mendershausen, "German Political Catholicism 1912–1919," Ph.D. dissertation, University of California, San Diego, 1972, pp. 118–28, correctly focuses his discussion on lower-class pressure within the Center, but is not very specific.

76. Westarp to Heydebrand, 13 April 1913, reprinted in Westarp, *Konservative Politik*, vol. 2, pp. 278–80.

77. *Ibid.* Both Witt, *Finanzpolitik des deutschen Reiches*, p. 369, and Rauh, *Parlamentarisierung des deutschen Reichstages*, p. 273, exaggerate the unwillingness of the Conservatives to accept the wealth tax.

When Wahnschaffe made no firm assurances to Westarp on these two points, the Conservative leader was unable to come to any decision concerning his party's stance.

The movement to force the government to accept a wealth tax was quickly undermined by the Kaiser. The king of Saxony, infuriated at the prospect of parliament bullying the Federal Council, drafted an angry letter of protest to William in early April. The malleable emperor quickly instructed Bethmann to put an end to all talk of wealth taxes by stating boldly in the Reichstag that the Federal Council would never accept them.[78] After another stern warning in May, Gröber and Erzberger completely abandoned the idea of wealth taxes and contacted the National Liberals concerning support for a capital gains tax which, among other things, would tax landed inheritances. Bethmann, who was favorably disposed to the plan, exerted pressure on the recalcitrant states in the Bundesrat, and by late June 1913, both houses had accepted the reform.

The bill was widely heralded in Liberal circles as a major step in the direction of progressivism, and Christian labor, too, could find some satisfaction in the fact that the Center had responded to the demand of the workers for a more equal distribution of the tax burden. The reform could not be seen, however, as a victory for the Christian labor movement, for its primary goal of uniting the bourgeois parties against the Socialists had not been achieved. The unions' agitation for the Reich wealth tax had been foiled by the Bundesrat in March and again by Bethmann's warnings in April and May. Thus the only direct tax which the Conservatives might have supported was cast aside. As had occurred so often in the past, a situation unfavorable to Christian laborers had been imposed on them by the arbitrary decisions of a few powerful individuals. This dilemma was compounded by the unions' decision to back the capital gains tax in June. The Conservatives were vehemently opposed to the idea of inheritance taxes in any form, and were appalled at the mere suggestion of bowing to the demands of a "leftist" Reichstag majority. By refusing to support the tax, even after certain concessions were made in the area of landed inheritances, the Conservatives had dealt a blow to the cause of anti-Socialist solidarity from which this cause would never recover.[79]

The indignation of Centrist and Conservative agrarians found quick expression that summer. On 6 July 1913 at Paderborn, representatives of the *Bund der Landwirte* and the National Federation of Christian Farmers' Associations met with officials of the Central Association of German Industrialists and the Reich Union of the Old Middle Class to discuss closer economic and

78. Hertling to his wife, Anna, 22 April 1913, Herling Papers 22, BA Koblenz.
79. Witt, *Finanzpolitik des deutschen Reiches*, pp. 370–71; Bassermann to Jacob Riesser, 18 July 1913, Stresemann Papers 429, H126142–44, BA Koblenz; Ernst Bassermann, "Die politische Bedeutung der Deckung der Heeresvorlage," as cited above in note 75; *Westdeutsche Arbeiter-Zeitung*, no. 28, 12 July 1913.

political cooperation. Further negotiations followed, and on 24 August the above organizations gathered in Leipzig to announce the formation of a "Cartel of the Producing Classes."[80] The new coalition advocated "the protection of national production," establishment of reasonable prices, maintenance of authority in all economic enterprises, protection of strike breakers, and opposition to "excrescences in the system of our economic life"[81] as well as the Social Democrats and false Socialist doctrines. To implement this program, the member organizations hoped to place enough pressure on the Center and National Liberals—the two parties that had played into the hands of "the Left" during the financial reform—so that radical elements in these parties would be suppressed and dragged along to the Right. Simultaneously, pressure would be exerted on Reich and Prussian leaders to support the Cartel's program.[82]

It must be emphasized, however, that the members of the Cartel held differing views over the term "Right." They were all determined to halt the trend toward "socialistic" property taxation and generally dedicated to the struggle against free trade unions, S.P.D., and bourgeois radicalism. But here agreement ended. The agrarian wing of the Cartel was primarily interested in securing a Reichstag majority for agricultural tariffs, while neither the Central Association nor the Reich Union warmed to the idea. Heavy industry and the small producer, on the other hand, wanted to crush the entire trade union movement and halt further social legislation, but these goals did not appeal to all Christian and Conservative farmers. Of the six organizations in the Christian Federation, for instance, only the Rhenish and Silesian were emphatically anti-union, and neither favored a rollback of social insurance legislation. The Westphalian association was even prepared to expand the Cartel to include the Christian trade unions.[83]

80. Stegmann, *Die Erben Bismarcks*, pp. 355–56; Saul, *Staat, Industrie, Arbeiterbewegung*, pp. 339–40.
81. For the proceedings at Leipzig, see the *Deutsche Tageszeitung*, no. 428, 25 August 1913.
82. Stegmann, *Die Erben Bismarcks*, pp. 415–21; Saul, *Staat, Industrie, Arbeiterbewegung*, pp. 340–41.
83. For the views of the Central Association, see the speeches of heavy industrialists Ferdinand Schweighofer and Julius Vorster, printed, respectively, in *Deutsche Tageszeitung*, no. 470, 16 September 1913, and *Westdeutsche Arbeiter-Zeitung*, no. 5, 31 January 1914; for the Imperial Union, see the report of its annual congress for 1913 printed in *Zentralblatt*, no. 22, 27 October 1913; for the views of Christian farmers, see the observations of Karl Herold, *Augustinus-Blatt*, no. 10, October 1913, Baron von Löe, printed in *Zentralblatt*, no. 23, 10 November 1913, and Silesian agrarians, discussed in the *Deutsche Tageszeitung*, no. 492, 28 September 1913; for an excellent discussion of the Christian farmer's view of society and other social groups, see David W. Hendon, "The Center Party and the Agrarian Interest in Germany 1890–1914," Ph.D. dissertation, Emory University, 1976; Timothy Nugent, "The Bourgeoisie Awakes: Socio-Economic Interest Groups in Germany 1909–1914," Ph.D. dissertation, University of Wisconsin, 1975, pp. 260–62, 287, exaggerates the anti-social views of Christian farmers by concentrating solely on Baron Löe's Rhenish organization.

Much the same can be said for the *Bund der Landwirte*. The League was prepared to accept new social insurance legislation, albeit at a slower pace than the labor movement desired. *Bund* leaders were also in favor of incorporating the Christian and "national" labor associations (yellow) into the emerging coalition. Before this could happen, however, Conservative agrarians wanted the unions to accept a slower social reform tempo and compromise on certain key legal issues such as the right to strike. Like Marx, ironically enough, they assumed that most workers could never get along with employers and that authoritarian institutions had to be maintained to keep this class conflict within manageable bounds. Once this dilemma was solved, League activists like Conrad von Wangenheim wanted to transform the cartel into a great right-wing *Volkspartei* encompassing agriculture, industry, handicraft, non-Socialist labor, and other associations such as the Pan-German League.[84] In the long run, the "egotistical tendencies" of heavy industry could be curbed by compromises within the party.[85]

Only League leaders were enthusiastic about these designs, significantly enough, for the Conservative Party was too attached to the past to warm to the idea of a radical party-political transformation. Most Conservatives were also wary of attenuating the property rights of industrialists for fear the same principles would be applied with equal force to landowners. The history of the Cartel thus provides added evidence in support of the thesis that the *Bund der Landwirte* was more attuned to the need for organization, somewhat more willing to make concessions, and hence more "modern" than the upper strata of the Conservative Party itself.[86] These developments also lend credence to the view that some right-wing politicians, by employing democratic techniques in pursuit of anti-democratic goals, were precursors of the fascists.[87] The *Bund*'s emphasis on militant nationalism, anti-Semitism, and new party formations, its criticism of the weakness of Kaiser and chancellor, and its desire to shackle *both* capital and labor place it squarely in this category. As argued at the beginning of this study, however, such comparisons should not be exaggerated.

Public response to the new coalition, meanwhile, was not at all what Cartel

84. Stegmann, *Die Erben Bismarcks*, pp. 356, 361, 379–90, 403–4, has uncovered the ambitious plans of Wangenheim *et al.*, but does not mention Christian labor as part of the design. That the unions were eventually to be included will be shown below.

85. See Rösicke's letter to Wangenheim of July 1912, cited above in note 61; Puhle, *Agrarische Interessenpolitik*, pp. 159–64, stresses the fact that the *Bund* wanted to dominate the Cartel, and also that the anti-Semitism took on definite anti-business tones, but does not link these facts to a desire to eliminate the social abuses of modern industry.

86. For Puhle's views, see his *Agrarische Interessenpolitik*, pp. 274–78. That the *Bund* was willing to pursue social reforms, however, is not mentioned by Puhle.

87. Puhle, *ibid.*, pp. 278–89, advances this view, as does Stegmann, *Die Erben Bismarcks*, pp. 449–522, and Eley, *Reshaping the Right, passim.*

leaders had hoped. National Liberal Reichstag leaders and the overwhelming majority of the party's press denounced Leipzig as a sellout to Junkers and Free Conservative industrialists.[88] The party's *actions* that fall, however, illustrate that the formation of the Cartel was not entirely without effect on the Liberals. The National Liberal convention at Wiesbaden in early October not only professed the party's reliability with regard to tariffs, but also established a special commission to investigate the question of protection for strike breakers.[89] The move was interpreted by right-wing National Liberals as a sign that the party was prepared to abandon its opposition to the demands of the Conservative Party and heavy industry. This was not exactly true, as the moderate Gustav Stresemann noted in a letter to Bassermann in late October.

> I'm not demanding a special piece of legislation [against unions] nor even a banning of pickets. I do feel that it's urgently necessary, on the other hand, that the National Liberal *Fraktion* advocate a law within the framework of present legislation that facilitates a quicker prosecution of strike excesses, introduces corporate status for trade unions, makes them responsible for damages, and further, [that we ask] state authorities to issue strike instructions which specify that more energetic use will be made of existing legal means . . . I feel these proposals hold out a way which the National Liberal *Fraktion* can go without damaging its status with labor organizations.[90]

Stresemann reinforced his bid to influence the Wiesbaden Commission in early November by obtaining the sanction of the *Hansabund*'s Industrial Council for the position outlined above.[91]

Bassermann's protégé fell between two stools. In numerous assemblies and petitions, the right wing of the party demanded entirely new legislation to crush the strike and warned of "weighty consequences"[92] should the Wiesbaden Commission fail in this mission. The howls of protest from the left were equally frightening. The white-collar employees associated with the *Hansabund* threatened to bolt unless the organization disavowed Stresemann's resolution. The executive committee obliged the clerks in late November by denouncing the Leipzig Cartel as one-sided and reactionary,[93] then buried the Industrial Council's resolution in a committee which never met. The Young Liberal Clubs and numerous district party organizations joined this protest,

88. See Stegmann, *Die Erben Bismarcks*, p. 399.
89. Saul, *Staat, Industrie, Arbeiterbewegung*, p. 357.
90. Stresemann to Bassermann, 31 October 1913, Stresemann Papers 135, H126169, BA Koblenz.
91. Nugent, "The Bourgeoisie Awakes," p. 289.
92. Quoted in Saul, *Staat, Industrie, Arbeiterbewegung*, p. 357. The warning may have referred to the agrarians' plan of forming a new right-wing party.
93. Nugent, "The Bourgeoisie Awakes," pp. 290–91.

insisting that the newly established commission abandon the anti-union cause. Adding to the pressure from the left wing of the party, Christian trade union and Hirsch-Duncker leaders warned National Liberal officials not to back the demands of heavy industry.[94]

The general threat of losing mass support soon forced party leaders to hedge on the question of strike breakers. In late October Karl Heckmann and George Ickler, two non-Socialist labor leaders elected in 1912, were co-opted into the Wiesbaden Commission. The move was clearly designed to lessen the chances of anti-labor findings once the commission began its work. In mid-November a number of other topics were added to the commission's agenda in the obvious hope of postponing the proceedings indefinitely. That Bassermann and the party leadership felt compelled to adopt expedients such as these was a good illustration of the fragile nature of National Liberal Party unity on the eve of the war. The left wing was much more pleased with the move than the right, however, which was good indication that the Cartel had lost the first round with the Liberals.[95]

The initial reaction in Center circles was much more positive. Christian agrarian and artisan groups were naturally in favor, as were the *Fachabteilungen* in Berlin, whose theological objections to the stike fit well into the Cartel's program. Matthias Erzberger, who sympathized with the Berliners, also pronounced a positive judgement in *Tag*. Much more surprising was the cautious, but by no means negative, response of Julius Bachem and the *Kölnische Volkszeitung*. The Center's leading journal in western Germany greeted the idea of bourgeois *Sammlung* and held out hope that the Cartel could develop in a more progressive direction. The *Essener Volkszeitung, Niederrheinischer Volkszeitung*, and *Schlesische Volkszeitung* expressed similar views.[96]

The only outright negative reaction in the Catholic camp came from the Christian trade unions and the western *Arbeitervereine*.[97] Throughout the fall of 1913 Christian labor leaders kept up a constant barrage of criticism, claiming that the Cartel would reduce the workers' standard of living by pushing for tariff increases on grain and, more importantly, that the allied organizations intended to stamp out trade unionism. The presence of Central Association

94. Saul, *Staat, Industrie, Arbeiterbewegung*, pp. 357–60.
95. *Ibid.*, pp. 357–58.
96. *Kölnische Volkszeitung*, no. 804, 16 September 1903; *Deutsche Tageszeitung*, no. 610, 2 December 1913; Stegmann, *Die Erben Bismarcks*, p. 398; Saul, *Staat, Industrie, Arbeiterbewegung*, pp. 342–43; *Essener Volkszeitung*, no. 254, 16 September 1913; *Niederrheinischer Volkszeitung*, no. 915, 20 September 1913.
97. See Giesberts's notes for a speech before Catholic artisans on 29 September 1913, Giesberts Papers 120, Bl. 1–9, ZStA Potsdam; *Zentralblatt*, no. 20, 29 September 1913; *Westdeutsche Arbeiter-Zeitung*, no. 39, 27 September 1913; and Giesberts's speech of 9 November before his constituents in Essen, printed in the *Kölnische Volkszeitung*, no. 970, 10 November 1913.

representatives at Leipzig offered some proof of this latter charge, but the unions could also point to a resolution passed by the Imperial Union in August 1913 which, if implemented, would have effectively excluded trade unions from negotiation of wage contracts. The most alarming, and surprising, aspect of these developments to Christian labor, however, was the wholehearted support German agrarians seemed to give to the anti-social demands of heavy industry and the old middle class. Stegerwald, Giesberts, and other Catholic laborers saw no reason why Christian and Conservative farmers had to join such a coalition to protect agriculture, for, with the exception of the Progressives, all bourgeois parties were willing to accept reasonable tariff increases. The only conclusion to be reached, therefore, was that farmers had joined the Cartel to oppose organized labor. If they did this, warned the Christian trade union *Zentralblatt*, they would arouse a "monstrous opposition" in labor circles. In order to oppose the anticipated demands of the Cartel for a rollback of social legislation and the shackling of unionism, Christian labor leaders decided to hold a third German Workers' Congress when the Reichstag convened in November.[98]

The unions' reaction, which was delayed for unknown reasons until late September,[99] gave rise to a long series of requests from Center and Cartel circles that Christian labor reconsider its stance. The *Deutsche Tageszeitung* was the first to speak out. The Agrarian League organ found the *Zentralblatt*'s article inexplicably harsh and based on a thoroughly false understanding of the Cartel. "It can only be hoped that the Christian trade unions quickly come to a calmer and more accurate interpretation of the goals discussed at Leipzig."[100] The *Kölnische Volkszeitung* was also quick to comment, advising the unions to wait and see what course the Cartel pursued. Not all member organizations, the paper pointed out, were opposed to social reform.[101] When the influential *Schlesische Volkszeitung* also challenged the union's viewpoint concerning the threat to social reform, the *Deutsche Tageszeitung* reprinted the article in its press review.[102]

The eagerness of the *Bund der Landwirte* to smooth relations with Christian labor spread to other Cartel members that fall. In mid-October the Rhenish Artisans' League, one of the more progressive members of the Reich Union, defended the idea of broadening the Cartel to include Christian labor.[103] Karl

98. *Zentralblatt*, no. 20, 29 September 1913.
99. Christian labor leaders probably wanted to observe Center Party reaction before speaking out. A *negative* response to the Cartel in Catholic circles might have obviated the need for a dramatic rejection by the unions.
100. *Deutsche Tageszeitung*, no. 492, 28 September 1913.
101. *Kölnische Volkszeitung*, no. 842, 28 September 1913.
102. *Deutsche Tageszeitung*, no. 495, 30 September 1913.
103. For the views of the Rhenish Artisans' League, see the *Zentralblatt*, no. 23, 10 November 1913; and the *Kölnische Volkszeitung*, no. 912, 21 October 1913.

Herold seconded the idea at the Westphalian Center Party's convention in Münster a month later. The Christian-national workers had to be included in the Leipzig initiative, argued the Center's leading agrarian, "in order to arrive at common action of *all* the great occupational estates which recognize the existing societal order."[104] Perhaps the most significant statement came from Dr. Hugo Böttger, one of the spokesmen for heavy industry in the National Liberal Reichstag *Fraktion*, who admitted during a speech in Duisburg that it had been a mistake not to invite the Christian trade unions to Leipzig.[105]

Baron von Löe, Catholic leader of the conservative Rhenish Farmers' League, joined the chorus in late November.

> The Christian trade unions called the meeting of the Cartel [in August] a storm-warning signal for the bourgeois labor movement. Nothing is more false than that. We have no intention of marching in double battle formation. We are content to move the battle line forwards. With this front we'll also acquire terrain for the [non-Socialist] working class.[106]

Löe's appeal for non-Socialist solidarity was printed in the morning edition of the *Deutsche Tageszeitung* on 2 December. That evening the *Bund der Landwirte* daily praised the remarks of the Catholic nobleman and extended its own olive branch to Christian labor.[107] The paper's editor, Georg Oertel, was even more explicit in the Reichstag ten days later. If German agriculture was to remain strong, he noted, "unity is needed—unity in the Reichstag and among the producing classes, including the workers."[108]

These pleas had no effect whatsoever. The answer of the German Workers' Congress was a defiant rejection of those elements in the Cartel that had urged the unions to moderate their demands and join the coalition. The Frankfurt program of 1903 was not diluted; rather it was expanded to include unemployment compensation, housing legislation, public works, the eight-hour day in certain industries, a resolution against higher tariffs, and a host of minor additions to Germany's social insurance laws. The offers of the fall concerning participation in the Cartel were also turned down on the grounds that no union could take part in a venture aimed primarily at eliminating the strike and collective bargaining.[109] Having drifted as far to the right as any bona fide

104. Quoted in *Bericht über die Verhandlungen des dritten Deutschen Arbeiter-Kongresses* (Cologne: Christlicher Gewerkschaftsverlag, 1914), p. 65.
105. *Kölnische Volkszeitung*, no. 1071, 11 December 1913.
106. Quoted in the *Deutsche Tageszeitung*, no. 610, 2 December 1913.
107. *Deutsche Tageszeitung*, no. 611, 2 December 1913.
108. Reichstag Debates, Period 13, Session 1 (11 December 1913), vol. 291, p. 6388.
109. *Bericht über die Verhandlungen des dritten Deutschen Arbeiter-Kongresses*, pp. 18–22, 291–317.

labor organization could be expected to over the last ten years, Christian labor was announcing that the time for concessions on its part was past. If the Leipzig Cartel was the only basis for bourgeois *Sammlung*, the movement for non-Socialist solidarity was bankrupt.

The presence of 28 Center deputies at the Congress was a good indication that the union's tough stand had not been in vain. Indeed in mid-December the *Kölnische Volkszeitung* admitted that many in Center circles had reconsidered their stance to the Cartel in the light of unionist arguments and revelations.[110] The political expediency of this turnaround was not mentioned by the paper, but there is no reason to doubt that fear of vote loss was the major motivating factor. Despite the fact that agrarian and middle-class elements in the Center still favored a closer relationship with the Cartel, it was clear that the Leipzig forces had lost another round.

However, as has been emphasized so often in this study, the Reichstag was not the real locus of power in Imperial Germany, even on the eve of the war. For this reason Cartel forces had divided their efforts from the beginning between parliament and highly placed individuals in state and Reich government. This pressure, together with the sympathy that most top civil servants felt for the conservative cause, resulted in an unmistakable shift to the right in these circles during the year before Sarajevo. Thus, in early July 1913 Bethmann Hollweg told Count Lerchenfeld that he supported Bavaria's desire to halt the movement toward direct Reich taxes.[111] With Saxony and Württemberg already on record as opponents of direct Imperial taxation, further reform of Germany's outmoded financial system seemed highly unlikely. In January 1914, moreover, Reich secretary of the interior Delbrück announced that the Imperial government would block all efforts to undermine the country's tariff system, and if need be, would even strive for "improvements"[112] in this system. The stance of the German Workers' Congress against tariffs had clearly been without effect. The rightward drift of German officialdom became even more evident in May 1914 when Prussian minister of the interior von Loebell categorically rejected the idea of a democratization of the three-class suffrage.[113]

Nor was there much hope in the area of social reform. In mid-January 1914 the hard-pressed chancellor spoke out against the workers' demand for unemployment compensation,[114] and on 20 January, Delbrück announced that the nation had reached "a definite standstill"[115] in social insurance legislation.

110. *Kölnische Volkszeitung*, no. 1071, 11 December 1913.
111. Lerchenfeld to Hertling, 7 July 1913, MAI 955 GStA München.
112. Reichstag Debates, Period 13, Session 1 (20 January 1914), vol. 292, p. 6647.
113. Bachem, *Zentrumspartei*, vol. 7, p. 123.
114. Saul, *Staat, Industrie, Arbeiterbewegung*, p. 382.
115. Reichstag Debates, Period 13, Session 1 (20 January 1914), vol. 292, p. 6637.

The prospect for bills guaranteeing the legal *rights* of labor organizations looked just as bleak. In mid-December 1913 Bethmann responded to Conservative demands for protection of strike breakers by declaring that this question would be handled in the upcoming reform of Germany's criminal code. Not content to wait, the Prussian and Saxon police were already in the process of issuing tough new regulations against the activity of workers on strike.[116] In Delbrück's speech of 20 January, moreover, the secretary held out no hope for legislation to ensure collective bargaining. "Gentlemen, after the experiences we've had in this house with deliberations over the [bargaining] question, it seems doubtful to me whether this goal will be reached in the foreseeable future."[117] It had clearly been a black day for the cause of social emancipation in Germany. Unable to influence Germany's bureaucratic elite as effectively as heavy industry and agriculture, Christian labor derived little satisfaction from blocking the Cartel's first Reichstag initiative.

Five days after Delbrück spoke, the Christian labor world was rocked by reports that the Prussian episcopate no longer stood behind the Essen interpretation of the encyclical *Singulari Quadam*. The news stemmed from a letter Cardinal Kopp had printed in the "Berlinist" organ *Klarheit und Wahrheit* on 25 January 1914.[118] Kopp noted that he had formulated the Essen interpretation jointly with Bishop Schulte of Paderborn and, further, that the bishops' conference had never formally debated the matter. The archbishop then disclosed the contents of a letter to Schulte of 1 December 1912 in which he had dissociated himself from the interpretation. With this letter, he asserted, the approval of the entire episcopate had been withdrawn. Kopp's claims were fraught with procedural errors, as Schulte pointed out in a lengthy article series in late January 1914,[119] but the unions took little consolation in this. As *Gesamtverband* leaders saw it, they were now faced with an even greater challenge from the entrenched forces of conservatism.

Coming at a time when the state and the German Right were tightening their grip on trade union freedoms, the specter of church control of the labor movement contained in Kopp's letter[120] aroused suspicion among Christian

116. Reichstag Debates, Period 13, Session 1 (10 December 1913), vol. 291, pp. 6341–43; Saul, *Staat, Industrie, Arbeiterbewegung*, pp. 381, 392–93.

117. *Ibid.*, p. 6640.

118. Kopp to Count Hans Oppersdorf, 21 January 1914, printed in *Klarheit und Wahrheit*, no. 4, 25 January 1914.

119. *Westfälischer Volksblatt*, 27, 29, 30, 31 January 1914 (clippings in: Brauweiler Papers 14, StA MG).

120. This was, in fact, exactly what Kopp had in mind. In late 1913 he had proposed that Christian trade union headquarters be moved from Cologne to Berlin—a city under his jurisdiction (Mühlberg to von Langwerth, 26 February 1914, Päpstl. Stuhl *secr.* 3, AA Bonn). Some months earlier, Kopp had rallied the Prussian bishops for another offensive against the *Volksverein* (Archbishop Hartmann to Pieper, 25 September 1913, Hohn Papers 15/2, StA MG).

labor leaders of a broad conspiracy. The mood was captured well by the *Leipziger Neueste Nachrichten*, which printed a letter from leading Christian trade union circles in early February 1914.

> The Essen Congress [of 1912] wrung attention from many sides for the Christian trade unions. We had refused to allow church authorities to interfere in our affairs. The reputation and influence of the Christian trade unions rose. This was not just a boon for us, but also for the progress of social-mindedness, for without a doubt the idea of social reform finds the best support today in the Christian-national labor movement . . . Now Cardinal Kopp's political sympathies do not lie with those circles which are pressing for the energetic continuation of social legislation. More than that, as a member of the Free Conservative faction of the [Prussian] House of Lords, he stands close to the very circles for which more vigorous social policies as well as a greater participation in political events on the part of the laboring masses is an abomination. Cardinal Kopp was the bridge over which the aversion to an independent labor movement in political circles was shifted to the side of the church. The most recent attacks made by Cardinal Kopp against the Christian trade unions must be viewed in this connection. His attacks are nothing more than a projection of all the reactionary socio-political measures observed of late. If the *Reaktion* succeeded in knocking out the best troops among the socially conscious patriotic workers, then it would have a much easier time implementing its plans.[121]

As explained elsewhere,[122] the immediate motivation for Kopp's letter was different. In a broader sense, however, the authors of the above letter were close to the truth. For both church and state regarded strike action on the part of independent, sometimes militant trade unions as a serious threat to the existing order of things that they were both pledged to uphold. The forces of change and resistance to change in Germany were coalescing, consciously and unconsciously, into two opposing fronts on the eve of World War I. The unionists had sensed this.[123]

Without an appreciation for these feelings, the unusually vehement protest of Christian labor during the month of February cannot be fully understood. On 3 February the Political Committee of the Catholic *Arbeitervereine* held a

121. Reprinted in *Badischer Beobachter*, 5 February 1914 (clipping in: Brauweiler Papers 14, StA MG).
122. See this author's dissertation, "Christian Labor and the Politics of Frustration in Imperial Germany," pp. 365–66.
123. The idea of conspiracy, though unfounded with regard to Kopp, did nevertheless have some basis in fact. Count Hoensbroech, a Catholic agrarian who stood behind the Cartel and for years had backed the demands of the *Osterdienstag* conference, planned to lobby against the Christian trade unions in Rome in April 1914. (Zimmermann to Mühlberg, 7 April 1914, Päpstl. Stuhl 26 *secr*. 3, AA Bonn.)

mass rally at Bochum which led to "deplorable"[124] outbursts against the church. On the tenth Archbishop Hartmann of Cologne tried in vain to halt a meeting of labor priests who sympathized with the workers' feelings. The *Arbeiterverein* leaders added insult to injury by submitting a nine-page protest resolution to Hartmann, then asking him to forward it to Rome! Despite the archbishop's efforts to halt another protest rally of workers at Essen on the fifteenth, this meeting, too, went ahead as planned. Pieper, Müller, and Giesberts finally responded to Hartmann's pleas in late February by urging Catholic workers to calm down. The rift between masses and hierarchy, however, was already too wide to close. Eight hundred thousand Catholic workers belonged to free trade unions by this time and many of those who remained loyal to the Christian labor movement were too radical for even the most sympathetic clergymen.[125] Bishop Faulhaber of Speyer, for instance, complained that "the trade union leaders speak in such an irreverent and impermissible way that without an express order from Rome one can't work with them anymore."[126]

Quotations such as these are part of a larger body of material—to be presented shortly—indicating a marked radicalization of the Catholic proletariat on the eve of World War I. This had not always been the case. The qualitative evidence introduced since the beginning of this study suggests that the radical consciousness was rare among Catholic workers before the turn of the century. Thus the majority of Catholic miners in the Ruhr sided with their priests, not Anton Rosenkranz, in 1878, while August Brust had a flock of timid *Gewerkverein* initiates to contend with in the mid-1890s. The emergence of a radical wing in that union by 1897 and the *Gesamtverband*'s flirtation with merger a few years later are illustrative of more aggressive tendencies. But the movement was still too reliant on the devout, malleable type of member, the reader will remember, to risk the danger of church condemnation. Thus the idea of union with the General Commission was quickly abandoned.

As Chapter 10 illustrated, susceptibility to manipulation by the hierarchy of the Catholic church remained a problem for the Christian trade unions well into the first decade of the new century. By approximately 1905, however, the temperament of the average Christian worker appears to have changed. Thus a brochure issued that year by the western and southern *Arbeitervereine* dis-

124. Hartmann to Otto Müller, 14 February 1914, *Archiv der katholischen Arbeitnehmerbewegung*, vol. 5, KfZG Bonn.
125. Hartmann to Müller, 10 February 1914, Müller to Hartmann, 12 February 1914, *Archiv der katholischen Arbeitnehmerbewegung*, vol. 5, KfZG Bonn; Hartmann to Wilhelm Marx, 11 February 1914, Marx Papers 219, HA Köln; *Westdeutsche Arbeiter-Zeitung*, no. 10, 7 March 1914; *Kölnische Volkszeitung*, no. 1099, 19 December 1913.
126. Faulhauber to Ritter, 24 February 1914, Ges. Päpstl. Stuhl 905, GStA München.

tinguished between "old style" Catholic workers of the 1880s who lacked a sense of class consciousness and self-achievement and "new style" Catholic workers who looked upon their organization as a "conquering troop, a battle brigade, a leadership troop."[127]

It was at about this time, moreover that the Christian rank and file began to express the desire for an independent Christian labor party. As the years drew on to the eve of the war, a number of dramatic incidents eroded even further the patience of these "new style" proletarians. The demonstration effect of the Russian Revolution of 1905, the failure of the Ruhr miners' strike of that year, the inequalities of the financial "reform" of 1909, the disappointing experience with reform of Prussia's plutocratic suffrage in 1910, the final collapse of the "Frankfurt initiative" (see Chapter 9), and the recession which descended on Germany in 1912/13 all helped darken the mood of Catholic workers. This was quite apparent during the *Gewerkverein*'s wage action in the Saar in December 1912 when union leaders could barely keep the rank and file in line. To *Singulari Quadam*, moreover, Christian unionists shouted that they "stood with Adam" and did not care what the pope thought. The protest against Cardinal Archbishop Kopp in February 1914 was therefore not an isolated development; Christian labor had radicalized.

Like the church, the Center Party was also injured by these trends. Alarmed by the loss of its two Munich seats, the party had adopted a different attitude toward the worker after 1900. Primarily this took the form of labor candidacies for the Reichstag and Landtage and parliamentary backing for the social demands of the German Workers' Congress. But the erosion of working-class support continued unabated. Strassburg (Stadt), Mühlhausen, Mainz, and Düsseldorf fell during the elections of 1903 and 1907, then came the deluge in 1912: Strassburg (Land), Freiburg, Bingen, Hamm-Soest, Osnabrück, and Cologne, the "Hochburg" of the Rhineland, were lost.

These setbacks, which saw the Center's strength in the Reichstag decline from 105 to 91, jolted the party into more far-reaching concessions to Catholic labor. Previous objections to the eight-hour day and unemployment insurance were dropped and, in the former case, a corresponding parliamentary resolution introduced.[128] For the Center, however, attention to social reform was no longer sufficient. By 1912/13 Catholic workers were beginning to *insist* that these concessions extend to financial, tariff, and electoral reform as well.

To be sure, the party's support for a Reich wealth tax in 1913 illustrated a wider pro-labor stance and helped counterbalance the effects of the unpopular tax increase of 1909. But there was only so far that an agrarian-oriented

127. Quoted in Lidtke, "Social Class and Secularization," p. 32.
128. Reichstag Debates, 10 February 1912, vol. 298 (bill no. 63).

institution like the Center could go. Thus in February 1914 the Prussian Center joined the National Liberals in a declaration for higher tariffs. Less dependent on labor votes, the Landtag *Fraktion* felt it could afford to ignore Christian labor on this issue. Even more bitterness was generated over the suffrage question. Despite a campaign against the three-class system that winter by the Political Committee of the Catholic *Arbeitervereine*, Herold announced in May that his party colleagues in Prussia had no intention of introducing a reform bill. Worried that an influx of Socialists and Progressives into the Landtag would mean an end to the confessional school in Prussia, Herold and others had little sympathy for the workers' demand for a voice in the government of Germany's largest and most powerful state.[129]

The pressures resulting from these differences of opinion were beginning to undermine Center unity on the eve of the war. As *Fraktion* leader Peter Spahn put it, "everything is as brittle as if it were made of glass."[130] Thus in October 1913 the noblemen who had abstained during the financial reform in June formed a "committee of the 22." Their goal was to prepare for the "hot struggles"[131] anticipated with Catholic labor over the tariff issue. The workers were sharpening their swords too. August Brust, former leader of the *Gewerkverein*, barked in November that "the workers can't be caught anymore by waving the bloody shirt and crying that the church is in danger. We can easily bring about a leftist majority [in the Reichstag], and we can vote 'no' just like the Center agrarians did over the capital gains tax."[132] In late September 1913, moreover, Stegerwald and Wilhelm Weyer, co-chairmen of the Political Committee of the Catholic *Arbeitervereine*, invited *Volksverein* and Christian labor leaders to a meeting in Cologne to discuss "the upcoming struggles in the area of tariff and commercial policies," creation of a political journal for the entire Christian-national labor movement, and the need "to make the parliamentary activity of Christian-national labor deputies more effective."[133] It is not clear what the Political Committee had in mind, for the minutes of the meeting itself are not extant. The strategy must have been similar, however, to one which emerged a few years later: all Christian labor

129. Bassermann notation of 25 February 1914, Kl. Erw. 303-17, BA Koblenz; Müller Manuscript, p. 31, KAB Haus Köln; Reichstag Debates, Period 13, Session 1 (19 May 1914), vol. 295, p. 9085.

130. Spahn made the statement to his son, Martin, who related the pre-war conversation to a special Reichstag committee in 1928. Cited in: *Die Ursachen des deutschen Zusammenbruches im Jahre 1918: Das Werk des Untersuchungsausschusses der Verfassungsgebenden Deutschen Nationalversammlung und des Deutschen Reichstages* 1919–1928 (Berlin: Deutsche Verlagsgesellschaft für Politik und Geschichte GmbH, 1928), vol. 7, part 2, p. 229.

131. Count Galen to Herold, 19 October 1913, Herold Papers 6, BA Koblenz.

132. See Chaplain Heinrich Wiedemann to Herold, 28 May 1914, and accompanying documents, Herold Papers 7, BA Koblenz.

133. See Stegerwald's and Weyer's invitation to the meeting, in *Archiv der katholischen Arbeitnehmerbewegung*, vol. 1, KfZG Bonn.

deputies would form an inter-party committee to pressure the various *Fraktionen.*[134] The fact that Christian laborers were talking that winter about prodding the Center into the mainstream of political life and purging it of "hyper-particularistic, purely religious, narrow-minded elements"[135] lends credence to the idea that such a committee was being planned. So too does evidence that Christian labor wanted to work, as its leaders put it, "with the utmost pressure and speed in order to carry through the interconfessionalization of Catholic Germany over the head of all resistance."[136] Giesberts, Schiffer, *et al.* would become, for all intents and purposes, representatives of the German Workers' Congress, not the Center.

This process of political fragmentation was not limited to the Center. Dissatisfied with the political inactivity of the Hirsch-Duncker unions and the lack of labor representations in the Progressive Party, for example, Anton Erkelenz had formed his own political organization during the summer of 1912. The Reich Association of Liberal Workers and Clerks, as the new group was called, was virtually a party within a party.[137] Labor and anti-labor factions could also be observed in the National Liberal Party, as witnessed by the debate over protection of strike breakers. Had it not been for the strong bond of imperialism and militant nationalism, in fact, the *Fraktion* would probably have split, with more than half going over to the Progressives, the others to the Conservatives.[138]

The Conservatives had avoided such problems over the years by refusing to admit workers to the party, but this was beginning to change in the two years before the war. The *Bund der Landwirte* had supported a number of Christian laborers during the elections of 1912 and was eager to develop closer ties with Christian labor during the following two years. As a result of these efforts, the Christian-Social metal worker Herman Wahlbaum was nominated by the Conservatives and elected to the Prussian Landtag in July 1913. When Archduke Franz Ferdinand was shot a year later, the Conservatives and Christian-Socials were about to sign a merger agreement.[139] The *Bund*'s views on more effective

134. See Stegerwald's outline for a presentation in July 1916 entitled "Fundamental Principles and Demands of the Christian-National Movement of Workers and Clerks," in the Bachem Papers 960, HA Köln.

135. Behrens to Wahnschaffe, 6 February 1914, Papstl. Stuhl 26 *secr.* 2, AA Bonn. Behrens's letter is significant because he summarizes the feelings of the *Gesamtverband* executive committee, which had met the night before.

136. Archbishop Hartmann of Cologne to Kopp, 10 November 1913, B III 15.9, Bd. 1, pp. 50–53, BisA Trier.

137. *Protokoll der Reichskonferenz liberaler Arbeiter und Angestellten (10–11 August 1912)*, Erkelenz Papers 117, BA Koblenz.

138. Stegmann, *Die Erben Bismarcks*, pp. 315–16.

139. Dieter Fricke, "Christlich-soziale Partei," in Dieter Fricke (ed.), *Die bürgerlichen Parteien in Deutschland*, vol. 1, p. 253. Fricke quotes the memoirs of Christian-Social party chairman Wilhelm Philipps.

political organization had begun to prevail, for the move was designed to win influence in western Germany and find "access to the working class."[140] That tensions lay ahead for any expanded Conservative Party, however, goes almost without saying.

While the bourgeois parties were being driven apart by the radicalization of the non-Socialist rank and file, working-class leaders were forced to put past differences aside. In the face of such serious challenges from the Right on issues which affected the very heart of trade unionism, continuation of past feuds appeared unbelievably foolish to many non-Socialist unionists. These grumbles of dissatisfaction and discontent played into the hands of Hans Berlepsch and Ernst Franke of the Society for Social Reform. As explained in earlier chapters, the two had tried for years to unite the Christian, Hirsch-Duncker, and Socialist unions within the framework of the Society. The frees had refused from the beginning on the grounds that bourgeois reform ideas would only compromise a true labor organization. The Christians and Hirsch-Dunckers had joined the Society, but there cooperation ended. Political and religious differences kept the liberal unions away from the German Workers' Congress in 1903 and 1907, and, despite a truce in May 1911 that was supposed to pave the way for Hirsch-Duncker membership, the Third Congress in November 1913 also saw a divided non-Socialist labor movement. The liberal miners were still infuriated with the *Gewerkverein* for refusing to strike in 1912, and the large Hirsch-Duncker machinists' union had severed relations with Franz Wieber's Christians only months before the Congress over another strike-related argument. The Christians had insisted, moreover, that participants to the Congress pledge their adherence to the Christian *Weltanschauung*. This the liberals felt had nothing to do with trade union affairs.[141]

The ominous socio-political signs of the winter of 1913/14 and the leftward drift of many non–Social Democratic workers facilitated the Society's mission. Following the German Workers' Congress, Anton Erklenz had wanted to unite all liberal workers and clerks in another great congress, but the idea never came to fruition. There is excellent reason to believe that Francke convinced Erkelenz to cancel the congress and work for the unity of labor, not promote further divisions.[142] The frees were also warming to the idea of

140. Westarp, *Konservative Politik*, vol. 1, p. 403.
141. Franz Schmidt, leader of the Hirsch-Duncker miners, to Erkelenz, 22 January 1913, Erkelenz Papers 8, BA Koblenz; Flugschrift Nr. 57 des Gewerkvereins der Deutschen Maschinenbau- und Metallarbeiter, in *Ein zweifelhafter Bundesgenosse* (Berlin: Goedecke und Gallinek, 1913), pp. 4–5; *Der Gewerkverein*, no. 91, 12 November 1913; *Die Wacht*, no. 47, 22 November 1913.
142. Dr. Ludwig Heyde of *Soziale Praxis* to Erkelenz, 8 November, 29 November, 1 December, and 10 December 1913, Erkelenz Papers 8, BA Koblenz.

cooperating with their rivals. At an executive council session of the General Commission in mid-January 1914, the various union chairmen expressed interest in an active role within the Society for Social Reform.[143] The Leipzig Cartel was not mentioned, but the threat of a social reform rollback was the only explanation for this sudden interest in Berlepsch's creation. This trend became more obvious in late April when free, Hirsch-Duncker, Christian, and other labor leaders joined Ernst Francke in Berlin to make a public stand for trade union rights. The General Commission's *Correspondenzblatt* felt compelled to point out the importance of this unique occasion.

> Of great significance was the fact that representatives of the free, Hirsch-Duncker, and Christian trade unions, as well as clerks and technical employees, stood as one behind the viewpoint: decisive struggle against the measures now threatening to limit coalition rights and ban the posting of pickets. All these measures are a barrier to the labor movement, whose healthy growth is absolutely necessary. All the above representatives spoke out against the yellow movement and expressed the desire to have nothing to do with these employer foundings. The pleasant result to be observed from all this is that, even if many other differences of viewpoint between the above organizations still exist, all are thoroughly united in the fight for the basic economic rights of the workers and white-collar employees.[144]

The paper's observations were confirmed three weeks later at a mass rally in Berlin convened by the Society. Berlepsch, Posadowsky, Hitze, Stegerwald, and spokesmen for the frees, Hirsch-Dunckers, and white-collar unions were on hand to demand rapid introduction of far-reaching social reforms.[145]

This was probably the first time Stegerwald had appeared on a speakers' platform next to a Socialist to argue the same point. But the prospect was obviously displeasing to him. Speaking at Aschaffenburg in early May 1914, for instance, the general secretary declared that "the hour has come for us to swing over to the attack against the S.P.D. and the Socialist trade unions."[146] Like Behrens, he considered the need for a *Volk* movement of bourgeois forces more urgent than ever before. Opposition to the Leipzig Cartel could not be taken too far. This strategy, however, was rapidly losing adherents in the Christian camp. In June 1911 Franz Wieber, leader of the Christian metal workers, admitted that it was almost impossible for small unions such as his to

143. *Protokoll der Konferenz von Vertretern der Zentralverbandes-Vorstände*, 13–14 January 1914, DGB Haus Düsseldorf.
144. *Correspondenzblatt der Generalkommission der Gewerkschaften Deutschlands*, no. 18, 2 May 1914.
145. See the report of the *Correspondenzblatt*, no. 21, 23 May 1914.
146. Police chief of Bochum to the *Regierungspräsident*, 19 June 1914, Reg. Arnsberg I 1476, StA Münster.

continue the struggle against the frees. "The miners can keep up this fight because they're the same strength—but what about us? What can we possibly do against the half-million [Socialist metal workers]?"[147] Indeed Wieber had no choice but to follow the lead of the free trade unions. Angered by declining real wages and an adverse political situation, the Socialist metal workers waged 447 strikes with 55,000 strikers in 1911, 402 strikes with 46,000 strikers in 1912, and 336 strikes with 60,000 strikers in 1913.[148] Given the mood of Christian workers, unwillingness to strike may have led to the collapse of the 43,000-member union.

Even the Christian miners were ready by 1913 to discontinue the anti-Socialist struggle so dear to the general secretary of the *Gesamtverband*. In March the *Gewerkverein* called for a joint strike with the *Alter Verband* in the Wurm district and, simultaneously, cooperated with the Socialists in a miners' election at the Hercules pithead in Essen.[149] The union's fiascoes in the Ruhr and Saar the previous year had begun to have an effect on wage movement strategy. These initial changes were followed in August 1913 with the announcement of a complete abandonment of the counterproductive feud with the Social Democrats. The union's general assembly elected Hermann Vogelsang, an advocate of inter-union cooperation, as chairman, called for a "community of labor" with the *Alter Verband*, and raised dues to fortify its "fight fund" (*Kampffond*)[150] for the tough times ahead. After learning of these developments the *Regierungspräsident* of Münster notified Berlin that the state should "reckon with the probability that all organizations will fight in unison during the next miners' strike, as they did in 1905."[151] The Ministry of the Interior was alarmed enough by this news to scold *Gesamtverband* leaders in Cologne, who in turn "took steps"[152] against the *Gewerkverein* leadership. The action was unwise, for Vogelsang and his colleagues were better informed about what steps were necessary to keep the union abreast of radical currents in the labor world.

This became obvious in early 1914 when the district leader of the

147. Fritz Kraus of the executive committee of the Christian metal workers' union, to district leader K. E. Weinbrenner, 13 June 1911, StA Duisburg. Kraus quotes Wieber.

148. Karl Koszyk, "Die Metallarbeiter-Zeitung am Vorabend des ersten Weltkrieges Zur Geschichte des Gewerkschaftspresse," in Vetter, *Vom Sozialistengesetz zur Mitbestimmung*, p. 177.

149. Police chief of Essen to the *Regierungspräsident*, 31 March 1913, Reg. D. 42813, and *Regierungspräsident* Aachen to the minister of the interior, 13 December 1913, Red. D. 42809, HSA Düsseldorf.

150. *Regierungspräsident* Münster to the minister of the interior, 27 October 1913, HSA Düsseldorf.

151. *Ibid.*

152. Behrens relayed the information to Wahnschaffe in the Reich Chancellery in late February 1914. See the latter's notes of 28 February 1914, Reichskanzlei, Nr. 2271, Bl. 44, ZStA Potsdam.

Gewerkverein in Recklinghausen attempted to stem the flow of workers who had been leaving the union with a tough-sounding letter.

> The times will become harder for the miner. Tough struggles, even fights to the finish, stand before us. I am not at liberty to say more about it today—only this would I like to say to you, the members, in your interests and the interests of your family: Stay in the union so that in the near future you won't rue the hour that you quit.[153]

The police chief of Bochum investigated the matter and was able to determine that top union leaders were definitely not planning an immediate strike. The letter was probably a recruiting ploy by a local leader knowledgeable about the disillusionment which many members felt over the inactivity of their union. It is noteworthy, however, that *Gewerkverein* officials in Essen refused publicly to rebuke the author for fear of provoking further membership loss.[154] This catering to the radical temperament of the rank and file and many of the non-organized would have placed the union squarely on the side of a strike, if it came, and in direct opposition to Stegerwald, who might have opposed it as detrimental to his *Volk* movement.

It is questionable, on the other hand, how long the general secretary would have been able to ignore mass sentiment in his federation. As observed in Chapter 9, Christian trade unions in the *Gesamtverband* not only were involved in a crescendo of strike activity since 1907/8, but were also striking more and more frequently with the Socialist unions after 1907/8. Stegerwald was also under pressure to change course as a result of membership drain from the *Gesamtverband* to the General Commission. A *rapprochement* with Legien and the possibility of a strong alliance between the organizations may have allayed the economic fears of those in the weaker union. Stegerwald and Behrens, furthermore, were increasingly isolated among Christian trade union *leaders* at all levels as the war approached. The last locally organized mass rally against the S.P.D. was held in late summer 1913 in Eschweiler.[155] Thereafter rallies were directed against the Leipzig Cartel or the Catholic church. Christian labor journalists illustrated the same leftist sympathies. Not one negative word against the Socialists was written in the *Zentralblatt*, for instance, after August 1913. Similarly, the editor of the *Westdeutsche Arbeiter-Zeitung*, Joseph Joos, held out an olive branch to the free trade unions at the

153. The letter was printed in the *Bergarbeiterzeitung*, 7 March 1914 (clipping: Reg. D. 15939, HSA Düsseldorf).
154. Police chief of Bochum to the *Regierungspräsident*, 28 March 1914, Reg. Arnsberg I 1476, StA Münster.
155. *Regierungspräsident* in Aachen to the *Oberpräsident*, 10 October 1913, 403/9037, LHA Koblenz.

third German Workers' Congress in December 1913, and in succeeding weeks his paper twice advocated a counter-cartel of the left.[156] The examples of the Christian miners and metal workers discussed above provide further evidence that Christian labor was indeed drifting toward a cartel of this sort in 1913/14. It was only a matter of time before die-hard anti-Socialists in the *Gesamtverband* fell in line.

That two opposing coalitions were just beginning to coalesce in Germany is thus abundantly clear. On the right were the most powerful governments and bureaucracies in the empire, the Prussian bishops, the organizations of the Leipzig Cartel, the yellow trade unions, and a rightist grouping of deputies that extended into the Center and National Liberal parties. On the left were the free trade unions, the Hirsch-Dunckers, the Christians, the member organizations of the German Workers' Congress and the Society for Social Reform, the Reichstag Left, and a large number of deputies in other parties who sympathized with the labor movement. Whether these two loose groups or coalitions would have solidified, creating what some historians have referred to as a "bi-polar" political alignment,[157] is highly doubtful. Germany was too fragmented and torn between worker and patrician, Catholic and Protestant, and Prussian and non-Prussian to permit this type of political evolution. The trend was sufficiently noticeable, however, to give influential military men, conservative politicians, and some statesmen an added incentive to desire a short, victorious war, for such a conflict, it was felt, would not only rid Germany of its jealous foreign enemies, but also purge the nation of dissent, or at least distract the masses from their domestic demands. Despite the fact that the old order was still well entrenched, unshaken by the radicalization of organized labor, many German leaders perceived the need for a *Flucht nach vorn*. Herein lies the tragedy of the developments described in this chapter.

156. *Bericht über die Verhandlungen des dritten Deutschen Arbeiter-Kongresses*, pp. 45–70; *Westdeutsche Arbeiter-Zeitung*, no. 52, 27 December 1913, and no. 4, 24 January 1914.
157. James C. Hunt, "The Bourgeois Middle in German Politics, 1871–1933: Recent Literature," *Central European History*, vol. 11, no. 1 (March 1978), pp. 83–106.

12

Christian Labor and the Collapse of the Old Order

To most casual observers during the early days of August 1914, the polarization of the German body politic disappeared in a wave of patriotism and nationalist hysteria. A closer examination indicates, however, that the problem of widening division between Right and Left remained during the month of August, then grew markedly worse during the succeeding fall and winter.

Trends in the Conservative camp provide evidence in support of this point. Even before the war broke out, Party leader Ernst von Heydebrand remarked to Bethmann Hollweg that a victorious military conflict would strengthen the workers' loyalty to the "patriarchal order."[1] Feelings such as this were apparently widespread in Conservative circles, for in August the party discontinued its merger negotiations with the Christian Socials;[2] total victory, it appears, would enable the Right to gain electoral popularity at a far cheaper price. One can imagine the consternation of the Conservatives later that month, therefore, when rumors began to circulate that Bethmann was anxious for a peace treaty and an alliance with England after the defeat of France. What was worse, as soon as the war against monarchist Russia were successfully terminated, he allegedly wanted to introduce electoral reforms in Prussia to reward the loyalty of the S.P.D., which was supporting the war effort.[3] The desire to preserve

1. Quoted in Karl Dietrich Erdmann, *Kurt Riezler Tagebücher Aufsätze-Dokumente* (Göttingen: Vandenhoeck and Ruprecht, 1972), p. 183.
2. See the minutes of the Political Committee of the Christian-Social Party, 29–30 November 1914, and Mumm to Behrens, 3 October 1914, Mumm Papers 1056, ZStA Potsdam.
3. Rosesicke to Wangenheim, 28 August 1914, Kl. Erw. 230–1, BA Koblenz.

Germany's "patriarchal order" intact and fight on for total victory, especially against democratic England, induced the agrarians to initiate intrigues against the chancellor in the Kaiser's entourage that fall,[4] establish even closer ties to the organizations of the Leipzig Cartel, and prepare to unleash an "elemental upsurge from the masses"[5] should Bethmann continue his peaceful, reformist plans.

Heavy industry sympathized with these views. In fact for years Germany's iron and steel magnates had anxiously awaited the coming of war.[6] Increased profits from armaments production and, more importantly, the more efficient economies of scale to be derived from annexation of mineral-rich territory west of the Reich explained this anticipation. But, unlike Heydebrand in July, big business realized that modern warfare, even if victorious, would greatly increase the desire of working-class veterans for more internal freedoms. Hence an additional reason for annexations, as Alfred Hugenberg, a member of the board of directors at Krupp, explained to his fellow industrialists in October 1914:

> The consequences of the war will in themselves be unfavorable for the employers and industry in many ways. There can be no doubt that the capacity and willingness of the workers returning from the front to produce will suffer considerably when they are subordinated to factory discipline. One will probably have to count on a very increased sense of power on the part of the workers and labor unions, which will also find expression in increased demands on the employers and for legislation. It would therefore be well advised, in order to avoid internal difficulties, to distract the attention of the people and give phantasies room to play concerning the extension of German territory.[7]

Armed with this logic, big business circles joined the agrarian intrigue against Bethmann, warning that internal concessions should be forgotten and the question of war aims publicly debated. These efforts culminated in early 1915 with an extreme annexationist declaration by the German Farmers' Association, the Manufacturers' League, and the four member organizations of the Leipzig Cartel.[8]

4. Erdmann, *Kurt Riezler Tagebücher*, pp. 206–7, 211, 219; Erich Matthias and Susanne Miller, *Das Kriegstagebuch des Reichstagsabgeodneten Eduard David 1914 bis 1918* (Düsseldorf: Droste Verlag, 1966), p. 69.
5. Wangenheim to Roesicke, 31 August 1914, Kl. Erw. 230–1, BA Koblenz.
6. See Karl Bachem's notes of a conversation with heavy industrialists, 22 June 1908, Bachem Papers 367, HA Köln.
7. See the minutes of the subcommittee of the Commission of German Industry during the War, 7 November 1914, Stresemann Papers 139, AA Bonn; this translation is taken mostly from Feldman, *Army Industry and Labor*, p. 136.
8. Matthias and Miller, *Kriegstagebuch David*, p. 36; Erdmann, *Kurt Riezler Tagebuch*, p. 219; Hans W. Gatzke, *Germany's Drive to the West* (Baltimore, 1950), pp. 38–47.

A similar process of consolidation was underway among the interest groups of the Left. The threat to coalition freedoms, it will be remembered, had sparked protest demonstrations by Socialist and non-Socialist labor organizations in the spring of 1914. The coming of war in August, particularly the national loyalty exhibited by the free trade unions in backing the war, strengthened the bonds between the various labor groups. The patriotism of the frees could no longer be doubted, and the war had created a whole set of social and economic problems—food shortages, inflation, unemployment, etc.—which labor did not want "solved" in a one-sided manner by employers, agrarians, and the state. There was, furthermore, the desire to prepare for those struggles with big business that both capital and labor expected after the termination of hostilities.

At the forefront of the movement toward greater cooperation on the Left stood the free trade unions. Karl Legien and his followers were so anxious to strengthen the position of labor, in fact, that for the first time a general *rapprochement* with bourgeois reform circles was sought. The Social Democratic workers established closer ties to Hans Berlepsch and his associates in August 1914 by joining the so-called Free Commission of the Society for Social Reform. This *de facto* membership in the Society was followed by formal adherence a few years later. In September 1914 the General Commission also encouraged its members to work for municipal unemployment relief programs, an action which resulted in a number of joint petitions by local branches of the free, Hirsch-Duncker, and Christian trade unions. At the top, the frees cultivated a cordial relationship with Clemens von Delbrück and the reform-minded staff of the Reich Office of the Interior. In return for backing the war, terminating strikes, and suppressing old, doctrinaire feuds, the frees wanted far-reaching social legislation and suffrage reform in Prussia. The anticipated struggles after the war would be fought on more even terms.[9]

As far as can be determined, free trade union leaders did not contemplate merger with their Christian rivals as part of this *rapprochement*. Although many individual members may have warmed to the idea, memories of old disputes over taxes and tariffs were too fresh in the minds of General Commission leaders to permit amalgamation into a single organization.[10] A similar situation existed in Christian trade union circles. Here, however, a lengthy debate over the question of merger was forced on *Gesamtverband* leaders by

9. Theodor Leipart, *Carl Legien: Ein Gedenkbuch* (Berlin: Verlag des allgemeinen deutschen Gewerkschaftsbundes, 1929), p. 32; Paul Umbreit, *Die deutschen Gewerkschaften im Kriege* (Stuttgart: Deutsche Verlagsanstalt, 1928), pp. 60, 165; Matthias and Miller, *Kriegstagebuch David*, pp. 22–25, 64; Kautsky to Adler, 28 November 1914, printed in Adler, *Victor Adler Briefwechsel*, p. 605.

10. See Legien's remarks to Bethmann, discussed in the *Zentralblatt*, no. 16, 31 July 1916.

the Christian rank and file, most likely by the miners, wood workers, and metal workers. These unions had been drifting toward the frees during the previous year and were eager to cooperate with the Social Democratic organizations after war was declared. The Christian wood and metal workers had actually joined cartels with the frees during the first weeks of the war to increase wages and deliberate over social questions. As Franz Behrens recalled, with the Socialists defending the fatherland and pressing social and political problems to solve, many asked whether there was any further necessity for a Christian, patriotic countermovement.[11]

Behrens, Stegerwald, and other Christian labor leaders who had vehemently opposed the Social Democrats before the war replied that the old reasons for independence were still valid. The frees advocated the socialization of the means of production, which the Christian labor movement had rejected for over a generation as a radical, "unnatural" solution to the social problem. Nor could one assert that Social Democratic views on religion and the monarchy were compatible with Christian thinking on these matters. The question of war aims was also problematic. Christian trade union leaders opposed the extreme imperialism of the Leipzig Cartel as a crude attempt to divert the interests of the masses, but found the idea of a peace without any annexations dangerous to Germany's future security.[12]

The merger debate in the Christian camp, which was "very serious for a long time at the beginning of the war,"[13] was settled in favor of the anti-merger faction during the winter of 1914/15.[14] What evidence there is suggests that the growing opposition to the war within the S.P.D. was the determining factor. With the frees hard-pressed by the anti-war radicals around Karl Liebknecht and Rosa Luxemburg, a countervailing force such as the *Gesamtverband* was considered indispensable.[15]

The rejection of merger, however, did not halt the pre-war drift of the

11. Walter Neumann, *Die Gewerkschaften im Ruhrgebiet* (Cologne: Bund Verlag GmbH, 1915), pp. 158, 161, 171; Franz Behrens and *Geheimrat* Dr. Stieda, *Das neue Program der christlich-nationalen Arbeiterbewegung* (Leipzig: A Deichert'sche Verlagsbuchhandlung, 1918), pp. 18–19; also see the remarks of Franz Wieber and one "Herr Arens" from Berlin before the *Augustinusverein* on 18 February 1915, *Augustinus-Blatt*, no. 2, 1915, StBib MG.

12. Stegerwald to Trimborn, 11 September 1915, Marx Papers 222, HA Köln; Behrens and Stieda, *Das neue Programm*, pp. 19–34; Giesberts before a meeting of Center Party Leaders, n.d., Marx Papers 222, HA Köln; *Westdeutsche Arbeiter-Zeitung*, no. 27, 3 July 1915; executive council meeting of the *Volksverein*, 30 August 1915, Hohn Papers 15/2, 1915, StA MG.

13. Behrens and Stieda, *Das neue Programm*, p. 19.

14. The end of the debate was followed almost certainly by the first deliberations over the Christians' so-called new program, discussed below. According to Giesberts, the program had been debated for almost two years when finally completed in the early fall of 1916. Giesberts to Stegerwald, 15 September 1916, Giesberts Papers 43, Bl. 46, ZStA Potsdam.

15. See Joos's articles in *Deutsche Arbeit*, February and May 1916, pp. 106–9, 222–29; and the *Zentralblatt*, no. 17, 16 August 1915, and no. 8, 10 April 1916.

Christian labor movement to the Left. For even Stegerwald and Behrens were sufficiently impressed with the General Commission's support for the war effort, the threat of socio-political *Reaktion*, and the need to appease the Christian miners and metal workers to warm to Joseph Joos's idea of a "counter-cartel" of the Left. Thus in late December 1914, the Christian trade unions and most of the member organizations of the German Workers' Congress joined the frees, the Hirsch-Dunckers, the Polish trade unions, and numerous white-collar unions in the so-called Committee for Consumer Interests during the War. A bona fide pressure group, the Committee was organized on the local, district, and Reich level to protect the small man against the spiraling inflation of food costs. In February 1915 the Left drew closer together when the frees invited Hans von Berlepsch and Ernst Francke of the Society for Social Reform along with leaders of all the non-Socialist unions to a conference to discuss implementation of labor exchanges. A joint petition was submitted to Bethmann Hollweg in early March. It should also be noted that later that month the S.P.D., Progressives, National Liberals, and Center passed a Reichstag resolution demanding reform of the *Vereinsgesetz* of 1908. That free, Hirsch-Duncker, and Christian trade union pressure lay behind this move goes almost without saying.[16]

The conflicting, irreconcilable demands of Left and Right created a dilemma for the government. As Fritz Fischer has shown, Bethmann's views on annexations were not unlike those of heavy industry,[17] and the Kaiser, too, was undoubtedly in favor of expanding the Reich's holdings. But such views could not be discussed openly for fear of alienating the anti-imperialistic S.P.D. and endangering the acceptance of war credits by the Reichstag. Far more problematic was the related question of domestic reform. Bethmann rejected as nonsense Heydebrand's opinions about strengthening the patriarchal order,[18] while William II was in no mood to listen to the sniping of right-wing intriguers. The "red varnish" had chipped away from the S.P.D., he proclaimed proudly, leaving only "good German wood."[19] An ambitious, reformist course, on the other hand, was equally out of the question. Conservatism was too firmly entrenched in the country's bureaucracies, churches, and right-wing lobbies to contemplate radical change. William, Bethmann, and Delbrück were far too patriarchal in their own views, moreover, to accept the trade unions as *equal* social and political partners.

16. *Zentralblatt*, nos. 3, 6–7, for 1 February, 15 February, and 29 March 1915; Umbreit, *Die deutschen Gewerkschaften im Kriege*, pp. 96, 165.
17. Fritz Fischer, *Germany's Aims in the First World War* (New York: Norton, 1967), pp. 103–5.
18. Erdmann, *Kurt Riezler Tagebücher*, p. 183.
19. Matthias and Miller, *Kriegstagebuch David*, p. 38. David obtained the information from a Westphalian industrialist.

Given the lack of a clearly workable compromise program, the Reich government chose a policy of evasion and postponement. It would be made clear to the Right that "this war has to change many things, including the area of domestic policies,"[20] but the decision to proceed with reforms, Bethmann made quite clear, would depend upon the complete transformation of the S.P.D. into a patriotic, monarchical party willing to support "the system previously branded as militaristic."[21] As the S.P.D. changed its attitudes, those reforms which were deemed permissible would be announced, preferably at a time which "promised the most political effect."[22] The Right would be appeased by the cautious nature of the reforms and the anticipated annexation of European and colonial territories.

This policy was bankrupt from the beginning. Had the war ended as quickly as everyone in Germany anticipated in 1914, the empire would have faced a greater polarization between Right and Left than had existed before the July crisis. And, with slight chances of the S.P.D. meeting Bethmann's requirements concerning the "system,"[23] and the Right opposed to *any* reforms, a new domestic crisis, if not outright violence, appeared likely. A lengthy war promised to lead to the same end. As the hostilities dragged on, Bethmann's "diagonal," evasive policy only increased the danger of a deterioration of the empire's social and economic fabric as interest groups insisted that their demands be fulfilled immediately.

Stegerwald, Behrens, and others in the German Workers' Congress had no intention of relieving the pressure on Germany's governing system. As they saw it, the war had created an opportunity to remodel the prejudicial, restrictive society of the empire and allow the workers, for the first time, to cooperate with the other classes on a basis of social and political equality.[24] Not long after the question of merger with the frees was rejected, therefore, plans were drawn up for an ambitious legislative initiative after the war.

The new "program" was completed during the winter of 1915/16. Along with the impressive list of social reforms demanded by the Berlin Congress of December 1913, the organization would work for suffrage reform in Prussia, progressive tax legislation, a consumer-conscious tariff policy, government housing programs, and increased educational opportunities. As they had since the days of Ketteler, the Christians also defended the "natural" institution of

20. Fritz Klein *et. al.*, *Deutschland in Ersten Weltkrieg* (Berlin: Akademie-Verlag, 1968), vol. 1, pp. 423–24, quotes the Delbrück–Bethmann Hollweg correspondence of September 1914.
21. *Ibid.*
22. *Ibid.*
23. Matthias and Miller, *Kriegstagebuch David*, pp. 15, 22–25, 36, 44, 50.
24. Porsch to Marx, 27 December 1915, Galen to Marx, 4 January 1916, Marx Papers 222, HA Köln; *Zentralblatt*, nos. 3, 6, and 7 for 1 February, 15 and 29 March 1915, and especially no. 17, 16 August 1915.

private property. Similarly, Christian workers supported Germany's constitutional monarchy as part of the divinely sanctioned order which had led to the nation's greatness. The only change required was a new attitude by officials towards workers' social rights. In short, the Christian trade unions called for the *Volksmonarchie*, a conservative political concept with very progressive social implications.[25]

While formulation of this program was underway in 1915, other preparatory steps for political action were taken. One of the first was the establishment of a special political office in Berlin. The General Secretariat in Cologne was considered too far removed from the nation's capital to lobby effectively for reforms. Equally pressing was the need for a new political journal to represent non-Socialist workers. The *Zentralblatt* was printed every two weeks, but was too burdened with organizational matters and questions of social reform to respond to all aspect of political life. Meeting only three or four times a year, moreover, the executive committees of the *Gesamtverband* and the German Workers' Congress could not make timely responses to new developments. By the end of 1915, both the Berlin office and the new journal, *Deutsche Arbeit*, had come into being.[26]

These accomplishments added greatly to the political arsenal of Christian labor, but after the frustrating political experience of the pre-war days Christian trade union leaders knew they could not rely solely on the Berlin office and *Deutsche Arbeit*, much less the German Workers' Congress, to implement the new program. The united trade union organizations, especially the frees, would have to stand behind these demands if the inertia of German officialdom and the unresponsiveness of the bourgeois parties were to be overcome. For this reason, the Christians joined free and Hirsch-Duncker leaders in calling for a continuation of their loose cartel after the war.[27]

In so doing, *Gesamtverband* leaders like Stegerwald were fairly confident that their organization would not merely be pulled in tow by the larger and now more influential General Commission. Part of this optimism stemmed

25. The earliest draft of the program dates from 8 July 1916, Bachem Papers 960, HA Köln. The executive committee of the *Gesamtverband* had agreed on the essentials, however, by November 1915. See Giesberts to an associate in Essen, one "Prokurist Weber," 24 November 1915, Giesberts Papers 43, ZStA Potsdam.

26. Giesberts to Otto Müller, 29 June 1916, Giesberts Papers 43, ZStA Potsdam; police commissioner Gelsenkirchen to *Regierungspräsident* Münster, 31 August 1915, and accompanying memorandum from Christian trade union leaders concerning *Deutsche Arbeit*, Reg. Münster VII 47, StA Münster; *The Program and Organization of the Christian Trade Unions of Germany*, International Labor Office, Studies and Reports, Series A, no. 21 (Geneva, 1921), p. 9.

27. *Correspondenzblatt*, nos. 14 and 48, 3 April and 27 November 1915; the articles in the *Zentralblatt*, nos. 8 and 10, 12 April and 10 May 1915, are rather skeptical about permanent cooperation, but by the time the new program was complete, the paper had swung around. See no. 9, 25 April 1916.

from a membership drive which was planned for state enterprises and large agricultural undertakings—both considered poor recruiting grounds for the frees. With a more equal relationship in terms of size, the spirit of Social Democracy would not dominate the post-war alliance. It was also hoped that the fighting at the front would be an ally of the Christian cause. Removed from the suggestive effect of party propaganda and locked in combat alongside workers of the most disparate political and religious beliefs, Social Democratic soldiers would begin to reassess their political views. Once home, the party rank and file would no longer be as susceptible to the theoretical articles of S.P.D. intellectuals. So strong would be the aversion to Marxist dogma, ran this scenario, that S.P.D. veterans would demand a definitive break with socialistic thinking.[28]

These calculations were based on a fairly sound assessment of the situation. Although Christian trade union membership had sunk from its pre-war mark of 350,000 to a level of 162,000 by late 1915, the General Commission had slipped from 2,500,000 to a little over 1,000,000—the most favorable ratio from the Christian's standpoint since the turn of the century.[29] With their bold new program and planned membership drive, the Christians stood a fair chance of narrowing the gap. Nor was it unrealistic, however belated, to envision an upsurge of anti-Marxism in General Commission ranks. In February 1915, for instance, Karl Kautsky, the party's most prominent theoretician, complained that the "rightist" group around Eduard David and the trade union functionaries "thinks the moment ripe to purify the party of all Marxism."[30] That same month David observed that the General Commission, in its turn, "is *forced*, purely and simply, to support reasonable, reformist policies."[31] Preferring visible, practical benefits, what was left of the free trade union rank and file was clearly in no mood for scientific socialism. Whether or not the mingling of Christian and free trade unionists at the front would accelerate this tendency was not clear in 1915.

To ensure that the General Commission became permanently committed to a policy of anti-Marxism and *rapprochement* with bourgeois Germany, the Christians planned to exact the support of the bourgeois parties for the new legislative program of the German Workers' Congress and force these parties, or as many individual deputies as could be recruited, into a progressive

28. For the Christian membership drive, see Stegerwald's "Materialen betreffend Verbesserung und Verbreitung der Organisationsbasis für die christlichen Gewerkschaften," Giesberts Papers 84, ZStA Potsdam; for the anti-Marxist scenario, see *Deutsche Arbeit*, May 1916, pp. 222–29, and the *Zentralblatt*, no. 17, 16 August 1915, and nos. 8–9, 10 and 25 April 1916.

29. *The Program and Organization*, International Labor Office, p. 21; Varain, *Freie Gewerkschaften*, p. 96.

30. Kautsky to Adler, 11 February 1915, printed in Adler, *Victor Adler Briefwechsel*, p. 611.

31. Matthias and Miller, *Kriegstagebuch David*, p. 105.

parliamentary coalition.[32] Cooperation with the former class enemy would be more palatable for the frees if a clear break were made by the bourgeois parties from the conservative orientation of pre-war days. To prod the Center, Conservatives, and National Liberals in the desired direction, the new program of the Congress called for the formation of special worker caucuses for each party. The labor caucus would "keep in close contact with party and *Fraktion* officials, submit at any given time its wishes to them, and recruit friends within the party for these demands."[33] The strain on the existing party system, which had already been in evidence shortly before the war, would be greatly increased.

Nowhere was this more the case than within the Catholic Center Party. Tensions arising from the leftist orientation of the Christian trade unions approached crisis proportions, in fact, as the second year of the war began. At no less than six meetings between union, *Arbeiterverein, Augustinusverein, Volksverein,* and Center Party spokesmen in the fall and early winter of 1915/16, Stegerwald and other Catholic trade union functionaries insisted that the party commit itself to a sincere and ambitious policy of social, financial, and electoral reform.[34] The tone of these meetings is best illustrated by a memorandum which Stegerwald distributed to the executive committee of the *Gesamtverband* shortly after the sixth session with Center leaders in January 1916:

> No one who considers [political] relations in Germany wants a special Christian labor party. What is necessary is that the Center Party reassess and reorient its overall policies such that secret forces do not determine Center policy behind the scenes. Rather, the voters must have a greater role [in these matters]. In short, Catholic feudal and agrarian circles will have to choose whether they want to go along with this new policy or if it wouldn't be better to beat a retreat to where they belong—namely, in the straight-out Conservative camp. The old middle class, moreover, must be openly confronted. After such a revitalization of the Center Party, party-political union between modern wage workers, small and middle-sized farmers, and the reasonable portion of the middle class could well be possible.[35]

32. Giesberts to Müller, 23 and 28 December 1915, Giesberts Papers 43, ZStA Potsdam; Johann Becker before the *Augustinusverein*, 18 February 1915, StBib MG; Carl Bachem to Erzberger, 8 January 1916, and Carl Bachem to Eisele, 3 May 1916, Bachem Papers 854, HA Köln; *Deutsche Arbeit*, May 1916, pp. 222–29.
33. See the July 1916 draft of the unions' program, Bachem Papers 960, HA Köln.
34. Stegerwald to Trimborn, 11 September 1915, and Stegerwald to Lensing, 28 September 1916, Marx Papers 222, HA Köln; also see the protocol of a conference of Catholic *Arbeiterverein* members of western Germany, 29 October 1915, Bachem Papers 854, HA Köln.
35. Stegerwald's memorandum is quoted by Giesberts in a letter to the *Gesamtverband* executive committee, n.d., probably late December 1915, Giesberts Papers 94, ZStA Potsdam.

The message was quite clear. Either the Center turned left, forcing its right wing to comply or get out, or else the workers, as Joos put it, "will have to consider whether *we* should migrate from the grounds of the Party."[36]

The unions' demands received a sympathetic hearing from the Center's Christian-social wing. August Pieper and Heinrich Brauns of the *Volksverein*, for example, not only were in agreement with Christian labor's legislative demands, but also wanted to steer the Center into a center-left parliamentary coalition. Catholics would be able to cooperate closely with Protestants, thus eroding many of the old prejudices, the isolation often imposed on the party in pre-war days would be overcome, and the government would be less able to resist the Center's demands for repeal of anti-Catholic laws. The *Volksverein* was determined, however, to prevent class tensions from tearing apart the party. Mönchen-Gladbach's impressive apologetic apparatus would be employed to avoid what was regarded as the worst possible setback for the Catholic cause.[37]

Father Otto Müller, who by 1915 had replaced Pieper as the dynamic force behind the Catholic *Arbeitervereine* of western Germany, reacted in a similar fashion to the escalating union demands. However, unlike the *Volksverein*, which was willing to let the unions speak for themselves politically, Müller wanted to place himself at the head of the reform movement. "The reforms must come from below," he told a colleague in November 1915, "but you know very well what I mean by that . . . The people must act as if they discovered for themselves the things we say to them."[38] The prospect of Catholic workers cooperating on their own with Social Democrats in the more democratic environment anticipated after the war was obviously unnerving to Müller. The guiding, manipulative hand of priests would be indispensable.

This was the rationale for the actions taken by Müller after the stormy sixth meeting of union and middle-class Catholics in January 1916. He reactivated the Workers' Political Committee, which Stegerwald had ignored since the beginning of the war because of its previous ineffectiveness, assumed the duties of chairman, and gave a few trusted *Arbeiterverein* priests an advisory voice. Henceforth only the Committee would speak for Center workers in western Germany, but in accordance with the patriarchal thinking described above, a special subcommittee more easily controlled by Müller was given the

36. See Bachem's notes to the sixth meeting, 7 January 1916, Bachem Papers 854, HA Köln.
37. See Pieper before the *Augustinusverein*, 18 February 1915, *Augustinus-Blatt*, no. 2, February 1915, StBib MG; and Brauns before the executive committee of the *Volksverein*, 30 August 1915, Hohn Papers 15/2, 1915, StA MG; also see Pieper to Bernhard Letterhaus, 30 January 1933, Pieper Papers 36, StA Münster.
38. Müller to Walterbach, 16 November 1915, *Archiv der katholischen Arbeitnehmerbewegung*, vol. 1, KfZG Bonn; Müller in a conversation with Archbishop Hartmann, August 1918, quoted in the Müller Manuscript, p. 98, KAB Haus Köln.

responsibility for preparing all statements. The Catholic workers in southern and eastern Germany would also be represented by a committee of workers and priests chaired by Müller. The *Arbeitervereine* were to have a special political program of their own, moreover, while the new organ of the German Workers' Congress, *Deutsche Arbeit*, would be complemented by another journal, *Glaube und Arbeit*, published by the Catholic labor associations.[39] By making many of the same radical demands as the Christian trade unions, Müller felt he could maintain the workers' trust and preserve their allegiance to Church and Center.

In light of the anti-labor views held by Felix von Hartmann, archbishop of Cologne, the political orientation of the *Volksverein* and western *Arbeitervereine* was remarkably bold. A few months before the war broke out, Hartmann had decided to seek a modus vivendi with the Christian trade unions, "because we can't supress them, at least for the time being."[40] The tough talk of the Christian leaders after the war broke out, and their determination to work hand in hand with "atheists," apparently convinced the archbishop that the *Gesamtverband*'s following was now lost to the Christian cause, for in early 1915 be began to move cautiously in the direction of suppression. The statutes of the Catholic *Arbeitervereine* of his diocese were revised in a conservative direction. The passage calling for schooling of members about their political rights and duties as citizens—Müller's rather vague reference to the Workers' Political Committee—was stricken in favor of a reminder that political efforts by the associations were forbidden. The passage calling for close cooperation with the Christian trade unions, moreover, was conspicuously absent from the new by-laws. Simultaneously, Hartmann intensified pressure on the *Volksverein*. The question of Mönchen-Gladbach's alleged subsidization of the unions was raised again, and a subtle campaign initiated to reduce the influence of the *Volksverein* with other Catholic social organizations. For Pieper, Brauns, and Müller to support the unions' new program, therefore, was a gesture of defiance. Not wishing, perhaps, to risk an open feud during Germany's hour of need, Hartmann decided to ignore the challenge to his authority, "at least for the time being."[41]

39. See the Müller-Walterbach correspondence of November-December 1915, the protocols of meetings of the *Arbeiterverein* priests of the diocese of Cologne, 6 March 1916 and 25 March 1918, and the protocol of a meeting of the *Kartelverband* of Catholic *Arbeitervereine* of western, southern, and eastern Germany, 3–4 December 1916, *Archiv der katholischen Arbeitnehmerbewegung*, vol. 1, KfZG Bonn.

40. Hartmann to a fellow bishop, 31 March 1914, quoted in Brack, *Deutscher Episkopat und Gewerkschaftsstreit*, p. 345.

41. Schäfers to Hohn, 13 March 1915, Hohn Papers 15/2, 1915, StA MG; Generalvikar Kreuzwald to Müller, 13 February 1915, *Archiv der katholischen Arbeitnehmerbewegung*, vol 5, KfZG Bonn; Herbert Gottwald, "Volksverein," in Fricke *et. al.*, *Bürgerliche Partein*, vol. 2, p. 822; *Tremonia*, no. 267 (2), 27 September 1918.

With the major exception of Julius Bachem, who agreed with Stegerwald and therefore encouraged him,[42] Center Party leaders reacted to the defiance of Christian union circles with the same fatherly restraint shown by Hartmann. The patronizing speech delivered by Carl Bachem to the angry laborers at a private meeting in December 1915 is an excellent example. The workers and urban inhabitants, he began, already represented a majority of the Center's voters. It was thus fitting that the party advocated social reform and generally work for the equal rights of the lower classes. But the Center could never represent the interests of the workers to the point of ignoring the other classes which made up the party. The farmer and small businessman were just as crucial as the worker. Certain reforms, moreover, the Center could never support. In the matter of electoral reform, Bachem explained, a democratic suffrage would bring attacks on the Church like those in France before the war. "What is more important, democratization or maintenance of the Christian state?"[43] The latter was surely most important, he concluded, and the need to protect the Church would necessitate a close political relationship with religiously tolerant Conservatives. A turn to the Left was out of the question.

Bachem repeated his message in January, and again at a seventh meeting in July 1916. When Center leaders requested another session with the workers in August, however, Stegerwald refused to comply. The general secretary was convinced that the Center had never had its heart in social reform and had only pursued these policies for opportunistic, tactical reasons. Now the party was criticizing the workers for trying to monopolize the party, while in truth it was the upper classes which wielded exclusive influence in the *Fraktion*.[44] By late summer 1916, moreover, the executive board of the German Workers' Congress had approved a final draft of the new program, and the unions' general secretary, as he told Giesberts in September, had "no desire to attend further conferences [with the Center]. Now I will attempt to work for our goals by means of pressure from outside."[45]

It was apparently at this time that Stegerwald, Julius Bachem, and Heinrich Brauns began to discuss plans for a total reconstruction of the Center along interconfessional lines after the war. These changes would provide the party with the broad base necessary to survive in freer times. If developments in late 1918 provide any indication of Stegerwald's thinking two years earlier, he may

42. *Augustinus-Blatt*, no. 2, February 1915, StBib MG; Julius Bachem, *Der Krieg und die politischen Parteien* (M. Gladbach: Volksvereins-Druckerei, 1915), pp. 15–16.
43. See Bachem's speech notes of December 1915 in the Bachem Papers 960, HA Köln.
44. See Bachem's notation of Stegerwald's remarks of July 1916 in the Bachem Papers 960, HA Köln.
45. Stegerwald to Lensing, 28 September 1916, Marx Papers 222, HA Köln.

have been prepared to go much farther in this direction than the other two, perhaps to the point of forming an altogether new party around the German Workers' Congress and allied bourgeois reform circles. The reaction of the Center to the aforementioned "outside pressure," the degree to which Stegerwald was willing to tolerate Otto Müller's progressive paternalism, and the perceived dangers of such action to the unity of the Christian labor movement would determine what steps, if any, were taken.[46]

The Center was not the only party to come under increased pressure from Christian labor in 1915/16. As cited above, the unions had not given up hope that the Conservatives could also be maneuvered into a more progressive position. Most optimistic in this regard were Franz Behrens and his fellow Protestant workers in the Christian-Social Party. The discontinuation of merger talks with the Conservative Party in August 1914 had not dampened their spirits, for in November they prevailed upon Reinhard Mumm and other more skeptical Christian-Social leaders to reopen the negotiations. After Count Westarp of the Conservatives agreed to the idea, discussions began in December 1914.[47]

The talks continued intermittently for about a year. Given the illusions of most Conservatives concerning the social impact of annexations, it is not surprising that little was accomplished. For purposes of Reichstag committee participation, Mumm, Behrens, and Dr. Burckhardt, Christian-Social deputy from Dillenburg, were allowed to join the Conservative Reichstag *Fraktion*. Rather far-reaching electoral agreements which promised to aid both parties politically were also made. However, in the area of social reform, where the Conservatives were asked to make more significant concessions, no progress was registered. The Conservatives refused even to commit themselves to the "radical" Frankfurt demands of 1903, let alone the more ambitious program which Christian labor was formulating in 1915. The unions' desire to work closely with the free trade unions and moderate elements of the S.P.D. found an equally icy reception. All talk of a new attitude toward the state among the Social Democratic workers was rejected as naive. Unable to compromise on these issues, both sides called off the negotiations in late 1915. In what was

46. Eisele to the editorial staff of the *Kölnische Volkszeitung*, 27 September 1916, Bachem Papers 932, HA Köln; Julius Bachem, *Der Krieg und die politischen Parteien*, pp. 15–16; Hugo Stehkämper, "Julius Bachem," in Rudolf Morsey (ed.), *Zeitgeschichte in Lebensbildern aus dem deutschen Katholizismus des 20. Jahrhunderts* (Mainz: Matthias Grünewald-Verlag, 1973), vol. 1, p. 37; alse see the activities of Stegerwald discussed at the end of this chapter. That Stegerwald was not alone among Christian workers in desiring a revamped party system in 1916 is indicated by the August 1916 issue of *Deutsche Arbeit*, pp. 397–401.

47. See the correspondence between Behrens, Mumm, Westarp, and other Evangelical unionists, Mumm Papers 1056, and Westarp Papers 4, ZStA Potsdam.

obviously a related move, the Christian-Socials exited the Conservative *Fraktion* in January 1916.[48]

Occurring at a time when Stegerwald was having similar difficulties with the right wing of the Center, the Christian-Social failure to maneuver the Conservatives into the progressive coalition undoubtedly encouraged the general secretary to think more in terms of preparing to restructure the party system. One of the major reasons for founding *Deutsche Arbeit*, for instance, was to gain sympathy for the movement among intellectuals and academicians who had hitherto supported the Conservative Party.[49] Stegerwald's reference in December 1915 to the advisability of Catholic noblemen migrating "where they belong, namely, in the straight-out conservative camp," is a clear indication that he had less desire to attract the support of the Conservative Party as such. During the spring of 1916, moreover, Stegerwald wrote about the need for Behrens to act as "a bridge of understanding to reasonable conservative elements," which are "not one and the same with the Conservative Party of today."[50]

Just as the Center, therefore, the Conservatives were being threatened with an insurrection in party ranks inspired by Christian labor. Such actions, of course, were not without definite risks. The lessons of the tariff controversy of 1902 and the election of 1907 were that the parties of Imperial Germany might be able to withstand the strains of political warfare more successfully than the Christian trade union movement. Even more likely, given the volatility of the wartime situation, was the possibility that both might collapse. It was for this reason, no doubt, that Stegerwald was so reluctant to discuss his views openly.

The National Liberals were also plagued by the mutually exclusive demands of extreme groups within the party. While the progressive wing entrenched in the Reichstag *Fraktion* looked forward to a post-war period of democratization and social reform, the Prussian-industrialist branch of the party anticipated a reactionary, military rule based on the popularity that the seemingly victorious army had gained during the war. And, while the industrialists prepared to resist change by clamoring for annexations and attempting to unseat Bethmann, the Reich party tried desperately to ready itself for the anticipated era of greater freedoms.

48. Minutes of the executive council of the Christian-Social Party for 25 October, 4 December, and 8 December 1915, Mumm Papers 401, ZStA Potsdam; Mumm to Westarp, 9 November 1915, and Westarp to Mumm, 13 November 1915, Mumm Papers 1056, ZStA Potsdam; Mumm and Behrens to Westarp, 17 January 1916, Westarp Papers 13, ZStA Potsdam; Westarp to Linde, 19 November 1917, Westarp Papers 21, ZStA Potsdam; *Die Arbeit*, no. 5, 29 January 1916.

49. Police commissioner Gelsenkirchen to *Regierungspräsident* Münster with accompanying memorandum from Christian trade union leaders concerning *Deutsche Arbeit*, Reg. Münster VII 47, StA Münster.

50. See Stegerwald's memorandum of spring 1916 as cited above in note 28.

Thus in May 1916, after a winter of pressure from the Christian trade unions and other non-Socialist labor groups, the National Liberals created a special fifteen-man commission attached to the central executive board of the party. Representing organized factory workers, white-collar employees, civil servants, artisans, and peasants, the new commission would work with party leaders to influence local nominating committees during elections. At the commission's first meeting in June, moreover, party officials encouraged the body to write a political program and delineate its own sphere of activity within the party. Rather than lose the increasingly crucial support of Germany's lower and lower middle classes, National Liberal leaders had opted to give these groups a much greater voice. Like the opportunistic Father Müller of Mönchen-Gladbach, however, one suspects that party leaders wanted to control the pace of political events.[51]

That this reform was made in mid-1916, observed Georg Streiter, leader of the Christian trade unions of Berlin and one of four non-Socialist unionists on the new National Liberal commission, was "extraordinarily timely, as certain symptoms [exhibited] by the labor representatives of the Center and Christian-Social parties would seem to indicate."[52] Streiter was probably referring to the growing disillusionment of Stegerwald and Behrens with the Center and Conservative parties and the threat of similar troubles for the National Liberals. But however timely from the workers' standpoint, the decision to create the special commission had not solved the problem of maintaining unity for the National Liberals. If anything, the new body would only hasten the exodus of the party's heavy-industrial wing as the workers pressed the leadership leftwards. Considering what has already been said here about Christian labor's relationship with the Conservatives and Center, this may have been exactly what some leaders in the Christian camp desired.

It seems reasonably clear, therefore, that the Christian trade unions' attempt to form a parliamentary alignment into which the frees could fit comfortably had placed a considerable strain on the existing party system. This development was highly significant, for, assuming that the government proceeded to introduce liberal political reforms, which seemed more and more likely for Prussia, the parties would play a somewhat more important role in the political

51. Minutes of the executive council of the National Liberal Party, 21 May 1916, pp. 377, 592–93, R 45 I-2, BA Koblenz; Stresemann to Bassermann, 31 December 1914, Stresemann Papers 135, and the *Protokoll der 1. Sitzung des Beirates des Centralvorstandes der Nationalliberalen Partei*, 6 June 1916, Stresemann Papers 154, AA Bonn; for evidence that the Christian trade unions sought to interest the National Liberals in the unions' new program, see Giesberts to Stegerwald, 15 September 1916, and Giesberts to Müller, 3 November 1915, Giesberts Papers 43, ZStA Potsdam.

52. *Protokoll der 1. Sitzung des Beirates . . . der Nationalliberalen Partei*, 6 June 1916, Stresemann Papers 154, AA Bonn.

process than before the war. And parties as unstable as Germany's bourgeois *Fraktionen* would either be prone to splinter, with the attendant damage to parliamentary efficiency, or else succumb to the demands of extreme factions and interest groups. This situation could lead to bitter inter-party fighting, parliamentary stalemate, and the temptation for authoritarian groups of the Left or Right—perhaps a Reich government disenchanted with reform—to seize power. The exacerbated class tension caused by the First World War was rapidly limiting the possibility of stable political development in Germany.

Hoping to preserve the possibility of a sound political evolution, Bethmann and Delbrück cast aside earlier plans to wait for a *complete* transformation of the S.P.D. into a loyal, nationalistic party before proceeding with their much-discussed *Neuorientierung*. Rather, they chose to grant a few minor concessions to the united trade unions. Thus in April 1916, after months of intense ministerial infighting in Prussia, it was agreed to submit a bill to the Reichstag that would end the treatment of trade unions as political organizations under the *Vereinsgesetz* of 1908, an interpretation which had made it illegal for youths to join unions.[53] It was also decided to extend the rights of the newly worded law to rural laborers, a provision which the Christian trade unions, who hoped to make great membership gains in the countryside, had insisted upon.[54] Even more important from the worker's standpoint, William II announced in January 1916 that some changes would be made in the Prussian suffrage after the war. William and Bethmann hoped that these reforms would keep the workers in line during the war and, even more importantly, insure the long-term political stability of the empire.

> What does [the fulfillment of these minimal demands] mean [wrote Bethmann] next to the Bismarckian concession of universal suffrage before the war of 1866 and his liberal bills of the 1870s, what comparison is there to the upheaval which the Stein-Hardenberg reforms brought! Mass wars lead necessarily to the need to fulfill the political wishes of the broad lower strata of society. When this fulfillment has occurred at the right time and out of the free will of the ruler, it has always strengthened the monarch. The years after the Treaty of Tilsit and the era of 1866 and 1871 have taught us that.

The alternative, concluded Bethmann and William, would be a revolutionary situation like that of 1848.[55]

53. Clemens von Delbrück to the Prussian *Staatsministerium*, 29 November 1915, and 3 February 1916, and the minutes of the Prussian cabinet sessions of 4 December, 11 December, 24 February, and 11 April 1916, Reichskanzlei, Nr. 224, Bl. 218, 219, 243, 280, 347, Nr. 2244, Bl. 35, ZStA Potsdam.
54. See the talks between Delbrück, Giesberts, and Behrens, March 1916, Reichskanzlei 2244, Bl. 9–20, ZStA Potsdam.
55. Bethmann to Valentini, 6 May 1916, and Valentini to Bethmann, 8 May 1916, Reichskanzlei 2244, Bl. 69–73, ZStA Potsdam.

As indicated above, however, expedient reforms would not guarantee a healthy body politic unless the country's political parties and the interest groups behind them also made a break from the class tension–ridden past. And in the spring of 1916, as the history of the *Vereinsgesetz* amendment illustrates, there was no sign that this would be the case. The Conservatives were the most problematic in this respect. Any strengthening of the trade union movement in the cities was dubious enough, it was argued, given the lack of concern of these organizations for the employer's rights. But the spread of unionism to the large estates of eastern Germany, where the masses of rural workers were still relatively docile, was a direct threat to the state. Neither the Socialist nor the Christian rural unions could be trusted to refrain from stirring up trouble at harvest time, and this would undermine the nation's security during times of peace or war. Equipped with these arguments, the Conservatives intensified efforts to oust Bethmann Hollweg, while also trying to mobilize other parties of the center-right against the *Vereinsgesetz* amendment.[56]

Joining the Conservative campaign of obstruction were the Free Conservatives, the heavy-industrial wing of the National Liberals, and a handful of anti-Semites and independent agrarian deputies—the nucleus of the reactionary German National People's Party formed in late 1918. Karl Liebknecht, the future leader of the revolutionary Spartacists, rejected the idea of collaborating with the government and was prepared to exit the chamber with his five to ten followers in the S.P.D. With only the Progressives, the leftist National Liberals, the bulk of the S.P.D., and a few others behind Bethmann, the Center Party was once again in a position to determine the outcome.[57]

And the Catholics, not surprisingly, were sorely divided. Like the Conservatives, most of the noblemen in the *Fraktion* were eager to weaken the trade unions. A second faction of clerical deputies was afraid the law would radicalize Germany's youth and impair the religious programs of the Catholic Church. Yet another group of South German zealots around Gröber and Erzberger was ready to vote against the *Vereinsgesetz* amendment if the government refused to lift the remaining restrictions against the Jesuits. All three of these groups were angry that the government was openly courting the S.P.D., whom most bourgeois deputies in the party still did not trust. The trade unionists and a large number of urban deputies from the Rhineland were

56. See Delbrück's discussion with Gustav Roesicke of the *Bund der Landwirte*, March 1916, and the remarks of Bethmann and Prussian minister of agriculture Schorlemer-Lieser in the Prussian *Staatsministerium*, 24 February and 11 April 1916, Reichskanzlei, Nr. 2243, Bl. 347, Nr. 2244, Bl. 9–20, 35, ZStA Potsdam; also see Eisele to the editorial staff of the *Kölnische Volkszeitung*, 9 May 1916, Bachem Papers 983, HA Köln.

57. Matthias and Pikart, *Reichstag Fraktion der deutschen Sozialdemokratie*, vol. 2, pp. 195–97, 204–6; Reichstag Debates, Period 13, session 2 (5 June 1916), vol. 307, pp. 1513–15.

behind the bill, regarding it as the first tangible evidence of the chancellor's intentions, but could not muster a majority.[58]

In a desperate attempt to tip the scales in their favor, therefore, the unionists threatened to bolt the party unless the law was supported. Given the radical drift of the Christian trade unions, it seems clear that this was no bluff. The threat, however, only angered the right wing of the *Fraktion*, increasing the Right's desire for a showdown with Christian labor. For the first time in its history, the Center seemed unable to resolve its differences through compromise. As Pieper recalled years later, despite the best apologetic efforts of the *Volksverein*, the party was dying in 1916.[59]

External developments saved the 56-year-old party from collapse. While the Center's opposing wings battled one another in mid-May 1916, word came that Archbishop Hartmann had sent a special petition to the Kaiser, supposedly with the backing of the entire episcopate. Probably spurred on by the disgruntled Prussian minister of agriculture, Clemens von Schorlemer-Lieser,[60] Hartmann asked William to intervene at the last minute to save the country from the serious danger posed by the *Vereinsgesetz* bill. It would destroy the friendly relationship between landowners and rural workers, while also "abandoning adolescents prematurely to the dangers of trade union life with its impassioned wage and class struggles."[61] In the event that William ignored this appeal, the archbishop urged Center leader Peter Spahn to maneuver the party into an oppositionist stance.

The petition played right into the hands of the beleaguered Bethmann Hollweg. Still fairly optimistic about the outcome of the war and patriotism of German workers, the Kaiser agreed with his chancellor that reforms such as the *Vereinsgesetz* were a cheap price to pay for domestic tranquillity and the survival of the monarchy. This left Bethmann free to use the petition as a lever against the Center. The National Liberals, who could be expected to condemn the Center as a church-controlled party should it now opt to oppose the bill, were given a copy of Hartmann's petition. The Catholic trade union deputies were then informed of the ire of the National Liberals. The unionists now had an additional argument to use against the nobles and artisans of the right wing, for it was hard to dispute the fact that the Center would be in an awkward position if it bowed to the bishops and rejected the bill. Mixing the carrot with

58. See Eisele's reports to the editorial staff of the *Kölnische Volkszeitung*, of 9 May, 20 May, 26 May, and 7 June 1916, Bachem Papers 983, HA Köln.

59. Giesberts to Michaelis, 8 August 1917, Reichskanzlei 1391/4, Bl. 34, ZStA Potsdam; Eisele to the *Kölnische Volkszeitung*, 9 May and 26 May 1916, Bachem Papers 983, HA Köln; *Rheinische Zeitung*, no. 189, 21 August 1916; Pieper to Letterhaus, 30 January 1933, Pieper Papers 36, StA Münster.

60. Schorlemer-Lieser to Bishop Korum, 28 April 1916, Korum Papers 378, BisA Trier.

61. Prussian episcopate to William II, 10 May 1916, copy in Bachem Papers 983, HA Köln.

the stick, Bethmann let it be known in early June 1916 that the Bundesrat would agree to the repeal of existing anti-Jesuit legislation. These ploys swung the South German Centrists into the Christian labor camp. Twenty-three Catholic noblemen angrily left the chamber before the vote, but the *Vereinsgesetz* amendment passed easily.[62]

Archbishop Hartmann would not accept defeat. In June 1916 he drew up plans to forbid Catholic youths in his diocese to join trade unions. Learning of the intended action, Dr. Karl Walterbach, a close associate of Otto Müller in the Catholic *Arbeiterverein* movement, formed a delegation of like-minded labor priests and urged Hartmann to reconsider. The archbishop was probably told that such a stern measure would only encourage defiance among German adolescents who were already prone to reject authority as a result of the tremendous rigors and losses of a war that the established order condoned. In early July the angry bishop once again canceled plans for energetic confrontation with the union movement, but his patience was clearly wearing thin.[63]

Almost a stillborn child, Bethmann's *Neuorientierung* had nevertheless managed to survive. Much of historical significance can be learned from this experience. As emphasized above, the parties were not ready to function in a parliamentary or semi-parliamentary system. The S.P.D., the National Liberals, and the Center had split to one degree or another over the bill, and these fissures showed every sign of widening in the months that followed. Stegerwald was thinking about the possibility of forming a new party, and Liebknecht had similar thoughts. Since his party began to vote for war credits and cooperate with the government in August 1914, in fact, Liebknecht's secession was just a question of time, "for the struggle against the ruling system in general, and militarism in particular, had always been the factor assuring the internal integration of the party."[64] A considerable number of middle- and upper-class deputies on the Right, moreover, were prone to rely on obstructionist tactics rather than compromise. The first attempt to block reform had failed, but, as all die-hards, German conservatives were determined to prevent any *further* encroachment on their rights, privileges, and prerogatives. Perhaps most important of all, the *Vereinsgesetz* debate had shown how far the Reich government was from alleviating the general problem of political polarization in Germany. The Prussian Cabinet of Ministers met in four turbulent sessions during the winter of 1915/16 before Bethmann and Delbrück were able to exact an agreement on the bill. Once this diluted

62. Valentini to Bethmann, 8 May 1916, Reichskanzlei, Nr. 2244, Bl 73, ZStA Potsdam; Eisele to the *Kölnische Volkszeitung*, 20 May, 26 May, and 7 June 1916, Bachem Papers 983, HA Köln.
63. Walterbach to Müller, 11 July 1916, *Archiv der katholischen Arbeitnehmerbewegung*, vol. 5, KfZG Bonn.
64. Groh, *Negative Integration*, p. 727.

amendment was introduced, it met fierce resistance from a coalition of political and religious forces in and out of parliament possessing a deep suspicion and fear of labor independence. The victorious Left, on the other hand, considered the bill merely a first step with more symbolic than substantive value. What were the chances, one must ask, of avoiding a more serious crisis over the highly controversial and complex issue of Prussian suffrage reform? Though alive at birth, the government's new orientation faced the prospect of a very grim childhood.

From the workers' vantage point, the *Vereinsgesetz* controversy underscored the need for labor unity. Few believed the war would last another winter, which meant that laborers had to make final preparations to mold post-war Germany into the desired progressive form. Thus in August 1916 the leaders of the free, Christian, Hirsch-Duncker, and Polish trade unions issued a sharp denunciation of the "yellow" factory associations which employers were promoting with renewed vigor in an attempt to break organized labor.[65] That fall witnessed further cooperation during the debates over the special Auxiliary Service Bill requested by the new military team of Hindenburg and Ludendorff. Originally designed to subject workers to the authority of the army and employers for the duration of the war, the proposal was amended in Reichstag committee to provide workers with substantial, albeit temporary, codeterminational rights.[66] "The idea for all improvements in the law," wrote Giesberts, "stemmed from the trade unions."[67] Much to the dismay of all opponents of labor who realized the precedent-setting importance of such a bill to the unions once the war was over, Bethmann Hollweg agreed to the changes. The four major union organizations celebrated their "triumph" with a mass rally in Berlin in early December 1916.[68]

Inter-union collaboration continued during the following winter. In fact, a significant transition was made in the relations between the various organizations. Although organized labor had drawn continually closer together since 1914, this cooperation was still of an *ad hoc* or temporary nature, as was the case with the *Vereinsgesetz*, the Auxiliary Service Bill, and the Committee for Consumer Interests during the War. In January 1917, however, union leaders began to hold *regular* meetings to discuss common political action. These deliberations resulted in petitions and declarations concerning the need for a more effective agricultural policy, elimination of abuses under the Auxiliary Service Law, and the willingness of the unions to continue to support the war.

65. Umbreit, *Die deutschen Gewerkschaften im Kriege*, p. 166.
66. For a detailed discussion of the bill, see Gerald D. Feldman, *Army Industry and Labor in Germany 1914–1918* (Princeton, New Jersey: Princeton University Press, 1966), pp. 197–252.
67. Giesberts to Müller, 29 November, Giesberts Papers 43, Bl. 67, ZStA Potsdam.
68. *Zentralblatt*, nos. 25–26, 4 and 18 December 1916.

Concerning the transition from war to peace, the united labor organizations called for the participation of capital *and labor* in the maintenance of strict governmental control of production and trade. Yet another petition made it clear that in the long run the unions did not envision a complete return to the market economy. The unionists wanted compulsory formation of state-regulated, state-taxed cartels for much of German industry. Enhancing the regular nature of these inter-union ties, the free trade unions joined the Society for Social Reform in March 1917. Praised in theory for over a generation by all union leaders, but heretofore rejected in practice, labor unity was beginning to become a reality.[69]

This is not to say, of course, that relations in the union camp were frictionless. Karl Legien and free trade union leaders advocated a more far-reaching program of socialized industry and were not as comfortable with monarchial institutions as the Christians. These differences kept alive the suspicions and mutual distrust which had characterized union relations before the war. Under tremendous pressure from the Liebknecht-Luxemburg faction, which was winning adherents among free trade unionists who felt the General Commission was sacrificing Social Democratic principles by cooperating with suspect bourgeois groups, the frees were also prone to boast publicly about their allegedly dominant influence in the union cartel. Christian leaders were naturally very sensitive to such statements and responded with an intense promotion of the new program of the German Workers' Congress, which, it will be recalled, was designed to provide the Christians with at least an equal position in the union camp. The arrogance of the frees, in fact, gave rise to a vocal minority of *Gesamtverband* leaders around Johannes Giesberts who wanted to break the pattern of ever-closer ties to the General Commission. Unlike the radical minority in the Social Democratic organization, Giesberts did not want to revert to the counterproductive hostility of prewar days, nor did he want to alienate the frees, thus endangering their willingness to cooperate with bourgeois Germany. He was primarily concerned with maintaining the distinctive identity of the *Gesamtverband*, an identity he felt Stegerwald would unwittingly ruin with concessions to the Social Democrats.[70]

69. Giesberts to Müller, 27 January 1917, and Giesberts to Stegerwald, 19 March 1917, Giesberts Papers 43, Bl. 90, ZStA Potsdam; "Forderungen der deutschen Gewerkschaften für die Umstellung der deutschen Wirtschaft nach dem Kriege," 30 June 1917, printed in Umbreit, *Die deutschen Gewerkschaften im Kriege*, pp. 263–73; *Zentralblatt*, nos. 3, 6, and 7, for 29 January, 12 March, and 26 March 1917, Reichskanzlei, Nr. 2272, Bl. 22, ZStA Potsdam; Leipart, *Karl Legien*, p. 32.

70. Brauer to Giesberts, 13 March 1917, and Brauer to Behrens, 4 April 1917, Kl. Erw. 461-6 (Otte Papers), BA Koblenz; Giesberts to Müller, 27 January and 10 March 1917, and Giesberts to Stegerwald, 19 March 1917, Giesberts Papers 43, Bl. 90, 100, 102, ZStA Potsdam; Giesberts before a meeting of Center Party leaders, n.d. (WWI), Marx Papers 222, HA Köln.

Giesberts and his followers were unsuccessful for a number of reasons. As in August 1914, there were tremendous pressures from the rank and file in the Christian camp against any loosening of the unions' alliance. The miners, metal workers, and wood workers had sat together with the frees in local wage cartels since the beginning of the war and had no intention of weakening labor's position vis-à-vis the employers. Christian workers, moreover, were in a very "proletarian" mood in January and February 1917. Harsh winter weather, a severe food shortage, and low coal rations for civilian use convinced most Christian laborers that they should operate in the closest possible manner with other workers to improve the lot of the lower classes.[71]

The anti-Socialist minority around Giesberts was also unable to prevail against the arguments of Stegerwald, Joos, and *Zentralblatt* editor Theodor Brauer concerning ongoing developments within the S.P.D. Throughout 1916 the free trade unions had placed demands upon Social Democratic leaders to continue to support the war effort in return for the reforms Bethmann seemed willing to implement. Legien and his associates insisted that the doctrinaire, orthodox Marxists around Liebknecht be displined or forced to leave. If not, the unions threatened to form their own party. By early 1917 the Liebknecht-Luxemburg faction and the so-called moderates around Hugo Hasse were no longer able to tolerate the "rightist" course of the unions and the majority of the S.P.D. These two groups seceded from the S.P.D. in March to form the Independent Socialist Party.[72] To break with the frees now, argued Stegerwald and the others, would be outright folly, for here was an opportunity which *Gesamtverband* leaders had eagerly anticipated since the turn of the century.

> The free trade unions can systematically take up their efforts for effective social reform without having to fear a hindrance of their policies every minute by radical intriguers who strive for a complete social upheaval. The other trade union groups can now cooperate with the Socialist organizations in many areas of practical politics where earlier such cooperation was not possible. The lead weight of radicalism, the greatest enemy of gradual, pragmatic politics, falls away from the mass of organized German workers.[73]

The frees would still have to compete with the Independent Socialists, but this reality made it even more essential that the influence of the Christian trade unions be felt in the union cartel. In return for certain concessions to the frees in the area of nationalizing industry, Stegerwald and his followers felt the

71. Giesberts to Müller, 22 January 1917, Giesberts Papers 38, Bl. 1, and Kloft to Giesberts, 17 February 1917, Giesberts Papers 64, Bl. 1, ZStA Potsdam.
72. Matthias and Miller, *Kriegstagebuch David*, pp. 152, 157; Kautsky to Adler, 7 August 1916, and 28 February 1917, reprinted in Adler, *Victor Adler Briefwechsel*, pp. 630, 635.
73. *Zentralblatt*, no. 3, 29 January 1917; also see Joos's articles in *Deutsche Arbeit*, January and April 1917, pp. 34–35, 186–88.

Gesamtverband could elicit free trade union backing for the essential aspects of the Christians' newly formulated program.[74]

Stegerwald's strategy was not an unrealistic one.[75] To be sure, the General Commission was exacting some tribute from the Christian trade unions. The petition of the united unions concerning the agricultural crisis was much more aggressively formulated than Stegerwald had wanted, and the whole concept of compulsory cartelization of industry by the state for tax purposes ran counter to Christian thinking on private property. But the Christian general secretary could point to important instances where his ideology had prevailed. The cartelization paper, for instance, included far-reaching demands for labor codetermination in industry. The unions asked that labor be given a legally specified number of representatives to participate in the management (*Verwaltung*) of each cartel.

> Our demand has significance in principle, but finds its justification in the heavy importance which the cartel will represent in the life of the workers. With participation in management through suitable representatives who are familiar with the details of practical relations in the cartelized industries, the workers will be able to exert a certain corrective influence in their own favor. That is true for questions that are directly or indirectly related to labor relations, but also for the setting of prices, which affects the workers as consumers. The fulfillment of our demand would also introduce an element of social harmony which must not be underestimated.[76]

For Social Democrats like Legien who had stated eight years earlier that social harmony was impossible unless workers alone controlled the means of production, this was a significant concession. Illustrating further desire to compromise—and admitting the tremendous practical benefits to be gained from *Mitbestimmung*—the frees agreed later in 1917 to support the longstanding Christian desire for management-labor chambers (as opposed to *Arbeiterkammer*).[77] Although not altogether unwarranted, therefore, Giesberts's concerns about a Socialist takeover of the *Gesamtverband* were surely exaggerated.

Stegerwald should also be given credit for realizing that the late winter and spring of 1917 was politically a very propitious time to concentrate the efforts of all organized labor groups in Germany. Indeed, under the impact of the harsh winter, the revolutionary upheaval in tsarist Russia, and a concomitant

74. Adam Stegerwald, *Arbeiter-Interesse und Friedensziele* (Cologne: Christlicher Gewerkschaftsverlag, 1917), *passim*; *Zentralblatt*, nos. 9, 11–13, for 23 April, 21 May, 4 and 18 June 1917.
75. For this paragraph, see the sources cited above in notes 69 and 70.
76. The union's petition is printed in *Zentralblatt*, no. 7, 26 March 1917.
77. Behrens to Brauer, 24 August 1917, and Brauer to Behrens, 17 September 1917, Kl Erw. 461–6 (Otte Papers), BA Koblenz.

wave of wildcat strikes in Germany, a worried Bethmann was trying against fierce resistance on the Right to increase the pace of internal reform. Thus without the Bundesrat or the Prussian ministers being consulted, word was passed to press and parliamentary circles in early April that the chancellor wanted to abandon the remaining anti-Jesuit legislation, introduce management-labor chambers, and reform the commercial code to strengthen the position of trade unions. The Kaiser made the most significant announcement on Easter Day. *After the war*, elections in Germany's largest state would be direct and secret. There was no more room, he stated, for a purely class suffrage. Although the Kaiser and the army obviously favored some form of plural, that is, *unequal*, voting system, the speech was heralded in the Christian camp as the first bloom of liberalization in Germany. As stated above, however, tough struggles against the Conservatives and most likely the Center were almost inevitable, even to pass a compromise bill. Thus Stegerwald and his cohorts felt they had added reason to join hands with the frees.[78]

Giesberts appreciated the need to reform the suffrage, but felt the Christians should break with the frees on this issue in order to avoid another damaging clash in Center ranks. Since 1915 the dedicated Centrist deputy from Essen had watched with dismay as the Christian trade unions, dominated by the intransigent Stegerwald, drifted closer and closer to the free trade unions and, consequently, to the point of breaking with the party. By late 1916 the first of the so-called worker caucuses described in the new program of the German Workers' Congress had been created by disgruntled rank and file unionists in western Germany. Ostensibly part of the web of Center Party organizations, these caucuses were really external pressure groups which functioned like a separate party. Should the Center join the Conservatives in blocking suffrage reform, or even try to avoid the issue with ambiguous resolutions, Giesberts feared the party would be torn asunder by Stegerwald and the vengeful workers.[79] Only the Social Democrats stood to gain from the destruction of their one great rival.

Determined to preserve his party, Giesberts urged party leaders to accept only meaningful reform proposals put forward by the government, then convinced Father Otto Müller to arrange a meeting in early February 1917 with Stegerwald, Joos, and other leaders of the recently revitalized Workers' Political Committee of the Center Party. At the session, Giesberts urged his col-

78. Erdmann, *Kurt Riezler Tagebücher*, pp. 378, 402, 407, 419–24; Eisele to the *Kölnische Volkszeitung*, 3 and 13 April 1917, Bachem Papers 940, HA Köln.
79. Giesberts to Müller, 22 May, 23 December, and 28 December 1915, and Giesberts to Weber, 24 November 1915, Giesberts Papers 43, Bl. 16–20, and Giesberts to the executive committee of the *Gesamtverband*, n.d. (probably late 1915), Giesberts Papers 94, Bl. 36, and Giesberts to Müller, 22 January 1917, Giesberts Papers 38, Bl. 1, ZStA Potsdam; *Westdeutsche Arbeiter-Zeitung*, no. 5, 4 February 1917, and no. 37, 15 September 1918.

leagues to adopt a flexible attitude toward the moderate reforms being considered by Prussian ministers and party politicians in Berlin, even to the point of accepting a plural suffrage based on age, education, or family status. His arguments appealed to *Arbeiterverein* colleagues Joseph Joos and Joseph Gronowski, but Stegerwald, Brauer, and representatives of the Christian miners and metal workers were unmoved. No position at all would be better than one which advocated something less than the Reichstag suffrage for Prussia.[80] Compromise would be not only suicidal for the Christian trade unions, which were fighting desperately to overtake the frees, but also humiliating. What Catholic worker did not feel just as much outrage over the three-class suffrage as his Social Democratic counterpart?

Giesberts's campaign of moderation crumbled completely during the following weeks. Driven forward by Müller, who decided to place himself at the head of the drive for electoral reform and thereby preserve some measure of control over the irate rank and file, the Workers' Political Committee inundated Center leaders with ambitious suffrage resolutions. Despite the Kaiser's Easter message, the Committee continued throughout April 1917 to press its demand for universal, direct, secret, and equal voting rights in Prussia. Publicly, Center spokesman equivocated, insisting the party would stay abreast of political currents, while also depicting the government's plural voting proposals as a definite improvement.[81] Privately, however, Catholic conservatives like Carl Bachem damned the workers and their mentors in Mönchen-Gladbach for "playing into the hands of the Social Democrats."[82]

To Stegerwald, the entire episode reemphasized the futility of working within the framework of the Center. Thus in early May 1917 he bypassed the Workers' Political Committee and the troublesome Müller and chose the more independent central committee of the German Workers' Congress as a platform to repeat his now-familiar political stratagem: close cooperation with the free trade unions to ensure the attainment of a progressive, popular monarchy after the war. The Center, and the nation, had to be dragged to the Left.[83]

The month of July 1917 brought this goal closer to realization. Under continuing pressure to relieve the political tension in Germany and thereby

80. Giesberts to Müller, 22 January 1917, Giesberts Papers 38, Bl. 1, and Giesberts to Müller, 27 January 1917, Bl. 90, ZStA Potsdam; Joos to Gronowski, 10 July 1918, and the Protocol of the Committee of *Arbeiterverein* Priests for the Archdiocese of Cologne, 13 March 1917, *Archiv der katholischen Arbeitnehmerbewegung*, vol. 5, KfZG Bonn; also see drafts of articles by Giesberts on the suffrage question dating from this time, Giesberts Papers 38, Bl. 4 and 8, ZStA Potsdam.

81. Müller Manuscript, p. 97, KAB Haus Köln; *Westdeutsche Arbeiter-Zeitung*, nos. 16, 18, and 21, for 22 April, 6 May, and 27 May 1917; Protocol of the Central Committee of the Rhenish Center Party, 19 April 1917, Marx Papers 222, HA Köln; *Augustinus-Blatt*, no. 3, March 1917, StBib MG.

82. Carl Bachem to Eisele, 4 May 1917, Bachem Papers 940, HA Köln.

83. Stegerwald, *Arbeiter-Interesse und Friedensziele, passim.*

preserve the monarchy, the Prussian government announced that a bill guaranteeing equal suffrage would be introduced in the next session of the Landtag. A few days later, the Reichstag passed its famous peace resolution. "The Reichstag strives for a peace of understanding and the permanent reconciliation of peoples. Forced territorial acquisitions and political, economic, and financial oppressions are irreconcilable with such a peace."[84] Like the concession of suffrage reform *during the war*, the peace resolution was primarily an attempt to prevent the lower classes from deserting the war effort. If the masses knew they were fighting a just, defensive struggle, not an imperialistic war of conquest as advocated by right-wing circles in Germany, the will to fight would not be undermined.[85] Occurring within the space of a week, these events came as a shock to conservatives in Germany. The intricate strategy of social imperialism had been dealt a solid blow.

The Christian trade unions reacted to these changes with less enthusiasm than might have been expected. There was no disagreement with the general motivation behind the peace resolution and it was defended both publicly and privately. With the exception of the faction around Giesberts, there was also renewed faith in the strategy of cooperation with the free trade unions. For it had been primarily the threat of losing General Commission and Majority S.P.D. support for the war effort that had forced the government to place suffrage on the agenda for the fall session in Prussia.[86] But the momentous events of July 1917 gave rise to grave concerns in the Christian camp too. For one thing, Bethmann Hollweg had fallen prey to the numerous intrigues around him shortly after the suffrage announcement, and the commitment of his successor (Georg Michaelis) to social reforms like management-labor chambers, which were being drawn up by subordinates in the Reich Office of the Interior, was not known. Secondly, there were worries that the specific wording of the peace resolution would severly limit the bargaining power of the German delegation at a peace conference, thus allowing other powers to make greater gains and perhaps cripple the future economic growth of the empire. And without growth, goals such as higher wages, contributory insurance programs, progressive taxes, and other social reforms designed to re-

84. Epstein, *Matthias Erzberger*, p. 202.
85. See Erzberger's memorandum of 15 July 1917, Erzberger Papers 18, BA Koblenz; Johannes Giesberts, "Zur Klarstellung der parlamentarischen Kriegszielaktion," *Düsseldorfer Tageblatt*, 14 July 1917; Adam Stegerwald, "Entscheidungsstunden," *Zentralblatt*, no. 16, 30 July 1917; and the analysis of Mendershausen, "German Political Catholicism," chapter 8.
86. See the Protocol of the Diocesan Committee of the Catholic *Arbeitervereine* of Cologne, 11 September 1917, Nr. 651, Münsterarchiv Essen; also see the articles by Giesberts and Stegerwald cited in note 85; J. K. Vietar to Mumm, 14 September 1917, Mumm Papers 1056, ZStA Potsdam; rough draft of a letter from the executive committee of the *Gesamtverband* to Giesberts, July 1918, Kl. Erw. 461-6 (Otte Papers), BA Koblenz; notation by Carl Bachem of 3 August 1917, Bachem Papers 854, HA Köln; *Augustinus-Blatt*, no. 7, July 1917, StBib MG.

distribute wealth and power would be impossible. Finally, Christian labor leaders were upset by the desire of Matthias Erzberger and other spokesmen of the parliamentary Left to move in the direction of British-style parliamentarism. At a time when the German empire was locked in a deadly struggle with the parliamentary monarchy of England it seemed somehow unpatriotic to want to strip the Kaiser of most of his constitutional powers and implement rule by inefficient Reichstag parties which rarely agreed upon anything. More importantly, Christian laborers suspected that the Progressives, the leftist National Liberals, and the "democratic" wing of the Center were only interested in constitutional changes. Once in power these middle-class democrats would pull the ladder up behind them and ignore the more crucial issue of social reform as British, American, and French examples from the nineteenth century demonstrated.[87] In the last analysis, then, it was the prospect of losing social-legislative momentum that worried the Christians in the summer of 1917.

The political activity of Christian labor in the late summer and early fall of that year reflected the concerns described in the preceding paragraph. In numerous speeches, articles, petitions, and private meetings with top government and army leaders, Christian trade unionists emphasized the necessity of social legislation and a moderate peace settlement that would allow Germany to continue the rapid industrial growth of pre-war decades. Erzberger was rebuked publicly, and the concept of parliamentarism branded as un-German. A fourth German Workers' Congress was held in late October to underscore this socially progressive, albeit constitutionally conservative, course. The Congress also served the ancillary purpose of accentuating the Christians' program of 1916 and strengthening the *Gesamtverband* in its muffled rivalry with the General Commission. Neither parliamentarism nor socialism would have a place in the *Volksmonarchie*.[88]

87. See the articles cited by Giesberts and Stegerwald in note 85; Mumm to Franz Herzberg, 20 February 1918; Mumm Papers 1056, ZStA Potsdam; Giesberts before officials of the Reich Chancellery, 24 September 1917, Reichskanzlei, Nr. 1843, ZStA Potsdam; *Westdeutsche Arbeiter-Zeitung*, nos. 30 and 34, for 29 July and 26 August 1917.

88. Giesberts before officials of the Reich Chancellery, 24 September 1917, Reichskanzlei, Nr. 1843, *Oberpräsident* Rheinbaben to von Graevenitz, 21 September 1917, Reichskanzlei, Nr. 1391/3, and Behrens to Michaelis, 9 October 1917, Reichskanzlei, Nr. 534, ZStA Potsdam; *Sitzung des Zentralvorstandes der Nationalliberalen Partei*, 23 September 1917, R 45/I-3, BA Koblenz; *Zentralblatt*, nos. 18, 19, 22, for 27 August, 10 September, and 22 October 1917; Behrens and Stegerwald to the Central Committee of the German Workers' Congress, 21 August 1917, Giesberts Papers 43, ZStA Potsdam; *Düsseldorfer Tageblatt*, no. 266, 26 September 1917; Erich von Ludendorff, *Urkunden der obersten Heeresleitung über ihre Tätigkeit 1916–18* (Berlin: Ernst Siegfried Mittler and Sohn, 1920), pp. 94–97; also see the notes of *Geheimrat* Seifart of the Reich Ministry of the Economy, December 1917, Reichswirtschaftsministerium, Nr. 2013, Bl. 103–4, ZStA Potsdam.

The peace resolution and the suffrage decree, meanwhile, had led to a further deterioration of relations between Right and Left in Germany. Encouraged by others at Supreme Army Headquarters, the Leipzig Cartel and a wide assortment of interest groups committed to foreign expansion for domestic reasons formed the so-called Party of the Fatherland (*Vaterlandspartei*) in September 1917. Although this supraparty organization has not found a modern-day historian, the general characteristics of its activity are well known. As army censors turned their heads, the new party flooded newspapers and journals with pan-German literature of the most extreme form. Victory and empire were of overridding importance, and the Bismarckian order that was able to produce these triumphs, the nation was told, should not be altered one iota. Illustrating the tremendous appeal of these arguments, well over a million Germans had joined the *Vaterlandspartei* by spring 1918.[89]

Under the weight of this proto-fascist creation, the structure of the old party system began to crumble. The Catholic community was so badly divided over the *Vaterlandspartei*, for instance, that Center leaders simply had to avoid the issue for fear of splitting their party.[90] In the Conservative, Free Conservative, and right-wing National Liberal camp, moreover, preparations were underway by fall 1917 to form an altogether new political party once victory was attained and the *Vaterlandspartei* had completed its work. Led by Count Westarp, Baron Klitzing, and Prince Donnersmarck of the Conservatives, Wilhelm Hirsch of the Prussian National Liberals, and others from Rhenish and Silesian industrial circles, the party would strive to retain the predominantly middle-class backing of its wartime predecessor.[91] But the thought of eliciting added support from the non-Socialist unions—a plan which still intrigued certain members of the *Bund der Landwirte*[92]—was considered hopeless.

> Whether or not we should also approach the workers—to the extent that they stand on monarchical footing—will have to be reserved for a later consideration. For the most part, I wouldn't promise much from it. As much as I'm convinced that anti-monarchical views are only held by a relatively small part of the working class, that is, when you look into the hearts of these people and are able to make sense out of their sorely confused political ideas, still one shouldn t forget on the other hand that the opposition between rich and poor is used more and more these days as an inflammatory means of

89. For general discussions of the *Vaterlandspartei*, see Stegmann, *Die Erben Bismarcks*, pp. 497–519; and Gordon Craig, *Germany 1866–1945* (New York: Oxford University Press, 1978), pp. 388–89.
90. Mendershausen, "German Political Catholicism," p. 348.
91. Klitzing to Westarp, 19 September 1917, Westarp Papers, Nr. 20, Bl. 158, ZStA Potsdam.
92. Franz Behrens to Theodor Brauer, 20 September 1916, Kl. Erw. 461–6 (Otte Papers), BA Koblenz.

> class struggle, and that compared to this conflict, which dominates everything, other political outlooks in the main pale in significance.[93]

Employer-controlled, "yellow" labor associations were regarded by most conservatives as much safer than the suspect Christian and Hirsch-Duncker unions, but for some industrialists, even these groups could no longer be trusted. Two of the most powerful Silesian businessmen, Privy Councilors Hilger and Williger, withdrew their support from the yellows that year, claiming that "all worker organizations must eventually turn on their employers."[94] Statements such as these illustrate well the extent to which the upper classes had hardened in their long-held, fatalistic view that struggle between classes was inevitable. The possibility of stable political development in Germany, it must be emphasized once again, was a slim one.

The *Vaterlandspartei* was soon joined by another supraparty group, the People's League for Freedom and Fatherland (*Volksbund für Freiheit und Vaterland*). Initiated by liberal intellectuals like Friedrich Meinecke and Ludwig Heyde, the *Volksbund* also wanted to impress the masses with the need for increased sacrifices on the way to victory. But the whole approach was different. Internal reforms, not annexations, were the only incentives which would convince the laboring masses to fight on. The workers had to realize that it was in *their* interests, not just the government's, to win the war, for defeat would surely eliminate the gains made by the labor movement. Meinecke and the others encouraged the trade unions to join as corporative members in the hope that these organizations would have the desired effect upon the small man.[95]

The Christian trade unions joined the Hirsh-Dunckers at the founding assembly in mid-November 1917. *Gesamtverband* leaders like Giesberts and Stegerwald saw the progressive federation as the only effective means to combat the radical *Vaterlandspartei*, whose goals of internal political stagnation and European hegemony were considered disastrous. If the Right were successful, the labor movement would be shackled and the delicate fabric of Europe's interdependent economy ruined. The workers would be socially and politically disenfranchised in a German-dominated Europe that was less productive and dynamic than it had been in 1914. Before the *Vaterlandspartei* obtained its goals, however, an alternative scenario might unfold: the workers

93. Klitzing to Westarp, n.d. (summer 1917), Westarp Papers, Nr. 20, Bl. 108, ZStA Potsdam; Westarp agreed: see Westarp to Linde, 13 November 1917, Westarp Papers, Nr. 21, Bl. 53, ZStA Potsdam.

94. Quoted in Feldman, *Army Industry Labor*, p. 374.

95. See the reports of Giesberts and Hirsch-Duncker leader Gustav Hartmann, both founders of the *Volksbund*, before the executive committe of the *Freie Väterlandische Vereinigung*, 27 November 1917, Giesberts Papers 32, Bl. 104, ZStA Potsdam.

could undermine the war effort through strikes, sabotage, or revolution, as had already occurred in Russia. The Christians were particularly concerned that the free trade unions, which were already losing some important local branches to the Independent Socialists, would harden their position to the war or, perhaps, revert to the intransigent opposition characteristic of pre-war decades. For a number of reasons, therefore, the Christian trade unions wanted to further the goals of the *Volksbund*.[96]

Much to the relief of Stegerwald and his comrades, the General Commission decided to join the new organization in late November 1917. Like the Christians, free trade union leaders were thinking in very pragmatic terms. The labor movement could simply not afford to divide ranks.

> Should the *Vaterlandspartei* dominate the field all by itself, the forces of the *Reaktion* will prevail and afterwards we will have ourselves to blame for not coordinating and organizing the forces of the people and throwing their weight into the balance for a peace of understanding and a new orientation internally. It is better, therefore, if we do not stand alone, rather that the great forces of the people, especially the working class, stand solidly behind our own demands . . . Even if the power of the Christian and Hirsch-Duncker unions by themselves is slight, it is still true that some positive progress is attainable due to their contacts with the political parties. It can not be a matter of indifference to the free trade unions, for instance, how the suffrage question in Prussia is solved . . . Too, if people see that large segments of the bourgeois labor movement stand on *our* ground, this will be of considerable help in keeping the bourgeois parties from turning away into the camp of the annexationists.[97]

Private expressions such as this make it fairly clear that the Christian trade unions were not alone in viewing labor solidarity as a means of furthering a partisan political program. Trade union unity was still a tenuous affair. With the addition of the frees to the *Volksbund*, nevertheless, it too could claim an impressive membership of well over a million. As the weary nation entered its fourth winter of the war, the political battle lines between Right and Left were clearly drawn.

As is well known, the domestic battle in 1918 was fought primarily over the issue of Prussian suffrage reform. With the *Vaterlandspartei* exerting internal and external pressure on Prussian politicians and the *Volksbund* issuing repeated declarations about the pressing need for universal suffrage, the government's moderate bill moved through the legislative machinery. By June it had

96. See the two private notations by Stegerwald of 10 and 15 January 1918, as well as Giesbert's speech at the *Volksbund*'s founding assembly of 14 November 1917, Giesberts Papers 40, Bl. 23–25, 36–43, ZStA Potsdam: also see Adam Stegerwald, "Volk und Frieden," *Zentralblatt*, 14 January 1918, and *Deutsche Arbeit*, August 1917, pp. 367–68.

97. *Protokoll der Konferenz der Vertreter der Verbandsvorstände*, 22–24 November 1917, DGB Haus Düsseldorf.

become clear just how impervious deputies elected on the basis of a plutocratic system were to pressure from the lower classes. A Landtag majority consisting of Conservatives, Free Conservatives, and many National Liberals and Centrists amended the government's proposals to ensure an even greater degree of upper- and middle-class influence in the nation's largest and most powerful state. Mesmerized by the drum-beating of the *Vaterlandspartei*, the Prussian legislature ignored the lessons of timely political reform pointed out by Bethmann Hollweg in 1916. Only in late October, after the ascension of the liberal government of Max von Baden, did the Landtag reverse itself, but by then the timeliest moment for reform had passed.

Developments in the socio-political arena did not augur well for the future of the empire either. Following the lead of the Christian trade unions, the united labor organizations presented the Reich government with demands for full-fledged management-labor chambers in the late fall of 1917.[98] The bill which emerged after a long, tough winter of ministerial bickering and quarreling, however, was unacceptable to the workers. Agricultural laborers were not included in the provisions of the proposed law, and the regional chamber concept dear to the unions had been discarded in favor of the idea proposed formerly by Bethmann Hollweg that the chambers be trade-oriented. The latter concept, it will be recalled, was thought by government circles to be less conducive to radical politicization. When the Reichstag commission insisted that the unions' demands be met, government and parliament became deadlocked, just as they had been seven years earlier over the same issue. Due to its influence in the bureaucracy, the *Vaterlandspartei* had again gained the upper hand. In late October 1918, with Germany's world crumbling about her, the new liberal government finally accepted the Reichstag's amendments.[99] But this should not obscure the fact that for decades, until it was probably too late, Imperial Germany had been unwilling to accommodate those social forces which were now threatening to sweep it away.

Still the major spokesman for the Christian labor movement, Adam Stegerwald addressed himself to this unfolding crisis with a flurry of rhetorical and journalistic activity. With the *Vaterlandspartei* ascendant in bureaucratic, business, and high church circles, the general secretary concentrated his criticism on the only area of German political life over which he had somewhat more control—the political parties. The malady of class prejudice and conceit

98. Theodor Brauer to Franz Behrens, 17 September 1917, Kl. Erw. 461–6 (Otte Papers), BA Koblenz; Stegerwald to Siefart, 30 November 1917, and the notes of a meeting between representatives of the united unions and spokesmen from the Imperial Ministry of the Economy, 5 December 1917, Reichswirtschaftsministerium, Nr. 2013, Bl. 106, 107–8, ZStA Potsdam.

99. The pertinent documents and protocols for the dispute over management-labor chambers in 1918 are located in Reichskanzlei, Nr. 534 and Reichswirtschaftsministerium, Nr. 2013/1, 2014, and 2015, ZStA Potsdam.

which plagued Germany's party system was condemned rightly as the potential harbinger of doom for the nation's war effort. In particular, the self-centered policies of the bourgeois parties, as evidenced by the suffrage vote in Prussia, were singled out for criticism. This behavior would have to give way to more-progressive parliamentary activities. In speech after speech, the general secretary warned the middle class *Fraktionen* that they could no longer take the working class for granted if they wanted to survive.[100]

Privately, Stegerwald did not view the survival of the bourgeois parties as possible *or* desirable. Along with sincere and well-justified concerns for the long-term social and political development of the fatherland, these feelings also disclosed serious apprehension concerning the progress of *his own movement*. It could not be disputed, argued Stegerwald, that the Christian labor movement had an important mission to accomplish. The *Gesamtverband* had not only to exert its energies to defeat reactionary elements in the *Vaterlandspartei*, but also to insure that a Christian, not a Socialist, regime emerged in the new Germany. In order for the Christian trade unions to fulfill this dual historical mission, an effective avenue of party-political influence was absolutely essential. But, surveying the bourgeois parties from Right to Left, the general secretary observed his movement everywhere relegated to a position of secondary or tertiary influence and hence with no real chance to ward off reactionaries or Socialists in the long run.[101] The solution, particularly after the precipitate increase of parliamentary influence under Max von Baden in October 1918, was obvious to the frustrated Stegerwald.

> The possibility is not to be excluded that the course of our state constitution which we have embarked upon will lead to a great shake-up [*Erschütterung*] of the existing political parties. The direction in this area which developments will take is still unpredictable. We only know that a great number of our fellow citizens, and not merely the worst, feel comfortable in none of the now-numerous party houses, and therefore prefer to move about outside without a political home. We know, furthermore, that even for many inhabitants of the various party houses, quarters have become too narrow, too musty, too dilapidated and out of repair. And finally, it seems to us as if the various party groups have more in common than they themselves know or are willing to admit. Should it for these reasons come to a reconstruction of the German party system, we do not need to regard this fearfully. It can definitely not get worse than it already is.[102]

100. *Düsseldorfer Tageblatt*, 31 July 1918, and *Kölner Local-Anzeiger*, 30 September 1918 (clippings: Marx Papers 1016, HA Kölner); *Westdeutsche Arbeiter-Zeitung*, nos. 29–30, for 21 and 28 July 1918.

101. Adam Stegerwald, "Das Alte Stürzt!" *Deutsche Arbeit*, no. 11, November 1918.

102. *Ibid*. In his recent article, "Adam Stegerwald und die Krise des deutschen Parteiensystems," *Vierteljahrshefte für Zeitgeschichte*, (Heft 1, 1979), p. 4, Larry Jones errs in dating Stegerwald's public announcement of plans for a new party in July 1917. This speech was given in July 1918

Although concerned, as will be seen, about the willingness of many Catholic workers to make a clean break from the *Zentrumsturm*, Stegerwald had nevertheless made *his* sentiments quite clear.

The momentous events of November 1918 temporarily interrupted such deliberations. Exhausted after fifty-one months of war, and frustrated by the apparent unwillingness of the Kaiser to sign an armistice, revolution raised its head in Germany. What began in Kiel on 30 October as a sailors' protest against the idea of a desperate sortie to save the honor of the navy soon spread to other parts of the nation. In Hamburg, Cologne, Dresden, Munich, and Berlin, workers' and soldiers' councils similar to those formed in Russia the previous year came into existence. Anxious to prevent the bolshevization of Germany, which appeared imminent when a Socialist Republic was proclaimed in Munich on the eighth, government leaders in Berlin took quick action. Without William's authorization, Max von Baden announced the abdication of the Kaiser on the ninth, then handed over the chancellorship to Majority Social Democratic leader Friedrich Ebert. The latter's colleague Philip Scheidemann proclaimed the new German Republic from the balcony of the Imperial Chancellery later that day. By the eleventh an armistice had been signed—the holocaust was finally over.

Although glad to see an end to the slaughter, Christian workers were soon faced with a very real problem at home. Not only was all hope for the *Volksmonarchie* dashed, but the Majority Social Democratic leaders of the new Republic had extended an olive branch to the Independent Socialists. The more radical faction was offered seats on an all-Socialist cabinet which set for itself the task "of realizing the Socialist Program."[103] Throughout Germany, moreover, the workers' and soldiers' councils had usurped many of the functions of local government. Given their minor voice in most of the old city councils, Christian workers might not have objected to this latter development were it not for the fact that everywhere the new institutions were dominated by Socialists who, despite the wartime alliance, refused to cooperate with Christian and Hirsch-Duncker unionists. At the trade union level, too, events were ominous. The free trade unions were taking full advantage of the collapse of the authoritarian political order and the weakness of employers by recruiting the now-emboldened proletariat at a frenzied pace. The Christian organizations made impressive gains too, but in the absence of a common reactionary enemy of labor, the wartime partnership among the various trade union groups

---

and did not mention anything more radical than internal reorganization of the Center Party. Only in October 1918 did Stegerwald publicize his views.

103. Quoted in Koppel Pinson, *Modern Germany* (New York: Macmillan Company, 1966), p. 365.

was falling apart, and with it, the Christians' strategy of drawing the free trade unionists and moderate Social Democrats into the bourgeois camp.[104]

It would have been a great tactical mistake, therefore, for the Christian labor movement to reject the newly proclaimed Republic. "If we return to an advocacy of the monarchy," explained Christian unionist Johann Becker, "then we make it almost impossible for the Majority Socialists to work with the progressive bourgeoisie in consolidating domestic relations."[105] Afraid of the more radical Independents and Spartacists, the moderates had already proclaimed the Republic and turned to the Left. Pro-monarchist sentiments among former allies like the *Gesamtverband* would isolate the moderates on the Left and prevent a reconstruction of the wartime alliance. For reasons like this Christian labor leaders ignored their emotional attachment to the monarchy and doubts concerning the efficacy of republicanism in federalist, particularist Germany. The call from non-Socialist circles for a national assembly to draft a democratic constitution received the Christians' full support.[106]

Stegerwald wanted to go one step further in the struggle to regain some measure of control over the moderate Social Democrats. As might have been expected, he viewed the situation as propitious for the establishment of a bourgeois party phalanx. Only with adequate *political* clout could the ideology of the non-Socialist workers and the progressive bourgeoisie prevail. The general secretary seems to have realized by this point that the predominantly political approach taken by the *Gesamtverband* and the German Workers' Congress *before* 1914 had been ineffective. In the conservative sociopolitical milieu of pre-war days, the labor organization with the most members and the greatest potential for winning strikes had been the most successful. By November 1918, however, union conditions had changed. The old order had collapsed, and barring further revolution from the streets, Germany's future would be determined politically, not at the trade union level. One had only to look to the new *Arbeitsgemeinschaft* agreed on by leaders of capital and labor a few days after the armistice. Not content with progressive, harmonious relations at the plant level, Germany's employers wanted to extend the community of interests to the political arena; all legislative matters affecting the socio-economic position of capital and labor would be dealt with in concert. But to insure that capital did not cooperate solely with the Social Democrats who were solidly entrenched in government, non-Socialist laborers needed a

104. Stegerwald to the executive committees of member organizations in the *Gesamtverband*, 30 November 1918, Giesberts Papers 94, ZStA Potsdam; *Zentralblatt*, nos. 24–25, for 18 November and 2 December 1918.
105. Johann Becker to Stegerwald, 19 November 1918, Marx Papers 222, HA Köln.
106. See the proclamation of the *Gesamtverband* central committee of 13 November, *Zentralblatt*, 18 November 1918.

political party as much their own as the S.P.D. was to the frees. There is some evidence to indicate that Stegerwald wanted a new party which would become the fulcrum of German political life, balancing the German business community and other conservatives on the one side and the Majority Socialists on the other. Radicals and extremists from Left and Right would fall into obscurity.[107]

A "bourgeois" response to the revolution had begun to take shape by 14 November. As Behrens informed his Christian Social colleagues that day, "a new non-Socialist trade union federation and, in connection with it, a new social *Volkspartei* is being formed."[108] The first initiative in this direction seems to have been taken by left-liberals like Gustav Hartmann of the Hirsch-Duncker unions and Theodor Wolff of the *Berliner Tageblatt*. Their plan was to create a large bourgeois party of truly progressive, republican politicians who would take up their position between the Socialists and the Catholics. Simultaneously, the progressive industrialist Walter Rathenau, one of the leading proponents of the new *Arbeitsgemeinschaft* between capital and labor, proposed the even more ambitious idea of uniting *all* disparate non-Socialist elements and pressing for far-reaching social reforms and the convocation of a constituent assembly which would decide Germany's fate in a democratic fashion.[109]

Because of his influence with the Center Party and the non-Socialist masses, as well as his preference for new party formations, the general secretary of the Christian trade unions was wooed from the beginning by Rathenau. As Stegerwald recalled in his memoirs, "my office [in Berlin] now became a much-frequented place for all those [like Rathenau] who were involved with shaping the new course of political events."[110] Already accustomed to widespread cooperation with these circles after the founding of the *Volksbund* in 1917, the Christian trade union leader joined the left-liberals in an almost instinctive effort to block the radicalization of the Socialists.

107. Stegerwald, Bechly, and Behrens to other leading members of the German Workers' Congress, 28 November 1918, and Stegerwald to the executive committees of member organizations of the *Gesamtverband*, 30 November 1918, Giesberts Papers 94, ZStA Potsdam; *Zentralblatt*, 6 January 1919; Eduard Stadtler, *Als Anti-Bolschewist* 1918/19 (Düsseldorf: Neuer Zeitverlag GmbH, 1934), p. 9; Stegerwald, "Adam Stegerwald," *25 Jahre christliche Gewerkschaftsbewegung*, p. 143.

108. Minutes of the Political Committee of the Christian-Social Party, 14 November 1918, Mumm Papers 401, Bl. 2, ZStA Potsdam.

109. Wilhelm Wallbaum to the executive committee of the Christian-Social Party, 27 November 1918, Mumm Papers 1056, ZStA Potsdam; F. Varnholt to Anton Erkelenz, 5 October 1918, Erkelenz Papers 12; BA Koblenz; Gustav Stresemann to Margarethe Dammann, 15 November 1918, Stresemann Papers 187, AA Bonn; *Freisinnige Zeitung*, no. 272, 19 November 1918; *Kölnische Zeitung*, no. 1080, 21 November 1918; and Harry Kesseler, *Walter Rathenau: His Life and Times* (New York: Harcourt, Brace and Company, 1930), pp. 259–61.

110. Stegerwald, "Adam Stegerwald," *25 Jahre christliche Gewerkschaftsbewegung*, p. 143.

The new "social *Volkspartei*," replete with a progressive program and an executive council, was christened on the sixteenth as the Democratic Party of Greater Germany. On the same day, Rathenau and Stegerwald called to life a "Democratic People's League," whose apparent purpose was to expand Wolff's creation to include all of bourgeois Germany. The related German Democratic Trade Union Federation, a politically-oriented *Bund* consisting of the Hirsch-Duncker unions and the unionized white- and blue-collar groups within the German Workers' Congress, emerged with Stegerwald at the helm on the twentieth.[111]

The political reaction to the embryonic bourgeois alliance was at first somewhat encouraging. There was some press and rank and file endorsement among former National Liberals for a union with the Progressives and the Center, and even the stubborn Wolff held a number of meetings where greater bourgeois union was discussed.[112] There were Catholics other than Stegerwald, moreover, who were also warm to the idea. The Erzberger Papers in Koblenz contain an interesting memorandum prepared for the political orientation of the controversial Württembergian upon his return from the armistice talks in Spa on the fourteenth. The memo was probably drafted by Maximilian Pfeiffer, one of the only leading Centrists left in Berlin after the revolution. Concerning the "merger of the bourgeois parties,"[113] he noted that the Progressives and National Liberals of Berlin had entered into negotiations which would soon result in a new union. "Under these circumstances the Center will have to consider whether it wants to join this union. The answer cannot be no, especially if we want to deny full power to the Social Democrats and avoid an isolation of the Center."[114] He recommended that the middle-class parties of Austria be included in the negotiations and that "a joint bureau and action committee of the cartelized bourgeois parties"[115] be formed without delay. The birth of the Democratic Party of Greater Germany and Rathenau's People's League a few days later fulfilled these conditions and seems to have found the backing of Erzberger, Pfeiffer, and the prestigious party organ *Germania*.[116]

111. *Germania*, no. 540, 18 November 1918; *Deutsche Arbeit*, no. 12, December 1918; *Zentralblatt*, no. 25, 2 December 1918; *Deutsche Tageszeitung*, no. 585, 16 November 1918.
112. See the numerous letters in the Stresemann Papers 187, AA Bonn; and Theodor Wolff, *Der Marsch durch zwei Jahrzehnte* (Amsterdam: Albert de Lange, 1936), pp. 207–9.
113. Pfeiffer (?) to Erzberger, n.d. (November 1918), Erzberger Papers 32a, BA Koblenz.
114. *Ibid.*
115. *Ibid.*
116. See Erzberger and Pfeiffer to the Austrian Christian-Social Party, 17 November 1918, printed in the *Kölnische Zeitung*, no. 1073, 18 November 1918; and *Germania*'s support (*Deutsche Tageszeitung*, press section, no. 592, 21 November 1918) for a union (*zusammenschliessen*) of the bourgeois parties and the formation of a joint bureau to ward off the Spartacists.

But the German bourgeoisie was not really unified. Stunned for days by the unexpected collapse of the empire, Conservative and Free Conservative circles overcame their demoralization and entered into negotiations to form a new union of largely anti-republican, conservative forces on 16 November. Coming on the day that the Democratic Party and the People's League were founded, the rallying of the Right may well have been a reaction to the plans of Rathenau, Stegerwald, and the more progressive non-Socialist elements in Berlin. Neither were all National Liberals pleased by the new developments, for Gustav Stresemann soon made preparations for a party of his own. The former helmsman of the National Liberals made some attempt to reconcile differences between the two liberal factions, but by the twentieth these talks had faltered over which candidates to run during the elections and also, one suspects, over programmatic points like the restoration of the monarchy, the degree of socialization of industry, and support for the "yellow" trade unions. The cracks and fissures which had weakened the bourgeois party edifice in Germany before the revolution had not taken long to reappear in the new structure.[117]

The bulk of the old Center Party soon rejected the idea of a bourgeois union too. Unaware of the undertakings in Berlin, the "Industry Committee," a caucus of Center Party officials, journalists, and Catholic interest group leaders from Rhineland-Westphalia, had agreed to a provisional program for the Center in Düsseldorf on 16 November. The new program called for maintenance of Germany's religious traditions, acceptance of the Republic, and a long list of social and political reforms which the workers had demanded. In order to prevent confusion among Catholic supporters, the name "Center" would be retained, but the party's doors were to be flung wide open to all socially progressive, religiously tolerant Protestants.[118]

The agreement represented a compromise between moderate Centrists primarily concerned with preserving the Center and protecting Catholic interests in the turbulent aftermath of the revolution, and those groups most exclusively concerned with molding a true interconfessional people's party. The driving force behind the new program was Father Heinrich Brauns of the *Volksverein*, who, like Otto Müller, August Pieper, and other socially activist clergymen in

117. Westarp to Count Behre, 30 November 1918, Westarp Papers 25, Bl. 137, ZStA Potsdam; *Freisinnige Zeitung*, nos. 272–73, for 19–20 November 1918; Stresemann to Margarethe Dammann, 15 November 1918, Stresemann to Stubmann, 15 November 1918, and Stresemann to Hugo, 18 November 1918, Stresemann Papers 187, AA Bonn; *Deutsche Tageszeitung*, no. 593, 21 November 1918; and *Kölnische Zeitung*, no. 1080, 21 November 1918.

118. Heinrich Brauns to Wilhelm Marx, 13 November 1918, and Johann Becker to Stegerwald, 19 November 1918, Marx Papers 222, HA Köln; Maximilian Pfeiffer, *Zentrum und Neue Zeit*, 5 December 1918, in the Herold Papers 9, BA Koblenz.

western Germany, was convinced that only a liberalized, nondenominational Center was capable of holding aloft the religious standard in Germany. Christian trade union circles in the western provinces were wholeheartedly behind Brauns, and with good cause, for, as the conservative Carl Bachem observed with alarm at the time, the *Volksverein* leader and his associates "want consciously or unconsciously to place Catholicism in the service of democracy; they begin with the interests and attitudes of the workers and want this to be the focal point of our entire modern political life."[119] In fact, when word of Stegerwald's association with Rathenau and the People's League reached Cologne on the eighteenth, Christian trade union leaders wired their colleague to shy away from the new party and join ranks with the reformed Center. The general secretary should also encourage the Protestant wing of the *Gesamtverband* and other bourgeois elements of the Right to follow suit.[120]

To many of Stegerwald's closest adherents who had experienced the excitement of the interconfessional German Workers' Congress of 1903, the frustrations of the campaign to forge a nondenominational "Christian-national Bloc" in the decade before 1914, and the bitterness of intra-Center relations during the war, Brauns's proposals for a reformed, expanded, interconfessional party must indeed have been irresistible. It no longer made sense to struggle against the Center Party or desire new party groupings; on the contrary, with religious interests threatened by the Socialists and Spartacists, there was every reason to back the "Christian" Center and its new platform. Thus the fiery August Brust, who as late as August 1918 had "drawn his sword"[121] during a caucus with party officials in the Ruhr, recalled that he hung "with every thread of my heart to the Center Party"[122] after the revolution.

There was great concern among many of those who had followed Stegerwald during the war, moreover, that the unity of the Christian trade union movement would crumble if the general secretary persisted with his plans. Memories of the Reichstag elections of 1907, when rival union organizations and unfriendly parties had tried to recruit factions within the *Gesamtverband* for purely political purposes, partially explain these worries. There was also a fairly strong contingent around Heinrich Imbusch of the Christian miners' *Gewerkverein* which disagreed vehemently with Stegerwald's assessment of the primacy of parliamentary politics. Just as before the war, argued this group, the movement which provided the workers with the best wage contract

119. Bachem to Hilngrainer, 20 January 1919, Bachem Papers 464, HA Köln.
120. Becker to Stegerwald, 19 November 1918, Marx Papers 222, HA Köln.
121. Brust to Brauer, 21 August 1918, Kl. Erw. 461-6 (Otte Papers), BA Koblenz.
122. Brust to Pieper, 30 March 1923, Pieper Papers 35, StA Münster.

would attract the most members. Politics would do nothing for the weak union, nor could weak unions exert great political influence.[123]

Within two weeks of its founding, therefore, the cause of the People's League had foundered. "The Democratic People's League gave us one more proof," observed Rathenau dryly, "of the distaste of the middle classes for considering social problems seriously, and that was why it failed; it could not be got to unite on anything more definite than the colorless demand for a national assembly."[124] In the meantime, he added, the old Catholic and Protestant interest groups of Imperial Germany were emerging under new party banners with the same demand for a constituent convention, thus effectively undermining the People's League. After further talks with Stegerwald in Berlin, it was agreed to scrap plans for a new party for the time being and concentrate on improving relations between non-Socialist labor and the bourgeoisie.[125]

The general secretary did not intend to wait any longer than the successful convocation of a national assembly, however, before moving ahead with new plans for a *Mittelpartei*. With the aid of middle-class intellectuals like Martin Spahn, he felt sure he could convince the unionists around Imbusch of the narrowness of their views. Once educated to the exigencies of a political situation which they did not thoroughly understand, the "*Nurgewerkschaftler*" would swing into line. Nor did the existence of a "new" Center Party deter Stegerwald. His disappointment with the Center was too deep for any great rekindling of party loyalty, and his long-held conviction that Brauns, Müller, and other priests in Mönchen-Gladbach were opportunists must have further prejudiced Stegerwald with regard to the new spirit in the Center. Nor could he have been unaware that the Evangelical unionists in the *Gesamtverband*, however eager for new political experiments, would never agree to join a party whose name for so many years had stood for the defense of the Catholic Church. The new Center would be left with a base of support as narrowly Catholic as the old *Zentrumsturm*. The general secretary hoped that he would have time to educate his Catholic comrades to these realities in the coming weeks before the elections and that when the time came the new bourgeois parties would also be ready for such an effort.[126]

123. Stegerwald to Christian trade union leaders, 30 November 1918, Giesberts Papers 84, ZStA Potsdam; Heinrich Imbusch, "Die Brüder Imbusch," *25 Jahre christliche Gewerkschaftsbewegung*, p. 204.
124. Rathenau to Robert Bosch, 27 November 1918, printed in Walter Rathenau, *Ein preussischer Europäer: Briefe* (Berlin: Käthe Vogt Verlag, 1955), pp. 288–89.
125. *Ibid.*
126. Brauns to Kastert, 19 November 1918, Marx Papers 222, HA Köln, *Germania*, no. 544, 21 November 1918; Stegerwald to Christian trade union leaders, 30 November 1918, Giesberts Papers 95, ZStA Potsdam; Stegerwald to Esser, 20 December 1934, Ritter Papers ER/D 27, KfZG

Stegerwald's resolve to postpone his plans for a month or more cannot be fully appreciated without a discussion of the political activity of other non-Socialist workers in late November 1918, for the Evangelical wing of the *Gesamtverband* and allied Protestant groups in the new German Democratic Trade Union Federation were pushing impatiently at that time for the very same type of party desired by their Catholic colleague. After frustrating years of minor influence within the Conservative, National Liberal, and Progressive parties, the prospect of a united bourgeois *Fraktion* relying to a great extent on the votes of the now-united non-Socialist unions was overpoweringly tempting to the Protestant unionists. The collapse of the bourgeois "front" was felt keenly by these groups, but they refused to abandon their efforts. Not long after the founding of the new union federation on 20 November, therefore, plans were laid for a second campaign to weld bourgeois unity.[127]

The guiding hand behind these designs seems to have been Adolf Damascke, a Conservative who leaned close to the Christian-Social Party. Joining him were Hans Bechly of the Association of Patriotic Clerks (*Deutschnationaler Handlungsgehilfenverband*) and Franz Behrens, Hermann Wallbaum, Wilhelm Gutsche, and Friedrich Baltrusch of the *Gesamtverband*. As far as can be determined, their plan was to recruit liberal white-collar organizations to take their places alongside the liberal Hirsch-Duncker unions in the German Democratic Trade Union Federation; simultaneously, pressure from the member organizations would be applied to the bourgeois parties, including the Center, to return to the path of merger begun with the People's League.[128]

One of the first steps was taken on or shortly before the twenty-seventh when Behrens and Wallbaum approached the Catholic wing of the *Gesamtverband* with the idea of a new bourgeois party based squarely on the German Democratic Trade Union Federation. There had apparently been no serious thought given to the proposal of Brauns and the western unionists that Behrens *et al.* join the newly reorganized Center. Available evidence suggests that Stegerwald had not yet decided to postpone his own plans and probably represented the Protestants at a meeting of the Catholic unionists held in

---

Bonn, Eduard Stadtler to his wife, 28 November 1918, printed in Stadtler, *Als Antibolschewist*, p. 1011; Brust to Pieper, 30 March 1923, Pieper Papers 35, StA Münster; Stadtler, *Als Antibolschewist*, p. 8.

127. Jones, "Adam Stegerwald," p. 6, errs in concluding that Behrens and his Evangelical colleagues were the stumbling block to Stegerwald's plans. On the contrary, the Catholic unionists formed the main element of resistance, while Behrens *et al.* wanted desperately to form a new party. See below.

128. Gustav Stresemann, "Die Entstehung der Deutschen Volkspartei," 1918, unpublished manuscript in the Stresemann Papers 186, and Gutsche, Bechly, and Baltrusch to Stresemann, 14 December 1918, Stresemann Papers 183, AA Bonn; Stegerwald, Bechly, and Behrens to the other leaders of the German Workers' Congress, 28 November 1918, Giesberts Papers 94, ZStA Potsdam; *Deutsche Arbeit*, no. 12, December 1918, p. 575.

Berlin circa the twenty-fifth. Just as they had a week earlier, however, the Catholics argued "for internal reasons"[129] against any political leap in the dark. It was agreed to reconsider the question after the election campaign, but for the time being the Protestant unions could count on no help from the Catholic camp.

Without this support, there was little chance of constructing a viable party out of the German Democratic Trade Union Federation. Nevertheless, they pushed ahead. On 28 November, 120 representatives from a wide assortment of labor, white-collar employee, and commercial interest groups met in Berlin to discuss "the restructuring of the bourgeois parties."[130] The assembly, which appears to have been jointly sponsored by the new federation of non-Socialist workers, the Young Liberals, and the commerce- and banking-oriented *Hansabund*,[131] spoke out for further negotiation between the German Democratic Party and Streseman's German People's Party. A few days later Damascke and Behrens met with Dr. Bruno Marwitz, a *Hansabund* official, who reported to Gustav Stresemann that "the two gentlemen want the [white- and blue-collar] organizations represented by them to found a new party in cooperation with [the German People's Party], the Young Liberals, the various associations which stand at the disposal [of the *Hansabund*], and all suffrage-conscious, socially-progressive Conservatives."[132] In essence, Behrens and Damascke wanted to move one step beyond the assembly of the twenty-eighth and unite the German Democratic Party, the German People's Party, and the emerging German National People's Party.

These grandiose plans came to nought. Talks between the two liberal parties were resumed as a result of interest group pressure, but by the second week in December the negotiations had again fallen apart. The views of men like Stresemann and Wolff concerning the future of Germany were too divergent for any compromise. Nor was there any desire to join hands with the German Democratic Trade Union Federation. Marwitz and the chairman of the *Hansabund*, Dr. Kurt Köhler, rejected the proposals of Damascke and Behrens out of fear that such a party would eventually be dominated by the workers. The anti-Semitism of Bechly and his patriotic clerks, it was felt, would also attract questionable elements to the anti-Socialist cause. By mid-December 1918 the

129. Wallbaum to the executive committee of the Christian-Social Party, 27 November 1918, Mumm Papers 1056, ZStA Potsdam.
130. Kaufmann and Thissen to the leaders of the German Democratic Party, 30 November 1918, R 45 II, p. 167, BA Koblenz.
131. *Ibid.*; also notice the striking similarity between the resolutions passed by the assembly of the twenty-eighth and the *Aufruf* of the German Democratic Trade Union Federation a few days earlier, *Zentralblatt*, no. 25, 2 December 1918.
132. Marwitz to Stresemann, 6 December 1918, R 45 II, pp. 189–90, BA Koblenz.

Protestant unionists had no alternative but to join the bourgeois party of their choice, as the Catholic workers had already done.[133]

Indeed by December and January 1918/19 the moment for welding bourgeois unity had passed. The centripetal forces at work in the bourgeois world in November were rapidly subsiding. Neither the Majority Socialists nor the soldiers' and workers' councils had proved as radical as they had appeared shortly after the armistice. The councils decided in December to place legislative authority in a national assembly, and Ebert, by then, had reestablished ties to the bourgeoisie. His cabinet was opened to Center and left-liberal politicians, the old Imperial Army was called upon to defend the Republic, and the Independent Socialists bolted in anger and disgust. January brought the suppression of the Spartacists in Berlin and election of the bourgeois-dominated Weimar Assembly. The shock and fear which for a few days had driven the middle-class parties together was no longer present. With the urgency of bourgeois consolidation less apparent, the remnants of the old parties quickly reshuffled themselves and slipped into the old patterns.

In late January 1919, nevertheless, Stegerwald returned to his plan of a new *Mittelpartei*. The result was another rebuff from Catholic colleagues in the *Gesamtverband*. The Center Party had elected 25 workers to the assembly, a development which elated the more "loyal" faction around Giesberts and appeased those unionists who had followed the general secretary during the war. The unpolitical faction around Imbusch was no doubt more than pleased. Realizing that further initiatives on his part would be to no avail, and might even split the movement, Stegerwald abandoned his efforts.[134] A final attempt in 1920 met with no more success.[135]

As discussed in the concluding chapter, the inability of Stegerwald, Rathenau, Damascke, and Behrens to forge a great party of the middle was tragic for the young republic and certainly helped pave the way for Hitler's rise to power. In early 1919, however, these crucial events still lay far in the future and the Christian trade union movement was increasingly preoccupied with the task of adjusting to the new realities of Republican Germany. An analysis of this effort, as well as a treatment of the social and political activity of Christian laborers in general from 1919 to 1933, awaits another study. For now our tasks will be to summarize the politics of Christian labor over the long history of Imperial Germany and attempt to elicit some of the broader implications of this experience.

133. *Kölnische Zeitung*, nos. 1116, 1120, 1150, for 3, 5, and 16 December 1918; Marwitz to Stresemann, 6 December 1918, R 45 II, pp. 189–90, BA Koblenz; Gutsche, Bechly, and Baltrusch to Stresemann, 14 December 1918, Stresemann Papers 183, AA Bonn.

134. Brust to Pieper, 30 March 1923, Pieper Papers 35, StA Münster; Stegerwald to Esser, 20 December 1934, Ritter Papers ER/D 27, KfZG Bonn.

135. See Jones, "Adam Stegerwald," pp. 1–29.

Summary and Conclusions

At the end of his political career, Bernhard von Bülow learned from Rudolf von Valentini, the Kaiser's chief political aide, that William II doubted that his chancellor of nine years was a "vigorous monarchist." "Where does he want to get," replied Bülow, "to a state of affairs like that in Russia?" Valentini's response could not have been too surprising to the chancellor who had known William so long. "Well, not precisely the same as in Russia, but more or less that sort of thing . . . Above all, we must bridle the Reichstag."[1]

Aside from the question of Prussian suffrage reform, anti-democratic feelings such as this were most pronounced in high circles when parliament raised the question of labor legislation. As long as the Reichstag was willing to accept new military increases, compromises on specific questions of taxation were tolerated by the chancellor, and sometimes by the Kaiser too. But trade union rights was another matter, for it was usually assumed that greater freedoms for the labor movement would weaken the state in its fight against the allegedly revolutionary S.P.D. This was essentially a condemnation of the entire working class, for it was often taken for granted that common laborers were too immature intellectually to avoid being swept along by the demagoguery of the Social Democrats. The worker, even if he claimed to be "Christian-national," could probably not be trusted with new legal rights.

There were only two periods before 1914, in fact, when the cause of Christian-social reform had the slightest chance of success—in the early 1890s, and in the aftermath of the Frankfurt Workers' Congress of 1903. In the former case the Kaiser's willingness to implement Mönchen-Gladbach's programs was undermined by the S.P.D.'s electoral gains in 1893. The "ungrateful" workers did not deserve legal equality. Christian labor leaders managed to revive William's interest in labor reforms after 1903, but when these

1. Bülow, *Memoirs*, vol. 2, pp. 571–73.

issues did not suit Bülow's or the Kaiser's political needs after 1907, a "slower tempo" of social reform was adopted. By 1914, despite constant pressure from the Reichstag left, this tempo had slowed to a standstill. Even during the First World War, a time when labor had the most bargaining power it had possessed since the founding of the Reich, unions made no substantial, permanent gains until the exceptional fall of 1918.

The Reichstag's inability to improve the rights of labor was a good indication that Valentini's comparison to conditions in tsarist Russia was very appropriate. Indeed the findings of the present study place it squarely in opposition to the views of those historians who believe that an institutional shift was underway between the centers of power created in 1871 and the Reichstag. Only during the First World War did it even begin to appear likely that parliament's influence would expand in the Reich and in Prussia. But this was a product of unusual wartime conditions *and did not*, as Chapter 12 makes clear, augur well for Germany's parliamentary future.

In another sense, however, Valentini's comparison to Russian conditions is not appropriate, for unlike the mailed-fist response to change which was so characteristic of the tsarist experience, German rulers displayed an impressive amount of shrewdness, cleverness and subtlety in dealing with serious challenges to the system. As Bethmann pointed out to the Kaiser in 1916, Prussia had met the Napoleonic threat, the revolutions of 1848, and the Liberal crisis of the 1860s with a profound sense of realism and flexibility that had enabled the old order to emerge restructured but largely intact. It is in this overall context that the phenomenon of political manipulation in Germany after 1871, to which the present work has paid considerable attention, can be most fully appreciated. After the period of social insurance concessions ended in the early 1890s—there were no major socio-political departures or innovations after William II's initiative of 1890 had run its course—the state adopted a variety of manipulative techniques (see p. 13) designed to guarantee relative stability and perpetuate the old regime.

This study has sought to add to our knowledge of this latter-day *Realpolitik* by delving deeply into the experience of one movement. We have seen that governmental manipulation was not usually a public policy imposed on a passive, unsuspecting populace but rather something that came frequently in response to pressure from below. Moreover, manipulation was sometimes poorly conceived, as in 1878 at the time of the anti-Socialist laws, was at times difficult to control, witness the nationalist hysteria during the 1906 elections, was sometimes only temporarily successful, as illustrated by the eventual rise of the *Gewerkverein* in the late 1890s and the radicalization of the German Workers' Congress by 1913, and was sometimes strikingly effective, as the blocking of union merger in 1900/1901. The effect of such policies by 1914, multiplied many times over for the other groups and organizations which experienced similar experiences, was a fairly solidly entrenched old order, its challengers frustrated and increasingly angered, but still far from their goals. Then came the war.

As this work has also stressed, political manipulation was not the exclusive preserve of the empire's patrician ruling elite. As will be reviewed later in this concluding section, many of the problems and frustrations encountered by Christian labor came at the hands of manipulating Catholic and Evangelical clergymen and party politicians at the local and national level. Significantly, these leaders were usually acting independently of one another and of any instruction from above. But there was enough unity of purpose here to justify labeling these groups "auxiliary elites," a term connoting a second line of defense, or back-up system, if you will. The Junker minister in Berlin, the Landrat in Altenkirchen, the mine owner in Essen, the parish priest in Steele, the church canon in Cologne, and the lawyer *cum* local party boss in Coblence—all were, despite many differences on other issues, reacting to the threat which labor represented to the non-proletarian world with which they were all inextricably linked. Even close supporters of the Christian trade unions and the German Workers' Congress in the *Volksverein*, the Rhenish Center, and other parties in the Reichstag were willing to back Christian labor only to a certain point. Beyond this, they too sought to restrain and manipulate the workers. As Marx reminded us, the distant pull of one's relationship to the means of production whether direct or quite indirect and circuitous, was always very strong.

> Marx . . . maintained that a man's purposes were made what they were by the social, that is economic, situation in which he was in fact placed, and were made so, whether he knew it or not. Whatever his opinions, a man's actions were inevitably guided by his real interests, by the requirements of his material situation; the conscious aims of at any rate the bulk of mankind did not clash with their real interests, although they sometimes appeared disguised as so many independent, objective, disinterested ends . . .[2]

There were many aspects of pre-war society which Marx did not see accurately, but one of the most unshakable observations which result from an analysis of Imperial *and* Weimar Germany, and from the present study in particular, is the loose but purposeful unity with which the most far-reaching demands of the working class were resisted by "the bulk" of patrician and auxiliary elites.

* * * *

Without the institutions which parliament and Christian labor wanted to create for trade unions, union organizers in Germany were at a tremendous

2. Isaiah Berlin, *Karl Marx* (New York: Oxford University Press, 1959), p. 134.

disadvantage. Collective bargaining was not included in the German Commercial Code of 1869 and employers took full advantage of this fact. Throughout the Imperial period entrepreneurs resorted to strike insurance, blacklists, company-run labor exchanges, and "yellow" labor associations to discourage employees from joining trade unions. The courts, the police, and the Prussian army could usually be counted on to back the owners in any tight situation. Faced with these restrictions, most workers, especially married laborers with families to support, refused to risk their jobs and carry a union card. Despite the best efforts of Germany's trade union functionaries, only three million out of a total of nearly fourteen million workers had signed up by 1914. In the freer atmosphere of 1919 and 1920, close to nine million flocked to union halls.

The fact remains, however, that within that 22 percent minority of German workers who had joined unions by 1914, the Christians were no match for the Socialist unions (2,500,000 vs. 360,000). Even among the 3.2 million Catholic workers in Imperial Germany, the free trade unions possessed a very substantial advantage (c. 800,000 vs. c. 275,000). The leaders of the Christian trade union movement added to their own membership woes, it must be said, with numerous tactical errors that played into Hirsch-Duncker and Socialist hands. The pro-tariff stance in 1901/2 was incomprehensible to most workers and led to bitter, counterproductive quarrels within the Christian camp. The Prussian suffrage issue at the second German Workers' Congress in 1907, the debacle over the *Vereinsgesetz* and the apparent surrender to the bishops in 1908, and the retreat from inheritance taxes in 1909 provided the free trade unions, the S.P.D., and the left-liberals with lethal propaganda material. In a desperate attempt to forge an anti-Socialist movement after 1909, Stegerwald, Behrens, and other Christian leaders made appeals to big business and the Conservatives which were easily depicted as betrayals of the working class. These mistakes lent credence to the exaggerated charge that the *Gesamtverband* was a pliant tool in the hands of the class enemy and compromised Christian leaders in the eyes of an increasingly impatient and surly rank and file (Chapter 11). When Bülow and Bethmann abandoned the German Workers' Congress, Christion labor brought its tactics into line with its Neo-Thomist ideology and adopted a tougher stance.

An explanation preferred by Christian leaders, in fact, for the inability of the *Gesamtverband* to overtake the free trade unions in the decade before World War I was the failure of the Frankfurt initiative of 1903. But it is unlikely that such labor legislation, even in the *absence* of tactical errors by Christian labor leaders, could have reversed the Socialist lead at that time. In the somewhat freer atmosphere after the *Vereinsgesetz* of 1908, for instance, free trade union membership exploded from 1.5 to 2.5 million. Moreover, in the early 1920s, a time of complete legal equality for labor, the Christian organization grew to over a million members, while the General Commission rose meteorically to approximately seven million—almost the same seven-to-one ratio that had existed before the war. As the *Regierungspräsident* in Düsseldorf observed in 1908, the boldest workers were flocking to the largest unions hoping for more strength vis-à-vis employers. And the frees, who had been building since the early 1880s, represented the largest and most solid organization in 1908. That relative organizational and financial weaknesses in the *Gesamtverband* underlay its failure to compete with the unions of the General Commission is one of the main conclusions of this study.

Compounding the woes of Christian labor, especially in the decades before the turn of the century, was the response of the Catholic church. In the 1860s and 1870s, activists like Cronenberg and Rosenkranz had to contend with prelates who considered labor independence "the storm-warning signal of the revolution" and were able to manipulate most Catholic workers into "safer" havens. During the 1880s and 1890s, *Arbeiterwohl* and *Volksverein* leaders like Hitze felt compelled to promote confessional *Arbeitervereine* and *Fachabteilungen* rather than outright labor organizations because the majority of priests and bishops still feared the unpredictability and potential radicalism of independent trade unions. Brust experienced the same stiff resistance in the Ruhr and later in the 1890s when trying to spread the Christian labor movement to other parts of the empire. In the meantime, the frees had recruited close to half a million members and possessed an irreversible lead. The years before 1900 were thus quite important in determining the future political composition of the organized labor movement in Germany.

After the turn of the century, most Catholic clergymen adopted a more expedient attitude toward Christian labor. But the craft sections of Berlin and their archconservative patrons in Trier and Breslau, opposed to the strike because it set one class against another and contradicted the harmonious relationships which God had envisioned for the "limbs" of the social body, formed a countermovement to oppose the Christian trade unions. The Berliners embarrassed the *Gesamtverband* in the eyes of its rivals by insisting that the church have control. Valuable time and energy which could have been used for Christian membership drives was sapped by the constant need to deal with the intrigues of Savigny and his associates. Even the pope could not be relied on for moral support. Convinced that interconfessionalism and increased secularism in the Catholic community were the first signs of another Reformation, Pius, too, attempted to shackle the Christian trade unions to the episcopate. For the Christian trade unions, the result of the church's manipulative policies was a loss of potential members. General Secretary Stegerwald estimated this loss at 300–400,000.

The conservatism of church leaders contributed to considerable ill-feeling among Catholic workers and, as far as many lower-class contemporaries were concerned, confirmed the Marxian view of the church as little more than a pillar of the bourgeois edifice. And yet, for all the anger generated in Christian labor circles—and *Schadenfreude* in the Socialist camp—such conservatism added to the overall institutional stability of the Second Reich by perpetuating proletarian division and thereby lessening the amount of pressure which could be brought to bear on the system from below by any one organization. Thus auxiliary elites in the church did indeed serve to prop up the old regime.

The workers, however, were not merely the victims of manipulation. It was most unfortunate for Christian labor, German labor, and Germany in general that for two generations before 1914 the workers themselves had been unable to devise a formula that would have enabled the competing, feuding labor organizations to set aside their numerous political, religious, and philosophical differences and unite, if only on an *ad hoc* basis, on those trade union goals that all had in common. This goal was temporarily realized during the war, but in the first months of the peace the unions were at one another's throats again. It would be inappropriate to place the blame for this on any one organization, for all, at one time or another, contributed to the perpetuation of proletarian division. It is more important to observe that as interest groups, the frees, the Hirsch-Dunckers, and the Christians expended a great deal of energy that could have been turned to more productive uses. It was no coincidence, therefore, that the occupation forces in Germany after World War II insisted on a unified trade union movement. For the divisions in worker ranks described in this study weakened the forces of both social reform and political freedom in the 1920s, facilitating the rise of fascism and the tragedies that came in its wake.

* * * *

Adding to the setbacks experienced by the Christian labor movement was the disappointing record of the bourgeois political parties. The quest to win support in the Conservative Party was historically more important than parallel efforts to gain influence with the National Liberals and Center, for the Conservatives were the only party whose opinions were seriously considered by the government. Like the government, however, the Right resisted the approaches of Christian labor. Although Conservatives advocated harmonious relationships between the various estates of society, there was little hope in rightist circles that such a development was possible. They assumed that authoritarian institutions had to be maintained to keep class conflicts within manageable bounds. There is good reason to believe that Conservatives, particularly the *Bund der Landwirte*, were beginning to adopt more positive views concerning the political efficacy of social reform just prior to the outbreak of World War I. But it is doubtful, despite the advanced stage of merger negotiations between the Conservatives and Christian-Socials, that any middle ground could have been found between non-Socialist workers and the agrarian Right. The leftist drift of Christian labor in 1913/14 would have prevented the establishment of any permanent *rapprochement.*

The National Liberals were predominantly an employers' party until the late 1890s when the Young Liberals prevailed in the Reichstag with their ideas of moderate social reform. After the turn of the century, Christian labor began to benefit from this trend, as witnessed by the presence of National Liberal deputies at German Workers' Congresses and crucial legislative support which ensured the success of some of Christian labor's demands in the Reichstag. But the party refused to nominate non-Socialist workers lest far-reaching social demands split apart the *Fraktion.* The pressure to stay abreast of the S.P.D. eventually led to three successful labor candidacies in 1912—victories which paid handsome dividends to Christian labor during the strike-breaker debate of 1913/14. Given the rightward drift in government circles, however, such successes provided little satisfaction.

Christian labor's relationship with the Center Party was much more complex. With the exception of the Westphalian faction, Christian-social demands for an attenuation of private property rights found little support within the party during the 1860s and 1870s. The opposition of Catholic employers, the fears of the church, the indifference of middle-class Catholics preoccupied with the *Kulturkampf,* the reluctance of persecuted Catholics to provoke the wrath of a *laissez-faire*–oriented government, and the fundamental agrarian orientation of the party during these early decades explain the social inertia of the Center at this time. Party unity was maintained only by a sometimes crude, sometimes clever manipulation of the Christian workers. The end of the *Kulturkampf,* the social insurance initiatives of Bismarck and William II, the growing prestige and influence of the *Volksverein,* and the dictates of political expediency gave rise to many *real* concessions by the Center to Christian labor after the late 1890s. Unionists were nominated to safe seats in the Reichstag and state parliaments, and the demands of the German Workers' Congress were adopted as the party's own. Considering, once again, the unresponsiveness of the government to the Congress's call for greater labor freedoms, these gains were a mere consolation.

Making matters worse was the fact that the Center was still not the genuine friend of Christian labor that Carl Bachem depicted in his nine-volume history of the party after World War I. The Center remained a party primarily of middle- and upper-class interests. The reaction of the Center to the Leipzig Cartel was a good example of the willingness of many Catholics to ignore the workers, while intra-party disputes over tariff, tax, and suffrage reform on the eve of the war complicated the relationship with Catholic labor still more. Nor was the "Berlinist" opposition to the Christian trade unions without sympathizers in the Catholic camp. An influential coalition of parliamentarians, agrarians, editors, and clergymen fought the *Gesamtverband* and succeeded in limiting the maneuvering room of the unions, the *Volksverein*, and the interconfessionalists in the party. Party unity was increasingly a thing of the past in 1914, and renewed manipulative efforts were not going to change this as easily as in previous decades. "The workers can't be caught anymore by waving the bloody shirt and crying that the church is in danger," barked Brust.

At the time of the outbreak of World War I the Christian trade unions were already beginning to despair of their strategy of encouraging electoral alliances and parliamentary compromise among the bourgeois parties. Under the leadership of an increasingly intransigent Stegerwald, the Christian trade unions attempted to prod the National Liberals, Center, and Conservatives into policies that would promote *Neuorientierung* and cooperation with the S.P.D. Much more abrasive and demanding, the Christians placed tremendous pressure on the existing party system, and in so doing, became a centrifugal force in the process of disintegration of German political life. A justifiable concern for progressive social legislation aside, these tactics must be seen as essentially destructive in nature, for the unions had abandoned compromise and were interested in merely exacting concessions.

Stegerwald's advocacy in 1918 of an altogether new party went one step further and finally offered a positive, constructive alternative. Fragmented elements of the bourgeoisie with an interest in social reform would be brought together under one roof. If successful, conservatives would be forced to join or, what was more likely, create their own rightist party. With only three or four parties in the Reichstag (Independents, Majority S.P.D., Christian Middle, and Conservative Right), parliamentary efficiency would be greatly improved. But the far-reaching concessions and manipulative efforts made by Otto Müller and Heinrich Brauns in a shrewd bid to preserve the workers for the Catholic cause succeeded, and Stegerwald's efforts were doomed. The other parties, too, proved unresponsive.

This was indeed tragic. With the numerous problems Germany had to face in the 1920s, she could ill afford to be burdened with an antiquated party system which often stood in the way of effective parliamentary rule. That Stegerwald and his followers failed was not surprising, however, for their efforts were plagued by the same contagion that had weakened parliamentary forces in the empire and the same disease which would enervate these forces in the republic. Class hatred, confessional suspicion, and political fragmentation were historical forces which were born in the social and economic upheavals of the mid-nineteenth century. Germany would produce no leader capable of dealing successfully with these problems before they ran their fatal course to 1933.

* * * *

There is one final statement to be made about the experiences of Christian labor which adds to our understanding of the further course of German history to 1933 and beyond. The most striking observation which emerges from this study, in fact, is the immense scale and magnitude of class division. That the nobleman, the middle-class entrepreneur, and the proletarian had their differences is hardly a revelation to the historian of modern Germany, but previous discussions of this problem have tended to focus exclusively on the tensions between a suspicious, phobia-ridden bourgeois world and its ideological foe, the "Marxist" S.P.D. The logical conclusion is that the middle and upper classes did not fear all workers, only the Marxists. In his commendable study of the Nazi takeover in one north German town, for instance, W. S. Allen observes that "the antipathy of the middle class was not directed . . . toward the working class as such, but only toward its political and social aspirations [i.e., Marxism]."[3] An analysis of the politics of Christian labor in Imperial Germany offers a new perspective on the great degree of social and political polarization in Germany, for it becomes apparent that both the non-Socialist unionist, the unorganized proletarian, and the small man were treated with the same suspicion and denigration as the Socialists by church, state, and middle-class politicians. "In the last few decades we have witnessed many great cultural achievements in Germany," observed a worried Stegerwald in July 1918 before the patricians and noblemen of the Prussian House of Lords.

> Where we have failed, where we have been negligent, however, is in the cultivation of human relations and the human disposition. We have not brought [the German] people closer together. The organs of state and those of the working folk exist next to one another as if in two foreign worlds. This caste spirit in political life has carried over into religious and economic life, and vice versa. After this war we will not be able to remain a people set apart in castes and classes.[4]

Unfortunately these problems only worsened after 1918 and a dangerously radical movement emerged whose ultimate aim was the violent destruction of the old world of class snobbery and elitism, the same world which Christian labor had confronted with painfully frustrating results from the days of Ketteler until the collapse of the empire in 1918.

3. William Sheridan Allen, *The Nazi Seizure of Power* (Chicago: Quadrangle Books, 1965), p. 275.

4. *Westdeutsche Arbeiter-Zeitung*, no. 29, 21 July 1918.

Glossary of German Words

Alter Verband—The Socialist miners' union
Arbeiterkammer—A chamber of labor
Arbeiterverein—A workers' club, usually under church patronage
Arbeitervereinler—The members of an *Arbeiterverein*
Arbeiterwohl—Workers' Welfare, an organization founded by Franz Brandts in 1880
Arbeitskammer—A management-labor chamber
Arbeitsgemeinschaft—The alliance of capital and labor formed in 1918
Aufruf—A proclamation
Augustinusverein—The German Catholic Press Association
ausschlaggebende—Decisive (adj.)
Ausschliessungspolitik—Isolationist politics
Block—A parliamentary bloc
Blockpolitik—The politics of parliamentary bloc formation
Bund—A league or confederation
Bund der Landwirte—The Agrarian League, a conservative pressure group founded in 1893
Denkschrift—A position paper
Drang nach Osten—Eastwardly expansion
Ehrenrat—An honorary council or advisory body
Erlass—A decree
Fachabteilung—A craft union under church patronage
Flucht nach vorn—A desperate attack
Fraktion—The parliamentary body of a political party
Freie Gewerkschaften—The free trade unions (General Commission of German Trade Unions)
Freie Kirchlich-soziale Konferenz—The Free Conference for a Social Church (Evangelical)
Freisinnige Volkspartei—The Progressive People's Party

Gesamtausschuss—A joint or general committee
Gesamtverband—The National Federation of Christian Trade Unions of Germany
Gesellenverein—A journeymen's club, usually under church patronage
Gewerkschaftshaus/Berlin—Free trade union headquarters in Berlin
Gewerkschaftsstreit—The quarrel over trade unions within the German Catholic community after 1900
Gewerkverein—The Christian miners' union
Gewerkvereinler—The members of the *Gewerkverein*
Glückauf—The short-lived Christian miners' union of 1890
Handelsvertragsverein—The left-liberal Commercial Treaty Association
Handwerkerbund—The German Artisans' League formed in the 1860s
Hansabund—The progressive alliance of businessmen formed in 1909
Hauptwahl—A preliminary election
Herr im Haus—The lord of the house
Hirtenbrief—A pastoral letter
Hochburg—A stronghold
Kampfverein—A union willing to strike
Katholikentag—The Catholic Diet, an annual political caucus for German Catholics
Kirchturmspolitik—Religiously motivated provincialism
Klassenkampf—The class struggle
Klassenkampfspolitik—The politics of class struggle
Knappenbund—A league of *Knappenvereine*
Knappschaftsverein—See Chapter 3, note 23
Knappenverein—A miners' club, usually under church patronage
Kölner Richtung—The Cologne faction in the *Gewerkschaftsstreit*
Kreisverband—A district association
Kulturkampf—The cultural struggle or persecution of the German Catholic Church in the 1870s and 1880s
Kulturkampfspartei—A party advocating persecution of the Catholic Church
Landesverein—A State party or association (e.g., in Saxony)
Landrat—A local magistrate of the Prussian government
Landtag—A State parliament (e.g., in Prussia)
Mainzer Leitsätze—The Mainz Guidelines, the original Christian trade union national program of 1899
Mitbestimmung—Codetermination for workers
Mittelpartei—A party uniting the political center
Mittelstand—The old middle estate of peasants, artisans, and tradespeople
Nationalverein—The National Association, a group of Prussian Liberals advocating German unification in the 1860s
Neuorientierung—Bethmann Hollweg's new political direction of World War I

Nichtkampfverein—A union or association not willing to strike
Oberkirchenrat—The High Church Council of the Prussian government
Oberpräsident—A provincial governor in Prussia
Osterdienstag—Easter Tuesday
Reaktion—Extreme conservatism
Rechtfähigkeit—Legal capacity or legal personality
Regierungspräsident—A district governor in Prussia
Reich—The empire
Reichsfeinde—The enemies of the empire
Reichspartei—The Imperial Party, one of two conservative parties in the Reichstag
Reichstag—The Imperial Parliament
Revolutionspartei—A party advocating revolution
Sammlung—A coalition
Sammlungspolitik—The politics of coalition, usually anti-Socialist coalition
Schadenfreude—Joy derived from the misery of others
schiedlich-friedlich—Separate but peaceful (e.g., relations)
schlagkräftig—Strong
Schwarzseher—A pessimist
Siebenercommission—The commission of seven miners formed after the Ruhr miners' strike of 1905
Soziale Geschäftsstelle—The Social Reform Center of the *Freie Kirchlich-soziale Konferenz*
Sozialkritik—Critique of society
Sozialpolitik—The politics of social reform
Staatsministerium—The Prussian cabinet of ministers
Stadtmission—A domestic missionary service of the Evangelical Church
Ständestaat—A state based on corporate or estatist representation
Stichwahl—A run-off election
Umsturzvorlage—William II's reaction Subversion Bill of 1894
Vaterlandspartei—The Party of the Fatherland
Verein—A club or association
Vereinsgesetz—A law governing associations
Vermögenssteuer—A tax on wealth
Volk—The people
Volksbüro—A local office or branch
Volksbund—The People's League for a Free Fatherland
Volksmonarchie—A popularly based monarchy
Volkspartei—A popularly based party
Volksverein—The People's Association for Catholic Germany
Weltanschauung—A world view or guiding philosophy
Zechenverband—An association of Ruhr mine owners

Zentralrat—The Central Committee of the Hirsch-Duncker trade unions
Zentrumspartei—The Center Party
Zentrumsturm—The Center Fortress or Center Tower, Bismarck's metaphor for the Center Party

Bibliography

Archival Sources

I. Archiv der evangelischen Kirche der Union, Berlin (EZA Berlin)
   A. Proceedings
      1. *Verhandlungen der V. Ordentlichen Generalsynode der Evangelischen Landeskirche Preussens*, 1903
   B. Organizational Files
      1. *Archiv der Geschäftsstelle für das Evangelische Deutschland*

II. Friedrich Ebert Stiftung, Bonn
   A. Newspapers
      1. *Die Arbeit*
      2. *Bergknappe*
      3. *Der Arbeiter* (Munich)
      4. *Der Gewerkverein*
      5. *Evangelischer Arbeiterbote*
      6. *Bergarbeiter-Zeitung*
      7. *Deutsche Metallarbeiterzeitung*
      8. *Correspondenzblatt der Generalkommission der Gerwerkschaften Deutchlands*

III. Archiv der Sozialdemokratie, Bonn (AdSoz Bonn)
   A. Personal Papers
      1. Ludwig Frank
      2. Hermann Molkenbuhr

IV. Kommission für Zeitgeschichte, Bonn (KfZG Bonn)
   A. Personal Papers
      1. Emil Ritter
      2. Wilhelm Ziebach Diary
   B. Organizational Files
      1. *Archiv der Katholischen Arbeitnehmerbewegung,* 5 volumes, presently with Herr Jürgen Aretz
   C. Unpublished Manuscripts
      1. Emil Ritter, *Die Männer aus Monchen-Gladbach,* n.d.

V. Politisches Archiv des auswärtigen Amtes, Bonn (AA Bonn)
  A. Prussian Diplomatic Correspondence
    1. Deutschland 123, volumes 1–3, 9; 125 Nr. 1, volumes 1, 5, 6; 125 Nr. 1 *secr.*, volumes 2–4
    2. Europa Generalia 82 Nr. 1 *secr.*, volume 4
    3. Päpstl. Stuhl 3 Nr. 2; 6 *secr.*, volumes 1–6; 13a Nr. 1, volumes 5–8; volumes 2–4; 24 *secr.*, volume 1; 26 *secr.*, volumes 1–6
    4. Preussen 2 Nr. 2b, volume 9; 2 Nr. 2h, volume 23
    5. Rom-Vatikan 180-14; 199 (309–312); 201–50
  B. Personal Papers
    1. Gustav Stresemann

VI. Institute fur Zeitungsforschung, Dortmund
  A. Newspapers
    1. *Tremonia*
    2. *Kölnische Volkszeitung*
    3. *Germania*
    4. *Kölnische Zeitung*
    5. *Rheinisch-Westfälische Zeitung*
    6. *Dortmunder Zeitung*
    7. *Frankfurter Zeitung*
    8. *Berliner Tageblatt*
    9. *Neue Preussische (Kreuz-) Zeitung*

VII. Stadtarchiv, Dortmund (StA Dortmund)
  A. Police Reports
    1. Bestand 3
    2. Bestand 17

VIII. Archiv des deutschen Gewerkschaftsbundes, Düsseldorf (DGB Archiv Düsseldorf)
  A. Organizational Files
    1. Minutes of the Executive Committee Sessions of the General Commission of German Trade Unions, 1899–1914

IX. Hauptstaatsarchiv, Düsseldorf (HSA Düsseldorf)
  A. Government Documents
    1. *Semester-, Sammel-,* and *Terminalberichte* from the files of the *Regierungspräsident* of Düsseldorf

X. Stadtarchiv, Duisburg (StA Duisburg)
  A. Personal Papers
    1. Karl Weinbrenner
    2. Biographical Collection Franz Wieber

XI. Stadtarchiv Essen
  A. Proceedings
    1. *Protokollbuch des katholischen Knappenvereins Essen-Ruhr*, 11 Rep. 103, E1, Nr. 25

2. *Protokollbuch des Bergmanns-Verein zu Überruhr*, 10 Rep. 103, E1, Nr. 23

XII. Münsterarchiv Essen
A. Organizational Files
1. *Akten der christlichen Arbeiterverin zu Essen 1892–1918*, Nr. 641–651

XIII. Registratur des erzbischöflichen Generalvikariats, Köln (Erzb. Registratur Köln)
A. Church Records
1. Gen. 23.61., volumes 1–2

XIV. Historisches Archiv, Köln (HA Köln)
A. Personal Papers
1. Carl Bachem Papers
2. Wilhelm Marx Papers

XV. Kettelerhaus der katholischen Arbeitnehmer-Bewegung, Köln (KAB Haus Köln)
A. Personal Papers
1. Wilhelm Ziebach
B. Unpublished Manuscripts
1. Otto Müller, *Eine Geschichte der katholischen Arbeitervereine*, n.d.
C. Proceedings
1. *Der erste Arbeitervereinskongress zu Frankfurt*, 1912
D. Newspapers
1. *Die Wacht*

XVI. Stegerwald Stiftung, Köln
A. Personal Papers
1. Adam Stegerwald

XVII. Bundesarchiv, Koblenz (BA Koblenz)
A. Personal Papers
1. Ernst Bassermann
2. Lujo Brentano
3. Bernhard Bülow
4. Hermann Cardauns
5. Anton Erkelenz
6. Matthias Erzberger
7. Thomas Esser
8. Fechenbach Colllection; Fechenbach Papers
9. Ernst Francke
10. Karl Herold
11. Georg Hertling
12. Jakob Kaiser
13. Bernhard Otte
14. Eugen Schiffer

15. Reinhold Seeberger
16. Gustav Stresemann

B. Proceedings
1. Stenographic Reports over the Christian Trade Union Congresses of 1901, 1902, 1904, 1906, 1909, 1912, and the Extraordinary Congress of November 1912
2. Stenographic Reports over the German Workers' Congresses of 1903, 1907, and 1913
3. Stenographic Reports over the General Commission of German Trade Union Congresses of 1899, 1902, 1905, 1906, 1908, and 1911

XVIII. Landeshauptarchiv, Koblenz (LHA Koblenz)
A. Government Documents
1. Files of the *Oberpräsident* of the Rhineland
2. Files of the *Regierungspräsidenten* of Trier, Koblenz, Cologne, Düsseldorf, and Aachen

XIX. Dom- und Diözesanarchiv Mainz (DDA Mainz)
A. Personal Papers
1. Wilhelm Emmanuel von Ketteler
2. Christoph Moufang

XX. Zentrales Staatarchiv, Merseburg (ZStA Merseburg)
A. Personal Papers
1. Hans von Berlepsch

XXI. Allgemeines Staatsarchiv, München (AStA München)
A. Government Documents
1. Ministerium der Arbeit 383–384

XXII. Geheimes Staatsarchiv, München (GStA München)
A. Bavarian Diplomatic Correspondence
1. Ges. Berlin, Pol. Schriftwechsel 1068–1086, 1897–1914
2. Päpstl. Stuhl 903–906

XXIII. Stadtarchiv, Mönchen-Gladbach (StA MG)
A. Personal Papers
1. Anton Heinen
2. Wilhelm Hohn
3. Heinz Brauweiler
4. Umberto Benigni Papers (in Brauweiler Papers)
5. Medard Hartrath

B. Organizational Files
1. Minutes of the Executive Council Sessions of the *Volksverein für das katholische Deutschland*, 1910–1914 (in Hartrath Papers)

C. Unpublished Manuscripts
1. August Pieper, *Die Geschichte des Volksvereins für das katholische Deutschland*, n.d.
2. Anton Heinen, *Mein Leben als Volksbildner: Worum es mir ging*, n.d.

XXIV. Stadtbibliothek Mönchen-Gladbach (StBib MG)
- A. Private Newsletters and Communiqués
  1. *Augustinus-Blatt*, 1897–1914
  2. *Kölner Correspondenz für die geistlichen Präsides katholischer Vereinigungen der Arbeitenden Stände*, 1887–1900
  3. *Präsides-Korrespondenz*, 1901–1914
  4. *Mitteilungen an die Präsides der katholischen Arbeitervereine der Erzdiözese Köln 1908–1914*
  5. *Christlich-soziale Blätter*
- B. Proceedings
  1. Stenographic Reports of the General Assembly of German Catholics (*Katholikentage*)
  2. *Offizieller Bericht über den 3. Delegiertentag der Katholischen Arbeitervereinigungen der Erzdiözese Köln zu Köln am 15. Juni 1897*
- C. Newspapers
  1. *Westdeutsche Arbeiter-Zeitung*
  2. *Mitteilungen des Gesamtverbandes der christlichen Gewerkschaften Deutschlands*
  3. *Zentralblatt der Christlichen Gewerkschaften Deutschlands*
  4. *Korrespondenz des Bundes der Landwrite*
  5. *Deutsche Tageszeitung*
  6. *Der Arbeiter* (Berlin)
- D. Miscellaneous
  1. Numerous rare books and pamphlets from the library of the old *Volksverein für das katholische Deutschland*

XXV. Staatsarchiv, Münster (StA Münster)
- A. Personal Papers
  1. August Pieper Papers
- B. Government Documents
  1. Files of the *Oberpräsident* of Westphalia
  2. Files of the *Regierungspräsidenten* of Münster and Arnsberg

XXVI. Zentrales Staatsarchiv, Potsdam (ZStA Potsdam)
- A. Personal Papers
  1. Johannes Giesberts Papers
  2. Reinhardt Mumm Papers
  3. Kuno von Westarp Papers
- B. Government Documents
  1. Files of the Reich Chancellery
  2. Files of the Reich Ministry of the Interior
  3. Files of the Reich Ministry of the Economy

XXVII. Stadtarchiv Recklinghausen (StA Recklinghausen)
- A. Newspapers
  1. Zeitungsarchiv

XXVIII. Hauptstaatsarchiv Stuttgart (HSA Stuttgart)
    A. Württembergian Diplomatic Correspondence
        1. Kgl. Min. der auswärtigen Angelegenheiten, E73a, verz. 12e

XXIX. Bistumsarchiv Trier (BisA Trier)
    A. Personal Papers
        1. Bishop Michael Felix Korum

XXX. Archiwum Archidiecezjalne we Wrocławie (AA Wrocławie)
    A. Personal Papers
        1. Bishop Adolf Bertram

Select List of Published Sources

Alexander, Edgar. "Church and Society in Germany," in Moody, Joseph N. (ed.), *Catholic Social and Political Movements*. New York: Arts, Inc., 1953.

Anderson, Margaret Lavinia. *Windthorst: A Political Biography*. New York: Oxford University Press, 1981.

Bachem, Karl. *Vorgeschichte Geschichte und Politik der deutschen Zentrumspartei*. Cologne: Verlag, J. P. Bachem, 1929. 9 vols.

Berger, Michael. *Arbeiterbewegung und Demokratisierung*. Freiburg i. Br.: Dissertationsdruck Johannes Kraus, 1970.

Blackbourn, David. *Class Religion and Local Politics in Wilhelmine Germany: The Centre Party in Württemberg before 1914*. Wiesbaden: Franz Steiner Verlag GmbH, 1980.

Böhme, Theodor. *Die christlichnationale Gewerkschaft*. Stuttgart: Verlag von W. Kohlhammer, 1930.

Bongartz, Arnold. *Das katholisch-soziale Vereinswesen in Deutschland*. Würzburg: Bonifacius-Druckerei, 1879.

Brack, Rudolf. *Deutscher Episkopat und Gewerkschaftsstreit 1900–1914*. Cologne: Böhlau Verlag, 1976.

Brügmann, Arnold. *Sozialer Katholizismus im 19. Jahrhundert*. Frankfurt a. M.: Deutsche Kunst und Verlagsanstalt, 1943.

Censarek, Franz-Maria. *Die christlichen Gewerkschaften in Deutschland*. Dissertation, Karl-Franzens-Universität zu Graz, 1967.

Cwiklinski, Bernhard (ed.). *August Brust: Gründer und Vorkämpfer der christlichen Gewerkschaftsbewegung Deutschlands*. Essen: Boners, n.d.

Denk, Hans Dieter. *Die christliche Arbeiterbewegung in Bayern bis zum Ersten Weltkrieg*. Mainz: Matthias Grünewald–Verlag, 1980.

Deutz, Joseph. *Adam Stegerwald*. Cologne: Bund-Verlag GmbH, 1952.

Dockhorn, Wilhelm. *Die christlich-soziale Bewegung in Deutschland*. Halle: Buchdruckerei des Waisenhauses, 1928.

Eley, Geoff. *Reshaping the German Right*. New Haven: Yale University Press, 1980.
Epstein, Klaus. *Matthias Erzberger and the Dilemma of German Democracy*. Princeton, New Jersey: Princeton University Press, 1959.
Erdmann, August. *Die christliche Arbeiterbewegung in Deutschland*. Stuttgart: J. W. H. Dietz, 1908.
———. *Die christlichen Gewerkschaften insbesondere ihr Verhältnis zu Zentrum und Kirche*. Stuttgart: J. H. W. Dietz, 1914.
Evans, Richard (ed.). *Society and Politics in Wilhelmine Germany*. London: Croom Helm, 1978.
Filthaut, Edgar. *Deutsche Katholikentage (1848–1958) und soziale Frage*. Essen: Hans Driewer-Verlag, 1959.
Frank, Walter. *Hofprediger Adolf Stöcker und die christlich-soziale Bewegung*. Berlin: Verlag von Reimer Hobbing, 1928.
Franz, Dr. Albert. *Der soziale Katholizismus in Deutschland bis zum Tode Kettelers*. M. Gladbach: Volksvereins Verlag GmbH, 1914.
Frey, Ludwig. *Die Stellung der christlichen Gewerkschaften zu den politischen Parteien*. Berlin: Christlicher Gewerkschaftsverlag, 1931.
Fricke, Dieter, *et al. Die bürgerliche Parteien in Deutschland*. Berlin: Das europäische Buch, 1968. 2 vols.
25 Jahre christliche Gewerkschaftsbewegung Deutschlands 1899–1924. Berlin: Christlicher Gewerkschaftsverlag, 1924.
Gasteiger, Michael. *Die christliche Gewerkschaften in Süddeutschland*. Munich: Verlag des "Arbeiter," 1908.
Gornik, Alfons. *Die Entwicklung der nichtsozialdemokratischen Arbeiterbewegung in Deutschland*. Halle: Hofbuchdruckerei von C. A. Kaemmerer und Co., 1909.
Hartmann, Albrecht. *Zentrum und christliche Gewerkschaften von 1900–1914*. Dissertation, Berlin, 1952.
Heitzer, Hortswalter. *Georg Kardinal Kopp und der Gewerkschaftsstreit*. Cologne: Böhlau Verlag, 1983.
———. *Der Volksverein für das katholische Deutschland in Kaiserreich*. Mainz: Kommission fur Zeitgeschichte, 1979.
Heuss, Theodor. *Friedrich Naumann*. Stuttgart: Rainer Wunderlich Verlag Herman Leins, 1937.
Hitze, Franz. *Kapital und Arbeit und die Reorganisation der Gesellschaft*. Paderborn: Bonifacius-Druckerei, 1880.
———. *Die sociale Frage und die Bestrebungen zu ihrer Lösung*. Paderborn: Bonifacius-Druckerei, 1877.
Hue, Otto. *Die Bergarbeiter*. Stuttgart: J. H. W. Dietz, 1910–13. 2 volumes.
Hull, Isabel. *The Entourage of Kaiser William II*. New York: Cambridge University Press, 1982.

Imbusch, Heinrich. *Arbeitsverhältnis und Arbeiterorganization im deutschen Bergbau*. Essen: Verlag des Gewerkvereins christlicher Bergarbeiter, 1908.

———. *25 Jahre Gewerkverein christlicher Bergarbeiter*. Essen: Verlag des Gewerkvereins christlicher Bergarbeiter Deutschlands, 1919.

Joos, Joseph. *Am Räderwerk der Zeit Erinnerungen aus der kath. und sozialen Bewegung und Politik*. Augsburg: Verlag Winfried-Werk GmbH, 1951.

———. *So Sah Ich Sie*. Augsburg: Verlag Winfried-Werk, 1958.

Kaelble, H., and Volkmann, H. "Konjunktur und Streik während des Übergangs zum organisierten Kapitalismus in Deutschland." *Zeitschrift für Wirtschafts- und Sozialwissenschaften*, vol. 92, no. 5 (1972), pp. 526-45.

Kalis, Alfred. "Die christlich-soziale Arbeiterbewegung in Essen," *Heimatstadt Essen*, 1965–66, pp. 60-70.

Kaster, Johannes. *Die christlich-sozialen Ideen und die Gewerkschaftsfrage*. Mönchen-Gladbach: Volksvereinsverlag GmbH, 1922.

———. *Die Stellung der deutschen Katholiken zur Gewerkschaftsfrage vor der Gründung der christlichen Gewerkschaften*. Mönchen-Gladbach: Volksvereinsverlag, 1921.

Ketteler, Wilhelm Emmanuel Freiherr von. *Die Arbeiterbewegung und ihr Streben im Verhältnis zu Religion und Sittlichkeit*. Mainz: Verlag von Franz Kirchheim, 1869.

———. *Die Arbeiterfrage und das Christenthum*. Mainz: Verlag von Franz Kirchheim, 1864.

———. *Deutschland nach dem Kriege von 1866*. Mainz: Verlag von Franz Kirchheim, 1867.

———. *Freiheit Autorität und Kirche*. Mainz: Verlag von Franz Kirchheim, 1862.

———. *Die Katholiken im Deutschen Reich*. Mainz: Verlag von Franz Kirchheim, 1873.

Kirchhoff, Hans Georg. *Die staatliche Sozialpolitik in Ruhrbergbau 1871–1914*. Cologne: Westdeutscher Verglag, 1958.

Kissing, Johannes B. *Geschichte der deutschen Katholikentage*. Münster: Verlag der Aschen'dorffschen Verlagsbuchhandlung, 1920. 2 vols.

Koch, Max. *Die Bergarbeiter im Ruhrgebiet zur Zeit Wilhelms II*. Düsseldorf: Droste Verlag, 1954.

Kosthorst, Erich. *Jacob Kaiser: Der Arbeiterfuehrer*. Stuttgart: W. Kohlhammer Verlag, 1967.

Kraneburg, Hans, *Hitzes sozialpolitische Forderungen und ihre Verwirklichung in der Gesetzgebung*. Mönchen-Gladbach: Volksvereinverlag, 1922.

Kudera, Lucian. *Der Gewerkschaftsstreit der deutschen Katholiken in der Publizistik 1900–1914*. Dissertation, Münster, 1967.

Kulemann, Wilhelm. *Die Berufsvereine*. Jena: Gustav Fischer Verlag, 1908. 2 vols.

———. *Die Gewerkschafts-bewegung*. Jena: Gustav Fischer Verlag, 1900.

Lidtke, Vernon. *The Outlawed Party: Social Democracy in Germany 1878–1890*. Princeton, New Jersey: Princeton University Press, 1966.

———. "Social Class and Secularization in Imperial Germany: The Working Classes," *Publications of the Leo Baeck Institute*, vol. 25 (1980), pp. 21–40.

Lepper, Herbert. "Kaplan Franz Eduard Cronenberg und die christlich-soziale Bewegung in Aachen 1868–1878," *Zeitschrift des Aachener Geschichtsvereins*, vol. 79 (1968), pp. 57–148.

Loth, Wilfried. *Katholiken im Kaiserreich*. Düsseldorf: Droste Verlag, 1984.

Mattheier, Klaus. *Die Gelben Nationale Arbeiter zwischen Wirtschaftsfrieden und Streik*. Düsseldorf: Padagogischer Verlag Schwann, 1973.

Mendershausen, Ralph Rene. "German Political Catholicism 1912–1919," Ph.D. dissertation, University of California, San Diego, 1972.

Metlake, George [pseud. Laux]. *Christian Social Reform Program Outlined by Its Pioneer Wilhelm Emmanuel Baron von Ketteler*. Philadelphia: Dolphin Press, 1912.

Meyer, Rudolf. *Der Emancipationskampf des vierten Standes*. Berlin: Verlag von August Schindler, 1874.

Mittmann, Ursula. *Fraktion und Partei: Ein Vergleich von Zentrum und Sozialdemokratie im Kaiserreich*. Düsseldorf: Droste Verlag, 1976.

Mockenhaupt, Hubert. *Katholische Sozialpolitik im 20. Jahrhundert: Ausgewählte Aufsätze und Reden von Heinrich Brauns*. Mainz: Matthias Grünewald–Verlag, 1976.

Moellers, Paul. *Die politische Strömmungen im Reichstagswahlkreis Essen 1867 bis 1879*. Dissertation, Bonn, 1956.

Mommsen, Hans, and Borsdorf, Ulrich. *Glückauf, Kameraden!* Cologne: Bund Verlag GmbH, 1979.

Mumbauer, Johannes (ed.). *Wilhelm Emmanuel von Ketteler's Schriften*. Kempten und München: Verlag der Jos. Kösel'schen Buchhandlung, 1911. 3 vols.

Müller, Franz. *Franz Hitze und sein Werk*. Hamburg: Hanseatische Verlagsanstalt, 1928.

Müller, Otto. *Die christliche Gewerkschaftsbewegung Deutschlands*. Karlsruhe: Druck und Verlag der Braunschen Hofbuchdruckerei, 1905.

Naujoks, Eberhardt. *Die katholische Arbeiterbewegung und der Sozialismus in den ersten Jahren des Bismarckschen Reiches*. Berlin: Junker und Duennhaupt Verlag, 1939.

Nitti, Francesco. *Catholic Socialism*. London: Swan Sonnenschein and Co., 1908.

Nolan, Mary. *Social Democracy and Society: Working-Class Radicalism in Düsseldorf 1890–1920*. New York: Cambridge University Press, 1982.

Oertzen, Dietrich von. *Erinnerungen aus meinem Leben*. Berlin: Verlag von Edwin Runge, 1915.

Pfülf, Otto. *Bischof von Ketteler: Eine geschichtliche Darstellung* Mainz: Verlag von Franz Kirchheim, 1899.

Raich, Dr. J. M. *Briefe von und an Wilhelm Emmanuel Freiherr von Ketteler*. Mainz: Verlag von Franz Kirchheim, 1879.

Rauh, Manfred. *Die Parlamentarisierung des deutschen Reiches*. Düsseldorf: Droste Verlag, 1977.

Reulecke, Jürgen (ed.). *Arbeiterbewegung an Rhein und Ruhr*. Wuppertal: Peter Hammer Verlag GmbH, 1974.

Ritter, Emil. *Die katholisch-soziale Bewegung und der Volksverein*. Cologne: Verlag J. P. Bachem, 1954.

Ross, Ronald J. *Beleaguered Tower: The Dilemma of Political Catholicism in Wilhelmine Germany*. Notre Dame, Indiana: University of Notre Dame Press, 1976.

Saul, Klaus. *Staat, Industrie, und Arbeiterbewegung im Kaiserreich*. Düsseldorf: Bertelsmann Universitätsverlag, 1974.

Schorr, Helmut J. *Adam Stegerwald—Gewerkschaftler und Politiker der ersten deutschen Republik: Ein Beitrag zur Geschichte der christlich-sozialen Bewegung in Deutschland*. Recklinghausen: Kommunal Verlag, 1966.

Schurmann, Karl Heinz. *Zur Vorgeschichte der christlichen Gewerkschaften*. Freiburg: Verlag Herder, 1958.

Shanahan, William O. *German Protestants Face the Social Question*. Notre Dame, Indiana: University of Notre Dame Press, 1954.

Sperber, Jonathan. *Popular Catholicism in Nineteenth Century Germany*. Princeton, New Jersey: Princeton University Press, 1984.

Tenfelde, Klaus. *Sozialgeschichte der Bergarbeiterschaft an der Ruhr im 19. Jahrundert*. Bonn: Verlag Neue Gesellschaft GmbH, 1977.

Vetter, Heinz Osgar (ed.). *Vom Sozialistengesetz zur Mitbestimmung*. Cologne: Bund Verlag GmbH, 1975.

Vieth, Otmar. *Die katholischen Knappenvereine im Bereich des heutigen Bistums Essen*. Unpublished seminar manuscript presented to the present author.

Vincke, Franziska. *Die Arbeitnehmer-Sozialpolitik des Zentrums*. Münster: Wirtschafts- und Sozialwissenschaftlicher–Verlag, 1933.

Wachtling, Oswald. *Joseph Joos, Journalist, Arbeiterführer, Zentrumspolitiker: Politische Biographie 1878–1933*. Mainz: Matthias Grünewald–Verlag, 1974.

Windolph, J. *Der deutsche Protestantismus und die christlichen Gewerkschaften*. Berlin: Kommissionsverlag des "Arbeiter," 1909.

Zeender, John K. *The German Center Party 1890–1906*. Philadelphia: American Philosophical Society, 1976.

Index